Crete

written and researched by

John Fisher and Geoff Garvey

roughguides.com

Contents

Introduction to
Crete

With its fabulous beaches and crystalline seas, Crete has everything you could want of a Greek island. But it also has a great deal more: as the birthplace of Zeus and cradle of Europe's earliest civilization Crete can boast a history longer even than classical Greece, and reminders of its extraordinary past are scattered all over the island. It's also a substantial and multifarious land in its own right, with cosmopolitan cities as well as unspoilt, hidden villages, dramatic gorges and mountains high enough to be snow-capped well into summer.

Because the island is so big, it is far from dominated by visitors. Indeed, thanks to a flourishing agricultural economy – including some surprisingly good vineyards – Crete is one of the few Greek islands that could probably support itself without holiday-makers. So although tourism is an important part of the economy, traditional life also survives, along with the **hospitality** that forms part of that tradition. There are plenty of visitors, of course, and the populous **north coast** can be as sophisticated as you want it; here you'll find every facility imaginable and, in places, crowds of package tourists determined to exploit them to the full. But in the less-known coastal reaches of the **south** it's still possible to escape the development, while the high mountains and agricultural plains of the interior are barely touched. One of the most rewarding things to do on Crete is to rent a car and head for remoter villages, often just a few kilometres off some heavily beaten track. Here the island's customs, its everyday life, dialects, song, traditional dress and festivals, and above all its welcome to strangers, survive to an extent that's exceptional in modern Europe.

The **mountains**, which dominate the view as you approach Crete, run from one end of the island to the other, and make all but the shortest journey inland an expedition. They are perhaps the island's greatest surprise and biggest reward, providing welcome relief in the heat of summer, giving Crete much of its character, and making the place feel much larger than it really is. Cut through by gorges and studded by caves, they offer fabulous **walking** too, from easy strolls to strenuous climbs, as well as a huge variety of habitats for

ABOVE MINOAN FRESCO, IRÁKLIO ARCHEOLOGICAL MUSEUM

CRETE

MEDITERRANEAN SEA

Metres
2000
1500
1000
500
200
100
0

E4 PAN-EUROPEAN
FOOTPATH

0   25
kilometres

N

Kássos, Kárpathos & Rhodes

Gulf of Mirabello

Spinalónga
Eloúnda
Áyios Nikólaos
Lató
Pláka
Neápoli
Mália
Sísi
Mílatos
Stalída
Hersónisos
Káto Goúves
Koútoulos
Goúves
Skalani
Myrtiá
Péza
Houdhétsi
Arhánes
Knossós
IRÁKLIO
Ayia Pelayía
Fódhele
Dhía
Paleókastro
Marathos
Angélia
Tílissos
E75

Xái
Toploú
Sitía
Palékastro
Áno Zákros
Zíros
Kató Zákros
Xerókambos

Mókhlos
Makbryialós
Pahiá Ámmos
Ayía Foú
Goúmia
Ierápetra
Gadhrounísi

LASÍTHI PLATEAU
Dhíkteon Cave
Dhíkti (2148m)
Áno Viánnos
Árvi
Myrtos
Tsoútsouros
Keratókambos

Ístro
Kritsá
Áyios Konstantínos
Tzermiádho
Pshró

Arkalohóri
Vathýpetro
Ayía Varvára
Áyii Dhéka
Gortys
Léndas
Pýrgos
Kalí
Limènes
Mátala
Pitsídhia
Festós & Ayía Triádha
Ayía Galíni
Kamáres
Idean Cave
Psilorítis (2456m)
AMÁRI VALLEY
Fourfourás
Throní
Spíli
Lefkóyia
Préveli
Plakiás
Mýrthios
Dhamnóni

Ayios Ioánnis
Vathýpetro
Mýres

Réthymno
Pérama
Pánormos
Bali
Dhamásta
Arkádhi
Pérama

Stavrós
Kalathás
Moni Ayía Triádha
Akrotíri
Sternes
Kalyves
Soúdha
Vámos
Vrýsses
Yeoryioúpoli
Kournás
Ímbros
Hóra Sfakíon
Frangokástello

Haniá
Plataniás
Ayía Marína
Alíkianos
Voukoliés
Kándanos
Oméla
Topólia
Kastélli
Kolymbári
Rodhopoú
Moni Goniá
Tavronítis

WHITE MOUNTAINS
Páhnes (2452m)
Omalós
Samariá Gorge
Ayía Rouméli
Loútro
Anópoli
Thríptí
Lefká Óri

Gramvoússa
Falássarna
Plátanos
Sfinári
Mília
Kámbos
Elós
Khrysoskalítissa
Elafonísi
Paleohóra

Soúyia

Gávdhos
Gavdhopoúla

E75
E4

MOUNTAIN HIKING

There are few places in the world where high **mountains** so close to the sea combine with an often perfect climate. This is a paradise for climbers, birdwatchers, botanists and nature lovers, but above all for **walkers** – whether on a brief stroll or a week-long hike. A network of ancient footpaths and shepherds' trails allows you to walk all day and barely see a soul. Yet, should you want to, you can always find a village, and Cretan hospitality ensures that almost wherever you end up you will eat well and spend the night in comfort. The daddy of Crete's treks is the **E4**, the long-distance European footpath that traverses the island, taking in many of the highest peaks en route. To walk the entire length takes weeks, but there are plenty of sections that are easily accessible and where you can hike for a few hours. Some of the best of these are in the southwest, where the path splits: one branch following the coast and another winding through the heights of the Lefká Óri; the magnificent Samariá Gorge links the two.

One striking feature of Crete's topography is the sheer number of spectacular **gorges** that slash their way through the mountains. In addition to Samariá, there are at least fifty more gorges in the Lefká Óri alone, many hardly visited at all. On a hot summer's day, heading down a gorge is the ideal hike: you're shaded from the sun's ferocity, with an empty beach and a welcome swim to reward you at the end. Arrange for someone to collect you so you don't have to toil back up, and you have the makings of a perfect day.

wildlife, including many large birds of prey. For birdwatchers and wildflower spotters, Crete has no end of treats in store.

Cretan **food** can also prove an unexpected bonus. There's an increasing awareness of culinary traditions based on magnificent sun-ripened fruit and vegetables, locally sourced, foraged herbs and home-reared meat, much of it organic. In fashionable city restaurants, grandma's recipes are being rediscovered to great effect, while in more rustic village or beachside tavernas, the age-old combination of superb ingredients, simply served, has never been forgotten.

An extraordinary **history** plays a large part in Crete's appeal, too. It was more than four thousand years ago that the island's story began to be shaped, when, from around 2000 BC, the **Minoans** developed an advanced and cultured society at the centre of a substantial maritime trading empire: the first real European civilization. The artworks produced on Crete at this time are unsurpassed anywhere in the ancient world, and it seems clear, as you wander through the Minoan palaces and towns, that life on the island in those days was good. For five hundred years, by far the longest period of peace the island has seen, Crete was home to a civilization well ahead of its time. The excavations of the great Minoan palaces are among the island's prime tourist attractions today.

The Minoans are believed to have come originally from Anatolia, and the island's position as strategic **meeting point** between east and west has played a crucial role in its subsequent history. The Greek flag was raised over Crete little more than one hundred years ago, in 1913. For two thousand years and more before that the island was fought over by others – subject to Rome, Byzantium and Venice before being subsumed into the Turkish Ottoman empire. During World War II Crete was occupied by the Germans and gained the dubious distinction of being the first place to be successfully invaded by parachute. Each one of these diverse rulers has left some mark, and more importantly they have imprinted on the islanders a personality toughened by constant struggles for independence.

OPPOSITE CLOCKWISE FROM TOP LEFT OCTOPUS DRYING IN THE SUN; FORTEZZA, RÉTHYMNO; PALM BEACH, RÉTHYMNO PROVINCE

Where to go

Every part of Crete has its loyal devotees who will argue fervently in defence of their favourite spot. On the whole, though, if you want to get away from it all you should head for the ends of the island – west, towards Haniá and the smaller, less well-connected places along the south and west coasts, or east to Sitía and beyond. Wherever you're staying, you won't have to go far inland to escape the crowds.

In the centre of the island the sprawling capital, **Iráklio** (Heraklion), is home to a magnificent **archeological museum** and lies just a few kilometres from **Knossós**, the greatest of the **Minoan palaces**. You'll find other reminders of history all over Crete, but the best known are mostly here, near the heart of the island; above all **Festós** and **Ayía Triádha** in the south (with Roman **Górtys** to provide contrast) and the palace of **Mália** on the north coast.

As for **beaches**, you'll find great ones almost anywhere on the north coast. From Iráklio to Áyios Nikólaos there's very heavy development, and most package tourists are aiming for the resort hotels in this region. These places can be fun if nightlife and crowds are what you're after – particularly the biggest of them, like **Mália**, **Hersónisos** and **Áyios Nikólaos**. The majority of the island's most luxurious **hotels** and **inclusive resorts** are near Áyios Nikólaos, especially around **Eloúnda**, overlooking the Gulf of Mirabello. Further east things get quieter: **Sitía** is a place of real character, and beyond it on the east coast are a number of laidback resorts as well as the beautiful palm beach at **Vái**, a favourite with day-trippers from across the island, and the relatively little-visited Minoan palace of **Zákros**. To the west there's more development around both **Réthymno** and **Haniá**, the most attractive of the island's big towns. Other places at this end of the island tend to be on a smaller scale.

Along the **south coast**, where the mountains frequently drop straight down to the sea, resorts are more scattered. Only a handful of places are really developed – **Ierápetra**, **Ayía Galíni**, **Mátala**, **Paleóhora** – with a few more, like **Plakiás** and **Makriyialós**, on their way. But the lesser-known spots in between, not always easy to get to, are some of the most attractive in Crete.

For many people, unexpected highlights also turn out to be the island's **Venetian forts** and defensive walls and bastions – dominant at Réthymno, Iráklio and Haniá, magnificent at **Frangokástello**, and found in various stages of ruin all over Crete. The **Byzantine churches** and remote **monasteries** dotted across the island, many containing stunning medieval **wall**

A RURAL ISLAND

Despite the rapid growth in the last fifty years of towns like Haniá, Réthymno and particularly Iráklio, Crete remains a land rooted in the **countryside**. Almost everyone seems to have some connection to the land – a smallholding where they grow fresh produce or a village where parents or grandparents still live. The villages, each with its own character and traditions, are the island's pulse, where the pace of the year is determined by the agricultural calendar. Here you can still find everyday life lived as it has been for centuries, where potters spin clay into ewers and jars, weavers make rugs in traditional patterns and farmers cart their olives to the local press.

Author picks

Our authors have explored every corner of Crete in order to uncover the very best it has to offer. Here are some of their favourite things to see and do.

Unspoilt villages You can escape the coastal crowds and heat by heading inland almost anywhere. Try these for starters: Aryiroúpoli (p.228), Áyios Yeóryios (p.219), Kamilári (p.113) and Kefáli (p.302).

Amazing adventures Bungee jump into a 140m gorge at Arádhena (p.284), windsurf at Koureménos (p.164), or trek down the sensational Samariá Gorge, Europe's longest (p.275).

Fresh from the sea Feasting on fish and crustaceans in sight of the sea is a tip-top Cretan treat. Four of the best places to do it are *Caravella* (p.311), *To Akrogiali* (p.247), *To Bogazi* (p.153) and *Hióna* (p.165).

Brilliant beaches Among hundreds of superb beaches standouts include tropical Elafonísi (p.303), the idyllic white-sand Balos Bay (p.297) and the Caribbean-style palm beach at Vái (p.161).

Cretan castles If castles are your thing Réthymno's Fortezza (p.193), Frangokástello (p.290) and the stirring island forts of Spinalónga (p.135) and Gramvoúsa (p.298) won't disappoint.

Caves and caverns Crete has thousands of caves, many of which can be explored. The Sendóni (p.205), Melidhóni (p.204) and Dhiktean (p.143) caverns are all well worth a trip.

Intriguing islands The seas surrounding Crete are dotted with dozens of offshore islands and islets. Spinalónga (p.135), Gramvoúsa (p.298), Gaidhouronísi (p.181) and Gávdhos (p.318) each have a unique character.

Magnificent museums Iráklio's magnificent Archeological Museum has reopened after a stunning makeover (p.52) but the museums at Haniá (p.241) and Sitía (p.156) are also well worth a visit.

Views to die for Mátala is famed for its crimson sunsets (p.109), hilltop Mírthios has a fabulous view over the Libyan Sea (p.222) and sunrise seen from the summit of Psilorítis is unforgettable (p.209).

> Our author recommendations don't end here. We've flagged up our favourite places – a perfectly sited hotel, an atmospheric café, a special restaurant – throughout the guide, highlighted with the ★ symbol.

FROM TOP VÁI; BUNGEE JUMPING, ARÁDHENA GORGE; SPINALÓNGA

paintings, are also unexpected treasures. Smaller Cretan **towns**, supply centres for the island's farmers, are always worth visiting for their vibrant markets, shops and tavernas, while Réthymno and Haniá boast atmospheric, cluttered old centres, whose narrow alleys are crammed with relics of the Venetian and Turkish eras.

The mountains and valleys of the interior deserve far more attention than they get, too. Only the **Lasíthi** plateau in the east and the **Samariá Gorge** in the west see really large numbers of visitors, but turn off the main roads almost anywhere and you'll find villages going about their daily agricultural routine, often in the midst of astonishingly beautiful scenery. This is especially true in the west, where the Lefká Óri – the **White Mountains** – dramatically dominate every view; but the **Psilorítis** range in the centre of the island also offers magnificent scenery and mountain villages, along with some of the island's finest walking, while the **Sitían mountains** in the east are far less explored.

When to go

The combination of high **mountains** and warm seas, together with a position as far south as any in Europe, makes for an exceptionally long season: you can get a decent tan in Crete right into October and swim at least from April until early November. **Spring** is the prime time to come: in April and May the island is relatively empty of visitors (except over Easter), the weather clear and not overpoweringly hot, and every scene is brightened by a profusion of wildflowers.

By mid-June the rush is beginning. **July** and **August** are not only the hottest, the most crowded and most expensive months, they are also intermittently blighted by fierce winds and accompanying high seas; the south coast is particularly prone to these. In September the crowds gradually begin to thin out, and **autumn** can again be a great time to visit – but now the landscape looks parched and tired, and there's a feeling of things gradually winding down.

Winters are mild, but also vaguely depressing: many places are shut, it can rain sporadically, sometimes for days, and there's far less life in the streets. In the mountains it snows, even to the extent where villages can be cut off; on the south coast it's generally warmer, soothed by a breeze from Africa. You may get a week or more of really fine weather in the middle of winter, but equally you can have sudden viciously cold snaps right through into March.

AVERAGE MONTHLY TEMPERATURES AND RAINFALL (IRÁKLIO)

	Jan	Feb	Mar	Apr	May	Jun	Jul	Aug	Sep	Oct	Nov	Dec
Max/min (°C)	15/9	15/9	17/9	20/12	23/15	27/19	29/22	29/22	27/19	24/17	20/13	17/11
Max/min (°F)	60/48	60/48	63/48	68/54	73/60	81/66	84/72	84/72	81/66	75/63	68/55	63/52
Rainfall (mm)	76	48	48	21	10	1	0.5	1	7	30	65	79

1 LOUTRÓ
Page 279

Accessible only by boat or on foot, this idyllic retreat on the edge of its own bay is the perfect place to get away from it all.

2 TRADITIONAL MUSIC AND DANCE
Page 206

Crete's musical traditions are thriving, and traditional music and dance is widely performed at tavernas, weddings, baptisms and saint's day celebrations across the island – often featuring the *lyra* and *laúto*.

3 KNOSSÓS
Page 66

Crete's biggest attraction, this 3500-year-old Minoan palace is a sprawling maze of royal chambers, grand staircases, storerooms and workshops.

4 ARCHEOLOGICAL MUSEUM, IRÁKLIO
Page 52

The finest collection of Minoan artefacts in the world, with a brand-new setting to do them justice.

5 LASÍTHI PLATEAU
Page 140

Traditional village life continues on this fertile mountain plateau, famed for its windmills, where you'll also see a riot of springtime wildflowers.

6 ELAFONÍSI
Page 303
Turquoise waters, rose-tinted sands and a shallow, warm lagoon make this coral-island beach one of Crete's most exotic locations.

7 WINDSURFING
Page 164
Koureménos Beach is Crete's top windsurfing spot, with constant winds almost year-round.

8 WILDLIFE
Page 347
Crete's spectacular flora and fauna ranges from ubiquitous vultures to rarities like the *kri-kri* wild goat and delicate mountain orchids. Many beaches are nesting sites for the endangered loggerhead turtle.

9 HIKING
Pages 6, 27 & 36
Crete's countless walking opportunities include spectacular gorge hikes that take you from the mountains to the sea.

10 HANIÁ
Page 237
Wander the streets of Haniá's old town to discover its beautiful harbour and haunting vestiges of a Minoan, Venetian and Ottoman past.

11 ÁYIOS NIKÓLAOS
Page 127
With no end of restaurants, bars and clubs, this is one of the island's most vibrant and picturesque towns.

12 LEFKÁ ÓRI
Page 272

The Lefká Óri, or White Mountains, snow-capped right through to June, dominate the western end of the island, offering some unbeatable walking, hiking and adventure.

13 BEACHES
Page 298

From great swathes of sand at the north-coast resorts to tiny pebble coves overshadowed by stunning mountains in the south, Crete has beaches to suit any mood.

14 CAVES
Page 204

The awesome Melidhóni Cave is just one of hundreds dotted around the island, many of which can be visited.

15 MONÍ ARKÁDHI
Page 202

The most celebrated of Crete's numerous monasteries has a fine Venetian church and is an emblem of the island's struggle for independence.

16 RÉTHYMNO
Page 191

Lose yourself in the old quarter of Réthymno, an elegant town dominated by its Venetian fortress and fine beach.

17 THE KAFENÍO
Page 31

Focal point of traditional Cretan life, the *kafenío* is a great place for lively discussions or games of *távli* (backgammon) while downing a coffee, an ouzo or a fiery *rakí*.

18 BYZANTINE FRESCOES
Page 78

Some of the finest Byzantine frescoes in Greece are to be found in Crete's country churches.

Itineraries

There are as many potential itineraries as there are visitors to Crete, and you'll no doubt want to create your own to reflect personal interests, whether those be mountain climbing, bird-watching or lying on the beach. The itineraries below should begin to give a flavour of what the island has to offer.

THE GREAT ISLAND

The Grand Tour, taking in the best-known destinations. Allow at least two weeks, taking time off for the beaches and hikes along the way.

❶ **Iráklio** The inevitable starting point, Crete's capital boasts a world-class archeological museum, and is the easiest base from which to visit the ruins at Knossós. **See p.46**

❷ **Áyios Nikólaos** Home to the finest of Crete's luxury resort hotels, this is a beautiful town with good restaurants and nightlife. **See p.127**

❸ **Sitía** Laidback capital of the far east, offering excellent food, subtle charms and an escape from mass tourism. **See p.154**

❹ **Zákros** A tiny, isolated seaside hamlet with a lovely pebble beach and one of the four great Minoan palaces. **See p.166**

❺ **Mátala** From hippy hideout in the 1960s to crowded resort today, Mátala and its beachside caves have managed to retain a unique charm. **See p.109**

❻ **Réthymno** A university city with an enchanting old town, a big sandy beach and beautiful countryside in easy reach. **See p.191**

❼ **Haniá** The island's second city is for many its most attractive; gateway to the mountains of the west and with plenty of sophisticated charm. **See p.237**

THE EAST: MINOANS, MOUNTAINS AND BEACHES

This itinerary offers a little of everything the east of the island has to offer, with ample opportunities for getting to the beach or hiking into the hills. You could easily do it in four days, or break the journey into day-trips from a base almost anywhere in the east.

❶ **Knossós** The greatest of the Minoan palaces, Knossós lies in the countryside just behind Iráklio. Partly reconstructed and with many of the original frescoes copied, it's an extraordinary sight. **See p.66**

❷ **Mália** Both the island's most notorious resort and an important Minoan palace, in a glorious seaside setting. Some of Crete's sandiest beaches lie between here and Knossós. **See p.89**

❸ **Kárfi** An ancient Minoan site on a limestone pinnacle, with spectacular views over the coast and the Lasíthi plateau. Little survives of the site itself, but the journey, the taxing hike up and the chance to visit the plateau afterwards are irresistible. **See p.143**

❹ **Spinalónga** This island and one-time leper colony can be reached only by boat, with swimming in crystal-clear waters along the way. **See p.135**

ABOVE OLIVE GROVES NEAR ZÁKROS

THE GREAT ISLAND

THE EAST: MINOANS, MOUNTAINS AND BEACHES

WALKING IN THE WEST: CASTLES AND CHURCHES

MEDITERRANEAN SEA

❺ Gourniá A unique Minoan town set on the isthmus at Crete's narrowest point, Gourniá allows a glimpse of the lives of ordinary Cretans four thousand years ago. **See p.148**

❻ Mýrtos A tranquil, laidback spot on the sunny south coast where there's little to do but lie on the beach, swim, eat and drink. **See p.182**

❼ Ayía Triádha Tiny and enigmatic, Minoan Ayía Triádha has glorious views of both mountains and sea, with easy access to both. It's also very near the major palace at Festós, and the Roman ruins of Górtys. See **p.106**

❽ Zarós A wholly traditional village in the shadow of the Psilorítis mountains, Zarós offers some great places to stay and to eat, as well as lovely walks. **See p.97**

WALKING IN THE WEST: CASTLES AND CHURCHES

The castles, monasteries and wonderful painted Byzantine churches that litter the west are set among some of Crete's finest hiking territory and most spectacular mountain scenery. This itinerary takes you to a selection; all of them also offer tremendous opportunities for short walks or day hikes.

❶ Moní Arkádhi The island's most important monastery – with a fine Venetian church – is a shrine to the nineteenth-century independence struggle. A branch of the E4 path passes the monastery, which is also close to superb walking in the Amári valley. **See p.202**

❷ Moní Préveli Another of Crete's great monastic settlements, Préveli played a heroic

role in World War II. Walk down to Palm Beach directly below, or longer hikes head up the river behind the beach. **See p.225**

❸ Frangokástello An imposing fourteenth-century Venetian fort between the beach and forbidding mountains. Two little-known gorges are nearby. **See p.290**

❹ Church of Panayía and Sotíra, Roústika Some of Crete's most spectacular mountain roads lie between Frangokástello and Roústika, a drive through great walking country. The Byzantine church has some of the finest ancient frescoes in Crete. **See p.228**

❺ Chapel of Metamórphosis Sotírou, Mesklá Hidden away in a mountain village close to Haniá, this chapel celebrating Christ's transfiguration has superb frescoes dating from the fourteenth century. **See p.270**

❻ Moní Goniá, Kolimbári On the coast at the base of the Rodhopoú peninsula, where few roads penetrate, this seventeenth-century monastery played a stirring role in Crete's wars against the Turks – and has cannonballs lodged in its walls to prove it. **See p.265**

❼ Topólia Fascinating village with a frescoed Byzantine church – several others are nearby – at the head of a lovely inland ravine. **See p.304**

❽ Moní Khrysoskalítissa Isolated in the southwest, almost at the end of the road, this much-venerated monastery, close to fine beaches, is reached through verdant countryside studded with ancient churches and chapels. **See p.302**

TOUR BOATS AT SPINALÓNGA ISLAND

Basics

Getting there

By far the easiest way to get to Crete is to fly. The vast majority of visitors are Northern Europeans on package tours that include a direct charter flight. Many of these charter companies sell flight-only tickets on their planes, and there are a limited number of direct scheduled flights too. Overland routes are long, tortuous and expensive, so we've included only the briefest details here.

Even if your starting point is outside Europe the most cost-effective way to reach Crete may well be to get to London – or Amsterdam, Frankfurt or another Northern European hub – and pick up an onward flight from there. The chief disadvantage of direct flights to Crete is a lack of flexibility; most companies have only one or two flights a week. For greater choice, you may have to fly to Athens and take a domestic flight or ferry from there (see p.23).

There are two main **airports**: at **Iráklio** (Heraklion) for the centre and east of the island, and at **Haniá** (Chania) for the west; both have scheduled international services with budget airlines, regular charters from across Europe and numerous daily flights from Athens. **Sitía** in the far east has just a few flights from Athens and regional Greek airports, though that may change.

When **buying flights** it always pays to shop around, and bear in mind that many websites don't include charter or budget airlines in their results. Be aware too that a **package deal**, with accommodation included, can sometimes be as cheap as, or even cheaper than, a flight alone: there's no rule that says you have to use your accommodation every night, or even at all.

Flights from the UK and Ireland

There are **direct flights** to Crete on British Airways (Ⓦba.com), with budget airlines easyJet (Ⓦeasyjet .com), Ryanair (Ⓦryanair.com) and Jet2 (Ⓦjet2 .com), or with charter airlines. Don't expect them to

be cheap though: unless you book far in advance, there are few bargains to be had. **Fares** depend on the season, with the highest in July, August and during Easter week. But May, June and September are also popular, and since no direct flights operate through the winter (most run from April to mid-October), bargains are rare at any time. In theory, you can fly from Gatwick to Iráklio for as little as £80 return, but you'll have to move very fast to find fares this low. Realistically you can expect to pay £180–400 return at most times of the year; more if you leave your booking late.

British Airways operates four flights a week from Gatwick to Iráklio. EasyJet flies to Iráklio from Gatwick (twice daily), Manchester (3 weekly), Edinburgh, Luton and Bristol (all twice a week); and to Haniá six times a week from Gatwick. Jet2 has flights to Iráklio from Leeds-Bradford, Glasgow and Manchester (2–3 weekly), and from Edinburgh, East Midlands and Newcastle (once or twice a week each). Ryanair flies to Haniá from Stansted (2–4 weekly), from Leeds, Manchester, Bristol and East Midlands (2 or 3 weekly) and from Glasgow once a week.

Most **charter operators** offer very similar flight-only deals, either through their own websites or through package and specialist operators; prices from airports outside London are generally somewhat higher. In summer there are direct charters to Iráklio from several UK regional airports; the biggest operators are Thomson (Ⓦflights .thomson.co.uk; they also have flights to Haniá), Thomas Cook (Ⓦthomascookairlines.com) and Monarch (Ⓦmonarch.co.uk).

If you can't find a direct flight, want more flexibility or are travelling out of season, consider travelling **via Athens** (some flights are also routed via Thessaloníki), with a domestic flight or ferry from there to Crete. Scheduled flights include Aegean (Ⓦaegeanair.com) from Heathrow, Birmingham and Manchester to Athens; British Airways from Heathrow to Athens and Gatwick to Thessaloníki; easyJet from Gatwick, Manchester or Edinburgh to Athens and Gatwick or Manchester to Thessaloníki;

A BETTER KIND OF TRAVEL

At Rough Guides we are passionately committed to travel. We believe it helps us understand the world we live in and the people we share it with – and of course tourism is vital to many developing economies. But the scale of modern tourism has also damaged some places irreparably, and climate change is accelerated by most forms of transport, especially flying. All Rough Guides' flights are carbon-offset, and every year we donate money to a variety of environmental charities.

and Ryanair from Stansted to Athens. From Athens you will then have to arrange onward transport to Crete (see opposite).

From Dublin there are direct charters to Crete through the summer (rarely less than €400). Aer Lingus (**W** aerlingus.com) also flies direct to Athens (April–Sept, 3 weekly) with fares starting at around €115 each way, though you can easily pay twice that, or more. At other times of year you'll have to make at least one stop en route to Greece, in London or elsewhere.

Flights from the USA and Canada

Delta (**W** delta.com) operates **direct nonstop flights** from New York JFK to Athens, daily for most of the year, while American Airlines (**W** aa.com) fly daily from Philadelphia to Athens between May and October. Code-sharing airlines can quote through fares with one of the above, or a European partner, from **virtually every major US city**, connecting either at New York or a European hub such as London or Frankfurt. From Athens there are reasonably priced add-on flights to the islands (see opposite).

Fares vary greatly, so it's worth putting in a little time on the internet, or using a good travel agent; book as far ahead as possible to get the best price. Round-trip prices range from US$900 out of season to $1400 in high summer; from the west coast, expect to pay ten to twenty percent more. Remember too that you may be better off getting a domestic flight to New York or Philadelphia and heading directly to Athens from there, or flying to London (beware of changing airports) or another European city and travelling on from there.

As with the US, airfares **from Canada** vary depending on where you start your journey, and whether you take a direct service. Air Canada rouge (**W** flyrouge.com) flies to Athens out of Toronto three to five times weekly, and from Montreal two to four times weekly, between May and October. Air Transat (**W** airtransat.com) also has summer-only flights from Toronto (weekly) and Montreal (twice a week) to Athens. Otherwise you'll have to choose among one- or two-stop itineraries on a variety of European carriers, or perhaps Delta via New York; costs run from Can$1000 round trip in low season from Toronto to well over double that from Vancouver in high season.

For all of the above, a **connecting flight to Crete** will add US$75–150, depending on season and airline.

Flights from Australia and New Zealand

There are **no direct flights** from Australia or New Zealand to Greece; you'll have to change planes in Southeast Asia or Europe. Tickets bought direct from the airlines tend to be expensive; travel agents or Australia-based websites generally offer much better deals on fares and have the latest information on limited specials and stopovers. For a simple return fare, you may also have to buy an add-on internal flight to get you to the international departure point.

Fares **from Australia** start from around Aus$1200, rising to around Aus$2600 depending on season, routing, validity, number of stopovers, etc. The shortest flights and best fares are generally with airlines like Singapore (**W** singaporeair.com), Etihad (**W** etihadairways.com) and Emirates (**W** emirates.com), that can fly you directly to Athens from their Asian or Gulf hubs, though you'll also find offers on Swiss (**W** swiss.com), KLM (**W** klm.com) and other European carriers. **From New Zealand**, prices are slightly higher: from around NZ$1800, rising to over NZ$3000 in high season.

If Greece is only one stop on a longer journey, you might consider buying a **Round-the-World** (RTW) fare, although Greece never seems to be included in any of the cheaper deals, which means you might have to stump up over Aus$3000/NZ$3500 for one of the fully flexible multi-stop fares from One World or the Star Alliance. At that price, you may be better off with a cheaper deal and a separate ticket to Greece once you get to Europe.

Flights from South Africa

There are currently **no direct flights** from South Africa to Greece. Alternative routes include EgyptAir (**W** egyptair.com) via Cairo, Emirates (**W** emirates.com) or Etihad (**W** etihadairways.com) via the Gulf, or just about any of the major European airlines through their domestic hub. Prices start at around R7000 for a good low-season deal, to double that in high season or if the cheaper seats have gone.

Overland from the UK, Ireland and the rest of Europe

As a result of the economic crisis, **Greek rail routes** have been greatly reduced, and for a while all international services were suspended. Once you reach Crete there are no trains at all. However, that doesn't necessarily mean that you can't travel most of the way to Crete by **train**, provided you have three or four days to spare and accept that it will almost always work out more expensive than flying. Travelling by train offers the chance to stop over on the way; with an InterRail (for European residents only) or Eurail (for all others) pass you could take in Greece as part of a wider rail trip around Europe. The most practical route from Britain crosses France and Italy before embarking on the ferry from Bari or Brindisi to Pátra (see below). If you're determined to go all the way by train, there are a number of alternative routes across Europe to either Belgrade or Sofia, each of which has connections to Thessaloníki, from where you can get an onward train to Athens. Booking well in advance (essential in summer) and going for the cheapest seats on each leg, you can theoretically buy individual tickets to Iráklio for around £180/€250/$280 each way. Using rail passes will cost you more, but give far more flexibility. For full details, check out the Man in Seat Sixty-One website (Ⓦseat61.com).

Driving to Crete can also be worth considering if you want to explore en route or are going to stay for an extended period. The most popular **route** is again down through France and Italy to catch one of the Adriatic ferries. The much longer alternative through Eastern Europe only makes sense if you want to explore the Greek mainland on the way.

Once in **Italy**, regular car and passenger ferries link Venice, Ancona, Bari and Brindisi with Pátra (Patras, at the northwest tip of the Peloponnese). From here you can cut across country to Pireás for daily ferries to Crete, or head down through the Peloponnese to Kalamáta or Yíthio, from where there are a couple of weekly sailings to Kastélli in western Crete.

Internal flights to Crete

Flying to Crete **via Greece** doesn't necessarily mean going through Athens, although the vast majority of people do so. **From Athens** Aegean (Ⓦaegeanair .com), Ellinair (Ⓦellinair.com) and Sky Express (Ⓦwww.skyexpress.gr) between them offer at least eight flights a day to Iráklio in peak season, while Aegean and Ryanair (Ⓦryanair.com) operate six times daily to Haniá, and Astra (Ⓦastra-airlines.gr) flies daily to Sitía. Journey time is less than an hour, and flying is good value when weighed against a ferry trip: one-way **prices** start from around €40. There are also daily direct flights **from Thessaloníki** to both Iráklio and Haniá with Aegean, Astra, Ryanair and Ellinair, and direct services in summer from some of the larger islands, as well as connections from every regional Greek airport. Local operators Sky Express and Minoan Air (Ⓦminoanair.com) also serve various smaller islands.

Ferries to Crete

There are overnight services every day throughout the year from **Pireás** (the port of Athens) to Iráklio and Haniá, plus daytime services in summer and at other peak periods. There are also much slower ferries, once or twice a week, to Kastélli and Sitía. Much the most useful of the other services is that from the **Peloponnese**. The schedule is somewhat confusing and varies according to the season, but generally there's at least one departure a week from Yíthio and one from Kalamáta to Kastélli.

Ferries are operated by ANEK (Ⓦanek.gr; Iráklio, Haniá and Sitía), Minoan (Ⓦminoan.gr; Iráklio) and LANE (Ⓦlane.gr; Kastélli and the Peloponnese route); information on all the routes can also be found at Ⓦopenseas.gr and Ⓦferries.gr.

Pireás is about an hour from Athens airport by bus (#X96; at least 2 an hour, day and night; €5), or easily reached on the Metro from central Athens. A taxi from the airport will cost around €45. You can buy **tickets** online, or from dozens of agencies in Pireás or in central Athens, as well as from booths on the docks near the boats. If you're taking a car or want a cabin it's worth booking ahead, but deck-class tickets are always available on the spot.

These cheapest tickets give you the run of almost the entire boat, excluding the cabins, some reserved seating and the upper-class restaurant and bar. Most of the ferries serving Crete are modern and reasonably luxurious, with plenty of café and "pullman seating" areas inside, though often without a huge amount of deck space. If you are travelling deck class, it's worth getting on board reasonably early to claim a good space. Cabins are also available, ranging from four-berth, shared cabins inside (all en suite and perfectly adequate) up to deluxe suites with huge picture windows.

Prices are similar on all the routes: around €40 deck class, €65 for a berth in a basic cabin, and €90–110 per person in a luxurious double, with cars going for €85 and motorbikes for €20.

Agents and operators

Just about every mainstream **tour operator** includes Crete in its portfolio. You'll find far more interesting alternatives, however, through small **specialist agencies**. As well as traditional village-based accommodation, many of these offer **walking** or **nature holidays** and cater for other special interests such as **yoga**, **art**, **kayaking** or **cycling**.

PACKAGE OPERATORS

Hidden Greece UK ☎ 020 8758 4707, ⓦ hidden-greece.co.uk.
Specialist agent putting together tailor-made packages to smaller destinations at reasonable prices.

Homeric Tours US ☎ 1800 223 5570, ⓦ homerictours.com. Hotel packages, individual tours, escorted group tours (though none exclusively to Crete), and fly/drive deals. Good source of inexpensive flights.

Olympic Holidays UK ☎ 020 8492 6868, ⓦ olympicholidays.com. Huge package holiday company specializing in Greece; all standards from cheap-and-cheerful to five-star, and often a good source of last-minute bargains and cheap flights.

Sun Island Tours Australia ☎ 1300 665 673, ⓦ sunislandtours .com.au. Good choice of hotel-based package holidays.

Sunvil Holidays UK ☎ 020 8758 4758, ⓦ sunvil.co.uk. High-quality outfit offering a wide range of small hotels, apartments and villas in western Crete.

True Greece US ☎ 1 800 817 7098, ⓦ truegreece.com. Upmarket escorted travel and custom-made trips catering for special interests such as cooking.

VILLA AND APARTMENT HOLIDAYS

Cachet Travel UK ☎ 020 8847 8700, ⓦ cachet-travel.co.uk. Attractive range of villas and apartments right across the island, plus some boutique hotels.

CV Villas UK ☎ 020 3811 1854, ⓦ cvvillas.com. Upmarket villas, mainly in Eloúnda and Áyios Nikólaos.

Freelance Holidays UK ☎ 01789 297705, ⓦ freelance-holidays .co.uk. Good-value apartment and villa holidays across Crete, mostly in the west.

Greek Islands Club UK ☎ 020 8232 9780, ⓦ gicthevillacollection .com. Upmarket villas with private pools, in the west.

Pure Crete UK ☎ 01444 880 404, ⓦ purecrete.com. Village villas and characterful converted cottages and farmhouses in western Crete, plus walking, wildlife and other special-interest trips.

Simpson Travel UK ☎ 020 3797 1935, ⓦ simpsontravel.com. Classy villas, upmarket hotels and village hideaways.

WALKING AND WILDLIFE TOURS

ATG Oxford UK ☎ 01865 315678, ⓦ atg-oxford.co.uk. Pricey but high-quality guided walks in the White Mountains.

Inntravel UK ☎ 01653 617001, ⓦ inntravel.co.uk. Hotel-to-hotel and single-centre self-guided walking holidays; also some small rural hotels.

Jonathan's Tours ☎ 335 6233 8790, ⓦ jonathanstours.com. Family-run walking holidays with a highly experienced guide – English, but based in France.

Naturetrek UK ☎ 01962 733051, ⓦ naturetrek.co.uk. Spring and autumn botanical and bird-watching tours.

Ramblers Holidays UK ☎ 01707 331133, ⓦ ramblersholidays.co.uk. Big, specialist walking-holiday company with a number of options on Crete.

SPECIALIST, ACTIVITY AND PERSONAL DEVELOPMENT TOURS

Andante Travels UK ☎ 01722 713800, ⓦ andantetravels.co.uk. Minoan archeology tours with leading experts as guides.

Astra US ☎ 303 321 5403, ⓦ astragreece.com. Very personal, idiosyncratic, two-week tours led by veteran Hellenophile Thordis Simonsen.

Classic Adventures US ☎ 1 800 777 8090, ⓦ classicadventures.com. Twelve-day biking tours.

Freewheeling Adventures Canada & US ☎ 1 800 672 0775, ⓦ freewheeling.ca. Eight-day cycling tours, escorted or self-guided.

Northwest Passage US ☎ 1 800 RECREATE, ⓦ nwpassage.com. Excellent sea-kayaking and hiking "inn-to-inn" tours of Crete, plus climbing, art and yoga holidays.

Sportif UK ☎ 01273 844919, ⓦ sportif.travel. Windsurfing packages and instruction in Palékastro.

Yoga Plus UK ☎ 01582 724214, ⓦ yogaplus.co.uk. Ashtanga yoga courses in a remote part of the south.

Yoga Rocks UK ☎ 020 3286 2586, ⓦ yogaholidaysgreece.com. Yoga courses in Triópetra, an isolated south coast location.

Getting around

Crete is, on the whole, pretty easy to get around. The main towns and resorts along the north coast are linked by an excellent road and a fast and frequent bus service. Elsewhere the road network has been extensively upgraded, and most villages see at least one daily bus. However, if you're keen to escape the crowds and experience some of Crete's remoter beaches and spectacular mountain scenery, you'll need to get off the main roads; for at least some of your time it's worth considering renting some transport or setting out on foot – or better still, a combination of the two.

By bus

The only form of public transport on Crete, **buses** cover the island comprehensively. Modern, fast and efficient services run along the main north-coast road every hour or more, though off the major routes standards vary. The ones used primarily by tourists (to Omalós and Hóra Sfakíon for the Samariá Gorge, for example, or to Festós and Mátala) tend also to be modern and convenient. Those that cater mainly for locals are often older vehicles that run once daily as transport to market or school – into the provincial capital very early in the morning and back out to the village around lunchtime, which means they're of little use for day-trips. There are few places not accessible by bus, though, and if you combine buses with some walking you'll get about extremely cheaply, if not always especially quickly.

Buses on Crete are run by a consortium of companies jointly known as **KTEL**. That this is not one single company is most obvious in Iráklio where there are two separate bus terminals, serving different directions. On the whole, buses to a given village run from the provincial capital – Iráklio, Réthymno and Haniá, or in Lasíthi province from Áyios Nikólaos and Sitía. There are also a number of small-scale services that cross inter-provincial borders. Current **timetables** are generally available from bus stations and tourist offices or online at Ⓦ bus-service-crete .com; you can also find timetables, fares and online booking for the west (Réthymno and Haniá) on Ⓦ e-ktel.com, and for the east (Iráklio and Lasíthi, no online booking) at Ⓦ ktelherlas.gr.

Prices remain reasonable: each hop between the major north-coast towns – Iráklio to Réthymno or Áyios Nikólaos, for example, or Réthymno to Haniá – costs €7–8 one way.

By taxi or tour bus

Local **taxis** are exceptionally good value, at least as long as the meter is running or you've fixed a price in advance; from the airport in Iráklio to Hersónisos, for example, would be about €35, or the 90km from Haniá airport to Paleóhora around €95. Much of their business is long-distance, taking people to and from the villages around the main towns (at some city taxi ranks and all major airports, there's a printed list of prices to the most common destinations). If you want to visit somewhere where there's only one bus, or spend some time hiking and get a ride back, it's well worth arranging for a taxi to pick you up: four people together in a taxi will pay little more per person than on the bus.

It's also quite easy to negotiate a day or half-day **sightseeing** by taxi, although this may require some Greek, and over long distances can become expensive. A simpler alternative for a one-off visit is to take a **bus tour**. Travel agents everywhere offer the obvious ones – the Samariá Gorge or Vái beach – and a few offer more adventurous alternatives: some of the best of these are detailed in the Guide.

By car or motorbike

Renting a **car** or **bike** (or bringing your own), will give you a huge amount of extra freedom to explore and to check out mountain villages and isolated beaches. Most people seem to do this for at least part of their stay, and there are numerous operators in every resort, the vast majority of them offering modern, reliable vehicles and competitive rates.

Do take the time, however, to check out any vehicle carefully before driving off. More importantly, take care while driving, as Greece has a very high **accident rate** compared with Northern Europe or North America. This is in part due to the state of the roads and the nature of the countryside: although many minor roads have been upgraded in recent years, they are still mountainous and winding, and you'll frequently pass without warning from a smooth, modern surface to a stretch of potholed track. Signage is also poor in many places, and road traffic rules often ignored. On the main north-coast highway – an excellent road for the most part – you're expected to drive with at least two wheels on the hard shoulder to allow faster vehicles to overtake.

Fuel costs are broadly similar to the UK, with regular unleaded (*amólyvdhi*) currently around €1.70 per litre on the north coast, but often €1.90-plus in more remote areas; diesel is a little cheaper. It's easy to run out after dark or at weekends, especially in the extreme east and west of the island; most rural stations close at 7 or 8pm and some shut at weekends. When touring in these areas it's wise to maintain a full tank, especially when a weekend or national holiday is approaching.

Rules of the road

EU **driving licences** are valid in Crete, and in practice you can rent a vehicle with almost any valid national licence; however, non-EU drivers are legally required to have an International Driving Permit (acquired before leaving home through organizations such as the AAA; Ⓦ aaa.com), and the lack of one could cause problems should you have a run-in with the police. It is compulsory to wear **seat belts**, and for motorcyclists to wear **helmets**, and children under the age of 10 are not allowed to sit in the front seats of cars. There has also been a major crackdown on **drink driving** in recent years, with random checks and roadblocks especially designed to catch clubbers heading home in the early hours of the morning around major towns and resorts. **Parking** can also be a headache, especially in the big towns, where it's rarely obvious where you are and are not allowed to park, or how to pay when you do so.

If you are involved in any kind of **accident** it's illegal to drive away, and you can theoretically be held at a police station for up to 24 hours. If this happens, ring your consulate immediately to get a lawyer, and don't make a statement to anyone who doesn't speak, and write, very good English. **On-the-spot fines** can be issued for minor traffic infringements such as speeding or crossing a central

SIX SCENIC DRIVES

The Far West A circuit from Kastélli Kissámou, down the west coast and back on the inland roads via Élos offers a bit of everything: stunning coastal vistas, traditional villages, mountains and gorges. See p.297

North to South West of Réthymno, a choice of roads crosses the island towards Frangokástello and Plakiás, each more spectacular than the next. See p.228

Amári Valley and Psiloritis Heading southeast from Réthymno, the Arkádhi monastery marks the entry to the Amári valley, whose east side, especially, offers glorious mountain scenery. See p.210

Iráklio to Réthymno Take the old road via Anóyia for a complete contrast to the coastal highway, or combine with the Amári route for a total circumnavigation of Crete's highest mountain. See p.80

Lasíthi plateau Beautiful, however you approach it: try a complete circuit, climbing up from the north coast and back through Neápolis. See p.140

The far east Barren and lonely: from Sitía, head east to Vái beach, south through Zákros and Xerókambos, then back on the inland road via Zíros. See p.160

double white line; from around €50 to €200 depending on the gravity of the offence. The address on the ticket will detail the office in the nearest town to which you should go to pay the fine.

Car rental

Car rental starts at around €35 a day or €200 a week in high season for the smallest model, including unlimited mileage, tax and insurance; outside peak season, prices drop by about 25 percent. An open-top jeep or a van will cost up to three times as much; jeeps can be fun, but there's little point going for a fancy vehicle – you'll rarely get a chance to drive at great speed, and small cars are an advantage when parking or negotiating narrow village streets.

Many package holidays will include a car, and if not there's a great deal to be said for organizing your rental in advance, when you may well get a much better deal. If you go for a Cretan company, pick one that is local to where you intend to head or, if you're touring around, one that has offices around the island to ensure that there's help available should you need it.

All agencies will require a blank **credit card** slip as a deposit (destroyed when you return the vehicle safely); minimum **age requirements** vary from 21 to 25. Be sure to check that full insurance and a **collision damage waiver** is included (or take out a separate car hire excess insurance in advance, generally far cheaper) and note that damage to tyres and the underside of the vehicle is usually excluded from the insurance, so take care on bumpy dirt roads.

Motorbikes and mopeds

Motorbikes, **mopeds**, **scooters** and **quad bikes** are also widely available to rent in Crete, at prices starting around €20 a day (€120/week) for a 50cc

moped, and €30 a day (€190/week) for a 200cc trail bike. Reputable establishments demand a full motorcycle driving licence for any engine over 80cc, and you will usually have to leave your passport (sometimes a valid credit card is acceptable) as security. For smaller models any driving licence will do.

The smaller bikes and scooters are ideal for pottering around for a day or two, but don't regard them as serious transport: Crete is very mountainous and the mopeds simply won't go up some of the steeper hills, even carrying only one person. Be sure not to run beyond the range of your petrol tank either, as they're not designed for long-distance travel and there are few filling stations outside the towns. For serious exploration, or to venture into the mountains, you really need a motorbike or a more powerful scooter.

Although motorbikes are enormous fun to ride around, you need to take more than usual care: there's an alarming number of **accidents** each year among visitors and locals because basic safety procedures are not followed. It's only too easy to come to grief on a potholed road or steep dirt track, especially at night. You should never rent a bike that you feel you can't handle, and always use a **helmet** (a legal requirement), despite the fact that many locals don't. Quite apart from any injuries, you're likely to be charged a criminally high price for any repairs needed for the bike, so make sure that you are adequately **insured**. Note that some travel insurance policies specifically exclude injuries sustained while riding/driving a rented vehicle.

CAR RENTAL AGENCIES IN CRETE

Alianthos ☎ 28320 32033, ⊛ alianthos-group.com. Cars and bikes, with offices at the airports and across western Crete.

Blue Sea ☎ 2810 221 215, **ⓦ** bluesearentals.com. Cars and bikes in Iráklio and elsewhere.

Clubcars ☎ 28410 25868, **ⓦ** clubcars.net. Áyios Nikólaos, Iráklio airport and other locations in the east.

Kosmos ☎ 2810 241 357, **ⓦ** cosmos-sa.gr. Iráklio, Réthymno, Haniá, Áyios Nikólaos.

Motor Club ☎ 2810 222 408, **ⓦ** motorclub.gr. Cars and bikes in Iráklio and resort locations.

Olympic ☎ 2810 220 678, **ⓦ** olympic-carhire.com. Inexpensive battered but serviceable cars in Iráklio, Réthymno and Haniá (off-airport sites).

Walking, cycling and local boats

The idea of **walking** for pleasure is a recent one in Crete, but there are plenty of opportunities for visitors. Choices range from local strolls inland from almost any resort to organized tours through the Samariá Gorge and the challenging E4 trans-European footpath, which crosses the island from west to east. If you have the time and stamina, walking is probably the single best way to see the island. There are suggestions for hikes, from easy strolls to serious climbing, throughout the Guide: check out, too, our list of specialist walking-tour operators (see p.24).

Cycling

The popularity of **cycling** is growing rapidly in Crete – **mountain bikes** can be rented in most resorts of any size, and many of the rental places offer organized local excursions. Any significant distance, however, generally involves steeply mountainous terrain and, in summer, fierce heat. Even so, provided you're reasonably fit, riding a bike offers an incomparable view of the island and guarantees contact with locals whom the average visitor could never meet. A number of companies offer tours involving group exploration of the island by bike (see p.24). If you're really keen you can bring your own bike by plane (it's normally free within your ordinary baggage allowance) or by sea if you're coming from Italy or Athens (in which case it should go free on the ferry).

Boats and local ferries

Around the island numerous **local ferry services** run to offshore islets and isolated beaches; these are detailed throughout the Guide. Where there is no ferry service you can often arrange a trip with local fishermen. Asking at the bar in the nearest fishing village will usually turn up someone willing to make the trip. Some adventure travel operators (see p.24) offer tours around the coast by **sea kayak**.

Accommodation

There are vast numbers of beds available for tourists in Crete, and most of the year you can rely on turning up pretty much anywhere and finding something. At Easter and in July and August, however, you can run into problems unless you've booked in advance, especially in the more popular resorts and cities.

The big **hotels** and self-catering complexes in the larger resorts are often pre-booked by package-holiday companies for the whole season. Although they may have vacancies if you just turn up, non-package visitors are far more likely to find themselves staying in smaller, simpler places which usually describe themselves simply as "**rooms**", or as apartments or studios. Standards here can vary from spartan (though invariably clean) to luxurious, but the vast majority are purpose-built blocks where every room is en suite, and where the minimal furnishings are well adapted to the local climate – at least in summer.

Single rooms are rare, and generally poor value – you'll often have to pay the full double-room price or haggle for around a third off; on the other hand, larger groups and **families** can almost always find triple and quadruple rooms or two-bedroom apartments, and fancier hotels may have family **suites** (two rooms sharing one bathroom), all of which can be very good value.

Hotels

The tourist police set official **star categories** for hotels, from five-star down; all except the top category have to keep within set price limits. You may still see the old letter system (L, luxury, is five-star, then

---

ACCOMMODATION PRICES AND SEASONS

There are typically three **seasons** that affect accommodation prices in Crete: October to April (low), May, June and September (mid) and July and August (high) – though Easter and the first two weeks of August may be in a higher category still.

The prices we quote in our accommodation reviews are for the establishment's **cheapest double room in mid-season** – there may well be other rooms that cost more.

A to E). Ratings correspond to the facilities available (lifts, dining room, pool etc), a box-ticking exercise which doesn't always reflect the actual quality of the hotel; there are plenty of 2-star hotels which are in practice smarter and more comfortable than nearby 3-star outfits. A new "boutique" category does allow some hotels to escape the straitjacket on the grounds of location or historical significance.

2-star hotels and below have only to provide the most rudimentary of continental **breakfasts** – sometimes optional for an extra charge – while 3-star and above will usually offer a buffet breakfast including cheese, cold meats, eggs and cereals.

Rooms and apartments

Many places categorized as apartments or rooms are every bit as comfortable as hotels, and in the lower price ranges are usually more congenial and better value. At their most basic, **rooms** (*dhomátia* – but usually spotted by a "Rooms for Rent" or *Zimmer Frei* sign) might be literally a room in someone's house, a bare space with a bed and a hook on the back of the door, and washing facilities outside. However, these days almost all are purpose-built, with comfortable en-suite accommodation and balconies; at the fancier end of the scale you'll find studio and apartment complexes with marble floors, pools, bars and children's playgrounds. Many have a variety of rooms at different prices, so if possible always ask to see the room first. Places described as **studios** usually have a small **kitchenette** – a fridge, sink and a couple of hotplates in the room itself – while **apartments** generally have at least one bedroom and separate kitchen/living room.

Rooms proprietors usually ask to keep your **passport**: ostensibly "for the tourist police", but in reality to prevent you leaving with an unpaid bill. Some may be satisfied with just taking down the

---

AIR CONDITIONING AND WI-FI

Almost all modern rooms and apartments have **air conditioning** (indicated by a/c in our listings), but it's sometimes an optional extra and you'll be charged an additional €5 or so a night for the remote so you can use it. **Wi-fi** is ubiquitous, and even the most basic places tend to have it; there's very rarely a charge (you're more likely to be charged extra, ironically, in more expensive hotels), but the signal may not extend to the rooms (or if it does, not to every room), and it's often pretty slow.

---

details, and they'll almost always return the documents once you get to know them. In the larger resorts, though, the only way to keep hold of your passport may be to pay in advance.

Villas and longer-term stays

Although one of the great dreams of Greek travel is finding an idyllic coastal **villa** and renting it for virtually nothing for a whole month, there's no chance at all of your dream coming true in modern Crete. All the best villas are contracted out to agents and let through foreign operators. Even if you do find one empty for a week or two, renting it in Crete usually costs far more than it would have done to arrange from home. Specialist operators (see p.24) represent some superb places, from simple to luxurious, and costs can be very reasonable, especially if shared between a few people.

Having said that, if you do arrive and decide you want to drop roots for a while, you can still strike lucky if you don't mind avoiding the coast, and are happy with relatively modest accommodation. Pick an untouristed inland village, get yourself known and ask about; you might still pick up a wonderful deal. Out of season your chances are much better – even in touristy areas, between October and March (sometimes as late as April and May) you can bargain a very good rate, especially for stays of a month or more. Travel agents are another good source of information on what's available locally, and many rooms places have an apartment on the side or know someone with one to rent.

Youth hostels

There are just four unaffiliated **youth hostels** on Crete, all of which must be among the least strictly run in the world. Long-standing hostels survive in Iráklio, Réthymno and Plakiás – the last two particularly good – and there's a new backpacker-style place in Haniá. Facilities are basic – you pay around €10 a night for a dormitory bed (twice that in Haniá) on which to spread your sleeping bag – but they offer cheap meals, kitchen facilities, a good social life and an excellent grapevine for finding work or travelling companions.

Camping

There are about fifteen official **campsites** in Crete – see ⓦwww.greececamping.gr for a list – and on the whole they're not very comfortable, tending to be dominated by camper vans and with very

SIX GREAT ESCAPES

Looking to get away from it all and escape the crowds? Look no further:

Akrogiali, Líkkos Rooms on the beach, accessed by boat. See p.283
Liviko View, Xerókambos Comfortable rooms in the island's empty and isolated far east. See p.174
Miliá Eco Village Abandoned mountain hamlet restored as lovely, candle-lit accommodation. See p.306
Moní Koudhoumá This remote seaside

monastery welcomes pilgrims and gives them a bed. See p.118
Vailakakis, Sarakiníko, Gávdhos The island of Gávdhos is about as far off the grid as you can hope to get in Europe. See p.322
Vilaeti Traditional Guesthouses, Áyios Konstantínos Night-time on the Lasíthi plateau is magical: a taste of timeless mountain Crete. See p.144

hard earth. Several do have spectacular seafront locations, though. Prices start at around €5/night per person, but they mount up once you've added a charge for a tent (generally about €3.50 for a two-person model or €5 for something larger), and the same again for a vehicle and for everyone in your group – you're looking at €18–25 a night for two people, tent and vehicle in high season.

Camping outside an official campsite (with or without a tent) is against the law – enforced in most tourist areas and on beaches. Nevertheless, with discretion and sensitivity it can still be done: the police crack down on people camping rough on (and littering) popular mainstream tourist beaches, but there are still places on the south and west coasts where the practice is fairly common.

From May until early September it's warm enough to **sleep out** in just a lightweight sleeping bag (though the nights can be chilly in mountainous zones). A waterproof bag or groundsheet is useful to keep out the late summer damp, and a foam pad lets you sleep in relative comfort almost anywhere.

Food and drink

Cretans spend a lot of time socializing outside their homes, and sharing a meal is one of the chief ways of doing it. The atmosphere is invariably relaxed and informal, with pretensions and expense-account prices rare outside the fancier hotels. Greeks are not prodigious drinkers – tippling is traditionally meant to accompany food – though there are plenty of bars in the tourist resorts and you can always get a beer, a glass of wine or an ouzo at a café.

The **food** in Crete may be simple, but at its best it is magnificent – vibrantly flavoured with the herbs that scent the countryside. Organic production,

local sourcing and foraging for ingredients are not fads or recent developments here, but central to the way people have always eaten; most Cretans have access to a smallholding of some kind, or if not to local markets where the island's superb agricultural produce is sold. In the better tavernas, the bulk of the produce used will be fresh, local and naturally organic. There's a **food and drink glossary** in our Contexts section (see p.359).

Breakfast, fast food and snacks

Greeks generally don't eat much in the way of **breakfast**, more often opting for a mid-morning snack from the bakery. Some of the best rooms places will serve up fresh fruit and yoghurt, eggs straight from the hen and home-made breads and pastries; more often, though, "continental" breakfast consists of cardboard-flavoured orange squash, stewed coffee, processed cheese and meats, plus pre-packaged butter, honey and jam (confusingly called *marmeládha*). In the resorts, there are plenty of places offering bacon and eggs too.

Picnics and snacks

Picnic ingredients are easily available at supermarkets, bakeries and greengrocers, most of which open early. Yoghurt, bread, eggs, fruit, cheese, salami, olives and tomatoes are always easy to buy. Note that Greek **cheese** isn't all feta (salty white sheep's cheese); tasty local varieties include creamy *mizíthra*, *káskavali*, *kritiko* and *graviéra*; the last – a peppery, mature, full-fat sheep's cheese – is particularly good.

At **bakeries**, you'll find oven-warm flaky pies filled with cheese (*tyrópita*), spinach (*spanakópita*), wild greens or sausage or, better still, stuffed with creamy cheese and sprinkled with icing sugar and cinnamon (*bougátsa*). In the tourist areas many bakeries also cater for northern European palates by turning out croissants, doughnuts and even wholemeal and rye breads.

OLIVE OIL AND THE CRETAN DIET

Great claims are made for the **Cretan diet** – comparative studies have shown that the island has (or had) one of the longest-lived and least diseased populations in the world – and any local will be happy to lecture you on the life-enhancing properties of good **olive oil** (plus a little wine or *rakí* in moderation). As increasing amounts of meat and dairy produce are added to the everyday diet, the health benefits are falling away, but with plentiful locally produced olive oil, cereals, and sun-ripened vegetables and fruit, this still feels like a very healthy place to eat.

Ubiquitous **fast-food** snacks include **souvláki** – small kebabs on wooden sticks, which as *píta-souvláki* are served stuffed into a doughy bread (more like Indian naan than pitta bread) along with salad and yoghurt – and, even better, doner-kebab-like **yíros píta**. You'll also find places serving **pizza** (usually excellent at specialist places and awful in tavernas) and **tost** (bland ham-and-cheese toasties).

Seasonal **fruits** are exceptionally inexpensive. Look out for what's on offer in the markets or by the roadside: cherries in spring; melons, watermelons, plums and apricots in summer; pears and apples in autumn; oranges and grapes most of the time. They even grow small bananas in the area around Mália – an endeavour heavily subsidized by the EU.

Tavernas and restaurants

Most Cretan restaurants describe themselves as **tavernas**, though you can also get a meal at an *estiatório* or a *psistariá* as well as in ouzerís and many others. **Estiatória** are very similar to tavernas but specialize in the baked dishes known as *mayireftá* (see opposite) and tend to be simpler, less expensive, and perhaps more traditionally Greek. **Psistariés** are restaurants that offer grilled or spit-roasted meat, usually over charcoal. A **psarótaverna** is a taverna that specializes in fish. **Ouzerís** are bars specializing in ouzo and mezédhes; a *rakádhika*, very fashionable these days, is the equivalent, but serving *rakí*. They are well worth trying for the marvellous variety of **mezédhes** (small plates of food) they serve, although the most authentic are to be found in the larger towns where there's a local customer base to keep them on their toes. At the better places several plates of mezédhes will effectively substitute for a meal (though it may not work out any cheaper if you have a healthy appetite, and mezédhes are also served at many tavernas). Wherever you eat, chic appearance is not a good guide to quality; often the most basic place will turn out to be the best, and in swankier restaurants you may well be paying for the linen and stemmed wineglasses.

Sometimes at traditional tavernas and *estiatória* there's no menu and you're taken into the **kitchen** to inspect what's on offer: uncooked cuts of meat and fish, simmering pots of stews or vegetables, trays of baked foods. Even where there is a **menu** (usually in English as well as Greek) it's often a standard printed form that bears little relation to what is actually on offer: again, check the kitchen or display case.

A basic taverna meal with house wine or beer will **cost** around €12–20 per person. Add a better bottle of wine, seafood or more careful cooking, and it could be €20–30 a head; you'll rarely pay more than that. If you're unsure about the **price** of something, ask before ordering since it always seems to turn out more expensive if you wait until after you've eaten. Fish is almost always priced by weight (see opposite). There's always a small **cover charge** (€0.50–1 per person), which includes the bread you'll inevitably be given.

Greek dishes and Cretan specialities

As Cretan restaurants increasingly adapt themselves to tourists, you'll find that some of the advice below no longer applies in the resorts, where you're more likely to get western European-style service (places

---

TAVERNA TIPS AND HOURS

Cretans generally eat late: **lunch** is served at around 2–3pm, **dinner** at 9–11pm. You can eat earlier than this, but you're likely to get indifferent service at a tourist establishment or find yourself eating alone everywhere else. If you can't wait that long, do what the locals do: take an aperitif along with a few mezédhes.

The **opening hours** we quote in our reviews throughout the Guide should be taken as indicative rather than set in stone; if you want to sit talking and drinking till the early hours (as many locals do), you'll rarely be thrown out. And if the proprietor has been up till 3am, it's no surprise if he should choose to open a little later than usual the next day.

Prices are supposedly inclusive of all taxes and service, but an extra **tip** of around five percent or simple rounding up of the bill is always welcome.

much patronized by the French, for example, offer fixed-price set menus). On the other hand, the better tavernas have started to recognize the value of their culture and serve more consciously **traditional foods** in traditional ways.

A typical Greek meal consists of shared salads and appetizers (often in the form of **mezédhes**) and a main meat or fish dish. They may be brought to the table at much the same time as there's no strict concept of courses – if you want the main course later, stagger your ordering.

Salads and vegetables are traditionally served as the first course and usually shared. If you ask for salad you'll invariably be brought *horiátiki saláta* – the so-called **Greek salad**, including feta cheese: wonderful as it is there are plenty of cheaper alternatives without cheese. Vegetable dishes are often very good in themselves and, if you order a few between several people, can make a satisfying meal. The **main dish** of meat or fish generally comes on its own except for maybe a piece of lemon or half a dozen chips (fries); lamb (or better still goat if it's available) is usually the best meat, local and excellent, if a little pricier than the alternatives. Check out the kitchen for **oven-baked dishes** (*mayireftá*, such as *moussaká*, *pastítsio* (macaroni pie), meat or game stews, *yemistá* (stuffed tomatoes or peppers), the oily vegetable casseroles called *ladherá*, and oven-baked meat and fish), which are generally delicious and less expensive than straight meat or fish dishes.

Traditionally, restaurants didn't serve much in the way of **dessert** – the Greek practice is to visit a *zaharoplastío* for pastries, coffee and liqueurs once the main meal is over – but these days more often than not you'll be offered something on the house: fresh fruit, halva or báklava, often accompanied by a phial of *rakí*.

In season, **fish** is varied and delicious, but in summer visitors get a relatively restricted choice as local trawling is prohibited from June to September. It is also relatively expensive: if the prices on the menu seem phenomenally high, that's generally because they are **per kilo**; €50 a kilo will work out at €15 or so

FABULOUS RURAL TAVERNAS
The best food is often found off the beaten track.
Kafenío Sto Scolio Anídhri. See p.314
Piperia Pefkí. See p.178
Taverna Plateia Mírthios. See p.224
Taverna Tzitzifia Tzitzifés. See p.259
Taverna Vilaeti Áyios Konstantínos. See p.144
Vegera Zarós. See p.99

a head. Most tavernas will encourage you to go into the kitchen to see what's available and when you've selected your fish they'll weigh it to determine the actual price (a larger fish, shared between two or more, is generally tastier and better value; don't leave it to the waiter to choose, or you may well get the biggest). Cheaper, tasty alternatives are small **sardine** or whitebait-style fish, eaten whole, fish soups and stews, and **squid**, octopus and shellfish.

Traditional **Cretan specialities** increasingly find their way onto menus too: some of the more common among dozens of typical dishes are snails and rabbit, both often served stewed with onions. Look out too for savoury stuffed pastries. Another speciality you shouldn't miss if you get a chance is *hórta* – the wild greens that grow in abundance on the Cretan hills. These are gathered and boiled to be served up lukewarm (or sometimes cold), dressed with olive oil and vinegar, and can be delicious – or at the very least good for you. Although you can eat them all year round, spring and autumn are the best times, when they grow vigorously in the damper climate.

Cafés and bars

The traditional Cretan coffee shop – the **kafenío** – filled with old men arguing and playing *távli* (backgammon, a national obsession; most places will lend you a set) is still found in every village, though

VEGETARIANS
Although there are scarcely any vegetarian restaurants, **vegetarians** can eat extremely well in Crete. Quite apart from the fact that meals based on eggs, pizza or pasta are available in all the towns and resorts, as are traditional snacks like *tyrópita*, the increased interest in local cuisine, as well as pressure from tourists, has seen far more vegetable dishes appear on local menus. Many mezédhes like tzatziki, *dolmádhes* (stuffed vine leaves) and *yígandes* (large haricot beans in tomato sauce) are naturally meat-free; you'll find excellent salads everywhere; *yemistá* (stuffed vegetables) are usually meat-free; and there are frequently vegetable-baked dishes including ratatouille-like *briám*, *imám bayaldí* (stuffed aubergine/eggplant) and *bouréki* (potato, courgette/zucchini and cheese bake) on the menu.

RAKÍ – A SHOT OF HOSPITALITY

Rakí, also known in Crete as *tsikoudhiá*, holds a special place in the Cretan heart, and is central to traditional Cretan hospitality. No matter the time of day, if you're invited into a Cretan home you'll be presented with a glass of water, a morsel of cheese or a home-made sweet, and a shot of *rakí*, the local firewater. Many tavernas will offer you a shot after your meal, too, though this may be a more commercial (and hangover-inducing) product. Distilled from grape must – the leftovers from winemaking – the real stuff is home-made in hundreds of tiny stills (and a few bigger, communal ones) in villages the length of the island. Each is unique – Cretans pride themselves on being able to detect the most subtle distinctions in taste and quality – all are fiercely potent, and the best have a wonderfully clean yet fiery effect. Accept it if you can; quite apart from the danger of causing offence if you refuse, you'll rarely regret saying yes – and this is a gesture of welcome that still marks Crete out as a uniquely hospitable place.

increasingly beleaguered under the onslaught of global mass culture. In the towns and resorts its place has largely been taken over by modern **cafés** and elegant **patisseries** (*zaharoplastía*).

Actual **bars** are rare except in the bigger resorts, but you can get a beer or glass of wine at almost any time in any café or taverna, and the modern cafés that proliferate in the major towns and cities generally become bars by night.

Coffee and kafenía

Traditional Greek **coffee** is what most Westerners would call "Turkish", tiny cups filled with a thick, black, heady concoction. It makes a great start to the day or a pick-me-up later – once you've acquired the taste and learned to leave the grounds behind in the cup. Most Cretans drink it medium-sweet or *métrio*; if you want no sugar at all, ask for *skéto*, while *glykó* is very sweet indeed. If you want Greek coffee, ask for a *kafé ellinikós* – many Cretan *kafenío* proprietors assume foreigners will want ordinary coffee (usually instant), so by choosing it you'll rise greatly in their estimation. *Kafenía* also serve ouzo, brandy, beer, various teas (*tsái*), soft drinks and juices. Some close at siesta time, but many remain open from early in the morning until late at night.

Cappuccino and other coffees, including iced *freddoccino*, are rarely available at *kafenía*, but are of course the staple of more modern cafés. The universal drink of young Greece, however, is **frappé**. This is simply instant coffee powder, ice and water, whizzed to a froth and served with a glass of cold water: but it is infinitely better than that makes it sound, and the quintessential taste of a Greek summer. Again, you can have it *skéto*, *métrio* or *glykó* and with milk (*me gála*) or without.

Ouzo and rakí

In a *kafenío* or ouzerí, the prime time for an **ouzo** is 6–8pm, before dinner and after the afternoon nap. Ouzo, an aniseed-flavoured spirit, is served by the glass or *karafáki* (a 200ml vial or miniature bottle); add water or ice to taste, and watch the clear liquid turn cloudy white. Traditionally every ouzo was automatically accompanied by a small plate of *mezédhes* on the house – cheese, cucumber, tomato, a few olives, sometimes octopus or a couple of small fish – and this is a tradition that has made a welcome comeback; if you want something more substantial, you can always order more. **Rakí** (see box above) is a burningly strong, flavourless spirit, usually consumed as a digestif.

Wine

Wine is the usual accompaniment to a meal in a restaurant or taverna. If you don't specify what you want, you'll be served the **house wine**, traditionally poured cold from the barrel into tin jugs (*kantária*) or carafes in either kilo (litre), half- or quarter-kilo measures. Often the wine is home-made and a source of great pride: this can be excellent, it's invariably interesting and it's always inexpensive. Increasingly, though, it is likely to be from a wine box or barrel produced by one of the big co-ops, and is almost always more than drinkable – which is more than can be said for the few bottles of overpriced wine stored on a hot, dusty shelf in the average taverna. If you want to taste the house wine before committing yourself to a *karáfa*, this should never be a problem.

Retsína is also produced locally, and always available. This resinated wine, which usually comes in half-litre bottles, is an acquired taste, but some varieties are extremely good (particularly those produced by the Central Union of Haniá Wine Producers). It's also exceptionally cheap: a half-litre generally costs less than €1 in the supermarket, much the same as a half-litre of beer.

CRETAN WINE

With the increase in tourism and a new breed of fancier restaurants has come a demand for a more polished product, and Cretan viniculture is developing rapidly; increasing numbers of vineyards even offer tastings (see p.74 and ⓦ winesofcrete.gr). **Cretan wines** come in many varieties; the hot, dry summers are more suited to producing dry red wines – dark and powerful – than whites. Six traditional grape varieties thrive on the island – *kotsifáli, thrapsathíri, liátiko, mandilariá, roméiko* and *vilána* – and there are four appellation wine-growing areas: Pezá, Dafnés, Sitía and Arhánes, the last still using some vineyards cultivated by the Minoans almost four thousand years ago.

Pezá brands like Minos red and white, which you can get everywhere, are generally palatable if rather boring. The **Arhánes** wine region also produces some pretty good red and white vintages, most notably by a co-operative that sells its wines under the Arhánes brand name. The **Sitian** wines Topiko (medium-dry with a hint of sherry) and Myrtos are both good everyday whites to drink with seafood. In the west, Kissamos red is another good bet. But the really interesting wines come from a proliferation of **smaller, boutique producers**: look out for names including Lyrarakis, Miliarakis (the Minos boutique range) and Michalakis from the Pezá region; Dafnés producer Douloufakis; Economou from Zíros in the far east; or in the west, Manousakis, near Vrísses, and Karavitakis, from the Kolymbári region.

The media

Greeks are great devourers of newsprint – although few would propose the Greek mass media as a paradigm of objective journalism. Papers are almost uniformly sensational, while state-run TV and radio are often biased in favour of whichever party happens to be in government. Foreign news is easily available in the form of locally printed newspaper editions and TV news channels.

Newspapers

British newspapers are widely available in resorts and the larger towns at a cost of €2–4 for dailies, or €4–6 for Sunday editions. Many, including the *Guardian*, *Times*, *Mail* and *Mirror*, have slimmed-down editions printed in Greece available the same day; others are likely to be a day old. The *International Herald Tribune*, which has the bonus of including an abridged English edition of the same day's *Kathimerini*, a respected Greek daily, is also sold widely, and in bigger newsagents you'll also be able to find *USA Today* and *Time*.

Radio

Crete's airwaves are cluttered with **local stations**, many of which have plenty of music, often traditional. In resort areas some have news bulletins and tourist information in English. The mountainous nature of much of the island,

though, means that any sort of radio reception is tricky: if you're driving around you'll find that you constantly have to retune. The two state-run networks are ER1 (a mix of news, talk and pop music) and ER2 (pop music).

The BBC World Service no longer broadcasts to Europe on short wave, though Voice of America can be picked up in places. Both of these and dozens of others are of course available as internet broadcasts, however, or via satellite TV channels.

Television

Even if your hotel advertises **satellite TV**, the only English-language channels usually included are CNN and BBC World. However, most evenings you'll find English-language films and mini-series, with subtitles, on at least a couple of the main Greek channels.

MOVIES

Cretan **cinemas** show the regular major release movies, which in the case of English-language titles will almost always be in English with Greek subtitles. In summer, **open-air screens** operate in all the major towns and some of the resorts, and these are absolutely wonderful. You may not hear much, thanks to crackly speakers and locals chatting away throughout, but watching a movie under the stars on a warm night is simply a great experience.

Festivals and cultural events

Most of the big Greek popular festivals have a religious origin, so they're observed in accordance with the Greek Orthodox calendar. This means that Easter, for example, can fall as much as three weeks to either side of the Western festival.

On top of the main religious festivals, there are scores of local fiestas, or **paniyíria**, celebrating the patron saint of the village church. Some of the more important are listed below; the *paramoní*, or **eve of the festival**, is often as significant as the day itself, and many of the events are actually celebrated on the night before. If you show up on the morning of the date given you may find that you have missed most of the music, dancing and drinking. With some 330-odd possible saints' days you're unlikely to travel for long without stumbling on something. Local tourist offices should be able to fill you in on events in their area. Twelve **public holidays** are dotted through the year (see box, p.41), during which banks and many shops and businesses close.

Easter

Easter is by far the most important festival of the Greek year. It is an excellent time to be in Crete, both for the beautiful and moving religious ceremonies and for the days of feasting and celebration that follow. If you make for a smallish village, you may well find yourself an honorary member for the period of the festival. This is a busy time for Greek tourists as well as international ones, though, so book ahead.

The first great ceremony takes place on **Good Friday** evening as the Descent from the Cross is lamented in church. At dusk, the *Epitáfios*, Christ's funeral bier, lavishly decorated by the women of the parish, leaves the sanctuary and is paraded

solemnly through the streets. **Late Saturday** evening sees the climax in a majestic mass to celebrate Christ's triumphant return. At the stroke of midnight all the lights in each crowded church are extinguished and the congregation plunged into darkness until the priest appears, holding aloft a taper to light the candles of the nearest worshippers. The flame is passed from person to person until the entire church – and the outer courtyard, standing room only for latecomers – is ablaze with burning candles. These are carried home through the streets and are said to bring good fortune to the house if they arrive still alight.

The lighting of the flames is the signal for celebrations to start, the Lent fast to be broken and, in many Cretan villages, for effigies of Judas to be burned. The traditional greeting, as fireworks and dynamite explode all around you in the street, is *Khristós Anésti* ("Christ is risen"), to which the response is *Alithós Anésti* ("Truly He is risen"). On **Easter Sunday** there's feasting on roast lamb.

The Greek equivalent of **Easter eggs** are hard-boiled eggs (painted red on Holy Thursday), which are baked into twisted, sweet bread-loaves (*tsourékia*) or distributed on Easter Sunday. People rap their eggs against their friends' eggs, and the owner of the last uncracked egg is considered lucky.

JANUARY

Jan 1: New Year's Day Also celebrated as the Feast of St Basil.
Jan 6: Epiphany Marks the baptism of Jesus and the end of the twelve days of Christmas. Baptismal fonts, lakes, rivers and seas are blessed, especially harbours, where the priest traditionally casts a crucifix into the water, with local youths competing to recover it.

FEBRUARY & MARCH

Carnival (Apokriátika) Festivities span three weeks, climaxing during the seventh weekend before Easter; big in Kalíves, Haniá and Réthymno.
Clean Monday (Katbará Dheftéra) The beginning of Lent, 7 weeks before Easter, is a traditional time to fly kites and to feast on all the things that will be forbidden over the coming weeks.

EASTER'S HOLY FLAME – A PAGAN RITE?

The flame from which all the Easter candles are lit has its source at Christ's Tomb in the Church of the Holy Sepulchre in Jerusalem; here the Patriarch of the Greek Orthodox Church celebrates the ceremony of the Holy Fire each Holy Saturday. From Jerusalem the flame is transported on a special flight to Athens, and within hours distributed by land, sea and air to churches throughout Greece and the islands.

These ceremonies around the rebirth of light closely mirror the ancient Greek worship of Persephone, daughter of Demeter, goddess of the earth. In legend, Persephone was banished to the darkness of Hades for the winter, returning joyously to the light of day every spring.

NAME DAYS

In Crete, everyone gets to celebrate their birthday twice. More important, in fact, than your actual birthday, is the "**Name Day**" of the saint that bears your name. Greek ingenuity has stretched the saints' names (or invented new saints) to cover almost everyone, so even pagan Dionysos or Socrates get to celebrate. If your name isn't covered, no problem – your party is on All Saints' Day, eight weeks after Easter.

The big name-day celebrations (Iannis/Ianna on January 7th or Yeoryios on April 23rd for example) can involve thousands of people, and traditional naming conventions guarantee that families get to celebrate together. In most families the eldest boy is still named after his paternal grandfather, and the eldest girl after her grandmother, so all the eldest cousins will share the same name, and the same name day. Any church or chapel bearing the saint's name will mark the event – some smaller chapels will open just for this one day of the year – while if an entire village is named after the saint, you can almost guarantee a festival. To check when your name day falls, see ⓦ namedays.gr.

March 25: Independence Day and the Feast of the Annunciation Both a religious and a national holiday, with military parades and dancing to celebrate the beginning of the revolt against Ottoman rule in 1821, and church services to honour the news given to Mary that she was to become the Mother of Christ. There are special celebrations in Paleóhora.

APRIL

Easter (Páskha) April 16, 2017; April 8, 2018; April 28, 2019. Widespread celebration for the most important festival of the year (see opposite); Good Friday and Easter Monday are public holidays.

April 23: Áyios Yeóryios St George, the patron saint of shepherds, is commemorated with big rural celebrations throughout Crete, with much feasting and dancing. There's a major celebration in Así Goniá.

MAY

May 1: May Day The great urban holiday – most people make for the countryside to picnic. In the towns, demonstrations by the left claim the day as Labour Day.

May 20–27: Anniversary of the Battle of Crete Celebrated in Haniá and a different local village each year, with veterans' ceremonies, sporting events and folk dancing.

May 21: Áyios Konstandínos The feast of St Constantine who, as emperor, championed Christianity in the Byzantine Empire, and his mother, Ayía Eléni (St Helena), with services and celebrations at churches and monasteries named after the saint, especially Arkádhi; also a very popular name day.

JUNE

Whit Monday (Áyion Pnévma) Seven weeks after Easter, this is both a religious holiday and a secular one marking the start of summer.

June 24: Summer Solstice/John the Baptist Bonfires and widespread celebrations.

Late June: Naval Week Naval celebrations culminating in fireworks – especially big at Soúdha.

JULY & AUGUST

Early July: Réthymno Cretan Diet Festival A week of celebration of Cretan food and wine, along with traditional music and dancing. ⓦ cretandietfestival.gr

July to mid-Aug: Sitía Kornaria Festival Concerts, dance, theatre and food.

July & Aug: Áyios Nikólaos Lato Festival Cultural and sporting events throughout the summer.

July to mid-Sept: Iráklio Festival A wide variety of cultural events from drama and film to traditional dance and jazz, at scattered sites through most of the summer.

Aug 6: Metamórfosi/Transfiguration Another feast day. Especially celebrated in Voukoliés (Haniá), Máles (Ierápetra) and Zákros.

Aug 12: Áyios Mathéos The feast of St Matthew sees celebrations in Kastélli Kissámou.

Mid-Aug: Sitía Sultana Festival An enjoyable, week-long celebration of the local harvest, with plenty of wine.

Aug 15: Assumption of the Virgin (Apokímisis tís Panayías) A huge holiday throughout Greece, the great feast of the Assumption is a day when people traditionally return to their home village, often creating problems for unsuspecting visitors who find there's no accommodation left. Services in churches begin at dawn, but latecomers usually arrive for the bread, lamb and wine served in the churchyard at the end of the service around lunchtime. Neápoli is a main centre for this feast.

Aug 24: Áyios Eftíhios Celebrated especially in the southwest corner of the island, where many infants are given this name; there are festivities at Kambanós near Soúyia (Haniá).

Aug 24: Áyios Títos The patron saint of Crete is celebrated all across the island, and with a big procession in Iráklio.

Aug 29: Áyios Ioánnis A massive name-day pilgrimage to the church of Áyios Ioánnis Giónis on the Rodhopoú peninsula in Haniá.

Late Aug: Kritsá Cretan Wedding A "traditional" wedding laid on for the tourists – quite a spectacle nonetheless.

SEPTEMBER & OCTOBER

Sept 14: Áyios Stavrós/Holy Cross Celebrated with festivities at Tzermiádho and Kalamáfka.

gelos The feast of the archangel is especially ...asíthi).

...**estival** Celebrated in Élos and other villages ...re chestnuts are grown.

...ational holiday with parades, folk dancing and speeches to commemorate prime minister Metaxas' one-word reply to Mussolini's 1940 ultimatum: Óhi! ("No!").

NOVEMBER & DECEMBER

Nov 7–9: Anniversary of the explosion at the monastery of Arkádhi One of Crete's biggest gatherings.

Dec 6: Áyios Nikólaos The patron saint of seafarers. Many chapels are dedicated to him around the island's coastline, including the one at the resort named after him, where processions and festivities mark the day.

Dec 25 & 26: Christmas It's less all-encompassing than Easter, but Christmas is still an important religious feast, and one that increasingly comes with all the usual commercial trappings: decorations, gifts and alarming outbreaks of plastic Santas on rooftops. Both Christmas Day and Boxing Day are public holidays.

Sports and outdoor activities

Although, not surprisingly, watersports are tremendously popular in Crete, there are perhaps fewer opportunities to take part than you might expect. Away from the coast, it's the mountains that are the great lure, with plenty of hiking options, from gentle strolls to long-distance mountain paths, and above all the great gorge walks, predominantly in the south. The mountains also offer the opportunity for more strenuous adventure activities.

Watersports

In all the resorts you'll find **waterski** boats that spend most of their time hauling people around on bananas or other inflatables, or towing parachutes for **parascending**. Sometimes there are jet skis too, but it's rare to find boats or windsurfers to rent. **Windsurfing** is particularly good in the far east, however, with a major centre at Kourémenos Beach (see p.164). **Scuba-diving** is also growing in popularity, largely due to the relaxation of government controls. There are centres where you can learn to dive in all the major north-coast resorts, but the best diving is probably off the south coast – especially around Plakiás – and in the far east,

where there are fewer facilities. There isn't much life left in the Mediterranean, but these waters have more than most, and they're also exceptionally clear, while the rocky coast offers plenty of caves and hidden nooks to explore. **Kayaking** is growing in popularity, too, especially around the southwest coast, where some tour operators offer kayaking and hiking holidays (see p.24)

Hiking, cycling and climbing

There are great **walks** everywhere inland, and many of the best are pointed out throughout the Guide. If you're planning any serious hiking – including any of the various gorges – stout shoes or trainers are essential and **walking boots** with firm ankle support recommended, along with protection against the sun and adequate water supplies. Walking is much better in the spring and autumn than in the fierce heat of midsummer, especially as there will be far more animal and plant life then. Be aware that paths are none too well marked, and even those that start out clear may peter out as you climb into the mountains – always try to get local advice before setting out on anything at all challenging, and never hike alone.

In most of the resorts you can rent **mountain bikes**, and many of the rental places lead organized rides, which vary from easy explorations of the countryside to serious rides up proper mountains.

Crete also offers some exciting possibilities for **climbers**: contacts for the local mountaineering clubs (EOS) in Iráklio, Réthymno and Haniá are given in their respective listings, or see Ⓦ climbincrete.com.

Horseriding and adrenaline sports

A handful of adventure operators offer **adrenaline sports** including climbing, canyoning, abseiling

---

FIVE GREAT GORGE HIKES
Arádhena A challenging and spectacular trek. See p.284
Áyio An easy path through a lonely gorge to a great beach. See p.114
Roúvas An inland gorge, climbing high into the mountains. See p.98
Samariá Always crowded, always extraordinary. See p.275
Zákros, Gorge of the Dead A straight-forward walk, rewarded with a Minoan palace and a welcome swim. See p.166

and bungee – the Arádhena Gorge (see p.284) offers Europe's second-highest **bungee jump**. There are also opportunities for **horseriding** and, believe it or not, it is even possible to **ski** in Crete in winter: there's a tiny ski lift on the Nídha plain above Anóyia, while the *Kallergi Refuge* in the White Mountains (see p.275) may also open for ski parties. Don't come specially, however.

ADVENTURE SPORTS OPERATORS

Crete is a great place for adventure holidays, and there are numerous companies across the island offering everything from mountain biking and canyoning to trekking and horseriding. Watersports and diving operators are also listed throughout the Guide.

CLIMBING/ADRENALINE SPORTS

Liquid Bungy ☎ 6937 615 191, 🔲 bungy.gr. White-knuckle bungee jumping at the Arádhena Gorge, Haniá.

Trekking Plan ☎ 6932 417 040, 🔲 cycling.gr. Rock climbing, mountaineering, skiing, canyoning, abseiling, kayaking and mountain biking in Haniá province.

HORSERIDING

Horse Riding Center ☎ 28320 31196, 🔲 cretehorseriding.com. Horse and donkey rides and instruction outside Plakiás.

Melanouri ☎ 28920 45040, 🔲 melanouri.com. Horseriding and instruction, from an hour-long jaunt to a week's riding holiday, at a stable near Mátala.

Odysseia ☎ 28970 51080, 🔲 horseriding.gr. One- to six-day guided horse treks from their base at Avdhoú near the Lasíthi plateau.

Zoraïda's Horseriding ☎ 28250 61745, 🔲 zoraidas-horseriding.com. Horseriding holidays and treks from their stables in Yeoryioúpoli, Haniá.

WALKING AND CYCLING

Cretan Adventures ☎ 28103 32772, 🔲 cretanadventures.gr. Hiking, cycling and a huge variety of other adventure and family activities throughout Crete.

Crete-Cycling.com ☎ 6986 927 706, 🔲 crete-cycling.com. Hardcore cycling with high-quality equipment from bases in Ayía Galíni and Mókhlos; spring and autumn training camps.

The Happy Walker ☎ 28310 52920, 🔲 happywalker.com. Walking tours ranging from day-hikes near Réthymno to ten-day mountain hikes.

Hellas Bike ☎ 28210 60858, 🔲 hellasbike.net. One- to seven-day bike tours at anything from family to committed mountain-biker level, from Ayía Marína in Haniá province.

Korifi Tours ☎ 28930 41440, 🔲 korifi.de. Hiking tours from a tiny village in southwest Crete; also climbing and enduro motorbiking.

Olympic Bike ☎ 28310 72383, 🔲 olympicbike.com. Gentle bike tours and serious mountain biking, mostly in central Crete from a base in Réthymno.

Strata Walking Tours ☎ 28220 24249, 🔲 stratatours.com. Guided treks and day-walks in the Kastélli area of the far west.

Travel essentials

Costs

The **cost** of travelling in Greece has dropped markedly since the economic crisis; nonetheless it remains an EU country and member of the euro, and prices in shops and cafés are broadly comparable to other EU countries (including the UK). In general, though, your needs are simple here and public transport, accommodation and taverna meals are among the less inflated items.

Average costs depend very much on where and when you go. The cities and major resorts are usually more expensive, and costs increase substantially in July, August and at Easter. A **budget** of €60/£45/$70 a day will get you a share of a plain double room with bath or shower, breakfast, a picnic or simple taverna lunch, bus ride, museum tickets, a couple of beers and a decent evening meal. You could save a bit on this by camping or staying at hostels and catering for yourself, while for €80–100/£60–75/$90–115 you could upgrade your room, squeeze in a few extra drinks, and share the rental of a motorbike or small car.

Entry charges for archeological sites and museums vary from €2 to around €6 for an important site such as Knossós; entrance to state-run sites and museums is **free** on Sundays and public holidays between November and March.

Most shops have fixed prices, so **bargaining** isn't a regular feature of tourist life. It is worth negotiating over rooms, though, especially off-season, or for vehicle rental, especially for longer periods.

Tipping is not essential anywhere, though taxi drivers generally expect it from tourists and most service staff are very poorly paid. Restaurant bills incorporate a service charge; if you want to tip, rounding up the bill is usually sufficient. If you are offered hospitality by a local they are likely to insist on paying – and offering cash can be seen as offensive. The best solution is to offer to reciprocate, making clear that it's on you next time.

Crime and personal safety

Crete, along with Greece as a whole, remains one of Europe's safest regions, with a low **crime** rate and a deserved reputation for honesty. If you leave a bag or wallet at a café, you'll most likely find it scrupulously looked after, pending your return. Nonetheless theft and muggings are becoming increasingly common, a trend only likely to be increased by the economic crisis. With this in mind, it's best to lock

---

DISCOUNTS AND STUDENT CARDS

State-run museums and archeological sites offer free entry to under-18s, senior citizens, students, teachers and journalists from the EU with proper identification, and substantial reductions for other nationalities; private attractions may also offer reduced prices, especially for children.

Full-time students are eligible for the **International Student ID Card** (ISIC; ⓦ isic.org), which entitles the bearer to special air and ferry fares and discounts at numerous shops and attractions. For Americans there's also a health benefit. You only have to be 26 or younger to qualify for the **International Youth Travel Card**, which costs the same and carries the same benefits – it's not strictly student ID, but will probably work. Teachers qualify for the **International Teacher Identity Card (ITIC)**, offering insurance benefits but limited travel discounts.

As well as the benefits listed above, **senior citizens** are entitled to cut-price fares on some buses, ferries and domestic flights. You'll need to have proof of age to hand.

---

rooms and cars securely, and to keep your valuables hidden, especially in cities. Civil unrest, in the form of strikes and demonstrations, is also on the increase but while this might inconvenience you, you'd be very unlucky to get caught up in any trouble as a visitor.

In more remote localities **women** may feel slightly uncomfortable travelling alone. The traditional villagers may not understand why you are unaccompanied, and might not welcome your presence in their exclusively male *kafenía* – often the only place where you can get a drink. Travelling with a companion, you're more likely to be treated as a *xéni*, a word meaning both (female) stranger and guest.

Police and potential offences

Though the chances are you'll never meet a member of the national **police force**, the *Ellinikí Astynomía*, Greek cops expect respect: in Crete, on the whole, they're pretty laidback, but they can be harsh if you cross them, and police practice often falls short of northern European norms. If you need to go to the police, always try to do so through the Tourist Police (❶ 171), who should speak English and are used to dealing with visitors. You are required to **carry suitable ID** on you at all times – either a passport or a driving licence.

The most common causes of a brush with the law are beach **nudity**, **camping** outside authorized sites, **public inebriation** or lewd behaviour. In 2009 a large British stag group dressed as nuns was arrested in Mália and held for several days, having managed to combine extreme drunkenness with a lack of respect to the church. Also avoid taking **photos in forbidden areas** such as airports.

Drug offences are treated as major crimes, particularly since there's a mushrooming local addiction problem. The maximum penalty for "causing the use of drugs by someone under 18", for example, is life imprisonment and an astronomical fine. Foreigners

caught in possession of even small amounts of marijuana get long jail sentences if there's evidence that they've been supplying the drug to others.

Electricity

The **electricity** supply – erratic at times, especially during peak summer demand – is 220 volt AC. Plugs are the standard European variety of two round pins and you should pick up an adapter before you leave home, as they can be difficult to find locally. North American appliances (unless they're dual voltage) will also require a transformer.

Entry requirements

UK and all other EU nationals need only a valid **passport** for entry to Greece, and are not stamped in on arrival or out upon departure (in other words, you can stay as long as you like). US, Australian, New Zealand, Canadian and most non-EU Europeans can stay as tourists for ninety days (cumulative) in any six-month period; make sure your passport is stamped to avoid problems on exit. Your passport must be valid for three months after your arrival date.

Visitors from non-EU countries, unless of Greek descent, are very rarely granted **extensions** to tourist visas. If you overstay you're liable to be deported (at vast expense) or will be hit with a large fine upon departure when you attempt to leave. A full list of Greek embassies and consulates overseas can be found at ⓦ mfa.gr.

Health

There are no required **inoculations** for Greece, though it's wise to ensure that you are up to date on tetanus and polio. The main **health risks** faced by visitors involve overexposure to the sun, overindulgence in food and drink, or bites and stings from insects and sea creatures. **Drinking water** is safe pretty much everywhere, though it doesn't always taste great; in the mountains, it often comes straight from the same spring used by the bottling factories. Despite this, almost everyone drinks the bottled stuff instead.

British and other EU nationals are entitled to free medical care upon presentation of a **European Health Insurance Card** (EHIC; free online at Ⓦ www.ehic.org.uk or Ⓦ ehic.ie). The US, Canada, Australia and New Zealand have no formal health-care agreements with Greece (other than allowing for free emergency trauma treatment), so insurance is highly recommended.

For serious medical attention you'll find English-speaking **doctors** (mainly private) in all the bigger towns and resorts. There are also hospitals in all the big cities. For an **ambulance**, phone ☎ 166.

Pharmacies, drugs and contraception

For minor complaints, head for the local pharmacy (**farmakío**). Greek pharmacists are highly trained and dispense a number of medicines which elsewhere could only be prescribed by a doctor. In the larger towns and resorts there'll usually be one who speaks good English. Pharmacies are usually closed evenings and Saturday mornings, but all should have a schedule on their door showing the night and weekend duty pharmacists in town.

If you regularly use any form of **prescription drug**, you should bring along a copy of the prescription, together with the generic name of the drug; this will help you replace it, and avoids problems with customs officials. In this regard, you should be aware that **codeine is banned** in Greece, and if you import any you might find yourself in trouble, so check labels carefully; it's a major ingre-dient of Panadeine, Veganin, Solpadeine, Codis and Nurofen Plus, to name just a few. If you have a prescription, you should be OK.

Contraceptive pills are sold over-the-counter at larger pharmacies, though not necessarily the brands you may be used to; a good pharmacist should come up with a close match. **Condoms** are inexpensive and ubiquitous – just ask for *profy-laktiká* (less formally, *plastiká* or *kapótes*) at any pharmacy, sundries store or corner *períptero* (kiosk).

Insurance

Even though EU health care privileges apply in Greece (see above), you'd do well to take out

insurance before travelling to cover against theft, loss, illness or injury. Before paying for a whole new policy it's worth checking whether you are already covered: some all-risks home insurance policies may cover your possessions when overseas, and many private medical schemes offer coverage extensions for abroad. There may be some form of insurance included if you paid for your holiday with a **credit card**, too.

For most, though, it is worth buying **specialist travel insurance**; there are plenty of deals online (it's rarely good value when bought from a travel agent), or consider the offer from Rough Guides (see box above). Most policies exclude so-called **dangerous sports** unless an extra premium is paid: in Crete this could include horseriding, windsurfing, jet skiing, mountaineering and motorbiking.

If you need to make a **medical claim**, you should keep receipts for medicines and treatment, and in the event you have anything stolen or lost, you must obtain an **official statement** from the police or the airline that lost your bags. With a rise in the numbers of fraudulent claims, most insurers won't even consider one unless you have a police report.

Internet

In the resorts and bigger towns there's **free wi-fi** in the majority of hotels and rooms places, as well as in most cafés and tavernas. **Internet cafés** are dying out as a result, though you can usually find something (often packed with local kids, gaming online): rates are around €2–4/hr.

LGBT travellers

There are no specifically **LGBT resorts** on Crete, and few gay holidays offered by tour operators, though a web search will turn up a number of gay-friendly accommodation options.

Homosexuality is legal in Greece over the age of 17, and (male) bisexual behaviour common but rarely admitted; the law code itself, however, still contains pejorative references to passive partners. Greek men are terrible flirts, but cruising them is a semiotic minefield and definitely at your own risk – references in (often obsolete) gay guides to "known" male cruising grounds should be treated sceptically. Out gay Greeks are rare, and out local lesbians rarer still; foreign same-sex couples will generally be regarded with some bemusement but accorded the standard courtesy as foreigners – as long as they refrain from indulging in displays of affection in public, which remain taboo in rural areas.

Living in Crete

Many habitual visitors fall in love with Crete and end up as part- or full-time residents, more likely buying property than renting it, and most probably retired or self-employed rather than working at relatively low Greek wages. EU citizens are entitled to stay indefinitely, and to work in Crete, but this is a highly bureaucratic society where getting a job (at least legally) is fraught with paperwork, as are the everyday needs of getting a phone, power and the like. It's beyond the scope of this book to go into detail, but there's plenty of assistance available locally, above all from the existing expat community who've done it all before. The website ⓦ livingin crete.net is also an excellent resource.

Work

Work opportunities in Crete are severely limited and, EU membership notwithstanding, **short-term unskilled work** is often badly paid and undocumented. The old standby of work on the harvests is now dominated by immigrants from Albania and Eastern Europe, and appallingly paid even if you can find it.

There's a far better chance of employment in **tourism**, or teaching English. Many bars, tavernas and hotels have seasonal jobs, for which you should turn up early in the season and ask around. Your chances will be better if you can speak more than one language (ideally including Greek!), and if you are female. Men, unless they are trained chefs, find it harder to find any work, even washing up.

On a similar, unofficial level you might be able to work in a **tourist shop**, or (if you've the expertise) helping out at a watersports centre. Perhaps the best type of tourism-related work, however, is that of courier/greeter/group coordinator for a **package holiday company**. Most of these jobs are filled well in advance, but people may leave or fall ill – get yourself known to the reps, locally or on their airport runs, and you may get lucky.

Teaching English is largely a winter job, in the big towns where the language schools are. It's relatively well paid, but almost impossible to get into without a bona fide TEFL certificate.

Mail

Post offices are open Monday to Friday from 7.30am to 2pm, though certain main branches are also open evenings and Saturday mornings. **Airmail letters** take 3–7 days to reach the rest of Europe, 5–12 days to North America, a little longer for Australia and New Zealand. As anywhere, post offices tend to have long queues, so if all you want is a stamp (*grammatósimo*) you're better off buying it when you buy your postcards, or from almost any *periptero* (kiosk) and most minimarkets. Postage for postcards and letters up to 20g is the same for all international destinations, currently €0.90. For about €3 you can use the express service (*katepigonda*), which cuts letter delivery time to two days for the UK and three days for the Americas.

Ordinary **postboxes** are bright yellow, express boxes dark red, but it's best to use those by the door of a post office if possible, since days may pass between collections at others.

Maps

Maps of Crete are easily available all over the island, but you'll almost certainly find a better one at home. Having said that, even the best maps seem to have a number of significant errors. For drivers this is rarely more than a minor irritation, but hikers should take care not to rely solely on a single map and to confirm directions locally wherever possible.

The best maps for **driving and general use** are the Terrain and Freytag & Berndt versions; some of the better free car-rental maps are also surprisingly useful – they may be small-scale and covered in adverts, but they tend to be updated regularly, which means that they often show the main roads

SHHHH! SIESTA TIME

The hours **between 3 and 5pm**, the midday *mikró ýpno* (**siesta**), are sacrosanct – it's not acceptable to visit people, make phone calls to strangers or cause any sort of loud noise (especially with motorcycles) at this time. Quiet is also legally mandated **between midnight and 8am** in residential areas.

more accurately than many more professional-looking rivals. The Greek tourist authorities also provide a downloadable map at Ⓦ visitgreece.gr.

If you want more detail, for **hiking** for example, the best maps are from Greek cartographer Anavasi (Ⓦ anavasi.gr), who cover the island in three GPS-compatible regional 1:100,000 maps and also produce seven excellent 1:25,000 or 1:30,000 hiking maps covering the most popular areas, including the White Mountains, Mount Psilorítis and the far east.

Money

Currency in Crete is the euro (€). Euro coins are issued in denominations of 1, 2, 5, 10, 20 and 50 cents and 1 and 2 euros; euro notes come in denominations of 5, 10, 20, 50, 100, 200 and 500 euros. Up-to-date exchange rates can be found on Ⓦ xe.com.

Banks and exchange

The airports at Haniá and Iráklio should always have an **exchange desk** operating for passengers on incoming international flights, as well as ATMs – but at peak periods there's often a queue and it's well worth taking some euros to tide you over the first few hours. You'll generally get a better rate if you buy euros at home, provided you shop around and pre-order, rather than waiting till you get to the airport.

Banks are normally open Mon–Thurs 8.30am–2.30pm, Fri 8.30am–2pm, while outside these hours larger hotels and travel agencies can often change money, albeit with hefty commissions. When using a bank, always take your passport with you and be prepared for at least one long queue – often you have to line up once to have the transaction approved and again to pick up the cash. Rates and commissions vary considerably, even between branches of the same bank, so ask first.

ATMs and credit cards

ATMs are plentiful, and can be found in all the resorts and towns of any size, though you shouldn't expect to find them in rural areas or the smaller resorts (especially on the south coast). They're easy to use, with your normal PIN, though you won't know exactly what exchange rate you're getting or how much you're being charged. In most cases rates and commission are no worse than the alternatives, however, and you can avoid some of the charges and uncertainty by using a prepaid holiday money card in euros.

Major **credit cards** are widely accepted, but only by the more expensive stores, hotels and restaurants: they're useful for renting cars, for example, but no good in the cheaper tavernas or rooms places. Using a credit card in an ATM (as opposed to a debit card) means you'll be charged interest from the moment you do so.

Opening hours and public holidays

It's difficult to generalize about Cretan **opening hours**, which are notoriously erratic. Nonetheless the general pattern is that on Monday, Wednesday and Saturday shops are open 8.30am–2.30pm, and on Tuesday, Thursday and Friday 8.30am–2pm and 5.30–9pm; offices will generally follow similar hours, but most reopen every evening. In tourist areas, though, stores and offices may stay open right through the day – certainly the most important **archeological sites and museums** do so. As far as possible, opening hours for these are quoted in the Guide, but they change with exasperating frequency, especially since the economic crisis. If you're planning a special journey try to confirm in advance, or time your visit for the core hours of 9am–2pm; many close on Mondays. **Churches and monasteries** are generally open through the day, though they, too, may well close for an afternoon siesta.

PUBLIC HOLIDAYS

Jan 1 New Year's Day
Jan 6 Epiphany
Feb/March Clean Monday, 7 weeks before Easter
March 25 Independence Day
April/May Good Friday and Easter Monday (see p.34)
May 1 May Day
May/June Whit Monday, 7 weeks after Easter
Aug 15 Assumption of the Virgin
Oct 28 Óhi Day
Dec 25/26 Christmas Day/Boxing Day

Phones

There's excellent **mobile phone** coverage throughout Crete, and you should be able to pick up a signal just about anywhere. To use your own phone you'll need to call your provider to ensure that you have international roaming switched on (US users should also check that their phone will work in Europe), and you should find out the cost of calls at the same time – most networks offer good-value European add-ons, essential if you plan to use data (otherwise, make sure data roaming is switched off). International charges are coming down, but they're still high; remember that you'll be charged for incoming as well as outgoing calls. If you plan to use a phone extensively for local calls you might well be better off buying a Greek **pay-as-you-go** SIM card (or even an entire phone, starting from around €15); you may have to have your phone unlocked to use this, but most Greek mobile shops can do this for a small fee.

Calling on regular phones is pretty straight-forward, and all the resorts and towns of any size will have **call boxes**, invariably sited at the noisiest street corner. These work only with **phonecards** (*tilekártes*), widely available from kiosks and newsagents in various denominations starting at €4. They offer fairly good value even for international calls, especially within Europe. A **calling card** may make international calls cheaper; either one provided by your own operator at home, accessed by a freephone number and charged directly to your domestic account (these are convenient, but rates vary), or a prepaid card which you can buy from many local kiosks and newsagents (compare rates, as different cards offer better value for different countries).

Avoid making calls from your **hotel** room, as a huge surcharge will be slapped on, though you shouldn't be charged to access a free calling card number.

Smoking

Greeks are among the heaviest **smokers** in Europe, and although legally you're not allowed to smoke indoors in restaurants, bars or public offices, in practice the law is widely disregarded. No-smoking areas are sometimes enforced these days, but they're still the exception.

Time

Greek **summer time** begins at 2am on the last Sunday in March, when the clocks go forward one hour, and ends at 2am on the last Sunday in October when they go back. This change is not well publicized locally, and visitors miss planes and ferries every year. Greek time is always 2hr ahead of Britain. For North America, the difference is usually 7hr for Eastern Standard Time and 10hr for Pacific Standard Time – but bear in mind that daylight saving starts 2–3 weeks earlier and ends a week later than in Europe.

Toilets

In **toilets** throughout Crete you're expected to toss paper in a wastebasket, not in the bowl: learn this habit, or you'll block the pipes. There's almost

---

PHONE CODES AND NUMBERS

The international dialling code for Greece is +30. To make an international call, dial the international access code (in Greece it's 00), then the destination's country code, before the rest of the number. Note that the initial zero is omitted from the area code when dialling the UK, Ireland, Australia and New Zealand from abroad.

Australia international access code + 61
New Zealand international access code + 64
UK international access code + 44
US and Canada international access code + 1
Ireland international access code + 353
South Africa international access code + 27

USEFUL PHONE NUMBERS

Ambulance ☎ 166
Fire service ☎ 199
Forest fire reporting ☎ 191
Operator (domestic) ☎ 132

Operator (international) ☎ 139
Police/emergency ☎ 100
Tourist police ☎ 171

always a sign to remind you, but even if not you should do so, except in the most modern and upmarket hotels. Public toilets are rare except in the towns, usually in parks or squares, often subterranean. Otherwise try a bus station or pay for a coffee somewhere. It's worth carrying toilet paper with you – though it's provided by the attendants at public facilities, there may be none in tavernas and cafés.

Tourist information

The **National Tourist Organization of Greece** (*Ellinikós Organismós Tourismoú*, or EOT; ⓦvisit greece.gr) maintains offices in major European capitals, and in New York.

On the island, **local tourist offices** in the major towns and many smaller resorts provide an array of maps, timetables and leaflets as well as details of local accommodation, sometimes offering a booking service as well. The economic crisis is taking a heavy toll, though, and most have drastically shortened their hours and reduced staffing; some have closed altogether. In their stead, local **travel agencies** are always helpful and many voluntarily act as improvised tourist offices; many of these are listed in the Guide. The **tourist police** may also be helpful: a branch (or often just a single delegate) of the local police, they should have some knowledge of English and deal with complaints about restaurants, taxis, hotels and all things tourist-related; call ☏ 171 for information and help, and see individual town accounts for local addresses.

Travellers with disabilities

It is all too easy to wax lyrical over the attractions of Crete – the stepped, narrow alleys, the ease of travel by bus and ferry, the thrill of clambering around the great archeological sites. Travellers who use a wheelchair or have limited mobility or vision may not be so impressed. Uneven pavements, steep streets, and lack of facilities in ancient towns will always be an issue. Few of the major archeological sites or museums are at all wheelchair-friendly and nor, on the whole, are the towns and resorts.

Having said that, new hotels and apartments, along with modern museums, are subject to **EU legislation** and increasingly take people with disabilities into account in their design. With a little forward planning, it's possible to enjoy an inexpensive and trauma-free holiday in Crete. A quick web search will find a number of organizations that can help, including numerous small specialist agencies. One resort hotel, the *Eria* (☏ +30 28210 62790, ⓦeria-resort.gr), in Maleme near Haniá, has been **designed specifically** for disabled visitors and their carers, with facilities including rental of most equipment you might need (from oxygen to hoists), physiotherapy, accessible airport transfers and so on. Inevitably, it's not cheap.

Many other hotels and apartments are accessible, and even mainstream operators and the large package companies now provide information on access, although such advice rarely extends to what happens when you venture beyond the front door.

A **medical certificate** of your fitness to travel, provided by your doctor, is extremely useful; some airlines or insurance companies may insist on it. You should also carry extra supplies of any required **medicines** and a prescription including the generic name in case of emergency. It's probably best to assume that any special equipment, drugs or clothing you may require is unavailable in Crete and will need to be brought with you.

Travelling with children

Children are worshipped and indulged in Crete, arguably to excess – wherever you go, your kids will be welcome. Greek children sleep in the afternoon and stay up late. You'll see plenty of kids at tavernas, joining in with the adult food and conversation.

While there's not much in the way of specifically child-oriented holidays to Crete, many hotels and newer apartment complexes have children's pools and small playgrounds, and most tour operators will be able to book you something suitable. Some of the fancier resort hotels have kids' clubs and activities, while almost all hotels and rooms places have three- and four-bed rooms (or can add a cot to a regular room, at minimal or no extra cost); many have small apartments with fridges and simple cooking facilities, too. There are several water parks along the north coast, and activities like gorge-hiking or boat trips can become real adventures (though don't be overambitious – they can also be really gruelling in the heat). Younger kids may also enjoy the "tourist train" rides that operate in and around many of the major towns and resorts. Under-18s get **free entry** into state-run museums and archeological sites, and reduced prices at most attractions.

Baby food and **nappies** (diapers) are readily available and reasonably priced.

Iráklio

MOROSINI FOUNTAIN, IRÁKLIO

1

Iráklio

The province of Iráklio sees more tourists than any other in Crete. They come for two simple reasons: the string of big resorts that lies to the east of the city, just an hour or so from the airport, and the great Minoan sites, almost all of which are concentrated in the centre of the island. Knossós, Mália and Festós are in easy reach of almost anywhere in the province, and there are excellent beaches all along the north coast.

Iráklio itself is a big, boisterous city – the fifth largest in Greece. Strident and modern, it's a maelstrom of crowded thoroughfares, building work and dust, and, in high summer, its great sites are packed. Penetrate this facade, however, and you can discover a vibrant working city with a myriad of attractive features that do much to temper initial impressions. **East of the city**, the startling pace of **tourist development** is all too plain to see. In peak season, it can be hard to find a room in this monument to the package tour, and expensive if you do, though some of the resorts, most notably **Mália** and **Hersónisos**, do at least have good beaches and lively nightlife. As a general rule, the further east you go, the better things get: even where the road veers briefly inland, a more appealing Crete – of olive groves, tidy villages and picturesque mountain vistas – reveals itself.

    West and south of Iráklio, the beaches are smaller and the coastline is less amenable to hotel builders. To the west, there's just one small, classy resort – in the bay at **Ayía Pelayía** – a few isolated hotels and, in the hills behind, a number of interesting old villages. **Mátala** is the only resort of any size in the south, and a day-trip route takes in the major archeological sites of **Górtys**, **Festós** and **Ayía Triádha**. The rest is traditional farming country; the **Messará plain**, in particular, has been a vital resource since Minoan times, and its importance is reflected in the number of large and wealthy villages here.

Iráklio city

The best way to arrive in **IRÁKLIO** (Ηράκλειο) is from the sea: the traditional approach and still the one that shows the city in its best light, with Mount Yioúhtas rising behind, the heights of the Psilorítis range to the west and, as you get closer, the great fortress guarding the harbour entrance and the city walls encircling and dominating the oldest part of town.

    The reality when you arrive is less romantic: modern ferries are far too large for the old harbour and dock at giant concrete wharves alongside, while on closer inspection what little remains of the **old city** has been heavily restored, often from the bottom up. The slick renovations often look fake, pristine and polished alongside the grime that coats

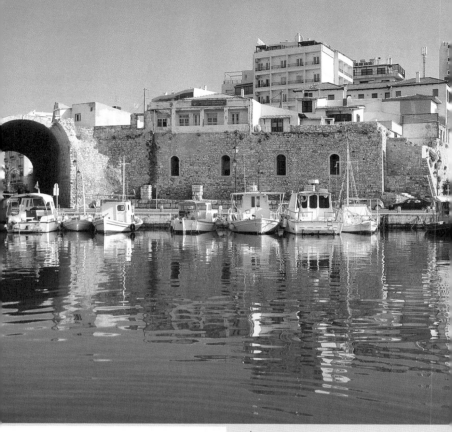

IRÁKLIO HARBOUR

Highlights

❶ **Iráklio** Crete's bustling capital boasts great restaurants and cafés, a vibrant market and an impressive harbour fortress, as well as an outstanding archeological museum with the world's finest collection of Minoan artefacts. **See p.46**

❷ **Knossós** Crete's major tourist attraction, the world-famous palace of Knossós remains the most impressive of the Minoan sites. **See p.66**

❸ **Górtys** Capital of Crete in Roman times, this site has plenty of ruins to explore, including the imposing remains of Áyios Títos, the island's first Christian church. **See p.100**

❹ **Festós and Mália palaces** These two outstanding ancient sites in picturesque locations are superb examples of Minoan architecture. **See p.103 & p.90**

❺ **Museum of Cretan Ethnology, Vóri** An outstanding folk museum in a mountainous, rural area of great beauty. **See p.108**

❻ **Mátala** In striking contrast to the brash north-coast resorts, Mátala is on a thoroughly human scale, though still with lots going on late into the night. Nearby are plenty of quieter escapes, and it's within easy reach of many of the major sights. **See p.109**

HIGHLIGHTS ARE MARKED ON THE MAP ON P.48

IRÁKLIO ORIENTATION

Virtually everything of interest in Iráklio lies within the old walled city, with the majority of the sights clustered in the northeastern corner. Despite the city's rather cheerless reputation, parts of the old town can be genuinely picturesque, not least the weighty **Venetian defences**: the harbour fortress and the massive walls framing the old quarters. Focal to this area are **Venizélou** and **Eleftherías** squares, and most of the churches and museums – including the **Archeological Museum**, with the world's foremost collection of Minoan antiquities – are just a few minutes' walk from either.

The most vital thoroughfare, pedestrianized **Odhós 25-Avgoústou** (see box, p.57), lined with banks, travel and shipping agencies and car rental outfits, links the harbour with the commercial city centre. West of here, behind Platía Venizélou, is the grandly named **El Greco Park**, which is in reality more of a garden. On the opposite side of 25-Avgoústou are some of the more interesting of Iráklio's older buildings, including the church of **Áyios Títos** and the Venetian Loggia. At its southern end, 25-Avgoústou opens into Platía Venizélou, which forms a junction for central Iráklio's other main arteries: **Kalokerinoú** heads westwards down to the Pórta Hioníon and out of the city; straight ahead, Odhós 1821 – a fashionable shopping street – heads southwest; and the adjacent Odhós 1866 is given over to the animated **market** (see p.58 & p.66).

even the most recent buildings – a juxtaposition that seems neatly to sum up much about modern Iráklio. While the city will never be one of the jewels of the Mediterranean, the ebullient friendliness of its people and an infectious cosmopolitan atmosphere may well tempt you into giving it more than the customary one-night transit.

Brief history

A Roman port, Heraclium, stood hereabouts and the city readopted its name only at the beginning of the twentieth century. Founded by the **Saracens**, who held Crete from 827 to 961, it was originally known as **El Khandak**, after the great ditch that surrounded it, later corrupted by the Venetians to **Candia** – or Candy, as Shakespeare titled it in *Twelfth Night* – a name also applied to the island as a whole. This Venetian capital was, in its day, one of the strongest and most spectacular cities in Europe; a trading centre, a staging-point for the Crusades and, as time wore on, the front line of Christendom. The **Turks** finally conquered the city after 21 years of war, which culminated in a bitter siege from May 1667 to September 1669. Under its new Turkish rulers, the city's importance declined in relation to Haniá's, but it remained a major port and the second city in Crete. It was here, too, that the incident occurred which eventually put an end to Turkish occupation of the island (see box, p.57). Finally united with **Greece**, Iráklio's future prosperity was assured by its central position.

Almost all that you see today dates only from the last sixty years or so, partly because of the heavy bombing the city suffered during World War II, but above all thanks to Crete's (until recently) booming agriculture, industry and tourism. In 1971, Iráklio regained the official title of island **capital**, and the city is now the wealthiest per head in the whole of Greece. In the boom years the authorities undertook ambitious projects to spruce up and refurbish the city centre, though many of these works have been abruptly put on hold as a result of the continuing economic crisis.

The harbour

The obvious starting point is the **harbour**, now home to fishing boats and a pleasure marina but still guarded over by an impressive sixteenth-century **Venetian fortress**, generally known by its Turkish name of **Koúles**, emblazoned with the Lion of St Mark. Though it withstood the 23-year Turkish war and siege, time has caught up with the underwater foundations and the building is closed to visitors pending restoration. Even

IRÁKLIO CITY

● SHOPS

Iráklio Market	3
Planet International Bookstore	1
Roadside Travel Bookshop	2

■ ACCOMMODATION

Atrion	2
Creta Camping	10
Heraklio Youth Hostel	5
Iráklion Hotel	9
Kastro	7
Kronos	4
Lato	3
Lena	8
Megaron	11
Olympic	6
Rea	

■ BARS, CLUBS & LIVE MUSIC

Akrotiri Envy	2
Central Park	8
Kafe Diartiriteo	4
Kafenion Fix	10
Island of Desire	1
Jailhouse	9
Pagopiion (Ice Factory)	6
Rolling Stone Rock Bar	7
Senses Club	3
Take Five	5
To Milon tis Eridos	11

● CAFÉS

Hatzaki	17
Kirkor	15
Mare	3
News Café	13
Utopia	11

● RESTAURANTS

Aztecas	12
Giakoumis	18
Hovoli	19
I Avli tou Defkaliona	6
Ippokampos	1
Katsinas	4
Ligo Krasi, Ligo Thalassa	14
Loukoulos	2
Meyeireuontas Me Ayapi	7
O Miltos	5
Opus	9
Pagopiion	8
Peri Orexeos	16
Peskesi	10

IRÁKLIO SUMMER FESTIVAL

The **Iráklio Summer Festival** runs from July to mid-September. Exhibitions, concerts and plays are put on by groups from around the world – some of which are top-notch – at venues across the city, mostly open-air. Details are available online at ⓦ nowheraklion.com/festival.html and from the tourist office (see p.62).

from the outside it is undeniably impressive, with sturdy walls protecting a series of chambers in which the defenders must have enjoyed an overwhelming sense of security. The causeway leading to the fort is a favourite place for a stroll and for locals to fish: at night, when the fortress is floodlit, it's a fine place to watch the ferries coming and going.

The Arsenali

On the landward side of the harbour, the vaulted **Arsenali** are marooned in a sea of traffic scooting along the harbour road. A typically ambitious Venetian military project, they were completed in four stages between the fifteenth and seventeenth centuries as this became the most important dockyard of the Venetian fleet in the eastern Mediterranean. The elongated ship sheds originally stretched to the water's edge – they were substantially shortened in order to build the road. Recently restored, in their heyday as many as fifty galleys at a time could be built here, or dragged ashore to be overhauled and repaired. They fell into disuse following the Turkish conquest.

The city walls

Iráklio's **city walls** were originally thrown up in the fifteenth century, the strongest bastion in the Mediterranean. They were constantly improved thereafter as Crete became increasingly isolated in the path of Turkish westward expansion; their final shape owes much to Michele Sanmicheli, who arrived here in 1538 having previously designed the fortifications of Padua and Verona.

Though well preserved and restored in parts, the walls are tricky to access. The easiest approach is to follow Odhós Pedhiádhos south from the back of Platía Eleftherías and find your way up one of the dusty tracks that lead to the top of the rampart. With luck and a little scrambling, you can walk all the way around from here, clockwise, to the **Áyios Andhréas Bastion** overlooking the sea in the west. To follow the walls in the other direction, simply head west along the coast for a little over 1km from the harbour until you reach this mighty bastion.

There are some curious views as you walk around, often looking down onto the rooftops, but the fabric of the walls themselves is rarely visible – it's simply like walking on a dusty path raised above the level of its surrounds. A word of warning, though: usually completely safe in daytime, the walls tend to attract less desirable types from dusk onwards.

Nikos Kazantzákis' tomb

On the **Martinengo Bastion**, facing south, is the **tomb of Nikos Kazantzákis**, Crete's greatest writer (see p.52). Despite his works being banned for their unorthodox views, Kazantzákis' burial rites were performed at Áyios Mínos Cathedral, although he was not permitted burial in a cemetery – hence the interment on the bastion – and no priests officially escorted his body up here. His simple grave is adorned only with an inscription from his own writings: "I hope for nothing, I fear nothing, I am free". When she died (on Kazantzákis' birthday) in 2004 aged 101, the author's wife Eleni Samiou Kazantzákis was buried in a grave alongside his on the bastion. At the weekend, Iraklians gather here to pay their respects – and to enjoy a free, grandstand view of the matches played by the city's once proud, but now second-string football team Ergotelis (see p.66) in the stadium below.

1

NIKOS KAZANTZÁKIS

Crete's best-known writer, **Nikos Kazantzákis**, was born in Iráklio in 1883 in the street now named after him. His early life was shadowed by the struggle against the Turks and for union with Greece. Educated in Athens and Paris, Kazantzákis travelled widely throughout his life, working for the Greek government on more than one occasion (serving briefly as Minister for Education in 1945) and for UNESCO, but above all writing. He produced a vast range of works, including philosophical essays, epic poetry, travel books, translations of classics such as Dante's *Divine Comedy* into Greek and, of course, the novels on which his fame in the West mostly rests. **Zorba the Greek** (1946) was his first and most celebrated novel, but his output remained prolific to the end of his life. Particularly relevant to Cretan travels are *Freedom or Death* (1950), set amid the struggle against the Turks, and the autobiographical *Report to Greco*, published posthumously in 1961 (Kazantzákis died in Freiburg, West Germany, in 1957 after contracting hepatitis from an unsterilized vaccination needle during a visit to China).

Kazantzákis is widely accepted as the leading Greek writer of the twentieth century, and Cretans are extremely proud of him, despite the fact that most of his later life was spent abroad, that he was banned from entering Greece for long periods, and that he was excommunicated by the Orthodox Church for his vigorously expressed doubts about Christianity. This last detail gained him more notoriety when his *The Last Temptation of Christ* was filmed by Martin Scorsese, amid much controversy, in 1988. The Church was also instrumental in working behind the scenes to deny him the Nobel Prize, which he lost by one vote to Albert Camus in 1957. Many critics now regard much of his writing as overblown and pretentious, but even they admit that the best parts are where the Cretan in Kazantzákis shows through, in the tremendous gusto and vitality of books like *Zorba* and *Freedom or Death*. Kazantzákis himself was always conscious, and proud, of his Cretan heritage.

City gates

For the most impressive views of the city's defences, stroll out through one of the elaborate gates, the **Pórta Haníon** at the bottom of Kalokerinoú or the **Pórta Kenoúria** at the top of Odhós Evans, and admire them from the outside. Both of these portals date from the second half of the sixteenth century, when the majority of the surviving defences were completed. At the Pórta Kenoúria, the walls are over 40m thick.

The Archeological Museum

Xanthoudhídhou 2 • April–Oct daily 8am–8pm; Nov–March Mon noon–5pm, Tues–Sun 8am–5pm • €6, joint ticket with Knossós €10 • ☎ 2810 279 000

Iráklio's **Archeological Museum** is one of the major reasons to visit the city. It houses far and away the most important collection of **Minoan art and artefacts** anywhere in the world, and a visit to Knossós or the other sites will be greatly enhanced if you've been here first. Recently reopened following a seven-year refurbishment, the end result is spectacular and places the museum at the forefront of Greek museums. The museum is almost always crowded (at least in summer) and often becomes overwhelmed by coach parties, with an endless procession of guided tours in all languages, monopolizing the major exhibits. Given this, it's advisable to visit early, late or around lunchtime.

Rooms 1–3: Prehistory and the early Minoans

The museum begins on the ground floor with the earliest signs of human settlement in Crete, around 6000 BC. The **Vasilikí pottery** here (Case 6), from an early Minoan site in the east (see p.149), is a foretaste of the more famous **Kamáres ware** (see p.209), with often elaborate white and red decoration on a dark background. There are also fine examples of stone vases and jars from Mochlos and elsewhere (Case 9), displaying an early mastery of the lapidary's craft. A tomb discovered at Malía unearthed the stunningly intricate **pendant of two bees around a golden disc** (Case 19); the disc is supposedly a drop of honey that they are storing in a comb. Among the miniature

1

sculpture, don't miss the **clay bull** (Case 22) with tiny acrobats clinging to its horns: an early sign of the popularity of bull sports. In Case 11 there is a display of intricately engraved seal stones, including one from ancient Mesopotamia, suggesting early contact between the island and its near eastern neighbours.

Room 3 is devoted to the **Old Palace period** (Protopalatial, 1900–1700BC) and the first palaces at Knossós, Festós and Malía, with displays on daily life, economy and administration. There is a stunning collection of Kamáres ware from the Festós palace (Cases 27–34) – regarded as the peak of this artistic development – exemplified by the so-called "**royal dinner service**" (Case 35) which includes a magnificent vase with sculpted white flowers in high relief. Finally, note the clay statuettes (Case 21) of sanctuary worshippers – their arms crossed or placed on the chest in reverential attitudes – as well as the *taxímata* (ex votos) representing parts of the human body the deity was requested to heal, a custom still followed in churches all over Greece today.

Rooms 4–5: the New Palace period

From the **New Palace period** (Neopalatial, 1700–1400 BC) the collection features the **Jug of Reeds** (Case 41), a superb and typical example of the new styles that that replaced Kámares pottery. Technological advances in material, higher temperature firing and faster pottery wheels also enabled an evolution in form and design. Vases became more slender and there was a move away from spiral designs as floral and marine decoration took centre stage. Other highlights include the fascinating "**Town Mosaic**" from Knossós (Case 37), consisting of a series of glazed plaques depicting multistorey Minoan houses, beautiful pieces that probably fitted together to form a decorative scene; and the celebrated **Festós Disc** (Case 51), a circular slab of clay upon which hieroglyphic characters have been inscribed in a spiral pattern. The disc is frequently described as the earliest-known example of printing, since the impressions of hieroglyphs were made with stamps before it was fired. The various signs are divided into groups, believed to be words; some are repeated, leading scholars to suggest that what is represented on the disc may be some form of prayer or hymn. In recent years a controversy has raged about the disc's authenticity, some scholars believing it to be a nineteenth-century hoax; only a thermoluminescence test will answer the question once and for all, but so far the museum authorities have been unwilling to allow this. Also here are a number of great bronze **double axes** erected on wooden poles. The double axe was an important cult symbol for the Minoans, and huge axes like these were placed in shrines and palaces.

A beautiful **gaming board** (Case 39) from the Corridor of the Draughtsboard at Knossós, made of ivory, blue paste, crystal, and gold and silver leaf, with ivory pieces, is a reminder of the luxurious life which some Minoans at least could enjoy. A fascinating example of domestic architecture comes at the end of the Neopalatial period in the form of a model of a modest **Minoan dwelling** (Case 36) from Arhánes; features include a light well, small rooms and tiny windows to keep out the bright Cretan sun and fierce winds, while the roof terrace above is similar to those seen on village houses throughout Crete today. Also worth a look here is the unique ceramic portrayal of lively dolphins plunging among cockles and seaweed (Case 41), perhaps originally the neck of a large vase. In the centre of Room 4 there is a wonderful wooden model reconstruction of the Palace of Knossós. Finally, two small **clay cups** (Case 53) may hold important clues to the history of Minoan writing, of which little survives. These vessels bear inscriptions written in Linear A script – developed from the cumbersome hieroglyphic – using cuttlefish ink. This use of ink suggests the existence of other suitable writing materials (possibly imported papyrus or even domestically produced palm-leaf paper) that have since perished in the Cretan climate.

Room 6: daily life

Room 6 displays artefacts attesting to the Minoan love of sports and spectacles. The famous "**Bull Leaping**" fresco from Knossós (Case 60) depicts acrobats performing

1

somersaults over the back of a charging bull, while a carved ivory **figurine of a bull-leaper** (Case 63) was part of an unusual sculpted composition with other figures. The **Boxers' Rhyton** (Case 62) is a black steatite vase from Ayía Triádha depicting gloved boxers (who appear to be wearing tassled helmets) and wrestlers in combat. A wonderfully vibrant set of ceramic **figurines of dancers** circling a lyra player (Case 59) from Palékastro is typical of the later Minoan period, influenced by Mycenean styles – with less naturalism and more stereotyped designs.

Rooms 7–8 Minoan Religion

The star exhibit in Room 7 is the famous **Harvesters Vase** (Case 75), the finest of a pair of stone (steatite, or soapstone) vases from Ayía Triádha. It depicts with vivid realism a procession returning home from the fields; the harvesters are led by a strangely dressed character with long hair and a big stick, possibly a priest, and accompanied by musicians, one of whom is waving a sistrum (a percussion instrument that sounds rather like a maraca). The other vase (Case 71) shows what appears to be a chieftan receiving a report from an official. Some **bronze figurines** (Case 74) depict worshippers making the ritual "salute" gesture to the deity while leaning backwards. Also of note here is the renowned **Bull's Head Rhyton** (Case 79), a sacred vessel used in religious ceremonies and found in the Little Palace at Knossós. Carved from black stone (steatite) with inlaid eyes and nostrils (the wooden horns are new), the bull is magnificently naturalistic. Another imposing alabaster rhyton, or libation vessel, is carved in the form of a lioness's head (Case 87).

Also here are two representations of the **snake goddess** (Case 83), both wearing tight-waisted, breast-baring dresses and decorated aprons, and each with snakes coiling around their hands; they may equally be priestesses engaged in sacred rituals. The so-called **"ring of King Minos"** (Case 78) was found seventy years ago close to the Knossós palace. After disappearing while in the possession of a local priest, the solid gold ring emerged again when one of the priest's descendants sold it to the museum. Highly important for its depiction of Minoan religion, the ring is engraved with a scene showing a goddess with worshippers as well as a sailing boat. Other items of note here include the magnificent **rock crystal rhyton** (Case 89) from the Zákros palace, with a handle of beads and a collar that hides a join between two pieces encased in gold. Its beauty aside, this exhibit is always singled out by the guides as an example of the painstaking reconstruction undertaken by the museum – when discovered, it was broken into over three hundred fragments.

Rooms 9–10: the Late Palace Period

Rooms 9–10 are devoted to the final period of the palace culture (1450–1400BC), mainly at Knossós, and the objects are considerably less exciting. In pottery, similar decorative themes continued to be used, but with a new formalism and on new types of vessel, which has been taken as a sign that Mycenaean influences were beginning to take hold. Items of note here include a small **group of clay figures** (Case 98) – from a tomb at Kamilári (see p.113) near Festós – taking part in what seems to be a ritual dance inside a circle decorated with the horns of consecration. It's a very crude work but wonderfully effective and reminiscent of the *pentozalis* danced by Cretan men today. The martial arts are represented by some fine gold sword hilts and a fabulous reconstructed **boar's tusk helmet** (Case 105) which also makes an appearance on an amphora from Arhánes (Case 108). Taken with the other weapons and military equipment displayed here, these items can be seen as further proof of the subordination of Minoan culture to the more warlike Mycenaean in this period.

Also from Arhánes comes a curious **horse burial** (Case 107) found in a fourteenth-century tholos tomb. The corpse of the horse is believed to have been a sacrifice in honour of the possibly royal personage buried in the same tomb. After slaughter the beast had been systematically dismembered and its parts carefully placed in the position in which they are now displayed. Equally striking is the **Peak Sanctuary Rhyton** (Case 90), a green stone vessel on which a low relief scene depicts a mountain shrine, with horns of consecration decorated with birds and wild goats. Originally covered in gold leaf, this discovery provided valuable information on Minoan religion.

Rooms 11–12: late settlements, sanctuaries and tombs

The final rooms in the ground floor's Minoan section deal with the artefacts from the palaces and tombs of the late and post-palatial periods. The outstanding exhibit here is the magnificent **Ayía Triádha sarcophagus** (Case 127), which, with its unique and elaborate painted-plaster ornamentation, is one of the masterpieces of Minoan art. Dating from the fourteenth century BC, it is the only stone sarcophagus to be found in Crete and was discovered in a tomb beside the palace at Ayía Triádha; it had probably been used for a royal burial. On one side is a depiction of an animal sacrifice, with a bull already dead on the altar and two goats tied up awaiting their fate. On the other are two scenes, perhaps of relatives making offerings for the safe passage of the deceased. The ends feature an image of goddesses riding in a chariot drawn by griffins, and of two women in a chariot pulled by goats above a procession of men. Unlike the palace frescoes (see below), nothing has been restored or reconstructed, making this in many ways even more striking.

Towards the end of the Bronze Age (c.1100–1000BC) the Minoans were fleeing from the coasts before successive waves of Dorian invaders, and attempted to maintain their culture in inaccessible parts of the island such as the settlement high above the Lasíthi Plateau at Karfí (see p.143). From this remote settlement came terracotta figurines, utensils and vessels as well as large figures of the "**goddess with raised hands**" (Case 117), their anguished features seeming to foreshadow the end. New types of ritual vessel are typified by the rhyton in the shape of a **chariot drawn by bodyless oxen** (Case 117), giving the work a somewhat abstract quality.

Much of the rest of these rooms is taken up with a collection of **lárnakes** (clay coffins) from various periods, their painted decoration reflecting the prevailing pottery style. The Minoan burial position of the knees drawn up to the chest explains the small size of the coffins – and also suggests that the bodies would have been placed in them soon after death, before the onset of rigor mortis. They come in two basic shapes: chests with lids and "bathtubs" (which may well have been used as such during their owners' lifetimes, as many have plugholes). From Room 12 stairs lead to the rooms on the second floor.

Room 13: Minoan palace frescoes

Room 13, the **Hall of the Frescoes**, is perhaps the most interesting in the museum, particularly now that the paintings are stunningly illuminated and displayed in the refurbished gallery. Only tiny fragments of original fresco survive, but they have been painstakingly reconstituted and mounted on matching backgrounds, giving as true an impression of the entire fresco as possible.

Frescoes are among the greatest achievements of Minoan art: they were originally painted directly onto wet plaster, using mostly plant dyes but also colours from mineral sources and even shellfish – a technique which has ensured their relatively unfaded survival. The job of the restorers was helped to an extent by knowledge of the various conventions, which matched Egyptian practice: men's skin, for example, was red, women's white; gold is shown as yellow, silver as blue and bronze, red.

Most of the frescoes displayed come originally from **Knossós**, and date from the Neopalatial period (1700–1400BC). Along the left hand wall as you enter (Cases 129–131) are four large panels from the enormous fresco which led all the way along the **Corridor of the Procession** at Knossós; an artist's impression shows how the whole might originally have looked. Two groups of youths are shown processing towards a female figure, presumably a priestess or a goddess. The **fresco of griffins** (Case 138) came from the throne room at the palace, while the elegant **Priest-King** (Case 137) – or Prince of the Lilies as

1

Sir Arthur Evans (see p.326) described him – once decorated a corridor near the palace's west entrance. A great painted relief of a **bull's head** (Case 139), transmitting agony and power, is flanked by a beautifully simple fresco of **swimming dolphins** (Case 142) from the queen's apartment, while nearby a heavily restored fresco depicts the elegantly attired **ladies of the court** (Case 140). Among other fresco fragments displayed, one of the most interesting is the **"Saffron Gatherer"** (Case 144). Originally reconstructed by Evans and his team as a boy, it has since been decided that this in fact represented a blue monkey; the two versions are shown side by side. Finally, one of the most celebrated fresco fragments is the so-called **"La Parisienne"** (Case 141), so dubbed for her bright red lips, huge eyes, long hair and fancy dress, but in reality almost certainly a priestess or a goddess.

Rooms 14–17: Early Iron Age
After the dazzling magnificence of the Minoan frescoes the post-Minoan period can seem like something of an anticlimax, but some of the exhibits are definitely worth a look. Highlights include, in Room 15, three large **bronze hammered figurines** of Apollo and Artemis with their mother, Leto, from the eighth-century BC sanctuary of Apollo Delphinius at Dréros (Case 159); Room 17 has a display of figurines and artefacts found at the remote mountain shrine of **Káto Sími** (Case 165) near Ano Viannos in the southeast of Iráklio province (see p.121). As the objects on view from Minoan, Greek and Roman periods demonstrate, this is one of the few shrines in Crete where worship continued without interruption from prehistorical times to the end of antiquity. Notable pieces include bronze figurines of worshippers and ivory-handled swords from the Minoan age, and a figurine from the Hellenistic period of a lyre-playing Hermes (to whom the Greeks dedicated Káto Sími).

Rooms 18–19: Late period cemeteries
Rooms 18–19 display finds from cemeteries in the period following the Dorian invasions to the fourth century BC. Finds include a fine collection of **jewellery and gold leaf** from Knossós (Case 187), as well as some wonderful animal votive vases depicting a rooster, a hare and an owl (Case 196).

Rooms 20–25: Classical and Roman periods
Displays of finds from Cretan city states, sanctuaries and cemeteries take up most of the rest of the collection. Highlights here include two recently discovered Roman mosaics from a villa at Hersónisos, one depicting a cock fight. Room 23 displays the accumulations of an Iráklio doctor and antiquities collector, the **Yiamalakis Collection**, which covers pieces from every Cretan historical period, from Neolithic to Roman. Among interesting items displayed are a collection of Roman oil lamps, on which are featured some fairly saucy erotic images as well as some stunning gold jewellery. From here, you can take the stairs to the ground floor.

Rooms 26–27: Archaic and Classical Sculpture
The collection concludes on the ground floor with a display of sculpture from the Archaic (Room 26) and Classical (Room 27) periods. The post-Minoan era in Crete tends to be overlooked due to the overwhelming interest in Minoan civilization, but there are some very fine pieces here including, from the Archaic period, a fine limestone lintel from a seventh-century temple at **Prinias** (Rizinia), with worshippers wearing sacred headdresses, and panthers parading beneath their feet. The Classical collection has a wonderfully executed **group of statues** from Górtys depicting Pluto, Persephone (holding a sistrum) and Cerberus, the triple-headed "hellhound" and guardian of the underworld. A marble statue of **Aphrodite** holding a bowl, a Roman copy of a fifth-century BC work by Alkamenes, comes also from Górtys. There's also a superbly carved second-century AD **Roman sarchophagus** found at Mália, as well as a number of other outstanding examples of the sculptor's craft including an imposing

image of a **bearded philosopher**, also from Górtys. Along the walls are a series of **portrait busts** of members of Rome's imperial families, including images of the emperors Augustus, Trajan and Marcus Aurelius.

The exit from here brings you to the **shop** and **café**, the latter with a pleasant shaded terrace. From here you can look down into the ruins of the seventeenth-century **Venetian monastery of St Francis**, the discovery of which delayed the progress of the museum's renovation.

Platía Eleftherías

The south wall of the Archeological Museum faces **Platía Eleftherías (Liberty Square)**, the city's biggest square. On its southern and western flanks, a line of pricey pavement cafés face a rather uninspiring central concourse dotted with gum trees and benches, and skirted by busy roads. Mainly due to its size the square is one of the city's most popular venues for political demonstrations, but most of the time is used by locals for strolling, chatting and sitting out. There's a small bust of Nikos Kazantzákis (see box, p.52) and a larger-than-life statue of Eleftherios Venizélos (the leading figure in the struggle for union with Greece), on the ramparts, looking remarkably like Lenin. Beyond the statue, you reach the entrance to the **public gardens**, as often as not half taken over by a funfair, but otherwise relatively peaceful. In the square's southeast corner, a flight of steps descends to a vaulted passage leading to the sixteenth-century St George Gate in the Venetian walls. The external side of the gate (on Ikarou) survives, but the inner gateway was levelled in the nineteenth century to build the Dhimokratías thoroughfare. On its western side the square is linked to Platía Venizélou by the pedestrianized street **Dedhálou**, lined with many of Iráklio's top designer clothing stores.

Odhós 25-Avgoústou

Pedestrianized **Odhós 25-Avgoústou**, which heads up from the harbour past or towards many of the city's major attractions, takes its name from one of the final acts in the ending of Turkish domination of the island at the end of the nineteenth century (see box below).

Áyios Títos

Platía Áyios Títou • Daily 7.30am–1pm & 4.30–7.30pm • Free

On the left of Odhós 25-Avgoústou as you climb, the church of **Áyios Títos** commands a lovely little square. Originally Byzantine, but wholly rebuilt by the Venetians in the sixteenth century, it was adapted by the Turks as a mosque and rebuilt by them after a

---

STREET OF THE AUGUST MARTYRS

The name of the city's major thoroughfare, in full **Odhós Martírion 25-Avgoústou** (the 25th of August Martyrs), commemorates a bloody incident at the very end of the period of Ottoman rule in Crete. In 1898 under the aegis of the great powers of post-Napoleonic Europe (France, Italy, Russia and Britain), an autonomous Cretan state with an Executive Council was formed under Turkish sovereignty, regarded by most Cretans as a prelude to union with Greece. On August 25 a detachment of British soldiers was escorting Council officials along this street from the harbour when they were attacked by a violent mob of Turkish Cretans, smarting at what they saw as the betrayal of their birthright. In the bloody riot that ensued, hundreds of Christian Cretans lost their lives as well as seventeen British soldiers and the British Honorary Consul. This stirred the British to take reprisals and, on the principle of an eye for an eye, they rounded up and hanged seventeen of the Turkish Cretan ringleaders and put many more in prison. Shortly after this, the British navy sailed into the harbour and the city was cleared of Turkish troops. The following November the last Turkish military forces left the island they had controlled for 230 years.

1

major earthquake in 1856. The Orthodox Church renovated the building after the Turkish population left Iráklio, and it was reconsecrated in 1925. A reliquary inside contains the skull of St Titus (see p.333), originally brought here from his tomb in Górtys; his body was never found. In the Middle Ages, the skull was regularly and ceremonially exhibited to the people of Iráklio, but was later taken to Venice, where it stayed from the time of the Turkish invasion until 1966, when it was returned. On August 25 each year, a major procession from the church marks St Titus' Day.

San Marco and around

Beyond Platía Ayíou Títou, at the northern end of 25-Avgoústou, stands the Venetian City Hall with its famous **loggia**, reconstructed after earthquake damage was compounded by the rigours of World War II. Just beyond here, at the entrance to Platía Venizélou, is the church of **San Marco**, its steps usually crowded with sightseers spilling over from the square. It was the city's cathedral in the Venetian era (two interesting carved gravestones survive in what was the altar area), and was later converted to a mosque. Neither building has found a permanent role in its refurbished state, but both are generally open to house some kind of exhibition or craft show.

Platía Venizélou

Platía Venizélou (also known as Fountain Square or Platía Liontária, Lion Square), formerly the Venetian Piazza San Marco, opens off 25-Avgoústou opposite San Marco church. Ringed by busy cafés, its focal point is the magnificent **Morosini fountain**, which dates from the final years of Venetian rule and upon its inauguration in 1628 became the city's main source of fresh water. Inspired by the city's governor, Francesco Morosini, the work took fourteen months to complete. The fountain was supplied with water from Mount Yioúhtas near Arhánes and reached the city along a 15km-long aqueduct. The fountain's basin is mounted on a circular base and is composed of eight lobes, thus enabling many people to fill their water-jars at the same time. The lobes are decorated with scenes from Greek mythology in carved relief, mainly Tritons, dolphins and nymphs as well as the arms of the Doge, the city councillors and Morosini himself. Originally the whole thing was topped by a giant statue of Poseidon, but even without him it's impressive: the lions on guard are two to three hundred years older than the rest of the structure.

Odhós 1866: the market

Daily 8am–8pm (though individual stalls vary; some close on Sun, while many take a siesta at around 2–5pm)

South of Platía Venizélou, across the busy Odhós Dhikeosínis, **Odhós 1866** is packed throughout the day with the stalls and customers of Iráklio's main **market**. This is one of the few living reminders of an older city, with an atmosphere reminiscent of an eastern bazaar. There are stalls piled high with luscious fruit and vegetables, as well as butchers' and fishmongers' stalls and others selling a bewildering variety of herbs and spices, cheese and yoghurt, leather and plastic goods, CDs, tacky souvenirs, an amazing array of cheap kitchen utensils, pocket knives and just about anything else you might conceivably need.

Platía Kornárou

At the top of the Odhós 1866 market, **Platía Kornárou** makes a pleasantly tranquil contrast. The focal point of the square is a beautiful hexagonal **Turkish pumphouse**, heavily restored, which now houses a café run by the municipality, a meeting place for elderly locals, who converse at the tables under the trees. The small sixteenth-century Venetian drinking fountain beside the café – the **Bembo fountain** (named after its designer Zuanne Bembo) – was the first to supply the city with running water. It incorporates a headless Roman torso imported from Ierápetra.

Platía Ayías Ekaterínis

Three churches ring the **Platía Ayías Ekaterínis**, a quiet escape from the busy shopping streets close by. The **cathedral of Áyios Minas**, a rather undistinguished nineteenth-century building, is notable mainly for its size and the gaudiness of its decoration. Just in front stands its tiny forerunner, the medieval **church of Áyios Mínas**, whose gilded and elaborately decorated altarpiece contains some interesting icons.

Ayía Ekateríni Museum

Platía Ayías Ekaterínis • Daily: April–Oct 9.30am–7pm; Nov–March 9.30am–3pm • €4 • ☎ 2810 336 316

The most interesting church on Platía Ayías Ekaterínis, **Ayía Ekateríni**, recently reopened after a five-year refurbishment and is now a wonderful **museum** dedicated to the Cretan School of **icon painting**. Originally part of the monastery of St Catherine, founded in the tenth century, this building – dating from the sixteenth century – was its main church. The monastery also incorporated a **monastic school** which, up to the end of Venetian rule, was one of the centres of the Cretan Renaissance, a last flourish of Eastern Christian art following the fall of Byzantium. Among the school's students were Vitzentzos Kornaros, author of the Cretan classic *Erotókritos*, and many leading Orthodox theologians; most importantly, however, it served as an **art school** where Byzantine tradition came face to face with the influences of the Venetian Renaissance.

Among the greatest of the school's pupils was the late sixteenth-century painter **Mihailis Dhamaskinos**, and six of his works – including the *Adoration of the Magi*, the *Last Supper* and *Christ Appearing to the Holy Women* – form the nucleus of the collection. It was the much-imitated Dhamaskinos who introduced perspective and depth to Byzantine art, while never straying far from the strict traditions of icon painting. The most famous Cretan painter of them all, Domenicos Theotokopolous, known today as **El Greco**, took the opposite course, wholeheartedly embracing Italian styles, to which he brought the influence of his Byzantine training. Although there is little evidence, it's generally accepted that these two – Dhamaskinos and El Greco – were near contemporaries at the school, though the only El Greco works now on the island are in the Historical Museum (see below).

Among the exhibits are examples of **Venetian arts and crafts**, including stone carving and wood sculpture, both of which display strong Byzantine overtones, as well as sections devoted to church vestments and plate.

The Priouli fountain

Northwest of Platía Ayías Ekaterínis close to Dermatás Bay lies the impressive **Priouli fountain**, built in 1666 at the very end of the Venetian period at the behest of city governor Antonio Priouli, during the long siege of the city by Turkish forces. Sited in what was then the old Jewish quarter, the fountain is based on the form of a Greek temple with Corinthian capitals and crowned with a triangular pediment. It used an underground source to supply the city with water after the Turks had destroyed the aqueducts. Following the Turkish conquest the fountain was restored, as a plaque bearing a Turkish inscription informs.

The Historical Museum

Sófokli Venizélou 27 • Mon–Sat: April–Oct 9am–5pm; Nov–March 9am–3.30pm • €5 • ☎ 2810 283 219, ⊛ historical-museum.gr

The **Historical Museum** is one of the most dynamic in Iráklio, with frequent events and interesting temporary exhibitions. The fascinating permanent collection – with many interactive displays – helps fill the gap which, for most people, yawns between Knossós and the present day, and since it's always virtually deserted, wandering around is a pleasure.

1

The ground and first floors

The **ground floor**, if you're working chronologically, is the place to start; it contains sculptures and architectural fragments from the Byzantine, Venetian and Turkish periods. There are some beautiful pieces, especially a fifteenth- or sixteenth-century tiered fountain from a Venetian palace. The **first floor** has religious art, wall paintings and documents from the same periods, plus a reconstruction of a typically domed Cretan church. Here also are two works by El Greco – the small *View of Mount Sinai and the Monastery of St Catherine* (painted around 1570) and the even smaller *Baptism of Christ* (1567). Sadly – considering the hundreds of canvases by El Greco displayed in the museums of Spain and elsewhere – these are the only works by Crete's greatest painter to be seen on the island of his birth (see p.59 & p.82).

The upper floors

The museum's **upper floors** bring things up to date with reconstructions of the studies of the writer Nikos Kazantzákis (see box, p.52) and of the Cretan statesman (and Greek prime minister) Emanuel Tsouderos; photos and documents relating to the occupation of Crete by the Germans, plus the odd helmet and parachute harness; and a substantial selection of folk art – particularly textiles. There's also the reconstructed interior of a Cretan farmhouse, and a small **café** with sea-view terrace.

The fountain of Idomeneus

Constructed in the late seventeenth century following the fall of the city to the Turks, the small but elegant Ottoman **fountain of Idomeneus** is set into a wall to the rear of the Historical Museum, partly obscured in the evening by diners on the terrace of a nearby taverna. It was a favourite location of Kazantzákis (who was born nearby); the author mentions it in his novel *Kapetan Michalis*. It's worth a look and consists of two columns with floral capitals flanking an arched niche. In the niche, a marble slab bears a Turkish inscription; the water fell into a marble basin below.

The Natural History Museum

Sófokli Venizélou • June–Sept Mon–Fri 9am–7pm; Sat & Sun 10am–7pm; Oct–May Mon–Fri 9am–6pm, Sat & Sun 10am–8pm • €9 • ☎ 2810 282 740, ⓦ nhmc.uoc.gr

Spectacularly housed in a converted power plant overlooking the Bay of Dermatás, the **Natural History Museum** examines the ecosystems of the eastern Mediterranean along with Crete's geological evolution, the arrival of man, and the environment as it would have appeared to the Minoans. Exhibits over four floors (with more planned in the coming years) display fossils, rocks, minerals and caves, and the flora and fauna of modern Crete. For kids there's the **Discovery Centre** in the basement, a wonderful hands-on interactive natural playground with microscopes and a mock-up marine exploration boat. There's plenty on dinosaurs too, including a huge 4.5m-high prehistoric Cretan mammoth, reconstructed from fossil remains; and there's an **earthquake simulator** and a planetarium. The latest addition is a **"Living Museum"** on Level 1, with live examples of frogs, reptiles and mice found in Crete. An emphasis on respect and care for the environment, and on species endangered by tourism and development, is a welcome reflection of the growing awareness of these issues on the island.

City beaches

It's easy to escape the city for a few hours to lie on the **beach**. The simplest course is to head east, beyond the airport, to the municipal beach at **Amnísos** or to the marginally quieter **Tobróuk** beach. Beaches to the west are less prone to aircraft noise but are also more commercialized. Turn to "Getting Around" (see p.62) for details of how to reach them.

Eastern beaches

To the east of the city, past the airport, the old road along the coast runs past a series of sandy strands. A few areas are fenced off as pay beaches with showers, changing rooms and other facilities, but between them are plenty of free spots. **Amnísos** is perhaps the pick here, with tavernas and food stalls immediately behind the beach, and showers and loungers for rent; there's good sand and clean water, too, although the stream of planes coming in to land directly overhead can be wearing. Amnísos itself is a famous name in Minoan archeology, and through a fence you can glimpse the remains of the small settlement here. This was apparently a port for Knossós, from which the Cretan forces engaged in the Trojan War are said to have set sail, and it was in a villa here that the unusual **Fresco of the Lilies** was found – now on display in the Archeological Museum.

Just beyond Amnísos, the beach at **Tobróuk** is arguably even better, with more tavernas and drinks stalls, slightly fewer people, and relative peace to be found if you walk a little way along the sand.

Western beaches

The beaches to the **west** of the city are less atmospheric and more exposed to the wind and waves than the eastern ones – which makes them popular with local surfers and kitesurfers. Cutting through Iráklio's prosperous western suburbs, you end up on a road which runs through the strip-development of **Amoudhára**, finally ending up at the luxury *Creta Beach* hotel complex, unappealingly sited immediately before the power station and cement works. **Amoudhára beach** lies on the other side of the many hotels along this road, and getting to it is not always easy; although the beach is open to the public, there are very few access roads. One is located just west of the *Creta Beach* hotel.

ARRIVAL AND DEPARTURE

IRÁKLIO CITY

BY PLANE

Iráklio airport The airport (Heraklion; ☎ 2810 397 800, ⓦ heraklion-airport.info) is right on the coast, 4km east of the city. Bus #1 leaves for Platía Eleftherías (every 20min until 11pm; €1.70) from the car park in front of the terminal; buy your ticket at the booth before boarding. There are also plenty of taxis outside, with prices to major destinations posted – it's €10–15 to the centre of town depending on traffic; agree on the fare first.

Airlines Aegean (☎ 2810 330 475, ⓦ aegeanair.com) and Olympic (☎ 2810 337 203, ⓦ olympicair.com) are the main scheduled airlines, with domestic flights to Athens and elsewhere, and international connections via Athens or Thessaloníki; Sky Express (☎ 2810 223 800, ⓦ www.skyexpress.gr) and Minoan Air, Vosporóu 1 (☎ 2810 333 183, ⓦ minoanair.com) also operate small planes to Athens and the islands. EasyJet, Jet2 and charter airlines have direct flights from the UK in summer.

Destinations Athens (12 daily; 50min); Kýthira (2 daily, 1hr 30min); Kós (2–4 daily; 1hr); Mytilíni (Lésvos, 2–3 daily; 1hr 15min); Rhodes (3–4 daily; 1hr); Thessaloníki (at least 2 daily; 1hr 15min).

BY FERRY

Ferry dock From the wharves where the ferries dock, the city rises directly ahead in steep tiers. If you're heading for the UK in summer.

the centre on foot, for the Archeological Museum or the tourist office, cut straight up the stepped alleys behind the bus station (from where there are buses to the centre) onto Doúkos Bófor and to Platía Eleftherías (about a 15min walk). For accommodation, though, and to get a better idea of the layout of Iráklio's main attractions, it's simpler to follow the main roads: head west along the coast, past Bus Station A and on by the Venetian harbour before cutting left towards the centre on Odhós 25-Avgoústou.

Operators and destinations Minoan Lines, 25-Avgoústou 17 (☎ 2810 229 602, ⓦ minoan.gr) and ANEK/Superfast, Dhimokratías 11 (☎ 2810 223 067, ⓦ www.anek.gr) have nightly ferries to Athens (9pm/9.30pm; 8hr 30min); ANEK also operate the *Prevelis*, departing Wed at noon to Sitía (3hr), Kássos (6hr), Kárpathos (8hr), Hálki (11hr) and Rhodes (13hr). Hellenic Seaways (ⓦ hellenicseaways.gr) run a daily fast catamaran (April–Oct) to Thíra (Santoríni; 2hr), Íos (2hr 40min), Páros (4hr) and Mýkonos (4hr 50min); Seajets (ⓦ seajets.gr) also run daily in summer to Thíra (Santoríni; 2hr 15min).

Tickets and timetables The local agent for Hellenic Seaways and Seajets is Paleologos Travel, 25-Avgoústou 5 (Mon–Fri 9am–8pm, Sat 9am–3pm; ☎ 2810 346 185, ⓦ ferries.gr), who have current timetables and can sell tickets for all ferries. You can also check timetables at ⓦ openseas.gr.

1

BY CAR

Arriving in town by car, the best bet is to head for one of the signposted city-centre car parks (€3–6/day depending on location). One of the best is the large museum car park on Doúkos Bófor, 70m downhill from the Archeological Museum, which uses space below the city walls and has plenty of shade.

BY BUS

You can check bus timetables at ⓦ bus-service-crete-ktel .com.

Bus Station A On the main road between the ferry dock and the Venetian harbour, Bus Station A serves all the main north-coast routes; west to Réthymno and Haniá and east along the coastal highway to Hersónisos, Mália, Áyios Nikólaos and Sitía, as well as southeast to Ierápetra and points en route. There's a left luggage office here (daily 6am–9pm; €2/bag/day).

Destinations Arhánes (14 daily, fewer at weekends; 30min); Ay. Nikólaos (20 daily; 1hr 30min); Ay. Pelayía (Mon–Sat 4 daily; 45min); Haniá (16 daily; 3hr); Hersónisos (every 30min; 45min); Houdhétsi (Mon–Fri 2 daily, noon & 2pm; 40min); Ierápetra (8 daily; 2hr 30min); Kastélli (6 daily, fewer at weekends; 1hr); Lasíthi plateau (Mon & Fri 2.15pm; 1hr 30min); Mália (every 30min; 1hr); Pezá (Mon–Fri 2 daily, noon & 2pm; 30min); Réthymno (16 daily; 1hr 30min); Sísi (daily 3pm; 1hr 30min); Sitía (7 daily; 3hr 15min).

Bus Station B Buses for the southwest (Festós, Mátala and Ayía Galíni) and along the inland roads west (Týlissos, Anóyia and Fódhele) operate out of Bus Station B just outside Pórta Haníon, a 15min walk from the centre down Kalokerinoú (or jump on any city bus heading along this street).

Destinations Anóyia (3 daily; 1hr); Ay. Galíni (5 daily; 2hr 15min); Festós (3 daily; 1hr 30min); Mátala (3 daily; 2hr); Míres (11 daily; 1hr 30min).

GETTING AROUND

By bus Only the further-flung sites and beaches really justify taking a bus. For the beaches, head for Platía Eleftherías; westbound bus #6 stops outside the *Capsis Hotel* and heads out through the Pórta Haníon (past Bus Station B); eastbound #7 departs every 15min or so from the tree-shaded stop opposite. Knossós buses start from the city bus stands alongside Bus Station A and pass through Platía Eleftherías; airport buses also pass through the square. It's easier to buy tickets (€1.70) before you board, from machines in Platía Eleftherías and elsewhere, or from the many kiosks.

Bike and car rental 25-Avgoústou is lined with rental companies, but you'll often find better deals on the

backstreets nearby; it's always worth asking for discounts. Try the reliable Blue Sea, Kosmá Zótou 7, just off the bottom of 25-Avgoústou (☎ 2810 241 097, ⓦ bluesearentals.com); Alianthos, Íkarou 97 and at the airport (☎ 2810 390 482, ⓦ alianthos-group.com); Kosmos, 25-Avgoústou 15 (☎ 2810 241 357, ⓦ www.cosmos-sa.gr); Caravel, 25-Avgoústou 39 (☎ 2810 245 345, ⓦ caravel.gr), or Ritz, in the *Hotel Rea*, Kalimeráki 1 (☎ 2810 223 638, ⓦ www.hotelrea.gr). All offer free delivery to hotels and the airport.

Taxis Major taxi stands are in Platía Eleftherías, Platía Kornárou, Odhós Dhikeosýnis by the market and at the bus stations; or call ☎ 2810 210 102 or ☎ 2810 210 168. Prices should be displayed on boards at the taxi stands.

INFORMATION AND TOURS

Tourist office The hi-tech Info Point, Platía Nikifourou Foka (effectively the east side of Platía Venizélou, Fountain Square), is currently the city's only tourist information office (Mon–Fri 8.30am–2.30pm; ☎ 2813 409 777; ⓦ www.heraklion.gr). The EOT office at Xanthoudhídhou 1, just below Platía Eleftherías opposite the Archeological Museum, is currently closed and it is unclear as to when or if it will reopen.

Travel agencies 25-Avgoústou is crammed with shipping and general travel agents; Paleologos Travel, 25-Avgoústou 5 (Mon–Fri 9am–8pm, Sat 9am–3pm; ☎ 2810 346 185,

ⓦ ferries.gr) sells tickets for all ferries.

Tours Two rival companies operate hop-on, hop-off bus tours, offering a good overview of the city with stops at all the major sights and museums. The route stays almost entirely outside the walls, so doesn't include the city centre, but they do go out as far as Knossós. In high season buses run every 40min or so – the red bus (ⓦ cretecitytour .com) is more frequent than the green (ⓦ her-openbus.gr); a 24hr ticket costs around €20, though if you hesitate their ubiquitous touts may offer you a better deal.

ACCOMMODATION

Finding a room can be difficult in high season. **Inexpensive places** are mainly concentrated in the streets above the Venetian harbour to the west of Odhós 25-Avgoústou. More **luxurious hotels** mostly lie closer to Platía Eleftherías and near Bus Station A. Noise can be a problem wherever you stay.

★**Atrion** Hronáki 9 ☎ 2810 246 000, ⓦ atrion.gr. This attractive, modern, business-style hotel, with all the comforts that implies – marble bathrooms, minibar, silent

a/c – combines luxury with a personal touch and a friendly welcome. Top-floor suites have stunning views. Breakfast included. **€96**

1

Heraklio Youth Hostel Vironos 5 ☎ 2810 286 281, ✉ heraklioyouthhostel@yahoo.gr. The youth hostel occupies a wonderful old building with high ceilings and tiled or wood floors, and you certainly can't complain about the price, though the dorms – single-sex, with 8 to 10 bunks – and bathrooms are very basic indeed. There are some simple private rooms too. Dorms €12, doubles €30

Iraklion Hotel Kalokerinoú 128 ☎ 2810 281 881, ⓦ iraklionhotel.gr. Newish and comfortable hotel close to the attractive Platía Ekaterínis, which has plenty of good breakfast bars. Rooms come well equipped with a/c, fridge and satellite TV, and many of the rooms on the third and fourth floors have fine views out to sea. Cheap parking (€5/day) on site. €55

Kastro Theotokopoúlou 22 ☎ 2810 284 185, ⓦ kastro-hotel.gr. Attractive and recently refurbished three-star hotel with elegant a/c rooms equipped with modern en-suite bathrooms, fridge and flat-screen TV. Handily located on a side street behind El Greco park. Breakfast included. €75

Kronos Agarathou 2 ☎ 2810 282 240, ⓦ kronoshotel .gr. This friendly two-star hotel is located on a busy street (so there's some traffic noise) by the central seafront. En-suite rooms with a/c, TV, fridge and balcony, some with wonderful sea views (at extra cost). €55

★ **Lato** Epimenídhou 15 ☎ 2810 228 103, ⓦ lato.gr. Stylish boutique hotel in a great central location opposite the Venetian harbour, with luxurious a/c rooms sporting fine balcony views over the port (the higher floors have better views). There's an excellent rooftop bar and restaurant, *Herbs' Garden*, in summer. Breakfast included. €90

Lena Lahana 10 ☎ 2810 223 280, ⓦ lena-hotel.gr. Likeable small hotel with friendly management in a quiet street. Simple en-suite or shared-bath rooms all have a/c and tea- and coffee-making facilities. The second floor is airier. €40

Megaron Doúkos Bófor 9 ☎ 2810 305 300, ⓦ www .gdmmegaron.gr. This imposing five-star directly above the bus station has lots of black marble in its public areas, and well-equipped a/c rooms with balcony (you pay extra for a sea view), plus a sauna, gym and rooftop pool. It's all a bit soulless, but the rooftop bar (open to all) has spectacular views over the Venetian harbour. Breakfast included. €142

Olympic Platía Kornarou ☎ 2810 288 861, ⓦ hotel olympic.com. Modern, business-style hotel in a great location. The a/c rooms, with laminate flooring and blonde-wood furnishings, are quiet and well equipped, if a little small. Breakfast included. €65

Rea Kalimeráki 1 ☎ 2810 223 638, ⓦ hotelrea.gr. A good budget option, this friendly, comfortable and clean *pension* is in a quiet area just off Hándhakos. Some rooms come with washbasin, others are en suite; there can be some internal noise, and wi-fi doesn't reach all rooms. €35

CAMPING

Creta Camping Káto Goúves, 16km east of Iráklio ☎ 2897 041 400, ✉ cretacamp@hotmail.com. The surroundings are bleak, but this is a big, well-organized site right on the seafront, with facilities including restaurant, minimarket, wi-fi, beach bar and beach loungers, as well as car rental and organized tours. Decent shady pitches and also tents to rent. Two people plus tent and car €22.50

EATING

There's no shortage of excellent places to eat in Iráklio, though **prices** are generally slightly higher than anywhere else on the island. For good quality and reasonably priced food, you need to get away from the more obvious tourist haunts, above all the main squares of Venizélou and Eleftherías (though the former is a great coffee stop). Another good way to cut costs is to do what the locals do – share. A couple of mezédhes starters and a shared main dish accompanied by a salad and a half-litre of house wine can work out at €20–30 for two. The **market** has plenty of fresh produce, and you can also find **picnic** food at the minimarkets in tourist areas, which are open every day, and at the supermarket on the north side of El Greco Park.

CAFÉS

Hatzaki Kazáni 5, Platía Ayía Ekateríni ☎ 2810 330 049. The most popular of a cluster of relaxing, traditional cafés on this quiet square with tables under the trees. Join the locals for a coffee, or something stronger, after a visit to the cathedral. Daily 8am–11pm.

Kirkor Platía Venizélou 29 ☎ 2810 242 705. The cafés fronting the Morosini fountain on Platía Venizélou specialize in luscious pastries to accompany a strong mid-morning coffee. *Kirkor* is *the* place to sample authentic Cretan *bougátsa* (a deliciously creamy cheese pie served warm and sprinkled with sugar and cinnamon – add ice cream and it becomes ambrosia); also excellent *loukoumádhes* (dough fritters in honey) and *tyrópita*. If you

can't get a table, *Fyllo...Sofies*, next door, is an excellent alternative; both claim to have been founded in 1922. Daily 6am–10pm.

Mare Sófokli Venizélou ☎ 2810 241 946. Stylish café-bar with a wonderful setting and spectacular glass seafront terrace. Serves a range of snacks, and good cocktails at night. Pricey, but worth it for the location. Daily 8am–2am.

News Café Minotaúrou 32 ☎ 2810 241 545. A modern café-bistro on the southwestern side of El Greco Park offering breakfast snacks and baguettes (€3.50–5), burgers (€5.50), salads, grills, pasta and risotto, as well as coffee, juices and ice cream. Very busy as a bar at night, too, when they go into cocktail mode. Daily 9am–2am.

1

Utopia Hándhakos 51 ☎ 2810 341 321. Locals flock here for the cakes and biscuits, served on fancy stands, and above all for the chocolate fondue and chocolate fountains – not cheap, but irresistibly indulgent. At night they also serve more than sixty different beers from all over the world, along with "beer meze" (sausages, mainly), but even then, most people are here for the chocolate and cake. Daily 9am–2am.

RESTAURANTS

Aztecas Hándhakos 22 ☎ 2810 220 334. The salmon-pink decor creates a warm atmosphere in this restaurant, which serves inexpensive Mexican tacos (€2.50 each), fajitas (€17 for two, with all the trimmings), beers and jugs of sangria. July & Aug daily 1pm–12.30am, Sept–June Mon–Sat 1pm–12.30am, Sun 5pm–1.30am.

★**Giakoumis** Fotiou Theodosaki 5 ☎ 2810 284 039. The little alley connecting the market with Odhós Evans is entirely lined with tavernas, catering for market traders and their customers as well as tourists. Established in 1935, *Giakoumis* retains its authenticity, and claims to be the city's oldest taverna. Locals still reckon it serves up some of the best *païdhákia* (lamb chops; €10) on the island – some tribute, given the competition. You can wash them down with the *hyma* (house) wine produced by Lyrarakis, a noted Pezá vineyard (€3.50/0.5l). Mon–Sat 10am–late.

Hovoli Platía Dhaskaloyiánni 3 ☎ 2810 220 320. If all you want is a *yíros* and a beer, or some plain grilled meat, this is the pick of several simple, inexpensive places on this leafy square just off Platía Eleftherías. *Yíros píta* €3, grilled chicken €7, *souvláki* €6. Mon–Sat 7am–11pm.

★**I Avli tou Defkaliona** Kalokairinoú 8 ☎ 2810 244 215. Highly popular (with locals) taverna-ouzerí with a great little terrace fronting the Idomeneus fountain, serving up excellent meat and fish dishes (mains €6.50–12). There's a long list of tasty *orektiká* (appetisers – try the *fáva*), and outstanding choices for main courses include succulent *païdhákia* (lamb chops); you'll probably get at least one dessert on the house to go with the complimentary *rakí*. In high summer, you may need to book to ensure an outdoor table; if you despair of getting one, you could try one of the other tavernas on the same square. Daily 5pm–1am.

★**Ippokampos** Sófokli Venizélou 3 ☎ 2810 280 240. The first of a row of places with glassed-in, sea-view terraces (there's also a pleasant dining room for cooler days) immediately west of the harbour, *Ippokampos* serves excellent fish at competitive prices (sardines €6.50, red mullet €11). Highly popular with locals, it's often crowded late into the evening, and you may have to queue or turn up earlier than the Greeks eat. Mon–Sat 1pm–midnight.

★**Katsinas** Marinéli 12, Platía Pireós ☎ 2810 221 027. A simple, economical and friendly ouzerí/grill serving tasty mezédhes and traditional dishes at outdoor tables. Genuinely home-made food, with hand-cut chips, good fish, and earthy mezédhes like snails (€5), tzatzíki (€3) and wild onion bulbs (€4). Daily 11.30am–1am.

Ligo Krasí, Ligo Thálassa Marinéli at Mitsotáki ☎ 2810 300 501. This ouzerí is very popular with locals and serves up a good selection of seafood mezédhes (seafood meze menu for two €39.80; individual dishes around €4), with a small street terrace on a busy corner facing the harbour. At the end of the meal there's a complimentary *loukoumádhes* dessert and *rakí* on the house. Daily noon–1am.

Loukoulos Koraí 5 ☎ 2810 224 435, ⓦ loukoulos -restaurant.gr. With a very attractive leafy courtyard terrace and an Italian slant to its international menu, this is one of the more elegant tavernas in Iráklio. Not as pricey as it looks (mains around €12, set menu €10–12), though if you go for the bottled vintages, rather than their acceptable *hyma* (barrelled) wine, things can get expensive. They bake their own bread in a wood oven and have a good selection of fish (as well as meat) dishes and salads. The soups are pretty tasty, too. Daily 1pm–1am.

Mayeireuontas me Ayapi Koroneou 21 ☎ 2810 335 119. Wonderful spick and span little diner – the name means "Cooking with Love" – run by the ebullient Sofía who prepares a range of *mayireftá* (oven-cooked dishes), including pasta bakes, at economical prices (€5–8). The *yemistá* (stuffed tomatoes) and *moskhári yálaktos* (beef stew) are recommended. Salads and pizzas are also on the menu, and the house wine is a mere €2.50 per half-litre. Mon–Sat noon–midnight.

O Miltos Linoperamata, 5km west of the centre ☎ 2810 821 584. Excellent, friendly and cheap fish taverna, one of a cluster owned by three competing brothers, with a terrace overlooking the sea. *Taverna Delfini* and *I Kalouba* are the others, but unlike *O Miltos*, they are open only in the evening. You'll need your own transport or a taxi to get here; they're 1km west of the power station, with its red-and-white chimney stacks, and close to the cement factory – but don't let that put you off. Daily noon–midnight.

Opus Kapetán Haralabí 3 ☎ 2810 225 151. Atmospheric wine bar with a cellar containing no less than 160 wines from the whole of Greece (€16–90 per bottle). The building is a superbly restored Venetian-Turkish structure, part of which was once a prison – hence the sturdy walls. Dishes to go with the wines range from *orektiká* like stuffed mushrooms and skewered prawns (both €6) to cheese boards to share (€8) and more elaborate dishes such as steak and salmon fillet (€12–18). Daily 10am–2am.

Pagopiion Platía Áyios Títos ☎ 2810 221 294, ⓦ pagopoieion.gr. With a makeover and new management, this is the pricier restaurant of Iráklio's most stylish bar (see opposite), with stripped stone walls, wooden tables and retro chairs. The menu offers international dishes and modern versions of traditional Greek food, with pasta, risotto and pizzas all costing around €10; an expansive wine list has bottles from little-known but excellent small vineyards. Daily noon–1am.

Peri Orexeos Koraí 10 ☎ 2810 222 679. This popular small taverna is a good bet for creative Cretan cooking, with generously portioned dishes such as burger stuffed with feta, red pepper and olives (€8.50). Mains €7–15; house wine €7 per litre. Daily 1pm–midnight.

★**Peskesi** Kapetán Haralabí 3 ☎ 2810 225 151. Traditional Cretan dishes concocted with a creative twist are served inside a beautifully restored mansion (menti̇̀ Kazantzákis's *Freedom and Death*) with pastel-tinted wai. delightful nooks and secluded patios. All the ingredients come from the restaurant's own farm and the wine list is exclusively Cretan. House specialities include *kolokoánthi* (courgette flowers stuffed with cheese) and *syglino* (pork ribs smoked with thyme and sage); mains cost €8–11. Cocktails (made with exclusively Cretan spirits, herbs and spices) are also served. Daily noon–1am.

DRINKING AND NIGHTLIFE

As a university town, Iráklio has plenty of places to let your hair down. Young Cretans tend to be more into sitting and chatting over background music than dancing; large areas of Koraí and the surrounding pedestrianized streets are packed with alfresco cafés that transform into **bars** as the lights dim and the volume ramps up. The bigger **clubs** are generally away from the central zone; they tend to play Western music (and lots of techno) interspersed with Greek pop. Most don't open their doors before 11pm, with the crowds drifting in after 1am and dancing until dawn. For livelier, and earlier, partying head to one of the nearby resorts or look out for posters advertising beach parties in summer. There are good listings for all sorts of events online at ⓦ nowheraklion.com.

BARS

Central Park Arkoléondos 19, El Greco Park ☎ 2810 346 501, ⓦ central-park.gr. Big, busy cocktail bar and café with one of the city's most popular terraces for those who want to see and be seen. There's a substantial menu (until midnight) that goes beyond the usual snacks, big screens, and an almost permanent crowd. Daily 8am–1am.

Kafe Diartiriteo Hándhakos 71 ☎ 6942 617 932. With its walls filled with old music and film posters, this a cosy, arty bar with an eclectic playlist, ranging from techno to blues and rembétika. Also has a pleasant street terrace. Daily 1pm–1am.

Kafenion Fix Aretoúsas 2 at Meramvélou ☎ 2810 289 023. Traditional café and bar, busiest in the evenings, with tables set out under the trees of an attractive platía. There's no music, so this is a popular place for a quiet, early drink and great if you want to make yourself heard. Daily 9am–1am.

Jailhouse Ayiostefanitón 19. Friendly rock bar in what turns out inside to be an ancient stone building on two levels; a gathering place for Iráklio's alternative crowd who can hang out here all day until the live music starts next door at *Rolling Stone* (see below). Daily 5pm–4am.

Pagopiion (Ice Factory) Platía Áyios Títos ☎ 2810 346 028. Stunning bar with arty decor inside Iráklio's former ice factory. Much of the old building has been preserved, including a lift for hauling the ice from the basement freezer and a fascistic call to duty in German Gothic script on one wall – a remnant of Nazi occupation of the factory in World War II. Be sure to visit the toilets, which are in an artistic league of their own. An outdoor terrace faces the church of Áyios Títos and an attractive square. Daily 11am–1am.

Take Five Arkoléondos 7, El Greco Park ☎ 28150 05650. One of the oldest bars in Iráklio, *Take Five* began as a rock bar in the 1980s and is now a slick pavement café with an indoor bar, playing jazzy music; it's a favourite late-night hangout for a slightly older crowd. Daily 10am–3am.

To Mílon tis Eridos Platía Koraí ☎ 2810 241 820. Café-bar and terrace that serves everything from twelve types of coffee to cocktails and herbal teas, including *diktamo* (Cretan dittany), a panacea the Cretans have been sipping for thousands of years. Live music at weekends. Daily 9am–3am.

CLUBS AND LIVE MUSIC VENUES

Akrotiri Envy Sof. Venizélou, on seafront 400m west of the Natural History Museum ☎ 6940 588 430. Expansive, swish seafront club with daytime bar, pool bar and day-glo cocktail bar, with frequent live acts in summer (mainly Greek *bouzoúki* big names). Thurs & Sun are international nights when DJs play modern and classic US and European tunes. Daily 9am–3am or later.

Island of Desire Makaríou 17 at Venizélou ☎ 6980 343 484. Dance club facing the sea that's part of a huge shopping complex. Cool lighting and DJs set the mood and dancing often lifts off in the small hours. The playlist features rock, Greek pop and international chart music, and weekends in summer feature live bands from the UK and the Netherlands. Daily 11pm–late.

Rolling Stone Rock Bar Ayiostefanitón 19 ☎ 6980 715 658. Attached to the *Jailhouse* bar (see above), this is a rock club with a great atmosphere, sweaty, late-night live rock and punk bands, and rock DJs – Wednesday is Greek rock night. Tues–Sat 10.30pm–4am; closed July & Aug.

Senses Club Papandréou 277, Amoudhára ☎ 6944 269 733. A lively, summer-only club with a party atmosphere, 5km west of the city by Amoudhára beach, playing various genres of music including dance and r'n'b. Good theme nights and special events. Summer daily 9pm–late.

ps, especially those selling jewellery, clothes and fabrics, head to Dedhálou, Odhós 1821 and Odhós est of the market respectively) and to Kalokerinoú heading west from here. There's a huge **street** turday in an open area at Itánou and Leonídhou, southeast of the centre, and a smaller, local one every ótou in the airport suburb of Alikarnassós.

Iráklio market Odhós 1866. One of the best markets on the island, good for food and herbs – bargain-priced saffron and unique Cretan dried thyme – as well as cheap practical goods, leatherware, hats and tourist items like beach towels and T-shirts. Daily 8am–8pm (though individual stalls vary; some close on Sun, while many take a siesta from around 2–5pm).

Planet International Bookstore Hándhakos 73

2810 289 605, ritio@otenet.gr. Excellent bookshop, with the best selection of English-language titles and maps. Mon, Wed & Sat 9am–2pm, Tues, Thurs & Fri 9am–2pm & 6–9pm.

Roadside Travel Bookshop Hándhakos 29 2810 344 610. Map specialist with a large selection of maps and guides, plus books in English. Mon, Wed & Sat 8am–2pm, Tues, Thurs & Fri 9am–2pm & 5.30–8pm.

DIRECTORY

Banks and money The main branches are on 25-Avgoústou, many of them with ATMs; there are more machines at banks along Dhikeosínis.

Football OFI Crete is Iráklio's and Crete's major team, until 2014 playing in the Greek Superleague (first division); financial irregularities led to the club being relegated to Division 3. Their matches take place at the Demótikou stadium, Platía Ayía Varvára in the Kaminia district on the west side of town (2810 283 920). The city's other team, Ergotelis (Division 2), play at the stadium below the Martinengo Bastion.

Hospitals The closest is the Venizéleio Hospital, on the Knossós road south out of town (2813 408 000); there are better facilities at the modern University Hospital at Voútes, the island's largest (2813 402 111), 6km southwest of the city.

Laundry Washsalon, Evgenikoú and Ayiostefanitón (Mon & Wed 9am–6pm, Tues, Thurs & Fri 9am–9pm, Sat 9am–3pm) and Wash Center, Epimenídhou 38, near the

Lato hotel (Mon–Fri 8.30am–3pm & 5.30–9pm, Sat 8.30am–3pm), both do good service washes.

Left luggage In addition to the left luggage in Bus Station A (see p.62), the youth hostel (see p.63) allows you to leave bags (€5/bag/day to non-residents, €3 to residents). Most hotels will look after your bags free for a few days if you've stayed, as will bike rental companies.

Mountaineering and hiking The local EOS is at Dhikeosínis 53 (2810 227 609, eos-her.gr).

Pharmacies Plentiful on the main shopping streets. At least one will be open 24hr on a rota basis; check the list on the door of any pharmacy. There are also traditional herbalists in the market.

Post office Main office in Platía Dhaskaloyiánnis, off Eleftherías (Mon–Fri 8.30am–7pm).

Public toilets In El Greco Park, the public gardens, Platía Kornárou, Platía Ayía Ekateríni, at the bus stations and at the Archeological Museum (no need to pay entrance charge).

Knossós

…a dancing place
All full of turnings, that was like the admirable maze
For fair hair'd Ariadne made, by cunning Daedalus

Homer, *The Odyssey*

KNOSSÓS (Κνωσός), 5km south of Iráklio on a low, largely artificial hill, was by far the largest of the **Minoan palaces**, thriving more than three and a half thousand years ago at the heart of a highly sophisticated island-wide civilization. Long after Minoan culture had collapsed, a town on this site remained powerful, rivalling Górtys well into the Roman era. Today it is the most famous – and most visited – of all Crete's tourist attractions. No matter when you come, you won't get the place to yourself, but with luck you will have the opportunity to appreciate individual parts of the palace during the brief lulls between groups. In summer the best time of day to avoid the crowds is in the last couple of hours before closing time, which also has the advantage of being cooler. If you get the opportunity to come back a second time, it will all begin to make a great deal more sense.

ARCHEOLOGICAL MUSEUM, IRÁKLIO (P.52) >

1

Brief history

The discovery and excavation of the palace is among the most amazing tales of modern archeology. Until the start of the twentieth century, Knossós was a place thought to have existed only in mythology. **Heinrich Schliemann**, the German excavator of Troy, suspected that a major Minoan palace lay under the various tumuli here, but was denied the permission to dig by the local Ottoman authorities. Today's Knossós, whose fame rivals any such site in the world, is primarily associated with **Sir Arthur Evans**, who excavated and liberally "restored" the palace at the start of the twentieth century and whose bust is one of the first things to greet you at the site. The autocratic control he exerted, his working standards and procedures, and, above all, the restorations he claimed were necessary to preserve the building have been a source of furious controversy among archeologists ever since (see box, p.326). It has become clear that much of Evans's upper level, the *Piano Nobile*, is pure conjecture. Even so, his guess as to what the palace might have looked like is certainly as good as anyone else's, and it makes the other sites infinitely more meaningful if you have seen Knossós first. Without the restorations, it would be hard to visualize the ceremonial stairways, strange top-heavy pillars and brightly frescoed walls that distinguish Knossós – and almost impossible to imagine the grandeur of the multistorey palace. To get an idea of the size and complexity of the palace in its original state, take a look at the cutaway drawings on sale outside; they may seem somewhat fantastic, but are probably not too far from reality.

The Palace of Knossós

Daily: May–Sept 8am–8pm; Oct–March 8am–5pm • €6; €10 joint ticket with Iráklio Archeological Museum • ☎ 2810 231 940

As soon as you enter the **Palace of Knossós** through its West Court, it is clear how the legends of the labyrinth grew up around it. Even with a map and description, it can be very hard to work out where you are.

The remains you see are mostly those of the **second palace**, rebuilt after the destruction of around 1700 BC (see p.330) and occupied – with increasing Mycenaean influence – through to about 1450 BC. At the time, it was surrounded by a town of considerable size. The palace itself, though, must have looked almost as much of a mess then as it does now – a vast bulk, with more than a thousand rooms on five floors, which had spread across the hill more as an organic growth than a planned building, incorporating or burying earlier structures as it went. In this, Knossós simply followed the pattern of Minoan architecture generally, with extra rooms being added as the need arose. It is a style of building still common on Crete, where finished buildings seem to be outnumbered by those waiting to have an extra floor or room added when need and finance dictate.

THE LEGEND OF THE MINOTAUR

Knossós was the court of the legendary **King Minos**, whose wife Pasiphae, cursed by Poseidon, bore the **Minotaur**, a creature half-bull, half-man (see p.345). The **labyrinth** was constructed by Daedalus to contain the monster, and every nine years (some say every year) seven youths and seven maidens were brought from Athens as human sacrifice, until finally **Theseus** arrived to slay the beast and, with Ariadne's help, escape its lair. Imprisoned in his own maze, Daedalus later constructed the wings that bore him away to safety – and his son **Icarus** to his untimely death. The legend has inspired writers from Homer to Dante, who famously depicts the beast in his vision of Hell:

Into the chasm was that descent: and there
At point of the disparted ridge lay stretch'd
The infamy of Crete, detested brood
Of the feign'd heifer: and at sight of us
It gnaw'd itself, as one with rage distract.

Dante, *Inferno*, Canto XII

PALACE OF KNOSSÓS

Royal Road

Theatral Area

North Entrance

Lustral Basin

Bull Relief

West Court

Storage Pits

Giant "Píthoi"

Site Entrance

Statue

Piano
Nobile

Throne Room

Storerooms

Workshops

Central Court

West Entrance

Grand
Staircase

Priest-King
Fresco

Royal Apartments

Corridor of the
Procession

South House

Southeast House

0   25
metres

N

The difficulty in understanding the site is not helped by the fact that you are no longer allowed to wander freely through the complex: instead, a series of **timber walkways** channels visitors around. This is particularly true of the Royal Apartments, where access to many rooms is denied or reduced to partial views from behind glass screens. Given the reluctance of Greek museums and archeological sites to use less disruptive audioguides, the walkways also make it almost impossible to avoid the guided tours that congregate at every point of significance en route. On the upside, wait anywhere long enough and a free tour will come along – you can always tag onto one of these for a while, catch the patter and then hang back to take in the detail when the crowd has moved on.

The West Court

The **West Court**, across which you approach the palace, was perhaps a marketplace or, at any rate, the scene of public meetings. Across it run slightly raised walkways, leading from the palace's West Entrance to the Theatral Area, and once presumably on to the Royal Road. There are also three large **circular pits**, originally grain silos or perhaps depositories for sacred offerings, but used as rubbish tips by the end of the Minoan era. When these were excavated, remains of early dwellings – visible in the central pit, dating from around 2000 BC and thus preceding the first palace – were revealed. The walls and floor surfaces were found to have been coated with red plaster, and these are among the earliest-known remains on the site.

Following the walkway towards the **West Entrance** nowadays, you arrive at stones marking the original wall of an earlier incarnation of the palace, then the facade of the palace proper, and beyond that a series of small rooms of which only the foundations survive.

1

The first frescoes

Anyone entering the palace by the West Entrance in its heyday would have passed through a guardroom and then followed the **Corridor of the Procession**, flanked by frescoes depicting a procession, around towards the south side of the palace; the walkway runs alongside. A brief detour down the stairway near the West Entrance would enable you to view the **South House** (see p.72) before entering the palace proper.

Following the walkway, you come to the reproduction of the **Priest-King Fresco** (which Evans dubbed the Prince of the Lilies, although some scholars are convinced the figure is female or not even a royal personage at all); the original of this and other Knossós frescoes are in Iráklio's Archeological Museum (see p.52). A revealing glimpse into Evans's mindset comes from an article he wrote in the London *Times* when this fragmentary figure came to light: "…the head is wearing a crown, which terminates in a row of five sloping lilies… That the *fleur-de-lis* of our Edwards and Henrys should find a prototype in prehistoric Greece is a startling revelation". The nearby viewing point offers a chance to look down over the palace. Apparently, a whole series of large and airy frescoed chambers, perhaps reception rooms, once stood here.

The Central Court

The **Central Court**, the heart of the palace, is aligned almost exactly north–south. The courtyard paving covers the oldest remains found on the site, dating back to Neolithic times. In Minoan times high walls would have hemmed the courtyard in on every side, and the atmosphere would have been very different from the open, shadeless space that survives. Some say this was the scene of the famous bull-leaping, but that seems unlikely: although the court measures almost 50m by 25m, it would hardly be spacious enough to accommodate the sort of intricate acrobatics shown in surviving pictures, let alone an audience to watch.

The Throne Room

The entrance to one of Knossós's most atmospheric survivals, the **Throne Room**, is in the northwestern corner of the central courtyard; you'll spot the room by the queues of people waiting to press their faces against the glass to view it. In the room, a worn stone throne sits against the wall of a surprisingly small chamber; along the walls around it are ranged stone benches and, behind, there's a copy of a fresco depicting two griffins. In all probability, this was the seat of a priestess rather than a ruler – there's nothing like it in any other Minoan palace – but it may just have been an innovation wrought by the Mycenaeans, since it appears that this room dates only from the final period of the palace's occupation. Opposite the throne, steps lead down to a lustral basin – a sunken "bath", probably for ritual purification rather than actual bathing, with no drain.

The Piano Nobile

Alongside the Throne Room, a stairway climbs to the first floor and Evans's reconstructed **Piano Nobile**. One of the most interesting features of this part of the palace is the view it offers of the palace storerooms with their rows of *píthoi* (storage jars). There's an amazing amount of storage space here, in the jars – which would mostly have held oil or wine – and in sections sunk into the ground for other goods. The rooms of the *Piano Nobile* itself are again rather confusing, though you should be able to pick out the Sanctuary Hall from stumps that remain of its six large columns. Opposite this is a small concrete room (complete with roof), which Evans "reconstructed" directly above the Throne Room. It feels entirely out of place; inside, there's a small display on the restoration of the frescoes, and through the other side you get another good view over the Central Court. Returning through this room, you could climb down the very narrow staircase on your right to arrive at the entrance to the corridor of storerooms (fenced off) or head back to the left towards the area where you entered the palace.

1

The Royal Apartments

On the east side of the central courtyard, the **Grand Staircase** leads into the **Royal Apartments**, clearly the finest of the rooms at Knossós, though sadly you can't enter any of them. The **staircase** itself is an architectural masterpiece, not only a fitting approach to these sumptuously appointed chambers, but also an integral part of the whole design, its large well allowing light into the lower storeys. Light wells such as these, usually with a courtyard at the bottom, are a common feature of Knossós and a reminder of just how important creature comforts were to the Minoans, and how skilled they were at providing them.

For more evidence of this luxurious lifestyle, you need look no further than the **Queen's Suite**, off the grand **Hall of the Colonnades** at the bottom of the staircase. The main living room is decorated with the celebrated dolphin fresco and with running friezes of flowers and (earlier) spirals. On two sides it opens to courtyards that let in light and air; the smaller one would probably have been planted with flowers. It is easy to imagine the room in use, scattered with cushions and hung with rich drapes, curtains placed between the pillars providing privacy and cool shade in the heat of the day. Guides will describe all this but it is of course almost entirely speculation – and some of it pure con. The dolphin fresco, for example, was found in the courtyard, not the room itself, and would have been viewed from inside or above as a sort of *trompe l'oeil*, like looking out of a glass-bottomed boat. There are many who argue, convincingly, that grand as these rooms are, they are not really large or fine enough to have been royal quarters. Those would more likely have been in the lighter and airier rooms that must have existed in the upper reaches of the palace, while these lower apartments were inhabited by resident nobles or priests.

Whether or not you accept Evans's names and attributions, the rooms remain an impressive example of the sophistication of Minoan architecture. The **Queen's Bathroom**, its clay tub protected behind a low wall (and probably screened by curtains when in use), is another fine example, as is the famous "flushing" lavatory (a hole in the ground with drains to take the waste away – it was flushed by a bucket of water).

On the floor above the queen's domain, the Grand Staircase passes through a set of rooms that are generally described as the **King's Quarters**. These are chambers in a considerably sterner vein. The staircase opens into a grandiose reception area known as the **Hall of the Royal Guard**, its walls decorated in repeated shield motifs. Opening off it is the ruler's personal chamber, the **Hall of the Double Axes** – a room that could be divided to allow for privacy while audiences were held in the more public section, or the whole opened out for larger functions. Its name comes from the double-axe symbol, so common throughout Knossós, which here is carved into every block of masonry.

The drainage system

From the back of the queen's chambers, you can emerge into the fringes of the palace where it spreads down the lower slopes of the hill. This is a good point at which to consider the famous **drainage system** at Knossós, some of the most complete sections of which are visible under grilles. The snugly interconnecting terracotta pipes ran underneath most of the palace (here, they have come more or less direct from the Queen's Bathroom), and site guides never fail to point them out as evidence of the advanced state of Minoan civilization. Down by the external walls you get a clear view of the system of baffles and overflows designed to slow down the runoff and avoid flooding.

The Palace Workshops

From the bottom of the slope, you get a fine impression of the scale of the whole palace complex and can circle around towards the north, climbing back inside the palace limits to see the area known as the **Palace Workshops**. Here, potters, lapidaries and smiths appear to have plied their trades, and this area is also home to the

1

spectacular **giant píthoi**; people queue to have their photograph taken with the jars towering over them. From here there's also a good view of the Bull Relief fresco in the restored north entrance.

Around the North Entrance

Circling around the palace, you can re-enter by the **North Entrance**. Beside the gateway is a well-preserved **lustral basin**, and beyond that, a guardroom. As you head up towards the central courtyard, a flight of stairs doubles back to allow you to examine the copy of the **Bull Relief** close up.

Just outside the North Entrance, the **Theatral Area** is one of the more important enigmas of this and other Minoan palaces. An open space resembling a stepped amphitheatre, it may have been used for ritual performances or dances, but there's no real evidence of this, and again there would have been very little room for an audience if that was its function.

Beyond it, the **Royal Road** sets out: originally this ran to the Little Palace (see below), perhaps with branches heading north to the palace's harbour at Amnísos and west across the island; however, nowadays it ends after about 100m at a brick wall beneath the modern road. Alongside are assorted structures variously interpreted as stores, workshops or grandstands for viewing parades.

The south side

Of the lesser structures that crowd around the palace, a number of houses on the south side are particularly worth noting. The one known simply as the **South House**, reconstructed to its original three floors, seems amazingly modern, but actually dates from the late Minoan period (c.1550 BC). The dwelling is believed to have belonged to an important official or noble, since it encroaches on the palace domain. In the **Southeast House** of the same period, a cult room with a sacred pillar was discovered, as well as stands for double axes and a libation table.

Outlying remains

Numerous small sites dot the fields surrounding the palace, most of them barely visited, perhaps because unless you get lucky all you can do is stare in through their fences.

Caravanserai

Across a little valley from the south side of the palace, accessed from the road south

The **Caravanserai** was where travellers visiting Knossós would rest and water their animals. The restored building contains two elegant rooms, as well as a large stone footbath still with running water from an ancient spring. There's a good view of the palace from the surrounding fields.

Little Palace and Royal Villa

Off the road to Iráklio • Both occasionally open for special visits; details from ticket office

Among the most important of Knossós' outlying buildings are the **Little Palace**, on a site which also contains a mansion and many Roman remains, and the **Royal Villa**, facing the palace from the slope to the northeast.

Villa Dionysos

300m up the road to Iráklio from the site entrance

The first-century **Villa Dionysos** lay near the centre of the Roman city of Cnossus. The villa has extremely fine polychrome mosaics, and once restoration work (which has been delayed by the economic crisis) is complete it is planned to open it up to the public. For details on the progress of the restoration, contact the Knossós ticket office or the Iráklio tourist office (see p.62).

Villa Ariadne

About 100m along the road to Iráklio from the site entrance • Not open to the public

The **Villa Ariadne** was built by Arthur Evans as his home-from-home during excavations. Later, the house served as a military hospital during the German siege of Iráklio and, following the city's fall, as the residence of the German commander of Crete. It was where General Kreipe was based when he was kidnapped (see p.338), and the villa's dining room was also where the German army signed the treaty of surrender on May 9, 1945. Although not open to the public, nobody seems to mind if you walk up the drive past the gatehouse to have a look at the house's exterior and lush gardens.

ARRIVAL AND DEPARTURE

KNOSSÓS

By bus Local buses #2 and #4 set off (every 10min; €1.50 each way) from Iráklio's city bus stands (adjacent to Bus Station A), then proceed to Platía Eleftherías and out of town along Odhós-1821 and Evans.

By taxi A taxi from the centre of Iráklio will cost around €12.

By car From the centre of Iráklio head out through the Pórta Kenoúria; from anywhere else on the island turn directly off the bypass onto the badly signed Knossós road. There's a free car park immediately before the site entrance; avoid paying exorbitant rates for the private car parks dotting the road immediately before this (whose touts will attempt to wave you in).

INFORMATION AND TOURS

Information The British School at Athens has a useful website dedicated to Knossós, with detail on its history and excavations in addition to a virtual tour; check out ⓦ bsa.ac.uk/knossos/vrtour.

Tours Official guides (there are no audio guides), who are self-employed, can be hired at the site entrance; the tour lasts 1hr 30min and the guide expects to receive a minimum of €100 per tour. This fee will be divided between the number making the tour (thus four people will pay €25 each). To get the lowest rate (€10 per person) you will need to wait until the guide has gathered ten customers. This can take up to 15min in high season, longer in slack periods. The maximum number of people allowed per tour is 14.

South of Iráklio: wine country

The countryside south of Knossós is dominated by the bulk of **Mount Yioúhtas** (811m), which rises alone from a landscape otherwise characterized by gently undulating agricultural country. Seen from the northwest, the mountain has an unmistakably human profile, and was traditionally identified with Zeus. The ancient Cretans claimed that Zeus lay buried underneath the mountain; given that the god is immortal, this furnished proof for other Greeks of the assertion that "All Cretans are liars" – it may even have been the original basis of this reputation.

As you leave Knossós behind, the nature of the journey south is transformed almost immediately: the road empties and the country becomes greener. Almost any of these roads makes a beautiful drive, past vineyards draped across low hills and through flourishing farming communities. Just a couple of kilometres from the archeological site, at the head of the valley, an extraordinary **aqueduct** arches beside the road. This looks medieval and was built on the line of an earlier Roman aqueduct, but is in fact less than two hundred years old, having been constructed during the brief period of Egyptian rule (1832–40) to provide Iráklio with water. A little further on, the junction where you turn right towards Arhánes seems a singularly unthreatening spot today, yet it was here, on April 26, 1944, that General Kreipe was kidnapped (see p.338). The site is now marked by a lofty modern monument.

Much of the interest in this region centres around **Arhánes**, where there's an **Archeological Museum** and easy access to three fascinating **Minoan sites** at Foúrni, Anemospília and on the summit of Mount Yioúhtas itself. Nearby at **Vathýpetro** the remarkable remains of a Minoan vineyard can be seen, at the heart of what remains one of the island's chief **wine-growing areas**: many winemakers open their doors to the public, especially at **Pezá**.

1

East of Pezá, the village of **Myrtiá** boasts a museum devoted to Crete's most famous literary name, Nikos Kazantzákis, and just south of here a road meanders through hilly farm country well inland from the big resorts, into a region known as the **Pedhiádha**. There's an important **pottery** centre at **Thrapsanó**, and other diversions include the ancient site of **Lýttos** and some notable **frescoed churches** around **Kastélli**.

Arhánes

ARHÁNES (Αρχάνες) is a large and prosperous agricultural centre, substantial enough to have a one-way traffic system and be served by hourly buses from Iráklio. The streets in the central area are narrow and confusing, and the best advice for drivers is to park up near the square and explore on foot. There are tavernas and cafés around the main square, as well as numerous flashy modern bars, reflecting the region's agricultural prosperity. In summer (mid-July to mid-August) a colourful daily **street market**, selling local crafts and delicacies, takes place in the old quarter.

The richness of the land around Arhánes is nothing new: this area was a major centre of **Minoan civilization**, and there are a number of important sites in and around town, including a hypothesized fifth palace to rival those at Festós and Mália. Most are relatively recent discoveries, having been excavated over the last few decades, and not all of the excavations have been fully published. Consequently, these sites are neither particularly famous nor especially welcoming to visitors, but many of the finds are nonetheless important; indeed, some of the greatest treasures of the Iráklio archeological museum come from this region. A site right in the heart of modern Arhánes is described as the **Summer Palace**, and may have functioned as such for Knossós in the way that Áyia Triádha apparently did for the Festós palace, but this is largely speculation. Still,

---

WINE TASTING AROUND PEZÁ

Locals claim, with some justification, that **wine** has been made in the area around Pezá for four thousand years (see p.77), probably using grape varieties not far removed from the Kotsifáli and Mandilariá (for red), Plytó and Vilána (white) that are extensively cultivated today. Cretan wines, traditionally very much *vin ordinaire*, are becoming increasingly sophisticated, and a number of wineries open their doors to visitors. Most require appointments, but all of the following allow unplanned visits. For more information there is a useful and detailed wines of Crete **map** available from vineyards and the Iráklio tourist office, as well as a website: ⓦ winesofcrete.gr.

Boutari Skaláni, on the Myrtiá road, 4km beyond Knossós ☎ 2810 731 617, ⓦ www.boutari.gr. Modern estate with state-of-the-art facilities and a fancy multimedia show. Boutari is a big, national company with an excellent reputation, though this Cretan operation is still in its early stages. Tours €5. Mon–Fri 9am–5pm.

Mesarmi Houdhétsi, on the left as you enter the village from Áyios Vasílios ☎ 6972 665 599. A wine shop which offers tastings of Pezá and Cretan wines as well as olive oil and cheese. The proprietor, Stella Vassilaki, is a Master of Wine. Tasting of six wines €12. Daily 11.30am–5pm.

Minos Pezá ☎ 2810 741 213, ⓦ minoswines.gr. On the main street in Pezá village, the epicentre of Cretan wine production, Minos is one of the island's biggest producers. There are tours of the winemaking plant, but at any time you can watch a video about the history of Cretan wine production, look at some traditional equipment, and taste

and buy the house brands. Tours roughly hourly (40min; €3). Mon–Fri 9am–4pm, Sat 10.30am–3pm.

Peza Union Pezá, on the Kastélli road at the eastern edge of town ☎ 2810 741 945, ⓦ pezaunion.gr. The union of agricultural cooperatives of Pezá produces olive oil as well as wine, from the vines and trees of many small producers. A tour of their exhibition centre is followed by wine tasting and a small portion of meze. Free. April–Oct Mon–Fri 9am–3pm.

Stilianoú Winery Kounavi, 3km north of Pezá and signed once you reach the village ☎ 6936 430 368, ⓦ stilianouwines.gr. A pleasant drive through the vines takes you to the welcoming Stilianoú family vineyard, where they have been producing wine for four generations. Following a tour you can taste their four wines (three reds and a white), as well as the family-produced olive oil, a wonderfully peppery number. Free. April–Oct daily 11am–7pm; Nov–March Mon–Sat 10am–3pm.

what remains is impressive and through the chain-link fence you can see evidence of a substantial walled mansion, representing only a small part of what once stood here. Piecemeal excavation is still going on at other sites in the centre too, but much is hidden beneath more modern buildings. If you make the Archeological Museum your first stop, you can find out more about the status of these sites, and pick up a leaflet (with town map) on things to do in the area.

Arhánes Archeological Museum

Miháli Kalohristianáki, an alley between the two one-way streets, about 80m north of the main square • Wed–Mon 8.30am–2.30pm • Free • ☎ 2810 752 712

Imaginatively laid out in a single room, the **Arhánes Archeological Museum** displays some exceptional finds from the town and surrounding sites. Near the entrance are some well-preserved Minoan **lárnakes** (clay coffins, complete with the bones found in them) from **Foúrni** (see below) dating from around 1800 BC. Displayed nearby is a replica of a **sistrum** (a simple, tambourine-like musical instrument; the original is in the Iráklio Archeological Museum), also from the cemetery at Foúrni, and dates from around 2000 BC; it may well be the oldest surviving musical instrument in Europe. A photo shows a detail of the famous Harvesters Vase from the Iráklio museum, depicting a sistrum in use.

There are fascinating finds, too, from **Anemospília** (see p.76), where human sacrifices appear to have taken place in the temple. A copy of the **dagger** found lying on the sacrificial victim is displayed here, with a curious motif of a hybrid animal – resembling a deformed boar – carved on the blade. There's also a copy of the seal stone that the priest was wearing on his left wrist, and of the terracotta feet of a wooden statue that was destroyed in the fire that followed the destruction of the temple; again, the originals are in the Iráklio museum.

Other items to look out for include small terracotta cups that contained the ochres used to paint frescoes on the walls in the palaces and villas, and an imaginative display of **pottery shards** that evidences five thousand years of human occupation in this town: crude works of the third millennium BC are succeeded by the various Minoan periods, then Greek, Roman, Byzantine, Venetian and Turkish pieces, down to broken pots of the present day. There are also fragments of Minoan wall painting and many everyday domestic objects, ranging from a wine-press and giant *píthoi* to jewellery and jugs.

Arhánes churches

Numerous ancient churches are scattered through the town, though there's no guarantee that you'll find any open. Right on the main square an incongruous whitewashed clock tower marks out one, with a fine collection of icons; elsewhere, there are Byzantine frescoes in the church of **Ayía Triádha** on the fringes of town and at the church of **Asómatos** to the east, where the superb fourteenth-century works include a horrific *Crucifixion* and a depiction of the fall of Jericho, with Joshua in full medieval armour.

Foúrni

Immediately west of Arhánes • July & Aug Tues–Sun 8am–3pm; at other times check with the Arhánes Archeological Museum (see above) • Free • Cross the bypass west of Arhánes and then walk for about 10min up a steep, very rocky trail

The size of the **burial ground at FOÚRNI** (Φούρνι) is evidence of the scale of the Minoan community that once thrived around Arhánes; the site was used throughout the Minoan period, with its earliest tombs dating from around 2500 BC (before the construction of the great palaces), and the latest from the very end of the Minoan era. The structures include a number of early tholos tombs – round, stone buildings reminiscent of beehives – each of which contained multiple burials in sarcophagi and *píthoi*. Many simpler graves and a circle of seven Mycenaean-style shaft graves were also revealed at Foúrni, making it by far the most extensive Minoan cemetery known. In "Tholos A", a side-chamber was found that revealed the undisturbed tomb of a woman

1

HUMAN SACRIFICE IN ANCIENT CRETE?

The temple at Anemospília appears to have been destroyed in the midst of a ceremony involving **human sacrifice** – the only evidence of such a ritual found in Minoan Crete. This came as a severe shock to those who liked to portray the Minoans as the perfect peaceable society, but the evidence is hard to refute. Three skeletons were found in the western room: one had rich jewellery, indicative of a priest; another was a woman, presumably a priestess or assistant; the third was curled up on an altar-like structure, and, according to scientists, was already dead when the building collapsed and killed the others. A large bronze knife lay on top of this third skeleton. Outside the western room, another man was crushed in the corridor, apparently carrying some kind of ritual vase. These events have been dated to roughly the time of the earthquakes that destroyed the first palaces and, in the circumstances, it seems easy to believe that the priests might have resorted to desperate measures in a final attempt to appease the gods who were laying waste to their civilization.

who, judging by the jewellery and other goods buried with her, was of royal descent and perhaps a priestess. Her jewellery is now on display at the Iráklio Archeological Museum, as is the skeleton of a horse apparently sacrificed in her honour.

Anemospília

2km northwest of Arhánes

ANEMOSPÍLIA (Ανεμοσπήλια) is enlivened by a spectacular setting and a controversial story, though the site itself can only be viewed through a fence. The approach road heads north from Arhánes: coming from Iráklio, you enter the one-way street and almost immediately turn sharp right, back on yourself, just past a small chapel. Following the road leading northwest out of the town, you begin to climb across the northern face of Mount Yioúhtas, winding around craggy rocks weirdly carved by the wind (Anemospília means "Caves of the Wind") until you reach the fenced site held in a steep curve of the road.

What stood here was a **temple**, and its interpretation has been the source of outraged controversy among Minoan scholars since its excavation at the beginning of the 1980s. The building, apparently destroyed by an earthquake around 1700 BC, is a simple one, consisting of three rooms connected by a north-facing portico, but its contents are not so easily described (see box above).

Mount Yioúhtas

A couple of kilometres south of Arhánes, a track leads towards the summit of **MOUNT YIOÚHTAS (Γιούχτας)**, a relatively easy drive. You can also climb the mountain in little over an hour from Arhánes, but it seems rather unsatisfying to do this only to discover other people rolling up on their motorbikes or in taxis (the summit is an optional diversion on the E4 European path as it crosses Crete: coming from the east it follows the track mentioned above, then winds steeply down to Arhánes, to rejoin the main route, via the footpath). At the summit, the **panoramic views** are the main lure, back across Iráklio especially, but also west to Psilorítis and east to Dhíkti. Up here, too, is a small chapel, and the trappings of the annual *paniyíri* (festival), which is celebrated on August 15 and attracts villagers from all around. The impressive remains of a **Minoan Peak sanctuary** dating from the early second millennium BC occupy the north side of the hill, partly built over by a telecommunications station. It very likely served as a cult centre, attracting pilgrims from Arhánes and Knossós, both of which can be seen from the summit. An enormous number of votive offerings, including jewellery, figurines and libation vessels, were unearthed in the excavations and are now on display in the museum at Iráklio. On the shoulders of the mountain, not easily accessible, are caves associated with the local Zeus cult.

Vathýpetro

4km south of Arhánes • Tues–Sun 8am–3pm • Free

The site of **VATHÝPETRO** (Βαθύπετρο) is well signposted off the road south of Arhánes, beneath Mount Yioúhtas. The remains of a large **Minoan villa**, which once controlled the rich farmland south of Arhánes, it was found when excavated to contain a remarkable collection of everyday items – equipment for making wine and oil, and other tools and simple requisites of rural life. Still surrounded by a vineyard with a valid claim to be the oldest in the world (wine has been produced here since the second millennium BC), the house was originally a substantial building of several storeys, with a courtyard enclosing a shrine, and fine large rooms – especially on the east side. The basement workrooms, however, were the scene of the most interesting discoveries, comprising agricultural equipment and a remarkably well-preserved **winepress**, which can still be seen in situ.

Houdhétsi

HOUDHÉTSI (Χουδέτσι) lies on a side road that links two major north–south thoroughfares, from Arhánes towards Pýrgos and the road through Pezá and Arkalohóri towards Áno Viánnos. The village is distinguished from its agricultural neighbours by the presence of the museum and music workshop, **Labyrinth**.

Labyrinth

Just off the main square • Mon–Sat: April–Oct 9am–2pm; Nov–March 10am–2pm • €3 • ☎ 2810 741 027, ✆ labyrinthmusic.gr

Labyrinth is partly a **museum of musical instruments** from all around the world and partly a music workshop with a programme of concerts and seminars throughout the summer. It was founded by Irish *lyra* player Ross Daly (see box below), who lives nearby, and is the focus for much of his musical energy. Housed in an elegant mansion, with a rare, emerald-green grass lawn, the museum consists of a collection of mainly string and percussion instruments (many very rare) from across the globe.

Myrtiá

The main reason to visit **MYRTIÁ** (Μυρτιά) is for the **Kazantzákis Museum**, dedicated to the writer and philosopher Nikos Kazantzákis (see box, p.52). Only the seriously committed will spend long here, but it's a lovely drive to the village on almost deserted roads. Myrtiá itself is larger than you'd expect – as are so many of these villages – and bright with flowers planted in old olive-oil cans.

THE IRISH LYRA PLAYER

One of the more remarkable stories of Cretan music is that an Irishman, **Ross Daly**, has become one of its most famous names. Born in England of Irish parents, he grew up in Asia and North America, the family settling wherever the work of his physicist father happened to take them. Daly first visited Crete in 1971 and was strongly attracted to its traditional music, studying in that same decade under master *lyra* player Kostas Mountakis, in Haniá. Part of his early career was spent in Anóyia teaching *lyra* to local children, but once he had become a *lyra* virtuoso he was not content to stay within the confines of Cretan music and began to synthesize what he had learned in Crete and Greece with music from other cultures such as Turkey, the Balkans, India and Afghanistan.

Daly now performs worldwide with his ensemble, Labyrinth, a unit comprising Russian, Greek and Cretan musicians, but always returns to his home in Crete. In addition to the *lyra*, he now plays a variety of instruments, including the *laoúto* (lute), *oud*, *rabab* (Afghan lute), *sarangi* (Turkish *bouzoúki*) and a special *lyra* with twenty-one strings instead of the usual three. More details, including a full discography, can be found at ✆ rossdaly.gr.

1

Kazantzákis Museum

In the village square • March–Oct daily 9am–5pm; Nov–Feb Sun 10am–3pm • €3 • ☎ 2810 741 689, ⓦ kazantzaki.gr

The **Kazantzákis Museum** occupies a cluster of buildings in the village square, where Nikos Kazantzákis's parents once lived. Its collection includes a vast quantity of ephemera relating to the great author and philosopher: diaries, photos, manuscripts, first editions, translations into every conceivable language, playbills, stills from films of his works, costumes and more. There's also a video documentary in Greek.

Thrapsanó

The large village of **THRAPSANÓ** (Θραψανό), 4km south of the Pezá–Kastélli road, has for centuries been an important **pottery-making** centre. Workshops still thrive in the village and along the roads out towards Vóni and Evangelismós, and many of them welcome visitors to admire the potters' skills, although there's not a great deal on offer to buy. There is, though, a good range of earthenware: *píthoi* are evident throughout Thrapsanó, not only in workshops but upturned in the main square and on the backs of parked pick-up trucks. Both Thrapsanó and Réthymno's pottery centre, Margarítes (see p.204), have found a new export market in recent years for these giant *píthoi*. In northern Europe, they have become popular decorative features for urban gardens, and both centres have been stretched to keep up with demand.

Kastélli and around

The chief village of the Pedhiádha, **KASTÉLLI** (Καστέλλι), or Kastélli Pedhiádhos, is a pleasant place to pause for a while. Chiefly an agricultural centre whose prosperity derives from the olive groves and vineyards spread across the surrounding hills, the town goes its own way, largely unaffected by the tourist zone on the coast below. There's a good taverna and peaceful accommodation, far from the madding crowd; otherwise the main attraction is the surrounding countryside, where winding lanes are traced by elderly oak and plane trees.

Áyios Pandeleímon

Less than 3km north of Kastélli, off the Hersónisos road, signed to "Paradise Tavern" • Daily 9am–3pm • Free

Should you decide to see only one of the many churches in this area, make it **Áyios Pandeleímon** (Άγιος Παντελεύμον), a large building set in a grove of oaks and planes around a spring which was very likely a sanctuary in ancient times. Inside the church are imposing though weathered frescoes of the soldier saints (on the north wall) and an unusual scene of Ayía Ánna nursing the infant Mary. The structure of the church, probably dating from the early thirteenth century, is interesting for the way it incorporates

---

FRESCOED CHURCHES AROUND KASTÉLLI

Many of the villages around Kastélli have frescoed medieval **churches**. Look out for signs as you drive around; they're usually worth seeking out simply for the journey off the main routes, even if you can't get in. In addition to the splendid **Áyios Pandeleímon** (see above), one of the more famous is the fifteenth-century **Isódhia Theótokon**, with fine Byzantine frescoes, near the village of **Sklaverohóri** just a couple of kilometres west of Kastélli. The key is available from the house with a vine trellis about 50m before the church, on the right. Some 6km further west, down a side road beyond Apostolí, **Moní Angaráthou** is in another pretty location. Although the monastery's church dates from the last century, the surrounding buildings date mainly from the sixteenth century and include a picturesque white-walled courtyard with palms, orange trees and cypresses. Another church is **Áyios Yeóryios** at **Ksidhás** (confusingly also known as Lýttos), about 3km east of Kastélli, which has frescoes dated by an inscription to 1321.

parts of the original tenth-century basilica and uses as columns some much older fragments, probably taken from Lýttos. The **aqueduct** that once transported water to the ancient city passes close by, and you may spot parts of it as you drive around. This idyllic spot also shelters the small *Paradise Taverna*, run by the eccentric Nikolaides family.

Ancient Lýttos

2km north of Ksidhás, east of Kastélli, between two small chapels that serve as useful landmarks as you approach

Ancient **LÝTTOS** (Λύττος), occupying a magnificent position in the foothills of the Dhíkti range, was a prominent city of Dorian Crete, mentioned by Homer as leading the Cretan contingent in the Trojan War. Later it was one of the most powerful city-states of Classical Greece during the centuries prior to the Roman conquest, and was the bitter enemy of Górtys, Ierápytna (modern Ierápetra) and especially Knossós. When Lýttos engaged these three in a **war** for control of the island (221–219 BC), it overreached itself; while its army was launching an attack on Ierápetra, Knossós seized the opportunity to destroy the unguarded city, leaving it in ruins and taking its women and children into captivity. The historian Polybius vividly describes how, on their return to Lýttos, the troops broke down in tears at the sight, refused to enter their devastated homes and went for succour to Lappa (see p.229) near Réthymno, one of its few allies. The city was eventually rebuilt, however, and enjoyed a small-scale renaissance under the Romans through to Byzantine times.

The site

Sadly, what is visible above ground today in no way reflects Lýttos's ancient status, as no systematic archeological exploration has yet taken place. Nevertheless what you can see underlines the fact that when the riches of Lýttos are finally excavated – including what is said to be the island's largest theatre, now lost – it will be an important site. Below the church of Tímios Stavrós, built over a large fifth-century basilica with stones from the ancient city, are the bastions and curtain of an enormous **city wall**. The church is believed to mark the centre, or agora, of Lýttos. The church of **Áyios Yeóryios** (which has fragmentary frescoes) is also constructed from stones scavenged from Lýttos: incorporated into the outer wall is a fine fragment of carved acanthus foliage. Nearby, the ancient city's **bouleterion** or council chamber has been excavated, with visible platforms and benches. Spend half an hour roaming through the vines and olive groves on the surrounding slopes and you'll come across partially excavated dwellings, delicately carved tombstones, half-buried pillars and the enormous foundation stones of buildings waiting to be unearthed.

ARRIVAL AND DEPARTURE

By car The old road out via Knossós is much the most pleasant route, but directions can be confused by the presence of the new road, which cuts across the island via Pezá and Houdhétsi, often extremely close to the older road. The loop via Kastélli and the coast makes for a satisfying circuit.

SOUTH OF IRÁKLIO: WINE COUNTRY

By bus Buses from Iráklio (Bus Station A) can take you into wine country.
Destinations Arhánes (Mon–Fri 14 daily, Sat 9 daily, Sun 3 daily; 45min); Kastélli (Mon–Fri 6 daily, Sat 4 daily, Sun 2pm; 1hr); Pezá & Houdhétsi (Mon–Fri 2 daily, noon & 2pm; 1hr).

ACCOMMODATION AND EATING

This is not remotely a touristy area, but you'll find somewhere to eat in most villages; if you stay you become very much part of the life of these thriving rural centres.

ARHÁNES

Arhontiko Villa On the edge of the village ☎ 2810 752 985, ⊚ arhontikoarhanes.gr. This mansion has been converted to provide four beautiful apartments for up to four guests. Furnished with antiques and with dark wood floors and ceilings and exposed brickwork, they also come with kitchenette, wi-fi, TV and a/c. **€70**

Kalimera Archanes Just north of the main square ☎ 2810 752 999, ⊚ archanes-village.com. Lovingly restored old house that offers four villas and studios for

1

two to five people around a tranquil, leafy courtyard. All have well-equipped kitchens and a/c; delicious breakfast included. Studios and villas €150

Lykastos Southwest corner of the main square ☎ 2810 752 433. Excellent and friendly taverna, with good prices – *païdhákia* (lamb chops) €7.50, *horta* (wild greens) €3. The wholemeal bread is outstanding and you'll get at least one tasty dessert on the house. With very good house wine at €3.50 per half-litre and an attractive terrace for people-watching, you couldn't really ask for more. Mon & Wed–Sun noon–1am.

HOUDHÉTSI

Petronikoli Traditional House In the centre of the village ☎ 2810 743 203, ⦿ petronikolis.info. Traditional building in the heart of the village, whose bare stone walls have been scrubbed to within an inch of their lives. Comfy studios and apartments are very well kitted out, with a/c, TV, wi-fi, CD players and more, and there's a café-restaurant and good-sized pool. Studios €60, apartments €70

KASTÉLLI

Hotel Kalliopi Off the main road, near the central crossroads ☎ 28910 32685, ⦿ kalliopi-hotel.gr. If you

want to stay entirely away from tourist centres and get a taste of modern agricultural Crete, you'd be hard-pressed to do better than this. Despite initial appearances the rooms, and a couple of apartments, are as rural as they get, especially if you are in the annexe at the back, amid kitchen gardens and olive groves behind the small pool. Simple but comfortable tile-floored rooms come with TV and a/c, and the proprietors are very friendly. Rooms €35 apartments €45

Taverna Irida Just off the west side of the square where you arrive coming from Iráklio ☎ 28910 32023. Authentic country taverna that serves up traditional dishes such as goat in tomato sauce (€6.50), or *mezédhes* (€3.50–7), along with plenty of seafood and salads. You can also simply stop in for coffee or a juice. Daily 8.30am–midnight.

MYRTÍA

Kampaeti Kazantzákis 48, 200m uphill from the Kazantzákis museum ☎ 28130 14051. Very welcoming and attractive taverna with a tree-shaded terrace, offering carefully prepared Cretan cuisine at bargain prices. A variety of *orektiká* (try the avocado vinaigrette) are priced at €2–5, while main dishes (including chicken with okra) go for €4–8; salads are also on the menu. House wine goes for €3 a half-litre. Daily 9.30am–midnight.

West of Iráklio

Heading west from Iráklio, the modern **E75 highway**, cut into the cliffs, is – in daytime at any rate – as fast a road as you could hope to find (see box below). In simple scenic terms it's a spectacular drive, but with very little in the way of habitation; there are only a couple of developed beach resorts and the "birthplace of El Greco" at **Fódhele** until the final, flat stretch before Réthymno. Once beyond the western city beaches, the highway starts to climb into the foothills of the Psilorítis range as they plunge straight to the sea. As you ascend, keep an eye out for the immaculately crafted medieval fortress of **Paleókastro**, built into the cliff right beside the road; it's easy to miss, so completely do the crumbling fortifications blend in against the rocks.

If you're in no hurry, try the **older roads west**, curling up amid stunning mountain scenery and archetypal rural Crete, with tracks tramped by herds of sheep and goats,

THE E75 HIGHWAY

The **E75 highway**, which crosses the north of the island, linking Haniá in the west to Sitía in the east, is one of the most **dangerous** in Greece. The fact that it is a two-lane road with a hard shoulder has not prevented local drivers from turning it into an unofficial four-lane highway: slow-movers are expected to straddle the line demarcating the hard shoulder, thus allowing faster cars to overtake at will. A reluctance by some tourists to follow this unwritten rule often leads to dangerous tailgating until the way is cleared for the driver in a hurry. Other hazards on this road are posed by small or badly positioned **signs**, frequently posted far too late. Missing your exit can mean travelling a considerable distance to the next one, as they are not as frequent as you might expect. Further dangers can include unexpected traffic lights where the highway passes close to a town, and **left turns**, which can be particularly scary at night when you must deal with the dual hazards of crossing the opposite lane of traffic and the possibility of someone ploughing into your rear while you're waiting to do so.

isolated chapels or farmsteads beside the road, and occasionally a village. There's a choice of routes at Arolíthos (see p.83); the road that goes further inland, through the village of Týlissos and on via Anóyia (see p.205), has more to see and passes through the **Malevísi**, a district of fertile valleys filled with olive groves and vineyards renowned in Venetian times for the strong, sweet Malmsey wine much favoured in western Europe. England became a major market for the wine, and the growth of the shipping trade between Candia (Iráklio) and English ports caused Henry VIII to appoint the first-ever British consul to the island in 1522.

Ayía Pelayía

AYÍA PELAYÍA (Αγία Πελαγία), some 15km from Iráklio, appears irresistibly inviting from the highway far above, a sprinkling of white cubes set around a deep blue bay. Closer up, the attraction is slightly diminished: development is rapidly outpacing the capacity of the narrow, taverna-lined beach, and is beginning to take its toll on the village. However, the water is clear and calm, the **swimming** excellent and there's a superb view, too, of all the ships that pass the end of the bay as they steam into Iráklio – spectacular at night, when the brightly lit ferries go by. Despite the development, and although the beach can get very crowded with day-trippers from Iráklio at weekends, Ayía Pelayía retains a slightly **exclusive** feel, partly thanks to a couple of upmarket hotels on the promontory immediately beyond the village.

    Waterskiing, parasailing and motorboats are all available on the town beach; if you feel in need of a little more space, you can head to one of several other small beaches nearby, though none could be described as empty or unspoilt. As you continue out of the far end of Ayía Pelayía it is possible to walk to three small coves on the coast as it curls around to the north and west: **Kladhisós**, **Psaromoúra**, with just a summertime bar, and finally **Mononáftis**. In the other direction, **Ligariá**, to the east, has a little harbour and a number of tavernas – most of the time it's very quiet, but summer weekends can get busy. There's a turning off the E75 signed directly to Ligariá, or you can get there off the road down into Ayía Pelayía.

ARRIVAL AND DEPARTURE AYÍA PELAYÍA

By car As it descends towards Ayía Pelayía, the road splits. The right-hand fork leads to a car park at the southern end of the beach; the other winds round to enter the town from the back, where there's an even larger car park (€2/day).

By bus There are four direct buses a day from Iráklio (30min; Bus Station A); if you take a long-distance bus bound for Réthymno or Haniá, you face a steep 3km walk down from the drop-off point on the highway.

INFORMATION AND ACTIVITIES

Travel agencies There's no tourist office here, but plenty of travel agencies who can help with rooms and general information as well as tours and car rental; JK Tours on Neofítou Pedhióti (the street between the northern corner of the car park and the beach; ☎ 2810 811 400, ⊛ jk-tours.gr; April–Oct) is particularly helpful.

See also the website ⊛ agiapelagia-crete.com.
Scuba-diving There are two good diving centres: Divers Club Crete (☎ 2810 811 755, ⊛ diversclub-crete.gr), in the middle of Ayía Pelayía's main beach, and the European Diving Institute (☎ 2810 811 252, ⊛ eurodiving.net) at Ligariá.

ACCOMMODATION

Almost every building in the centre of Ayía Pelayía seems to offer rooms, studios or apartments, but even so in peak season it can be hard to find anywhere. The greatest concentration of places is immediately **behind the beach**, especially on the road down from the car park by Vassilis supermarket ("Beach Road").

Creta Sun Hotel On the road behind the village ☎ 2810 811 626, ⊛ www.cretasunhotel.gr. Pleasant studio complex with friendly proprietors and a pool, offering well-kept a/c rooms with fridge and balcony

(sea view extra). €41
Irini Beach Road ☎ 2810 811 455. Cheery two-room apartments above *The Home*, a lurid pink ice-cream parlour/café, just a few metres from the beach. Apartments

1

sleep 2–6, with a/c, balcony, TV and kitchen. Rates rise by about 40 percent in Aug. **€45**

Out of the Blue East of the centre ☏ 2810 811 112, ⓦ capsis.com. This five-star luxury resort complex sits on a private peninsula, comprising five hotels, seven pools, luxury villas with private pools and three private beaches. It even has its own zoo. Minimum 3-night stay. **€235**

Renia Beach Road ☏ 2810 811 349, ⓦ renia.gr. Modern block comprising studios and apartments with a/c, TV and fridge overlooking a decent-sized pool. The decor is a little spartan, but there's a tiny gym (and fish spa), and breakfast is included. Rates go up by €20 in Aug. Studios **€35**, apartments **€40**

Zorba's Beach Road ☏ 2810 811 074, ⓦ zorbas.gr. Decent apartments and studios with balcony – many of which offer a sea view – above a shop just seconds from the beach. Facilities include a/c plus kitchen (apartments) or kitchenette (studios). Studios **€55**, apartments **€70**

EATING AND DRINKING

For food, it's hard to look past the obvious attractions of Ayía Pelayía's seafront **tavernas**, which stretch in a solid row behind the beach, broken only by the odd bar. There are plenty of cheaper options in the village, including a number of takeaways and small supermarkets for the makings of a picnic on the beach. Nightlife is mostly based at the numerous waterfront **bars**.

Mouragio Towards the southern end of the beach ☏ 2810 811 070. Also known as *Stella's* after its ebullient owner, this is among the better-value beachfront restaurants. It serves much the same Greek menu as all the others, with an emphasis on seafood, but is distinguished by the warmth of the welcome.

April–Oct daily noon–11.30pm.

Taverna Lygaria Ligaria beach ☏ 2810 811 242, ⓦ lygaria.gr. A good choice for plain, if rather touristy, food (mains €7–12), in a great location right above the beach. They have loungers for customers' use and also some simple rooms. April–Oct daily 10am–10.30pm.

Fódhele

FÓDHELE (Φόδελε) is firmly established on the tourist circuit as the birthplace of the painter **El Greco** (1541–1614), although there's virtually no hard evidence to substantiate the claim, and most experts now believe that he was born in Iráklio. Nonetheless, it's an enjoyable place to visit: Fódhele is a lovely village in a richly fertile, peaceful valley, surrounded by orange and lime groves. On the far side of the river as you drive up are a couple of small Byzantine chapels, and there's an ancient church in the village, a number of craft shops and some tavernas with riverside terraces. While you're here, take a few minutes to study the plaque in the main square, made of stone from Toledo (where Domenico Theotokopoulos settled, produced the bulk of his most famous works and earned the name El Greco). The plaque was presented to Fódhele in 1934 by the University of Valladolid as an authentication of the locale's claim to fame, which must be responsible in some measure for its current prosperity, whatever the scholars may say now.

Museum of El Greco

Overlooking the valley, about 1km from Fódhele up a signed track • April–Oct daily 9am–7pm • €2.50 • ☏ 2810 521 500, ⓦ psfodele.gr

They used to claim that the ancient building housing the **Museum of El Greco** was the artist's birthplace; without that excuse the museum is, frankly, a waste of time. Given his status in the history of art, there is a niche in the museum market for a venue dedicated to the life and history of this Cretan genius; unfortunately this is an opportunity missed. What you get are a few very poor reproductions and a tedious amount of "evidence" attempting to fix the artist's birthplace as Fódhele. That said, it is a pleasant spot, and directly opposite is the impressive church of the Panayía.

Church of the Panayía

Opposite the Museum of El Greco • Fri–Sun 8am–3pm, but call to check for changes to opening times • Free • ☏ 2810 288 484

The mainly fourteenth-century **Church of the Panayía** is charming. This exquisite, drum-domed church was built over an eighth-century basilica, and the baptismal font in the floor beside the church (deep enough for total immersion) dates from the earlier building. There are also a number of fine thirteenth- and fourteenth-century frescoes. Beneath the orange groves surrounding the church are the remains of the medieval village it once served.

Rodhiá and around

RODHIÁ (**Ροδιά**) is a sizeable village looking back down over Iráklio; looking up from the city at night, you can see its twinkling lights on the hillside. Travelling on the old road west from Iráklio, you pass under the highway, and immediately start to climb south into the hills. Almost straight away, there's a right turn signed to Rodhiá, where a couple of *kafenía* allow you to rest up and enjoy the views.

Convent of Savathianá

5km northwest of Rodhiá · Daily 8am–1pm & 4–8pm · Free

The isolated **Convent of Savathianá** (**Σαββαθιανά**) is set amid barren mountaintops, reached only by narrow tracks. It's an extraordinary place, a lush oasis filled with flowers and birdsong, redolent of a more tranquil age. Founded in the Venetian period, the settlement is beautifully kept by its diligent nuns, who cultivate fruit trees and sell home-made jam to visitors. There are three small chapels within the complex, which gained further celebrity in 1991 when an eighteenth-century icon entitled *Lord Thou Art Great*, identical to the one at Tóplou (see p.160), was discovered; both were painted by Ioannis Kornaros.

Márathos and around

Just beyond **Arolíthos** (**Αρολήθος**) – a tacky and artificial "traditional village" aimed squarely at tourists – the road forks; the route to the right seems far less used, though it used to be the main route from Iráklio to Réthymno. Some 9km northwest of Arolíthos this road passes through **MÁRATHOS** (**Μάραθος**), famous for the honey that seems to be on sale at every house. Márathos is an attractive place with a couple of *kafenía* where you can break the journey (this road runs through very few other villages of any size); not far beyond the village, it's possible to cut down by an unpaved but reasonable track to Fódhele (see opposite).

Týlissos

15km southwest of Iráklio; the archeological site is signed to the left as you approach the village from the east and is fronted by a car park · Daily 8am–3pm · €2 · There are four daily buses to Týlissos village (a few minutes' walk from the site) from Iráklio's Pórta Hanión (Bus Station B); buses continue towards Anóyia

TÝLISSOS (**Τύλισος**) is a name famous in the annals of Minoan archeology as one of the first sites to be excavated, and the thriving modern village has a fair claim to four thousand years of continuous human occupation. Local archeologist Joseph Hatzidhakis, working at the beginning of the twentieth century, revealed evidence of structures from the early Prepalatia period (c.2000 BC), but interest focuses primarily on three large villas (known as Houses A, B and C) from the **Neopalatial** era. They were probably not as isolated in the country-house sense as they seem today, but may well have been part of a thriving community, or even a staging post on the route west towards as yet undiscovered centres. The existence of a rather simpler villa at Sklavókambos, on the road halfway from here to Anóyia, may lend weight to this latter theory. Týlissos shared in the destruction of the palaces in about 1450 BC, but new buildings then arose, among which was the cistern in the northeast corner of the site. Following the arrival of the Dorians, Týlissos developed into a Greek city of the Classical period, issuing its own coinage. This later construction tends to make it a bit harder to get a clear picture of the form of the Minoan structures.

TÝLISSOS

Light Well

Lustral Basin

Entrance

Central Room

Paved Court

Storerooms

Pillar Crypt

Colonnaded Court

Cult Room

Stairway

Cistern

House A

House C

House B

Light Well

Storerooms

Main Room

Altar

Site Entrance

0   10
metres

The site

While it's not always the easiest of sites to interpret, Týlissos is a lovely place to wander round, with few visitors, pine trees for shade, and some evocative remains, including staircases and walls still standing almost 2m tall. Immediately beyond the fence, vineyards and rich agricultural land suggest a seductive, but probably illusory, continuity of rural life. **Houses A and C** are of extremely fine construction and design (C is the more impressive), while little remains of **House B** apart from its ground plan, although it does contain some of the oldest relics.

House A

A building of finely dressed ashlar stone, **House A** has a **colonnaded court** at its heart with a window lighting the staircase to the west side of this. In storerooms on the north side, some large reconstructed *píthoi* can be seen with holes near their bases for tapping the contents (probably oil). A number of Linear A tablets also came to light in this area. In the south wing, the main rooms open onto a light well, with the central room having a **lustral basin** – in this case more like a sunken bath – just off it. A stand for a double axe, similar to finds from Knossós, was found in the **pillar crypt**, along with the three enormous bronze cauldrons (now in the Iráklio Archeological Museum) that originally prompted the site's excavation. Throughout the house, fragments of painted stucco were found, leading archeologists to postulate the existence of a luxurious second storey to this dwelling, which had fallen in over time.

House C

House C, with a fair amount of concrete reconstruction, contains a **cult room** with a central pillar, storerooms and, at its northern end, the living area, where a paved main room would have been illuminated by a light well on its eastern side. At the end of one of many corridors (a Minoan speciality), a staircase would once have led to an upper floor. There is also evidence of a drainage system, while outside the house, beside the cistern, is a **stone altar** from the Classical period.

East of Iráklio

East of the airport and the city beach at Amnísos there's almost continuous development all the way to Mália, as what little remains of the coastal landscape is torn apart to build yet more hotels, apartments and beach complexes. You're in package-tour country here and the resorts of **Hersónisos** and **Mália**, above all, are big, brash and packed with visitors all summer long. There are one or two highlights and escapes along the way, though: the isolated **Skotinó Cave** near Goúves, the impressive **Cretaquarium** at Goúrnes, the **old villages** in the hills behind Hersónissos, and, just beyond the clubs of Mália, a fine **Minoan palace** that will transport you back three and a half millennia. From Hersónisos or Mália, you can also head inland to climb towards the **Lasíthi plateau**.

GETTING AROUND   EAST OF IRÁKLIO

By bus Buses from Iráklio (Bus Station A) serve the coastal resorts, running at least every 30min through Háni Kokkíni and Káto Goúves. Káto Goúves is the coastal offshoot to Hersónisso and Mália, with stops near all the major hotels. All the resorts also put on tours to big attractions like Cretaquarium and Water City.

By car The new E75 Highway runs a short way inland, bypassing all the major attractions and resorts; you'll need to turn off onto the old road to access any of them.

Háni Kokkíni

The first distinct centre east of Iráklio is **HÁNI KOKKÍNI** (Χάνι Κοκκίνι), a grubbily nondescript resort with a long but rather pebbly beach. There's a **Minoan villa** at the western end of town (Tues–Sun 8.30am–3pm; free) – known as Nírou Háni or simply Niros. Dating from the Neopalatial period, it must have been beautifully sited above the water when it stood alone. With the road now cutting it off from the beach, it is harder to appreciate; what you see is a site the size of a large modern house (stairs on the south side led to an upper storey), with walls standing to around waist height.

In the hills behind – a few kilometres to the southwest – is the locked **Cave of Eileíthyia**, which gets a mention in the *Odyssey* as one of Odysseus's stopovers on his way home from Troy. Eileíthyia was the Minoan goddess of childbirth and this cave was used as a place of worship and pilgrimage from the late Neolithic to the fifth century AD. Many figurines and votive objects were found in the cave, and its central stalagmite, a metre and a half high, is thought to have played some role in ceremonies here, perhaps as an altar. The Minoan villa and the cave share the same guardian and if free, he may be willing to accompany those with their own transport to open the cave. Information on both sites is available from the friendly *Taverna To Kyma*, almost opposite the villa, who also have the guardian's number.

Goúrnes and around

At **GOÚRNES** (Γούρνες), 15km from Iráklio, there's a break in the overdeveloped coastal strip where, just west of the village, a mammoth former US air force communications base awaits redevelopment. The one thing that has been built here, and currently stands surrounded by broken fences and crumbling buildings, is the **Cretaquarium**, a spectacular marine aquarium extensively signed from the highway.

Cretaquarium

Goúrnes • Daily: May–Sept 9.30am–9pm; Oct–April 9.30am–5pm • €9, children 5–17 €6 • ☎ 2810 337 788, ⓦ cretaquarium.gr

Boasting thirty tanks (some huge), the **Cretaquarium** houses everything from menacing sharks to dazzling jellyfish. Part of the Hellenic Centre for Marine Research, the venture is purely educational, scientific and non-profit-making. Most of the island's fish and crustaceans are included among the 250 species and more than 2500 specimens on

1

display, and unless you're a marine biologist the audio-guide (easily shared between two or three) is pretty well indispensable, giving loads of fascinating background information on the creatures you're looking at.

Water City water park

Anópoli, 4km inland from Goúrnes and Háni Kokkíni, 15km from Iráklio • May–Oct daily 10am–6.30pm • €25, children 90–140cm €17 • ☎ 2810 781 317, ⓦ watercity.gr

The giant **Water City** is the largest and probably the most impressive water park on the island, with many of the rides taking advantage of the natural hillside over which the place is built. There's the usual array of slides, pools, snack bars and fast-food outlets, though they can struggle to cope with the crowds in high season.

The Skotinó Cave

About 6km inland from Káto Goúves, 3km by road from the village of Skotinó • Open daylight hours • Free

The **Skotinó Cave** is one of the largest and most spectacular on the island. It's an uphill hike from the coast (get detailed directions before you set out), or an easy drive, passing through **Goúves** village, which makes an encouraging contrast to the coastal strip and is a good spot to pick up refreshments – there are a couple of decent tavernas. The cave itself is well signed from the village of **Skotinó** (Σκοτεινό), which means "dark", the last part on a rough track where the cave entrance is marked by a pair of chapels".

Some 160m deep, the cave is divided into four levels, with an awesomely huge main chamber; it's unattended and you can scramble down as far as you dare, with plenty of natural light at first, though you'd be brave to explore the further recesses alone. It was first investigated by Arthur Evans and more scientifically explored in the 1960s by French and Greek archeologists. A considerable number of bronze and ceramic **votive offerings** were found (the earliest dating back to early Minoan times), suggesting that this was an important shrine. The cave remained in use well into the Greek and Roman eras, when the fertility goddess Artemis was worshipped in what is thought to have been a substitution for an earlier Minoan female fertility deity, possibly Brytomartis. In the chapel of Ayía Paraskeví above, *tamata* (ex votos) left by pilgrims continue a tradition of supplication to the (now Christian) deity that has persisted on this same spot for well over four thousand years.

Hersónisos and around

HERSÓNISOS (Χερσόνησος) – more correctly **Límin Hersonísou**, the Port of Hersónisos; Hersónisos is one of the villages in the hills just behind – is the first of the big resorts east of Iráklio, a boisterous, sprawling and rather seedy place catering to mainly Dutch, Irish and Italian package tourists, replete with all the trappings of mass tourism. If you're looking for tranquillity and Cretan tradition, forget it; this is the world of concrete high-rise hotels, video bars, fast-food shops and eurodiscos. The town's main artery is a 2km-long street (Odhós Venizélou) parallel to the sea, a seemingly endless ribbon of bars, travel agents, amusement arcades, tacky shops, car and bike rental dealers and traffic jams. That said, the resort has plenty of life, lots of competition to keep food and drink prices down, and some really attractive rooms and restaurants in the hill villages behind; there are also decent sandy **beaches** both to the west and to the east. The one thing you may struggle to find in July or August is a room.

The esplanade

Along the modern seafront, a solid line of restaurants, bars, bars and more bars is broken only by the occasional souvenir shop or fish spa. In their midst you'll find a small **pyramidal fountain** with broken mosaics of fishing scenes. This dates from the Roman era and is the only real relic of the ancient town of **Chersonesos**, a thriving port from

Classical Greek through to Byzantine times, handling trade from Lýttos (see p.79). The busy pleasure **harbour** to the west of the fountain is built over the ancient Roman one, and in odd places along the seafront you can see remains of Roman harbour installations, mostly submerged. The headland above the harbour is a popular spot to watch the sun set; you can explore the excavated remains of an impressively large, early Christian basilica here, complete with mosaic floors, while on the far side the remains of ancient Roman fish tanks can be seen cut into the rock. Other than these, most daytime interest is on the fringes of Hersónisos.

Star Beach Water Park

On the beach immediately east of Hersónisos • Daily: April & May 10am–6pm; June–Sept 10am–7pm • Free entry, but charges for most activities • ☎ 28970 29351, Ⓦ star-beach.gr

Star Beach Water Park hugs the coast immediately east of town, with some fine beach areas as well as pools, slides, bars and restaurants, and a wide range of watersports from banana boats to kitesurfing. Activities for young children are generally free, as are the pools and wi-fi, but everything else has to be paid for, from loungers to bungee jumping.

Lychnostatis Open-Air Museum

On the eastern edge of Hersónisos, beyond Star Beach • Mon–Fri & Sun 9am–2pm; guided tours every hour on the half-hour • €5; tours €1 • ☎ 28970 23660, Ⓦ lychnostatis.gr

The entertaining **Lychnostatis Open-Air Museum** of folk culture is worth a visit, particularly if you haven't had a chance to see the "real thing" inland. Set in a reasonably authentic-looking recreation of a traditional Cretan village in a pleasant location next to the sea, the various exhibits relate to a way of life rapidly disappearing from the island. There are orchards and herb gardens, and live displays of local crafts, such as ceramics and weaving, as well as collections of lace, embroidery and traditional costumes within the main house. Concerts of traditional music and dance are frequent, and they occasionally stage more elaborate "dance spectaculars" in the evening, as well as seasonal special events like grape-treading in the autumn.

Aqua World

Just off Venizélou in Hersónisos, at the bottom of the road to Piskopianó • April–Oct daily 10am–6pm • €8, children €4 • ☎ 28970 29125, Ⓦ aquaworld-crete.com

A small aquarium displaying many of the fish and sea creatures found off the island's coast, **Aqua World** also has a selection of snakes, lizards and tortoises outside in the reptile garden. Scots-run, Aqua World has an environmental ethos, and many of the creatures it houses have been rescued or were unwanted pets.

Acqua Plus

3km inland from Hersónisos on the route to the Lasíthi plateau, by the golf club • May–Oct daily 10am–7pm • €26, children 5–12 €17; cut-price late-entry deals available • ☎ 28970 24950, Ⓦ acquaplus.gr

Acqua Plus is a big water park that comes close to rivalling Water City (see opposite), but doesn't quite match up in terms of size or number of slides. It's a good day out nonetheless, with an attractive setting in a natural bowl of hills and a fair amount of shade.

Piskopianó and around

In the hills immediately behind Hersónisos, the three pretty **hill villages** of **Piskopianó** (Πισκοπιανó), **Koutoulafári** and **"old" Hersónisos** present a glimpse of a more traditional Crete. They're far from unspoilt – Piskopianó is directly above the harbour and an easy walk, with Koutoulafári a little further, so plenty of people come up here in the evenings to the pretty tavernas and to nights of Cretan dancing – but they're certainly more peaceful than the coast.

1

Museum of Rural Life

Piskopianó • Mon & Wed–Sat 10am–6pm • €4 • ☎ 28970 23303, ⓦ historical-museum.gr

The one real sight in the villages around Hersónisos, the impressive **Museum of Rural Life**, is one of the best of its kind. It's housed in a nineteenth-century village mansion with attached olive mill, modernized to form the bulk of the museum, and a more traditional workshop/barn; displays cover all aspects of rural life from carpentry to olive-oil and *rakí* production, and above all there are some very fine examples of traditional weaving.

ARRIVAL AND DEPARTURE

HERSÓNISOS AND AROUND

By bus Buses run between Hersónisos and Iráklio (Bus Station A) virtually every 30min (45min), and to Áyios Nikoláos only marginally less frequently. Buses make stops along the main street (Odhós Venizélou).

By taxi For short hops around town, or up to the hill villages, there's a taxi stand at the western end of Venizélou. You can also call on ☎ 28970 22098.

INFORMATION AND ACTIVITIES

Travel agencies In the absence of a tourist office, travel agencies are the best source of information; they're everywhere, offering a huge variety of local tours as well as horseriding, scuba, boat trips and car rental.

Boat trips A wide variety of boat trips to local beaches and islands are on offer from the harbour; it's around €25

for the popular day-trip to Sísi (see p.138). Fishing trips are also on offer (tackle provided) for around €30 (3hr).

Horseriding Finikia (☎ 6945 924 112, ⓦ hersonissos -horseriding.com) offer riding tours into the hills (around €60) and on the beach, and lessons from their base close to Star Beach.

ACCOMMODATION

Although you should have little problem finding somewhere to stay outside the peak season of July and August, much accommodation is allocated to package-tour operators and what remains is not cheap. Hotels in the centre are subject to a fair amount of **noise** both from traffic and – after dark – the vibrant nightlife. If you have a car or don't mind a short taxi ride or 20min walk, it's best to head inland to the hill villages for better quality and more peaceful surroundings.

Caravan Camping On the beach at the eastern end of Hersónisos, by Lychnostatis ☎ 28970 22025, ⓦ camping -caravan.doodlekit.com. Small campsite in a brilliant location right on the water. Not much room, so pitches for tents can be tight-packed; they also have hexagonal concrete "bungalows", with just enough space for a double bed, sink and fridge. April–Nov. Two people plus tent and vehicle **€21.50**, bungalows **€33**

Creta Maris On the coast northwest of the centre ☎ 28970 22115, ⓦ maris.gr. The ritziest place in town, hogging the best part of the beach, with every facility you'd expect from a vast, luxury, all-inclusive resort (a wrist bracelet serves as ID), including bungalows designed to mimic a traditional village, seven pools, gym, spa and a wedding chapel. August rates add an extra €125. April–Oct. **€176**

Elgoni Apartments Piskopianó, right at the top of

the hill above the museum ☎ 28970 21237, ⓔ elgoni _apartments@hotmail.com. Welcoming, good-value, family-run place offering well-equipped studios, apartments and maisonettes in a lovely setting with pool and bar, and great views. The decor is looking a bit tired but it's still a good deal. April–Oct. Studios **€30**, apartments **€40**

Galaxy Villas Koutouloufári, towards the eastern end of the village near the Sports Café ☎ 28970 22910, ⓦ galaxy-villas.com. Comfortable, well-equipped modern a/c villa/apartments with kitchens, in a complex with pool and bar, and views down over the coast. Rates go up by €25 in Aug. April–Oct. **€55**

Ilios Omirou 2, on the western edge of Hersónisos just back from the main road ☎ 28970 22700, ⓦ hotelilios .gr. Standard hotel in a relatively quiet area with a rooftop pool; there's an extra charge for a/c. As good as you'll find in this price range in Hersónisos itself. May–Oct. **€45**

EATING AND DRINKING

There's no shortage of places to eat and drink in the resort, although quality is not always a priority, especially among the **waterfront** places, whose location is so irresistible that they don't need to try too hard. Better food and a more relaxed atmosphere is to be found out of town in the **hill villages**, where many tavernas have roof terraces with views towards the coast.

Argo Navárhou Neárhou 26, round the corner from the harbour ☎28970 22134. Much quieter and with a more personal welcome and traditional Greek feel than anywhere on the main seafront. They offer home-made Greek classics plus an international menu, and there's also a tranquil bar, popular with an older crowd. May–Oct daily 10am–12.30am.

★**Elliniko Estiatorio** Kaniadáki 4, off the south side of Venizélou slightly east of the church ☎28970 24138. The name means simply "Greek Restaurant", and that's exactly what it is – a place where locals come (many have takeaways) for a daily selection of freshly made *mayireftá* (trays baked in the oven, €6–7.50 for a main). There is a menu but no one uses it; simply look at the day's dishes displayed behind glass and tell chef Yiannis what you want; very little English is spoken. Come at lunchtime, because many dishes run out early. Mon–Sat noon–10pm.

La Scala Ayía Paraskeví 83, at the heart of the waterfront ☎28970 24777. The most glamorous of the central seafront restaurants, with candlelit tables right down on the sand as well as on a terrace above it, serving a huge menu of fresh fish, pizza (€6–12), pasta (from €10)

and Greek standards at much the same prices as its neighbours. April–Oct daily noon–midnight.

Nikis 25 Mártiou 12, at the eastern end of the seafront ☎6987 022 093. The international menu is not significantly better (or cheaper) than elsewhere, but it's a little further from the centre so less manic than other places, with great views and a totally irresistible line in chat to draw in the punters. April–Oct daily 9am–2am.

Oniro Koutouloufári, on the lower street through the village ☎28970 23840. The terrace here has some of the best coastal views of all, which is reflected in the prices (main dishes €11–15). Specials such as pork or lamb shanks are slow-cooked in a wood oven; try also the aubergine stuffed with veal and cheese or *exohikó* (lamb in filo; €11.90). April–Oct daily 11am–midnight.

★**Pithari** Koutouloufári, at the crossroads on the upper street through the village ☎28970 21449. Touristy, like everywhere up here, but with well-prepared authentic Cretan dishes and a large roof terrace. Try the likes of rabbit *stifádho* (€12.90) or lamb Pithari (baked in filo with potato and spinach; €14.50). April–Oct daily 11am–midnight.

NIGHTLIFE

Hersónisos is renowned for its **nightlife** and there's certainly no shortage of it. A night's partying kicks off around the many **bars** ringing the harbour; this is dancing on tables territory, so if you fancy a quiet drink, head for the fringes of town or to the hill villages. Later on, the larger **disco-pubs** and **clubs** in the streets leading up to and along Elefthériou Venizélou are the places to be seen.

El Paradiso Ayía Paraskeví 83. This late-night club right at the heart of the waterfront sees occasional appearances by visiting DJs, playing predominantly house and club tunes. May–Oct daily 11pm–dawn.

New York Ayía Paraskeví 30, right on the water ☎28970 23415, ⓦnew-york.gr. Glitzy club that's also a café and beach club, with sunbeds, by day, and a

sophisticated cocktail bar. DJ Yiannis plays funk, Greek pop and techno. May–Oct daily 11pm–5am.

Star Beach Water Park On the beach immediately east of the resort ⓦstar-beach.gr. The water park (see p.87) houses a megaclub, with wild foam parties on Sunday nights (free) and frequent appearances by international DJs. May–Sept daily 11pm–late.

Mália

MÁLIA (Μάλια) is, perhaps, the most notorious resort in Crete: brash, commercial, with a reputation for wild nightlife. The **beach**, long and sandy as it is, becomes grotesquely crowded at times. Having said that, it can be a great place to stay if you're prepared to enter into the spirit of things – party all night and sleep all day – with the bonus of a genuine town that existed before the tourists came, and a fabulous **Minoan palace** just down the road.

The beaches

Beaches stretch either side of Mália. If you're prepared to walk a bit you'll be rewarded with better sands and fewer people, though solitude is a distant dream. The **central beach** stretches east from the bottom of Beach Road; in summer, you'll need to walk through the mass of bodies for about another fifteen minutes before you find somewhere to spread out. At this eastern end of the beach is a small **church** backed by dunes and patches of marshy ground alive with frogs. You can also swim out to a tiny **offshore islet**: the rocks here are sharp for barefoot exploring, but your efforts will be

MÁLIA ORIENTATION

Mália consists of two distinct parts, lying on opposite sides of the old highway (Venizélou). The heart of tourist life lies to the north towards the **beach**, where two main streets snake for a good kilometre towards the sea: one, **Zahariádhi**, from the major junction near the western end of town; the other, **Dhimokratías**, a little further east. The streets merge into one after about 300m, and along them you'll find supermarkets, souvenir shops, travel agents, cafés, restaurants, video bars and nightclubs. To walk the length of this will take you about fifteen minutes – longer if you allow yourself to be enticed by the sales patter along the way, or after midnight, when it's at its busiest. At the end there's a car park, a small harbour and access to the beach.

South of the main road is the **old town**, with its narrow, twisting alleyways and whitewashed walls. Here you can still find traces of traditional life, as Mália determinedly clings to what remains of its self-respect.

rewarded by a (perpetually locked) white chapel and rock pools alive with crabs, shellfish and sea urchins on the islet's seaward side.

There are beaches west of the resort centre, but the most tempting lie to the east: **Sun Beach**, about 2.5 km from the centre, where there are free trampolines and pools, plus plenty of loungers, drinks, amusements and watersports; **Tropical Beach**, with more loungers but fewer buzzing banana boats and parascenders; and finally **Potamos**, at the mouth of a small river very close to the palace, with loungers and a café.

The Palace of Mália

3km east of Mália, just off the old highway • April–Sept daily 8am–5pm; Oct–March Tues–Sun 8am–3pm • €4 • Any bus from Iráklio bound for Áyios Nikólaos will stop at the turn-off on the main road; moving on, buses pass on the main road at least hourly throughout the day – west towards Iráklio and east to Áyios Nikólaos

Though much less imposing than either Knossós or Festós, the **Palace of Mália** in some ways surpasses both. For a start, it's a great deal emptier, and you can wander among the remains in relative peace. And while no reconstruction has been attempted, the palace was never reoccupied after its second destruction, so the ground plan is virtually intact. The excavations are by no means complete; inside and beyond the fenced site to the north and west, digs are still going on, as an apparently sizeable town comes slowly to light.

Of the **ruins** you see today, virtually nothing stands much more than 1m above ground level apart from the giant *píthoi* that have been pieced together and left about the place like sentinels: the palace itself is worn and brown, blending almost imperceptibly into the landscape. With the mountains behind, it's a thoroughly atmospheric setting. It's also easier to comprehend than Knossós, and if you've already seen the reconstructions there, it's easy to envisage this seaside palace in its days of glory. Basking on the rich agricultural plain between the Lasíthi mountains and the sea, it retains a real flavour of an ancient civilization with a taste for the good life.

Though the palace is accessible by bus, it's also easily reached on foot – a 40min **walk** from Mália – or you could rent a **bike** for the easy, flat ride out to the site, and stop for a swim on the way back.

Brief history

First discovered by Joseph Hatzidhakis early in the twentieth century, the site's excavation was handed over to the French School at Athens in 1922. As at Knossós and Festós, there was an earlier palace dating from around 1900 BC, which was devastated by the earthquake of about 1700 BC. The remains you see today are those of the palace built to replace this, which functioned until about 1450 BC, when it was destroyed for the last time (see p.130). From this site came the famous **gold pendant** of two bees that can be seen in the Iráklio Archeological Museum and on any local postcard stand. It was

PALACE OF MÁLIA

0		25
	metres	

allegedly part of a hoard that was plundered; the rest of the collection now resides (as the "Aegina Treasure") in London's British Museum. The beautiful **leopard's-head axe**, also in the museum at Iráklio, was another of the treasures found at Mália.

The West Court

The main palace is to the right of the site entrance, approached through the **West Court**. As at the other palaces, there are raised pathways leading across this, with the main one heading south towards the area of the eight circular **storage pits**. These probably held grain; the pillars in the middle of some would once have supported a protective roof. In the other direction, the raised walkway takes you to the building's north side, where you can pick up the more substantial paved road that apparently led to the sea.

The North Court

Entering the palace itself through a "door" between two rocks and jinking right then left, you arrive in the **North Court**, by the storerooms and their elaborately decorated, much-photographed giant *pithoi*. Off to the right are the so-called Royal Apartments, on the far side of which is a well-preserved lustral basin or bath. Nearby lies the

1

Archive Room, where a number of Linear A tablets were unearthed. Straight ahead is the **Pillared Hall**, which the excavators, encouraged by the discovery of some cooking pots, think may have been a kitchen (the relative location is almost exactly the same as that of the palace kitchen at Zákros). Above the hall, a grand dining room would have looked out over the courtyard.

The Central Court

Mália's **Central Court**, a long, narrow area, about 48m in length by 22m wide, is only slightly smaller than the main courtyards at Knossós and Festós. Look out for the remains of the columns that once supported a portico at the northern end, and for traces of a similar portico down the eastern side. Still-visible post-holes were discovered between these columns by the excavators, suggesting that the court could be fenced in – possibly to protect the spectators during the bull-jumping games that may have been held here. Behind the eastern portico are more storerooms, now under a canopy. In the centre of the court is a shallow pit that may have been used for sacrifices; if this was indeed its purpose then, along with Anemospília (see p.76), these are the only such Minoan sacrificial areas to have been discovered.

On the west side of the courtyard are the remains of two important stairways. The first led to the upper floor beside what is termed the **Royal Lodge** or Throne Room, which overlooks the courtyard. The second, in the southwest corner, comprises the bottom four steps of what was the main ceremonial staircase to the first floor, still impressive in its scale. Beside this is the curious *kernos*, or **altar**. The purpose of this heavy limestone disc, with 34 hollows around its rim and a single bigger one in the centre, is disputed: one theory suggests an altar where, at harvest time, samples of the first fruits of the Cretan crops would be placed in the hollows as offerings to a fertility goddess, while other theories have it as a point for tax collecting or even an ancient gaming board.

The rooms along the west side of the court also merit exploration. Between the two staircases ran a long room that may have gone straight through to the upper floor, like a medieval banqueting hall. Behind this is the **Pillar Crypt**, where the double-axe symbol was found engraved on the two main pillars. Behind the Pillar Crypt runs yet another corridor of storerooms; only accessible through areas which had some royal or religious significance, these would doubtless have been depositories for things of value – the most secure storage at the palace.

Agora and Crypt

Beneath a canopy to the west of the northern end of the palace lies the **Agora** (or Hypostyle Hall). This building consists of a number of rooms – apparently shops or market stalls – and two interconnected halls of uncertain function, described as the **Crypt**. Benches run round three sides of the Crypt, leading some to speculate that this was some form of council chamber.

Area "M"

A gate from the Crypt leads to **area** "M" (or Mu – the site is divided up by archeologists using the letters of the Greek alphabet), in a second fenced area almost as large as the palace itself. Here a large section of the town dependent on the palace is protected by a spectacular canopy. You can walk above and around it on a suspended walkway, looking down on workshops, dwellings, some preserved up to roof level, and streets that give a clear idea of the considerable scale of the complex community that surrounded the palace. In one small area a section of wood-beamed roof has been reconstructed, and there's a series of what are believed to have been ritual or **cult rooms**. Several of the other cult rooms yielded statuary, libation vessels and other artefacts connected with religious ceremonies.

1

Archeologists are still trying to piece together exactly what connection this complex had with the palace. Was it possibly the "monastery" of a priesthood serving the palace but living separately from it, or could it have served as a temporary home for the whole palace elite while some restoration or repair was carried out to the palace proper? Many of the most interesting finds from this area are displayed in the museum at Áyios Nikólaos, but at the site entrance there's a small **exhibition** on the excavations (especially the more recent ones) which is well worth a look, and includes a model of area "M" as it might have looked.

The Golden Pit

Turn right (west) on leaving the palace site, and then right again along a dirt track that heads northeast towards the sea; the fenced pit lies some 300m down the track, just before the islet of Ayía Varvára, visible offshore

Some 500m north of the palace, close to the sea and outside the main fenced area, is the *Chrysolakkos* or **Golden Pit**, apparently a large, multi-chambered mausoleum dating from the Protopalatial period. Its elaborate construction suggests a royal burial-place, as does the wealth of grave goods discovered here, among them the gold honeybee pendant now at the Iráklio Archeological Museum.

Area "E"

Along the entry road leading back to the main road, on the east side there are **new excavations** (fenced off) in a zone designated **area** "E", which further underline the scale of the urban area surrounding the palace. There are many substantial buildings here, including a large mansion where fragments of painted plaster were discovered, suggesting a sumptuously decorated interior.

ARRIVAL AND INFORMATION

By bus Arriving by bus you'll be dropped at the central junction on the main road (Venizélou) heading through the town. There are services to and from Iráklio (Bus Station A) virtually every 30min (1hr), and to Áyios Nikoláos at least hourly (40min).

Travel agencies Travel Deals, Venizélou 172, near the junction with 25 Martíou in the heart of town (☎28970 33324), can provide a town map and bus timetable as well as help with rooms and advice on local tours and car rental. Sunny Holidays, 25 Martíou 41 in the old town (☎28970 32120), are also helpful.

MÁLIA

ACCOMMODATION

Many **rooms** are taken up by the package industry, and in peak season finding somewhere to stay may not be easy. Your best bet if you want any sleep is to avoid the Beach Road area: try one of the numerous rooms signed in the old town or on the fringes of the new. You'll save a lot of schlepping around by booking though a travel agent (see above).

EATING AND DRINKING

Mália's **restaurant** owners jostle for your custom at every step, especially along Beach Road; none is particularly good, but they know their clientele – *moussaká*, pie and chips and all-you-can-eat Mexican, Indian or Chinese places abound. You're far better off in the **old town** where, around the Platía Ayíos Dhimítrios, you can choose from a variety of more elegant bars, tavernas and restaurants. If you're shopping for picnic food, look out for the tasty bananas sold at stalls throughout the centre: chances are they'll have been grown in the fields around the town.

Elizabeth and Stablos Platía Áyios Dhimítrios, old town ☎28970 31320. Elegant decor, decent mezédhes (mixed meze for two €12), fresh fish and good barrel wine, plus an attractive upstairs terrace opposite the little church, make this a popular and appealing spot. April–Oct daily 6.30pm–midnight.

Kalesma Omiroú 8, off the top of 25 Martíou, old town ☎28970 33125. Located in a quiet backstreet with a classy terrace and blown-glass light fittings, this is Mália's most stylish restaurant. Famous for its meze (€3–7), it also offers well-prepared traditional dishes (*kleftikó* €11.50) and a good selection of Cretan wines. Daily 5pm–12.30am.

Pizza Zorbas 25 Martíou 20, near the town hall ☎28970 32433. Attractive, economical old-town pizzeria with a wood-fired oven and roof terrace; there are also simple grills, *yíros* and salads at this popular late-night spot. Daily 5pm–1am.

NIGHTLIFE

Beach Road is transformed during the hours either side of midnight, when the profusion of **bars**, **discos** and **clubs** erupt into a pulsating cacophony. Most of them have touts outside trying to lure you in, and in most you can see through glass doors what you'll be letting yourself in for. The bigger, better clubs cluster around the point where the two beach roads meet. There are plenty of "English pubs", too. Vast crowds of 18–30s – many in organized groups – stagger between the bars and clubs, and while the worst excesses of past years have been left behind, you do still get the odd confrontation.

Camelot Castle Dhimokratias 82, at the junction on Beach Road ☎ 6944 285 769. Right at the heart of the action, this is the daddy of the Mália clubs, with big-name DJs (Judge Jules and Westwood), foam parties and more. May–Oct daily 11pm–4am.

Candy Club Beach Road ☻ facebook.com/malia.candy.

club. With a dress code above the door stating "less is more," this place lies at the throbbing heart of the Beach Road madness. A huge venue with three bars, two dance stages, VIP area and more, playing house and electro, and performances featuring the likes of Ms Dynamite. May–Oct daily midnight–dawn.

Towards the Lasíthi plateau

The one inland route that visitors follow in any numbers is the drive up to the **Lasíthi plateau** (see p.140). The main route heads inland from Hersónisos, initially towards Kastélli (see p.78), and then east through the Aposelémis valley to Potamiés and Goníes. The attractions are charmingly simple: scenery that becomes increasingly mountainous as you climb towards the plateau; old trees spreading beside the road, and still older churches in the villages. Alternative routes – dramatically wild and lonely, with spectacular views – wind up from Stalídha and Mália.

Panayía Gouverniótissa

The monastery of **Panayía Gouverniótissa** (Παναγία Γκουβερνιώτισσα; Assumption of the Virgin) is one of the oldest in Crete. The buildings are gradually being restored, and there's likely to be a workman or caretaker around to open any locked doors (if not, the key to the chapel is available from the *kafenío* at the edge of Potamiés). The tiny **chapel** stands close by in a peaceful garden with a lemon tree; inside are restored **frescoes** dating from the fourteenth century, with a fine *Pandokrátor* adorning the dome.

Avdhoú

In the village of **AVDHOÚ** (Αβδού) there are fine, very faded frescoes from the fourteenth and fifteenth centuries in three **churches**: Áyios Andónios, Áyios Konstantínos and Áyios Yeóryios. The churches should be open; if not, enquiries in the village cafés should produce the necessary keys.

Krási

The village of **KRÁSI** (Κράσι), just off the main road on the route to Mália, is curiously named – curious because Krási translates as "wine", but the village's fame is in fact based on water, in the form of a curative spring that is reputed to be especially good for stomach complaints. This is situated under stone arcading in the shade of an enormous **plane tree**, which is claimed to be two thousand years old and the largest in Europe, with a girth that cannot be encircled by twelve people. Flanking the tree are a couple of **tavernas**.

Panayía Kardhiótissa

3km south of Krási • Daily 8am–6pm • €2

The convent of **Panayía Kardhiótissa** (Παναγία Καρδιώτισσα) – Our Lady of the Heart – is one of the most important places of worship on Crete, with an annual celebration on September 8. The buildings date from the twelfth century, and though the heavily refurbished exterior of the monastery looks like whitewashed concrete, the interior is undeniably spectacular, with restored **frescoes** throughout. These came to light only in the 1960s, when they were discovered beneath accumulated layers of paint.

1

There is also a copy of a famous twelfth-century icon of the Virgin, the original of which was taken to Rome in 1498. According to legend, successive attempts by the Turks to steal this copy were thwarted when it found its way back to Kerá, despite being chained to a marble pillar; the pillar is now in the monastery yard, while the chain (kept inside the church) is believed to alleviate pain when wrapped around the bodies of the afflicted. There's an attractive little museum too.

The ascent to Séli Ambélou

Beyond the village of Kerá, the road winds on into the Dhiktean mountains, and the views become progressively more magnificent. To the left, **Mount Karfí** looms ominously, its summit more than 1100m above sea level. This spire-like peak (*karfí* means "nail" in Greek) was one of the sites where the Minoan civilization made its last stand, following the collapse of the great centres after the twelfth century BC. There's a scary-looking track to the site of **ancient Karfí** (see p.143), some 5km away, from the car park at the ludicrous **Homo Sapiens Village**.

The road continues to climb to the dramatic pass of **SÉLI AMBÉLOU** (Σέλι Αμπέλου), flanked by ruined stone windmills. Beyond, the Lasíthi plateau suddenly unfolds before you. Almost straight ahead, on the far side of the plateau, the highest peaks of the range dominate the landscape, with **Mount Dhíkti** – all 2148m of it – at their heart.

Southwest from Iráklio

Crossing the island on the southwest route is not, on the whole, the most exciting of drives: on the western outskirts of Iráklio you turn south, under the highway, following the signs to Festós and Míres. From the beginning, the road climbs, heading up to the island's spine through agricultural country renowned for its vineyards. In the Middle Ages this was traditionally the **Malevísi**, or Malmsey, wine-producing region (see p.81): though some wine is still made, most of the grapes you'll see now are grown for eating rather than pressing or for turning into sultanas. Highlights along this route include an ancient site at **Rizinía**, as well as picturesque medieval **monasteries** at Veneráto and **Zarós**, the latter a particularly pleasant village with great accommodation choices, surrounded by fine **walking country** and with a small lake nearby.

GETTING AROUND   SOUTHWEST FROM IRÁKLIO

By car The main road is the fast route via Veneráto and Ayía Varvára, but you can also follow a scenic detour via Voutés, Áyios Míronas and Pírgou, a wonderful undulating ride through some lovely out-of-the-way villages.
By bus Buses from Iráklio's Bus Station B (Mon–Sat 11 daily; fewer on Sun) follow the main road across the island,

heading for Festós and Mátala or Ayía Galíni via Tymbáki. Míres, in the heart of the Messará plain, is the southern junction for switching between these various routes. Ano Asítes (5km north of Priniás) also has a bus service from the same station (Mon–Fri 4 daily; Sat 2 daily, 7am & 2.30pm; 50min).

Ancient Rizinía

To visit the site, continue south beyond the hairpin bend 3km south of Ano Asítes to where a sign (to "Prinías archeological site") directs you up a short, just about driveable track, with the acropolis and chapel of Áyios Pandeleímon visible above

On a hairpin bend, 3km south of Ano Asítes and 2km north of Priniás, a pair of remarkable **rock-cut tombs** can be seen, part of the cemetery of **Ancient Rizinía** (Ριζινία), which occupied the flat-topped hill to the east. Founded at the end of the Bronze Age, possibly by Minoans fleeing the Dorian invasion of the north coast, Rizinía later flourished as a Greek city and the remains of two temples have been discovered on the acropolis. Although not a lot remains of the ancient town, the sheer quantity of broken shards littering the ground is evidence that this was once a substantial conurbation. Nosing around, you'll come across the footings of ancient dwellings, with steps and porches clearly identifiable. When you eventually reach the landmark whitewashed **chapel of Áyios Pandeleímon**, at the northern tip of the peak, you're greeted with astonishing **views** in all directions, especially north towards Iráklio, with the island of Dhía beyond.

Moní Palianí

MONÍ PALIANÍ (Παλιανή) is a well-signed 2km detour from the village of **Veneráto**. An ancient monastic foundation (dating perhaps from as early as the seventh century) and now a thriving convent, Palianí has at its heart a sacred ancient **myrtle tree** (said to be as much as a thousand years old), its every twig hung with *tamata* (ex votos) and credited with healing powers. There's a powerful feeling that the rituals centred on the tree predate the monastery, and even Christianity itself, by some centuries. Around the tree is a tranquil, plant-filled courtyard with a thirteenth-century chapel to one side. You can also buy lace, embroidery and other items hand-crafted by the nuns in a small shop.

Ayía Varvára

AYÍA VARVÁRA (Αγία Βαρβάρα) is the chief village of this region, a place known as the **omphalos** (navel) **of Crete**. The great chapel-topped rock that you see as you arrive is held to be the very point around which the island balances, its centre of being – not that this makes for any great tourist attraction. There are plenty of cafés and shops along the main street, but they cater mostly for local farmers in search of a bag of fertilizer or a tractor part.

Zarós and around

As a village, **ZARÓS** (Ζαρός), 14km west of Ayía Varvára, is attractive enough, but at first sight little different from many others nearby. A number of things distinguish it, however. For locals, it is known above all for its **spring waters**, which are bottled and sold all over Crete (the bottling plant is at the far edge of the village); the waters also feed a small artificial lake. It's also an excellent **walking** centre, within easy reach of a couple of interesting **monasteries**, and has some excellent accommodation and food. To the west, a beautiful drive on relatively good, empty roads follows the flank of the Psilorítis range towards Kamáres (see p.209) and eventually on to Réthymno or down to Ayía Galíni.

Folklore and Geological Museum

Just off Zarós' main street near the church of Áyios Yeóryios • April–Sept Tues–Sun 10am–noon & 4–6pm • €3

Zarós' new **Folklore and Geological Museum**, housed inside a restored mansion, is a labour of love realized by the village's Folklore Association. In addition to the usual collection of furnishings, tapestries and antique household implements the upper floor has a huge geological collection, assembled by a local geologist, displaying stones and fossils as well as a few Minoan and Roman artefacts.

Lake Vótomos

Just 1km or so out of Zarós, well signed for both walkers and drivers, deep-green **Lake Vótomos** (Βότομος) is overlooked by rocky heights. Tiny as it is, it's a lovely setting, and the lake, full of trout, is the starting point for numerous hikes. The lakeside bar and taverna *Limni* is run by the same family as the *Eleonas Resort* (see p.98), and they are also responsible for much of the excellent waymarking that helps walkers find their way around.

Moní Áyios Nikólaos

The pick of the well-marked paths that start at Lake Vótomos is the climb past **MONÍ ÁYIOS NIKÓLAOS** (Άγιος Νικόλαος; 1km) and through the Roúvas Gorge (2.5km) to the chapel of Áyios Ioánnis (5.2km). You can also drive to the monastery by heading west on the main road out of Zarós, and then 2km up a signed road. The monastery itself is now dwarfed by a vast blue-domed concrete church, which seems totally out of place here. Nevertheless, the older institution behind remains very welcoming, and the elderly monks will usually offer some refreshment to passers-by as well as opening the chapel so you can view the fourteenth-century paintings within.

Roúvas Gorge

Above Moní Áyios Nikólaos, the track snakes back and forth across an increasingly steep mountainside before reaching the entrance to the **ROÚVAS GORGE (Ρούβας)**. The gorge is a spectacular walk on a good path, tough going at times despite the wooden walkways that help in the steeper sections. At the top lies the chapel of **Áyios Ioánnis**, on the main E4 trans-island walking route (the gorge walk itself is signed as the E4, but it's certainly not part of the main path). Here the easy option is to turn around and head down the way you came for a well-earned drink by the lake, a couple of hours away. With an early start and plenty of provisions you could take a more ambitious course and head east on the E4 to Áno Asítes, picking up a taxi back from there; but be warned that this is a good 20km of high-altitude mountain walking on rough paths – the rewards are spectacular views and plenty of bird and plant life.

Moní Vrondísi

3km west of Zarós; some signs read "Áyios Antónios" • Daily 8.30am–3pm

Fourteenth- to seventeenth-century **MONÍ VRONDÍSI (Βροντύσι)** is a gloriously peaceful foundation overlooking the Koútsoulidi valley with views towards Festós and the Gulf of Messará. Beyond the entrance, guarded by a pair of prodigious plane trees, a tranquil courtyard surrounded by monks' cells (mostly empty) fronts the monastery's simple limestone **church**. Inside are some fine fourteenth-century **frescoes**, including a moving depiction of the Last Supper, and a collection of icons taken from the nearby church of Áyios Fanoúrios (see below). Vrondísi itself has given up the finest of its artworks, including the six great panels by Dhamaskinos, to the icon museum of Ayía Ekateríni in Iráklio (see p.59). For most locals, however, the attraction of Vrondísi is not art, but the cool water gushing from a fifteenth-century Venetian fountain, with figures of Adam and Eve, near the entrance. Here you can fill up your empty bottle with fine mountain spring water (the same stuff that's bottled down the road) for free.

Moní Valsamónero

Signed from the village of Vorizia • Official opening hours Mon–Fri 8am–3pm; occasionally it does not open so enquire at the Moní Vrondisi (see above) to save a wasted journey

All that survives of **MONÍ VALSAMÓNERO (Βαλσαμόνερο)** is its church, Áyios Fanoúrios. It's some survival though; it houses some of the best **frescoes** in Crete, painted in the fifteenth century by Konstantinos Rikos and depicting scenes from the life of the *Panayía* (Virgin Mary), images of various saints and a fine *Pandokrátor*.

ARRIVAL AND ACTIVITIES

ZARÓS AND AROUND

By bus One bus daily from Iráklio's Bus Station B (Mon–Sat 1.30pm, Sun 7am; 50min).

Cookery lessons The *Vegera* restaurant (see opposite) in Zarós offers cookery lessons, during which you prepare a five-course classic Cretan meal, then sit down and eat it (11am; 4hr; €25 including food and drink); call ☎6970 579 395 the day before to confirm.

ACCOMMODATION

★Eleonas Traditional Resort In the hills behind Zarós – follow signs from the bottling plant or from the lake ☎28940 31238, ⌨eleonas.gr. The traditionally built villas here are set in gardens, where native plants are labelled, at the base of the mountains. Built to resemble a village, facilities include kitchen, a/c, TV, DVD and CD player and a fireplace; the more attractive (and more expensive) original villas are slightly larger, with galleried bedrooms. There's also an excellent taverna using local produce (breakfast is included) plus a pool and five-a-side football pitch. Produces its own hiking map and rents mountain bikes. Daily 12.30–3pm & 7–11pm. **€95**

Idi Hotel On the road to Lake Vótomos ☎28940 31301, ⓦidi-hotel.gr. A comfortable place to get away from it all with a big garden pool (and indoor pool in winter) and tennis court, though the pine-panelled rooms are a little old-fashioned. There's a roaring spring directly outside the hotel, and an abandoned watermill, while the hotel's taverna makes a speciality of the trout that splash around in the trout farm behind. Breakfast included. April–Oct. **€48**

★ **Rooms Keramos** Zarós village, signed off the main street ☎28940 31352, ⓦstudiokeramos-zaros.gr. A bourgeois house in the village has been converted into a warren of individually decorated rooms with fridge, a/c and heating. Most have balconies with village and mountain views, and some have fine brass bedsteads. It's the exceptional warmth of the old-fashioned welcome that makes this place really special, though; that, and the amazing breakfasts with home-made pies and pastries. **€35**

EATING AND DRINKING

Limni Lake Vótomos ☎28940 31338. The only restaurant actually on the lakeside, *Limni* serves excellent food, beautifully presented; earthy bread comes with sage-flavoured olive oil, tzatziki, olives and tomato salsa. The lake trout is the inevitable special (€9.50), and tasty it is too, for it could hardly be fresher. *Orektiká* (€3–7) include a trout carpaccio (€6). Evenings here can be magical (providing you remember to bring mosquito repellent) and it's perhaps the only place in Crete where you'll have geese begging for food alongside the usual

cats. April–Oct daily 11am–11pm.

Vegera Main street, Zarós village ☎6970 579 395, ⓦvegerazaros.gr. From the same hospitable family as *Keramos* (see above), and with an all-female kitchen, *Vegera* offers traditional, local food. As well as a 10-dish menu (€7–8), there's also a special menu (€12) with a selection of dishes to share, based on whatever is fresh and in season; it's usually excellent and there are plenty of interesting veggie dishes too, but despite the name, this is not a vegetarian restaurant. April–Oct daily 10am–9pm.

The Messará plain

South of Ayía Varvára the road becomes genuinely mountainous until, at the Vourvoulítis Pass (650m), you enter the watershed of the Messará. The **MESSARÁ PLAIN** (Μεσσαρά), a long strip running east from the Gulf of Messará, is the largest and most important of Crete's fertile flatlands. Bounded to the north by the Psilorítis range and the lower hills that run right across the centre of the island, to the east by the Dhiktean mountains, and to the south by the narrow strip of the Asteroússia and Kófinas hills, it is watered, somewhat erratically, by the Yeropótamos. Heavy with olives, and increasingly with the fruit and vegetable cash crops that dominate the modern agricultural economy, the plain has always been a major centre of population and a mainstay of the island's economy. There is much evidence of this, not only at the ancient sites of **Górtys**, **Festós** and **Ayía Triádha**, but at a wealth of lesser, barely explored sites; today's villages exude prosperity, too, surrounded by neat and intensive cultivation.

GETTING AROUND

THE MESSARÁ PLAIN

By car As you descend to the plain by a series of long, looping curves, the main road heads west through Áyii Dhéka towards Míres, Festós and Mátala. A left turn eastwards takes you across far less travelled country (see p.117) and all the way to Ierápetra.

By bus Buses from Iráklio's Bus Station B (Mon–Sat 11

daily; fewer on Sun; 1hr 30min) head for Míres, the transport hub of the Messará plain. From here they continue variously to Mátala, Lendás or Ayía Galíni via Tymbáki; the majority of these buses call at Áyii Dhéka and Górtys before Míres, and many continue via Festós.

Áyii Dhéka

ÁYII DHÉKA (Άγιοι Δέκα) is the first village you reach on the Messará and the most interesting. The place takes its name from ten early Christians who were martyred here around 250 AD, at the behest of the Emperor Decius. The **Holy Ten** are still among the most revered of Cretan saints: regarded as martyrs for Crete as much as Christianity,

1

they were the first in a heroic line of Cretans who laid down their lives to oppose tyrannical occupation.

On the west side of the village are two churches associated with the holy ten: the older, originally Byzantine **church** is signed to the south of the main road. Inside, there's an icon portraying the martyrdom of the saints and the marble block on which they are supposed to have been decapitated, complete with the imprints of their knees. Signed from here is a relatively modern **chapel** on the edge of the village beneath which, visible from the exterior, is a crypt where you can see six of their tombs. Both churches are generally open in daylight hours; it's well worth taking the short walk between them to get a sense of how close to the busy main road rural Crete remains. You'll see reminders of the village's ancient past everywhere: Roman statues, pillars and odd blocks of masonry are reused in modern houses, propping up walls or simply lying about in yards.

Górtys

2km west of Áyii Dhéka • April–June, Sept & Oct Mon–Sat 8am–6pm, Sun 8am–3pm; July & Aug daily 8am–8pm; Nov–March daily 8am–3pm • €4 • ☎ 28920 31144

The remnants of the ancient city of **GÓRTYS** (**Γόρτυς**), known traditionally as Gortyn or Gortyna, are scattered across a large, fragmented area, covering a great deal more than the fenced site beside the road that most people see. One of the mightiest states of classical Crete, it reached the peak of its power in Roman times when it grew to become the island's largest city, as well as a provincial capital. The best way to get some idea of the ancient city's scale is to follow the path through the fields from the village.

This heads out more or less parallel to the road, opposite the chapel of Áyii Dhéka, and is an easy walk of less than 1km to the main site; along the way you'll skirt most of the major remains.

Brief history

Settled from at least Minoan times, when it was a minor subject of Festós, Górtys began its rise to prominence under the **Dorians**. By the eighth century BC it had become a significant commercial power and in the third century BC it finally conquered its former rulers at Festós. The society was strictly regulated, with a citizen class (presumably Dorian) ruling over a population of serfs (presumably "Minoan" Cretans) and slaves. Even for the citizens, life was as hard and orderly as it was in Classical Sparta.

Evidence of early Górtys has survived thanks largely to the remarkable **law code** found here, and to a lesser extent through treaties known to have existed between the Górtys of this era and its rivals, notably Knossós. **Hannibal** fled to Górtys, where he stayed briefly after his defeat by Rome, and later the city helped the **Romans** to conquer Crete. This enabled it to avoid the fate of many other cities that opposed the invaders (such as Knossós) and were destroyed. It was during the Roman era that the city reached its apogee, from 67 BC onwards. As the seat of a Roman praetor with a population estimated at 300,000, it was made the capital of the province of Crete and Cyrenaica, ruling not only the rest of the island but also much of Egypt and North Africa. It was here that **Christianity** first reached Crete, when St Titus was despatched by St Paul to convert the islanders, but after the **Saracen** invasion in the ninth century, when much of the city was razed, Górtys was abruptly abandoned.

South of the road: the Roman city

In the fields en route to the site, it is the **Roman city** that dominates: this once stretched from the edges of Áyii Dhéka to the far banks of the Mitropolitanos (then known as the Lethe) and from the hills in the north as far south as the modern hamlet of Mitrópolis, where a Roman basilica with good mosaics (now covered) has been excavated. For most people, though, the ruins along the main path, with others seen standing in the distance, and the tantalizing prospect of what lies unexcavated beneath hummocks along the way, are quite enough. Individually, or in another setting, these might seem unimpressive, but with so many of them, abandoned as they are and all but ignored, they are amazing – you almost feel as if you've discovered them for yourself. The sites that have been excavated here are mostly seen only through locked fences, but the ground everywhere is littered with pillars and broken masonry.

The **Praetorium** (the Roman governor's palace) has the most extensive remains, a vast pile built originally in the second century, rebuilt in the fourth, and occupied as a monastery right up to the time of the Venetian conquest. Excavations in this area have revealed impressive foundations, flights of steps, walls and marble columns once belonging to imposing buildings, all indicating how much more still lies beneath the olive groves waiting to be discovered. Within the same fenced area is a courtyard containing fountains and the **Nymphaeum**. Somewhere near here, too, was the terminus of the main aqueduct that brought water from the region of modern Zarós. About 100m to the west of the Praetorium area is the **Temple of Pythian Apollo**, the most important of the Roman city's temples, later converted to a church, while the nearby **theatre**, though small, is very well preserved. Some 50m north of here are the substantial remains of the **Temple of Isis and Serapis**.

The main site

Directly opposite the entrance to the main, fenced site, be sure not to miss the 1600-year-old **olive tree** that has grown around pillars from the ruins of the ancient site – a surreal attraction in its own right. Plenty of other trees that seem almost as venerable surround it;

1

the bus stop sign is nailed to one. As you enter the site, there's an impressive collection of **statuary** in a small pavilion backing onto the **café**, demonstrating the high standard of work achieved here during the city's halcyon days.

Áyios Títos

The apse of the church of **Áyios Títos** is much the most famous image of Górtys, and the thing that immediately grabs the eye. This is the only part of the church that has survived intact, but the shape of the whole structure is easy enough to make out. When it was built (around the end of the sixth century), it would have been the island's chief church, and it is the best remaining example of an early Christian church in the Aegean: you can see the extent to which it is still revered from the little shrine at the end of one of the aisles. The church's capitals bear the monogram of the sixth-century Byzantine emperor Justinian.

The Odeion

Beyond the church lies an area that was probably the ancient forum, and beyond this the most important relic of ancient Górtys, the **Odeion** (or covered theatre) and its **law code**. The law code – a series of engraved stones some 9m long and 3m high – dates from around 500 BC, but it presumably codified laws that were long established by custom and practice. It provides a fascinating insight into a period of which relatively little is otherwise known; the laws are written in a very rough Doric Cretan dialect and inscribed alternately left to right and right to left, so that the eyes can follow the writing continuously (a style known as boustrophedon, after the furrows of an ox plough). The code is not a complete system of law but rather a series of rulings on special cases, and reflects a strictly hierarchical society in which there were at least three distinct classes – citizens, serfs and slaves – each with quite separate rights and obligations. Five witnesses were needed to convict a free man of a crime, while one could convict a slave; the rape of a free man or woman carried a fine of a hundred *staters*, while the same offence committed against a serf was punishable by a mere five-*stater* fine. The laws also cover subjects such as property and inheritance rights, the status of children of mixed marriages (that is, between free people and serfs) and the control of trade.

The panels on which the law is inscribed are now incorporated into the round Odeion, which was erected under Trajan in around 100 AD and rebuilt in the third or fourth century (the brick terrace which protects the inscriptions from the elements is modern). The Odeion is just the latest incarnation of a series of buildings on this site in which the code has apparently always been preserved – obviously, this was a city which valued its own history.

The acropolis

With your own transport, you can reach the acropolis by following the road across the river towards Míres and Festós, taking a fork on the right signed "to the Acropolis of Górtys"; this road goes through the village of Ambeloúzos, where you should turn right immediately after the village sign; the route then climbs and you shortly need to turn right along a road signed to Apomarmá and Gérgeri; soon, a sign on the right will alert you to the acropolis, visible off to the right, a 5min walk away uphill

Beside the fenced site, the **river** runs by an abandoned medieval mill and on the far bank you can see a much larger **theatre**, in rather poor repair, set against the hillside. In Roman times, the river ran through a culvert here and you could have walked straight across; nowadays, you have to go back to the road-bridge to explore this area.

The guardians at the site will provide information on exploring the outlying areas, and will give directions to the easiest path up to the **acropolis** on the hilltop above the river. Hardly anyone makes the hike up there, shying away from such a stiff climb in the heat, but the ruins are surprisingly impressive, with Roman defensive **walls** and a building known as the *kástro* (though apparently not a castle) still standing to a height of 6m in places. The lesser remains are among the earliest on the site and include scant relics of a Greek **temple** that was later converted to a church. From this hilltop vantage point, you also get a fine overview of the layout of Górtys and the ongoing excavations, and it's possible to trace the line of the aqueducts coming in from the north.

Míres

The large market town of **MÍRES** (**Μοίρες**), 10km west of Áyii Dhéka, serves as a transport hub for buses further west and to the beaches of the south coast; if you're travelling to Mátala, or west beyond Festós then you'll normally switch buses here. There are good facilities including a **bank**, a few **restaurants**, a couple of **rooms** places and a handy **internet** café right opposite the bus stop, though there's no particular reason to stay unless you are stranded while waiting for a bus.

ARRIVAL AND DEPARTURE   **MÍRES**

By bus The bus station is at the western end of town: actually a patch of ground behind a *períptero* (kiosk). You may need to change here for Léndas and Mátala on the coast, Zarós and Kamáres in the mountains, Tymbáki and Ayía Galíni, or Réthymno.

Destinations Ayía Galíni (5 daily; 2hr 15min); Festós (6 daily; 20min); Iráklio (11 daily; 1hr 30min); Mátala (3–4 daily; 45min).

Festós

7km west of Míres • Daily: April–Oct 8am–8pm, Sun 8am–3pm; Nov–March 8am–3pm • €4, joint ticket with Ayía Triádha (see p.106) €6; note the latter's differing opening hours • ☎ 28920 91315

In a wonderfully scenic location on a ridge at the eastern end of the Messará plain, the **palace of FESTÓS** (**Φαιστός**) enjoys a stunning setting, overlooked by the snowcapped

PALACE OF FESTÓS

Tourist Pavilion

Entrance

Lustral Basin

Royal Apartments
Archive

Peristyle Hall

Peristyle House

North Court

Theatral Area
and West Court

Propylon

Storage
Pits

Grand
Stairway

Workshops

Storerooms

Office

Furnace

Prince's
rooms

Steep bank

Central
Court

First Palace Remains

N

Classical
Greek
Temple

Steep bank

0   25
metres

1

peaks of Psilorítis and with magnificent views east across the plain. While no traces of frescoes were found here, and few other artworks, this doesn't mean that the palace wasn't luxurious: the materials (marble, alabaster, gypsum) were of the highest quality, there were sophisticated drainage and bathing facilities, and remains suggest a large and airy dining hall on the upper floors overlooking the court. Bear in mind, as you explore, that part of the palace is missing: there must have been more outbuildings on the south side of the site, where erosion has worn away the edge of the ridge, and a corner of the Central Court itself has collapsed.

The West Court
You enter the palace from above, approaching the northwest corner of the complex through the Upper Court, then into the **West Court** and integral **Theatral Area**. There are raised walkways leading across the courtyard, and one of them runs right up the steps that form the seats of the Theatral Area (accorded this title by archeologists who supposed it was used for viewing some kind of performance or spectacle). On the west side of the court are circular walled pits, probably for storing grain. The West Court itself is a rare survival from the original palace; the main walkway leads not up the stairs into the new palace but past them and into the entrance to the old palace. From there, much of the facade of the old palace can be seen as a low wall in front of the Grand Stairway which leads into the newer building. When the palace stood, of course, this would not have been apparent; then, the court was levelled at the height of the bottom step of the stairway.

The Grand Stairway and storerooms
The **Grand Stairway** was a fitting approach to Festós, a superbly engineered flight of twelve shallow stone steps, 14m wide. Some of the steps are actually carved from the solid rock of the hill, and each is slightly convex in order to improve the visual impact. This remarkable architectural innovation anticipated similar subtleties of the Parthenon at Athens by twelve centuries. The entrance facade was no doubt equally impressive – you can still see the base of the pillar which supported the centre of the doorway – but it's hard to imagine from what actually survives. Once inside, the first few rooms seem somewhat cramped: this may have been deliberate, either for security purposes or as a ploy to enhance the larger, lighter spaces beyond. At the end would have been a blank wall, open to the sky, and a small door to the right that led onto stairs down towards the grand Central Court. Standing in the entrance area now, you can look down over the **storerooms**, and going down the stairs, you can get closer to them through a larger room that once served as an office. Exposed here is a storeroom from the old palace, with a giant jar still in place and another barred cellar to the right lined with more amphorae. At the far end, more *píthoi* stand in a room apparently used to store olive oil or other liquids; there's a stool to stand on while reaching in and a basin to catch spillage, while the whole floor slopes towards a hole in which slops would have collected.

EXCAVATING FESTÓS
In legend the home of Rhadamanthys, brother of King Minos, **Festós** was excavated by Federico Halbherr (also responsible for the early work on Górtys) at almost exactly the same time as Evans was working at Knossós. The style of the excavations, however, could hardly have been more different. Here, reconstruction has been kept to an absolute minimum, to the approval of most traditional archeologists: with the exception of the Royal Apartments in the site's northeast corner, it's mostly foundations that scarcely rise above ground level.

As at Knossós (see p.66), most of what survives is what the excavators termed the **Second Palace**, rebuilt after its destruction around 1700 BC and occupied until c.1450 BC. But at Festós, the first palace was used as a foundation for the second, and much of its well-preserved floor plan has been uncovered by the excavations. Fascinating as these superimposed buildings are for the experts, they can make Festós confusing for casual visitors to interpret.

The Central Court

From the stores "office", quite an elaborate room, you pass into the **Central Court**, which is by far the most atmospheric area of the palace. In this great paved court, with its scintillating **views**, there is a rare sense of Festós as it must have once been. Look north from here in the direction of the Psilorítis range and you can make out a black smudge to the right of a saddle between the two peaks. This marks the entrance to the Kamáres Cave (see p.209), a shrine sacred to the Minoans and the source of the famous hoard of elaborate Kamáres ware pottery. Even without the views – which would have been blocked by the two storeys to either side when the palace was standing – the courtyard remains impressive. Its north end, in particular, is positively and unusually grand: the doorway, flanked by half-columns and niches (possibly for sentries) covered in painted plaster, can be plainly made out. To the left as you face this are a couple of *píthoi* (left there by the excavators) and a stepped stone that some claim was an altar, or perhaps a block from which athletes would jump onto bulls, or maybe just a base for a flowerpot.

Along each of the lengthy sides of the courtyard ran a covered **portico** or veranda, the bases of whose supports are still visible. In the southwest corner are various rooms that probably had religious functions; beyond these are parts of the old palace that are mostly fenced off. Also here, right at the edge of the site, are the remains of a **Greek temple** of the Classical era, evidence that the site was occupied long after the Minoans and the destruction of the palace.

The Royal Apartments

Heading up through the grand north door – notice the holes for door pivots and the guardroom just inside – a corridor leads through the **North Court** towards the **Royal Apartments**. These have been covered and shut off to prevent damage from people walking through, and it's hard to see a great deal of the queen's rooms, or the king's rooms behind them. Above the king's quarters is a large **Peristyle Hall**, a colonnaded courtyard much like a cloister, open in the centre. On the north side, this courtyard was open to take in the view of Psilorítis: it must have been a beautiful place, and perhaps also one of some religious significance. Staircases linked the hall directly with the Royal Apartments (and the **lustral basin** on the north edge of the king's rooms); nowadays it's easier to approach from the palace entrance, turning left up the stairs from the Propylon.

Palace dependencies

Continuing past the royal quarters on the other side, you come to a series of buildings that almost certainly predate much of the palace. Among the first of these is the so-called **Archive**, where the famous **Festós Disc** (see p.53) was discovered in one of a row of mud-brick boxes. A little further on is the **Peristyle House**, probably a private home, with an enclosed yard similar in design to the Peristyle Hall. From here, stairs lead back down to the level of the Central Court, into the area of the palace **workshops**. In the centre of another large courtyard are the remains of a furnace, probably used for metalworking or as a kiln. The small rooms roundabout were the workshops, perhaps even the homes, of the craftsmen. As you walk back to the Central Court, another suite of rooms – usually described as the **Prince's Rooms** – lies on your left, boasting its own small peristyle hall.

ARRIVAL AND INFORMATION   FESTÓS

By bus Bus services to Festós are frequent, with 6 a day from Iráklio; there are also direct buses to and from Mátala and Ayía Galíni, or you can head back to Míres (see p.103) for more frequent connections.

ACCOMMODATION AND EATING

As you enter the site there's a **tourist pavilion** that serves drinks and food. **Rooms** can be found in villages such as Vóri (see p.107) and Kamilári (see p.113), as well as in Míres or Tymbáki. A major bonus of staying in the area is that if you get to the site early you may have a couple of hours of relative peace before the coaches start rolling in, some time after 10am. Áyios Ioánnis (see p.108), not far away on the Mátala road, makes a good **lunch stop** after or between sites.

1

Ayía Triádha

4km west of Festós on the far side of the hill • Daily: April–Oct 9.30am–4.30pm; Nov–March 9am–4pm • €3, joint ticket with Festós €6 •
An easy drive from Festós or a walk of about 45min by a well-signed road around the south slope • ☎ 27230 22448

In sharp contrast with unadorned Festós, **AYÍA TRIÁDHA** (Αγία Τριάδα) has provided some of the finest known Minoan **artworks**. These include frescoes, three famous vases of carved black steatite – the "Harvesters Vase", the "Boxers' Rhyton" and the "Chieftain Cup" – and a unique painted sarcophagus, all of which are on display in the Iráklio Archeological Museum. Yet the site – discovered and excavated at the beginning of the twentieth century by the Italian School under Federico Halbherr – remains something of an enigma. Nothing exists to compare it with, in what is known of Minoan Crete, nor does it appear in any records; even the name has had to be borrowed from a nearby chapel.

As ever, the ruins enjoy a magnificent **location**, looking out over the Gulf of Messará. The modern view takes in the coastal plain, with Tymbáki military airstrip in the foreground, but in Minoan times the sea would have come right up to the base of the hill, very close by. Despite this beauty and wealth, Ayía Triádha is clearly not a construction on the same scale as the great palaces: the most commonly accepted explanation is that it was some kind of royal villa, but it may equally have been the home of an important prince or a wealthy ship-owing merchant, a building of special ceremonial significance, or even (as more recent theories have it, based on the quantity of records and storage found here) simply an administrative centre.

The remains, in which buildings of several eras are jumbled, are confused and confusing. This matters little, however, for it is the **atmosphere** of Ayía Triádha that really makes the place – the absence of crowds, the beauty of the surroundings and the human scale of the villa.

1

The site

To your left as you climb down to the site are the bare ruins of a **Minoan house** older than most of the other remains (the villa was broadly contemporary with the new palace at Festós), and beyond them a **shrine** that contained a frescoed floor and walls now on show in the Iráklio Archeological Museum. If you keep to the higher ground here, you come into the courtyard of the villa, perhaps the best place to get an impression of its overall layout. The L-shaped building enclosed the courtyard only on its north and west sides, and the north side is further muddled by a much later hall – apparently a Mycenaean *megaron* – built over it. To the south of the courtyard is the early fourteenth-century chapel of **Áyios Yeóryios**, in which there are fragments of some fine frescoes.

The Royal Villa

The **Royal Villa** now lies under covers below the level of the courtyard, but in Minoan times it would not have appeared this way: the builders made use of the natural slope to create a split-level construction, and entrances from the courtyard would have led directly into upper levels above those you see today. The finest of the rooms were those in the corner of the "L", looking out over the sea; here, the best of the frescoes were found, including the famous "Stalking Cat". The quality of workmanship can still be appreciated in these chambers, with their alabaster-lined walls and gypsum floors and benches. Beside them to the south is a small group of storerooms with a number of *píthoi* still in place; some bear scorch marks from the great fire that destroyed the palace about 1450 BC. From the hall and terrace out front, you can walk around the **ramp** that runs beneath the north side of the villa. The Italian excavators named this the *Rampa al Mare*, and it seems that it would have once run down to the sea.

The town area

By far the most striking aspect of the **town area**, which occupies the slope below the villa, is the **market**, a row of stores that are once again unique in Minoan architecture. The stores, identically sized and fronted by a covered portico, run in a line down the hill; in front of them is an open space and, across that, the houses of the town. There's only one problem with the easily conjured image of the Minoan populace milling around the market while their rulers looked benignly on from above: this area dates from the declining years of the Minoan culture and is contemporary not with the villa, but with the Mycenaean *megaron* erected over it. Beyond the stores (and outside the fence) lies the **Cemetery**, where remains of two tholos tombs and many other graves were found, including the one containing the Ayía Triádha sarcophagus.

Tymbáki

West of Festós the final stretch of the Messará plain, with its acres of polythene greenhouses and burgeoning concrete sprawl, must be among the ugliest places in Crete. **TYMBÁKI** (Τυμβάκι) may also be the island's drabbest town. It's a sizeable place, which means there are cafés and restaurants along the main street, stores and banks, and even a couple of hotels, but there's no reason to stay longer than you have to. Just beyond, a turning leads to **Kókkinos Pírgos** on the coast. Here, too, plastic and concrete are the overwhelming images, and more inviting **beaches** in this area are to the south around Kalamáki (see p.113), Kommós (see p.112) and the developed resort of Mátala (see p.109).

Vóri

The road **north from Festós** confirms the rule that on Crete all you have to do is turn off the main road to escape into almost another world. **VÓRI** (Βόροι) is a sizeable place, very close to Festós and barely 1km off the main highway, yet it's almost entirely off the

1

beaten track, a pleasant working village going about its daily routine. That some tourists do come here is largely due to its outstanding ethnology **museum**. If you're heading for the Amári Valley and Réthymno from Vóri, you can spurn the main road and take a lovely, climbing drive via Kalohorafitís and Grigoría to **Kamáres** (see p.209); this also offers an alternativwe route back to Iráklio via Zarós (see p.97).

Museum of Cretan Ethnology

Hidden away in a pedestrian backstreet behind the church • April–Oct daily 11am–5pm • €3 • ⓦ cretanethnologymuseum.gr

Though much copied, Vóri's **Museum of Cretan Ethnology** is still probably the best example of its type on the island, worth seeking out for a comprehensive survey of traditional country life in Crete. In 1992 it won the European Museum of the Year award and in 2011 made the London *Daily Telegraph*'s list of Europe's Top 50 small museums. Sadly, all is not well with the museum: as a private foundation, it has been stripped of support by the Greek government as part of the budgetary cuts caused by the financial crisis; now reliant on private donors, it is struggling to avoid closure.

The museum's collection is a fascinating miscellany of agricultural implements, building tools and materials, domestic utensils, furniture, pottery, musical instruments, weaving and embroidery, all well labelled. There are sections on the production of olive oil, winemaking and the distillation of *rakí*, as well as a display of the myriad herbs and medicinal plants used by Cretans since ancient times. A collection of baskets is especially interesting, the various designs including beehives, eel traps, cheese-drainers, animal muzzles and snail containers. The section on social organization has a case dedicated to the islanders' valiant struggle against Nazi occupation during World War II.

ACCOMMODATION AND EATING   VÓRI

Pension Margit Signed towards the western edge of the village ☎ 28920 91129, ⓦ pension-margit.messara.de. Simple en-suite rooms in a modern house on a quiet street; very much away from it all. There's a communal kitchen, and breakfast available at extra cost; call ahead to ensure there's someone here to meet you. **€35**

★**Taverna Alekos** Well signed close to the centre of the village ☎ 28920 91094. Great little taverna with an enchanting courtyard planted with pomegranate and olive trees, serving straightforward Cretan village food, including snails, as well as pizzas for the tourists. There's a variety of salads on offer, and house specials include tasty *païdhákia* (lamb chops, €8.50) and succulent oven-baked chicken (€8). You can also stop in just for a drink, as an alternative to the *kafenía* in the village square. Daily noon–11pm.

Áyios Ioánnis

The road **south from Festós** passes the Ayía Triádha turn-off and soon approaches the village of **ÁYIOS IOÁNNIS** (Άγιος Ιωάννις) at the bottom of the hill. It's a handy stop for food or drinks, and it's worth taking the time to look at the venerable church of **Áyios Pávlos**. Right opposite the chapel a minor road heads west towards Kamilári and Kalamáki (see p.113), while the main route continues south towards Mátala.

Áyios Pávlos

500m beyond the Taverna Ayios Ioannis in a walled cemetery on the left side of the road • Normally open

Encircled by cypresses, the tiny, drum-domed church of **Áyios Pávlos** is one of the oldest on the island. Parts of it, in fact, date back to pre-Christian times, perhaps part of a Roman shrine to a water deity focused on the **well** at the back of the graveyard. The area to the rear of the church is the most ancient, with the dome probably added in the fourteenth century and the narthex, or porch – with its Venetian pointed arches – in the sixteenth. Inside, some interesting **frescoes** are dated by a frieze to 1303 and have images of the Evangelists Matthew and Luke, as well as a lurid representation of the punishments of Hell with souls being molested by serpents. This is one of the very few churches on Crete dedicated to St Paul, who was none too taken with the islanders, describing them in one of his epistles as "liars, evil beasts and lazy gluttons".

To the side of the church, a charnel house contains the (visible) bones of corpses removed from the nearby tombs after a period of time to "free up" space.

EATING ÁYIOS IOÁNNIS

Taverna Ayios Ioannis On the main road ☏ 28920 42006. Picturesque roadside taverna serving excellent food at tables set under a shady vine trellis; the house speciality of charcoal-grilled rabbit is recommended, and the lamb is tasty, too. Service tends to be slow at busy times. April–Sept daily noon–10pm.

The southwest coast

The best known of the beach resorts in the south of Iráklio province is **Mátala**, but this is far from the end of the story for this part of the coastline. There are much less crowded sands at nearby **Kommós** with its fine Minoan site, and **Kalamáki**, and alternative bases just a short way inland at **Pitsídhia**, a well-established overflow for Mátala, and **Kamilári**, a charming hill village. Throughout this corner of Crete many properties have been bought by foreigners (Germans especially in this area), and many of the small villages have incongruously fancy villas in their midst. Nonetheless, head inland and you'll find lovely, quiet countryside, the villages surrounded by their crops of oranges, pomegranates or olives. One excursion well worth making is to the **Moní Odhiyítrias** and **Áyio Gorge**, where you can follow a verdant ravine down to the sea.

South of the Messará, two more beaches beckon – **Léndas** and **Kalí Liménes**. In an undeveloped way, Léndas is quite a busy place. Kalí Liménes, 20km south of Míres, is hardly visited at all, perhaps due to its role as a bunkering station for off-loading oil tankers. The roads around here are all passable but mostly very slow: the Asteroússia Hills, which divide the plain from the coast, are surprisingly precipitous. The only completely paved **routes** to this part of the coast are from Áyii Dhéka or Górtys to Léndas, and from Míres to Kalí Liménes via Pómbia. Both itineraries offer great views back over the Messará plain before toiling on through a quintessentially Cretan mountain landscape, where clumps of violet-flowering wild thyme cling to the verges in early summer, and shepherds slow your progress as they herd their flocks of goats along the road at dusk.

Mátala

You may still meet people who will assure you that **MÁTALA** (**Μάταλα**), with its cave-dwelling hippy community, is *the* travellers' beach on Crete. But that history bears about as much relation to modern reality as Mátala's role in legend as the place where Zeus swam ashore in the guise of a bull with Europa on his back, or its former glory as one of the chief ports of ancient Górtys. The entry to the village should prepare you for what to expect: a new road littered with very un-Cretan roundabouts, followed by a couple of kilometres of new hotels, "Welcome to Mátala" signs and extensive car and coach parking areas. In fairness it's far quieter at night, once the tour buses have paraded home, but the town never feels anything other than touristy. On the plus side, there's a spectacular **beach**, the atmosphere is boisterous and you'll never be short of

MÁTALA ORIENTATION

For all its fame, Mátala is a very small place – you can walk through town and see all it has to offer in ten minutes. It consists basically of a single pedestrian street, running behind the **beach**: the **market** (where tourist tat has almost squeezed out the fruit and veg stalls) and many of the places to eat lie to the right, while the "**old town**", such as it is, is crammed against the rocks to the left. Car and bike rental, ATM and currency exchange can all be found on the first part of the street as you enter town. A widening of the main road close to the entrance to town we call the "first square"; the town's **main square** is immediately behind this.

THE MÁTALA CAVES

Nobody knows quite who originally built the **Mátala caves**, which are entirely artificial, but it seems likely that they were first hollowed out as Roman or early Christian **tombs**: they have since been so often reused and added to that it is virtually impossible to tell. The cliff in which they are carved is soft enough to allow surprisingly elaborate decor: some caves have windows and doorways as well as built-in benches or beds (which may originally have been grave slabs), while others are mere scooped-out hollows. Local people inhabited the caves, on and off, for centuries, and during World War II they made a handy munitions dump, but it was in the 1960s that they really became famous, attracting a large and semi-permanent foreign community. Name a famous hippy, and there'll be someone who'll claim that they lived here – the most frequently mentioned are Cat Stevens, Bob Dylan and Joni Mitchell ("they're playin' that scratchy rock and roll beneath the Matala moon" crooned the latter on *Carey*, from her 1971 album, *Blue*).

It has, however, been a very long time since the caves were cleared, and nowadays they're a fenced-off **archeological site** (April–Oct daily 10am–7pm, Nov–March 8am–3pm; €2), open by day to visitors but patrolled by the police – and floodlit – every night.

somewhere to enjoy a cocktail at sunset; with the caves lit up at night, the beach is an impossibly romantic setting.

Red Beach

When the crowds on the town beach get too much, you can scramble over the hill for twenty or thirty minutes to **Red Beach**, which, with its reddish-gold sand, nudists and scruffy, seasonal *kantína*, does its best to uphold Mátala's traditions (see box above). To get there, simply follow "Hotel Street" away from town, where a track becomes obvious; it can be quite hard going in parts. There's a slightly longer, easier route from town – look for the white-painted arrows pointing up from the main street.

ARRIVAL AND DEPARTURE   MÁTALA

By car Coming in by car you'll need to use the car park by the beach (€2), signed on the right as you enter the resort; if this is full (as it often is in high season) there's limited paid parking in Hotel Street (€3), or you can retrace your route and seek a place on the entry road.
By bus Arriving by bus you'll be dropped right at the entrance to town.
Destinations Iráklio (3 daily; 2hr); Míres (3 daily; 20min).

INFORMATION AND ACTIVITIES

Travel agencies Cretan Travellers (📞 28920 45732, 🌐 cretantravellers.gr) offers car and bike rental, ATM, currency exchange and information on rooms and excursions.
Horseriding Melanouri Stables (📞 28920 45040, 🌐 melanouri.com), on the western edge of Pitsídhia (see p.112), offers a variety of rides, from a 1hr trip to the beach (€25) to a 6hr ride to the Odhiyítrias monastery and beach (€70).

ACCOMMODATION

Finding a room should be no problem and, out of season, you may well be in a position to bargain. Most of the options below are on **"Hotel Street"**, left off the main road as you enter town, which is almost entirely lined with purpose-built places, all of them with parking and a/c.

Camping Kommos Off the seaward side of the road, roughly halfway between Pitsídhia and Mátala 📞 28920 42596. If you don't mind being further from the action, this is a better site than *Matala Camping*, with a swimming pool and taverna. May–Sept. Two adults plus tent and vehicle €15
Fantastic Hotel St 📞 28920 45362, 🌐 hotel-fantastic.gr. Good-value studios, rooms and apartments, some recently refurbished. It's on the town side of the street, with a private entrance at the back almost directly on the town square. April–Nov. Doubles €40, studios €45, apartments €70
Matala Bay Hotel On the entry road 📞 28920 45300, 🌐 matalabay.gr. One of many bigger hotels that have sprung up along the road into town, this is within easy walking distance of the beach, with a good-sized pool, pool bar, and comfortable rooms and apartments. Room rates rise by 20 percent in Aug. April–Oct. Doubles €40, apartments €50

1

Matala Camping Above the car park, close to the beach ☎ 28920 45720. This campsite with shady tamarisk trees is fine if you don't mind camping on sand; there's a busy bar, and August can bring a rowdy party atmosphere. May–Sept. Two adults plus tent and vehicle €15

Matala View Hotel St ☎ 28920 45114, ⊚ matala-apartments.com. Simple rooms, mostly with small balconies, as well as some larger studios and apartments, on the quiet side of Hotel St. Breakfast available at extra cost. Room rates go up by 25 percent in Aug. March–Nov. Doubles €35 studios €45, apartments €65

Nikos Hotel St ☎ 28920 45375, ⊚ matala-nikos.com. The fanciest of the places on Hotel St, with very well kept

rooms and studios around a charming plant-filled courtyard, plus one "penthouse" with a sea view. Direct access to town from the back. May–Nov. Doubles €40, studios €60

★ **Sunshine Matala** Hotel St ☎ 28920 45110, ⊚ matala-holidays.gr. Friendly, comfortable *pension* with classily renovated rooms, with a/c, fridge and TV, plus one- and two-room apartments with kitchens, on the quieter side of the street. Doubles €40, studios €70, apartments €85

Zafiria On the main street as you enter Mátala ☎ 28920 45366, ⊚ zafiria-matala.com. The largest hotel in town. The balcony rooms can be a little dark and old-fashioned, but they're comfortable and there's a good pool. Breakfast included. April–Oct. €45

EATING AND DRINKING

Eleni Behind the central section of the beach. One of the smaller places with a terrace hanging over the beach, they produce a list of daily specials (fresh grilled sardines or traditional lamb casserole, for example, for around €7), often just scrawled on a notepad, and these are the ones to go for. Exceptionally welcoming too. April–Oct daily 10.30am–11pm.

Giannis Main street beyond the market ☎ 6983 619 233. Usually one of the busiest places in town (partly because of a reputation for being inexpensive), this is an earthy, family-run taverna specializing in grilled meats and fish (mixed fish plate €11). You may have to wait, though they can often find space to set up another table somewhere. April–Oct daily noon–midnight.

La Scala Far end of the beach above the harbour ☎ 6981 388 135. Atmospheric little fish restaurant with a wonderful terrace overlooking the bay; more elegant than most and only marginally more expensive. Fish dishes €7.50–15, *kakaviá* (traditional fish soup) €8. April–Oct daily noon–midnight.

Petra and Votsalo Beyond the market, and close to Giannis (above) ☎ 28920 45361. Attractive taverna above the beach with a good reputation for fresh fish and a loyal clientele. Slightly pricier than places nearby, but worth the extra and has a nice line in creative salads with pasta and seafood. Meze €2.50–8, main dishes €6–17. Daily 11am–11pm; Nov–March Fri–Sun only.

Zouridhakis Alley leading up to the main square ☎ 28920 45352. There appear to be two bakeries here but in fact it's just one big place, with bread, ice cream, cakes and fresh rice pudding. Good for a breakfast of pastries, juice and coffee – they also serve eggs. Daily 8am–10.30pm.

Zwei Bruder First square ☎ 28920 45252. Perhaps the swishest place in town, with bare-stone walls, candles, tablecloths and proper glassware. Lovely setting, even if, underneath it all, the food is standard Greek cooking (meze €2.50–5, mains €6–14). There's also a café-bar area with comfy seating serving coffee and ices. April–Oct daily 11am–midnight.

NIGHTLIFE

The chief entertainment in the early evening is watching the invariably spectacular crimson **sunset** from the beach or one of the beachfront cafés. Later on, the main square is ringed with quiet bars, while livelier places are crammed together at the far end of town, where on busy nights they merge into one big party.

Akuna Matata Main street at far end of town ☎ 6947 343 688. This bar/café/taverna is distinguished by the pirate ship's prow hanging out over the water, and by the fact that you have to walk through the place to reach the far

end of town. There's plenty of choice of food, but that's not really the point; the place really comes alive at night, serving cocktails (mojitos €7), and with dancing and regular live bands. April–Sept daily 11am–4am.

MÁTALA FESTIVAL

Honouring its hippy past, on the third weekend in June the town launches into the three-day **Mátala Festival** (⊚ www.matalabeachfestival.org), when thousands of local and foreign hippies descend on the town to paint it all the colours of the rainbow (mainly road surfaces and street furniture, plus any convenient bits of naked flesh). The rest of the weekend is spent gyrating to "days of yore" tribute bands on the beach stage – don't forget your bell-bottoms and kaftan.

1

Marinero Main street at far end of town ☎6993 477 836. Next door to *Akuna Matata*, and also open all day, though with less emphasis on food; the music here tends to be more rock-oriented and they also have frequent live music, often in competition. April–Sept daily 11am–sunrise.

Port Side Main street ☎6945 983 886. A cocktail bar with an enviable location, its candlelit tables on a terrace hanging over the beach just at the start of the nightlife zone. April–Sept daily 5pm–3am.

SHOPPING

Carrefour Express Off the car park below the Hotel Zafiria. Foreign newspapers, along with picnic supplies and beach accoutrements, are sold at this supermarket. Daily 8am–10pm.

Fanourios On the main road close to the start of the market. Sells English-language books as well as maps, guides and gifts. Daily 9am–9pm.

Pitsídhia

An alternative base to Mátala, marginally cheaper and certainly more peaceful, **PITSÍDHIA** (Πιτσίδια) sprawls around the main road about 5km inland. This is already a well-used option, and far from unspoilt, but it's a congenial Greek village with plenty of rooms, decent places to eat and an affable young international crowd. Head up the hill away from the main road for more peace and atmosphere – there are numerous rooms places and tavernas up here, and a **traditional Cretan night** in the square every Tuesday.

ARRIVAL AND DEPARTURE PITSÍDHIA

By bus All Mátala-bound buses pass through Pitsídhia, and on the return journey to Míres and Iráklio.

ACCOMMODATION

Pension Nikos Inland from the town square ☎28920 45130, ◍pitsidia-nikos.gr. It's less fancy than it looks from the outside, but this is a tranquil spot with comfy rooms and two-room apartments with balcony, fridge and a/c. There's a communal kitchen supplied with coffee and the basics, and a roof terrace with fabulous views. The same owners have a couple of villas in the countryside nearby. March–Oct. Doubles €35, apartments €40

Vrisi Studios Just off the main road, near the bakery ☎28920 45114, ◍pitsidia-studios.com. Modern, a/c studios and one- and two-bedroom apartments accommodating up to five people, around a small pool; they also rent some nearby houses. April–Oct. Studios €40, apartments €45

Kommós

The archeological site of **KOMMÓS** (Κομός), a Minoan harbour town that was probably the main port for Festós and Ayía Triádha, lies on the coast west of Pitsídhia, at the southern end of a sandy shore that extends all the way to Kalamáki (see opposite). The northwesterly winds that often lash the beach and fill the sea with whitecaps would suggest that this was not the best place for a harbour, but the sea level would have been a couple of metres lower in Minoan times, when a reef, still just about visible offshore, provided shelter. On calm days, the **beach** here is lovely, with great views, a taverna at one end, a few loungers, and plenty of room to escape the crowds.

Ancient Kommós

Though it's clear that this is a major site, and visitor facilities have been built, the excavations remain closed – though you can get a pretty good view through the fence. There are three main **excavation areas**, none of them more than a stone's throw behind the beach. The **northern area**, on a low hill close to the sea, contains domestic dwellings, among which is a large house with a paved court and a limestone winepress. The **central group** – behind a retaining wall to prevent subsidence – has houses from the Neopalatial era, with well-preserved walls and evidence, in the fallen limestone slabs, of the earthquake of around 1700 BC. A rich haul of intact pottery was found in this area, much of it in the brightly painted Kamáres style.

The most remarkable finds, however, came in the **southern sector**. Minoan remains here include a fine stretch of **limestone roadway**, 3m wide and more than 60m long, rutted from the passage of ox-drawn carts, heading away inland, no doubt towards Ayía Triádha and Festós. To the south of the road, one building contains the longest stretch of **Minoan wall** on the island: over 50m of dressed stone. The function of this enormous structure isn't known but it could conceivably have been a palace, or it may have had a storage purpose connected with the port. Some of the nearby dwellings to the north of the roadway were also of elaborate construction, and a substantial number of fresco fragments unearthed by the excavators hint at sumptuous interior decorations. Just south of here another large building was a ship shed or **dry dock**, 30m long and 35m wide, with its seaward end open to the sea; it's now partly overlaid by a later Greek structure – probably a warehouse.

Kamilári

The attractive hill village of **KAMILÁRI** (Καμιλάρι) has numerous attractive **accommodation** options, plus plenty of **bars, cafés and tavernas**, some of which, thanks no doubt to the expat community, are surprisingly sophisticated. As you approach the village on the Festós road, you'll see signs (hard to follow; the final stretch is on foot, and the tomb is at the top of a hill) to an early **Minoan tomb**, one of the oldest and best preserved in Crete. Dating from about 1900 BC, the tomb was a circular structure with a large dome, inside which communal burials took place, while cult rituals were carried out in adjoining rooms. The stone walls still stand 2m high in parts; important clay models depicting worship at a shrine and a circular group of dancers unearthed here are now in the Iráklio Archeological Museum.

ACCOMMODATION AND EATING   KAMILÁRI

Acropolis Main Street, in the centre of the village ☎ 28920 42582. One of a number of tavernas in and around the main street, this is not that far above the rest in terms of its kitchen, but does have the most attractive terrace. House specials include lamb in the oven (€8) and there's decent barrelled house wine. May–Oct daily 3–11pm.

★ **Apartments Ambeliotissa** On the hill as you climb towards the village from the Festós road ☎ 28920 42690, ⊛ ambeliotissa.com. A very welcoming, child-friendly place with excellent a/c studios and apartments, some with mezzanine sleeping areas, in and around a house in its own grounds, with excellent pool and playground, café, communal barbecue and TV room. Studios **€30**, apartments **€50**

Kafeneio Kentriko Main Street, in the centre of the village ☎ 28920 42191. This *kafenío* opened its doors almost a century ago and is now run by an ebullient female proprietor. It serves mezédhes as well as breakfast snacks, and there's a little terrace almost opposite. Daily 4pm–1am.

Sifogiannis In the heart of the village ☎ 28920 42410, ⊛ sifogiannis.com. This flower-bedecked building has simple rooms that come with a/c, coffee-making facilities and fridge. There's also a roof terrace and communal kitchen. **€25**

Xenonas Apartments In the village ☎ 28920 42811, ⊛ xenonas.com. Four apartments sleeping two to four people, classily decorated in a traditional, blue-and-white Greek style. Potted plants and flowers abound in the outdoor areas. **€45**

Kalamáki

Some 3km from Kamilári, **KALAMÁKI** (Καλαμάκι) is a small beach resort, popular with locals, with a rather unfinished look. Though not particularly attractive, Kalamáki does have a large, uncrowded, windswept beach that stretches right down to Kommós, plenty of good-value seafront **accommodation**, almost all of it in four- or five-storey blocks, and a pleasantly backwater atmosphere.

ACCOMMODATION AND EATING   KALAMÁKI

For food, it's hard to look beyond the **seafront tavernas**, especially as eating there will allow you to use their loungers and parasols. All have standard Greek menus with an emphasis on fish.

1

Alexander Beach At the southern end of the seafront ☎ 28920 45195, ⓦ alexandros-kalamaki.com. In a quiet spot on the edge of town, this beachfront hotel has a/c rooms with fridge and balcony, plus its own restaurant. A recent addition is a stone-built villa complex on the hill behind with fully equipped apartments (sleeping up to 5) and great views. Free beach loungers and breakfast included at hotel. Aug rates add €15 to each category. April–Oct. Doubles **€45**, villa apartments **€70**

★ **Kiknos Studios** Beachfront in the centre of town ☎ 28920 45466, ⓦ kiknos.org. Exceptionally well-run place with classy touches that you'd expect in a far pricier establishment. Studios have kitchenette, fridge and big balconies, most with sea view (the few that don't cost less); there's also a great rooftop room, with the entire roof and its fabulous views to yourself, for an extra €10. Free loungers on the beach. April–Oct. **€35**

Rooms Psiloritis Set back a little from the northern end of the main beach ☎ 28920 45693, ⓦ psiloritis -hotel.com. Great value – a rambling, slightly ramshackle hotel with numerous sea-view terraces and plain en-suite rooms with fridge. Mar–Oct. **€30**

Taverna Avra Northern end of the beach ☎ 28920 45052. A good choice if you want to use the sun-loungers, as it's in a quieter part of the beach away from the centre. Fresh fish and good Cretan standards are served on tree-shaded waterfront and roadside terraces. April–Oct daily noon–11.30pm.

Taverna Delfinia Central beachfront ☎ 28920 45697. Small, popular fish taverna with a bright, modern look – stripped pine tables, white chairs – serving excellent fresh fish (gilt head bream is often on offer for €28 per kilo), plus locally sourced meat and veg. April–Oct daily 11.30am–11.30pm.

Inland from Mátala

Though there's not a great deal to seek out, it's enjoyable simply to drive around the villages of the southern Messará. Just north of Pitsídhia you can turn off the main road towards **SÍVAS** (Σιβας), a lovely village, but one of the most obviously affected by visitors, largely thanks to the rather bizarrely located *Shivas Village Resort*, a luxury resort on the edge of the village. Beyond Sívas you can continue to wander the back roads through villages like **Kousés**, where there are more rooms and places to eat, and on to the large agricultural centre of **Pómbia**, from where you can head south to the coast at Kalí Liménes (see opposite).

Moní Odhiyítrias

7km south of Sivas • Daily during daylight hours • Free, though you're encouraged to buy their excellent oil, honey or *raki* (all €5) • Just beyond Sívas, a paved road is signed south to Moní Odhiyítrias and Kalí Liménes – while the first half of this road, as far as the monastery, is excellent, the second half is a rough, mountainous dirt track

Even with excellent road access, **MONÍ ODHIYÍTRIAS** (Οδηγύτριας), founded in the fourteenth century, exudes a powerful sense of isolation, and except on summer weekends it sees few visitors. They make those visitors welcome, though, and there's usually someone to show you round this little walled oasis in the midst of the bare mountains: there's a flower-filled courtyard, fifteenth-century icons and frescoes in the church and a horse-powered olive-press, as well as a small collection of ancient agricultural implements and a crumbling tower to climb.

The Áyio Gorge

Opposite the Moní Odhiyítrias entrance you'll see signs for a track leading south to the Áyio Gorge • It's 1hr of relatively easy walking from Moní Odhiyítrias to the gorge entrance; you can also reach the gorge from a spot further down the (now unpaved) Kalí Liménes road, about 25min from the gorge entrance

ÁYIO GORGE (Άγιο) offers a lovely and relatively easy hike of about an hour (once you're in the gorge) down to a welcoming beach. The name ("Holy Gorge") refers to the fact that many of the caves that pockmark its sides are said to have been occupied by Christian hermits, especially during the period of the Turkish occupation. One of them, just 250m from the sea, was a site of early Christian worship, later enclosed in the fourteenth- to fifteenth-century church of Áyios Andónios. This is a beautiful building, with an ancient well outside (whose water, sadly, is not drinkable); the cave itself is not visible, locked within the inner sanctum of the church. Finally, the **beach** is ample reward for the walk, an expansive semi-deserted pebble cove with beautifully clear, calm water.

You'll find places to eat and tastefully restored houses, some of them for rent, in many of the villages you pass through. **Sívas** in particular has a couple of excellent tavernas on the main square, and some good accommodation options.

Horiatiko Spiti (Village House) 150m west of the main square ☎ 28920 42004, ⓦ horiatiko-spiti.de. A converted old house with beautiful, fully equipped studios and a duplex apartment sleeping up to four, all with full kitchen, a/c and wi-fi. In high season (July–Aug) there may be a minimum stay required. Studios **€43**, apartments **€70**

Kalí Liménes and around

KALÍ LIMÉNES (Καλοί Λιμένες) was an important port in Roman times, the main harbour of Górtys (see p.100) and the place where St Paul put in as a prisoner aboard a ship bound for Rome, an incident described in the Bible in Acts 27. Paul wanted to stay the winter here, but was overruled by the captain of the ship and the centurion acting as his guard; on setting sail, they were promptly overtaken by a storm, which drove them past Clauda (the island of Gávdhos) and on, eventually, to shipwreck on Malta. Today, Kalí Liménes is once again a port, for oil tankers this time, which – despite a sweeping beach to the east – has rather spoilt its chances of becoming a full-blown resort. It also has a real end-of-the-road feel, especially out of season, though summer weekends can see crowds of Irakliots descend.

A village of less than fifty souls, it must be said the isolation and loneliness does have a certain appeal, and the procession of tankers gives you something to look at as they discharge their loads into bunker tanks on an islet (named Áyios Pávlos after St Paul) just offshore. There's a solitary **taverna** on the harbour, but the nearest accommodation is at Khrysóstomos, 4km east (see below). Some small cove beaches are accessible beneath the cliffs to the west – on foot only – while to the east is the kilometre-long, pebbly Makriá Ámmos beach where people camp out around the *Taverna Gorgona*. Beyond here, the eastern end of the beach is nudist. With a full day you could also hike up to Moní Odhiyítrias and down through the gorge to Áyio beach (see opposite), having made arrangements at the harbour for a boat to pick you up at the end; you can also get a taxi-boat from Léndas (see p.116).

ACCOMMODATION AND EATING AROUND KALÍ LIMÉNES

Palio Limani Harbourside, Kalí Liménes ☎ 28923 00634. Kalí Liménes once again has a taverna after the other places closed down. The "Old Port" has a pleasant raised terrace with harbour view, serves economical Cretan standards and fresh fish and has wi-fi. Daily 8am–11pm.

Villa Koutsakis Khrysóstomos, 4km east of Kalí Limenes ☎ 28920 97468, ⓦ villakoutsakis.com. Just twelve rooms in a modern building, with restaurant, immediately above the beach, with balconies overlooking the sea, kitchenette, fridge and a/c (but no wi-fi). Very isolated, but very comfortable. **€40**

The coast road

Leaving Kalí Liménes to the east, a road follows the coast for 18km all the way to Léndas. Smooth and tempting at first, it later it becomes an extremely rough dirt track and although passable with a standard car, you'll need to take it very slowly. In the first few kilometres, still on asphalt, you'll pass a few small tavernas, a couple of which have rooms, around the village of **Lassaia**, tumbling down a hill to a bay with a good sandy beach, and **Khrysóstomos**, the next bay. Beyond there are plenty more scruffy beaches, but the coast is blighted by plastic greenhouses and there's only one place with any sort of permanent habitation: **Platía Perámata**, a sandy little village with a couple of stores, a few basic rooms and usually the odd camper.

1

Léndas

The reputation of **LÉNDAS** (Λέντας) as a hippy resort, a fishing village where you can hang out by the beach and camp for free, is somewhat outdated: these days it's a tidy whitewashed seaside village with an easygoing air. For a quiet break, you could hardly choose better: it's still small, low-key and a little alternative, but it's no longer especially cheap, nor the sort of place where campers are welcomed on the beach. Having said that, scores of people *do* camp on the sand at **Dytikós**, just over the headland to the west, a predominantly nudist beach where the old ethos is still very much alive and where there are some good taverna/bars with rooms. Most of the facilities you'll need, including a couple of supermarkets and internet cafés, are located on the main square. There are few other facilities: no fuel or ATM, for instance.

Léndas beaches

The **beach** in Léndas itself is narrow and grey: for better alternatives you can take the obvious path over the headland from the western end of the town beach to the 1km-long stretch of sand at **Dytikós** or head east, where a rough path or a dirt track (signed from the bend on the road) will take you towards **Petrákis Beach**, with rooms and taverna, and **Loutrá**, a bay 5km to the east with a decent beach, small fishing boat harbour and more places to stay and eat. From Loutrá you could take a more ambitious hike, 6km inland up the scenic **Trakhoúla gorge** to Krótos. From here you may find a bus (check the times in the village before leaving), or you can take a taxi the 10km back to Léndas.

Ancient Levín

Just above the village, right on the main road • Tues–Sun 8.30am–3pm • Free

Ancient Levín (or Leben) was an important centre of healing, with an *asklepion* sited by a spring of therapeutic waters – at its height, from the third century BC onward, the sanctuary maintained an enormous temple and was a major centre of pilgrimage. The ruins spread over an extensive area (not confined to the fenced site – you'll see remains throughout the village) and include a temple and a bath complex with tunnels and arches through which the water once flowed. Above all, there's a lovely third-century BC Hellenistic black, red and white pebble mosaic (beneath a canopy) depicting a mythical creature: half horse, half sea-monster. Adjacent to the site are the more substantial remains of an early Christian basilica, with a much smaller eleventh-century chapel still standing in their midst.

ARRIVAL AND DEPARTURE

LÉNDAS

By bus Bus service to Léndas is uncertain, so you'll need to check; usually there is a weekday bus from Iráklio via Míres, leaving Iráklio around noon: the return, from Léndas to Míres, leaves around 7am, a bit later on Saturdays. The bus stop is a dusty square on the east side of the village – from

here, a number of cobbled paths lead down towards the beach and the village's central platía.
By car The bus stop square also serves as a car park.
By taxi If there's no bus you'll have to take a taxi from Áyii Dhéka or Míres, for around €30–40.

ACTIVITIES

Boat trips Trips to local beaches can be arranged on the *Sandokan* (☎ 28920 95345, ⓦ petrakisbeach.gr), which is based at the *Petrakis Beach* hotel (see opposite). There are also regular full-day trips (€30 including lunch and drinks) to beaches not accessible by car, plus the isolated seaside

Koudhoumá monastery (see p.118).
Cretan Outdoor Adventures Based at Dytikós, in the laid-back *Café Relax*. They organize adventure activities including trekking, canyoning, climbing and abseiling, from around €50 (☎ 6909 008 502, ⓦ cretan-outdoor-adventures.com).

ACCOMMODATION

There's plenty of accommodation – most of it in good, modern studio-style **rooms** – though in peak season space can be at a premium. Unless stated, all of the following have a/c.

Casa Doria Loutrá beach at the end of a rough, unpaved road ☎ 28920 95376, ⍵ casadoria.net. Italian-run "slow life" hotel and restaurant right above the beach, with simple, brightly decorated rooms, a laidback atmosphere and Italian-influenced food. A fabulous place, but very isolated and relatively pricey for what you get (rooms have neither fridge nor TV). Breakfast included. March–Oct. Rates go up by €10 in Aug. **€60**

New Levin Apartments Immediately to the east of the main part of the village ☎ 28920 95237. Lovely modern studios and (pricier) apartments, some with two bedrooms and big balconies overlooking the sea. Rooms **€30** apartments **€45**

Nikis Rooms Centre of Léndas, behind Zorbas and El Greco ☎ 28920 95246. Super-friendly place with inexpensive rooms equipped with kettle and fridge, around a lovely flower-filled courtyard; a couple of upper-floor ones have views (at extra cost), but there's a shared roof terrace for those that don't. **€25**

Petrakis Beach Petrákis Beach, 2km east of the village ☎ 28920 95345, ⍵ petrakisbeach.com. Welcoming taverna-rooms place with excellent-value rooms all of which have sea view, terrace and fridge; there are also two rooms in the round tower alongside the main building. Free beach loungers, and Aris, the proprietor, also organizes boat trips (see opposite). **€25**

Studios Gaitani Western end of the beach ☎ 28920 95341, ⍵ studios-gaitani.gr. Studios and apartments with kitchenette and satellite TV immediately above the beach, with huge, rickety-looking balconies hanging over it. Loungers for guests' use on the beach. The same owners have a more modern apartment complex (with pool) in the hills immediately above town. Studios **€45**, apartments **€55**

Villa Tsapakis Dytikós Beach ☎ 28920 95378, ⍵ villa-tsapakis.gr. These bougainvillea-fronted rooms come with fridge and TV, and some with sea view. They also have studios (with kitchenette) and apartments, and their taverna, *Odysseas*, is the meeting point for everyone staying or camping at Dytikós. April–Oct. Doubles **€30**, studios **€35**

Zorbas Towards the eastern end of the beach ☎ 28920 95228, ⍵ zorbas-lentas.gr. Balcony rooms and studios directly above the beach, most with sea views, above a decent taverna, in conjunction with which they offer very good-value half-board deals. They also have a stone-built apartment complex overlooking the village with great views. Doubles **€30**, studios **€40**

EATING AND DRINKING

Tavernas in Léndas are generally very good, serving above-average Greek food with great **sea views**. Léndas' **nightlife** is confined to a handful of bars, although in summer there are frequent beach events at Dytikós or Petrákis Beach (the latter often lays on minibus transfers from town) – look out for the posters.

Blue Café On the rocks past the western end of the beach ☎ 6942 768 903. A romantic spot to lounge over evening drinks while watching the moon rise over the bay, as people have been doing here since the resort's earliest days. May–Oct daily noon–2am.

Lions On the square ☎ 28920 95208. By day a quiet café with internet access and a pleasant garden terrace at the side; at night it revs up (a little) with louder music and dancing (from 9pm), plus cocktails. This is about as wild as Léndas gets. April–Oct daily 9am–2am.

Pink Panther On the square ☎ 28920 95389. A long-time Léndas favourite, *Pink Panther* has a sea-view roof terrace for breezy cocktails, and cranks up the music (rock, reggae, jazz and Latin) inside as the evening wears on. April–Oct daily 9pm–4am.

Pylorus Towards the western end of the beach ☎ 6987 855 691. Good and friendly taverna in a great location on the beach; check out the day's dishes in the kitchen, and the not-too-pricey fresh fish. Mezédhes €2.50–4. April–Oct daily noon–11pm.

★ **Taverna El Greco** ☎ 28920 95322, ⍵ lentas-elgreco .com. An excellent restaurant with a large leafy terrace above the beach. The food is mostly traditional Greek – the day's baked dishes are on display in the kitchen – but cooked with exceptional care using the best local ingredients. There's an unusually good wine list, too, and they also have rooms. April–Oct daily 11am–11pm.

The southeast coast

East of Léndas there's barely any access to the coast before the far east of the province, where there are low-key beach resorts at **Tsoútsouros** and **Keratókambos**, though for hardy walkers the secluded monastic community at **Moní Koudhoumá** is an escapist's dream. The road that gives access to these places, east across the Messará from Áyii Dhéka through Asími to Áno Viánnos, is an enjoyably solitary drive through fertile farming country in the shadow of the **Dhiktean mountains**. There's not a great deal to stop for along the way, but there are plenty of solid traditional villages with *kafenía* and

1

places to eat. The more substantial village of **Áno Viánnos** has plenty of spots for a lunch break, as well as some ancient churches.

| GETTING AROUND | THE SOUTHEAST COAST |

By car The direct route from Iráklio to Áno Viánnos is via the featureless farming town of Arkalohóri, joining the west–east route at Mártha. Alternatively, you can head south from Houdhétsi (see p.77), joining the west–east road near Pýrgos.

By bus Buses run from Iráklio via Arkalohóri to Áno Viánnos (Bus Station A; Mon–Fri 9.30am, 1.15pm & 3pm, Sat 9.30am & 3pm, Sun 7.30am), but none follow the route across the Messará.

Moní Koudhoumá

The remote **MONÍ KOUDHOUMÁ** (**Κουδουμά**), on the coast almost due south of Iráklio, nestles in a seaside cove with an inviting pebble beach at the foot of a cliff, surrounded by pinewoods. Arriving here is a distinctly end-of-the world experience, and the handful of remaining monks spend most of the year alone. Donations by pilgrims and benefactors have financed a considerable rebuilding programme since the turn of the millennium and facilities for both monks and pilgrims have vastly improved. The monks see few visitors outside of the feast of the Panayía Koudhoumá in August (when up to fifteen thousand pilgrims descend on the monastery), but are extremely welcoming to those that do turn up, and will offer you food and a mattress in one of the dormitories set aside for "pilgrims". While the monks will not accept payment for their hospitality, a donation to monastery funds is unlikely to be refused. If you think the magic of the place may persuade you to prolong your stay, you should bring supplies with you. The nights here are exquisitely serene, broken only by the sound of the sea splashing against the rocks. While you're visiting the monastery, be sure to make the fifteen-minute walk west along the coast to the spectacular **cave** ("Avakospilios") where the founder monks lived during the building of the first monastery in the eighteenth century.

ARRIVAL AND DEPARTURE   MONÍ KOUDHOUMÁ

By car You can drive the 24km to the monastery on a reasonable unpaved road south from Stérnes, but the final switchback cliff face section is scary, with no barriers – allow at least 1hr 30min for the journey each way.
On foot It's possible to reach the monastery on foot, most easily by heading south from Hárakas on a paved road to

the hamlet of Paranímfi, where you can get local directions onto the path that leads directly to the monastery, or continue on a reasonable dirt track to Trís Ekklisíes (with tavernas and rooms), from where it's 7km or so along a coastal path. Alternatively, you can hike all the way from Pýrgos via Priniás (20km; 4–5hr).

Pýrgos

PÝRGOS (Πύργος) is the biggest village in these parts, with plenty of facilities. Along the main street – which sees a lively **market** take place every Tuesday morning (all over by noon) – you'll find a couple of decent **tavernas** and, at the eastern end of the thoroughfare, the fourteenth-century **church** of Áyios Yióryios and Áyios Konstantínos, with some superb fresco fragments. The key is available from the house (no. 137) to the right of the church gate.

ACCOMMODATION   PÝRGOS

Hotel Arhontiko On the main road into town ☎ 28930 23118. Comfortable, modern hotel mostly used by local

business travellers, hence plenty of parking and extras including a/c, TV and kitchenette. **€45**

Tsoútsouros

Some 11km of asphalt road winds alarmingly down from Káto Kasteliandá, on the highway, to **TSOÚTSOUROS** (Τσούτσουρος). Despite the drama of the approach, Tsoútsouros itself is not immediately attractive; the central beach is narrow, rocky and grey, while the village straggles in an untidy line behind it, with an ugly concrete harbour/marina as a focus. Nonetheless the place is growing into a small resort, and the little bay does have its attractions – it's peaceful, with good stretches of beach backed by shady tamarisks in both directions. On summer weekends, and in the first two weeks of August, it can be very busy with local tourists; out of season, from October to April, most places close.

ACCOMMODATION AND EATING   TSOÚTSOUROS

For **accommodation**, the best places are at the eastern end of the village, where there's a better beach and it's generally more attractive despite the new development; prices tend to be dramatically lower out of season.

Mouratis Eastern end of seafront ☎ 28910 92244, ⓦ mouratis.gr. A large, modern place above a taverna with good value a/c studios and apartments with cooking

facilities for up to six people, many with big seafront balconies. Aug rates increase by €10. April–Oct. Studios **€25**, apartments **€35**

1

Petra & Fos Western end of the seafront near the harbour ☎ 28910 92345. Good pizzas from a wood-fired oven, plenty of well-prepared Greek dishes (*païdhákia* €8, *mezédhes* €3.50–5) plus fresh fish and good barrelled wine. There's also a comfortable café which is lively throughout the day, with breakfast until noon and cocktails after sundown. April–Oct daily 10am–midnight.

Phaedra Apartments Far eastern end of seafront, beyond *Zorba's* ☎ 28910 92311, ⓦ www.faidras apartments.com. Simple two-room a/c balcony apartments with kitchenette, some with sea view. If there's no one around, ask at *Zorba's*. Aug rates go up by €10. April–Oct. €30

San Georgio Central seafront, by the harbour ☎ 28910 92322, ⓦ sangeorgio.gr. Sizeable hotel (by Tsoútsouros standards) with simple, smallish a/c rooms with fridge; some have a balcony and sea view. There's a pleasant garden at the back and the hotel's café has wi-fi. €35

★**Zorba's** Eastern end of seafront ☎ 28910 92277, ⓦ zorbas-taverna.com. The pick of the resort's tavernas, with an attractive terrace and food and wine that's home-produced or locally sourced. Main dishes include daily specials (€7–9) such as pork with tomato and feta. Its two excellent-value rooms – only available outside July and August (when they're needed for staff) – are generously proportioned, with fridge, kettle and sea-view balconies. Daily 10am–midnight; Nov–Feb Fri–Sun only. €25

Keratókambos

KERATÓKAMBOS (Κερατόκαμπος), 10km east of Tsoútsouros, is accessed by a spectacularly winding mountain road from Hóndhros, near Áno Viánnos, or on a good paved road along the coast from Tsoútsouros. Though you would not at first sight describe Keratókambos as a pretty place – a single street of mismatched houses interspersed with cafés and tavernas facing a narrow, grey, shingly beach – it grows on you if you stay long enough to get over first impressions; it's peaceful and friendly, with good food and rooms. The beach, too, is better than it appears, with sandy, shallow water for a long way offshore.

In theory Keratókambos is three separate villages, though in practice they run into one another. Keratókambos itself, with the best of the beach, is immediately east of the junction where the Hóndhros road meets the coast; **Kastrí**, immediately west, has most of the facilities, on the shore close to the junction; and **Pórto Kastrí**, where an ugly modern concrete harbour has been built, lies a couple of hundred metres west of here.

ACCOMMODATION AND EATING ⸻ KERATÓKAMBOS

Filoxenia Kastrí ☎ 28950 51371. Clean, modern en-suite rooms for two to three people, right on the seafront behind a lovingly tended, flower-filled garden. Studio-style rooms come with a/c, TV and kitchenette. €30

Komis Studios In Keratókambos proper ☎ 28950 51390, ⓦ komisstudios.gr. These lovingly designed, multi-level studio apartments in a garden setting come equipped with antique furnishings, minibar and TV. There's also a larger suite sleeping up to five. Breakfast included. May–Sept. €40

Pan Apartments Above the village and around the road down from Hóndhros ☎ 28950 51220, ⓦ pan-appartments.de. There are numerous rooms places attractively sited above the village, with fine views out to the Libyan Sea. *Pan* is a good choice: modern studios and apartments come with kitchenette, spectacular sea view and a pretty garden. Minimum three-night stay. March–Nov. Studios €30, apartments €40

Taverna Kriti Kastrí ☎ 28950 51231. One of the best local tavernas, serving good, earthy, traditional Cretan food; try the "special omelette", for example, with tomato, onion, potato and pepper (€4.50). They also serve meat dishes (*païdhákia* €7) and fresh fish at good prices, and have simple rooms. Daily 9am–midnight. €25

Áno Viánnos

ÁNO VIÁNNOS (Άνο Βιάννος), clinging to the southern slopes of the Dhíkti range, is a large village where almost everyone seems to pull over to break their journey. Given the narrow streets and lack of parking this can be unfortunate, but the air of busy chaos – with farmer's pick-ups the vehicle of choice – seems appropriate, somehow, in what was traditionally the administrative and market centre of this part of southeastern Iráklio province. Its importance has waned as the coastal settlements have grown but it's still a busy place, and there are some interesting churches to see as well as plenty of places to eat and drink. The sharper, cooler air up here is refreshing too.

The **churches** are signed from the main street, up the narrow alleys in the upper part of the town. The most interesting is fourteenth-century Ayía Pelayía, with a magnificent, if damaged, fresco of the Crucifixion on the back wall.

EATING	ÁNO VIÁNNOS

Kafenion 0 Platanos On the through road at the east end of the village. The most atmospheric of the local places to eat, serving mezédhes at tables under an ancient and gigantic plátano (plane tree). Daily 7am–midnight.

Káto Sými

East of Áno Viánnos the road to Árvi turns off at **Amirás**, alongside a giant memorial to the Cretans killed in World War II. A few kilometres further, 1km beyond Péfkos, you can turn left for a scenic detour to the village of **KÁTO SÝMI** (Κάτο Σύμη) and its atmospheric **ancient sanctuary of Hermes and Aphrodite**. The trip is worth it for the adventure as much as anything – an intimidating drive up into the mountains round first-gear hairpins, all on asphalt, with a rocky scramble around the site, surrounded by pine forest, to reward you at the end.

Káto Sými itself has another **war memorial**, commemorating five hundred people put to death in 1943 when it and six other settlements were destroyed in retaliation for an attack on a German patrol.

The Sanctuary of Hermes and Aphrodite

Known locally as **Kryá Vrísi** (cold spring), the **Sanctuary of Hermes and Aphrodite** is laid out on a series of broad ledges on the mountainside where a prodigious spring gushes clear, ice-cold water all year round. There is evidence of a **shrine** here dating back to prehistoric times. Adopted by the **Minoans**, it became a holy place of overwhelming importance, as evidenced by the thousands of votive clay and bronze figurines and vases brought here by pilgrims, many of which are now on display in the Iráklio Archeological Museum. In Greek and Roman times the shrine continued to be an important centre of pilgrimage, now to Hermes Dendrites and Aphrodite.

The spring still flows high up on the eastern side of the site, just outside the fence. Here too is an enormous hollow plane tree, which seems old enough to have witnessed many of the sacrifices and ceremonies that took place here in ancient times. The most obvious remains are in this corner of the site, including vestiges of temples, altars and cult rooms dating from all periods. Today most of the spring water disperses down the mountainside via plastic pipes to irrigate the olive groves below, but enough escapes to create several small waterfalls that you'll have passed on the way up.

ARRIVAL AND DEPARTURE	THE SANCTUARY OF HERMES AND APHRODITE

By car Start the ascent to the ancient site near the *Taverna Afrodite* (see below) in the village's main street. Uphill beyond the taverna follow wooden signs to Omalos Kristos, a chapel much higher in the mountains. You may be confused by turnings and junctions as you climb higher, but always stay on the asphalt. Eventually, some 3km above the village, a sign in Greek announces the site; the sturdy fence should be visible just above you, and although the site is almost always locked, the remains can easily be viewed by making a circuit of the exterior.

EATING	KÁTO SYMI

Taverna Afrodite Main street in Káto Sými (lower village) ☎ 28950 31463. A good taverna for a meal before or after you visit the site; waters from the ancient spring splash in troughs at the entrance. It has a fine terrace looking out over stands of plane trees, and serves a variety of salads as well as the usual Cretan standards (mains €6–10). They also sell home-made mountain honey. April–Oct daily 9am–10pm.

Lasíthi

VÁI

Lasíthi

Eastern Crete is dominated by the elegant resort of Áyios Nikólaos and the exclusive tourism it attracts, but get beyond "Ag Nik" (as it's known to the majority of English-speaking visitors) and its environs and you can experience some of the most striking highlands and wilderness coastlines on the island. Áyios Nikólaos itself, along with the pretty neighbouring resort of Eloúnda, is lively and cosmopolitan and has some of the most luxurious hotels on the island, although budget travellers are also catered for with a range of economical rooms and apartments. It's easy to escape into the surrounding hills and mountains, too. North beyond Eloúnda and its beaches, you come to the brooding islet of Spinalónga, once a redoubtable Venetian and Turkish fortress, later a leper colony. The town of Kritsá, with its famous frescoed church and textile sellers, and the imposing ruins of ancient Lató, also make for an enjoyable short excursion, while slightly further afield the Lasíthi plateau – a high mountain plain with picturesque villages and abundant greenery – makes a great day-trip from the coast, even better if you stay overnight.

The **far east** of Crete marks a dramatic change in scenery and tempo. Although much of it is rocky, barren and desolate, it is an area of great natural beauty, and on the whole the towns and villages are slower and quieter, with life conducted at an easier pace than in the rest of the province. The main town in the area, **Sitía**, is an attractive, traditional place where tourism has had little visible effect. The Minoan workers' village at **Gourniá** is definitely worth a stop en route while, at the island's eastern tip, the famed palm-studded beach at **Vái** and the Minoan palace at **Káto Zákros** are the major tourist attractions. **Palékastro**, between the two, has plenty of accommodation within easy reach of isolated beaches while the island's southeast corner is about as escapist as you could wish.

Along the south coast, there is generally far less development. **Ierápetra** is the major town in these parts, with a scenic harbour from where boats sail to the offshore desert island of **Gaidhouronísi**. In both directions from here, towards **Mýrtos** and **Makríyialos**, is a string of low-key resorts.

WINDMILLS ON THE LASITHÍ PLATEAU

Highlights

❶ Áyios Nikólaos A centre of upmarket tourism and one of the most attractive towns on the island, with good restaurants and buzzing nightlife. **See p.127**

❷ Spinalónga Fortified island whose impregnable isolation later made it an ideal location for a leper colony, chilling to visit even today. **See p.135**

❸ Lasíthi plateau This spectacular highland plateau is a verdant farming area, where cloth-sailed windmills, multicoloured wildflowers and soaring eagles compete for your attention. **See p.140**

❹ Kritsá Home to one of Crete's most famous frescoed Byzantine churches, this traditional

village is also a centre of weaving and lacemaking. **See p.147**

❺ Sitía Set around a beautiful bay is this attractive and easy-going resort with a couple of interesting museums and plenty of after-dark diversions. **See p.154**

❻ Koureménos Beach Not far from the exotic palms and crowds of tourists at Vái, the island's best windsurfing spot offers simpler beach pleasures, with plenty of more sheltered sands nearby. **See p.164**

❼ Káto Zákros With a romantically sited Minoan palace flanked by a cluster of fish tavernas and simple places to stay, Káto Zákros is a delightful seaside hamlet. **See p.166**

HIGHLIGHTS ARE MARKED ON THE MAP ON P.126

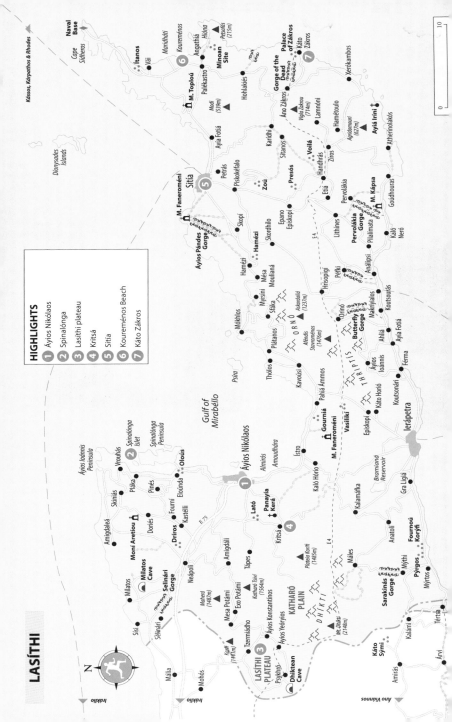

LASÍTHI

HIGHLIGHTS

1 Áyios Nikólaos
2 Spinalónga
3 Lasíthi plateau
4 Kritsá
5 Sitía
6 Kouréménos Beach
7 Káto Zákros

Kássos, Kárpathos & Rhodes

Naval Base

Cape Sídheros

Dionysades Islands

Gulf of Mirabello

Iráklio

Áno Vianós

Áyios Nikólaos

The capital of the province of Lasíthi, with a population of ten thousand – which more than doubles in the summer season – the coastal town of **ÁYIOS NIKÓLAOS** (**Άγιος Νικόλαος**) has obvious attractions. Set on a hilly peninsula around a supposedly bottomless **lake**, in a lovely setting overlooking the **Gulf of Mirabéllo** ("Beautiful View"), it is wonderfully picturesque, with dozens of excellent cafés, restaurants and bars around the lake, the harbour and the nearby coast. Curiously, what the town doesn't have is an outstanding beach, so the five-star hotels are all some way out – mostly to the north, around Eloúnda – where they have private access to the coast.

By day, things to do in town are pretty limited – most people simply spend the day recovering from the night before. For the majority of visitors the days are taken up strolling the area around **Lake Voulisméni**, nosing around in the shops, or heading to one of the local **beaches**, all of which have Blue Flag status. There's also a wide choice of **boat trips** around the bay (see p.129).

Brief history

In antiquity, Áyios Nikólaos was the port for the city of **Lató** (see p.146), though this settlement faded in the Roman period and seems to have been abandoned in Byzantine times. The Venetians built a fortress – of which nothing remains – and gave the surrounding gulf its name, Mirabéllo. In succeeding years the town came slowly back to life, and by the nineteenth century the port was again busy; following union with Greece in 1913, Áyios Nikólaos was confirmed as the **capital** of Lasíthi province. A quiet harbour town for most of the last century, Áyios Nikólaos was discovered in the 1960s by international tourism, and has barely looked back since.

Áyios Nikólaos beaches

The beach closest to the heart of things is the shingly little cove of **Kitroplatía**, surprisingly pleasant despite being right in the heart of town, though invariably crowded. The main **municipal beach** (with entry fee), beyond the marina on the southwest side of town, is no less busy. Beyond here there's a constant stream of people walking to the excellent sandy beach at **Almirós**, 2km to the south, or using bus or bike to reach the good beaches at Kaló Hório and beyond (see p.147). In the other direction, heading north, many locals simply dive off the rocks along Aktí Koundoúrou, though the first real sand in this direction is at tree-shaded **Ammoúdi**, another municipally run beach about 1km out of town – again, usually packed. Beyond are more little beaches en route to Eloúnda.

Folk Museum

Paleológou 1, near the bridge • May–Oct Tues–Sat 10am–2pm & 5–7pm • €3

The **Folk Museum** has a small but interesting display of handicrafts (especially embroidery), costumes, pottery, cooking utensils and old Cretan goat-leather bagpipes. The displays include a recreation of a traditional Cretan bedroom, and a collection of weaponry with numerous revolution-era firearms.

The Archeological Museum

Paleológou 74, at the top of the hill north of the lake • Currently closed; contact the tourist office (see p.129) for the latest

The town's **Archeological Museum** holds a great deal of interest, but is currently closed for renovation and is scheduled to reopen in 2016. Highlights include the extraordinary **Goddess of Mýrtos**, the museum's star exhibit, a goose-necked early Minoan clay jug (c.2500 BC). There's also gold jewellery from early Minoan tombs at Mohlós (2300–2000 BC) and some fine examples of Vasilikí ware, named after the early Bronze Age site on the isthmus of Ierápetra where it was first discovered. Recent finds from the palaces at Mália and Zákros are also displayed, though the major original discoveries are at the Iráklio Archeological Museum. Those on display include a curious **model house** from Mália with a pitched roof and chimneys – both foreign concepts in Minoan architecture – and a beautiful **gold pin** (of unknown provenance) bearing an intricately crafted bramble motif and a tantalizingly long inscription in the undeciphered Linear A script on the reverse. There are fine late Minoan **clay sarcophag**i, or *lárnakes*, too, decorated with birds, fish and the long-tentacled octopus that seems to have so delighted Minoan artists. There's also a rare Minoan **infant burial** displayed exactly as found at its site at Kryá, near Sitía.

▲ Tourist Police (150m)   ▲ ◪ (1km), Ammoúdi (1km) & Eloúnda

ÁYIOS NIKÓLAOS

● SHOPS

| Bibliopoleío Karterí | 2 |
| World Press | 1 |

● CAFÉS & RESTAURANTS

Aoúas	2
Asteria	6
Avlí	4
Du Lac	9
Hrisofílos	11
Itanos	12
Karnáyio/Píta Tou Riga	3
La Strada	10
Migomis	7
Ofou To Lo	13
Pelagos	5
Sarrí's	14
Toedeledoekie	1
Twins	8

■ BARS

Alexandros Rooftop Bar	2
Molo	4
Pier Bar	3
Yanni's Rock Bar	1

■ ACCOMMODATION

Angelos	4
Aphrodite	5
Coral	2
Doxa	12
Du Lac	7
El Greco	8
Hermes	3
Mary	10
Mediterranean	6
Mylos	9
Minos Beach Art Hotel	1
Sgouros	11

Áyios Nikólaos church

1km north of town in the grounds of the *Minos Palace Hotel* • Daily 4–8pm • Free • Ask for the key at the hotel's reception desk, leaving passport or driving licence as deposit

The Byzantine church of **Áyios Nikólaos**, from which the modern resort takes its name, is, perhaps appropriately, stranded in the grounds of a five-star hotel. It's worth the effort to get there, though, to see some of the earliest **fresco** fragments found in Greece, dating back to the eighth or ninth century. The geometric patterns and motifs that survive are the legacy of the Iconoclastic movement, which banned the representation of divine images in religious art.

ARRIVAL AND DEPARTURE   ÁYIOS NIKÓLAOS

By bus The bus station is north of the centre in the new town. There are local buses to the centre (July & Aug only) roughly every 30min (7.15am–10pm), or it's a short taxi ride. On foot, it's a steep up-and-down walk; head uphill and turn right along Knossoú and its continuation Kornárou, which will bring you out high above the lake; taking a left here to join Paleológou will lead you back down to the harbour area. Check timetables on ⓦ bus-service-crete-ktel.com.

Destinations Eloúnda (hourly; 20min); Ierápetra (6 daily; 1hr); Iráklio (20 daily; 1hr 30min); Kritsá (Mon–Fri 8 daily,

Sat & Sun 4 daily; 15min); Pláka (6 daily; 30min); Sísi (Mon–Sat 2.15pm; 45min); Sitía (7 daily; 1hr 45min).
By car If you're driving in, follow the one-way system up the hill to Platía Venizélou, and then down into the picturesque areas past the souvenir stores that line Koundoúrou and parallel 28 Oktovríou. Parking in the central areas is a nightmare, so you're better off leaving your vehicle in the car parks near the marina or at the harbour; parking spaces are often to be had heading north along Aktí S. Koundoúrou near the *Coral* hotel.

GETTING AROUND AND INFORMATION

Bike rental There are dozens of outlets, mainly in the harbour area. For scooters, small motorbikes and high-quality mountain bikes, try the friendly and reliable Manolis, Aktí S. Koundoúrou 11, facing the waterfront (☎ 28410 24940; April–Nov daily 8am–10pm).
Car rental Clubcars, 28-Oktovríou 24 (daily 8am–9pm; ☎ 28410 25868, ⓦ clubcars.net).
By taxi There are ranks in Platía Venizélou and outside the Folk Museum; or call ☎ 28410 24000 or ☎ 28410 24100.

Tourist information The tourist office (April, May, Oct & Nov daily 10am–6pm; June–Sept daily 8am–9pm; closed Dec–Feb; ☎ 28410 22357, ⓦ aghiosnikolaos.eu), by the bridge, is particularly helpful. They have lots of maps and brochures, as well as currency exchange at good rates and cheap internet access.
Tourist police The tourist police are at Eríthrou Stávrou 47 (☎ 28410 91409).

TOURS AND ACTIVITIES

Boat trips Trips to points around the Gulf leave from all around the harbour. There are daily trips to Spinalónga (€12–17), and various fishing, barbecue, beach and sunset tours, often with meals included. Longer trips to Mókhlos (see p.151) and the island of Psíra (see box, p.151) are also sometimes available. Sail Crete (☎ 28410 24376, ⓦ sail crete.com) offers small-group trips to Spinalónga and Mókhlos as well as private charter of a small yacht.

Scuba diving Happy Divers (☎ 28410 82546, ⓦ happy divers.gr) are based on the beach in front of the *Hermes* hotel; they can pick you up from your hotel. Pelagos Dive Centre is at the *Minos Beach Hotel* (☎ 28410 24376, ⓦ divecrete.com), while Underwater Crete is based in the *Hotel Mirabello* on the Eloúnda road (☎ 28410 22406, ⓦ creteunderwatercenter.com).

ACCOMMODATION

Except in peak season you're unlikely to have a problem finding a **room** in Áyios Nikólaos; however, with accommodation scattered on hilly streets all over town you may get footsore. If you haven't booked, start at the tourist office, which has information on current availability.

★**Angelos** Aktí S. Koundoúrou 16 ☎ 28410 23501. Welcoming small hotel on the seafront, offering excellent a/c balconied rooms with TV and fridge plus fine views over the Gulf. No breakfast, but you're a mere 50m from *Toedeledokie* (see p.130). The supermarket, owned by the same family, directly underneath, has information on the rooms. **€35**

Aphrodite P. Yeoryíou 34 ☎ 28410 28058. Cheap and cheerful, old-school rooms place with shared bathrooms, lots of plants, a rooftop terrace and the use of a communal fridge. Little has changed here in twenty years. **€25**
Coral Aktí S. Koundoúrou 17 ☎ 28410 28363, ⓦ mhotels .gr. Comfortable three-star sister hotel of the nearby *Hermes*,

2

with great sea views from rooms at the front (worth paying the extra); there's also a rooftop saltwater pool and bar. Breakfast included. May–Oct. **€80**

Doxa Idomenéos 7, close to the town beach ☎ 28410 24214, ⊛ doxahotel.gr. This rather old-fashioned hotel is not bad value for a/c balcony rooms with satellite TV and fridge. It often has rooms available when other places are full. Breakfast included. **€45**

★**Du Lac** 28 Oktovríou 17 ☎ 28410 22711, ⊛ dulac hotel.gr. Perhaps the most unexpected bargain in Áyios Nikólaos, with rooms and studios classily renovated in designer style with facilities including balcony, a/c, fridge and TV (the studios also have a kitchenette) in a prime location overlooking the lake. Not all rooms have lake views (€15 extra), however, and night-time noise can be a problem, as you're right in the heart of things. July & Aug rates increase by 25 percent. **€36**

El Greco Aktí Themistokleous 1 ☎ 28410 28894, ⊛ hotel elgreco.eu. This elegant seafront hotel has modern, refurbished rooms with fabulous sea views from their balconies (it's worth paying the extra; inland-facing rooms are gloomy). Rooms come equipped with fridge, minibar and tea-making facilities, and Kitroplatía beach is just 50m from the entrance. Aug rates increase by 50 percent. April–Oct. **€50**

Hermes Aktí S. Koundoúrou 21 ☎ 28410 28253, ⊛ dessolehotels.com. Luxurious four-star seafront hotel with a large rooftop saltwater pool and every facility, from minibar to satellite TV. Frequent online discounts. Breakfast included. **€80**

Mary Evans 13 ☎ 28410 23760. Very friendly place with

basic, inexpensive en-suite rooms with fridge and use of communal kitchen, some with a sea view and balcony. There are also some good-value apartments nearby sleeping up to four. Rooms **€35**, apartments **€40**

Mediterranean S. Dhávaki 27 ☎ 28410 23611, ✉ mannyspension@yahoo.com. On a hill between the lake and the seafront, these clean, economical rooms (most en suite, some with separate, private bath, some with balcony) are run by a welcoming Anglo-Greek couple. They come with fridges, a/c, TV and use of a communal kitchen. **€30**

★**Mylos** Sarolídi 24 ☎ 28410 23783, ⊛ pensionmylos .com. Sweet and welcoming little *pension* east of Kitroplatía, with some of the best rooms in town for the price. Spotless, en-suite a/c balcony rooms (no. 2 is a dream) with TV, fridge and spectacular sea views over the Gulf. Can advise on parking. April–Nov. **€35**

Minos Beach Art Hotel On the promontory 1km north of town ☎ 28410 22345, ⊛ bluegr.com. One of the first of the luxury hotels to be built – in the 1960s – which means its rooms and bungalows enjoy a setting and spaciousness that younger rivals can only dream of, with almost 1km of private coastline just outside town. Original artworks sprinkle the grounds, and there's every facility you could hope for, including private pools in the fancier villas. Online discounts on the quoted rates most of the year. **€378**

Sgouros Nikoláou Pagálou 3 ☎ 28410 28931, ⊛ sgouros grouphotels.com. Modern hotel overlooking Kitroplatía beach, with a/c balcony rooms (sea view €10 extra) with fridge and TV, and plenty of tavernas nearby. Rates go up by 20 percent in Aug. April–Oct. **€45**

EATING

There are tourist-oriented **tavernas** (invariably employing zealous greeters) all round the lake, with little to choose between them apart from the different perspectives you get on the passing fashion show. Have a drink here, perhaps, or a mid-morning coffee – but choose somewhere else to eat. The places around Kitroplatía are generally fairer value, but again you pay for the location – the more authentic and better-value establishments tend to be less obvious, tucked away in the backstreets behind the tourist office or close to Platía Venizélou.

CAFÉS

Asteria Aktí I. Koundoúrou ☎ 28410 22452. Nicely old-fashioned café with a waterfront terrace fronting the harbour, and another on the second-floor balcony. One of the oldest in town and great for people-watching. Daily 7.30am–1am.

Migomis Nikoláou Plastíra 22 ☎ 28410 23904. High above the bottomless lake, *Migomis* has a matchless view, arguably the best in town, and prices not significantly higher than any other fancy café; a great place for afternoon or evening drinks. Their elegant piano restaurant next door is a little over-the-top in terms of both price and decor, but perhaps worth it if you've booked a terrace-edge table to feast on that view. April–Oct daily noon–midnight.

★**Toedeledokie** Aktí S. Koundoúrou 19 ☎ 28410 25537. Café "toodle-oo" is a friendly, low-key bar run by

Lucia, a Dutch artist whose works decorate the interior. There's a great parasol-shaded terrace above the sea opposite, and in addition to (fast) wi-fi there are international papers to read. To go with the drinks and creamy milkshakes you can choose from freshly-made toasties, baguettes and great sandwiches (the tuna salad is tasty). At night it morphs into a chilled bar with ice cream and cocktails (try the strawberry daiquiri). April–Oct daily 10am–2am.

RESTAURANTS AND TAVERNAS

Aoúas Paleológou 44 ☎ 28410 23231. Very good, inexpensive traditional Cretan food (*païdhákia* €7.50), served in a plant-covered, trellissed courtyard. A bit out of the way, so can often be half-empty and lifeless. April–Oct daily noon–midnight.

★**Avlí** P. Yeoryíou 12 ☎ 28410 82479. Delightful garden ouzerí offering a wide mezédhes selection (with plenty of vegetarian options), as well as more elaborate dishes such as pork in wine, or lamb with artichokes slow-cooked in a traditional oven (both €9.50). Booking advisable in July & Aug. Daily 12.30–3pm & 7–11pm.

Du Lac By the lake ☎ 28410 22414. Probably the best of the lakeside restaurants, with a local as well as tourist clientele and good, fresh fish. It's expensive (mains €14–23) though, and you may need to book in the evening. The café upstairs offers if anything better views, with music and drink. April–Oct daily 9am–midnight.

Hrisofilos Aktí Pangálou ☎ 28410 22705. Attractive, stylish and creative *mezedhopolío* with reasonably priced fish, meat and veggie mezédhes served on a sea-facing terrace close to Kitroplatía beach. Has a varied wine list. Meze €3–8. March–Dec daily 4pm–midnight.

Itanos Kýprou 1 ☎ 28410 25340. Popular with locals, this traditional taverna serves reasonably priced Cretan food such as *yemistés* (rice-stuffed vegetables; €5) – check what's on offer from the trays in the kitchen (8 daily dishes €5–10) – and barrel wine. The surroundings don't match up to the food, sadly, with a choice of tables on the street or in the cavernous, dark interior, decorated with huge barrels. Daily 11am–11pm; Nov–April closes 6pm.

★**Karnáyio/Píta Tou Ríga** Paleológou 24 ☎ 28410 25968. What appear to be two separate establishments in fact share a colourful terrace above the lake, where you can order from either menu. *Karnáyio* is a modern incarnation of a traditional ouzerí serving tasty mezédhes (€4–5 each, or order the excellent value wine- or ouzo-meze combos), while *Píta tou Ríga* is an upmarket kebab joint – their speciality *píta tou ríga* (€3.80) comes with added bacon and cheese. The place attracts a young, local crowd and

there's *lyra* and *laoúto* (lute) music most Fri & Sat evenings. Daily 9am–3am.

La Strada N. Plastíra 5 ☎ 28410 25841. There's decent risotto, pizza and pasta (€7–11) plus reasonably priced fish dishes at this popular, Greek-Italian restaurant. Tables on the street are not in the prettiest setting, though, so you may want to eat inside. March–Dec daily 11am–11pm.

Ofou To Lo Kitroplatía ☎ 28410 24819. Best of the moderately priced places on the waterfront here, with consistently good food served on a lively terrace; it's usually crowded. Try their lamb "Anóyia style": baked in the oven with potatoes or stuffed courgette flowers. Mains around €9.50. Daily April–Oct 10am–midnight.

★**Pelagos** Stratígou Kóraka and Kateháki 10 ☎ 28410 25737. Housed in an elegant mansion, this stylish (mainly) fish taverna has an attractive leafy garden terrace that complements the excellent food. Fish is good but pricey, while meat dishes like *païdhákia* (€9.50) or seafood pasta (€14) are easier on the wallet. House wine €7.50 a half-litre. Booking advisable. April–Oct daily noon–midnight.

★**Sarri's** Kýprou 15 ☎ 28410 28059. Wonderful little economical neighbourhood café-diner-taverna in a quiet corner, with a shady terrace across the road overlooking an ancient church (with frescoes). Great place for veggies, and the vegetarian meze (€8) is easily enough for two. The range of mezédhes is very tempting, and a *megáli* (big) and terrific *vroutosaláta* (fruit salad – €5) makes the perfect finish to a meal. It also makes a good breakfast stop, and offers grills and *souvláki*. Low-priced barrelled wine. April–Oct daily 9am–4pm & 6pm–midnight.

Twins Aktí I. Koundoúrou ☎ 28410 28201. Large and always-busy pizzeria with tables right on the harbour and a busy takeaway business. The pizzas (€7–10) are good, and they also have sandwiches, salads, burgers and the like. Daily: April–Oct 9am–1am; Nov–March noon–11pm.

DRINKING AND NIGHTLIFE

One thing that Áyios Nikólaos undeniably does well is **nightlife**. A string of bars along the pedestrianized Aktí I Koundoúrou on the east side of the harbour play cool sounds to customers chatting on their waterside terraces, many with dancefloors inside that fill as the night wears on. There are bars on the opposite side of the harbour too, though fewer of them. More raucous music venues and clubs crowd the bottom of 25-Martíou (known as "Soho Street") as it heads up the hill – though few seem to survive in the same incarnation for long.

Alexandros Rooftop Bar Kondhiláki ☎ 28410 24309. The name says it all; a great eyrie for a relaxed drink overlooking the lake, becoming increasingly rowdy as the cocktails take effect. The music playlist dates from the 60s to the present day but is mostly oldies, and gets louder later, encouraging punters to take to the small dancefloor. Happy hour till 10.30pm. April–Oct daily 8pm–5am.

Molo Aktí I Koundoúrou 6 ☎ 28410 26250. One of a string of harbourside cafés with waterside terraces, *Molo* rarely closes; it's a café and local hangout by day and a cocktail bar in the evening; later on the action moves inside

for dancing, club nights and occasional live music. Daily 8am–early hours.

Pier Bar Aktí I. Koundoúrou 4, on the east side of the harbour ☎ 28410 82775. A new and popular venue along this strip, playing a rock, jazz and modern Greek soundtrack. As well as cocktails there's food too: salads, filled pitas and ices. Daily 10am–midnight.

Yanni's Rock Bar Aktí I Koundoúrou 1 ☎ 28410 23581. Long-running classic rock music bar, with a party atmosphere and a soundtrack of 70s and 80s music, blues, hard rock and heavy metal. Daily 10pm–4am.

THE MIRABELLO FESTIVAL

Each year, Áyios Nikólaos mounts a summer-long cultural festival, **"The Mirabello"**, which includes music, dance and theatre from Crete, Greece and other parts of Europe. Keep an eye out for posters advertising the various events, or ask at the tourist office.

SHOPPING

The prime shopping street in town is Koundoúrou as it heads uphill from the harbour: head up to Platía Venizélou and then back down on 28-Oktovríou and you'll have seen most of what's on offer – from jewellery and fashion to souvenirs and sponges, photography to pharmacies and dive gear to delis.

Bibliopoleio Karteri Koundoúrou 5 and 28-Oktovríou 4 ☎ 28410 22272. Near Platía Venizélou, has a good selection of books in English, and there are other bookshops nearby. Daily 9am–10pm; Nov–March closed Sun.

World Press On the harbour next to Twins pizzeria. The place for foreign newspapers. Daily 9am–10pm.

DIRECTORY

Banks and money Banks and exchange places are mostly found along Koundoúrou and 28-Oktovríou, where there are several ATMs. The tourist office also changes money at reasonable rates.

Hospital The town hospital is at the northern end of Paleológou, one block beyond the Archeological Museum (☎ 28413 43000).

Post office 28-Oktovríou, above the lake (Mon–Fri 7.30am–2.30pm).

The Gulf of Mirabéllo

North of Áyios Nikólaos, the swankier hotels are strung out along the **Gulf of Mirabéllo** coast road, especially as you approach the busy little resort of **Eloúnda**. The gulf's best-known attraction is the islet and former leper colony of **Spinalónga**, easily accessed from either Eloúnda or the hamlet of **Pláka**. Leaving Áyios Nikólaos, the road soon begins to climb; looking across the bay, you can make out the islands of Psíra and Mókhlos against the stark wall of the Sitía mountains, while nearer at hand mothballed supertankers are moored among the small islands sheltering in the lee of the peninsula.

Eloúnda

ELOÚNDA (Ελούντα) is a town with a split personality: surrounded by the most expensive hotels in Crete, and by fancy apartment and villa developments, it has plenty of jewellery and fashion stores and some pricey seafront restaurants; on the other hand, on the fringes there's a much more earthy resort, with plenty of inexpensive rooms and cafés that compete to provide the biggest, cheapest English breakfast. At the heart of town is an enormous seafront square ringed by cafés and restaurants, banks and post office, stores and hotels; virtually everything is here, or within a short walk. There are small beaches all around, though many of the best are monopolized by the big hotels; a good, sandy **municipal beach** stretches out north from the centre, and there are numerous popular swimming spots further out in this direction, along the road to Pláka.

ARRIVAL AND INFORMATION ELOÚNDA

By bus Buses stop on the main square, where tickets can be bought from the kiosk.

Destinations Áyios Nikólaos (hourly; 20min); Pláka (6 daily; 10min).

By car The seafront square is the best place to park.

Travel agents The continued closure of the municipal tourist booth in the harbour square due to financial constraints means that travel agencies are the only source of information. A good one, Olous Travel (☎ 28410 41324, ⓦ olous-travel.gr), is located on the seafront square next to the post office and can provide general information and assist with finding accommodation, as well as changing money and arranging tours and car rental.

ACTIVITIES AND TOURS

Boat trips Boats leave the harbour every 30min from 9.30am for the trip to Spinalónga (€10 return; ☎ 6976 683 597, ⓦ eloundaboat.gr); longer day-trips taking in local beaches are also available.

Train trips Two rival tourist trains offer local trips, some

of which venture way up into the hills (from €10), starting from the harbour square.

Walking tours Rambles to discover the flora of Crete (from €45 including refreshments) are run by Julia Jones (☎ 28410 42177, ⓦ flowersofcrete.com).

ACCOMMODATION

Many of the most **exclusive hotels** in Crete – and security-conscious, with guarded entry gates – are sited around Eloúnda, offering **spectacular villas** with private pools costing thousands of euros a night; these are almost always far less expensive booked as part of a package. As for more ordinary accommodation, if you're having problems finding somewhere, try Olous Travel (see opposite) or one of the other agencies in the centre of town.

Akti Olous On the road to the causeway ☎ 28410 41270, ⓦ eloundaaktiolous.gr. An attractive seventy-room three-star seafront hotel where comfortable rooms come with balcony, a/c, TV and fridge; many have a sea view across the bay (extra). There's a bar and pool on the roof, with great views, and a seashore terrace café flanked by a small beach. Breakfast included. Aug rates increase by 25 percent. April–Oct. €65

Corali Studios Behind the far end of the town beach ☎ 28410 41712, ⓦ coralistudios.com. A sizeable complex, *Corali* (together with neighbouring *Portobello Apartments*, under the same management) has good, modern a/c studios and apartments with cooking facilities, all with a sea view, and a pool and bar in the garden area behind. €65

Delfinia Rooms On the waterfront just south of the centre ☎ 28410 41641, ⓦ pediaditis.gr. A/c rooms, studios and apartments in a great position right at the heart of things and directly above the sea (most have balconies with views). The decor is simple, but it's reasonably priced. You can get information at the Pediaditis Bookshop on the main square. Doubles €45, apartments €60

Elounda Peninsula 2km south of Elounda ☎ 28410 68250, ⓦ eloundapeninsula.com. Spectacular gated hotel draped across its own private peninsula. Accommodation is in suites or larger villas, most with private pools, with virtually every imaginable facility including spa, tennis courts, 9-hole golf course, sandy beach and kids' clubs. It shares the complex (plus facilities) with the *Elounda Mare* and *Porto Elounda* hotels, which offer some more standard hotel rooms. €580

Marin Studios Behind the town beach, close to town ☎ 6972 314 067, ⓔ marinporoshotel@yahoo.gr. Bigger and better than they appear from the front, these quiet apartments and studios, set well back from the road, are well equipped – with kitchens and a/c – and run by a helpful family. Studios €35, apartments €50

Milos Rooms In the upper part of town south of the centre ☎ 28410 41641, ⓦ pediaditis.gr. Under the same management as the *Delfinia*, this is a more modern apartment complex with pool and bar. Rooms, studios and apartments are all a/c, and larger units have kitchens. You can get information at the Pediaditis Bookshop on the main square. May–Oct. Doubles €45, studios €50, apartments €60

Olive Grove Just off the square, on the road heading inland ☎ 28410 41448, ⓦ olivegrove.com.gr. Big, modern two-bedroom apartments with a/c, wi-fi and full kitchen in a complex with pool and pool bar. The latter is open to non-residents and hosts occasional music nights. €60

Paradisos Taverna 2km out of town, poorly signed down a dirt track off the Áyios Nikólaos road ☎ 28410 41631. Offering rural simplicity, this is an exceptionally quiet spot with an idyllic setting on the landward side of the Oloús lagoon and a very warm welcome. Simple rooms come with fridge and a/c. It also has an excellent garden taverna (see p.134). €45

Traditional Homes of Crete ☎ 28410 41717, ⓦ traditional-homes.gr. Excellent restored stone-built houses (many ancient with original features), sleeping up to four, on the heights in and around the village. All come with parking, wi-fi, a/c, kitchen, terraces, views and private or shared pool. €70

EATING AND DRINKING

Eloúnda has a good choice of **tavernas** and restaurants in all price categories, and just off the square you'll also find a couple of excellent bakeries. **Nightlife** is quiet, centring on the cafés and bars around the main square; for anything wilder, head to Áyios Nikólaos (see p.131).

Babel West side of the main square ☎ 28410 42336. A large and busy bar/café/pub with big-screen sports, wi-fi and internet; one of the liveliest spots in town, with music and

dancing as the night wears on. April–Oct daily 9am–late.

Dimitris On the square facing the church ☎ 28410 41822. It has all the atmosphere of a transport café, but

2

Dimitris' kitchen serves up good grilled meat dishes, as well as Greek standards, at economical prices; *moussaká* €6.50, *kléftiko* €8. Jan–Oct daily noon–11pm.

Ergospasio Waterfront, close to the Ferryman ☎ 28410 42082. Elegant ouzeri-taverna inside an old stone-built carob factory. The interior is bright and stylish and there's a choice of seafront terrace or another on the first floor. The menu is short, with a mixture of Italian and Greek dishes such as saffron, prawn and mussel risotto or stuffed lamb roll with feta. Prices are slightly above the norm (mains €16–22), although *mezédhes* cost €3–6 per plate. April–Oct daily 11am–11pm.

★**Ferryman** Waterfront, south of the harbour ☎ 28410 41230. This glitzy place is named after the 1970s BBC TV series *Who Pays the Ferryman?* in which it featured: ebullient owner and chef Akis Sfirogiannakis saw the series being filmed as a child (his grandmother founded the restaurant). It's pricey, but the kitchen – under noted chef Yiannis Baxevanis – offers interesting variations on traditional Greek recipes, and the waterfront terrace is a delight. Highlights include smoked aubergine *salata* (paté), tomato "balls" with aromatic herbs, mussels cooked in oúzo, and sea bass baked with Cretan herbs. Mains (excluding fish) €8–15. Booking advised. May–Oct daily noon–4pm & 7–11pm.

Katafygio On the main road above the Ergospasio restaurant ☎ 28410 42003. Snazzy new bar and club also serving snack food, ices and juices. A range of music – from classic rock to modern Greek – is played by resident DJs, and live bands also feature in high summer. April–Oct daily 11pm–6am.

Megaro Waterfront, south of the harbour ☎ 28410 42220. This friendly place serves fresh, well-prepared fish, seafood (mussels €12) and steaks, inside or on a pontoon terrace on the water; it's notably cheaper than its fancier neighbours. Salads and starters are delicious too – try the halloumi and aubergine salad (€8.50). April–Oct daily 11am–midnight.

★**Okeanis** Far end of the town beach ☎ 28410 42246. A very attractive terrace overlooking the town beach, with classy table settings, is matched by the quality of the cooking. Try the *lagudopaximádo* (stuffed cabbage leaves) or a mouthwatering lamb cooked in the oven with wine and garlic. Three-course menus for €9.90–16.90. Daily noon–4pm & 6–11pm; Nov–March Fri–Sun only.

Paradisos Taverna 2km out of town, poorly signed down a dirt track off the Áyios Nikólaos road ☎ 28410 41631. This taverna/rooms place (see p.133) is a wonderful place to eat – especially at lunchtime when you can appreciate the garden – and the welcome from Kostas and Dimitra makes it very special. Prices for fish are very reasonable, with *tsipoúra* (bream) for €13, as are meat dishes like *païdhákia* (€10). There's a range of *mezédhes* (€3–6), plus daily fish and meat specials for two, chalked up on the blackboard (€20–33). April–Oct daily noon–10pm.

Vritomartes Waterfront, main square ☎ 28410 41325. Occupying a plum spot on a floating pontoon in the centre of the harbour, this is one of the more expensive places in town, with a heavily marked-up wine list. Fish is excellent, though pricey, in this location (fish platter for two €47). April–Oct daily 11am–11pm.

SHOPPING

Eklektos A. Papandréou 13 ☎ 28410 42086. A great little English bookshop 50m uphill from the square in the direction of Áyios Nikólaos, on the steps down to the water and *Poulis* restaurant; they sell new and secondhand books, offer credit for your old books, and stock guides, maps and gifts. April–Nov daily 9.30am–2pm & 3.30–8pm.

The Spinalónga Peninsula

The barren **SPINALÓNGA PENINSULA** (**Σπιναλόγκα**) – often known as "big Spinalónga" to distinguish it from the more famous island of the same name – lies directly offshore from Eloúnda, forming a huge sheltered bay in front of the resort. It is linked to the mainland only by a narrow causeway, all that remains of a once-substantial sunken isthmus less than 2km from the centre of Eloúnda; it's an easy walk along the coast or short drive (though the sharp turning off the main road can be hard to spot). Protected by the causeway are the remains of Venetian salt pans, now fallen into disrepair, which are worth checking for migrating birds in the spring. Also here are the remains of stone windmills and the "French" canal, while all around on both sides you'll find people swimming from small patches of **beach** or basking on flat rocks. On the far side of the peninsula there are more tiny patches of sand – you can walk across to the nearest in a further thirty minutes or so. These are lovely spots, and apparently isolated, but become horrendously overcrowded in the middle of the day when boat tours make their lunch stops here.

Oloús

The ancient "sunken city" of **OLOÚS** (Ολούς) lay around the far end of the causeway to Spinalónga, mainly to the south and east, where a number of structures can be made out beneath the waves. Though it is known chiefly for having been the port of Dríros (see p.137), what little remains is **Roman**: there's a fenced enclosure behind the *Kanali* bar-restaurant in which you can see the floor of a fourth-century Roman **basilica** with an odd, almost patchwork-style black-and-white mosaic, and among the rocks a little further round (watch out for sea urchins) are traces of harbour installations, now submerged as a result of the rise in sea level over the past couple of millennia. The site has never been excavated, and this is about the extent of what is visible, but it's a worthwhile trip for the setting, especially if you combine it with a swim and a drink at the *Kanali*.

2

Spinalónga

Daily 9am–7pm • €2 • Boats run here every 30min in season (April–Oct) from both Eloúnda (€10 return) and Pláka (€8); most give you 1hr on the island, though you can take a later boat if there's room; it's also on many day-trips from Áyios Nikólaos (€12–17)

The imposing fortress rock of **SPINALÓNGA** (Σπιναλόγκα), at the northern end of the bay protected by "big Spinalónga", is a prime target for boat trips from Áyios Nikólaos, Pláka and, above all, Eloúnda. The **fortress**, which entirely covers the island, was founded by the **Venetians** in 1579 to defend the approach to the gulf and the sheltered anchorages in the bay. With its battlements, guard towers and seemingly impregnable walls, it bears all the hallmarks of the Italian republic's brilliant military architecture. Like their other island fortresses, it proved impregnable and was only handed over to the Turks by treaty in 1715, some fifty years after the rest of Crete had surrendered.

The infamous part of the island's history is much more recent, however. For the first fifty years of the twentieth century, Spinalónga was a **leper colony**, the last in Europe. Lepers were sent as outcasts – long after drugs to control their condition had rendered such measures entirely unnecessary – to a colony that was primitive in the extreme and administered almost as if it were a detention camp. Its jail was frequently used for lepers who dared complain about their living conditions.

Even today, if you can escape the visitors, there's an unnerving sense of isolation when the boat leaves you here, at a jetty from which a long tunnel leads up into the fortified centre. There are still just two easily sealed entrances: this tunnel, and a jetty on the seaward side (which you see if you approach from Áyios Nikólaos) leading up to the old **castle gate** with its lion of St Mark. Inside the castle a real town grew up – Turkish buildings mostly, adapted by the lepers using whatever materials they could find. Although everything is in decay, you can still pick out a row of stores and some houses that must once have been quite grand. A couple have been restored to make a small **museum**, with photos and artefacts outlining the island's history.

Pláka

PLÁKA (Πλάκα), about 5km north of Eloúnda, lies directly opposite Spinalónga and was once the mainland supply centre for the leper colony. Boats still make the short trip across, nowadays carrying tourists, and the formerly decaying hamlet has become quite chichi, overlooked by a vast luxury hotel and with many of its houses done up by foreign owners or villa companies. It's still an attractive, tranquil place, though, with a couple of excellent tavernas and crystal-clear water – though the beach is made up of large, uncomfortable pebbles.

ARRIVAL AND DEPARTURE	PLÁKA

By bus There are six daily buses to and from Eloúnda (10min).

2

ACTIVITIES AND TOURS

Boat trips Boats cross to Spinalónga from the quaysides beside the *Gorgona* and *Spinalonga* tavernas (April–Oct every 30min 9am–6pm; €8 return); the *Spinalonga*'s boat also does a complete circuit of the island – allowing a fuller appreciation of the impregnable bastion – and offers fishing trips (€80/hr for up to four people) with the catch cooked up at the taverna on your return.

Watersports A cabin on the beach is the headquarters of a watersports centre (☎ 6944 932 760, ⍟ spinalonga -windsurf.com), offering everything from windsurfing and ringos to kayaking and motorboat rental.

ACCOMMODATION AND EATING

Athina Villas In the heart of the village ☎ 28410 41342, ⍟ spinalonga.eu. A modern complex of comfortable a/c studios and apartments with kitchens and balconies, wi-fi and TV, many with sea views. Contact the owner for winter stays. May–Oct. Studios €40, apartments €50

Blue Palace Immediately south of the village ☎ 28410 65500, ⍟ bluepalace.gr. Spectacularly sited on a slope above the bay, the *Blue Palace* offers sybaritic luxury in its 250 suites and villas – many with private pool – although the guarded security gate at the entrance is slightly off-putting. Watersports, tennis courts, gym, spa, five restaurants and numerous bars are all on site. €543

Taverna Giorgos Southern end of village ☎ 28410 41353. The best setting in town, with a large terrace facing

out to sea opposite Spinalónga island. The fish is caught with their own boat but is pricey (mixed fish plate €30 per person), although there's a seafood *souvláki* for €15; meat and traditional Cretan dishes are less expensive. Daily 11am–midnight.

Taverna Spinalonga At the far end of the village ☎ 28410 41804, ⍟ tavernaspinalonga.com. With an outdoor terrace facing the sea and Spinalónga, this is Pláka's oldest taverna and bar (founded 1930) and has perhaps the most economical fish meals, fresh from the day's catch; the grilled octopus, *kalamária* (squid) and *tsipoúra* (bream) are all excellent. The owners are very helpful and also have en-suite rooms in the main building or in a new one across the road. Daily 11am–midnight. €30

The Áyios Ioánnis peninsula

The triangular **Áyios Ioánnis peninsula**, north of Áyios Nikólaos, inland from Eloúnda, is surprisingly wild and little travelled, with narrow roads running through remote farming hamlets with few facilities; the only sight of any significance is the remains of the ancient city of **Dríros**. The E75 north-coast highway delineates the northern edge of the peninsula; coming from the west it leaves Mália behind and embarks almost immediately on a long climb inland – rising at first through the **Selinári Gorge**, where travellers would traditionally stop at the chapel and pray to St George for safe passage. It's a tremendously engineered road, but bypasses the major town of **Néapoli** and anywhere else of note, and there's little to see until you emerge high above Áyios Nikólaos to spectacular views of the Gulf of Mirabéllo.

If you've time to dawdle, consider the minor roads across the peninsula: they make a great alternative route from Eloúnda to the west or to the Lasíthi Plateau. There's little specific to see, but there are wonderful views of the Gulf of Mirabéllo, while the larger villages offer plenty of places to eat and drink. A steep, narrow lane winds up from Eloúnda through **Páno Eloúnda** and **Pinés** towards **Fourní** and **Kastélli**, meeting up with the E75 highway outside Neápoli.

GETTING AROUND   THE ÁYIOS IOÁNNIS PENINSULA

By bus There's a steady stream of buses heading to and from Áyios Nikólaos along the E75 highway, most of which call at Neápoli (around 17 daily in each direction), but otherwise virtually no public transport on the peninsula; Sísi has just one bus a day in each direction, to Áyios Nikólaos and to Iráklio.

By car Road maps of Crete, unreliable at the best of

times, seem particularly hopeless on the peninsula; the Anavasi 1:100,000 Lasíthi map (see p.41) is the most trustworthy. Most significantly, there is no direct route around the coast, even on dirt roads, though some maps mark one. Follow the signposts and the asphalt, however, and you should eventually reach your destination.

Vrouhás and around

Beyond Pláka, the road leaves the coast and starts to climb towards **VROUHÁS** (Βρουχάς). Here, and in the surrounding country, you'll see many traditional stone windmills, mostly ruined: the winds that drove them are now being harnessed by a substantial **wind farm** on the ridges above. From Vrouhás and nearby **Skiniás**, rough tracks are signed to local **beaches**, plunging steeply down to isolated but unattractive pebble coves in a jagged, rocky coastline; there are small, seasonal tavernas at both.

   Inland just beyond Skiniás, a signed, paved road climbs towards the lonely, fortress-like, sixteenth-century **Moní Aretíou**, surrounded by cypresses and cedars. Recently restored, it often appears deserted, though a couple of monks do remain and the gate and church of Ayía Tríadha are usually open. Beyond, you can continue, on a paved road that initially winds through utterly barren mountain tops, to **Doriés**, where the church of Áyios Konstantínos holds an icon of the *Panayía* (Virgin), the oldest known on the island, dating from the fourteenth century. The church is sited near the heart of the village, and lies down a little path off the main road (marked by a small monument in the form of a church). The cream-and-brown-painted house next to it is that of the *papás*, who may be available to open the church for you.

Dríros

3km east of Neápoli • Open daylight hours • Free • On the northeastern edge of Neápoli, on the old road as it goes under the E75, is a road signed to Kouroúnes, Nofaliás and Skiniás; after 2km, a signed turn-off on the right leads a further 1km to a dead end beneath a rocky hillside – the stepped path up to the site can clearly be seen from the parking area inside the fence

The earliest remains found at ancient **DRÍROS** (Δρήρος) date back to the eighth century BC, and the city flourished for the next seven hundred years as an important ally of Knossós, but a deadly enemy of Lýttos (see p.79). Dríros declined in importance prior to the end of the second century BC, when many of its citizens emigrated to Miletus in Asia Minor (see p.140).

The site

Scrambling over piles of collapsed stones – ruins of the ancient city – you come eventually to a stone building under a corrugated canopy: the eighth-century BC **Temple of Apollo Delphinios**, one of the earliest known temples in all of Greece, in the centre of which can be seen the remains of a sunken hearth. Among the discoveries here were three hammered bronze statuettes (some of the earliest known, now in the Iráklio Archeological Museum) and two Eteocretan inscriptions – Greek letters used to write a Cretan, possibly Minoan, tongue. The temple was dedicated to a cult that celebrated Apollo transformed into a dolphin, a guise the god used when guiding Greek sailors; that the chief sanctuary of Miletus in Asia Minor was devoted to the same cult is further evidence of a link between this area and the founding of the colony there. As you look around today, it's hard to believe that this temple once lay on the edge of the bustling **agora**, or market square. This was approached by a flight of steps – visible on the west side of the canopy, to the left of the doorway. Another flight of steps joined the temple on the east side, and to the south is a huge **cistern** constructed in the third century BC, now crammed with fig trees.

Neápoli

Despite its size, strategic location and history – it was the birthplace of Pope Alexander V – **NEÁPOLI** (Νεάπολη) sees virtually no tourists other than those who stop for a coffee in the square between buses or as they drive through. A charming provincial town, it was formerly the capital of Lasíthi (a role now usurped by Áyios Nikólaos) and remains the seat of the local government and of the provincial courts;

it's a peaceful place for a stopover, and it is from here that one of the roads up to the Lasíthi plateau sets out. Around the expansive, sleepy main square, where the buses stop, are a post office, banks, tavernas and *kafenía*. You'll also see signs to both a folklore and an archeological museum, but both have been closed for some time and show no signs of reopening.

Sísi

SÍSI (Σίσι), a fair-sized resort on the western edge of the Áyios Ioánnis peninsula, in many ways has more in common with the nearby holiday centres of Iráklio province than with the rest of Lasíthi. Certainly during the day it can be crowded with day-trippers from Hersónissos and Mália, whose tour boats moor up in the harbour. That gloriously picturesque **harbour**, overlooked by a string of cafés, bars and tavernas, is the chief attraction here, though there are also some attractive cove **beaches** to the east. The best of these has been taken over by the *Kalimera Kriti* resort, but you can still get there by going to Avláki beach (itself very pleasant), and following the path round the rocks from there.

ARRIVAL AND INFORMATION   SÍSI

By bus A single bus leaves Sísi daily at 9.15am, headed for Áyios Nikólaos and Iráklio – passengers for the latter change buses at the highway; there are return journeys from each of those towns in the afternoon. If you walk or get a taxi the 2.5km to the highway junction, you can also pick up buses there (at least 17 daily in each direction).

Travel agents AIS Travel (☎ 28410 71712, ⬤ sisi-crete .com), 50m up the main street from the seafront, is a helpful travel agency that can provide a village map, bus timetables and assistance with everything from accommodation to tours.

ACCOMMODATION

Many of Sísi's visitors stay in modern **apartment complexes** scattered about the surrounding countryside. Because these are so widespread – and mostly pre-booked in high season – the best tactic is to ask around at the tavernas near the harbour or at AIS Travel (see above). There are also plenty of "Rooms for Rent" signs along the roads as you approach the village.

Bella Vista Overlooking the sea from the hills just over 1km west of town ☎ 28410 71370, ⬤ bellavistasisi .com. Large, modern complex of a/c studios and apartments with balconies (many with sea view), fully equipped kitchens and wi-fi in communal areas. In the gardens there's a big pool and pool-bar. Studios €30, apartments €40

Camping Sisi On the rocky shore just over 1km west of town ☎ 28410 71247, ⬤ sisicamping.gr. Campsite with a fabulous seafront location (though you can't actually swim from the shore here), shady pitches, and excellent facilities including swimming pool, restaurant, kitchen, laundry and wi-fi. Two people plus tent and car €17.50

Porto Sisi Hotel On the seafront, east of the harbour ☎ 28410 71385, ⬤ portosisi.com. Luxurious hotel/ apartment complex with the best location in town, right on the seafront. Comfortable, well-equipped and recently refurbished apartments come with kitchen and pool, though you pay for the privilege, especially if you want a sea view. April–Nov. €93

EATING AND DRINKING

Angistri Facing out to sea, round the corner from the main harbour ☎ 28410 71794. With the inevitable international menu featuring pizza and pictures of food to point at, *Angistri* also attracts locals for its competitively priced home-made food and fresh fish. Daily April–Oct noon–11pm.

Hemingway's Bar Above the harbour ☎ 28410 71068. With an immaculate setting above the harbour, *Hemingway's* is a great place to admire the sunset over a cool drink, to a mostly oldies soundtrack (60s and 70s); it's also something of an expat hangout, with quizzes, live music and the like. Daily noon–late.

Mike's Place Down a side street behind the AIS travel agency (see above) ☎ 6946 506 623. Despite the anglicized name this is a thoroughly Greek taverna, tucked away down a backstreet and serving fish and meat dishes on a pleasant terrace shaded by a rubber tree. You could try the *tsipoúra* for €14 or there's a daily plate for €10. Good local barrelled wine and free ouzo and *rakí*. April–Oct daily noon–11pm.

FROM TOP PANAYÍA KERÁ, NEAR KRITSÁ (P.145); SPINALÓNGA (P.135) >

2

Mílatos

An unpretentious settlement with a line of tavernas fronting the sea, **MÍLATOS** (**Μίλατος**) is very little developed, possibly because of its uncomfortable pebble beach and its relative isolation – a good twenty-minute drive from the highway. Although you'd never guess from what remains today, the place has a distinguished past; **ancient Miletus** even earns a mention in Homer's *Iliad* as one of the seven Cretan cities that sent forces to fight at Troy. In mythology – backed up by recent archeological finds – it was from Mílatos that Sarpedon (King Minos's brother, whom the king had defeated to take the throne) sailed to found Miletus, which was destined to become one of the greatest of all cities in Asia Minor. The site of the ancient city lies to the east of the beach, but there's little to see there: the place faded into obscurity in antiquity and by Roman times no longer existed.

Mílatos Cave

3km east of Mílatos village • Open daylight hours • Free

More a series of caverns than a single cave, the **Mílatos Cave** is something of a place of pilgrimage for Cretans. It appears to go back indefinitely, and with adequate lighting (bring a torch) you might be able to discover just how far. Less adventurously, there's a small chapel to explore right at the entrance, a memorial to the events that earned the cave its notoriety. In 1823, during one of the early rebellions against the Turks, some 2700 Cretans (that, at least, is the number claimed) took refuge in the cave, were discovered and besieged. Eventually, having failed to break their way out, they were offered safe conduct by the Turkish commander – only to be killed or taken away into slavery as soon as they surrendered.

ARRIVAL AND DEPARTURE   MÍLATOS

By car Mílatos is pretty much a dead end. Beyond the cave there are dirt roads that continue east, but there's no through route to the eastern half of the Áyios Ioánnis peninsula. What you can do, though, is zigzag up towards Neápoli, a beautiful drive on mostly good paved roads.

ACCOMMODATION AND EATING

Much of the accommodation is in **apartments** in the surrounding countryside, but there are also some excellent beachfront rooms. Almost everything clusters near the small church at the junction where the main road hits the waterfront: shops and car and bike rental places as well as tavernas, cafés and rooms.

Akrogiali Seafront, right by the junction ☎ 28410 81343. The tavernas lined along the seafront are almost all excellent; they're popular weekend outings for locals. *Akrogiali* is a particularly good spot, specializing in fish but with a broad menu for all tastes. April–Oct daily 11am–11pm.

Porto Bello Villas At the western end of the seafront ☎ 28410 81001, ⓦ portobello-villas.gr. Simple a/c apartments and studios in a lovely seaside setting close to the harbour with saltwater pool and satellite TV; there's an exceptionally friendly welcome from Johanna and Paris. April–Oct. **€50**

★ **Taverna-Apartments Sokrates** East along the waterfront ☎ 28410 81375, ⓦ socrates-rooms.gr. This excellent seafront taverna serves a range of mezédhes and Cretan dishes on a spacious terrace. There's good charcoal-grilled meat (try the *païdhákia*) or oven-baked lamb, as well as fish landed by the village boats. Accommodation consists of bright and airy modern apartments and studios with kitchen, a/c, balcony and sea view. April–Oct daily 9am–midnight. **€45**

The Lasíthi plateau

Every day, scores of bus tours toil up to the **LASÍTHI PLATEAU** (**Λασίθι**) to view what is promoted as a sea of white-cloth-sailed windmills. In reality there are very few working mills left, and those that continue to operate do so only for limited periods; others are marketing features next to tavernas. Nevertheless, the trip is well worth making, even if you don't see a single unfurled sail.

    If you **stay overnight** you'll see far more than on a day-trip, as the tour parties leave
and a great peace settles over the plateau. The excesses of Mália or Hersónissos seem a
world away as you climb into your bed to the sound of braying donkeys and a tolling
church bell, and wake to the cock's crow the next morning. Early in the day you'll often
see a diaphanous white mist floating over the plain and its windmills sparkling in the
sun. The winters are severe here – up to 50cm of snow is not unusual – so the **best time
to visit** is at either end of the summer season. In late spring, the pastures and orchards
are almost alpine in their covering of wildflowers, an impression reinforced by the snow
lingering on the higher peaks, while in autumn, the fruit trees can barely support the
weight of their crop. Whatever time of year you come, though, bring some warm
clothing, as the nights can get extremely cold.

Tzermiádho

TZERMIÁDHO (Τζερμιάδο), on the plateau's northern edge, is the largest village and one
of the least touristy; in the village centre old shops that seem virtually unchanged in
fifty years include sellers of hand-loom weaving and embroidery. There's also a post
office and bank (with ATM) as well as an excellent old-fashioned bakery, several *kafenía*
and good tavernas. In addition, Tzermiádho offers access to the Minoan site of Karfí
and the Kronos Cave.

LASÍTHI PLATEAU

Iráklio & Mália

Panayía Kardhiótissa

Kerá

Karfí

NÍSSIMOS PLATEAU

Áyios Timios Stavros

Séli Ambélou

Kronos Cave

Lagoú

Tzermiádho

Moní Vidianí

Pinakianó

Farsáno

Káto Metóhi

Marmakéto

Áyios Harálambos

Áyios Konstantínos

Pláti

Psykhró

Áyios Yeóryios

Dhiktean Cave

Magoulás

Koudoumaliá

Avrakóndes

Kamináki

0   2
kilometres

Áyios Nikólaos & Neápoli

2

THE LASÍTHI PLATEAU WINDMILLS

When you finally come upon the Lasíthi plateau laid out below you, it seems almost too perfect – a patchwork circle of tiny fields enclosed by the bare flanks of the mountains. Closer up, it's a fine example of rural Crete at work, with every centimetre given over to the cultivation of potatoes, apples, pears, cereals and almost anything else that could conceivably be grown in the cooler climate up here. The area has always been fertile, its rich alluvial soil washed down from the mountains and watered by the rains that collect in the natural bowl. In spring, there can be floods, which is why the villages all cluster on the higher ground around the edge of the plain, but in summer, the **windmills** traditionally come into use, pumping the water back up to the drying surface. Although the plateau was irrigated in Roman times – and inhabited long before that – this system was designed by the Venetians in the fifteenth century, bringing the plain back into use after nearly a century of enforced neglect (during which time cultivation and pasture had been banned after a local rebellion). Where they survive, the windmills have barely changed, and although many have been replaced by more dependable petrol-driven pumps, they have been making a comeback in recent years, thanks to EU funding and tourism. The 26 stone windmills standing guard on the ridges above the plain, also mostly ruined, were traditional grain mills.

Kronos Cave

Follow signs from the centre of Tzermiádho or from the edge of Marmakéto, on the main road southeast of Tzermiádho; a path and stone steps take you the final 500m to the narrow cave entrance • Open daylight hours • Free, though there's often a guide to show you around and lend out torches, who will expect a small payment

In the **Kronos Cave**, known to archeologists as Trápeza, Evans and Pendlebury discovered remains and tombs dating back to Neolithic times. Though the cave is small, footing is slippery and treacherous, so a guide (and torch) comes in handy. In any event it helps to have someone point out the ancient tombs: in Minoan times, communal burials took place here, and many funerary offerings were discovered.

Áyios Konstantínos

ÁYIOS KONSTANTÍNOS (Άγιος Κονσταντίνος) lies close to the point where the Neápoli road emerges onto the plain. As a result, it is the first (and last) village many people visit when doing a plateau circuit, and is therefore packed with souvenir stores. Some of the embroidery and weaving is very fine; in the best, natural dyes from onions, walnuts and other sources are still used. There's also an excellent taverna.

Áyios Yeóryios

ÁYIOS YEÓRYIOS (Άγιος Γεόργιος) is one of the largest and least touristy of the plateau villages, with a lovely, little-visited **Folk Museum** (April–Oct Mon–Sat 10am–4pm; €1.50). Housed in a low-ceilinged, windowless farmhouse preserved much as it would have been in the early twentieth century, it's full of rural tools and artefacts including a great winepress, which doubled as the family bed. Below is a bourgeois house of the same period with displays of old pictures, including many photos of Cretan author Nikos Kazantzákis (see p.52), and between the two a section on shops and trade, including old barbers' and blacksmiths' equipment.

Psykhró

PSYKHRÓ (Ψυχρό), a simple community strung out along a tree-lined street, is the plateau's chief destination: the base for visiting the **Dhiktean Cave**, legendary birthplace of Zeus. There are tavernas along the main street, but in practice hardly anyone stops, preferring to continue straight to the cave itself.

The Dhiktean Cave

1km southwest of Psykhró • Daily: April–Oct 8am–8pm; Nov–March 8.30am–3pm • €4 • From Psykhró a signed side road takes you up to a car park (the €2 parking charges are strictly enforced) from where the cave is a 10m climb away on a steep, rocky path, or a longer but easier walk up a paved track; you can also go up by mule (€10 one way, €15 return)

According to legend, it was in the **Dhiktean Cave** that Zeus was born to Rhea. Zeus's father, Kronos, had been warned that he would be overthrown by a son, and accordingly ate all his offspring. On this occasion, however, Rhea gave Kronos a stone to eat instead and left the baby Zeus concealed within the cave, protected by the Kouretes (see p.344), who beat their shields outside to disguise his cries. From here, Zeus moved to the Idean Cave, on Psilorítis (see p.208), where he spent his youth. This, at least, is the version generally told here, and though there are scores of variations on the myth, it is undeniable that the cave was a cult centre from the Minoan period onwards, and that explorations around the start of the twentieth century retrieved offerings to the Mother Goddess and to Zeus dating through to Classical Greek times.

Concrete steps and electric lighting have made the cave an easy place to visit, although some of the magic and mystery has inevitably been lost. The steps lead you on a circular tour, passing the bottom of the cave where you are confronted with an artificial lake. The one experience that has survived the alterations is the view back from the depths of the cave towards the peephole of light at the entrance, framed in

2

THE ASCENT TO KARFÍ

From Tzermiádho, there's an ascent to the ancient Minoan site of **Karfí** (**Καρφί**) one of the most dramatic places in Crete, perched on the southeast slope of Mount Karfí with an opportunity to see some of the area's spectacular birds of prey. The climb, some 6km, takes around 2hr on foot from Tzermiádho, less than half that if you drive as far as you can; you'll need sturdy footwear and, in summer, plenty of water. There are a number of shady places for a picnic on the way up, or even at the site itself.

The start of the route up is located on Tzermiádho's western edge at the side of the district health centre, opposite a blue sign marked, in English, "To the Timios Stavros church". Follow the road as it winds gently for the first couple of kilometres up to the Níssimos plateau. On this miniature plateau, turn left onto a dirt track and keep left, aiming for a small, whitewashed chapel. Leave any transport near the chapel, from just to the right of which the ascent begins, a final 30min through a rocky landscape patrolled by agile goats; there are no signs at the bottom, but the way is obvious and once climbing you'll come across numerous battered waymarkers.

THE SITE

At the end of the climb the **archeological site**, with magnificent views over the coast, spreads across the saddle between the summit of Mount Karfí (the location of an ancient peak sanctuary), to the west, and the pinnacle of Mikrí Kopróna (topped by a trig point), to the east. In this cluster of crude, stone-built, single-storey dwellings, founded in the twelfth century BC, Minoan refugees fleeing from the Dorian advance attempted to preserve vestiges of their ancestral culture. For the three thousand or so inhabitants who lived here prior to the site's peaceful evacuation around 1000 BC, life must have been a grim struggle, lashed by the winds and prey to the vicious winter elements. But this very inaccessibility was of great defensive value and preserved the settlement from attack, while the cultivation of the Níssimos plateau below provided food and pasture for livestock.

Among the ruins, excavated in the 1930s by John Pendlebury, it's hard to make out anything other than a mass of fallen stones intersected by paved alleyways. The most substantial structure is what the archeologist described as the **Great House**, an important building still retaining its walls and where a number of bronze artefacts were discovered. Behind this, just to the north, a **shrine** was located, containing remarkable, metre-high terracotta goddesses with arms raised in blessing (now in the Iráklio Archeological Museum).

While you're up here there's a good chance you'll see the odd griffon vulture gliding majestically overhead, or maybe even the much rarer lammergeier, or bearded vulture, now down to a handful of isolated pairs.

a blue haze caused by the damp atmosphere. It's not hard to believe the tales that this was the infant Zeus's first sight of the world destined to become his kingdom.

To avoid the crowds and savour the cave's mystical qualities to the full, try to arrive early (coaches start to arrive around 11.30am) or after 5pm.

Moní Vidianí

Beyond Psykhró, you can complete a circuit of the plateau on a far less travelled road via the villages of Pláti, with its many tapestry sellers, Áyios Harálambos and Káto Metóhi, to meet with the direct route back to the coast at Pinakianó. Between Káto Metóhi and Pinakianó is the **Moní Vidianí**, one of whose restored buildings houses the tiny **Natural History Museum of Dhíkti** (aka Bearded Vulture Information Centre; erratic hours, but usually open in summer; €1). Though not wildly inspiring, the informative display, well labelled in English, covers local fauna, concentrating especially on the lammergeier or bearded vulture, with many stuffed specimens.

ARRIVAL AND GETTING AROUND   THE LASÍTHI PLATEAU

By car The quickest and easiest routes up to the plateau are from the north and northwest, from Mália and Hersónissos (see p.95). The approach from Neápoli is far slower – a tortuous 30km climb, first south and then west into the mountains that ring the sunken plateau. Once you do finally make it, you'll find a circular road linking the villages on the plateau's edge.

By bus There are plenty of tours, but just two public buses a week between Iráklio and the plateau (where they circle the villages). These are designed to take villagers to town and back, rather than for tourists, so they leave the plateau at 5.45am on Mon & Fri, returning at 2.15pm from Bus station A.

On foot Once on the plateau, you can easily walk through the fields from one village to another – the paths between Áyios Yeóryios and Káto Metóhi via Psykhró even form part of the E4 Pan-European walking route. Whichever route you choose the path is rarely direct, but it's easy enough to pick your way by the trails: crossing the whole plain, from Psykhró to Tzermiádho, takes 1hr 30min or less. More ambitiously, you can also hike up to the plateau, most directly from Kritsá in the east, or on the E4 path from Kastélli in the west. A good time to take a walk here is the early evening, when you'll encounter the villagers on their carts, donkeys and pick-ups making their way back home.

ACCOMMODATION AND EATING

TZERMIÁDHO

Hotel Kourites On the eastern edge of the village ☎ 28440 22054. One of the larger options on the plateau, with reasonably modern balcony rooms above a taverna, in a quiet setting on the edge of the village. **€40**

★**Kronio** Village centre ☎ 28440 22375, ⓦ kronio.eu. Traditional Cretan dishes come with a French twist here, thanks to the proprietor's Gallic wife. It's very good value – if you're hungry and in no hurry, try the meze selection, with 18 dishes and dessert for around €20 for two – with excellent cooking. They do get the occasional coach party, though. Also rents a couple of modern apartments with pool just outside the village (available April–Oct). Daily 8.30am–11pm. **€40**

ÁYIOS KONSTANTÍNOS

★**Taverna Vilaeti** On the main street ☎ 28440 31983, ⓦ vilaeti.gr. A welcoming taverna in a beautifully restored old stone building, much more elegant than you'd expect in this setting, serving exceptionally good traditional food (most of it local and organic) at standard prices (mains €10–14). They also serve pasta topped with truffles found on the plateau by their own trained dog. Daily 9am–10pm; Nov–March Fri–Sun only.

Vilaeti Traditional Guesthouses Information at Taverna Vilaeti on the main street ☎ 28440 31983, ⓦ vilaeti.gr. Lovely, fully equipped restored village apartments and stone-built cottages, all with fireplaces for winter

---

CLIMBING MOUNT DHÍKTI

A former guardian of the Dhiktean Cave, the genial Petros Zervakis leads regular ascents (May–Sept) of **Mount Dhíkti** (Δίκτι), which include an overnight stay at a refuge, supper under the stars and a 5am start for the summit. It's not a terribly difficult climb, but you'll need stout walking boots or shoes and a sleeping bag. The cost (around €50 per person) depends on the number of people in the group; Petros also organizes hikes to spot wildflowers (mid-April to mid-June) and birds (April–Sept). For details, ring or call in at his family's taverna *Petros*, facing the car park (☎ 6972 442 293 or ☎ 28440 31316).

MINOANS ALIVE AND WELL ON THE LASÍTHI PLATEAU

A genetic study carried out in 2013 into the **origins of the Minoan civilization** has gone a long way to undermining Sir Arthur Evans' belief that the Minoans had a north African or Nile delta origin. The study – by a team from Greek and US universities – compared the **DNA** of four-thousand-year-old ancient Minoan skeletons buried in a cave ossuary near to the village of Áyios Harálambos with those of the modern inhabitants of the Lasíthi plateau and Crete, as well as north Africa and other parts of Europe. The results of the genetic analysis showed little connection with African populations and a remarkably strong affinity with **modern Cretans**, particularly those living on the Lasíthi plateau. This may in part be due to the plateau's isolation (the first road did not arrive here until the 1970s), and the use of the heights above the plateau as a refuge by late Minoan groups fleeing the Dorian invasions (see p.332). Researchers also found that the skeletons were similar to those of modern-day Cretans, suggesting that the Minoans would have been similar in build and body size to today's islanders.

Evans believed the civilization had been introduced by a group that had migrated from a superior culture elsewhere, most likely Egypt; the new research, however, seems to suggest that the Minoans were descended from Neolithic populations that migrated to Europe from the Middle East and Anatolia, and created what we now call Minoan civilization once established on the island.

and full kitchens, with breakfast basics supplied daily. Larger cottages sleep up to seven. Two-night minimum. **€65**

ÁYIOS YEÓRYIOS
Hotel Maria Hidden away in the backstreets; information at Hotel Rea on the main street, run by the same family ☎ 28440 31774. A sweet, old-fashioned rooms place with framed embroidery on the walls and tiny bathrooms. Some of the double beds are on the Lilliputian side too – they also have three- and four-bed rooms. April–Sept. **€30**

PSYKHRÓ
Stavros Taverna centre of the village ☎ 28440 31497. Friendly and economical taverna serving traditional Cretan staples and grills (mains €6–9) with produce from the family farm. Also open for breakfast. Daily 7am–midnight.

Taverna Dionysos Magoulás, around 1km east of Psykhró ☎ 28440 31672. Roadside taverna with quiet en-suite rooms with balcony (a couple at the back have a great view over the plain) and good food. April–Oct daily 8am–11pm. **€30**

Taverna Halavro Above the Dhiktean Cave car park ☎ 28440 31402. Better than you'd expect, considering the captive audience, providing fresh juices and snacks for cave visitors, as well as meze (€3–5), and lamb (€12) and pork (€10) roasted in a wood oven. April–Oct daily 9am–6pm.

Zeus On the western edge of the village; enquire at Taverna Halavro (see above) ☎ 6972 981 782. This small, seven-room hotel offers simple rooms, with balcony views across the plateau. **€30**

Kritsá and around

The "traditional" village of **Kritsá**, 9km inland of Áyios Nikólaos, is a popular destination for tour buses and day-trippers. Despite some commercialization this is a trip well worth making, offering as it does a break from the frenetic pace of the coast; buses run frequently from the main station in Áyios Nikólaos. Along the way you'd do well to take a look at the remarkable church of **Panayía Kerá** and the ancient site of **Lató**, both of which are worthwhile sights in their own right.

Panayía Kerá

About 1km before Kritsá on the Áyios Nikólaos road • Tues–Sun 8am–3pm • €3

Inside the lovely Byzantine church of **PANAYÍA KERÁ (Παναγία Κερά)** is preserved perhaps the most complete and certainly the most famous set of **Byzantine frescoes** in Crete. They're originally from the fourteenth and early fifteenth centuries, though all have been retouched and restored to such an extent that they're impossible to date accurately. Those in the **south aisle**, through which you enter, depict the life of Anne,

2

mother of Mary – her marriage to Joachim and the birth of Mary – and the early life of the Virgin herself up to the journey to Bethlehem. In the **centre** of the church, the oldest part, dating originally from the twelfth century, Mary's story is continued and there are scenes from the life of Christ, including the Nativity, Herod's banquet and a superb Last Supper. And in the **north aisle** there are vivid scenes of the Second Coming and Judgement, along with the delights of Paradise and assorted interludes from the lives of the saints (especially St Anthony). Throughout, the major scenes are interspersed with small portraits of saints and apostles.

Lató

4km north of Kritsá • Tues–Sun 8.30am–3pm • €2

Just outside Kritsá a surfaced road leads off for about 4km to the archeological site of **LATÓ** (Λατώ). The city, originally Doric, flourished through to Classical times but its ruins are little visited, presumably because visitors and archeologists on Crete are more concerned with the Minoan era. That it was an important place is clear from the sheer extent of the ruins, which spread in every direction. It is also a magnificent setting, sprawled across the saddle between the twin peaks of a dauntingly craggy hill. Standing on the southernmost peak you get magnificent views down onto the white cluster of **Áyios Nikólaos** (Lató's ancient port), with the gulf and Oloús (a major rival of Lató in its heyday) beyond, as well as inland to the valleys and climbing peaks of the Dhiktean mountains.

The site

You enter the site 200m or so below the ruins, following a rough path up to a rectangular area with a **gateway**, which would have been the city's original entrance. Continuing to climb up the street from here, you can see stores and workshops abutting the city wall on the right, with defensive towers and gateways into residential areas on the left. Higher up still, the pentagonal space of the **agora** was a meeting place for citizens that incorporates a tier of steps on its northern side, reminiscent of the theatral areas at Minoan sites such as Knossós and Festós. The steps ascend between the remains of two towers to the **prytaneion**, or town hall, with small rooms at the rear that held the city's archives. In the centre of the agora are a deep square cistern and a shrine, flanked on the western side by a colonnaded **stoa**, a shady place to shelter from the elements. The southern end of this has been cut through by a relatively modern circular threshing floor. The **exedra** nearby was a sort of public seating area, and in the southeast corner of the site is another exedra and a further broad flight of steps in the Minoan style, here officially dubbed the "Theatral Area". This leads to a raised terrace containing a well-preserved fourth-century BC temple.

THE KATHARÓ PLAIN

If you have a couple of hours to spare, take the magnificent drive up to the **Katharó plain** (**Καθαρό**), 16km above Kritsá. From the top of the village, a winding asphalted road ascends steeply through woods of holm oaks where the air soon becomes sharper, even in summer. There are plenty of potential picnic spots, and roadside boards display maps of the various areas, some marking the routes of amazingly well-preserved Minoan trading paths, no doubt used to access the plateau in ancient times. When you finally reach the plain – a fertile upland similar to Lasíthi (see p.140), though far smaller, less intensely cultivated or visited and, at 1150m, some 300m higher – you will find a few scattered dwellings occupied in summer by farmers and shepherds.

INFORMATION AND TOURS

On the Katharó plain itself, the unexpected and welcome **Kafeníon Zervas** (open all year except when snowed in, daily 9am–8pm) run by the amiable Yiannis Siganos, an expert on all aspects of the plateau, displays photographs of the plateau's flora and fauna, as well as information about the fossils of large mammals found here: 500,000 years ago this was apparently the preserve of hippos and elephants.

The plateau's **flowers**, including spectacular orchids, are exceptional; local expert Steve Lenton conducts **guided walks** to look at them, also taking in local wildlife, history, geology and paleontology; he also leads an 8km walk over the mountain from Katharó to Áyios Yeóryios on the Lasíthi plateau (all walks March–Nov pre-booked only; ☎ 28410 28263, ⓦ exploringkatharo.com).

Kritsá

KRITSÁ (**Κριτσά**), known as "the largest village in Crete", actually feels more like a small town, its main street lined with tourist stores selling local weaving, ceramics, carved olive wood, leather goods and embroidery. It enjoys a splendid **setting**, with views back over the green valley up which you arrived and the mountains rising steeply behind. You get little impression of this at street level, other than an awareness that you are climbing quite steeply, so try to get out onto one of the balconies or roof terraces of the *kafenía* and tavernas along the main street, from where you can look back over the town and towards Áyios Nikólaos. The more attractive part of the village is the upper half, beyond the square; this is also where you'll find the bulk of the better shops.

ARRIVAL AND DEPARTURE

KRITSÁ AND AROUND

By bus Buses from Áyios Nikólaos to Kritsá (8 daily Mon–Fri, 4 daily Sat & Sun; 15min) terminate in the village square (they also drop off and pick up outside Panayía Kerá) and immediately turn round for the return journey.

By car If you arrive by car, use the signed car park on the way into the village, as there's no chance of finding a parking place in the narrow streets.

ACCOMMODATION

Argyro Main road as you enter Kritsá ☎ 28410 51174, ⓦ argyrorentrooms.gr. Clean, pleasant and economical en-suite rooms (plus a couple with shared bath), some with TV, and many with views across the olive-tree-lined valley. There's a small courtyard café too. **€35**

East of Áyios Nikólaos: the isthmus

The main road south and then east from Áyios Nikólaos is not wildly exciting – a drive through barren hills dotted with new developments and villas above the occasional sandy cove – though in places the engineering of the new road (an ongoing process still years from completion) is breathtaking. Beyond the reed-fringed beaches at Almirós and Amoudhára (with watersports and giant inflatables) there's little temptation to stop until you reach the cluster of increasing development around **Kaló Hório**, 10km south of Áyios Nikólaos, which has tavernas and minimarkets, and paths winding steeply down to a couple of excellent small **beaches**. The next village is **Ístro**, soon followed by a turn-off to the isolated hilltop **Moní Faneroméni**. The route then passes a remarkable Minoan site at **Gourniá**. Just beyond, the road south across the isthmus towards Ierápetra turns off, allowing detours to another important early Minoan site at **Vasilikí** and the ancient village of **Episkopí**, with its splendid Byzantine church.

2 Ístro and around

ÍSTRO (Ίστρο), a strip of development along the road, offers scattered accommodation and superb **beaches**: follow the signs from town to Voúlisma or Áyios Pandelímon (or simply "to the beach"), down a variety of dusty tracks, for some lovely stretches of sand and crystalline water. There's a good beach café at Áyios Pandelímon.

Moní Faneroméni

5km east of Ístro, take the signed exit on the left; the route, asphalted in its early stages, later a track, climbs dizzily inland for 6km • Free

It's a bit of an effort to get to **MONÍ FANEROMÉNI (Μονή Φανερωμένη)**, but the **view** when you finally arrive must be among the finest on Crete. To get into the rather bleak-looking monastery buildings, knock loudly. When you gain entry you will be shown (by one of the two monks currently in residence) up to the **chapel**, built into a cave sanctuary where a sacred icon of the Virgin was miraculously discovered – the reason for the foundation of the monastery in the fifteenth century. The **frescoes**, although seventeenth-century and quite late, are impressive – especially that of the *Panayía Theotókou*, the Mother of God.

Gourniá

Signed off the E75 • Tues–Sun 8.30am–3pm • €2

GOURNIÁ (Γουρνιά), slumped in the saddle between two low peaks on a dusty track by the highway, is the most completely preserved **Minoan town** in Crete, and in its small scale contains important clues about the lives of ordinary people and the nature of the communities from which the Minoan palaces evolved. A look at the map tells you much about ancient Gourniá's strategic importance, controlling the narrow isthmus and the relatively easy communication this gave with the southern seaboard at modern Ierápetra. The overland route avoided a hazardous sea voyage around the eastern cape – a crucial factor in ancient times, especially in winter when sailing usually stopped because of rough seas.

As you leave Gourniá, it's tempting to cross the highway and take one of the paths north through the wild thyme to the sea for a swim. Don't bother – this seemingly innocent little bay acts as a magnet for every piece of floating detritus dumped off Crete's north coast. Do be sure to look back at the site, though; as the E75 climbs the hill opposite, its street plan is laid out like a map.

Brief history

There is evidence of occupation at Gourniá as early as the third millennium BC, but the remains you see today are those of a town of the **Neopalatial** period (c.1500 BC). Around 1450 BC, as happened elsewhere, the town was destroyed by fire. Limited rebuilding occurred during the era of **Mycenaean** rule at Knossós – and the shrine may date from this late period – but the site was soon abandoned again and disappeared beneath the soil where it lay unsuspected until the awakening of archeological interest in the nineteenth century. Arthur Evans, as usual, was the first to scent Minoan occupation of this area, and then a young American, Harriet Boyd-Hawes, started digging in 1901. The site, a budding archeologist's dream, made her reputation.

The site

Gourniá's narrow, cobbled alleys and stairways – built for pack animals rather than carts – intersect a throng of one-roomed houses centred on a main square and the house of a local ruler or, more likely, governor. The settlement is not a large place, nor impressive by comparison with the palaces at Knossós and elsewhere, but it must have been at least as luxurious as the average Cretan mountain village of as little as fifty years ago. Among the dwellings to the north and east of the site are some that have been clearly identified, by tools or materials discovered, as the homes of **craftspeople**: a carpenter, a smith and a potter. It's easy to imagine a cramped and raucous community here three and a half thousand years ago, though worth remembering that the rooms may not have been as small as they appear – many of them are in fact basements or semi-basements reached by stairs from the main rooms above, and the floor plans of those did not necessarily correspond with what you see today. The houses themselves were mainly built of stone on the lower courses and mud-brick above, with plaster-daubed reeds for roofing.

The Palace and shrine

The **palace** (or governor's quarters) occupied the highest ground, to the north of a courtyard containing a familiar L-shaped stairway. With a smaller court at its heart, the whole is a copy in miniature of the palaces at Knossós and Festós. About 20m to the north of the palace, a **shrine** was discovered. It is easily identified by the sloping approach path paved with an intricate pattern of evenly matched cobbles, and the shrine itself, up three steps, is a small room with a ledge for cult objects. Here, a number of terracotta goddesses with arms raised were unearthed, as well as snake totems and other cult objects, now on display in the Iráklio Archeological Museum.

Pahiá Ámmos and around

PAHIÁ ÁMMOS (**Παχειά Άμμος**), a rather windswept little place 2km east of Gourniá, makes for a good lunch or coffee stop, with a string of waterfront tavernas. There's a grey, pebbly beach, protected by a floating boom from the worst of the plastic rubbish that blights this stretch of coast. To the south, a fast road heads across the narrowest part of the island towards Ierápetra, with the awesome slopes of the Thriptís range bearing down from the east.

Vasilikí

3km south of Pahiá Ámmos • Daily 8.30am–3pm • Free

The Prepalatial settlement of **VASILIKÍ** (**Βασιλική**) dates from about 2650 to 2200 BC. The site may not be much to look at, but it's vitally important for the light that it throws upon the hazy millennium preceding the period of Minoan greatness. Remains from this period occur at Knossós and other palaces but cannot be properly excavated because of the important buildings constructed on top of them: Vasilikí was found in pristine condition, having being abandoned after a fire around 2200 BC. The **pottery** known as Vasilikí ware – ochre or red with dark, blotchy decoration – is named after this site, where the fine examples on display in the archeological museums at Iráklio and Áyios Nikólaos were discovered.

The site contains two main buildings, originally surrounded by numerous smaller (and simpler) dwellings. The remains of the edifice nearest to the entrance, on the lower slope of the hill, are slightly earlier than those on the crown. The **Red House**, as the former is named, has a number of interesting features. It is oriented with its corners towards the cardinal points of the compass, a practice normal in Mesopotamia and the Near East but alien to Egypt and the Aegean (and thus possibly a clue to Minoan origins). In the southern corner, deep basement rooms allow you to gain an idea of early Minoan building techniques: holes to support the absent wooden beams are visible as well as large patches of hard, red lime plaster, the forerunner of what later

2

artists were to use as the ideal background for the wonderful palace frescoes. On the southern flank of the Red House, excavations have revealed a bath, a stretch of roadway, more dwellings and quite a few hand-grindstones.

If you continue on up the lane into the **village** of Vasilikí, you'll find a friendly bar and a glimpse of traditional rural Crete well off the tourist trail.

Episkopí

Almost exactly halfway across the isthmus, **EPISKOPÍ (Επισκοπη)** makes a worthwhile diversion. Below the road, beside a raised platía where old men play *távli* in the shade of lofty eucalyptus trees, lies a charming **Byzantine church** dedicated to Áyios Yeóryios and Áyios Harálambos. The arched drum dome with elaborate blue-tile decoration, together with an unusual ground plan, make this church unique on the island. You may not be able to get in, but in any case it's the church's restored exterior that gives it its standing in Byzantine architecture.

ACCOMMODATION AND EATING	EAST OF ÁYIOS NIKÓLAOS: THE ISTHMUS
Istron Bay Hotel 1.5km east of Ístro ☎ 28410 61303, 🌐 istronbay.gr. Exclusive, long-established hotel hanging from the cliff above a spectacular cove with a fine sandy beach; extensive facilities include tennis courts, watersports and diving centre. Rates increase by 30 percent in Aug. **€75** **Zorba's Taverna** Pahiá Ámmos waterfront ☎ 28420	93455. This simple, very friendly Cretan restaurant serves well-prepared local food at reasonable prices. Both fish (try the sardines) and grills are on offer and the taverna uses olive oil from its own trees; you can also buy the oil here. There's also the usual array of coffees and juices, and breakfast is on offer too. Daily 7.30am–midnight.

The road to Sitía

The tawny bulk of the Ornó range of the Sitía mountains makes a formidable barrier to progress beyond the isthmus, and the road at first is carved into the cliff face, teetering perilously above the gulf. There's just one resort of any significance, at **Mókhlos**. Beyond here, lined in summer with a riot of pink and white oleander flowers, the road runs mostly a little further from the coast, toiling through villages clinging to the mountainside until the final approach to Sitía and a descent in great loops through softer hills. As you progress, the familiar olive groves are increasingly interspersed with **vineyards**, and there are some highly regarded local wines to be had in the village cafés, especially in **Mésa Moulianá** and its neighbour **Éxo Moulianá**. Most of the grapes, however, go to make sultanas; in late summer, when they are laid out to dry in the fields and on rooftops all around, the various stages of their slow change from green to gold to brown make a bizarre spectacle.

Kavoúsi

KAVOÚSI (Καβούσι), less than 6km from Pahiá Ámmos yet already high above the coast, is a pleasant village with Byzantine churches and a main street lined with oleanders and mulberry trees; at the far end of the village a map shows walks to various nearby places of interest, including a Minoan farmhouse and a vast, ancient olive tree. Many of the tempting **beaches** visible from on high are inaccessible, but **Thólos** – a quiet pebble-and-sand beach backed by tamarisk trees and a chapel, 3km below the village – can be reached by a good paved road.

Plátanos

As you travel east, the views back across the Gulf of Mirabéllo become more expansive all the time, until at **PLÁTANOS (Πλάτανος)**, some 6km from Kavoúsi, you reach a famous viewpoint, with a couple of tavernas – *Panorama* and *Pixida* – where you can

PSÍRA

The island of **Psíra** (**Ψείρα**), in the Gulf of Mirabéllo west of Mókhlos, is archeologically important, though these days it's almost impossible for tourists to visit. Like Mókhlos, Psíra was first excavated in 1907 by an American, Richard Seager, who revealed a Minoan port, occupied from the early Minoan era, with the remains of a town a little like Gourniá built amphitheatrically around a natural harbour. In one of a number of substantial dwellings – many containing hearths and with walls still standing up to 2m high in places – a fine relief **fresco** was found depicting female figures wearing richly embroidered dresses, the only known example outside Knossós.

No palaces or obvious public buildings were discovered, but the site did produce rich finds of **painted pottery**. One jar, now on display in the Iráklio Archeological Museum, is noted for its decoration of bulls' heads interspersed with the double-axe symbol. The remains of what is thought to be an ancient **well** have also been found, although the island is completely dry these days; even in ancient times, the islanders must have been heavily dependent on trade, with mainland Crete and further afield. The site was another of those destroyed about 1450 BC, though the **Romans** later used the island for strategic and navigational purposes, and the remains of their **lighthouse** and military settlement survive on the island's crown.

2

look down on the island of Psíra (see box above) and west across the gulf to Áyios Nikólaos to watch the sunset.

Mókhlos

MÓKHLOS (**Μόχλος**) lies way below the main road via 5km or more of dusty hairpin bends, but in a sleepy way it's a surprisingly developed spot. Small as it is, almost every house seems to advertise rooms for rent, and there are at least half a dozen good tavernas, and as many cafés. The whole place, in fact, is much fancier and more upmarket than you might expect, which is largely due to the presence of Minoan sites on two offshore **islets**. Not only do these attract tourists, but also American and Greek archeological teams, who often spend whole summers here.

There's not a great deal to do in Mókhlos – swim out to the islet from the rocky foreshore or hang out in the cafés – but it's a place where it's very easy not to do a great deal.

Mókhlos islet

Ⓦ uncg.edu/arc/Mochlos/first.html

When the weather is calm it's a reasonably easy swim across to the **islet of Mókhlos** – plenty of people do it – or you can arrange a ride across (see p.153). This barren rock, inhabited from the Prepalatial period, was in Minoan times almost certainly a much less barren peninsula, and the sandy spit linking it to the mainland would have been used as a harbour (anchorages which could be approached from either side were a great advantage for boats that could sail only before the wind). You can see remains of **late Minoan houses** on the south side of the island, and there are more below the current sea level where recent excavations have also identified remnants of the ancient harbour. But the important discoveries at Mókhlos were in the much more ancient **tombs** built up against the cliff. Here, very early seal stones were found (including one from Mesopotamia), as well as some spectacular gold jewellery now in the Iráklio Archeological Museum and a fine collection of marble, steatite and rock-crystal vases on display in the Áyios Nikólaos and Sitía archeological museums.

Myrsíni

MYRSÍNI (**Μυρσίνι**) is a resolutely traditional village whose attractive church is built around, and entirely encloses, a frescoed fourteenth-century chapel – fascinating, but you'll need to find the priest if you want to look inside; ask at the *Taverna Kathodon* (see p.153).

Hamézi and around

The sleepy village of **HAMÉZI** (Χαμέζι) spreads uphill to the north of the road some 10km west of Sitía. In the narrow streets (don't try to bring a car up here) plants are festooned over buildings and down whitewashed steps. The local **folk museum** (daily 9am–1pm & 5–8pm; €1) is worth a visit for its collection of ancient farm implements and rooms filled with furniture and utensils from the nineteenth century. To get there, walk up the main street, passing the brilliant-white **church**, and turn left up a charming stepped street. For the path through the Áyios Pándes Gorge (see box below), ask for directions locally.

Hamézi Minoan House

1.5km west of Hamézi village, near the ruined stone windmills on the final crest before the Bay of Sitía, a track on the right is signed "Middle Minoan House"; follow this winding track (driveable, or about a 15min walk), keeping right at a restored windmill, to the site • Unfenced • Free

The grey-stone **Minoan house** at Hamézi, dating from the Prepalatial period (c.2000 BC), is the only known Minoan structure to have had an oval ground plan, possibly dictated by the conical shape of the hill. It was thought at first to be a peak sanctuary, but the discovery of a **cistern** made a dwelling, or even a fortress, seem more likely. The ground plan sketched out by the walls – more than 1m high in places – consists of a number of rooms grouped around a central courtyard, where the cistern is located. A paved entrance is visible on the south side. Whatever the building's function, it certainly had a commanding view over the surrounding terrain from its spectacular hilltop setting. While you're taking this in, keep an eye out for the rare **Eleonora's falcon** that breeds on the offshore island of Paximádha – the valley to the east is one of its favourite hunting grounds.

Moní Faneroméni

About 6km west of Sitía, immediately east of the village of Skopí, a track heads north towards the **MONÍ FANEROMÉNI** (Μονή Φανερωμένη). This partly asphalted 5km road leads, via some alarming hairpin bends, to a picturesque rocky cove lapped by a turquoise sea. From the cove, the track climbs inland to the monastery. If you're coming from Sitía, you can join this route by following the signs down a narrow lane shortly after you leave the town.

The charming **monastic church** stands at the heart of a tiny, isolated community, built into the rock on the very lip of a gorge. Standing as a metaphor for recent Cretan history, the church has been battered but still stands unbowed. In 1829, monastery and church were looted and burned by the Turks, and most of the frescoes destroyed. They're now blackened and graffitied, but the beauty of what was lost can be glimpsed in one remaining fragment, depicting a saint reading. Behind the church, shoals of silver *taxímata* (ex votos), hung on the icon of the Virgin in a small cave, attest to the continuing importance of the shrine.

ARRIVAL AND INFORMATION   THE ROAD TO SITÍA

By bus If you're hoping to get to Mókhlos by bus, be warned that you'll be dropped on the main road, a full hour's walk above the village (and a sweaty slog back up); there's a good chance of getting a lift, however. Seven daily buses from Áyios Nikólaos (1hr) bound for Sitía pass the entry road.
Tourist information Ⓦmochlos.eu is an informative local website.

HIKES AROUND HAMÉZI AND MONÍ FANEROMÉNI

There are a number of attractive **hiking** possibilities in the area around Moní Faneroméni. A well-marked path leads from the coast (there's a parking area by the road), up the Áyios Pándes Gorge beneath the monastery, and eventually to Hamézi, from where you should be able to get a bus back to Sitía. You can also walk to Sitía in 2–3hr, or walk the whole way from Hamézi, via the gorge, to Sitía.

ACTIVITIES AND TOURS

Boat trips Mochlos Boat Tours (☎ 6977 837 803) – a rather grand name for one tiny fishing boat – takes people to and from the islet for €5 per person. The boat and captain (Yiannis) are usually in Mókhlos harbour; if not ask at one of the nearby tavernas.

Walks and tours Anne le Brun and Yannis Petrakis (☎ 28430 94725, ⓦ kastelas.com) run botanical guided walks in the vicinity (from €15–25/half-day including lunch), as well as trail bike and 4WD tours (from €75/day). There are also guided walks with donkeys (☎ 6992 574 134, ⓦ mochlos.eu).

ACCOMMODATION

KAVOÚSI

Tholos Beach Taverna Halfway down the Thólos road, 1.5km from Kavoúsi ☎ 28420 94785, ⓦ tholos-kavousi .info. There are several rooms places on the main road in Kavoúsi, but this modern block with simple, good-value a/c rooms offers peaceful nights, isolated in the middle of nowhere. There's decent taverna food too. **€30**

MÓKHLOS

Attractive rooms, studios and apartments around the village are also listed on ⓦ kastelas.com.

Blue Sea Coast road, less than 1km east of the village ☎ 28430 94237, ⓦ blueseamochlos.com. Sparkling a/c rooms and apartments with fridge, satellite TV and balcony overlooking the sea and small pool. Be aware that on Saturdays in July and August the pool bar is a meeting place for locals, and music goes on till the early hours. On other nights and rest of year it finishes at 10pm. **€40**

★ **Limenaria** On a rise overlooking the new harbour, 600m west of town ☎ 6972 441 703, ⓦ mochlos-crete .gr. A tranquil hideaway with attractive, fully equipped sea-view terrace apartments sleeping up to four; big balconies front and back allow you to appreciate the view. **€60**

Meltemi By the road as you enter the village ☎ 28430 94200. Attractive studios with kitchenette and sea view just above the village. The same owner has a couple of wonderful recently built apartments right on the harbour, with full, modern kitchens (including washing machine)

and big balconies looking over the action; get information at *Taverna Bogazi*. April–Oct. Studios **€40**, apartments **€60**

Mochlos Set back from the waterfront in the heart of the village ☎ 28430 94240, ⓔ hotel.mochlos@gmail .com. This welcoming hotel has undergone a complete refit, with sparkling en-suite rooms equipped with a/c, kitchenette and fridge, and most with balcony offering sea views. A few simpler rooms are also available. A top-floor suite with an expansive sea-view terrace sleeps up to five (€80). There's also a charming plant-filled patio for breakfast or late night drinks. April–Oct. **€35**

Mochlos Mare Coast road 500m east of the village ☎ 28430 94005, ⓦ mochlos-mare.com. Peaceful, well-equipped one- and two-bedroom apartments with kitchen for up to six people, set back from the road in the midst of the owner's lovingly tended kitchen garden. There's a separate lounging area above the sea. **€50**

Sofia On the harbour ☎ 28430 94554, ⓔ sofia-mochlos @hotmail.com. This friendly hotel has simple rooms with a/c, fridge, TV and sea views from the balcony, and is situated above a harbourfont taverna; they also rent studios and apartments nearby. Doubles **€30**, studios **€35**, apartments **€60**

To Kyma Beyond the harbour ☎ 28430 94177, ⓔ soik @in.gr. A new block of modern, good-value a/c studio rooms with kitchen, satellite TV and balcony, just round the corner from the harbour. Ask at Minimarket Anna, next door, for information. April–Oct. **€35**

EATING AND DRINKING

MÓKHLOS

Food is excellent at almost all of Mókhlos' tavernas. Many places feature *achinosálata*, something of an acquired taste, made from the roe of the sea urchins that flourish in the clear, unpolluted water here (most people wear plastic shoes or flippers, sold at the local minimarkets, when they swim).

Mesostrati On the harbour ☎ 28430 94170, ⓔ mesostrati@yahoo.gr. Traditional Cretan cuisine from family recipes, as well as fresh fish, served on a pretty seaside terrace; they also do good breakfasts. Meze €3–6; mixed meze €10. Cook Marianna also offers cookery classes (May–July & Sept) – call or email for details. March–Nov daily 9am–late.

The Rocks Waterfront, east end of harbour ☎ 6977 675 076. There's little in the way of nightlife in Mókhlos, but this easy-going cocktail and snacks bar-café is a prime spot

for a sundowner on the terrace. Daily 10am–2am.

★ **To Bogazi** On the harbour ☎ 28430 94200. With an unbeatable seafront position, *To Bogazi* is run by a Greek-Swiss couple; the shortish menu, heavy on fish (caught by the taverna's fisherman, Stavros), includes interesting "specials" such as rabbit in wine, grilled octopus and a delicious *skoumbrí* (grilled mackerel). The *mezédhes* list (€3–5) has plenty of vegetarian options and the barrel wine is from noted Pezá grower Lyrarakis. There's live music Thurs & Sun evenings in summer. April–Oct daily 9am–midnight.

MYRSÍNI

Taverna Kathodon Immediately above the road in Myrsíni ☎ 28430 94766. A classic Cretan taverna whose menu has everything from snails (€6) and *souvláki* to burgers and baked aubergine, plus – on the *mezédhes*

2

menu (€2.50–4.50) – a tasty *fáva*. Food is served on a terrace with stunning views across the coast – down to Mókhlos and out across the Gulf – where there are also tremendous sunsets. April–Oct daily 9am–11pm.

Sitía and around

After the excesses of Mália or Áyios Nikólaos, arriving in **SITÍA** (**Σητεία**) can seem something of an anticlimax. But allow yourself to adjust to the more leisurely pace of life here and you may, like many other visitors before you, end up staying much longer

SITÍA

Airport

Venetian Fortress

Roman Fish Tanks

ODHOS N. PLASTIRA

SFAKIANAKI

I. SFAKIANAKI

E. ROUSELAKI

PAPADAKI

R. FEREOU

P. METAHAKI

V. ARKADHIOU

KAZANTZAKIS

I. KONDHILAKI

Folk Museum

FOUNDALIDHOU

V. KORNAROU

EL. VENIZELOU

KAPETAN SIFI

MYSONOS

PLATÍA IROON POLYTEHNIOU

Sitía Bay

I. KONDHILAKI

MYSONOS

N

G. VOURLIDAKI

V. KORNAROU

ELEFTHERIOU VENIZELOU

4–SEPTEMVRIOU

DIMOKRITOU

PAPANASTASIOU

ANDHREA PAPANDHREOU

Bus Station

KARAMANLI

Archeological Museum

MERKOURI

KALOGERIDI

VARTHOLOMAIOU

ITANOU

Áyios Nikólaos & Tourist Police

0   100
metres

Makriyialós, & Ierápetra

Ayia Fotiá, Vái, Zákros, Petrás (300m) & Trypitos (1.5km)

BARS, CLUBS & LIVE MUSIC

Black Hole	1
Dal Mare	2
Nouvelle Boutique	3

ACCOMMODATION

Arhontiko	1
El Greco	2
Flisvos	4
Itanos	3
Porto Belis Apartments	5
Sitia Bay	6

CAFÉS & RESTAURANTS

Balcony	1
I Plateia	7
Meraki	2
Mitsakakis	4
Taverna Fengarapsaro	6
To Steki	5
Zorba's	3

than intended. An ideal base from which to visit the local attractions, Sitía hasn't entirely escaped the tourist boom; many of the visitors are French or Italian (as they are, in fact, throughout the far east of Crete), a legacy perhaps of the French troops who garrisoned the place under the Great Power protection at the end of the nineteenth century, and the Italians who occupied it during World War II.

The town is set on a hill tumbling down towards the western end of the picturesque **Bay of Sitía**. Its oldest sections, hanging steeply above the harbour, look east over the bay and the ribbon of new development along the coast. For visitors, life concentrates on the **waterfront**. A seafront promenade crowded with the outdoor tables of rival tavernas and cafés spreads in either direction from Platía Iróon Polytehníou, in the corner of the bay; northeast towards the port and ferry dock, south towards the town beach. The narrow streets behind the seafront feature the everyday scenes of a Cretan provincial town: villagers stocking up on news and necessities, and stores catering to their every conceivable need, from steel drums to wooden saddles, seed to pick-up trucks.

Brief history

This area was settled, as Eteia, in Classical times, but may be identified with the **Minoan** *se-to-i-ja* inscribed on clay tablets found locally. That there was a substantial Minoan presence hereabouts is borne out by the excavations at **Petrás** (see p.157), the town's southern suburb, where a settlement dating to the early second millennium BC has been unearthed and where, in the later Neopalatial period, there is evidence for what is believed to be a palace as well as a town with sophisticated buildings and roads (see ⊕petras-excavations.gr). A couple of **Minoan villas** have also been excavated immediately south of the city (see p.157). Knowledge of the subsequent Greek and Roman settlements is sketchy, although a substantial chunk of **Hellenistic Sitía** has recently been discovered on the outskirts (see p.157). Apart from some tombs and fish tanks (now incorporated into an artificial pond on the harbour promenade), little tangible survives from the **Roman** town.

It was under the **Venetians** that the port really took off (they called it *La Sitia* – hence Lasíthi), as part of a conscious attempt to exploit the east of the island. For all their efforts, the area remained cut off by land from the rest of Crete and, although what was in effect a separate fiefdom developed here, it never amounted to a great deal. Perhaps the most significant event of this era was the birth of Vitzentzos Kornaros, author of the epic Cretan poem, the *Erotókritos*. More physical remains are few, due to earthquakes and the raids of **Barbarossa**. Where once there was a walled city, now you'll find only the barest remains of a fortress.

The beach

Sitía's **town beach** is surprisingly excellent; sandy, with beautifully clear water, and stretching far into the distance south of town. In summer the heat eventually seems to draw half the town's population down here by late afternoon, but it's never unbearably crowded, and there's room to escape if you walk far enough along.

The Folk Museum

Kápetan Sifí 28 • Mon–Sat 10am–2pm • €2 • ☎ 28430 28300

The **Folk Museum** offers an entertaining look at traditional life, with displays of antique furniture, costumes, kitchenware and ceramics from the region, and above all textiles and embroidery. There's a working loom on which museum staff demonstrate; the finished items are on sale in the little shop. A fascinating recent addition is a reconstructed schoolroom using desks and furniture acquired from a number of old village schools. The end result is disturbingly reminiscent of the school attended by

Kazantzákis in the 1880s, to which his father (in *Report to Greco*) delivered him with the words "His bones are mine, his flesh is yours. Thrash him and make a man of him."

The Venetian fortress

On the hill above the harbour • Tues–Sun 9am–4pm • Free

The restored **Venetian fortress**, known as Kazarma (from Casa di Arma) dominates the town from its hilltop setting. Now used as an open-air venue for concerts, theatre, lectures and exhibitions, it doesn't offer a great deal to see, but the views are superb.

The Roman fish tanks

Seafront, north of the centre

The seafront promenade north of the centre – heading towards the vast concrete ferry jetty – leads past the ruined remains of some **Roman fish tanks**: freshly caught fish were kept in these semicircular constructions until they were needed. The tanks have been incorporated into an artificial **pond** along the concrete promenade, and are used as a preening perch by the resident colony of swans, ducks and geese.

The Archeological Museum

400m south of the centre on the Ierápetra road • Tues–Sun 8am–3pm • €3 • ☎ 28430 23917

Eastern Crete is rich in ancient peak sanctuaries and Minoan villas or country houses. Many finds from these, as well as from the palace at Zákros and from excavations in and around Sitía itself, are gathered in Sitía's little-visited **Archeological Museum**, a modern building surrounded by construction and new development.

The museum's greatest treasure, the **Palékastro koúros**, is on display as you enter. This little male figure is an exquisitely delicate work dating from c.1500 BC, made from eight interlocking pieces of hippopotamus ivory; when complete it would have been decorated with a gold Minoan belt, bracelets and shoes. Note that the left leg is placed slightly forward, following the Egyptian convention for the portrayal of this form of statue.

Right from here – circling an atrium – the cases progress chronologically through the **Neolithic and Prepalatial periods**, including finds from cemeteries, such as jewellery and household goods. Here also are a collection of seals found at the Petrás cemetery, some early ones made of hippopotamus ivory, and later ones made from agate, carnelian and jasper. Further cases display artefacts connected with peak sanctuaries and daily life, including a fascinating section on eating and drinking: look out for an oval-mouthed wine amphora from Mókhlos and terracotta grills used to prepare the ancient version of *souvláki*. In one excavated tripod pot were the remains of a rabbit stew (the bones of two hares were found inside as well as a lizard and sea snails); in the same pot was discovered a crystal lens that may have been used to start the fire.

A later case devoted to Minoan ritual and religion displays some intricate examples of Minoan painted decoration, depicting narcissus flowers as well as the **Mókhlos pyxis**, an ivory jewellery case with a delicately carved epiphany of a Minoan goddess. There's also a case devoted to finds from a perfume workshop at Mókhlos and its intriguing production process, which involved using wool as a filter. Dotted around the museum are numerous painted Minoan burial chests, and great *píthoi* (earthenware jars) – many from the palace at Petrás – used for storage.

The **Protopalatial and Neopalatial** cases display tools from the palaces as well as weaving utensils and a set of weights conforming to a Minoan metric system. Later cases deal with the mysterious Linear A script, with inscribed clay tablets found at the Petrás and Zákros Minoan palaces. The visit concludes with the **Late Minoan and Eteocretan** periods, after which there is a small section devoted to **Hellenistic and Roman** Lasíthi.

Petrás Minoan Palace

The site was closed in 2015 but is expected to reopen in 2016; enquire at the tourist office (see p.158) • Follow the Beach Road towards Vái–Tóplou for 300m beyond the *Sitía Beach* hotel; the road for the archeological site is signed on the right

A little over a kilometre to the southeast of the centre are the remains of **Petrás (Πετράς)** **Minoan Palace**, where excavations have been ongoing since its discovery in 1985. A palace structure – smaller in scale than the palaces at Zákros and Mália – was built here in the early second millennium BC but this building was destroyed by fire in around 1700BC, along with many other Minoan palaces across the island. Because of this, the palace's hieroglyphic archive (written on clay tablets) was fired and preserved. The palace was subsequently rebuilt on a grander scale before suffering two further destructions, probably by natural causes, around 1500BC and the mid-fourteenth century BC, when the palatial system collapsed. The palace seems to have served as an administrative, commercial and religious centre for the lands around the gulf of Sitía, and employed a large group of artisans producing stone vases, pottery and textiles. Many of the finds from the palace are displayed in the town's archeological museum (see opposite).

Access to the site is via a Venetian watchtower once owned by the sixteenth-century Cretan poet Vitzentzos Kornaros (see p.354). Information boards guide you around. The first structures are **House I and House II**, large two-storey Neopalatial buildings dating from the seventeenth century BC with typical Minoan architectural features such as light wells. The main **palace building** has many of the features associated with Minoan palaces elsewhere – central court, monumental staircase, complex drainage system, storage magazines, archives – but on a lesser scale. The **central court**, for instance, measures some 17.5m by 7.6m, less than half the area of the courts at Knossós, Festós or Mália. The court would have been enclosed on four sides with walls of fine ashlar masonry; as at other palaces these blocks bear masons' marks of double axes and stars. Excavation work continues both at the palace site and the remains of the town that once surrounded it.

Trypítos Hellenistic settlement

2km east of Sitía • Open daylight hours • Free • Off the main coast road, a signed track marked "Archeological Site" leads 100m to a farm building where you can park

The recently discovered remains of a **Hellenistic settlement**, at a site named **Trypítos**, dating from the third century BC and later, are substantial. Remains so far unearthed include easily identifiable ruins of dwellings, rooms and streets, and the remains of a remarkable 30m long "ship shed" with a sloping ramp for hauling ships ashore. Continuing excavations will no doubt add to these in the years ahead.

The Minoan graveyard

Ayía Fotiá, about 4km east of town: follow signs at the eastern edge of the village • Open daylight hours • Free

In 1971, the largest **Minoan graveyard** yet found in Crete was excavated, close to the sea on the edge of the village of Ayía Fotiá. More than 250 chamber tombs from the early Prepalatial period were revealed; among the outstanding finds of vases, fish hooks, daggers and stone axes (now in the Sitía and Áyios Nikólaos archeological museums) were a number of lead amulets, which suggests that these early Minoans regarded lead as a precious metal, as well as silver.

Piskokéfalo Minoan villa

Well signed 2km south of Sitía on the Ierápetra road • Open daylight hours • Free

Near the village of **Piskokéfalo**, the main road cuts straight through a **Minoan villa**. Dating from the late Neopalatial period (1550–1450 BC), it had two floors and is terraced into the hillside, with a well-preserved staircase giving access to an upper floor.

2

The villa's view would have encompassed the river valley below the road, where its farmlands were probably located.

Zoú Minoan villa

6km south of Sitía • Unfenced • Free • From Piskokéfalo a road is signed to the village of Zoú; 2km before the village the Minoan villa (signed) lies on a high bank to the right of the road

The **Minoan villa** at Zoú, dating from the late Neopalatial period (1550–1450 BC), was excavated by Nikolaos Platon, the archeologist who unearthed the palace at Zákros. This one is more a farmhouse – cultivating the land in the valley to the east – than simply a country dwelling, with rooms that appear to have been divided between those for domestic life and others for work and storage of farm equipment. A pottery kiln (perhaps used for making olive-oil containers) was discovered in one room, while two deep pits near the entrance probably stored grain. On the south side there is a well preserved "L"-shaped bench.

ARRIVAL AND GETTING AROUND

By plane Sitía Airport (☎ 28430 24424), catering for the occasional charter flight, lies immediately north of town. There's no public transport, but it's a taxi ride of just 5min (€5 with baggage). Although it can cater for international flights, so far there's only a very occasional charter. Astra Airlines (☎ 23104 89392, ⌨ astra-airlines.gr) fly daily to Athens; Olympic (☎ 801 801 0101, ⌨ olympicair.com) fly daily in summer to Kássos, Kárpathos and Rhodes; and Sky Express (☎ 2810 223 800, ⌨ skyexpress.gr) have flights on Sun, Wed & Fri to Alexandhroúpoli and Préveza.

By bus The bus station (☎ 28430 22272; timetables on ⌨ bus-service-crete.com) is on the southwest fringe of the centre; head north along Odhós Venizélou to get into town.

Destinations Ay. Nikólaos (6 daily; 1hr 45min); Ierápetra (3 daily; 1hr 30min); Iráklio (5 daily; 3hr 15min); Káto Zákros (Mon, Tues & Fri 2.15pm; 1hr); Makríyialos (4 daily; 1hr); Palékastro (3 daily; 30min); Vái (Mon–Fri 10.15am, 12.30pm & 2.15pm; Sat 10.15am, 12.30pm & 4pm; Sun

SITÍA AND AROUND

10.15am & 4pm; 30min).

By ferry The ferry dock is 500m northeast of the centre. Just one ferry currently calls at Sitía, the *Prevelis* (☎ 28430 28555, ⌨ anek.gr). Check timetables on ⌨ openseas.gr or ⌨ ferries.gr.

Destinations The *Prevelis* departs Wed & Sat to Kássos (3hr), Kárpathos (5hr), Hálki (8hr) and Rhodes (10hr); Sun to Anáfi (7hr), Santoríni (9hr), Mílos (13hr) and Pireás (19hr); Wed to Iráklio (3hr).

By car You're required to display a card to park anywhere in the centre Mon–Sat; cards (€1) can be purchased from kiosks and some shops. Most of the hotels on the Beach Road have off-street parking. For car rental, try Club Cars, Papandréou 3 (☎ 28430 25104, ⌨ clubcars.net) or Petras, Papandréou 8, a reliable local outfit (☎ 28430 24849; ⌨ petras-rentals.gr).

By taxi There's a rank at the corner of the harbour by the *Hotel Itanos*, or call ☎ 28430 22700.

INFORMATION

Tourist office The municipal tourist office, on the seafront along the Beach Road (May–Aug Mon–Fri 10am–2pm & 6–8pm; ☎ 28430 28300, ⌨ www.sitia.gr) can supply accommodation lists, town maps and a free guide to the region that also describes some walking routes.

Tourist police Therisou 39 (open 24hr; ☎ 28430 22259).

Travel agents Agents for ferry and airline tickets are mostly on Kornárou, one street inland from the harbour. Try Dikta Travel, Kornárou 150, corner of Filellínon (☎ 28430 25080), or Sitian Holidays, Kornárou 83 (☎ 28430 28555, ⌨ sitianholidays.gr). They can also help with accommodation, but the seafront *Porto Belis*, Karamánli 34 (☎ 28430 22370, ⌨ portobelis-crete.gr) is better for that.

ACCOMMODATION

★**Arhontiko** Kondhiláki 16 ☎ 28430 28172. The pick of the budget places, in a lovely, little-modernized traditional house with a shady garden. Only one of the rooms is en suite, but they're spotless and attractive with a charming proprietor. April–Oct. **€30**

El Greco G. Arkadhíou 13 ☎ 28430 23133, ⌨ elgreco -sitia.gr. Charming small hotel in the upper town with an old-fashioned feel; en-suite, a/c balcony rooms have fridge

and TV, and a couple have sea views. They also offer studios and apartments sleeping up to five. April–Nov. Studios **€40**, apartments **€50**

Flisvos Karamánli 4 ☎ 28430 27135, ⌨ flisvos-sitia .com. Small hotel fronting the sea at the start of the Beach Road. A/c rooms with TV and fridge face either the sea or a patio garden behind; those at the back are larger and more modern, and cost the same as the sea-view option.

Breakfast included. €50

Itanos Platía Iróon Polytehníou ☎ 28430 22900, ⓦ itanoshotel.com. This smart hotel just off the town's main square has light and airy a/c balcony rooms with sea views either to the side or front (€10 extra), and are equipped with plasma TV and fridge. There's also a rooftop bar. Breakfast included. €44

Porto Belis Apartments Karamánli 34 ☎ 28430 22370, ⓦ portobelis-crete.gr. Studios and two-room apartments with kitchens for up to four people, plus some

rooms. All are modern and well equipped, and half have sea-view balconies, while the rest overlook a small garden. Doubles €38, studios €42, apartments €65

★ **Sitia Bay** Trítis Septemvríou 8 ☎ 28430 24800, ⓦ sitiabay.com. Purpose-built apartment complex overlooking the town beach, with a large pool. Lovely modern studios and apartments, all with sea-view balconies and fully equipped kitchens (restocked daily), plus a very warm welcome. Aug rates increase by 40 percent. Studios €70, apartments €100

EATING AND DRINKING

SITÍA

★ **Balcony** Foundalídhou 19, corner of Kazantzákis ☎ 28430 25084, ⓦ www.balcony-restaurant.com. A meal at this restaurant – occupying the upper floor of a stone-built town house and run by accomplished chef, hostess and all-round "grande dame" Tonya Karandinou – is a memorable experience. The cuisine (using organic ingredients) is creative Greek (rooster cooked in wine with pasta and rosemary, or pork fillet with yoghurt and pilaf rice, both €14), with Cretan specials like lamb in lemon sauce, and herb and cheese pastry parcels (€10.95). A four-course meal – with a fish or meat main (€32 for two) – is a bargain. Good selection of Greek and Cretan wines. April–Oct Mon–Sat noon–3pm & 7–11pm.

★ **Meraki** Venizélou 151 ☎ 28430 23640. The first of a group of fashionable *rakádhika* (like an ouzerí, but serving *raki*) to open on the seafront, and the best. You can order (by ticking items off on a sheet) from a substantial meze menu (€3–8) combining modern and traditional, but the best deal is go for a *rakí* (or ouzo) with meze (around €7), which will come with about five small dishes of whatever is fresh that day; not quite a meal, but you can order a few extras. The barrel wine from Toploú monastery is also excellent. Daily 10am–1am.

Mitsakakis Karamánli 6, at 4-Septemvríou ☎ 28430 22377. Wonderful traditional *zaharoplastío* with a terrace facing the harbour, always busy with locals. Try their mouthwatering *loukoumádhes* (dough fritters) with vanilla ice cream; they also have sandwiches and crêpes. Daily 6am–midnight.

Taverna Fengaropsaro Karamánli 20 ☎ 6970 141 551. Excellent little seafront ouzerí/taverna with great-value fish and seafood – you can get a whole *fangrí* (bream) for €9 and a plate of grilled *kalamária* (squid) for €6.50. With good barrel wine from Pezá at €3.50 a half-litre and a pleasant shaded terrace, this is a winner. Daily 10am–midnight.

To Steki Papandréou 10 ☎ 28430 223857. Traditional place popular with locals for its good-value *souvláki*, grills and *mezédhes*; maybe not the prettiest setting, but this is more than compensated for by the warm hospitality. Has a small terrace on a grassy centre-strip of the road outside. Daily noon–11pm.

Zorba's Venizélou 56 ☎ 28430 22689. Occupying the prime position in the corner of the harbour, this is the biggest and busiest place on the seafront, with far more authentic food than you might expect from the touristy appearance. Decent selection of pasta and Greek standards and freshly caught fish, and economical menus for two. Daily 11am–midnight.

PISKOKÉFALO

I Plateia Main square ☎ 28430 22644. An excellent taverna 3km south of Sitía whose specialities include *kolokithóanthi* (stuffed courgette flowers), along with a good variety of meze and traditional baked dishes. Sit on the terrace and watch village life go by. Parking is difficult, so park on the village edge and walk in. Daily 3pm–midnight.

NIGHTLIFE

Black Hole Karaveláki 7, on the continuation of Venizélou ☎ 28430 20422. A meeting place for Sitía's alternative crowd, this is a rock music bar in an old harbour building with exposed stone walls. Loud rock and

occasional live performances as the action moves inside from around 10.30pm. April–Oct daily 9am–3am.

Dal Mare Venizélou 193 ☎ 28430 23640. Big café-bar with three separate seaside terraces, open most of the day

KORNARIA FESTIVAL

Sitía's **Kornaria cultural festival**, from the beginning of July to mid-August, features concerts, dance and theatre by Greek and international performers. Many events take place in the castle, and there are also "traditional feasts" staged in nearby villages; ask at the tourist office (see opposite) for details.

and night. By day there's coffee, snacks – burgers, club sandwiches – and sofas for lounging, and at night there's cocktails and music (including Greek, house and techno). Daily 9am–7am; Nov–March Thurs–Sun only.

Nouvelle Boutique Venizélou 161 ☎ 28430 26598. One of the liveliest bars in town, with a big dancefloor and a terrace, mainstream music, lurid pink decor and a young crowd. Daily 9am–4am.

SHOPPING

A colourful weekly **market** (Tues 7am–2pm) takes place along Odhós Itanou near the archeological museum. The **minimarket** at Karamánli 22 (daily 8am–2pm & 5–9pm), on the corner of Kaloyerídhi, stocks foreign newspapers and paperbacks.

DIRECTORY

Banks and money There's a bank with ATM at the bottom of Kápetan Sifi, facing Platía Iróon Polytechníou, and others inland along Venizélou.

Hospital Off the Áyios Nikólaos road on the town's western edge (☎ 28433 40100).
Post office Dhimókritou 10 (Mon–Fri 7.30am–2.30pm).

The northeast

Crete's northeast corner is among its most tempting destinations, at least if it's beaches and isolation you're after. Outside the winter months, though, you won't find much solitude at **Vái beach** which, with its famous grove of palm trees and silvery sands, features alongside Knossós, the Lasíthi plateau and the Samariá Gorge on almost every Cretan travel agent's list of excursions. But it remains a beautiful spot, and there are plenty of escapes nearby. If you're planning to stay at this end of the island, **Palékastro** is a lovely small town within easy reach of many less well-known beaches, as well as some of Crete's best windsurfing. There are also small **archeological sites** at Ítanos and Palékastro, as well as the ancient monastery of **Toploú**, one of the most revered on the island.

Leaving Sitía, the road runs along the coast for about 10km, turning inland by the extraordinarily ugly and misguided *Dionysos Village* holiday complex – now derelict following the financial crash. Here you start to climb into deserted, gently hilly country, the slopes covered in thyme, heather and sage with the occasional cluster of strategically sited beehives. In summer, the sweet-scented, deep-violet thyme flowers prove an irresistible attraction for the bees that feed on them almost exclusively, thus creating the much-sought-after **thimarísio** (thyme honey).

Moní Toploú

15km east of Sitía · Daily 9am–1pm & 2–6pm; Oct–March closes 4pm · €3 · Not long after the main road leaves the coast a side road switchbacks steeply up to the left, signed to Vái and Moní Toploú

Standing defiant in a landscape that is empty, save for a line of wind turbines along the ridge behind, **Moní Toploú** (Τοπλού) looks more like a fortress than a religious institution. Which is appropriate: the name Toploú is Turkish for "with a cannon", a reference to a giant device with which the monks used to defend themselves and uphold the Cretan monastic traditions of resistance to invaders. Highlights of the monastery's adventures include being sacked by pirates and destroyed in 1498; captured by the Turks in the 1821 rebellion, when twelve monks were hanged from the gate as an example; and serving as a place of shelter for the resistance in World War II. Forbidding exterior and grim history notwithstanding, Toploú is startlingly beautiful within. The monastery is reputed to be incredibly wealthy – it owns most of the northeastern corner of the island – which is no doubt how they can afford the extensive restorations that render the place so spotless. Stairways lead up from the flower-decked, cloister-like **courtyard** to arcaded walkways, off which lie the cells. The blue-robed monks stay out of the way of visitors as far as possible, and in quieter periods their cells and refectory (with spectacular modern frescoes) are left discreetly on view. In the **church** is one of the masterpieces of Cretan art, the eighteenth-century **icon** *Lord Thou*

Art Great by Ioannis Kornaros. This marvellously intricate work incorporates 61 small scenes full of detail, each illustrating, and labelled with, a phrase from the Orthodox prayer that begins with this phrase. There's a small **museum**, too, and a shop where you can buy expensive reproductions of the famous icon, as well as postcards, books and the monastery's own wine and olive oil. The monastery has recently added a tasting room for visitors to sample (and buy) its wines.

As you leave the church, take a look at the **inscription** set into the exterior wall. It records an arbitration by Magnesia, a city in Asia Minor, dating from the second century BC, concerning a territorial dispute between nearby Ítanos and Ierápytna (modern Ierápetra). At this time, when the Romans held sway over Crete, these deadly rivals clashed constantly, and finally Rome, unable to placate the two, called in the Magnesians to act as honest brokers. The inscription records part of their judgement (in favour of Ítanos) and was placed in the monastery wall at the suggestion of the English traveller and antiquarian Robert Pashley (see p.354), who found it being used as a gravestone in 1834.

Beyond Toploú, the road descends towards Vái through the same arid, rock-strewn landscape as before. There's a chance here that you could spot the rare **Eleonora's falcon**, which breeds on the Dionysádes islands to the north – Toploú and Cape Sídheros (a closed military zone) are its regular hunting grounds.

Vái

The beach at **VÁI (Βάι)**, famous above all for its **palm trees**, makes for a thoroughly secular contrast to the spiritual tranquillity of Toploú – and the sudden appearance of what is claimed to be Europe's only indigenous wild date-palm grove (the palms here are a local species, present on the island for millennia) is indeed an exotic surprise. As you lie on the fine sand in the early morning, especially in early spring or late autumn, you could almost imagine yourself to be on a Caribbean island.

In summer, however, the beach fills to overflowing as buses – public ones from Sitía and tours from all over the island – pour into the car park (€2.50), and cars unable to squeeze in line the access road for hundreds of metres. On the beach itself, only the boardwalks guarantee a route through the mass of baking bodies. Pricey sun-loungers are available and a watersports centre offers waterskiing, ringos and other high-speed rides. There's a café and expensive taverna, and you'll pay again to have a shower or use the toilet. That said, for a couple of hours at each end of the day, you should be able to enjoy Vái the way it ought to be. For a bit more peace you can climb the steps cut into the rock behind the taverna to the less shaded cove to the south or, with rather more difficulty, clamber over the rocks to the north.

Ítanos

The sand may not be as good as at Vái, but the relative emptiness of the three small beaches at **ÍTANOS (Ίτανος)**, 1.5km north of the turning to Vái, makes them far more enjoyable. There's still the odd palm tree scattered around here, and you can explore the remains of the **ancient city** too; there are no facilities of any sort, though.

Ancient Ítanos
Scattered over the hill above the beach • Free

Inhabited from Minoan times, **ancient Ítanos** became important later, flourishing through the Classical Greek and Roman eras, when it vied with Ierápytna (modern Ierápetra) for control of eastern Crete. One twenty-year squabble between these two led to the arbitration of Magnesia in 132 BC, part of the stone record of which is preserved at Toploú Monastery (see above). The settlement here remained prosperous until the medieval Byzantine era, when it was destroyed, most likely by Saracen pirates. All sorts of messy ruins strewn with potsherds survive beneath the twin acropolises, but

2

CAPE SÍDHEROS: A WILDERNESS UNDER THREAT

The wilderness of **CAPE SÍDHEROS (Σίδερος)**, Crete's northeastern tip, lies to the north of Ítanos. At the end there's a naval base, strictly off-limits and no photography permitted, but you can drive quite a way up the excellent asphalted road towards it, across a wild and craggy peninsula where there are coves with tempting beaches and some likely places to snorkel. This area, owned by the Touploú monastery, is under threat from international developers who – with the consent of the monks and the Greek government – drew up plans for a mammoth 7000-bed **tourist "village"** with casinos, yacht harbour, golf courses and luxury hotels. Despite a chorus of protest from environmental and political groups, construction work was supposed to start in 2009. This was finally stalled when the Greek Supreme Court intervened at the eleventh hour, putting a stop to the project. In September 2012, however, the government used emergency powers introduced as a result of the financial crisis to give fast-track approval to a slightly reduced development plan. A new decree confirming this was issued in March 2015 and at the time of writing the project appears set to go ahead, despite fierce local opposition.

little that retains any shape. You might be able to make out two early **basilicas** (one is signed), as well as the beautifully cut lower courses of a **Hellenistic wall**, near a guardian's hut on the western hill.

Palékastro and around

A substantial village with easy access to numerous excellent beaches, and with plenty of accommodation both in town and in the surrounding area, **PALÉKASTRO (Παλαίκαστρο)** makes an excellent, quiet base. There are several good tavernas and just about every other facility you might need, but just one real sight, an interesting little **folk museum** (Tues–Sun 10am–1pm & 4pm–7.30pm; €2), housed in a restored traditional cottage. Inside, rooms are decorated with period furnishings, and there are the usual displays of tools and agricultural equipment plus an interesting DVD on traditional crafts and customs.

Angathiá

The hamlet of **ANGATHIÁ (Ανκαθιά)**, barely ten minutes' walk east of Palékastro, is smaller and even quieter than its neighbour. There are good rooms and tavernas here, but little else – though it is convenient for Hióna beach, the Palékastro archeological site and the Petsofás peak sanctuary.

Ancient Palékastro

Close to Hióna beach, about 20min walk from Palékastro village • Tues–Sun 8am–3pm (but often left open during daylight hours) • €2

For archeologists the Minoan site of **Palékastro** (aka Roussólakkos) is a very significant excavation: the largest Minoan town yet discovered and a rich source of information about everyday Minoan life. It may seem disappointing for the casual visitor when compared with the spectacular palace sites elsewhere on the island, but there's still plenty to see (though signage could be improved), and continuing excavation means that new finds are still coming to light. Recent explorations on the site's northern side, for example, have revealed a road leading from the town to the nearby harbour (no trace of which has yet been found), while beneath the olive groves to the south and west more of the Minoan town lies waiting to be revealed – geophysical surveys have indicated the existence of a very large building, maybe a palace.

Set on a fertile agricultural plain on a bay offering harbourage beneath the protection of the high, flat-topped bluff of Kastrí, this is an obvious place to settle – and indeed the area was extensively inhabited both before and after the Minoan era. Water was available too; the site is dotted with deep wells, so superbly constructed that they still contain water today. **Building 5**, now under cover to protect its plaster walls, lies at the heart of a complex of streets, dwellings and small squares around the harbour road.

Here archeologists discovered the **Palékastro koúros** (see p.156), a stunning ivory statuette now in the Sitía archeological museum. To the south, the limestone-paved "**main street**" was the town's principal artery; around it a number of impressive dwellings with stone walls and column bases have been revealed, and the fine, Marine-style vases found in the ruins of some of them are evidence of the status and wealth of the owners. **House N**, at the site's western end, is dated to the late Neopalatial period, and excavations revealed horns of consecration and double-axe stands that had fallen from a shrine room on an upper floor. The room at the rear produced hundreds of cups as well as jars and cooking pots, suggesting that it may have been some form of communal eating club, or perhaps an early taverna.

Hióna beach

A good stretch of EU blue-flagged pebble and sand, **HIÓNA (Χιώνα)** is the closest beach to Palékastro, less than 2km east, or fifteen minutes' walk beyond Angathiá. Consequently it's often relatively busy, though still far from crowded. A couple of the region's finest tavernas overlook the beach (see p.165), and to the south a rough track follows the coast past more lovely little beaches, where for most of the year you can easily claim a cove to yourself.

Petsofás peak sanctuary

The summit of **PETSOFÁS (Πετσοφάς)** gives you a great overview of the ancient Minoan town of Palékastro, and was itself the site of a Minoan **peak sanctuary**, the most important in eastern Crete. Many small clay figurines were found here, representing the people that made offerings at the sanctuary, and these have provided a great deal of information about the dress and hairstyles of the period. Today there's not a great deal to see, but it's an enjoyable hike of some 3km on a path signed either off the road south of Angathiá or from the coastal path south of Hióna.

PALÉKASTRO ARCHEOLOGICAL SITE

HARBOUR ROAD

Square

Domestic Dwellings

← To Entrance

Building 5

Well

Domestic Dwellings

Well

MAIN STREET

House 'N'

Domestic Dwellings

0 — 10 metres

Koureménos Beach

You can get to Koureménos on a sandy track from Hioná, but if you're starting from Palékastro head out on the Vái road and follow the signs; it's barely a 30min walk

KOUREMÉNOS BEACH (Κουρεμένος), north of Hióna beyond the flat-topped hill of Kastrí, is one of Crete's top **windsurfing** spots. Not surprisingly, it can be windy (a funnel effect creates ideal windsurfing conditions; Hióna is far more sheltered), but it's a fine, long sand-and-pebble beach, with several tavernas and rooms places – even a bar – directly behind. There's also quite a community of camper vans in summer, and an excellent windsurf centre, too.

GETTING AROUND   THE NORTHEAST

By bus There are buses from Sitía to Vái via Toploú (Mon–Fri 3 daily; 10.15am, 12.30pm & 2.15pm; Sat 10.15am, 12.30pm & 4pm; Sun 10.15am & 4pm; 30min); Sitía to Palékastro (Mon, Tues & Fri 2.15pm; 45min) continuing to Zákros.

By car Watch where you park in Palékastro – they give tickets for parking around the main square.

INFORMATION AND ACTIVITIES

Tourist information Palékastro's tourist office remains closed at the time of writing, but a number of locally run websites have details of attractions and accommodation: check out ⓦpalaikastro.com, ⓦeastcrete-holidays.gr and ⓦwww.eastern.cretefamilyhotels.com.

Bike and scooter rental and tours Moto Kastri (☎28430 61477), on the eastern edge of Palékastro along the Vái road, also has quad and mountain bikes. Freak at Koureménos beach (see below) rents out mountain bikes and offers mountain-bike tours.

Windsurfing Freak (☎6979 253 861, ⓦfreak-surf.com), an excellent if pricey windsurf centre at Koureménos beach, rents high-quality equipment for all levels by the hour (€40), day (€100) or week (€250) and offers lessons (from €60) and other activities.

ACCOMMODATION AND EATING

As well as plenty of **rooms** in Palékastro itself (you'll see signs throughout the village), there are many apartment complexes in the surrounding countryside and at the nearby beaches. July and August get very busy here, so advance booking is advisable. See also ⓦpalaikastro.com, ⓦeastcrete-holidays.gr and ⓦeastern.cretefamilyhotels.com.

VÁI

Metohi Vai Village Taverna On the Palékastro road about 15min walk from the beach ☎28430 61071, ⓦmetohi-vai.gr. Former shepherds' shelters, owned by the Monastery of Toploú, have been converted into well-furnished, traditional-style apartments, which retain many original features including fireplaces and wooden beams. Rooms come with a/c, fridge, cooker and TV; there's an excellent garden taverna attached. April–Oct daily 1–3.30pm & 7–10pm. **€55**

PALÉKASTRO

Hellas On the main square ☎28430 61455, ⓦpalaikastro .com/hotelhellas. Simple a/c rooms come with balcony, TV and fridge. There's an excellent traditional taverna on the terrace beneath the hotel, in the heart of the village, serving Greek and Cretan dishes made from locally sourced ingredients; try the tasty oven-baked chicken with lemon and rosemary (€8.50). April–Oct daily 8am–midnight. **€30**

House Margot Set back from the Sitía road on the edge of the village ☎28430 61277, ⓦpalekastro.gr. Family-run accommodation in a garden setting, with en-suite, a/c balcony rooms with fridge. Clean, welcoming and good value. **€32**

Mythos On the main square ☎28430 61243. This friendly, family-run taverna serves good traditional food at cheap prices on a streetside terrace, with meat, fish and a vegetarian menu. Five-plate meze for two €4.90. March–Oct daily 10.30am–midnight.

Ostria Outskirts of the village on the Vái road ☎28430 61022, ⓦostria-itanos.gr. An incongruously modern, brightly furnished hotel in a garden setting. The tile-floored rooms have a/c, fridge and balcony. **€35**

Sticky Minds On the Zákros road, 50m from the square ☎28430 61528. As wild as Palékastro's nightlife gets: a café-bar with a classic 60s and 70s rock soundtrack and a courtyard shaded by mulberry trees. Daily 4pm–early hours.

ANGATHIÁ

Taverna Vaios Up the hill from the bridge leading into the village, on the right ☎28430 61043. A very popular place (you may need to book in high season), with traditional food and charcoal-grilled meats (from €5.50), plus mezédhes, oven-cooked daily specials and chicken on the spit (€6) served on a large roadside terrace. April–Oct daily 6pm–midnight.

HIÓNA

Hiona Hióna beach ☎ 28430 61228. Stunningly beautiful spot on a promontory at the northern end of the beach, a touch more formal than anywhere else in the area and a little pricier, but worth it. Fresh fish and seafood are the specialities; try the *kakaviá* traditional fish stew (€32 for two). Great shaded seafront terrace with fine views. April–Oct daily noon–11pm.

Kakavia Hióna beach ☎ 28430 61227. A less glamorous setting than nearby *Hiona*, but locals reckon that the fish here is even more expertly cooked. It's also marginally less expensive, and more likely to have a table. Daily noon–midnight.

Marina Village Off the Hióna beach road, about 600m from Hióna, 800m from Kouroménos ☎ 28430 61284, ⓦ marinavillage.gr. A peaceful haven whose well-furnished rooms come with a/c and balcony, surrounded by olive groves and a garden of bougainvillea and banana plants; there's a pool and tennis court too. They also have a tiny house (for up to four people) right by Hióna beach. Buffet breakfast included. April–Oct. **€58**

KOUREMÉNOS

Grandes Apartments Kouroménos beach ☎ 28430 61496, ⓦ grandes.gr. A small group of simple a/c apartments with attractive terraces, right behind the beach. Each can sleep up to four, with bedroom, sitting area with sofabeds, and kitchen. There's a taverna out front. April–Oct. **€50**

Kouremenos Beach Apartments Kouroménos beach ☎ 6932 356 825, ⓦ kouremenosbeach.gr. A couple of small studios for two in the olive groves immediately behind the beach, as well as some larger apartments for up to six people, all with a/c, TV and fridge, the larger ones with separate kitchen. April–Oct. Studios **€40**, apartments **€50**

★ **Kouremenos Villas/Panorama Apartments** On the hillside beyond Kouroménos beach ☎ 28430 61370, ⓦ palaikastro.com/kouremenos_apts. A glorious setting with great views over beach and countryside, and an exceptionally friendly welcome, make this place special; the apartments themselves are very comfortable, with modern kitchen, a/c, satellite TV and a pool. April–Oct. **€50**

Porto Heli apartments Inland from the Váï road, 1km from Palékastro, 450m from Kouroménos ☎ 28430 61275, ⓦ porto-heli-crete.gr. Two-room apartments, sleeping up to five, in a tranquil garden setting (no. 5, with sea view, is a peach), with a/c, TV and well-equipped kitchen. **€40**

To Votsalo Kouroménos beach ☎ 28430 61282. The pick of several tavernas behind the beach, *Votsalo* serves good Cretan dishes, fish and grills on a large terrace facing the sea, shaded by tamarisk trees. May–Oct daily 9am–late.

SHOPPING

Terra Elaía Not far from Palékastro's square on the road signed to Zákros and Hióna ☎ 28430 61305. This shop sells high-class souvenirs, the arty photos of co-owner Manolis Tsantakis, regional products plus books and foreign press. Daily 9am–10pm.

Zákros and around

South of Palékastro, a winding road offers a beautiful drive through countryside where the soil is a strange pinkish-purple colour, as if indelibly stained with grape juice (although actually it's olives, which grow around here). The few hamlets you pass along the way are so tiny that they make **Áno Zákros** seem positively urban when finally you get there. This is the point where you turn off for **Káto Zákros**, the tiny seaside village that's home to the magnificent **Minoan palace of Zákros** (see p.166), either walking down the gorge or by a spectacular cliff road.

Hohlakiés Gorge

For the one-way walk, you could get dropped at Hohlakiés by the afternoon Zákros bus (Mon, Tues & Fri); drivers in small cars (only a small car will squeeze through the village streets) can follow a track 200m from the main road to a parking place at the start of the trail

For a fine **gorge walk**, make a stop at tiny **HOHLAKIÉS** (Χοχλακιές), halfway between Palékastro and Áno Zákros, from where you can follow a well-signed route through the gorge to Karoúbes Bay and beach, 3km below. From the bottom you can either return up the gorge or strike out along the coast in either direction; north to Palékastro, south to Káto Zákros, each about 6km further.

2

Áno Zákros

A slow-moving little country town, **ÁNO ZÁKROS** (Άνω Ζάκρος) – "Upper" Zákros – boasts three or four tavernas around its central square which, throughout the summer at weekends, host numerous wedding feasts accompanied by dancing to *bouzoúki* and *lyra*; should you arrive then, you'll most likely have a glass of wine thrust into your hand by one of the multitude of smartly dressed revellers filling the square. The little trade these establishments see the rest of the time, however, is almost exclusively passing through, since the far more obvious attractions of Káto ("Lower") Zákros and the celebrated palace are on the coast 8km further southeast.

Locally, Áno Zákros enjoys a certain fame for the numerous **springs** that feed the lush vegetation hereabouts and which were also an attraction for the Minoans. If you follow the sign up to the right as you come into the town, or simply climb the hill from the centre, you'll reach a little **chapel** from where, in five minutes' walk, a path leads beside the stream to its source and some shady picnic spots. Information on how to get to it or to reach the start of the "Gorge of the Dead" walk (see below) is available from the town's small central hotel, the *Zakros*.

The Gorge of the Dead

There are plenty of ways to get to Káto Zákros, but perhaps the most satisfying is to walk, in about two hours altogether, via a beautiful ravine known as the **Gorge of the Dead** (but just as likely to be signed "Zákros Gorge" or "Dead's Gorge"). This path is also the final stage of the E4 trans-European footpath, so it's pretty well marked, at least once you get out of Áno Zákros. The easiest way to get on to it is to follow the signs from the south end of the village, opposite the *Napoleon* taverna. Alternatively there's a parking place beside the road about halfway to Káto Zákros, from where a steep path plunges down into the gorge, cutting off half the distance but still giving you the most spectacular portion of the hike.

Leaving from Áno Zákros, the first half-hour or so is through olive groves and lovingly tended smallholdings, gradually becoming lonelier and wilder as the valley closes in. The trail for the most part is easy to follow beside the stream bed, marked by the usual red waymarks and the occasional signpost in case of confusion. It's a solitary but magnificent walk, brightened especially in spring by plenty of plant life. High in the cliff walls you'll see the mouths of **caves**: it is these, used as tombs in Minoan times and earlier, which give the ravine its name. At the bottom you join a dirt road, which runs through groves of bananas and olives past the palace and into Káto Zákros.

Káto Zákros

From the first spectacular view as you approach along the clifftop road, **KÁTO ZÁKROS** (Κάτω Ζάκρος) – "Lower" Zákros – is a delight. There's a pebbly sand beach, half a dozen waterfront tavernas and café-bars, and a few places offering rooms and apartments; along with a tiny harbour with a few fishing boats, this is about all the place amounts to. It's best to bring cash and anything else you might need: there's a cardphone kiosk on the seafront and they'll change money and offer local information in the tavernas, but there's no shop, or anything else much. If it's laidback tranquillity you're after, you've come to the right place.

The Palace of Zákros

500m inland from Káto Zákros • Daily 8am–3pm • €3

Though the **Palace of Zákros** is small, it is full of interest, and can match any of the more important Minoan centres for quality of construction and materials. It's also much easier to understand than many of the other sites: here, the remains are of one palace only, dating from between 1600 and 1450 BC. Although there is an earlier settlement at a lower level, it is unlikely ever to be excavated – mainly because this end of the island is gradually sinking. The water table is already almost at the palace level, and anything deeper would be thoroughly submerged. Even the exposed parts of the palace are marshy and often waterlogged: there are terrapins living in the green water in the cistern. When it's really wet, you can keep your feet dry and get an excellent view of the overall plan of the palace by climbing the streets of one of Zákros's unique features: the **town** – a place very like Gourniá (see p.148) – that occupied the hill above it.

The destruction of the palace appears to have been very violent, with only enough time for the inhabitants to abandon it, taking almost nothing with them. This contributed to the enormous number of artefacts found here, but more importantly the nature of the destruction, in which the palace was flattened and burned, is an important prop in the theory that it was the explosion of Thíra (see p.330) that ended the Minoan civilization. Large lumps of **pumice** found among the ruins are supposed to have been swept there by the tidal wave that followed the eruption. However, many archeologists take issue with this hypothesis and question both its chronological accuracy and the type of destruction, seeing the palace's demise as more consistent with human than natural causes.

2

EXCAVATING ZÁKROS

The valley behind Káto Zákros was explored by a British archeologist, **David Hogarth**, at much the same time as the other great Cretan palaces were being discovered, around the beginning of the last century. But Hogarth gave up the search, having unearthed only a couple of Minoan houses, and it was not until the 1960s that new explorations were begun by a Cretan archeologist, **Nikolaos Platon**. Platon found the palace almost immediately, just metres from where Hogarth's trenches ended. The Palace of Zákros thus benefited from modern techniques in its excavation and, having been forgotten even locally, it was never looted. As a result, the site yielded an enormous quantity of treasures and everyday items, including a religious treasury full of stone vases and ritual vessels, and storerooms with their giant *píthoi* still in place.

The harbour road

The **site entrance** is on the south side, but the following description starts on the **east side** along the harbour road. This would have been the traditional approach used by visitors to the palace who arrived by sea. Following the road west leads to the palace's main gateway. The **harbour**, now lost beneath the sea, was the chief reason why a palace existed here at all; this must have been a significant port, the first landfall on Crete for trade from Egypt, the Nile Delta and the Middle East. Among the ruins were found ingots of copper imported from Cyprus, elephant tusks from Syria, and gold and precious materials from Egypt.

Before entering the palace, the harbour road passed various dwellings on each side as well as a **foundry** dating from the Protopalatial period; the remains stand beneath a protective canopy on the left. The road (part of which has been reconstructed) then curves round into the town, passing the palace entrance on the left.

The Central Court

As you enter the **palace**, the **main gate** leads to a stepped ramp, followed by a **courtyard** that may have served as a meeting place between the palace hierarchy and the townspeople. Here, in the northeast corner beneath another canopy, is a **lustral basin** where visitors to the palace may have been required to wash or purify themselves before proceeding. To the west of the courtyard lies the main or **Central Court**, a little over 30m by 12m, or about a third of the size of that at Knossós. Crossing the north edge of the court, you come to an **altar base**, with the lower courses of the west-wing wall in grey ashlar stone beyond.

The west wing

The **west wing** (actually the northwest, as Zákros is not truly aligned north–south), entered between two pillars, is where, as usual, the chief ceremonial and ritual rooms were located. A **reception room** leads into a colonnaded **light well**, the hallmark of Minoan architecture. The light well's black stone crazy paving survives, as do the pillar bases and a drain in the northwest corner. It was here that the excavators unearthed what was arguably Zákros's single most important find: the **Peak Sanctuary Rhyton**, a carved stone vase depicting a peak sanctuary with wild goats, from which valuable information about Minoan religion was gleaned. The light well illuminated the **Ceremonial Hall**, beyond which lay the **Banqueting Hall**, originally a lavish room with frescoed walls and an elaborate floor. Platon gave the room this name because of the large number of cups and drinking vessels discovered scattered about the floor.

At the heart of a complex of rooms behind the Banqueting Hall is the **Central Shrine** (with a canopy), which contains a ledge and niche, similar to the shrine at Gourniá, where idols would have been placed. Nearby is the **lustral basin**, necessary for purification before entering the shrine. Here, too, was the **Treasury** – probably the most important discovery from the excavators' viewpoint as it is the only one so far

FROM TOP THE PERVOLÁKIA GORGE (P.176); SITÍA HARBOUR (P.155) >

positively identified. In a number of box-like compartments (which have been partially restored), almost a hundred fine stone jars and libation vessels were discovered, including the exquisite rock crystal rhyton with its delicate crystal bead handle and collar – found crushed into more than three hundred fragments – that the Iráklio Archeological Museum is so proud of (see p.54).

Next to the Treasury, in the **Archives Room**, hundreds of Linear A record tablets were stored in wooden chests. Sadly, only a handful of the top layers survived the centuries of rain and flooding; the rest solidified into a mass of clay, depriving the archeologists of potentially priceless clues in their attempts at deciphering the script. On the opposite side of the treasury is a **workshop** where pieces of raw marble and steatite were found. The remaining stone slabs probably supported a craftsman's workbench. More workshops and storerooms lay to the west of the shrine – one of these has been identified as a **dye-house** – and a **latrine** with a cesspit outside the wall was found nearby. Further west, beyond the palace confines, new excavations are still going on.

The kitchen and south wing workshops
On the north side of the Central Court was the palace **kitchen**, the first to be positively identified at any of the palaces. Bones, cooking pots and utensils were found strewn around the floor both here and in the storeroom or pantry next door. The south wing was devoted to **workshops**: for smiths, lapidaries, potters and even, according to Platon, perfume-makers – possibly a borrowing from Egypt. The **well** that serviced this area still flows with drinkable water, and an offering cup was found close by, containing olives preserved by the waters. Platon and his team devoured the 3500-year-old olives, which shrivelled upon contact with the air, and said that they tasted as fresh as those in the nearby tavernas.

The royal apartments
Two large rooms regarded as **royal apartments** flank the east side of the Central Court behind a portico. The larger of the two, to the south, is called the King's Megaron or chamber and the smaller is described as that of the queen. However, one of these may have been the throne room, and there would have been elaborate rooms on the upper floor, possibly with verandas overlooking the courtyard below where the rulers may have lived. Next to a light well in the eastern wall of the King's Megaron lay the colonnaded **Cistern** with eight steps leading down to water contained in a plaster-lined basin, which may have served as a royal aquarium or even a swimming pool (if so, the only one known). It is ingeniously designed to maintain the water at a constant level, with the excess draining into the well to the south, which, being outside the palace wall, was probably used by the townsfolk. The water from the spring was, as at Knossós, piped throughout the palace, and traces of the pipework can still be seen.

Residential areas
Beyond the royal apartments lay other **residential areas**, though much has been destroyed by centuries of ploughing combined with frequent waterlogging of the land here, partly caused by the silting up of the cistern's outflow. In the steep **upper town** more survives and, close to the perimeter fence, a **narrow street** running east to west passes an impressive doorway and gives you some idea of how the town may have looked when twin-storey buildings overlooked these narrow thoroughfares. Quite a few grindstones found in the excavations are to be seen here, and nearby there's also a charming **stone bench**, now exposed, which would have looked into a light well. It's not hard to imagine someone sitting here, enjoying the cool shade of a summer evening. Near to the bench, there's a well-preserved stairway climbing tantalizingly a couple of metres towards the now disappeared second storey. Both the stairway and the bench are close to the perimeter fence on the eastern (or seaward) side of the upper town.

By bus Buses run from Sitía to Káto Zákros via Palékastro and Áno Zákros (Mon, Tues & Fri 2.15pm; return journey at 3.30pm).

On foot The gorge walk between Áno and Káto Zákros (see p.166), about 2hr each way, is just the start of the local hiking possibilities: the owner of *Terra Minoika* (see below), qualified mountaineer Ilias Pagiannidis, has waymarked several other 3–4hr walks in the surrounding hills;

information is available both here and at *Stella's* (see below). A good map to bring if you're thinking of doing a lot of walking is the *Anavasi* 1:25,000 Zákros–Vái map (also worked on by Ilias), widely available from bookshops on Crete and at Orange Books on the square in Áno Zákros.

Tourist information *Taverna Akrogiali* (see below) is a handy source of local information, and acts as agent for a number of rooms places nearby.

2

ACCOMMODATION AND EATING

The most attractive places to eat are in Káto Zákros. If you have trouble finding somewhere to stay – August can be very busy – try at the various waterfront tavernas, especially *Akrogiali*, which act as agents for many of the local places, or check out ⓦ eastcrete-holidays.gr.

★ **Akrogiali** End of the beach road ☎ 28430 26893, ⓦ kato-zakros.gr. The last of the places on the waterfront, with a particularly attractive waterfront terrace away from the road. Excellent food – including fresh fish and grills – and helpful management. April–Oct daily 8am–midnight.

Coral & Athina On the rise immediately beyond Taverna Akrogiali ☎ 28430 26893, ⓦ kato-zakros.gr. Rooms right above the beach, with great sea views from large communal terraces; clean and simply furnished, with a/c, fridge and TV. Breakfast included. April–Oct. €̶5̶5̶

Kato Zakros Palace Apartments On the entry road above the village ☎ 28430 29550, ⓦ katozakros-apts .gr. Perched high above the coast with spectacular views, this complex of a/c rooms and studios has terraces overlooking both the bay and the gorge. Facilities include TV, fridge (kitchenette in studios) and communal utility room. Doubles €̶5̶0̶, studios €̶6̶0̶

★ **Stella's Traditional Apartments** About 500m inland, beyond the palace ☎ 28430 23739, ⓦ stelapts.com. Large, elegantly decorated, stone-built a/c apartments, with hammocks and lovely views in the verdant gardens, and some slightly simpler studios. Exceptionally well equipped, well run and friendly. Studios €̶6̶0̶, apartments €̶7̶0̶

Terra Minoika On the entry road above the village ☎ 28430 23739, ⓦ terraminoika.com. A new complex of stone-built luxury apartments (sleeping up to 4) with terraces and fine views (from the upper apartments; €30 extra). Each comes with a fully equipped kitchen, tiled floors, beamed ceilings, top-quality furnishings and satellite TV. There's a small gym too. €̶8̶0̶

Yianni's Retreat About 500m inland, beyond the palace ☎ 28430 25726, ⓦ katozakros-rooms.com. Sharing a site with sister *Stella's* (see above), *Yianni's* offers simpler, smaller a/c studios, with slightly less magical views, though they're still classily fitted out. €̶6̶0̶

The southeast

Few tourists venture south of Zákros, and indeed there's little in the way of habitation in the whole of the southeastern corner of the island, and barely any public transport. The effort of getting to these remote parts is rewarded with a barren, empty landscape and numerous excellent **beaches** – mostly deserted. Along the road from Áno Zákros to **Xerókambos**, agricultural country of olive groves and plastic greenhouses gradually gives way to a harsher mountain environment until finally you emerge high above the coast, and a brilliant turquoise sea and white sandy beaches divided by rocky outcrops appear below. Beyond Xerókambos you can circle back round to Sitía, taking in an archeological site at **Presós** along the way, or on towards the south coast.

Xerókambos

Straggling across a little coastal plain in the lee of the Sitían mountains, the tiny hamlet of **XERÓKAMBOS** (Ξερόκαμπος) is not especially attractive, but it's as isolated and peaceful as you could wish for. There's no real centre, just a street along which, between fields of olive groves, are spaced some houses, a few tavernas and a couple of basic minimarkets, with rooms and apartment places scattered along the road and down by the beach. Despite the stirrings of development, this **main beach** is more than long enough to find seclusion if you want it, and there are isolated coves either side where you might never see another soul. The crystal-clear waters here are great for **snorkelling** too – the minimarkets sell the basic equipment.

Away from the sea, you could stretch your legs with a walk to the tiny chapel on a low hill to the south of the beach. Surrounding this are the ruins of an extensive **Minoan settlement** not yet fully explored or documented.

Hamétoulo

A good paved road – populated by herds of goats who, despite the arrival of the asphalt, still regard it as their domain – switchbacks up into the barren, desolate mountains behind Xerókambos, offering dramatic views before heading down towards Zíros. Almost at the highest point lies the primitive hamlet of **HAMÉTOULO** (Χαμαίτουλο), a piece of living Cretan folklore with twenty dwellings, a cobbled street and a church. Beyond here all views are dominated by a giant radar dome on the mountaintop, and the road itself is dotted with "No Photography" signs – this is a military zone and the site of NATO's main intelligence-gathering post for the eastern Mediterranean.

Zíros

The farming village of **ZÍROS** (Ζίρος), in the midst of a high inland plain, is the administrative centre of this region. That doesn't amount to a great deal, but it's a fair-sized place, tumbling down a hillside towards a neat platía circled by willow and acacia trees with whitewashed trunks. Facilities here include banks and fuel, and should you come in late July you might be lucky enough to catch the annual **festival**, when the women of the village produce huge trays of delicacies that are laid out on tables in the square and washed down with gallons of *rakí* to the accompaniment of *bouzoúki* and *lyra*. For quieter times, there are sixteenth-century frescoes to be seen in the church of **Ayía Paraskeví**, or you may prefer simply to soak up the atmosphere with a drink at a table in the square. In the early evening, when the rocky heights seem to crowd in on all sides, places like Zíros feel like the real heart of Crete.

Handhrás

The olive groves and vineyards around Zíros are said to be among the best on the island; the villages are still prosperous, though you feel that their best days are several hundred years behind them. **HANDHRÁS** (Χανδράς), another tidy farming village, is entered past its sail-less and derelict irrigation windmills whose modern counterparts – a phalanx of mammoth wind turbines spaced out along the ridge above the village – make a surreal addition to the landscape.

Etiá

At **ETIÁ** (Ετιά), a **Venetian mansion** (Tues–Sat 9.30am–4pm; free) stands in memorial to the glory days of the Italian city's power in Crete. Built by the Di Mezzo family (whose arms decorate the doorway) in the late fifteenth century, this once elegant edifice was badly damaged in 1828 when the local populace vented their rage on the Turks who had been using it as an administrative base, and later fell into almost complete ruin, along with the rest of the village. The completely refurbished mansion – often used for concerts and exhibitions – is one of the very few Venetian buildings to survive outside the cities. Around it is effectively a ghost town of one-room stone shacks; the last of what were once over five hundred permanent residents left in the 1970s. Only a seasonal roadside taverna, a Byzantine chapel and the church of **Ayía Katerína** (open daily during daylight hours), with an elegant carved stone belfry, show any signs of life.

Voilá

The ruined medieval village of **VOILÁ (Βοιλά)** is signed up a lane just outside Handhrás. With its Gothic arches and silent paved streets, this is a distinctly eerie place to wander round; two ornamental drinking **fountains** with beautiful brass taps still function, one at each end of the village, a Turkish contribution to this Venetian stronghold. The only building still standing with a functional roof is the twin-naved **Áyios Yeóryios** church (open daylight hours), inside which you can see an interesting sixteenth-century gravestone fresco. The church and a tower of the Turkish period dominate the site; you can also climb to a ruined Venetian fort above the village.

Ancient Presós

6km northwest of Handhrás • Open daylight hours • Free • From the centre of the village of Néa Presós, opposite a *kafenío* with a raised terrace, a dirt road is clearly signposted downhill; after about 2km you'll come to a signed gate for the "Archeological sites", where you can park

The archeological site of **PRESÓS (Πραισός)** is another of those sites where what you see – in this case very little – cannot begin to match the interest and importance of the history. When eventually it is excavated it will undoubtedly become one of the most important sites in the east of the island. But even without ruins, it would be worth taking the walk around the site for the **scenery** alone.

Brief history

Presós first came to light in 1884, when the Italian archeologist Federico Halbherr turned up a large number of clay idols and some unusual inscriptions written in an unknown tongue – very likely the same as that of the Linear A tablets – using Greek characters. Set out with lines reading alternately right to left and left to right, these **Eteocretan** (true Cretan) inscriptions are now believed to be evidence of the post-Bronze Age Minoans who fled from the Dorian invasions to remote locations in the east of the island in an attempt to preserve their civilization. Presós seems to have been one of their principal towns, controlling the sanctuary of Dhiktean Zeus at Palékastro, probably an earlier Minoan shrine. With harbours on the north and south coasts of the island, its power eventually led to conflict with the leading Dorian city of the region, Ierápytna (modern Ierápetra). Following final victory about 155 BC, Ierápytna razed Presós to the ground and the city was never rebuilt. With this defeat, the long twilight of Minoan civilization, lasting more than a thousand years after the palaces had fallen, came to an end.

The site

From the entrance, follow the signed path west to a saddle between the two hills where the ancient city lay; the defensive wall that encircled these two hills can still be made out in places. On the summit of the **First Acropolis** are the foundations of a temple. Further on, the path forks and to the right – on the western slope of the same hill – are the remains of a substantial **Hellenistic house**. Dating from the third century BC, the outer walls of superbly cut stone define the main living rooms at the front of the house, with workrooms at the rear. In the largest workroom, an olive press was found together with a stone tank for storing the oil. A stairway to the left of the main door led down to a cellar. Turning left at the fork brings you – after a hundred-metre walk across the saddle – to the **Second Acropolis** where cuttings in the rock on the south side formed the foundations of dwellings.

2

ARRIVAL AND GETTING AROUND

By bus The only buses in this region, apart from those that run along the main road from Sitía to the south coast, are a twice-weekly service from Sitía to Zíros (Tues & Fri at 1pm with an awkwardly timed return on the same days at 7am; 1hr).

By car Approaching the region directly from Sitía, the main road across the island to the south coast cuts high between the east and west ranges of the Sitía mountains. Along the way are a number of sturdy agricultural hamlets where you can stop for a snack and a drink, and short detours will take you to Presós or Etiá, and to Zíros beyond. From Xerókambos

THE SOUTHEAST

there are three potential routes. On the outskirts of Zíros, a paved road heads directly for the south coast at Goúdhouras (see opposite), through very lonely country. Continue through Zíros and the older road divides at Handhrás, both picturesque branches continuing to meet the main Sitía–Ierápetra road; the southerly route, the logical direction if you're heading for Makríyialos, Ierápetra and the south coast, goes via Etiá; the northerly, back toward Sitía, passes Voilá and ancient Presós.

On foot The E4 path passes through Handhrás and Zíros, before turning northeast to end at the Gorge of the Dead and Zákros.

ACCOMMODATION AND EATING

The only reliable accommodation in the region is at **Xerókambos**, where it's scattered across the countryside behind the beach; many local options are listed at ⊛ xerocamboscreta.com and ⊛ eastcrete-holidays.gr.

HANDHRÁS

Taverna Katerina Main Square ☎ 28430 72059. A simple taverna with a terrace on the square offering grills, *souvláki*, omelettes, salads and a few *mezédhes*. April–Sept daily 7am–midnight.

XERÓKAMBOS

Akrogiali On the beachfront, at the south end ☎ 28430 26777. This taverna serves up fresh fish, seafood, salads and Cretan dishes on a large terrace set back from the beach with good sea views. April–Sept daily 9am–midnight.

Asteras In the hills above the main road ☎ 28430 26787, ⊛ asterasapartments.gr. Set in their own garden above the olive groves, these modern a/c studios and two-room apartments all come with kitchenette, fridge and good sea views. April–Sept. Studios €40, apartments €45

Faros On the main road ☎ 28430 25612. Pleasant a/c rooms, studios and apartments with TV, and some with sea view. There's also a bar, and a garden with children's play area. April–Sept. Doubles €30, studios €35, apartments €45

Lithos Main road towards the south end of Xerókambos ☎ 28430 26729, ⊛ lithoshouses.gr. The village's most luxurious option, whose elegantly furnished stone-built

sea-view apartments (bedroom upstairs, living quarters below) come with kitchen, satellite TV, sound system, wi-fi and woodburning hearth for winter; free olive oil, wine and *raki* are provided. €75

★ **Liviko View** On main street, near the turn-off to the beach and chapel ☎ 28430 27000, ⊛ livikoview.gr. These excellent rooms, run by a couple of Greek-Australians, come with a/c and sea view from the balcony; there are also some apartments sleeping up to four. The taverna below offers great food, made from organic ingredients grown on the family farm, and a wonderful terrace. Try the house special, *kounéli krasato* (rabbit stewed in wine; €8); they also offer fresh fish, *mezédhes* (€2.50–7) and vegetarian dishes from €4. April–Sept daily 10am–midnight. Doubles €30, apartments €35

ZÍROS

Taverna Karkionakis Main street, opposite the dhimarhío (town hall) ☎ 28430 91266. Superb and friendly village taverna with an atmospheric bar-dining room. This is meat country, and the succulent *païdhákia* are a bargain (lamb chops; €6.50). Meze includes *loukánika* (spicy sausage; €2.50) and *spanakopitakia* (spinach pies). Daily 8am–midnight.

The south coast

There are three main approaches to Lasíthi's south coast: the long haul across the centre of the island from Iráklio via Áno Viánnos to approach from the west; the short cut across the isthmus from Pahiá Ámmos to **Ierápetra**; or the road south from Sitía that emerges on the coast at **Pilalímata**, close to **Makríyialos**.

Makríyialos and around

At first sight, **MAKRÍYIALOS** (Μακρύγιαλος) seems just another example of ruinous strip development, and even on better acquaintance it's never wildly attractive. However, it does have its compensations: the development is almost exclusively along the road, so get away from that and there are some quiet corners and congenial places to stay; there's an attractive little harbour, and right in town is one of the best **beaches** at this end of Crete, with sand that shelves so gently you might imagine you could walk the 320km to Africa. There are plenty of other beaches nearby, too, and attractive walks into the hills behind.

Much the most appealing part of town is in the west, where the **harbour** shelters under a little bluff, just off the main road. There's a patch of beach right by the harbour, and another around the corner of the bluff, to the west, but the main sands stretch out eastwards, where Makríyialos merges almost imperceptibly into **Análipsi**.

2

Beaches around Makríyialos

Should the town beaches get too crowded, there are plenty of alternatives nearby. To the west, the village of **Koutsourás** is effectively part of the same resort (albeit the poor relation), and though its beach may not be the most attractive, it does offer some excellent places to eat right by the water. Better places to swim and to escape the crowds lie to the east. The first of them, **Dhiaskári**, is at the eastern edge of town just beyond the *Sunwing Hotel*, an easy walk. The taverna here rents out little shelters with hammocks for a truly sybaritic experience, or walk further along the sand to get away from people altogether. Further east, there are numerous attractive little coves along the road to Moní Kápsa; to find them, simply look out for where the locals have parked alongside the road. A couple of the better ones are at **Kaló Neró**, where there are two small cafés, not far beyond the large *Dragon's Cave Taverna*, whose signs you can't miss.

Makríyialos Roman villa

On the bluff above the harbour, at the western end of the village • Open during daylight hours • Free

The extensive and impressive remains of Makríyialos's **Roman villa** are a reminder that this was an important trading port in Roman and Byzantine times. The trade was based on **Koufonísi**, an island to the southeast that's currently off-limits, and on the murex, a type of sea-snail found there from which valuable purple dye was extracted. As you stroll around the neglected site enjoying the sea views you can make out the remains of mosaic floors and – at the southern end – an elaborate suite of bathing rooms complete with hypocaust and furnace to provide underfloor heating. In other rooms, traces of plasterwork are visible on the walls along with fragments of the original marble that would have covered them. On the villa's west side, an atrium or ornamental garden underlines the fact that the owner was a person of elevated status.

Moní Kápsa

8km east of Makríyialos • Daily 6.30am–12.30pm & 3.30–7pm • Free • Modest dress required

MONÍ KÁPSA (Μονή Κάψα) enjoys an abiding reputation for miracles as well as a spectacular setting on a ledge in the cliffs where a gorge emerges into the sea (see p.176). You can easily imagine the isolation of this place when no real coast road existed, and even the paved road and extensive restoration can't entirely destroy the romance. The original monastery, probably founded in the early Venetian period, was destroyed by **Turkish pirates** in 1471. It was rebuilt, but most of the present buildings were constructed in the nineteenth century, thanks to the energies of **Yerontoyiannis**, a monk who earned himself a name as a Robin Hood-style hero as well as a healer. Locally he is revered as a saint, and although he never conducted a single service due to his illiteracy and is denied canonization by the Church, Cretans flock to leave offerings beside his silver-encased cadaver and skull in the monastery chapel. You can also visit a **cave** behind the church to which he often retreated and from where there's a fine view towards the island of Koufonísi.

Goúdhouras

The village of **GOÚDHOURAS (Γούδουρας)** marks the end of the coast road, though you can continue inland to Zíros (see p.172). Numerous grandiose modern villas in finest mock-Classical style attest to a recent local economic boom, thanks in part to the dusty plastic greenhouses scattered along the coast, and in part to the small fishing fleet, but above all to the new oil- and gas-fired power station in an isolated spot 5km further round the coast, at Atherinolakós. There's a long stretch of pebbly, rather windswept beach.

Pervolákia Gorge

The **Pervolákia Gorge** emerges at the sea by Moní Kápsa (see p.175) where there's a tiny pebble beach offering a chance to cool off. This is the deepest and most spectacular of the gorges around Makríyialos, and a slightly more challenging hike; two hours for the 3.5km up to the village of **Káto Pervolákia** (**Κάτω Περβολάκια**), a little less back down. Since there's no transport at either end, you'll need to walk both ways or arrange a taxi at the *Aposperida kafenío* (see p.178) when you reach the village.

Péfki Gorge

The hike up the **Péfki Gorge** to the village of Péfki is the most straightforward of several gorge walks you can make from Makríyialos, and the easiest. It starts up the valley of the Áspros Potámos (White River), on the track past *White River Cottages* (see p.178) towards the eastern edge of town; the gorge starts where the track ends, and though rocky in places a relatively straightforward hike will see you at the top in around two hours. **PÉFKI** itself (**Πεύκοι**) is a lovely village, where a number of houses have been bought and done up by foreigners. There are relaxing places to sit and eat, drink and take in the views and, right at the top of the village, a little **folklore museum** (Mon–Fri 9am–1pm; €1) is housed in the old schoolhouse, full of traditional artefacts including a working loom.

Butterfly Gorge

West of Koutsourás, keep an eye out on the right for the poorly signed **Koutsourás Communal Park**. This is at the bottom of **Butterfly Gorge**, and the start of a three- to four-hour walk up to the village of Orinó. Despite the name, the butterflies (Red admiral and Vanessa atalanta) have not been much in evidence in recent years, perhaps because the slopes higher up and the gorge itself were devastated by a massive fire in 1993. Although the woodland has grown back since then, and butterflies have been spotted, they have not yet recovered to the numbers preceding the blaze. Some believe that the fire was not the accident it appeared at the time (see box below); many of the nearby villagers would prefer to see olives planted here or some other "sensible" use of the land.

THE FIRES OF CRETE

Forest fires are an all-too-common occurrence in Crete. Understandable, perhaps, given the summer heat and tinderbox conditions but, depressingly, not all are the accidents they seem to be. Figures from the Greek Agricultural Ministry attribute no less than 57 percent of all fires to unknown causes or arson; the number also increases prior to general elections. This, of course, is when the politicians – in a desperate scramble for votes – are willing to recognize the claims to land of those who may have started the fires in the first place. Under Greek law, there is no organized system of land registry for publicly owned land, which means that if an area of woodland is burned down, the barren territory left behind becomes a no-man's-land that can be claimed under squatters' rights. Once olives or other crops have been planted, a foothold towards possession has been attained, with local politicians often smoothing over the obstacles to the land transfer. This callous attitude to the environment, where trees are little regarded for their beauty and their environmental benefits ignored or not understood, has a long history. In his book *Wild Flowers of Crete*, biologist George Sfikas writes of the Greek view that "a green wood is useless because the trees drink valuable water and don't produce anything". Attitudes are slowly changing as environmental awareness grows, especially among the young, but for now fires continue to plague the island.

It's easy enough to stroll a short way into the park (which, since it's on the main Ierápetra road, can be reached by bus), but the finest scenery, flora and fauna are to be found further up. In effect there are two gorges here: set out from the park through the first one, then across flatter, cultivated land to a final steep climb. In this last section there are waterfalls (in spring these can become torrents that make the way impassable, so check before setting out) and spectacular mountain scenery.

Orinó

The village of **ORINÓ** (Ορεινό) lies 2km further up the road from the top of Butterfly Gorge – you can also drive up there, on a road west of the park. Surrounded by lush greenery and wildflowers and at a height of nearly 1000m, the village is noticeably cooler than the coast; there's an excellent *kafenío* as well as a couple of rustic bars where you can slake your thirst after the climb.

Ayía Fotiá

AYÍA FOTIÁ (Αγία Φωτιά) is almost exactly halfway between Makríyialos and Ierápetra, where a poorly signed turning (hazardously situated halfway round a bend) leads down to an excellent small, sandy **beach** hidden from the road in a wooded valley. The tiny resort here is quiet at night, but the beach can get very crowded on summer weekends, when parking is also a nightmare. Nearby **Ahliá**, with a taverna and other facilities, is another lovely cove beach.

ARRIVAL AND DEPARTURE
MAKRÍYIALOS AND AROUND

By bus Four buses a day run between Makríyialos and Ierápetra (40min); there are 4 to Sitía (1hr) that stop at various points on the main road behind the beach; get off at the harbour for the western end of town, or near the *Villea Village Hotel* for Áspros Pótamos and places at the eastern end of town.

By boat In summer, there are daily trips from Makríyialos to Gaidhouronísi – Chrissi Island (see p.181) – on the *Sofia* (☏ 6974 409 511).

ACCOMMODATION

Thanks to its popularity with the package holiday market (generally the more exclusive end of it), Makríyialos is not overflowing with accommodation for anyone on a modest budget. There are some very good midmarket choices, though; many more can be found on ⑳ makrysgialos.com.

MAKRÍYIALOS

★ **Aspros Potamos Traditional Houses** 600m up a signed track at the eastern end of town (with a vehicle take the Pefkí road) ☏ 28430 51694, ⑳ asprospotamos .com. This back-to-nature version of *White River Cottages* (see p.178) is slightly further up the valley. Here another group of tiny stone houses cut from the rock has been delightfully converted into studios and apartments, but in this case there's only solar power; rooms have a fridge, single bathroom light and LED reading lamp (plus solar hot water), and in reception there's wi-fi and power for rechargers, otherwise you are reliant on oil lamps and candles for lighting, and a fireplace to warm you in winter (extra charge for firewood). **€45**

Asteria Studios Beachfront west of the harbour, close to the Roman villa ☏ 28430 51926, ⑳ relaxincrete .com. English-run a/c studios right by the beach: bright, airy and exceptionally well kitted out with everything from toasters to hairdryers. **€40**

Maria Tsankalioti Apartments Seaward side of the main road, halfway through town ☏ 28430 51557, ⑳ makrigialos-crete.com. The very friendly proprietor offers bright beachfront studio rooms and apartments – some with sea view and terrace – with kitchenette, a/c and TV. April–Sept. **€40**

Miramare Studios Eastern end of the town beach, down a track opposite the turning to Áspros Pótamos ☏ 28430 51049, ⑳ miramare-studios.gr. Bright, blue-and-white a/c studios with kitchenette, TV and large balconies directly above the beach, where they have free sunbeds. **€55**

Oasis Rooms Beachfront west of the harbour, close to the Roman villa ☏ 28430 51918. Spacious, simple and clean studios with a/c (€5 extra), kitchenette, fridge, terrace and balcony with sea view, right on the beach. Easy parking. **€30**

★ **White House** On the harbour ☏ 28430 29183, ⑳ makrigialos.com. Three houses and two apartments in beautifully restored harbour buildings, each one architect-designed and unique. The rooms are attractively decorated

2

with antiques, and the well equipped kitchens come with washing machine. Apartments €95, houses €225

White River Cottages 500m up a signed track at the eastern end of town ☎ 28430 51120, ✉ wriver@otenet .gr. An abandoned hamlet of traditional stone dwellings has been restored as a warren of studios and apartments (for up to four people) around a small pool. Built partly into the rocks, with the original stone floors and whitewashed walls, they come with a/c, kitchens and private terraces. Minimum three-night stay. April–Oct. Studios €80, apartments €104

AYÍA FOTIÁ

Markos Studios Built into the cliff on the east side of the bay, overlooking the beach ☎ 28420 61906, 🌐 markos-studios.com. Modern a/c studios and apartments for up to four people, with kitchenettes and balconies with awesome views. April–Sept. Studios €39, apartments €44

Taverna Agia Fotia Right by the beach ☎ 28420 61288, 🌐 agiafotia.gr. These simple a/c studios are set back a little from the beach, behind the taverna, which is probably the best of the places to eat here. April–Sept. €35

EATING AND DRINKING

The majority of **tavernas** in Makríyialos itself offer fairly standard, touristy food; options improve if you're prepared to travel a bit further. There's not much in the way of nightlife, but a number of **bars** on the harbour play soft music and serve cocktails.

MAKRÍYIALOS

Cafe Olympio Overlooking the beach beside the harbour ☎ 28430 52135. Friendly bar-café that's a good source of local information, with sunbeds on a sandy strip of beach. Breakfasts, light lunches, and draught beer in the daytime give way to creatively named cocktails ("Bloody Troika" and "Lost in Crisis" are typical) after dark. April–Sept daily 8am–1am.

Ilios Overlooking the beach beside the harbour ☎ 28430 51280. Housed in a refurbished carob warehouse, this bar-café serves breakfast but is better later on, when it's the perfect place for a sundowner. Daily 9am–2am.

Mina's Place Overlooking the harbour near the White House ☎ 28430 51949. Friendly and economical little taverna which uses the harbour jetty as its terrace. Fresh fish is the house speciality – try the tasty *gávros* (fried anchovies; €8) – but they also do meat grills and a range of *mezédhes* (€3–5). Your order will probably be supplemented by "on the house" offerings from "Mama" in the kitchen. April–Oct daily noon–midnight.

★Olive Tree Overlooking the beach beside the harbour ☎ 28430 51910. Excellent new taverna in a great position with a creatively slanted menu. There's a pleasant waterfront terrace, and the bread, dips and *mezédhes* (€3–7) are all superb; they also do fresh fish. Standouts include the *graviéra* goat's cheese (€4), *païdhákia* (€9) and risotto with scallops (€13). Daily noon–midnight.

KOUTSOURÁS

★Kalliotzina Towards the western end of the village ☎ 28430 51207. An absolutely classic old-fashioned taverna, serving home-cooked food and excellent fish on

a tree-shaded terrace right by the sea. There's no written menu, so check out what's on offer in the kitchen or listen carefully as the day's dishes are reeled off at speed; mains are around €5–7, or less for the veggie options. There's often musical accompaniment at weekends in summer. April–Oct daily 1.30pm–midnight.

Votsalakia In the middle of the beach by the mouth of the stream, 250m east of Kalliotzina ☎ 28430 51247. Old-fashioned food, fresh fish and barrel wine, but smarter than average decor, with cream-coloured awnings and dark-blue check tablecloths. April–Oct daily noon–midnight.

PERVOLÁKIA

Aposperida Káto Pervolákia ☎ 28430 31010 or ☎ 6937 819 269. Arriving at this *kafenío* – a simple place run by ex-sea captain Manolis Contolemakis and his wife Antonia – is a worthwhile reward for climbing the Pervolákia Gorge. It's a good place for a drink and a few *mezédhes* or Antonia's home-cooked food (including a delicious "village chicken" with tagliatelle). Call ahead to check they're open; they can arrange a taxi for the gorge walk (see p.176). Daily 8am–11pm.

PEFKÍ

★Piperia Upper part of the village ☎ 28430 52471. A lovely spot under a spreading pepper tree, with authentic, traditional food and great views over the coast. Mains like *païdhákia*, okra with lamb or rabbit in wine sauce go for around €9, and don't miss their *portokalópita* (orange cake dessert), which is a triumph. Live Greek music is put on some summer evenings, and they sell their own jams, olives and liqueurs. Daily noon–midnight.

Ierápetra and around

IERÁPETRA (Ιεράπετρα) has various claims to fame – the southernmost town in Europe, the most hours of sunshine, the largest town on the south coast of Crete – but until recently, charm was not one of them. Though there's an excellent Blue Flag **beach**, it's a big, sprawling place and a major supply centre for the region's numerous farmers who have grown rich on the year-round cultivation of cucumbers, tomatoes and peppers in the plastic greenhouses that scar the landscape along this coast. In recent years some resources have been devoted to smartening the town up, and, on the **seafront**, where a string of restaurants and bars stretches out in either direction, Ierápetra can be genuinely picturesque. However, tourism seems very much an afterthought, and things to do by day – apart from lie on the beach – are limited.

2

Brief history

Although you'd hardly know it to look at the town today, Ierápetra has quite a history. Early knowledge is sketchy, but it's almost certain that there was a settlement here, or at least a port, in **Minoan** times. A look at the map suggests a link across the isthmus with Gourniá, and it was probably from Ierápetra and other south-coast harbours that the Keftiu, as the Egyptians called the Cretans, sailed for the coast of Africa.

IERÁPETRA

SHOPS
Artopoleio Niki	2
Market	1

ACCOMMODATION
ByCaptain's	7
Camping Koutsounari	2
Coral Boutique Hotel	5
Cretan Villa	1
Erotokritos	6
El Greco	4
Katerina	3

CAFÉS & RESTAURANTS
Gorgona	5
Napoleon	6
Oxo	4
Parados	2
Tsi Tsi	3
Veterano	1

2

However, it was as a **Doric** settlement that **Ierápytna**, as the place was then known, grew to real prominence. By the second century BC it occupied more territory than any other Cretan city and had become a bastion of the Greek Dorians against their bitter enemies the Eteocretans: the final victory over Eteocretan Presós in 155 BC ended the last Minoan presence in eastern Crete. Only Ítanos, near Vái, now stood between Ierápytna and the complete domination of the eastern end of the island. Prolonged wars and disputes rumbled on for almost a century, and were finally brought to an end only by Rome's ruthless conquest of the entire island. Even then, Ierápytna stubbornly resisted to the last, becoming the final city to fall to the invading legions.

When **Rome** then joined Crete to Cyrene in northern Libya, forming the province of Cyrenaica, Ierápytna embarked on a new career as an important **commercial centre**, trading with Greece and Italy as well as Africa and the Near East. During this period, much impressive building took place – theatres, amphitheatres, temples – of which virtually nothing survives today, save for piles of fractured pillars and column capitals scattered in odd corners around the town.

From the Romans to the tourists is a chronicle of steady decline. The Venetians (who favoured Sitía as their administrative centre in the east) left behind a small **fortress**, now restored, defending the harbour entrance. The Turks, under whom Ierápetra languished as a backwater, are represented by a nineteenth-century **mosque** and nearby Ottoman fountain.

The Archeological Museum

Just off Platía Kanoupáki • Tues–Sun 8.30am–3pm • €2 • ☎ 28420 28721

Ierapetra's **Archeological Museum**, housed in the former Turkish school, is poorly labelled and doesn't take long to see, but does boast some high-quality exhibits. Among the highlights are numerous Minoan **lárnakes**, or clay coffins, the finest example of which was excavated at nearby Episkopí. Dating from the very end of the Neopalatial period (c.1300 BC), it has fascinating painted panels, one of which depicts a mare suckling her foal; other scenes revel in the stalking of the *kri-kri*, or wild goat, by hunting dogs. Look out too for some interesting **Vasilikí ware** (see p.149), including typical jugs and vases, as well as some potters' turntables from the early Minoan settlement at Fournoú Korýfi (see p.183). The Greek and Roman section contains a selection of statuary, mostly headless because iconoclastic Christians tended to regard the stone craniums as places where the spirit of the devil was lurking. One more recent discovery, a wonderful second-century statue of **Persephone**, holding an ear of corn in her left hand, managed to hang on to hers, which is crowned by a small altar encoiled by two serpents, symbols of her divinity.

The Kalés

East side of the harbour • Tues–Sun 8.30am–3pm • Free

A restored fortress known as the **Kalés** guards the harbour. Reputedly built by the Genoese pirate Pescatore in 1212, the present structure is basically a seventeenth-century Venetian defence, later used and modified by the Turks. Atmospheric as it is, it's simply an empty shell, with no signage or anything else apart from some public toilets.

The old quarter

A labyrinth of narrow streets inland from the harbour constitutes the **old quarter**. You'll almost certainly get lost here, but it's so tiny that a couple of minutes later you'll emerge at some recognizable landmark. Places to look out for include **Napoleon's House** (Káto Merá 9), where Napoleon Bonaparte allegedly spent a night in 1798, and the twin-domed church of **Aféndis Christós**, a fourteenth-century building with a fine carved and painted wooden iconostasis. In a small square opposite a Turkish fountain the **Tzami**, or mosque, has been painstakingly restored (it had been converted to a church). It retains a substantial chunk of its minaret and – inside – the original m

Beaches around Ierápetra

Much the best beaches accessible from Ierápetra are on Gaidhouronísi (see below), but there's a small **town beach** right in the centre in front of the old quarter, and more along the coast in either direction, with good bus services along the main road behind them. Most of the tourist development lies to the east, where aptly named **Long Beach**, a windswept line of sand (and the wind can really blow here) stretches virtually unbroken for 5km from the edge of town. There's more sand at **Koutsonári**, just beyond.

The Roman fish tank

Between Koutsonári and Férma, about 9km east of Ierápetra • Look for a sign for "Roman Fish Tanks" in front of the *Kakkos Bay Hotel*

The remarkable **Roman fish tank**, carved out of the rock near the village of Férma, is some 4m square, with the sea still sloshing through an ancient sluicegate in the bottom. The carved steps leading down into the tank would have been used by the fish sellers to net the fish demanded by their customers; the pools in the surrounding rocks were no doubt used for the fish to be sold that day, while the smaller ones could be fattened up in the larger tank below.

Gaidhouronísi

The most popular way to escape Ierápetra's often stifling summer temperatures is to take a boat trip (see below) to **GAIDHOURONÍSI (Γαιδουρονήσι)** – Donkey Island, more often known locally as **Chrissi** – some 10km offshore. A real desert island a little over 4km in length, with a fine cedar forest and a couple of tavernas, Gaidhouronísi has some excellent sandy **beaches** and plenty of room to escape – although you wouldn't want to miss the boat back. There's a waymarked **walking route** around the island on which you should spot quite a few examples of the varied flora and fauna, as well as fossils and the fabulous "**Shell Beach**" (Belegrina), covered with discarded shells from countless generations of molluscs (no souvenir-taking allowed).

ARRIVAL AND DEPARTURE   IERÁPETRA AND AROUND

By car Ierápetra has a complex one-way system and the usual shortage of parking. The easiest plan is to follow the signs for the "Archeological Collection" and from there to the seafront, where there's a large car park.

By bus The bus station (☎ 28420 28237) is on Lasthénous – the Áyios Nikólaos road. The centre lies to the southwest,

a 5min walk away.

Destinations Ay. Nikólaos (8 daily; 1hr); Iráklio (8 daily; 2hr 30min); Makríyialos (Mon–Fri 7 daily, Sat 4 daily, Sun 2 daily, 9.30am & 2.30pm; 30min); Mýrtos (Mon–Fri 5 daily, Sat 2 daily, 8am & 12.30pm; 30min); Sitía (Mon–Sat 4 daily; Sun 2 daily, 9.30am & 2.30pm; 1hr 30min).

GETTING AROUND AND INFORMATION

By boat Two competing companies, Chrysi Cruises (☎ 28420 20008, ⓦ cretandailycruises.com) and Zanadu (☎ 6937 811 095), run daily trips to Gaidhouronísi, on large boats with on-board bars, from the jetty on the seafront (May–Oct; peak-season departures 10.30am, 11am & 12.30pm, returning 4pm, 5pm & 6pm; 55min). Tickets are sold by agents throughout town, or at the boat; officially they cost €20 but off-season, or if you bargain with the agents, you may get them for as little as €10. From the harbour, small boats offer more personalized trips and private charters; they include a traditional fishing *kaïki*

(the *Nefeli*; ☎ 6942 791 474, ⓦ bateaucrete.canalblog .com) and a fast modern motor-yacht (the *Nautilos*; ☎ 6972 894 279, ⓦ nautiloscruises.com), both of which charge €45 a head for the day-trip to the island.

By taxi There's a taxi rank on Platía Kanoupáki, or call ☎ 28420 26600.

Tourist information The only current source of tourist information is the helpful Ierapetra Express travel agency (Mon–Fri 8am–2pm & 5–9pm, Sat 9am–2pm; ☎ 28420 28673), on Platía Eleftherías (opposite the *Veterano* café); they can also advise on accommodation and car rental.

ACCOMMODATION

ByCaptain's Stratigoú Samouíl 54 ☎ 6979 080 154, ☎ bycaptains.ierap@gmail.com. Newly converted a/c studios above a seafront souvenir shop, close to the town beach, with TV, modern kitchenette, and big seafront

balconies (in rooms 4 & 8). April–Oct. **€40**

Camping Koutsounari Koutsounári, off the coast road 7km east ☎ 28420 61213, ⓦ camping-koutsounari.gr. The only campsite on this stretch of the south coast, with a taverna, store and pool, and although the ground is a bit gritty there's a good beach and plenty of shade. May–Oct. Two people plus tent and car €18

Coral Boutique Hotel Platía Eleftherías 19 ☎ 28420 20444. Swish new small hotel with luxuriously decorated and furnished balcony rooms and suites (the higher ones come with sea views), kitted out with fridge, plasma TV and tea-making facilities. €45

★**Cretan Villa** Lakérda 16 ☎ 28420 28522, 🌐 cretan-villa.com. Close to the bus station on a pedestrianized street, this is a gem offering sparkling a/c rooms with TV and fridge overlooking the flower-bedecked patio of a beautiful two-century-old stone-built house. They've recently added some equally attractive apartments. Doubles €44, apartments €60

Erotokritos Paradós Stratígou Samouíl, signed off the seafront beyond Taverna Napoleon ☎ 28420 28151. Decent, old-fashioned en-suite rooms and apartments with kitchenette, fridges and fans (some with a/c), tucked away in the old quarter. €30

El Greco Kothrí 42 ☎ 28420 28471, 🌐 elgreco-ierapetra .gr. Refurbished beachfront hotel with harmoniously toned rooms and suites; balconies at the front have great sea views (extra), while inland-facing rooms are cheaper. Also has its own café and restaurant (discounts for guests). Breakfast included. €60

Katerina Markópoulo 95, on the seafront ☎ 28420 28345, 🌐 katerina-hotel.gr. Refurbished inside (but in need of a lick of paint outside), offering smart rooms and studios with a/c, TV, fridge and balcony with sea view. Rooms €45, studios €55

EATING AND DRINKING

Along Markópoulou, the seafront promenade stretching behind the beach northeast of the town hall, there's a string of **café-bars** with outdoor seating, many of which serve breakfast. Samouíl, the promenade south of the ferry terminal, has a number of more traditional **tavernas** facing the sea. In town itself there are plenty of more basic café and fast-food options between Platía Kanoupáki and Platía Eleftherías. Nightlife is pretty quiet, though there are lots of late-opening **bars** in the centre, especially around Platía Kanoupáki, by the Archeological Museum and south along Kírva.

Gorgona Stratígou Samouíl 12 ☎ 28420 26619. Near the harbour and fort, directly on the beach, this reliable, well-known and locally popular taverna serves good fish and seafood; try the octopus (€8) or a whole *tsipoúra* (bream) and Greek salad for €10, or a mixed fish platter for €12. Daily 11am–midnight.

★**Napoleon** Stratígou Samouíl 26 ☎ 28420 22410. One of Ierápetra's oldest tavernas, usually busy with locals at lunchtime. Freshly cooked dishes include oven-baked mountain lamb (€8), and there's a good choice of mezédhes (€2.50–7) – try a mixed plate of their cheese and vegetable pies or delicious courgette fritters. The wholemeal bread – baked daily by the proprietor's wife – is outstanding. Daily 12.30–6pm & 8pm–midnight.

Oxo Kírva 15 ☎ 28420 80089. This colourful *rakádhiko* (like an ouzerí, but with *rakí*) is packed late at night with young locals; it's one of a number of fashionable restaurants here, with tables looking out towards the harbour jetty. Good, inexpensive meze (€1.50–5), plus souvláki, panséta (pork ribs) and meat or mushroom pies (€4). Daily 7am–2am.

Parados Off Platía Kanoupáki, by the Archeological Museum ☎ 28420 27878. A lovely bar-café with an ambience as laidback as the jazz that's played here; it also sells arty books. Live traditional Greek music on Fri–Sat eve. Daily 10am–3pm & 6pm–late.

Tsi Tsi Behind the Archeological Museum ☎ 6972 166 219. Great new high-ceilinged *mezedopolío* (mezédhes bar) with original decor – the name means "chi-chi" – and an attractive outdoor terrace next to the museum. A good meze selection (€3–8) includes pork with cinnamon and a tasty *fáva*, and there's a varied wine list. Live Greek music is often put on at weekends. Daily 6pm–2am.

★**Veterano** Northern end of Platía Eleftherías ☎ 28420 23175. An elegant and excellent bakery/ *zaharoplastío* with an outdoor terrace where you can sit and watch the world go by. Great cakes and pastries, plus ice cream, coffee and sandwiches. Daily 7.30am–11pm.

SHOPPING

Artopoleio Niki Houta 2 ☎ 28420 27566. Foreign newspapers are available from this bakery facing the archeological museum. Mon–Sat 8am–2pm & 5–8pm.

Market Psilinaki to the northeast of the centre. An excellent Saturday street market and farmers' market with plenty of fruit and veg, plus local cheeses and spicy sausages (*lasithiotika*) as well as clothes, tools and flowers. Sat 8am–2pm.

Mýrtos and around

The coastline west of Ierápetra is, even more than usual, swathed in plastic, and holds plentiful signs of the wealth this form of agriculture has brought to the region: gleaming car and kitchen showrooms line the road. At the end of this stretch **MÝRTOS** (**Μύρτος**) lies just off the main road, which here turns inland, heading up towards Áno Viánnos. Razed to the ground by the German army in 1944 as a punishment for resistance activities, Mýrtos today is an unexpected pleasure after the drabness of what has gone before; a charming, white-walled village with a long shingle beach. Even in August, when the place can get pretty full, the pace of life remains slow, the atmosphere pleasantly laidback.

Apart from topping up your tan, swimming, renting a boat or lingering over a drink, there's not a great deal to do in Mýrtos, but the surrounding countryside offers a couple of important **Minoan sites**, as well as the opportunity for mountain **hikes**. Above the beach at the western edge of the village there's evidence of a **Roman-era settlement**: a brick-built circular tank construction that may be part of a Roman baths complex, walls and, closer to the water, harbour installations – all awaiting archeological investigation.

Mýrtos Museum
Western side of the village, beside the church • Mon & Fri 10am–2pm, Wed 5–8pm • Free

Mýrtos Museum was put together by a much-loved and respected local schoolmaster, Yiorgos Dimitrianakis, who taught most of the older folk in the village prior to his death in 1994. Throughout his life, he spent much of his free time wandering the fields and hills around Mýrtos collecting a wealth of finds, including ancient statuettes and vase fragments, and it was he who brought the Fournoú Korýfi and Pýrgos sites (see below) to the attention of archeologists. Inside are minor finds from those sites, as well as a folklore section with tools, kitchen and farming implements once used by the villagers. There's also a superb clay model of the site at Fournoú Korýfi created by John Atkinson, a British potter who now looks after the museum.

Pýrgos
Immediately east of Mýrtos, just beyond the bridge over the Mýrtos River; take the signed track and follow a waymarked footpath to the right, which climbs to the site, atop a low hill

The Minoan villa at **PÝRGOS** (**Πύργος**) was inhabited, like nearby Fournoú Korýfi (see below), in the early Prepalatial Period (c.2500 BC), and destroyed by fire around 2200 BC. Unlike Fournoú Korýfi, however, Pýrgos was reoccupied and rebuilt following its destruction, when it appears to have incorporated the former's lands. By the time of the Neopalatial Period (c.1600 BC), the community occupying the lower slopes was dominated by a two- or three-storey country villa spread over the crown of the hill.

The path up circles around the back of the hill and past the remains of an enormous plastered **cistern**, the largest found in Minoan Crete, dating from the Prepalatial era (c.1900–1700 BC). When it burst over the northern side of the hill in ancient times, it was not repaired. Beyond this, a fine stretch of **paved road** survives from the early period: this led to a burial pit, now excavated. Continuing up, a **stepped street** flanked by some well-cut lower courses of the villa's outer wall leads into a **courtyard**, partly paved in the purple limestone of the region. At the rear of the villa (furthest away from the sea) on the west side, it's possible to make out a **light well** floored with the same purple limestone. Many of the walls carry marks of the ferocious blaze which destroyed the villa around 1450 BC, lending credibility to the Thíra explosion theory (see p.330), especially since volcanic material was discovered amid the rubble. But it now seems that while the villa was burned, the surrounding settlement was untouched – another puzzle to contemplate as you savour the magnificent sea view from the courtyard.

Fournoú Korýfi
Signed inland a couple of kilometres east of Mýrtos, near the village of Néa Mýrtos • The gate is generally left open • The site is on the peak, reached by scrambling up a gully (signed), then heading towards a stand of pine trees just before which a path heads to the right across a flat expanse of brush towards a hill, where the fenced site is clearly visible

At **FOURNOÚ KORÝFI** (**Φουρνού Κορύφι**) – Kiln Hill, also known as **Néa Mýrtos** – a Minoan site excavated in the 1960s by a British team yielded important evidence

2

concerning early Minoan settlements. The excavations – which are not always easy to make sense of – revealed a **stone-built village** of nearly one hundred rooms, spread over the hilltop. Probably typical of numerous other settlements sited on the coast of eastern Crete during the early Prepalatial Period (c.2500 BC), these rooms contained stone and copper tools, carved seals and over seven hundred **pottery vessels**. Some of these were Vasilikí-type jugs (see p.149), and many were no doubt used to store the produce of the surrounding lands, then less arid than today.

In a room in the southwest corner of the site was located the oldest known Minoan domestic shrine, which produced the most important of the finds here: the **goddess of Mýrtos**, a clay idol with a stalked neck carrying a ewer (it's now in the Áyios Nikólaos museum, along with most of the other finds from this site and Pýrgos). Around the goddess, broken offering vessels were strewn about the floor, many of them charred by the fire that destroyed the site in about 2200 BC. The riddle of the fire, which seems to have left no casualties and provoked no rebuilding, is yet another of the unresolved Minoan questions.

ARRIVAL AND INFORMATION

By bus There are 5 buses to and from Ierápetra on weekdays, just two on Sat (8am & 12.30pm) and none on Sun.

Travel agencies Several travel agencies in Mýrtos offer local information and help with rooms, villas for rent, money exchange, car rental and the like. Perhaps the most helpful is the friendly Prima Tours (☎ 28420 51530,

MÝRTOS AND AROUND

ⓦ sunbudget.net), on a side street near the beach towards the eastern end of the village where the bus timetable and lots of other information is posted; they also run a used book exchange, lead guided walks and produce their own walks leaflet (€3.50) describing seven waymarked hiking routes.

ACCOMMODATION

Big Blue Apartments West side of village ☎ 28420 51094, ⓦ big-blue.gr. Lovely, recently refurbished rooms with fridge, studios with kitchenette, and larger two-bedroom apartments with stunning views ("Heaven" and "Myth" are the ones to go for), all with a/c and sea-view balconies in a stunning position high above the beach. Doubles **€35**, studios **€45**, apartments **€60**

Hotel Myrtos On the main street behind the beach ☎ 28420 51227, ⓦ myrtoshotel.gr. Friendly and good-value little hotel in the heart of the action. Recently refurbished rooms come with a/c, fridge and balcony, some of which on the second floor have a sea view. There's an excellent taverna below, too. **€35**

Nikos House At the heart of the village near Hotel Myrtos ☎ 28420 51116. Very simple studios and two-room apartments with a/c, bath and kitchenette; the upstairs studio, especially, is the one to go for, and you feel very much part of village life here. May–Oct. **€35**

Panorama At almost the highest point at the west end of the village, above Big Blue ☎ 28420 51556. Studios with kitchenette, TV, a/c (€3 extra) and balconies; there

are exceptional sea views from those at the front. March–Oct. **€35**

★**Villa Mala** Malés village 12km north ☎ 28420 91382, ⓦ villamala.gr. Very pleasant rural luxury hotel in Malés (see box opposite), whose extremely comfortable and tastefully furnished beamed rooms come with four-poster beds, snazzy bathrooms and terrace balconies. There's a/c and heating (for winter lets) and it's located next to a very good taverna. Breakfast included. **€70**

Villa Myrthe Towards the back of the village near the church ☎ 28420 51331, ⓦ villamyrthe.com. Pretty, new apartment complex where the ample ultra-modern apartments (sleeping 2–5) come with terrace, marble bathrooms and kitchen. Facilities include a/c and satellite TV. The minimum stay is seven days but this may be negotiable in slacker periods. **€50**

Villa Nostos Eastern edge of the village, signed as you enter from the main road ☎ 28420 51569, ⓦ villanostos .nl. Welcoming garden complex, right behind the beach, with plain but very good-value studios and apartments with a/c, fridge and balcony, some with sea view. **€35**

EATING AND DRINKING

Beach Café Western end of the promenade ☎ 6995 434 848. The last spot at the western end of the village, right above the beach. It's all too tempting to linger here for hours over a drink; they also serve breakfast and full meals. April–Oct daily 10.30am–11pm.

Katerina's On a pedestrian alley in the heart of the

village ☎ 28420 51451. Self-described as "the only gourmet restaurant in the region", *Katerina's* attempts to be a cut above the rest, and often succeeds, although things can sometimes be hit and miss. Specialities include Martini-marinated pork filet mignon as well as old favourites such as *kléftiko*, and there are plenty of veggie

INLAND ESCAPES FROM MÝRTOS

The **mountainous terrain** behind Mýrtos offers plenty of opportunity to escape the crowds and heat of the coast, or to stretch your legs, as well as some spectacular scenery. If you're driving to or from Ierápetra, the route through **Mýthi** and **Máles** to Gra Ligiá offers a beautiful, if extremely slow, alternative to the plastic-strewn coast road.

SARAKINÁS GORGE

The scenic, 150m-deep **Sarakinás Gorge** starts close to the village of **Mýthi**, some 5km north of Mýrtos. To reach the start of the walk, drive or take a taxi to the village and then follow the signs to the gorge; there's a small parking place five minutes downhill, just before the bridge, where the walk begins. Depending on the rains, the water level in the gorge may mean you'll have to do some wading in parts, so waterproof footwear would be useful. It's about 2km or one hour's climb to the top of the gorge and a little less coming back down, by which time the *kafenío* in Mýthi will be an irresistible stop. Should you not wish to repeat the scramble back down, it's possible to pick up an asphalt road back to Mýthi by following the river a further 300m upstream from the top of the gorge to where it's feasible to wade across. A path heads off from the opposite bank to meet the road.

MÁLES

Above Mýthi, with transport, you can continue to climb to **Máles**, a village clinging to the lower slopes of the Dhíkti range. The climb takes in some stunning rock formations and – as you get higher – there are views of Chrissi Island (see p.181) far out to sea, as well as the expanse of plastic greenhouses along the coastal strip. Máles would be a good starting point if you wanted to take a **walk** through some stunning mountain terrain (the E4 Pan-European footpath passes just 3km north of here) and it now has a comfortable hotel and taverna (see opposite).

choices; unsurprisingly, it's more expensive than elsewhere (allow at least €40 for two with wine). Chef Yiannis Zervakis also runs half-day cooking workshops and excursions into the mountains to forage for herbs and wild greens. April–Oct daily 6–11pm.

Myrtos Taverna Main thoroughfare, below Hotel Myrtos ☎ 28420 51227. An excellent, economical family-run taverna offering a range of *mayireftá* home-cooked dishes (€7–12) – try the *kounéli krasáto* (rabbit stewed in wine) – as well as

fresh fish and tasty mezédhes, with outdoor tables on a pleasant terrace. Daily 9am–midnight.

Votsalo Seafront in the middle of the beach ☎ 28420 51457. A likeable place with a great position at the centre of the beachfront promenade; hand-painted menus detail a good traditional set of dishes (meze €3–5, mains €7–10), washed down with home-produced wine. They also do breakfast, and coffee and drinks throughout the day. April–Oct daily 9am–midnight.

Tértsa

The narrow coast road west from Mýrtos runs for some 6km, past some tempting cove beaches, to the tiny resort of **TÉRTSA** (Τέρτσα). Technically, this is in Iráklio province, and there is a paved road that winds inland to meet the main Áno Viánnos road, but practically everyone who gets here has come from Mýrtos. There's an excellent long beach, partly nudist, a couple of fine tavernas, and some get-away-from-it-all apartments.

ACCOMMODATION AND EATING

Lambros Apartments Set back down a side road from the centre of the village ☎ 28950 61437, ⓦ tertsa.gr. Modern a/c studios and apartments with kitchenette and TV, in a rural setting at the back of the village. Information is available from *Lambros Taverna*. April–Oct. Studios €30, apartments €40

Lambros Taverna Seafront in the centre of the village ☎ 28950 61437, ⓦ tertsa.gr. Family-run taverna with a beachside terrace serving home-made traditional food plus daily fresh fish, a good meze selection (€3–6) and veggie options. There's also a Sunday barbecue with *souvláki* and lamb on the spit (€8–10). The taverna acts as an unofficial rooms information centre and provides free sunbeds on the beach for customers. April–Oct daily 9am–midnight.

Réthymno

THE AMÁRI VALLEY

Réthymno

The province of Réthymno has something for everyone. The island's intellectual and cultural capital, Réthymno itself is a relaxed university town overlooked by one of the most imposing Venetian fortresses on the island. It also retains a picturesque old quarter, redolent of traditional urban life, plus a fine beach. Probably the greatest attraction of the province, however, is its interior, dominated by mountains that provide stunning vistas at almost every turn. The provincial borders are defined by the island's loftiest peaks; in the east the looming mass of Psilorítis, Crete's highest mountain, and to the west the far reaches of the Lefká Óri, the White Mountains. The villages ranged around the Psilorítis massif provide ideal bases for spectacular wilderness hikes, highly recommended for casual ramblers and committed hikers alike.

The peaks themselves are approached most easily from **Anóyia**, a high mountain town known for its sheep-breeding, weaving and embroidery. From here, you can hike across to the south side of the mountains or down, via the summit of Psilorítis, to the pretty villages of the lushly fertile **Amári valley** – some of the least visited and most traditional places in Crete. Southwest of Réthymno town you're on the fringes of the Lefká Óri, studded with traditional hill villages such as **Aryiroúpoli** and **Así Gonía**, surrounded by more magnificent **hiking** country. In both directions, the mountains and valleys also offer spectacular **driving routes** across the island.

Not far out of Réthymno en route to the Amári valley is the revered **Moní Arkádhi**, a beautiful, ancient monastery whose history makes it the emblem of Crete's nineteenth-century struggle for independence against the Turks. The main road towards the south, meanwhile, heads via the Minoan cemetery at **Arméni** to the attractive hill town of **Spíli**, another centre for walkers with many fine hikes in the surrounding hills.

Réthymno's **south coast** has no fancy hotels, but if all you want is sea and sand it's a far more attractive prospect than the north. There are two sizeable resorts, crowded **Ayía Galíni** and its more easy-going rival, **Plakiás**. Along the coast between them is a string of secluded pockets of sand – sometimes with a village attached – often hard to access but well worth it for a few lazy days. One of them, **Palm Beach**, is among the most picturesque on Crete, though far from undiscovered. Above it is **Moní Préveli**, an illustrious seaside monastery that played a pivotal role during the Battle of Crete.

Highlights

❶ Réthymno The provincial capital has fine Venetian and Turkish monuments and an atmospheric old quarter, as well as a great beach, fine food and buzzing nightlife. **See p.191**

❷ Moní Arkádhi and Moní Préveli Two of Crete's most important monasteries, the imposing Moní Arkádhi and the seaside Moní Préveli are inextricably bound up with the island's history. **See p.202 & p.225**

❸ Margarítes A major centre of ceramics production, this is the place to buy anything from an egg cup to a massive Minoan-style *píthos*. **See p.204**

❹ Mount Psilorítis Dominating the province, Crete's highest peak provides some challenging hikes. **See p.208**

❺ Amári valley White-walled villages with frescoed Byzantine chapels surrounded by orchards, vineyards and olive groves, all with a spectacular mountain backdrop. **See p.210**

❻ Plakiás and Ayía Galíni The province's twin but contrasting south-coast resorts are ideal seaside getaways. **See p.221 & p.217**

❼ Mountain roads West of Réthymno, the mountain roads to the south coast offer some of Crete's most enthralling drives. **See p.228**

HIGHLIGHTS ARE MARKED ON THE MAP ON P.190

Réthymno town

Although it's the third largest town in Crete, **RÉTHYMNO** (Ρέθυμνο) never feels like a city, as Haniá and Iráklio do. Instead, it has an easy-going provincial air; it's a place that moves slowly and, for all the myriad bars springing up along the seafront, the **old town** still preserves much of its Venetian and Turkish appearance. Here the streets are a fascinating mix of generations of **architecture**, the Venetian buildings largely indistinguishable from the Turkish and all of them adapted by later generations. Ornate wooden doors and balconies and ancient stonework crop up everywhere, and there are a number of mosques and elaborate **Turkish fountains** hidden in obscure corners. A few traditional stores survive too, where craftsmen still make *lyras* (the Cretan "violin") or sharpen knives by hand. Arriving, especially if you approach from the east in the evening, the town looks exactly as it does in old engravings or in Edward Lear's watercolours – dominated by the bulk of a colossal **Venetian fortress**, the skyline picked out with delicate minarets.

All of this is increasingly under commercial threat – there are hundreds of tavernas, bars, cafés and clubs – but on the whole the big hotels are out of town, stretching away along the shore to the east. The town centre remains a very enjoyable place to spend some time, with a wide, sandy **beach** and palm-fringed promenade in front of the tangled streets of the old town.

The harbour

The Venetian or inner **harbour** is the most attractive part of Réthymno's waterfront, although these days its elegant sixteenth-century lighthouse looks down on a line of quayside fish tavernas, rather than the sailing ships and barges of bygone eras. The impressive breakwaters delineating the outer harbour see little use: ever since the Venetians built the harbour it has had an irresistible tendency to silt up, and few big ships now call here. The inner harbour and the new marina under the eastern breakwater are instead given over to small fishing *kaikia*, pleasure craft and tourist cruise boats.

The old town

Wandering through the old town is a large part of the pleasure of visiting Réthymno; there's little specifically to visit, but plenty to look out for as you stroll. At its heart are two Venetian survivals – the seventeenth-century **Rimóndi fountain**, whose lion-head spouts look out over **Platía Petiháki**, one of the liveliest areas in town, and the sixteenth-century **Loggia**, currently without a function. Not far away is the restored **Neratsés Mosque** (used for concerts but not otherwise open to the public), whose iconic minaret dominates the skyline.

The Historical and Folk Art Museum

Vernárdhou 28 • Mon–Sat 9.30am–2.30pm • €4 • ☎ 28310 23398

The little-visited **Historical and Folk Art Museum**, in a beautifully restored seventeenth-century Venetian mansion near the Neratsés Mosque, is among the best of its kind.

> ### RÉTHYMNO CITY CENTRE ORIENTATION
>
> Réthymno **city centre**, at least as far as tourists are concerned, is the largely pedestrianized old town bordered by the fortress, harbour and beach in the north, and the traffic-filled streets that run through the busy **Platía Tessáron Martíron** to the south. The fortress also delineates the western limit of the ancient streets, while to the east the beach and main roads converge around **Platía Stratióti** and the new marina. The major thoroughfares are **Ethníkis Andistásis**, the **market** street, leading from the heart of the old town south to the **Porta Guora**, the only surviving remnant of the city walls, and **Arkadhíou**, running parallel to the shore, a more commercial and touristy shopping street.

RÉTHYMNO TOWN

● SHOPS

Atelier	1
Bibliopoleío	5
Lyranthos	8
Mediterranean Editions	6
Nikos Siragas	7
Raw Materials	2
Vasilis Psiharaki	4
Yeoryios Papalexakis	3

● CAFÉS & RESTAURANTS

Akros Ikoyeniakon	14	Retro Café	6
Alana	8	Samaria	15
Avli	4	Stella's Kitchen	10
Bakalogatos	7	Sunset Taverna	2
Kyria Maria	9	Taverna Zambia	1
Melina	3	To Pigadi	5
Mesostrati	12	Zefyros	13
Mojo Burgers	11	Zisi	16

■ ACCOMMODATION

Atelier	3	Leo	14
Avli	5	Makri Steno	2
Barbara Studios	9	Olga's Rooms	10
Byzantine	11	Palazzino di Corina	8
Camping Elizabeth	18	Palazzo Vecchio	1
Caramel	17	Sea Front	16
Casa Moazzo	13	Vecchio	7
Castello	15	Veneto	4
Ideon	6	Youth Hostel	12

■ BARS & CLUBS

Figaro Social	2
Fraoules	7
Galero	3
Ice Club	4
Metropolis	6
Nuvel	5
O Kipos tou Ali Vafi	1

Starting with the inevitable Independence and Battle of Crete weaponry and memorabilia, it moves on to an exceptional depiction of traditional life, including a comprehensive weaving and embroidery display, a reconstructed sitting-room with all its furnishings, musical instruments (including the *lyra* of Nikos Piskopakis, one of its greatest-ever exponents), basketry, farm tools, traditional costumes, jewellery, pottery and more. At the back is a recreation of a typical city street including a *kafenío*, pharmacy, barber, tailor and blacksmith. It's a fascinating insight into the island's fast-disappearing lifestyles, many of which had survived virtually unchanged from Venetian times to the 1960s.

The Contemporary Art Museum

Mesolongiou 32 • Tues–Fri 9am–2pm & 7–9pm, Sat & Sun 10am–3pm • €3, free on Thurs • ☎ 28310 52530, ⓦ cca.gr

Réthymno's **Contemporary Art Museum** has a small permanent collection of works by Greek and Cretan sculptors and painters, with oils and watercolours by Réthymno-born artist Lefteris Kanakakis (1934–85) forming the core of the collection. Mostly, though, they stage challenging special exhibitions, both in the main building and at other venues across town, including places you might not otherwise be able to visit, such as the Kara Pasha mosque and the Ibrahim Khan mosque inside the Fortezza.

The Fortezza

Entrance from Odhós Katehàki • Daily: April–Sept 8.30am–8pm; Oct–March 8am–6pm • €4

Looking down on the old town from a lofty hill at the western end of the seafront stands the massive **Fortezza** or **Venetian Fortress**. Although much is ruined now, the fort remains thoroughly atmospheric (even more so if you catch an evening concert here), with **views** from the walls over the town and harbour, or in the other direction along the coast to the west. The chief impression once you're close up, inside or out, is of its vast scale – it's easy to imagine the city's entire population sheltering here.

Brief history

Said to be the largest Venetian castle ever built, the Fortezza was a response, in the last quarter of the sixteenth century, to a series of **pirate raids** (by Barbarossa in 1538 and Uluch Ali in 1562 and 1571) that had devastated the town. Designed by the Italian engineer Sforza Pallavicini, the mammoth edifice took a full ten years to build, at crippling cost. Whether it was effective is another matter; in 1645 the Venetian city fell to the Turks in less than 24 hours (they simply bypassed the fort), and when the English writer Robert Pashley visited in 1834 he found the guns, some of them still the Venetian originals, to be entirely useless.

Within the walls

As you walk through the impressive gateway in the walls you pass what must have been some sort of **guardhouse** within the bastion, and then emerge into the vast open interior space, dotted with the remains of barracks, arsenals, officers' houses, earthworks and deep shafts. At the centre is a large domed building which was once a **church** and later – following the fall of the town to the Turks – converted into a **mosque** dedicated to the then ruling sultan, Ibrahim. The renovated interior has a truly fabulous **dome** and a pretty, polychrome mihrab (a niche indicating the direction of Mecca), both of which are Turkish additions. Just north of the church/mosque are some fine arched foundations and a **stairway** leading down to a gate in the seaward defences. Among the most impressive remains are the **cisterns** where rainwater would have been collected: they are deep and cool, and dimly lit by slits through which shafts of sunlight penetrate.

The Archeological Museum

Odhós Katehàki • Tues–Sun 8am–3pm • €3 • ☎ 28310 54668

The **Archeological Museum** lies almost directly opposite the entrance to the Fortezza, in a building constructed by the Turks as an extra defence, and which later served as a prison. It's now entirely modern inside – cool, spacious and airy – and well worth a visit. There's an interesting collection of Minoan pottery and sarcophagi, mainly from Arméni (see p.215), as well as Roman coins, jewellery, pots and statues, all of them from Réthymno province. Take a look beneath the central atrium at an unusual unfinished Roman **statue of Aphrodite**, with the sculptor's chisel marks still plain to see, allowing you to glimpse the goddess's features – never completed – emerging from the stone.

The beach

Réthymno's **beach** is an invitingly broad swathe of tawny sand, right alongside the old town. There are showers and cafés, and the waters protected by the breakwaters are dead calm (and ideal for kids). Sadly, they're also crowded and often none too clean. Outside the harbour, less sheltered sands stretch for kilometres, only marginally less crowded but with much cleaner water and all sorts of watersports. Interspersed among the hotels along here is every facility you could need – travel agents, bike rental, bars and restaurants.

ARRIVAL AND DEPARTURE

RÉTHYMNO TOWN AND AROUND

BY BUS

Bus station Réthymno's bus station is west of the centre, on the Periferiakos. There's left luggage available (Mon–Fri 9am–11pm, Sat & Sun 9am–5pm). There's bus information and timetables at ☎ 28310 22212, ☜ e-ktel.com.

Destinations Amári (Mon–Fri 2 daily, 5.30am & 2pm; 1hr); Anóyia (Mon–Fri 2 daily, 5.30am & 2pm; 1hr 30min); Arkádhi (3 daily, 6am, 10.45am & 2.30pm; 50min); Ay. Galíni via Spíli (5 daily; 1hr–1hr 30min); Haniá (17 daily; 1hr); Hóra Sfakíon (change at Vrísses; 3 daily, 8am, 2pm & 3pm; 2hr); Iráklio (17 daily; 1hr 30min); Moní Préveli (2 daily, 9am & 11am; 1hr); Omalós (daily at 7am; 1hr 45min); Pánormos and hotels en route (at least 20 daily; 1hr); Plakiás (5 daily; 1hr).

BY CAR

Parking is even more tricky in Réthymno than elsewhere, especially as most of the old town is pedestrianized. Some hotels have spaces, or try the streets near Platía Plastíra by the outer harbour (where there is also a public pay car park), around the public gardens (with another pay car park) or in the streets surrounding Platía Stratióti at the east end of the seafront.

BY PLANE

The nearest airports to Réthymno are at Haniá (60km, see p.244) and Iráklio (78km, see p.61).

GETTING AROUND AND INFORMATION

By bus Once in Réthymno you'll mostly be walking, but if you're staying in the hotel strip east of town, you can take advantage of the excellent bus service along the coast road (every 30min 6.30am–midnight), and there are local buses, too, to nearby villages, detailed in the text where relevant.

By taxi There are ranks in Platía Tessáron Martíron and Platía Stratióti, or call ☎ 28310 25000 or ☎ 28310 35000.

Car and bike rental Arkadi, Venizélou 22 (☎ 28310 29134, ☜ arkadi-rental.com), have good modern cars, scooters and bikes. There are plenty of others nearby on this section of the seafront close to the marina, many with pedal bikes too. Stavros, Paleológou 14, in the heart of the old town (☎ 28310 22858), offer mountain bike rental from €7/day.

City tours Open-top bus and "Little Train" tours of the city are generally a waste of time, as they can't go into the old

town; some do take you a long way out into the countryside, though, and can be handy for hikes or visiting villages. One way you can explore the old town is on a Segway, with BestRide, Venizélou 4 (☎ 6948 175 785, ☜ bestride.gr).

Tourist information A municipal information booth operates in season from a booth in Platía Tessáron Martíron (Mon–Fri 9am–2pm). The municipal website, ☜ rethymno .gr, has good maps.

Travel agents There are numerous travel agents in the centre, especially on Venizélou near the marina. The following can all arrange excursions and domestic flight and ferry tickets: Cool Holidays, Melissinoú 2 (☎ 28310 35567, ☜ coolholidays.gr); Klados Travel, Platía Stratióti 14 (☎ 28310 54428, ☜ kladostravel.gr); Apoplous Travel, Yiamboudháki 11 (☎ 28310 20476, ☜ greentour.gr).

TOURS AND ACTIVITIES

Boat trips Dolphin Cruises (☎ 28310 29134, ☜ dolphin -cruises.com) runs a variety of day-trips and short cruises from the harbour, including a "pirate" boat, fishing trips and sunset cruises. There are also day-trips (or longer) to Thíra (Santoríni) with Seajets (☜ seajets.gr), most easily booked through a local travel agent.

Diving Paradise Dive Center (☎ 28310 26317, ☜ diving -center.gr), 10km west of town off the E75 highway, offers PADI-certificated scuba courses for beginners and facilities for certified divers. They will collect you and return you to your hotel. Kalypso Dive Centre (☎ 28310 74687, ☜ kalypso divecenter.com) also offers PADI beginners and advanced courses. Prices include transfers to and from their dive

centre near Plakiás on the south coast.

Mountain climbing The local EOS mountain climbing club is at Dhimokratias 12 (☎ 28310 57766, ☜ www .eosrethymnou.gr; office open Tues 9–11pm); besides offering advice on climbing, it also organizes walking tours and easy climbs that anyone can join.

Walking tours The Happy Walker, Tombázi 56 (☎ 28310 52920, ☜ happywalker.com; office daily 5–8.30pm, closed weekends in July & Aug), a long-standing Dutch operation near the youth hostel, offers walking tours from one to ten days. Single-day guided walks cost €32 (lunch €11 extra), including transport to and from your hotel to the start point.

3

ACCOMMODATION

The greatest concentration of **rooms** lies in the tangled streets west of the inner harbour, between the Rimóndi fountain and the museums. There are also quite a few places on and around Arkadhíou, behind the town beach, while the resort hotel zone stretches for kilometres eastward along the coast.

AROUND THE HARBOUR AND FORTRESS

Atelier Himáras 25 ☎ 28310 24440, ⊚ frosso-bora.com. This small place near the fortress is run by a talented potter with a studio in the basement. The attractive en-suite a/c rooms come with kitchenette and satellite TV. **€45**

★ **Avli** Xanthoudhídhou 22 ☎ 28310 58250, ⊚ avli.gr. Luxury apartments and suites from the people who run arguably the best restaurant around (see p.196). They're located in a couple of lovingly restored old town houses, with a rooftop terrace and hot tub, free wi-fi and a superb breakfast. **€140**

★ **Barbara Studios** Platía Plastíra 7/Dhamvérgi 14 ☎ 28310 22607, ⊚ barbarastudios.gr. This rambling old building with two entrances shelters beautifully done-up studios sharing a roof garden and various communal areas. **€55**

Ideon Platía Plastíra 10 ☎ 28310 28667, ⊚ hotelideon. gr. Upmarket modern hotel in an excellent location just north of the harbour – try to get a balcony room with a sea view. Rooms come with a/c, TV and internet and there's a pool. Breakfast included. **€80**

Makri Steno Nikifórou Foka 56 ☎ 28310 55465, ⊚ info @makristeno.gr. A somewhat chaotic but welcoming and nicely renovated mansion, with airy a/c studios with TV, huge roof terrace, and washing machine for guests' use. Some slightly more expensive apartments are also available. **€40**

Palazzino di Corina Dhamvérgi 7–9 ☎ 28310 21205, ⊚ corina.gr. Sumptuous luxury rooms and suites in a stunningly restored Venetian palace; rather formal and old-fashioned in atmosphere. The charming patio squeezes in a small pool. Breakfast included. **€100**

Palazzo Vecchio Corner Iróon Politehníou and Melissinoú ☎ 28310 35351, ⊚ palazzovecchio.gr. A delightful small boutique hotel in a restored Venetian mansion, where the elegantly furnished suites and maisonettes all come with cooking facilities, a/c and TV; there's also a small pool. Breakfast included. **€90**

Vecchio Daliáni 4 ☎ 28310 54985, ⊚ vecchio.gr. Hidden away in a narrow alley close to the Rimóndi fountain, this Venetian mansion was one of the city's first boutique hotels, and remains a haven of peace. Rooms, with a/c, balcony and fridge, are set around a courtyard pool; they're showing their age, but this is reflected in the price. **€65**

Veneto Epiménidhou 4 ☎ 28310 56634, ⊚ veneto.gr. Venetian-era monastery lovingly converted to a boutique hotel and restaurant. Each room or suite is unique, but most are furnished with antiques and have hefty beamed ceilings; one, in the basement, occupies a stone monk's cell. **€95**

EASTERN OLD TOWN

Byzantine Vospórou 26 ☎ 28310 55609, ⊚ hotel byzantine.com. Big, if rather basic, a/c rooms in a renovated Byzantine palace, hidden away down an alley, which also has a tranquil patio bar and a roof terrace. Breakfast included. **€65**

Casa Moazzo Tombázi 57 ☎ 28310 36235, ⊚ casa moazzo.gr. Delightful boutique hotel offering six luxurious and stylish suites with king-size beds, jacuzzi, and coffee-and tea-making facilities. Breakfast included. **€135**

Castello Karaolí 10 ☎ 28310 23570, ⊚ castello -rethymno.gr. A very pleasant small *pension* in a 300-year-old Turkish mansion; a/c en-suite rooms come with fridge, TV and cooking facilities and there's a delightful patio garden for taking breakfast (extra), plus a tiny subterranean jacuzzi pool. **€50**

Leo Vafé 2 ☎ 28310 26197, ⊚ leohotel.gr. Elegant boutique hotel in another restored Venetian mansion with eight luxurious and individually styled rooms featuring lots of exposed stonework. All are equipped with fridge and satellite TV and some come with jacuzzi. Breakfast included. **€110**

Olga's Rooms Soulíou 57 ☎ 28310 28665, ⊚ rethymno guide.com/olgas. This rooms place is redolent of an earlier era, though a/c, tv and wi-fi have been added. Basic, but exceptionally friendly and good value, given its location on this touristy street right at the heart of the action. There's even a tiny roof garden. They also have more modern studios in a separate building nearby. Excellent breakfast (€5) served next door in *Stella's Kitchen* (see p.196). **€35**

Sea Front Arkadhíou 159/Venizélou 45 ☎ 28310 24533, ⊚ rethymnoatcrete.com. Attractive a/c rooms in a water-front house, some with sea-view balconies (worth it, for an extra €10), and all with fridge and TV. The welcoming owners also have a number of excellent sea-view apartments nearby. Doubles **€45**, apartments **€50**

★ **Youth Hostel** Tombázi 41 ☎ 28310 22848, ⊚ yhrethymno.com. The cheapest beds in town, in six- to eight-bed dorms. Large, clean, very friendly and popular, it has a café, laundry facilities, free wi-fi, internet access and a multilingual library. **€10**

HOTEL ZONE

Caramel About 7km east of town ☎ 28310 71803, ⊚ caramel.grecotel.com. Classy, all-inclusive luxury on one of the finest stretches of beach; suites with retro, Italian-tiled floors, seafront maisonettes and bungalows with private pool. Usually better value as part of a package. **€360**

3

3

CAMPSITE

Camping Elizabeth About 3km east of town, near the highway junction ☎ 28310 28694, ⊛ camping -elizabeth.net. A large, appealing beachfront site with all facilities, plenty of shade, and regular connections to the city using the hotel zone bus (see p.194). Two people plus tent and car €21.50

EATING

Immediately **behind the town beach** are arrayed the most obvious of Réthymno's restaurants, all with illustrated menus out front and most with waiters who will run off their patter in a variety of languages. These places are sometimes reasonable value – especially if you hanker after an "English breakfast" – but they are all thoroughly touristy. Around the inner harbour there's a cluster of rather more expensive and intimate fish tavernas with annoyingly persistent greeters. The more authentic places are found away from the waterfront, in and around the **old town**.

OLD TOWN AND HARBOUR

★**Alana** Salamínos 15 ☎ 28310 27737, ⊛ alana -restaurant.gr. An attractive, tree-filled courtyard provides the setting for very good, adventurous Cretan-inspired cuisine. Interesting salads and starters followed by the likes of lamb with artichokes in an egg and lemon sauce (€10.30) or sea bass in a citrus sauce with sea fennel (€18.50). Also very good house wine and a range of bottled vintages. May–Oct daily noon–2am.

★**Avli** Xanthoudhídhou 22 ☎ 28310 26213, ⊛ avli.gr. Probably Réthymno's finest restaurant; an upmarket place in a Venetian mansion with an exquisite garden patio serving top-notch food. Traditional Cretan dishes are updated with wider Mediterranean touches: for lunch try the *moussaká* (€11.20) or *Avli* salad (€8.50), or if you're settling in there are excellent three-course menus (€29–39). There's also an extensive wine list. Daily 8am–midnight.

Bakalogatos Petiháki 15 ☎ 28310 20550. Arguably the best place on this crowded, touristy street, *Bakalogatos* serves food *mezedhopolío* style – you tick the items you want on a list – though the menu is actually fairly standard; mains €8–10. Daily noon–2am.

Kyria Maria Moskhovítou 20 ☎ 28310 29078. Tucked down an alley behind the Rimóndi fountain, this unassuming little taverna serves tasty *mezédhes* and good-value fish and meat dishes (chicken *souvláki* €7.50, rabbit in lemon sauce €9, set menu for two with wine from €23); after the meal, everyone gets a couple of Maria's delicious *tyropitákia* with honey, on the house. Daily 8am–midnight.

Melina Hímáras 22 ☎ 28310 21580, ⊛ melina -rethymno.gr. Traditional café/taverna handy for the fortezza, specializing in meat from the outdoor barbecue (€12–18); give them an hour or so's notice and they'll barbecue an entire joint for you. There are great views over the town from the terrace. Daily 10am–1am.

Mojo Burgers Dhamvérgi 38 ☎ 28310 50550. If you need a break from Greek food, *Mojo* serves up excellent burgers (from €3 to €10 for a double with everything) and hot dogs in a diner-style space. Daily noon–1am.

Retro Café Kefaloyiánnidhon 14 ☎ 28310 42269. Retro-style *mezedhopolío* with a seafront terrace just off trendy Platía Plastíra. Meze €4–6 each, or a menu for two with wine and dessert for €18. Daily noon–1am.

Samaria Venizélou 40 ☎ 28310 24681. One of the few seafront places patronized by locals, especially late at night, this place offers simple Greek food, specializing in meat barbecued over a charcoal grill (pork fillet or lamb chops €9). Daily 24hr.

★**Stella's Kitchen** Soulíou 55 ☎ 28310 54896. A great-value and welcoming little diner run by the eponymous and ebullient proprietor. Stella serves up half-a-dozen fresh, home-made daily specials each day (€6–8; at least two are vegetarian); it's also a good spot for breakfast. Mon–Sat 8am–8pm.

To Pigadi Xanthoudhídhou 31 ☎ 28310 27522. An attractive courtyard containing an ancient well (*pigadi*) houses this taverna, where the sometimes wacky flavour combinations (*moussaká* with shrimps and feta €9.40) can be hit and miss, but the traditional staples (like rabbit *stifádho* €12) are usually reliable. April–Nov daily noon–1am.

Zefyros Inner harbour ☎ 28310 28206. If you're determined to eat by the water, you could do worse than this, one of the more reliable of the harbourside fish tavernas, offering reasonably priced (for this location) fish and seafood such as sole fillet stuffed with prawns (€18.50) or fisherman's spaghetti (€17.50). March–Oct daily 10am–midnight.

NEW TOWN

Akros Ikoyeniakon Moátsou 40 ☎ 28310 55403. Modern-style *estiatório*, entirely off the tourist trail, serving hearty daily specials (€5–7) that you choose from the heated trays behind a glass display. Busiest at lunchtime. Mon–Sat noon–10pm.

★**Mesostrati** Yerakári 1 ☎ 28310 29375. An economical neighbourhood taverna-ouzerí serving well-prepared country dishes including tasty *apákia* (smoked pork) or *loukánika* (sausage; both €6). The main reason to come, though, is that there's excellent live Cretan *lyra* and *laoúto* (lute) music Wed–Sat from 9pm. Mon–Sat 10am–3pm & 6pm–2am, Sun 10am–3pm.

Sunset Taverna Periferiákos ☎ 28310 23943. Frequented more for its spectacular sunset views than its food, but the

RÉTHYMNO'S SUMMER FESTIVALS

The **Cretan Diet Festival** (ⓦwww.cretandietfestival.gr) is a week of celebration of Cretan food and wine, along with traditional music and dancing, held in the public gardens in July – it's a fun event with plenty to eat and drink. Later on, at the end of August or early September, the **Renaissance Festival** (ⓦrfr.gr) sees the fortress and venues around the old town host folk and classical music concerts and theatrical events, as well as performances of Classical tragedies and comedies.

meals aren't bad value (menus for two €20 and €25), there's usually a decent selection of fish, and often freshly caught octopus drying on the line. The terrace tables are right by the shore, and it's an ideal place for an ouzo and mezédhes at sunset with the breakers splashing over the rocks below. April–Oct daily 9am–11pm.

Taverna Zambia Stamathioudháki 20 ☎28310 24561. Popular – and good-value – local taverna with a seafront terrace, specializing in fish (sea bream €15, grilled octopus €9, fisherman's spaghetti €9.50) and serving delicious lunchtime *mayireftá* (traditional baked dishes). Daily 11am–midnight.

★**Zisi** Mákhis Krítis 63, Misíria, on the main road in the hotel zone 3km east of town ☎28310 28814, ⓦtaverna-zisis.gr. *Zisi* is one of the great Réthymno institutions, where local families get together for celebrations, especially on Sunday lunchtimes, when booking is advised. The place is large and elegant with real table linen, *mayireftá* (traditional baked dishes) laid out in heated display cabinets and a menu filled with other tempting fish and meat dishes; and it's exceptionally good value (*yemistá* – stuffed vegetables – €4.40; roast beef with lemon, wine and olive oil €7). It's a short taxi or bus ride from the centre. Daily 11am–midnight.

DRINKING AND NIGHTLIFE

Réthymno's **bars and nightlife** are concentrated on the seafront – especially either side of the inner harbour around Venizélou and Platía Plastíra – and up Salamínos and Melissinoú heading inland. The café-cum-cocktail places around the Rimóndi fountain are great for people-watching, but the cacophony of late-evening noise from competing bars is less than relaxing. Summer-only **clubs** operate to the east, among the big hotels, and it's also worth looking out for posters advertising beach parties.

Figaro Social Vernárdhou 23 ☎28310 50797. Arty café-bar that hosts frequent events, from Sunday afternoon jazz to stand-up comedy. Daily 10am–3am.

Fraoules Venizélou 62 ☎28310 24525. One of several lively all-day bar-cafés on this stretch of Venizélou that are especially busy late in the evening with a pre-club local crowd. Occasional events or live music, and good cocktails. Daily 9am–2am.

Galero Platia Petiháki ☎28310 54345. Large beers, toasted sandwiches and snacks served on a terrace overlooking the Rimóndi fountain right at the heart of the action make this one of the most popular places in town for an older generation of tourists, and deservedly so. Daily 8am–2am.

Ice Club Salamínos 22 ☎6949 986 294. One of half a dozen clubs around the junction of Salamínos, Mesolongíou

and Melissinoú, *Ice* is popular with young locals, especially in winter. Daily midnight–early hours.

Metropolis Neárchou 15 ☎28310 56854. Mainstream club in an alley off the inner harbour; it's a relaxed place playing techno and Greek and international pop to a mixed crowd of tourists and locals. They also have regular karaoke nights. Daily 11pm–late.

Nuvel Inner harbour ☎28310 52478. Chic café-bar, open all day, with a large terrace by the harbourfront. The music gets louder as night falls. Daily 9am–late.

O Kipos tou Ali Vafi Vounialí 65 ☎28310 23238. A vaulted tunnel off the street leads to a hidden garden and a cool café-bar with shisha pipes, board games, and events including live Cretan music on Sunday afternoons. They also serve good food. Daily 10am–2am.

SHOPPING

There are interesting **shops** throughout the old town; in general crafts and touristy stores cluster in the area around the Rimóndi fountain and along Ethníkis Andistásis, with boutiques and leather goods on and around Arkadhíou. There's a big **flea market** every Thursday in the car park by the Platía Tessáron Martíron, and on Mondays in the suburb of Kallithéa, just beyond the bus station.

Atelier Himáras 27 ☎28310 24440, ⓦfrosso-bora.com. Studio-workshop selling creative modern ceramics from local potter Frosso Bora. Mon–Sat 10am–9pm.

Bibliopoleío Souliou 43 ☎28310 54307. A handy place for secondhand English-language books in the old town. Mon–Fri 9am–2pm & 6–9pm, Sat 9am–2pm.

Lyranthos Arkadhíou 66 ☎ 28310 29043. Réthymno is a centre of *lyra* and *laoúto* (lute) production, and this is the shop of craftsman Mihailis Katsantonis; they sell CDs of traditional music and gifts as well as musical instruments. Mon–Sat 9am–2pm & 5.30–9pm.

Mediterranean Editions Paleológou 41 ☎ 28310 23398. A good selection of books in English, as well as many foreign newspapers. Mon–Sat 8am–9pm.

Nikos Siragas Kallérgi 38 ☎ 28310 50505, ⓦ www .siragas.gr. Gallery-shop of an internationally recognized wood-turner who produces creative sculptures in olive, eucalyptus, walnut and carob woods, as well as plenty of smaller items at souvenir prices. He also runs wood-turning classes. April–Oct Mon–Sat 10am–2.30pm & 6–10pm.

Raw Materials Arabatsoglou 40 ☎ 28310 58250. The elegant speciality Cretan and Greek food shop of the *Avli*

restaurant (see p.196) stocks many of the island's best wines and olive oils in addition to herbs, cheeses and lots more; all beautifully packaged, if at premium prices. Mon–Sat 10am–2pm & 5.30–9.30pm.

Vasilis Psiharaki Ethnikís Andistásis 41 ☎ 28310 23315. A lovely old-fashioned survivor of a shop selling worry beads, traditional handmade knives and more. Mon–Sat 9am–2pm & 5.30–9pm.

Yeoryios Papalexakis Dhimakópolou 6 ☎ 28310 50842. An extraordinary traditional *lyra*-maker's shop and workshop, apparently little changed since it opened in 1947. Most of the instruments are now crafted by Yeoryios's son Nikos, whom you can watch while he works. Prices for these stunningly crafted instruments range from €150 to more than €1000. Mon–Sat 9am–2pm & 6–9pm.

DIRECTORY

Banks ATMs can be found throughout the centre, but bank branches are mainly in the new town, especially along Koundouriótou east of the Platía Tessáron Martíron.

Laundry Iris, Melissinoú 36 (daily 9am–8pm, service wash from €8; ☎ 28311 04444).

Post office The main post office (Mon–Fri 7.30am–8pm) is on Moátsou, opposite the *Brascos* hotel.

Tourist Police In the waterfront Delfini building, by the marina (☎ 28310 28156).

East of Réthymno: the coast road

Leaving Réthymno to the east you can strike almost immediately onto the **coastal highway**, which runs fast, flat and dull along the coastal plain, or follow the old road, squeezed into the narrow gap between this and the sea. On the latter route you'll pass through a string of village suburbs, connected now by almost continuous hotel development for some 10km. In the hills behind the resort zone a few attractive villages survive, above all **Hromonastíri**, where the nearby **gorge at Míli** offers one of the best walks in the region. Around 15km from Réthymno the nature of the coast changes as you approach the Psilorítis massif: here the small resorts of **Pánormos** and **Balí** occupy coves beneath the road.

Hromonastíri and around

No regular public transport, but several of the bus and Little Train tours of Réthymno wind their way up here daily; the Rethymno City Tour bus (ⓦ rethymnocitytour.gr), for example, is a hop-on, hop-off service that passes through several times a day

One of the most attractive drives you could take out of Réthymno is to **Míli** and **HROMONASTÍRI** (Χρομοναστήρι), hill villages to the southeast of town, with the chance to walk down the Míli gorge on the way back. The road up to Hromonastíri winds attractively up the side of the gorge to arrive at the ancient and beautiful village. Its sights include **Prinari's mill** (daily 10am–5pm; €2), an old olive mill restored as a tiny folk museum, a couple of Byzantine churches, and the **Villa Clodio**, a striking Venetian mansion now run by the Greek army as a military museum, with all sorts of hardware parked outside (Tues–Fri 8am–2pm, Sun 10am–2pm; €1.50).

The Míli Gorge

The entry to the **Míli Gorge** is signed off the road below Hromonastíri, just beneath the village of **Míli**. Considering that you're barely 5km from the centre of Réthymno here, the gorge is pretty impressive, though it can't compare with the great south-coast

SAVE THE TURTLE

The beaches east of Réthymno make up the second largest nesting area in the Mediterranean for the endangered **loggerhead sea turtle**. Loggerheads, once common throughout the Mediterranean, are today under serious threat from the damage wrought by tourism and industry on their breeding habitats.

A seagoing creature for most of its life, the turtle must return to a beach – always the same one – in order to lay its eggs. Unfortunately, nesting occurs from early June to the end of August, coinciding with the high tourist season. Once the female has buried her eighty to a hundred eggs on a nocturnal visit to the beach, the eggs must then remain undisturbed for a period of two months before the hatchlings emerge to head for the sea. But even if they avoid being skewered by a beach umbrella or crushed by the feet of bathers – both common hazards – further dangers lie ahead for the newborn turtles. When they emerge, many of them, instead of heading for the sea, are lured inland by artificial lights from hotel and tourist developments. Emblematic of Crete's and Greece's problem of balancing tourist development and the needs of the environment, it remains to be seen whether the loggerhead turtle will avoid the fate of the dodo.

For **information** on programmes to protect the turtle, making donations or becoming a volunteer, contact the Sea Turtle Protection Society of Greece (☎6937 352 379, ⓦ www .archelon.gr).

ravines. Starting the descent to the bottom of the gorge, you'll find a friendly café-snack bar from where the path down is well signed. In the early sections you'll see the abandoned buildings of an old hamlet, including the mill from which the gorge takes its name; there's plenty of water in the stream, so this is a lush and shady walk. After about an hour, you arrive at the bottom. Here you can either walk back up, or if you walk about twenty minutes more, taking minor roads along the bottom of the gorge, you will come to the main road outside Perivólia, where you can pick up a bus or taxi.

Pánormos

PÁNORMOS (Πάνορμος), 22km east of Réthymno, marks a distinct break in topography: to the west is a long stretch of level coastline, to the east a spectacular, swooping mountain drive on the E75 highway which continues virtually all the way to Iráklio. The village is just a short (poorly signed) detour off the road, a pretty little place with pedestrianized streets and a tiny harbour, with a couple of small beaches either side. Perhaps because the beaches don't amount to much, Pánormos does not attract big crowds even in high season, and as a result holds on to its appealing tranquillity; many visitors rent apartments and stay for weeks or months. The better of the beaches is to the west of the harbour, with a bar-café and sunbeds. Surprisingly, this is also an ancient settlement (a minuscule river runs through to the sea) with the ruins of what was once a large sixth-century **basilica**, probably destroyed in the ninth-century Saracen invasion, and of a later **Genoese castle**.

ARRIVAL AND ACTIVITIES

PÁNORMOS

By bus The Réthymno hotel zone bus runs as far as Pánormos (at least 20 daily; 1hr); there are also fatser highway buses.

Boat trips and tours Most of the boat trips from Balí

call at Pánormos (see p.201); buy tickets at the harbour or from travel agents in town. There's a tourist train that runs to villages way up in the hills, including Margarítes (see p.204).

ACCOMMODATION

Asterion On a low hill above the village ☎28340 51081, ⓦ asterion-panormo.gr. Modern, purpose-built studio and apartment complex on the edge of the village; a family-run, family-friendly place with pool and comfortable units, all with kitchen, balcony, TV and a/c. Studios

€45, apartments €60

Captain's House On the harbour ☎28340 51352, ⓦ captainshouse.gr. Comfortable seafront studios and apartments with the best location in town, directly above the water, though those on the harbourside can be noisy;

there's also a beautiful luxury three-bedroom apartment. Studios €50

Lucy's Pension In the middle of the village ☎ 28340 51212, ⚲ lucy.gr. Excellent and good-value a/c studios, apartments and two-bedroom "maisonettes", all well-equipped with cooking facilities, balcony and TV. The friendly eponymous proprietor lives in an apartment below, and they have a fabulous five-bedroom luxury villa nearby, with pool and sea views. Studios €50, villa €280

EATING AND DRINKING

Places round the harbour have a lovely setting but are mostly very touristy, with international menus; on the whole you'll eat better for less at places on the small section of pedestrianized street immediately inland.

Ankyra East side of the harbour ☎ 28340 51022. The classiest of the harbour tavernas, *Ankyra* (anchor) specializes in fresh fish (mixed grilled fish for two €23; whitebait €6.60) but also has plenty of straightforward Greek and international food. Daily 11am–11pm.

Geronymos Pedestrianized street, directly up from the harbour ☎ 28340 51338. Popular taverna serving quality Cretan food, with well-priced fish, on an atmospheric street terrace beneath a spreading vine. Try the seabass (€10), beef *stifádho* (€8) or lamb in white wine sauce (€8). Daily 1.30–11pm.

Oasis Pedestrianized street, by Steki tou Sifaki ☎ 28340 51390. This very pleasant garden café makes an ideal place for breakfast or a nightcap. They show occasional original-version films on a screen in the garden and host frequent live guitar music. Daily 9am–1am.

★**To Steki tou Sifaki** Pedestrianized street, east of the centre ☎ 28340 51230. Good taverna with an attractive terrace serving delicious family-style traditional food such as stuffed peppers with meatballs (€6.80) or lamb baked with potatoes in lemon sauce (€8). Daily noon–11pm.

Balí

BALÍ (Μπαλί) is a resort set around a series of little coves, 9km east of Pánormos. The place is much bigger than it first appears, especially as the streets are winding and hilly – it's a couple of kilometres from the main road to the village, more to the best beach. Sadly, although the beaches are spectacular, they're very much overrun, and Balí has become a package resort too popular for its own good. It's lively and friendly, but only really tempting out of season, when there are bound to be bargains given the number of rooms.

Balí's beaches

The first beach, immediately below the road, is **Livádhi** (aka Paradise Beach). An extensive stretch of sand, with a row of bars and tavernas behind, it's the biggest, most recently developed and busiest of the beaches, lively at night as well. Balí proper is centred around three west-facing **coves** with pebbly beaches on the promontory beyond. The first is known as **Varkótopos**, with an inflatable fun park offshore and good bars behind; the second, at the centre of the old village, is itself divided in two by a rocky outcrop into **Limáni**, where the harbour is, and Limanákia beaches; a long loop of road then winds round to the final cove (there are short cuts if you walk), generally known as **Evita Beach** after some apartments behind it. This is barely developed and much the most pleasant place to swim – with a patch of sand and, on either side, crags of rock with level places to sunbathe – but still very crowded and overlooked. Two shady **tavernas** just above the beach make reasonable lunch stops.

Moní Áyios Ioánnis

Sat–Thurs 9am–noon & 6–8pm • Reached by turning inland on a good road (though a dangerous exit from the E75) that turns off the highway a short distance west of the resort

A wonderful viewpoint to appreciate Balí's setting is the tiny, part-restored seventeenth-century **Moní Áyios Ioánnis**. The monastery church has some fragmentary seventeenth-century frescoes and mosaics and there's a serene garden fronting the monks' cells (only a couple of monks now remain), but its reputation among Cretans today is for its energetic role in the struggle against Turkish rule, for which it was bombarded in 1866 by the Turkish navy.

ARRIVAL AND DEPARTURE

By bus Buses will drop you by a large service station at the junction with the road into town. It's quite a walk to the centre, so it may be worth considering a taxi (€5; ☎ 28340 23000 or 6987 963 238) or jumping on the tourist train that meets many of the buses and trundles into town.

INFORMATION AND ACTIVITIES

Boat trips and watersports There are day-trips to Réthymno via Pánormos aboard the *Calypso* (Mon, Thurs & Sat; €25; tickets from any travel agent or at the harbour). Captain Lefteris (☎ 28340 94102) offers a daily sail (€70 including lunch and drinks) or sunset cruise (€35 including drinks) in a catamaran, plus motorboat, kayak, pedalo and jet ski rental from the harbour.

Diving Just behind the harbour, Hippocampos (☎ 28340 94193, ⓦ hippocampos.com) is a PADI dive centre offering courses, trial dives and more.

ACCOMMODATION

Bali Beach Hotel Behind Limanákia ☎ 28340 94210, ⓦ balibeach.gr. Taking over much of Limanákia beach, with rooms tumbling down the slope behind it, this is among the fanciest hotels in town, and certainly has the best location. With two pools and balcony rooms with sea view, a/c, TV and fridge it's quite a bargain, especially out of season. Buffet breakfast included; but avoid all-inclusive deals and the rooms in the "Village", much higher up the hill. Free wi-fi in lobby only. April–Oct. **€85**

Bali Blue Bay Hotel On the ridge between Varkótopos cove and Limáni ☎ 28340 20111, ⓦ balibluebay.gr. Friendly, family-run, modern hotel with great views from most rooms and even better ones from the rooftop pool. Buffet breakfast included. Free wi-fi in lobby. April–Oct. **€55**

Dimitris Apartments High above the north side of the harbour ☎ 6973 352 714, ⓦ apts-dimitris.gr. Simple but well-equipped modern studios and two-room apartments, with good views from their balconies. April–Oct. **€35**

Mira Mare Above Varkótopos cove ☎ 28340 94256. Handily located above a supermarket, these en-suite rooms with a/c, fridge and sea views from the balcony are basic but excellent value. April–Oct. **€30**

EATING AND DRINKING

There are supermarkets, cafés and tavernas throughout the resort. A couple of the best **tavernas** are in the old village by the harbour. **Nightlife** tends to consist of late-night drinks at a number of music bars behind the beaches.

La Vida Loca Livádhi Beach ☎ 6940 726 780. Beach bar at the end of the beach where they can make some noise; free loungers for customers by day and a busy dancefloor at night. April–Oct daily 9am–4am.

Panorama In the old village by the harbour ☎ 28340 94217. Occupying a renovated old warehouse, with a superb view from its terrace overlooking the water, *Panorama* has an international menu, though you're best sticking to Greek standards. Specialities include a good-value assorted mezédhes plate (small €9, large €17) and grilled fresh octopus (€8.50). April–Oct daily 9am–11pm.

Porto Paradiso Varkótopos cove ☎ 28340 94201. A good spot for an early or late-evening cocktail, with the waves lapping the shore a mere 20m from the terrace tables. April–Oct daily 9am–2am.

Valentino In the old village by the harbour ☎ 28340 94501. Pleasantly situated harbourfront taverna with a lively terrace serving up the usual standards (*kléftiko* €7.90) as well as fresh fish (mixed plate €10.50). April–Oct daily 8am–11pm.

The foothills of Psilorítis

Taking the old roads east from Réthymno, through the **foothills of the Psilorítis** range, there are a variety of routes to choose from or combine. On the whole, the higher you head, the more interesting and scenic the road, though also more twisty and tortuous. The low road, through Dhamásta, has least to offer, though it's a pretty enough drive and takes you close to the historic cave at **Melidhóni**. If you head inland earlier, the **monastery of Arkádhi** is an obvious first stop – gateway both to the highest roads around the northern edge of the massif, and to the route south through the Amári valley (see p.210) on its western flank. This will take you through the potters' village of **Margarítes** and scenic archeological site of **Arhéa Eléftherna**, and on towards **Anóyia** via the remarkable caves at **Sfendóni**. The northern branch of the **E4 footpath** winds through this area, offering numerous attractive short walks.

Moní Arkádhi

25km southeast of Réthymno • Daily: April–Oct 9am–7pm; Nov–March 9am–4pm • €2.50 • ⓦ arkadimonastery.gr

MONÍ ARKÁDHI (**Μονή Αρκαδίου**) is, for Cretans, a shrine to the nineteenth-century struggle for independence. Historical resonance apart, the monastery's striking architecture and highly scenic location are reason enough to visit. It won't take you long to see the place: you can peer into the roofless **vault** beside the cloister where the 1866 explosion (see box below) took place, and wander about the rest of the well-restored grounds. The bulk of the buildings were relatively unscathed by the explosion and Arkádhi is still a working monastery. Of the surviving buildings the **church** is the most impressive, its rich mix of styles placing it among the finest Venetian structures left in Crete. The rest of the monastery is mainly seventeenth-century (though it was originally founded as early as the eleventh). A small **museum** and Gallery of Cretan Warriors (wielding rifles and fierce moustaches) is devoted to the exploits of the defenders of the faith, with a variety of mementoes and tributes, blood-stained clothing and commemorative medals. Opposite the monastery (next to its cafeteria-taverna) is a monumental **ossuary** where skulls and bones of a few of the explosion's victims are displayed behind glass.

ARRIVAL AND DEPARTURE

By bus From Réthymno there are 3 daily buses (2 at weekends; 40min), as well as countless tours.

By car If driving, watch out for the road layout: the Réthymno–Amári road passes the monastery on one side,

the route east towards Anóyia starts on the other; they're connected only by the unpaved track through the monastery's car park.

ACCOMMODATION AND EATING   MONÍ ARKÁDHI

Food is available from the monastery's cafeteria-taverna, and there are plenty of picnic spots nearby, but more attractive places to eat can be found in almost any direction, especially in the Amári valley (see p.214) or Margarítes (see p.204). Nearby is a unique hotel, though.

Kapsaliana Village Hotel Kapsalianá, 4km north of Arkádhi ☎ 28310 83400, ⓦ kapsalianavillage.gr. The monastery's former olive oil factory, abandoned in 1955, along with most of the homes of the hamlet that grew up around it, have been transformed into a chic boutique hotel. Luxurious rooms and suites, each unique, feature plenty of exposed beams and stonework, and are surrounded by gardens containing a pool and high-class restaurant. **€155**

A SHRINE TO CRETAN INDEPENDENCE

Historically, Arkádhi was one of the richest monasteries in Crete and a well-known stopover for travellers, as well as a centre of resistance. In the 1820s eighty Muslims, who had occupied the monastery to pacify local rebels, were captured and put to death; in retaliation, many of the buildings were burned.

It is the events of **1866**, however, which guarantee Arkádhi a place in history. In the rebellion of that year the monastery served as a Cretan stronghold in which, as the Turks took the upper hand, hundreds of Cretan guerrillas and their families took refuge. Here they were surrounded by a Turkish army until, after a siege of two days, the defences were finally breached on November 9, 1866. As the attackers poured in, the ammunition stored in the monastery exploded – deliberately fired, according to the accepted version of events, on the orders of the abbot. Hundreds were killed in the initial blast, Cretans and Turks alike, and most of the surviving defenders were put to death by the enraged assailants. This incited a wave of international sympathy for the cause of **Cretan independence**. Figures as disparate as Victor Hugo, Garibaldi and the poet Swinburne were moved to public declarations of support, and in Britain money was raised for a ship (the *Arkádhi*) to run the Turkish blockade. Though Crete's liberty was still some way off at that stage, the monastery remains the most potent symbol of the struggle (and the anniversary of the blast is commemorated on November 7–9 each year). More recently the monastery lent assistance to guerrilla fighters during **World War II**: George Psychoundakis (see p.353), for example, describes handing over supplies from a parachute drop to the monks.

Arhéa Eléftherna

From Arkádhi a lovely, lonely road winds through the village of Néa Eléftherna to the far more interesting hamlet of **ARHÉA ELÉFTHERNA** (Αρχαία Ελεύθερνα) and the spectacular acropolis of ancient **Eléftherna**. The ancient city that stood here was one of the most important in eighth- and seventh-century BC Dorian Crete; when the Romans came in search of conquest in 67 BC it put up a stiff resistance, and later flourished as the seat of a Christian bishop. The Saracen invasions finished it off, however.

Acropolis of Eléftherna

Signed from the centre of the village • Free

The **acropolis of Eléftherna** enjoys a magnificent defensive position on a steep-sided spur of rock surrounded by narrow ravines. It is approached via a narrow, natural causeway, carved in ancient times to resemble paving stones, at the end of which a hefty *pírgos* or **tower** (which in large part still stands) protects the narrow entrance to the acropolis itself. The E4 path (which seems blocked on the east side) climbs out of the western valley onto the acropolis – immediately below the point where it joins the main path, remarkable **Roman cisterns** are carved into the hill's west side, with enormous pillars of solid rock supporting a cavernous interior. Further out along the promontory (it's a good fifteen-minute walk to the end) are numerous scattered fragments of massive walls and ancient buildings, not always easy to make sense of, as well as the roofless ruined ancient church of **Ayía Ánna**, still revered as a shrine by locals.

In the valley below you can see both the **main site of ancient Eléftherna**, to the east, and, to the northwest, its **necropolis**. Both have impressive-looking visitor facilities but (see below) are currently closed. At the necropolis, archeologists made a potentially very significant discovery: traces of a **human sacrifice** made in front of the funeral pyre of some local magnate. It apparently dates from the late eighth century BC, about the same time that Homer was describing very similar sacrifices of Trojan prisoners in front of the funeral pyre of Achilles. The victim, who was bound hand and foot before ritually having his throat cut, may well have been expected to serve the dead man in the next world: also found in front of the pyre were sacrificed animals and offerings of perfume and food. Other cremations on the site (some twenty have been found, though only one human sacrifice) had offerings including gold, jewellery and fine pottery, as well as four tiny, superbly crafted **ivory heads** which are among the best work of their time (c.600 BC) yet discovered anywhere. A futuristic-looking **museum** for finds from the site has been built just outside Néa Elefthérna and was due (along with the sites) to open in 2016; given the continuing economic crisis it seems unlikely that it will.

Sotíros Chrístos

Signed where the road from Margarítes heads out of Arhéa Eléftherna • Usually unlocked in daylight hours

Sotíros Chrístos is a beautiful tenth-century Byzantine chapel in a picturesque setting beside a spring-fed pool. Inside there's a fine twelfth-century *Pandokrátor* in the dome, the only surviving **fresco** of what must once have been a glorious painted interior.

The Hellenistic bridge

On the river north of the acropolis • Easiest approach is from Néa Eléftherna, where a track and the E4 path head steeply downhill towards the Necropolis archeological site; from here on foot you can follow the track north along the valley for 15min or so to the bridge; the track can also be reached on the E4 descending from the acropolis

The remarkable stone-built **Hellenistic bridge**, standing 5m high and 3m deep, dates from roughly 300 BC. Its vaulted arch is almost perfectly intact and still capable of carrying traffic across the river. Beneath the arch is a washing and bathing place cut into the rock, probably dating from the same era.

Margarítes

A very pretty place on the edge of a ravine, with views back towards the coast, **MARGARÍTES (Μαργαρίτες)** has a long tradition of making **pottery**. A hundred years ago there were as many as eighty sizeable workshops here, producing all sorts of items for everyday and agricultural use. Today, smaller artisan producers are scattered throughout the village, and you can buy their work in a dozen or more outlets along the steep main street. Off the village's lower square, a well-signed path leads to **Moní Sotíros Chrístos**, or Áyios Gedeón, a ruined monastery that has been partly restored by its last remaining monk. The ancient church is usually open and the beautifully tended grounds are a flowery haven of peace and birdsong (from caged songbirds) – all the work of the same monk.

ARRIVAL AND DEPARTURE   MARGARÍTES

By bus On weekdays there are two daily buses to and from Réthymno (40min), at 6am and 2pm, returning

as soon as they arrive.

ACCOMMODATION AND EATING

Irini Apartments At the northern end of the village ☎ 28340 92494, ⊛ irini-apartments.com. Welcoming proprietors with two simple but well-equipped apartments in the lower village. €30

★**Kouriton House** In the hamlet of Tzanakianá, immediately north of Margarítes ☎ 6945 722 052, ⊛ kouritonhouse.gr. An eighteenth-century stone-built house, creatively converted to rooms, each unique and furnished in traditional style. Owner Anastasia is an expert on the local area – which she promotes as an open-air "ecomuseum" – and also runs activities including local walks, cookery classes and harvesting olives. Wonderful

Greek breakfast included. €55

★**Taverna Mantalos** Main square ☎ 28340 92294. On the village's attractive upper platía, this great little taverna has a shady terrace offering fine views over the valley. The friendly proprietors cook up tasty traditional Cretan food including delicious *kolokithoánthi yemistá* (stuffed courgette flowers, €5); daily specials are €7–9. Daily 9am–10.30pm.

Taverna Velanidia Just above the village, almost opposite Tsikalario ☎ 28340 92520, ⊛ belanidiahotel.gr. Good-value, a/c, en-suite rooms with balcony, fridge and TV above a decent taverna in a tranquil, leafy setting. €30

SHOPPING

E&A Main street just below the main square ☎ 6932 384 054, ⊛ eaceramicstudio.com. Arty, handcrafted earthenware based on a modern interpretation of traditional forms. Daily 10am–6pm.

Kerameion Main street above the main square ☎ 28340 92015, ⊛ keramion.gr. Creative potter Yiorgos Dalamvelas derives inspiration for his traditionally made ceramics from Minoan and Byzantine originals; lovely plates

and bowls with fish and olive motifs. Daily 10am–5pm.

Tsikalario Just above the village, by the road junction ☎ 28340 92000, ⊛ tsikalario.gr. The workshop of Nikos Kafgalakis is one of the largest and most traditional in town, turning out enormous *píthoi*, similar to those found in the Minoan palaces and still used throughout agricultural Crete today, as well as plenty of smaller and more decorative items. Daily 9am–6pm.

The Melidhóni Cave

Signed from the village of Melidhóni, 4km from the substantial town of Pérama, on the lower road • Daily: June–Sept 9am–8pm; April, May & Oct 9am–7pm • €3.50

The **Melidhóni Cave** was the setting for one of the most horrific **atrocities** in the struggle for Cretan independence (see box opposite). In terms of sheer size, it is also one of the most impressive on the island, and one can easily imagine the refugees sheltering in its cathedral-like space. Mythology holds that the cave was the home of **Talos**, a bronze giant who protected the coasts of Crete by striding around the island hurling rocks at unfriendly ships; the Argonauts were greeted thus when they approached. Excavations in the cave have shown that it was inhabited during the Neolithic period and later was an important shrine for the **Minoans**, who may have worshipped their fertility goddess Eileithyia here. The Greeks and Romans transformed it into a shrine to the god **Hermes Tallaios**, evidenced by thousands of inscriptions etched into the walls of one of the cave's inner chambers.

THE MELIDHÓNI MASSACRE

In 1824, during one of the early rebellions against Ottoman dominance, around three hundred villagers took refuge in the Melidhóni Cave, as they had often done before at time of war. This time, however, the Muslim commander demanded that they come out. When the Cretans refused, and shot two messengers sent to offer safe conduct, he tried to force them out by blocking the mouth of the cave with stones and cutting off the air supply. After several days of this, with the defenders opening new air passages every night, the troops changed their tactics, piling combustible materials in front of the cave and setting light to them; everyone inside was asphyxiated. The bodies were left where they lay for the cave to become their tomb; ten years later traveller and historian Robert Pashley, one of the first to enter after the tragedy, found "the bones and skulls of the poor Christians so thickly scattered, that it is almost impossible to avoid crushing them as we pick our steps along". This grisly event was far from unique: numerous other caves around the island have similar histories, although none claimed so many victims.

Today, the awesome **central chamber** shelters a shrine and ossuary commemorating the victims of the massacre, along with petrified "draperies", spectacular curtain-like folds formed by the calcium deposits, and hefty stalagmites and stalactites, though most of the latter have long since been broken off. Outside, the owners of the site run a friendly café.

The Sfendóni Cave

Signed from the village of Zoniá, or from Axós on the lower road • April–Oct daily 10am–5pm; Nov–March Sat & Sun 10.30am–2.30pm; guided tours every 40–50min • €4

The **Sfendóni Cave**, also known (and signed) as the Zonianá Cave, is the largest cave complex in Crete that's open to the public: local legend has it that the cave was discovered by an eight-year-old girl who, lured away by fairies, was later found dead in its darkest recesses. Today, enthusiastic and knowledgeable guides conduct you along walkways through a series of caverns, extending some 500m into a spur of Mount Psilorítis. There are magnificent displays of stalactites, stalagmites and petrified waves, many more than five million years old. At the entrance there's a giant visitor centre with a café and shop, where you may have to wait some time for a tour.

Anóyia

ANÓYIA (Ανώγεια), a small town perched beneath the highest peaks of the Psilorítis range, is the obvious place from which to approach the **Idean Cave** (see p.208) and, for the committed, the **summit of Psilorítis** itself (see p.209). The weather, refreshingly cool when the summer heat lower down is becoming oppressive, is one good reason to come, but most people are drawn by the proximity of the mountains or by a reputation for some of the best woven and embroidered **handicrafts** in Crete. The last is greatly exaggerated but this exceptionally friendly town still makes a pleasant break from the coast. The town also has a reputation as a centre of **lyra** playing and has a buoyant **sheep farming** sector; don't miss the local cheese, or the spit-roast lamb if you're carnivorously inclined.

On first impression it seems that Anóyia has two quite distinct halves: coming from the west you enter what appears to be the older, lower town, before the road takes a broad loop around to re-emerge near the upper town's large, modern-looking **Platía Meídani**, lined with youthful bars. The upper town has almost all the accommodation as well as the bank (with ATM) and post office, police and most of the non-tourist stores. In many ways this appearance is deceptive. A series of steep, sometimes stepped alleys connect the two directly, and however traditional the buildings may look, closer inspection shows that most are actually concrete. This reflects a tragic history – the village was one of those destroyed in 1944 as a reprisal for the abduction of **General Kreipe** (see p.338), when all the men who could be rounded up here were executed. Their names are chillingly recorded on the war memorial by the upper town's church.

Skoulas Museum

Signed from Platía Livádhi • Mon–Sat 9am–6pm • Free

The Skoulas family is one of Anóyia's biggest, and the one-room **Skoulas Museum** is dedicated to local artist Alkiviades Skoulas, who took up painting in his late 60s, sculpture in his 70s, and died in 1996 aged 94. As well as guiding visitors around his father's striking, naive works, museum curator Yeoryios Skoulas frequently treats visitors to a deft performance on the *lyra*; if the museum is closed, simply ask around for Yeoryios.

ARRIVAL AND DEPARTURE   ANÓYIA

By bus Three buses a day (one on Sun) run between Iráklio and Anóyia (1hr), and on weekdays there are two daily buses to and from Réthymno (1hr 30min).

ACCOMMODATION

Anóyia sees a lot of day-trippers, but most stay only an hour or so. Linger a while, or stay overnight, and it's surprisingly uncommercial. It shouldn't be hard to find a **room** in the upper town, where the best places line the ring road (Periferiákos) that climbs parallel to the main road on the east side of the village.

★ **Hotel Aristea** Periferiákos ☎28340 31584, ⍵hotel aristea.gr. Lovely room and apartment complex run by the irrepressible Aristea, her daughter and granddaughter (both also called Aristea). There's a beautiful maisonette for up to six people, as well as family duplex apartments and simpler rooms, all with sensational views.Good-value breakfast available. Doubles **€35**, apartments **€50**

Hotel Marina Periferiákos ☎28340 31817, ⍵marina hotelanogia.gr. Three-star modern hotel with studio rooms with kitchenette; most with fabulous views from their balconies. Enquire at *Rooms Aris* if no one's around. **€40**
Rooms Aris Periferiákos ☎28340 31817, ⍵arishotel anogia.gr. A pleasant flower-bedecked place with cosy, en-suite rooms with balcony views, TV and fridge. **€30**

EATING AND DRINKING

The speciality of most local tavernas is huge, fatty cuts of lamb (and other meats), grilled outdoors over wood or charcoal. This is best at lunchtime – in the evening you'll be eating whatever is left over.

Aetos Main street, upper village ☎28340 31262. Famous local taverna with a wood-fired grill and spacious terrace. Traditional specialities include goat dishes and local yoghurt and cheese, as well as a mouthwatering *ofto* (wood-fire-roasted lamb; €9 a portion). Daily 11am–11pm.
Arodamos Upper village, on the Psilorítis road ☎28340 31100. Exceptionally friendly place with a limited menu of local dishes, all of it sourced locally and some from their own farm and dairy; great lamb, and *saganáki* with their own cheese. Mains €7–9. Daily 10am–11pm.
Mihalos Platía Livádhi ☎28340 31396. Tavernas in the lower town are on the whole not great value, but this retro *kafenío* right on the square is a perfect people-watching spot serving breakfast, drinks, snacks and delicious *galaktoboúreko* (traditional custard pie). Daily 8am–midnight.

SHOPPING

Tarrha Glass Upper village, on the Psilorítis road ☎28340 31357, ⍵tarrhaglass.com. The studio-shop of creative glass designers Marios Chalkiadakis and Natasha Papadogamvraki, who, besides glasses, vases

---

THE LYRA IN ANÓYIA

Anóyia is a noted centre of **lyra music** – many of the greatest performers on the instrument have come from here. Among them, the late, self-taught Nikos Xylouris was a shepherd who made his own *lyra*, and whose performances and compositions made him a Cretan legend in the 1960s and 1970s. The house where he was born, on Platía Livádhi, is now the tiny *Kafenion Xylouris*, where you can get a glass of *rakí* or house wine, and here, or more frequently in the music cafés of the upper town, you may well have the chance to hear local performers.

EMBROIDERY IN ANÓYIA

Shops and stalls bedecked with local embroidery line the streets leading off **Platía Livádhi** in the lower town. This local handicraft tradition arose in part from bitter necessity, with so large a proportion of the local men killed in 1944. As a way of surviving it seems to have worked, and a few elderly widows (accompanied now by their daughters and granddaughters) remain anxious to subject any passing visitor to their aggressive sales techniques. The traditional feel of the lower town is reinforced by the elderly men, baggy trousers tucked into their black boots, moustaches bristling, who sit at the *kafenía* tables around the square.

---

and the like, also produce larger exotic glass sculptures. An immaculate two-tone 1968 Triumph Herald usually stands outside. Mon–Fri 9am–2pm & 5.30–9pm, Sat 9am–2pm.

Mount Psilorítis

At 2456m, **MOUNT PSILORÍTIS (Ψηλορείτης)**, also known as Mount Ida, is the highest mountain in Crete. It's 21km from Anóyia to the **Nídha plateau** (1400m) at its base – a steady climb most of the way, along a road travelled little except by the shepherds who pasture their sheep up here. In late spring, as the snow recedes, you'll see myriad wildflowers and, at all times, quite a few birds, including vultures and magnificent golden eagles. The *mitáta* or stone huts near the roadside – many of them ruined – are former shepherds' dwellings; many are now used as dog kennels and chicken coops.

Somewhere near the highest point a signed road leads off left for 3km to the **Skínakas Observatory**, sitting atop the peak of the same name (open on occasional weekends in summer – dates should be posted on a board at the start of the road or at Ⓦwww .skinakas.org.gr). A little further along, a track to the right goes to the **ski area**, which sees plenty of snow in season. Soon after, the small plateau and its bare summer pastures fan out below you, and the road drops to skirt around its western edge. At the end of the road, overlooking the plain, stands a crumbling and abandoned **visitor centre** and the *Taverna Nida* (see p.210).

The Idean Cave

A 15min climb on a well-signed path opposite the *Taverna Nida* • Visitor facilities have been built at the cave, but have never opened and show no sign of doing so; for the moment you can approach the mouth for free, but not go far in; in spring, and even early summer, the entrance can be blocked with snow

The celebrated **Idean Cave** rivals that on Mount Dhíkti (see p.143) for the title of **Zeus's birthplace**. Although scholarly arguments rage over the exact identity of the caves in the legends of Zeus, and over interpretation of versions of the legend, locals are in no doubt that the Idean Cave is the place where the god was brought up, suckled by wild animals. Certainly this hole in the mountainside, which as Cretan caves go is not especially large or impressive, was associated from the earliest times with the cult of Zeus, and at times ranked among the most important centres of pilgrimage in the Greek world. Pythagoras visited the cave, Plato set *The Laws* as a dialogue along the pilgrimage route here, and the finds within indicate offerings brought from all over the eastern Mediterranean. First signs of occupation go back as far as 3000 BC, and though it may then have been a mere place of shelter, by the Minoan era it was already established as a shrine, maintaining this role until about 500 AD.

Climbing Psilorítis

The *Taverna Nida* (see p.210) and visitor centre mark the start of the way (now forming a stretch of the E4 path) to the **summit of Psilorítis**. Though it's not for the unwary or unfit, the climb should present few problems to experienced, properly equipped hikers, and there are also **guided ascents** (including by moonlight) from Thrónos (see p.210). The route, which diverts from the path to the Idean Cave just beyond the small spring and chapel, is marked with red arrows in addition to the E4 waymarkers – a guide who knows the mountain would be useful, since it's not always obvious which is the main trail, but is by no means essential. The *Anavasi Psilorítis* map (see p.41) is the best available for this area and clearly marks the routes described here. Don't attempt the ascent alone, however, as you could face a very long wait for help if you were to run into trouble. If you do make the climb, allow for a six- to eight-hour return trip to the chapel at the summit, and be prepared in spring for thick snow to slow you down. Carry enough food, water and warm gear to be able to overnight in one of the shelters should the weather turn; a night at the top, with the whole island laid out in the sunset and sunrise, is a wonderful experience.

Only in the last twenty minutes or so of the climb does the peak of Psilorítis itself become visible and the ground start to fall away to reveal just how high you are. The **summit** is marked by a shelter and the chapel of **Tímios Stavrós** ("Holy Cross" – a name by which the peak is sometimes known locally), inside which Nikos Kazantzákis famously claimed to have lost his virginity. Nearby there's water in a cistern, which you should boil or purify before drinking. On a (rare) clear day the spectacular **panoramas** from the summit – including the Lefká Óri (White Mountains) rising in the west and the Dhíkti massif to the east – make the climb well worthwhile.

3

Alternative routes

There are any number of **alternate routes** up and down the mountain. From the west the obvious departure point is Fourfourás in the Amári valley, along the route of the E4. This is relatively straightforward in the sense that you can see the peak almost all the way, though it can be hard to find the start of the path, or to work out which is the main trail at times, despite the waymarking: it's also much further, a 2000m ascent and at least five or six hours climbing. There's a mountain hut about halfway up, run by the EOS in Réthymno (see p.194). The proprietors of the *Windy Place* taverna-rooms in Fourfourás (see p.214) can provide details of a short cut, which involves taking your car a good way up the mountain. With care you can take a vehicle to the tree line (about 1hr), from where it's about a three-hour trek to the summit, two hours back down. South of the mountain, **Kamáres** is another possible trailhead, on yet another branch of the E4. Again,

---

THE DESCENT FROM NÍDHA TO KAMÁRES

While most people are here to climb **Psilorítis**, there is also a good 5hr hike down from Nídha to Kamáres, via the huge **Kamáres Cave**, where the first great cache of the elaborate pottery known as Kamáres ware was found – it's now in the Iráklio Archeological Museum. You can either follow the E4 towards the summit for around an hour and a half, until you reach a basin (Kollita) where the trails meet, and descend south from there, or you can take the track which heads south from the *Taverna Nida* (see p.210). This is a much flatter route, but also significantly harder to follow in the later stages, so you're advised to check directions first; get it right and you will eventually approach the cave (a short detour off the E4) from the east. The track initially leads to a gully, which shortly after becomes a considerable ravine. Here, large red arrows direct you towards Kamáres and the cave. For **Vorízia**, follow the ravine for about an hour until a faint trail climbs out on the left (soon after this, the stream bed becomes impassable). Above the ravine there are fine views and a heady drop for another hour, when you must turn left (east) again. This is not obvious, but you should begin to see signs of life – goat trails and shepherds' huts. You cut past the top of a second, smaller ravine to a stone hut and then descend, zigzagging steeply, to a dirt road and Vorízia village.

Neither Kamáres nor Vorízia has a lot to offer when you arrive. In Kamáres the trail emerges at the eastern end of the village, opposite a very basic taverna. Ask here and you may be able to find a room; the only other facilities are a couple of old-fashioned *kafenía*. Vorízia has neither food nor accommodation.

3

THE WILDEST CAT IN CRETE

In Cretan myth and legend there have long been told tales of the **fourokattos** ("furious cat"), a mountain wildcat. Although in 1905 two skins from such a beast were bought at the market in Haniá by a British woman attached to a scientific mission, for most of the last century scientists regarded the existence of such a creature as unlikely. They also dismissed the stories of shepherds and goatherds who claimed to have seen this wild cat.

Then, in 1996, an Italian university team studying the carnivores of the Cretan mountains were astonished when they returned to their traps one morning to find they had snared a 5.5-kilo wildcat. The news created a sensation as the beast was taken to the University of Crete for study before being released back into the wild equipped with a radio tracking device. Tawny and with small lynx-like tufts, the cat does not belong to the subspecies of cats on the mainland of Greece and the rest of Europe; its nearest relative is a species inhabiting North Africa and Sardinia. Scientists believe that it is an extremely reclusive and nocturnal animal, which explains why it is so rarely seen.

The cat's discovery has not only proven generations of Cretans right, but has turned the zoological history of the island upside down. Recent research has produced evidence of more wildcats, but there are serious concerns for the future as its natural environment is encroached upon by development. Scientists are now puzzling over how the animal got to Crete in the first place – was the cat perhaps brought over as a domesticated beast by the ancestors of the Minoans, or has it been on Crete since the island became separated from the mainland?

---

this is a much more substantial ascent than from the plateau, starting from around 900m, and with some stiff climbing in the early stages.

ACCOMMODATION AND EATING   MOUNT PSILORÍTIS

Taverna Nida End of the road, Nidha plateau ☎ 28340 31141. Almost as run-down as the adjacent visitor centre, the taverna serves hearty Greek standards (mains €7–9) and has a couple of basic rooms sharing a bathroom. Stelios Stavrakakis, the proprietor, is a fount of information on the plateau and can advise (in Greek only) on the viability of walking routes in the mountains, as well as likely weather conditions. April–Sept daily all day; Oct–March Sat & Sun only. **€25**

The Amári valley

The **Amári valley** is one of those areas, like Sfakiá, which features prominently in almost everything written about Crete – especially in tales of **wartime resistance** – yet which is hardly explored at all by modern visitors. Shadowed by the vast profile of Psilorítis, its way of life survives barely altered by the changes of the last twenty or even fifty years. Throughout the valley, isolated hamlets subsist on the ubiquitous olive, with the occasional luxury of an orchard of cherries (especially around Yerakári), pears or figs, and throughout there are a startling number of richly frescoed **churches**. It's an environment conducive to slow exploration, with a climate noticeably cooler than the coast, and in midsummer the trees, flowers and general greenery make a stunning contrast to the rest of the island.

Coming from Réthymno you can either turn south at the first highway junction or take a slightly more circuitous route via the monastery at Arkádhi (see p.202). There are two **roads** through the valley, too, one following the **eastern** side and clinging to the flanks of the Psilorítis range, the other tracing the edge of the lesser Kédhros range on the **western** side. Both are scenically spectacular, but the eastern route probably has the edge in terms of beauty. On a day-trip, of course, you can do a complete circuit of both routes.

Thrónos and around

The first of the real Amári villages, at the head of the valley and close to the junction of both the routes in, is **THRÓNOS** (Θρόνος). Thrónos stands on the site of ancient Syvritos, and like so many of these villages seems lost in the past, with its beautifully frescoed eleventh-century **church of the Panayía** and majestic views. In the Byzantine era this was the seat of a bishop (hence *thrónos*, throne) and these early Christian days are recalled by the remains of the mosaic floor of the much larger original (fourth-century) church which spreads around the current building, with brightly-coloured traces both inside and out. Someone will usually appear with the key as soon as you start to take an interest in the church; if not enquire at either of the *kafenía* next door or at *Rooms Aravanes*.

The acropolis of Sývritos

On the hill above the village are the remains of the **acropolis of ancient Sývritos**, easily reached by following a path signed on the left beyond the church. Founded in the twelfth century BC in the troubled Late Minoan period, the original settlement seems to have been more a refuge from mainland invaders (similar to those at Karfí and Présos in eastern Crete) than a real town. Most of the remains visible today, however, date from the substantial Greco-Roman town that flourished from the fifth century BC into the early Byzantine period, when the modern resort of Ayía Galíni served as its port. The town was destroyed by the Saracens in the ninth century. At the top of the hill is a radio mast and plenty of ancient ruins, but above all there are spectacular views in all directions.

Moní Asomáton

Outside Thrónos, a confusing slew of roads converge at a junction by the **Moní Asomáton**, just a couple of kilometres away. The *Kafenio Klados* here is a wonderfully old-fashioned place, full of local farmers. A palm-lined drive leads into an agricultural school (which occupies the monastery's lands) and the abandoned monastery, mostly crumbling but whose church has a beautiful carved and painted iconostasis (altarpiece). Between Thrónos and Asomáton you'll see signs to the "**Monumental Olive of Jenna**", an olive tree said to be well over two thousand years old, and to the church of **Ayía Paraskévi**, a beautiful dome-in-cross church now isolated in the middle of nowhere. Both are in fields off a very rough track, and most easily reached on foot.

Monastiráki archeological site

Just outside the village of Monastiráki, 3km from Asomáton • Tues–Sun 8am–3pm • €2

The archeological site of **Monastiráki**, though little known or visited, is an important and substantial one: a Middle Minoan settlement that may have been an important trading and agricultural centre. Indeed the archeologists currently working here apparently believe that it may even have been a palace to rival Knossós or Festós – though little of their work has so far been published. At any rate it has a gorgeous setting beneath Psilorítis and there's plenty to see, including a maze of little rooms or storage areas, hefty

---

HIKES FROM THRÓNOS

The proprietor of *Rooms Aravanes* (see p.214) conducts **guided treks** to the peak of **Mount Psilorítis** (€70, including meals). Although he does take groups up in the daytime, his preferred approach is during the full moons of June, July and August, which avoids the extreme summer temperatures. Phone in advance for details; it's not a difficult climb, but you'll need sturdy footwear and a sleeping bag. On the **night walks**, the summit is reached at around dawn, and the sunrise is always spectacular. On the route down, you'll visit a goatherd's *mitáto* (stone mountain hut) where you can sample delicious cheese made on the spot.

You can also get details at *Aravanes* of other **hikes** from Thrónos; again, guided tours are available (€20/hr). These include a relatively easy route north through the foothills in a couple of hours to the monastery of **Arkádhi** (see p.202). The first half of this follows the road, before you head off cross-country to the east. South from Thrónos an extremely easy stroll on a paved road runs into the main valley via **Kalóyeros**. Fifteen minutes' walk beyond Kalóyeros, a narrow path on the left leads uphill to the small stone church of **Áyios Ioánnis Theológos**, whose fine but decayed frescoes date from 1347 – the church should be open. This walk can be extended into a two-hour trek back to Thrónos.

walls, lime-plastered floors and some larger, later Hellenistic buildings. In the village of **MONASTIRÁKI (Μοναστηράκι)** stands a giant plane tree allegedly blessed by Zeus never to lose its leaves, and beneath it an ancient washing-place and a cistern full of frogs.

Amári

The village of **AMÁRI (Αμάρι)** lies right at the heart of the valley, easily reached from either the eastern or the western roads, and has fair claim to be the valley's prettiest: it looks like nothing so much as a perfect Tuscan hill village – note the steeply sloping roofs to cope with the winter snows, and the chimneys for wood fires. There's very little to do here – though the *Café Petrakeion*, on the central platía, serves good, simple food – but there are scintillating views across to Psilorítis and west towards Méronas. For a bird's-eye view, climb the **Venetian clock tower** that dominates the narrow alleyways (the door is always open). Just outside the village, the church of **Ayía Ánna**, reached down a lane on the western edge opposite the police station, has some extremely faded **frescoes** – dating from 1225, they are among the oldest on Crete.

The eastern Amári valley

The eastern side of the valley, with the peak of Psilorítis almost directly above and the softer lines of Mount Kédhros facing you, is much less populated than the west. After Asomáton there's little on the road until you reach **Fourfourás**, some 10km away, a substantial village with facilities including an ATM and a friendly, excellent-value **taverna** and **rooms** place. From here the E4 heads up to the summit of Psilorítis (see p.208) and it's also the trailhead for some arduous hikes to the lesser peaks.

Kouroútes, 15km southeast of Amári, is a tiny place with two things going for it: hereabouts you get your first views of the south coast, and there's an excellent **place to stay** (see p.214). From here another just about driveable track heads up towards the peaks – this one going to the mountain hut at Prínos, the halfway point of the E4.

At the small village of **Níthavris**, 4km south of Kouroútes, the road divides. South, you can continue to the village of **Apodhoúlou** (a worthwhile 3km detour even if you're not continuing this way) and then on to circumnavigate Psilorítis or cut down to the south coast and Ayía Galíni. Head west and you can again choose to head to Ayía Galíni, or curve round to complete a circuit of the Amári valley. These roads divide at the hamlet of **Áyios Ioánnis**; on the route south, **Ayía Paraskeví** has fine sixteenth-century **frescoes** in the small **church of the Panayía**. The road to Hordháki, on the western side of the valley, is narrow, winding and neglected.

Apodhoúlou

On the way into the village of **APODHOÚLOU (Αποδούλου)** there's a Late Minoan **passage tomb**, signed on the left, with its lintel still intact. Beyond here – opposite a fountain – lies an interesting, partly ruined mansion known as the **House of Kalitsa Psaraki** (see box below).

THE HOUSE OF KALITSA PSARAKI

Apodhoúlou's once substantial **House of Kalítsa Psaraki** gets its name from the daughter of a local official who, in the 1821 rising against Turkish rule, was abducted by Muslims and sent to the slave market at Alexandria. By chance she was seen there by Robert Hay, a wealthy Scottish gentleman traveller and Egyptologist, who secured her freedom and – after he had paid for her to be educated in Britain – proposed. They married in Malta, after which Kalitsa accompanied him on his archeological trips to Egypt. Later, when they returned to Crete, an overjoyed family built this house for them to live in. Now a crumbling pile, it's nevertheless possible to see evidence of former grandeur. The stone lintel of a window facing the road bears both Hay's and Psaraki's initials and the date of 1846, when the house was completed.

WAR IN THE AMÁRI

The Amári villages suffered gravely during **World War II**, particularly towards the end of the German occupation in the latter part of 1944 when – with an Allied victory assured – the occupiers carried out many wanton atrocities. George Psychoundakis (see p.353) watched the outrage from a cave on the slopes of Psilorítis:

I stayed there two or three days before leaving, watching the Kedros villages burning ceaselessly on the other side of the deep valley. Every now and then we heard the sound of explosions. The Germans went there in the small hours of the twenty-second of August and the burning went on for an entire week. The villages we could see from there and which were given over to the flames were: Yerakari, Kardaki, Gourgouthoi, Vrysses, Smiles, Dryes and Ano-Meros. First they emptied every single house, transporting all the loot to Retimo, then they set fire to them, and finally, to complete the ruin, they piled dynamite into every remaining corner, and blew them sky high. The village schools met the same fate, also the churches and the wells, and at Ano-Meros they even blew up the cemetery. They shot all the men they could find.

Other villages around Psilorítis, from Anóyia to Kamáres, were also burned and destroyed. Officially these atrocities were in reprisal for the kidnap of General Kreipe, four months earlier. But Psychoundakis, for one, believed that it was a more general revenge, intended to destroy any effective resistance in the closing months of the German occupation. Today the villages of Méronas, Elénes, Yerakári, Kardháki and Vrísses mark the southward progress of the German troops with etched stone **memorials** dated one day apart. Áno Méros has a striking war memorial of a woman wielding a hammer and chisel as she carves the names of the dead into the monument.

The church of **Áyios Yeóryios**, signed from the village centre and currently undergoing restoration, lies around 1.5km from the village along a lane and dirt track (the latter is best done on foot, and takes about ten minutes). Inside are some damaged but wonderful **frescoes** from the fourteenth century by Iereas Anastasios, one vigorously portraying George slaying the dragon, while outside are perfect vistas of the south coast and the high mountains. Around 1km beyond the turn-off for the church the **Minoan site of Apodhoúlou** with its protective metal canopies can be seen; sometimes there is an attendant, but the gates seem to be left open even when he's absent. With no signage or information it's hard to make out what you're looking at, but excavations here have revealed impressive remains of a settlement dating from the early second millennium BC, with substantial dwellings and all the familiar features of Minoan architecture, including light wells, benches and narrow corridors.

The western Amári valley

The **western** side of the Amári valley is more populous, but the traditional-looking villages here are in fact almost entirely **modern** – rebuilt after their deliberate destruction during World War II (see box above).

Méronas

Arriving from the north, **MÉRONAS (Μέρωνας)** is the first substantial village you reach. Here, the soft-pink Venetian-style **church of the Panayía** (daily 10.30am–3pm) shelters frescoes from the fourteenth century. It takes time for your eyes to adjust to the dim interior and take in the painstaking detail of the artwork, darkened with age: a torch would allow you to see a great deal more than the candles or nightlights that usually provide illumination. There's an excellent **taverna** here too (see p.214), and a side road that cuts across the valley through Amári.

Yerakári and around

YERAKÁRI (Γερακάρι) is a bigger, more modern and prosperous-looking village than most, with several places to stop for a drink, food and accommodation. The village's

FESTIVITIES AND DANCE IN THE AMÁRI VALLEY

Whenever you come to the Amári valley, but in July or August especially, you may be lucky enough to stumble on a village wedding or a **festival** in honour of the local saint, the harvest or some obscure historical event; the latter are worth going out of your way for, so keep an eye out for notices pasted in *kafenío* windows. Beginning with a distorted cacophony of overamplified Cretan music, *lyra* and *laoúto* to the fore, the celebrations continue until the participants are sufficiently gorged on roast lamb and enlivened by wine to get down to the real business of **dancing**. Cretan dancing at an event such as this is an extraordinary display of athleticism and, as often as not, endurance – and if the party really takes off, locals will dig out their old guns and rattle off a few rounds into the sky to celebrate.

cheeses, *thimarísio* (thyme honey) and pickled cherries are all for sale on the main square and recommended, although their cherry brandy is probably an acquired taste. A spectacular road heads west from here to Spíli (see opposite), offering tremendous views along a valley between the heights of Kédhros and Sorós towards the distant Lefká Óri. Continuing south, though, the road beyond Yerakári narrows and is increasingly neglected. Just outside the village is the unusual thirteenth-century church of **Áyios Ioánnis Fótis**, with a spreading oak tree providing shade for a tapped spring – a beautiful spot to stop for a breather, or a picnic. The church has been painstakingly repaired and restored and its remaining **frescoes** preserved for posterity. Traces of the medieval stone road on which the church was originally aligned can still be made out behind it.

ARRIVAL AND DEPARTURE
THE AMÁRI VALLEY

By bus On weekdays there are two daily buses from Réthymno to Amári via Thrónos and along the western edge of the valley to Áno Méros.

ACCOMMODATION AND EATING

Alexander Hotel Main street, Yerakári ☎ 28330 51160, ⊛ alexanderhotelgerakari.gr. Indubitably the poshest place in the valley, this sprawling four-star hotel complex is full only in August. Out of season it's an extraordinary bargain, if eerily deserted. Built by a local boy made good, it hopes to become an outdoor activity (including hiking) centre and there's a large pool (open to all for the price of a drink) and tennis court in its ample grounds. It also has its own bar and taverna. Breakfast included. **€40**

Elia Hotel Above Méronas, signed from the northern edge of the village ☎ 28330 22229, ⊛ eliameronas.gr. Incongruously fancy apartment complex with fabulous views, pool and bar. Well-equipped rooms, studios with kitchens and two-bedroom apartments; all with a/c and heating, some with working fireplaces. Breakfast included. Doubles **€40**, studios **€50**

★ **Moskhovolis** Main street, Merónas ☎ 28330 22526. Excellent taverna offering a limited range of dishes served with organic veg from their own smallholding; there's no menu, just a few daily specials (€6–7). Daily 8am–11pm.

Studios Kourites At the northern edge of Kouroútes village ☎ 28330 41305. Modern rooms with kitchenette, balcony, TV and fans, some with spectacular south coast views. Some larger apartments are also available, sleeping up to four. **€35**

★ **Taverna/Rooms Aravanes** Thrónos ☎ 28330 22760, ⊛ aravanes-rooms-taverna.gr. Signs in Thrónos will guide you to this welcoming bar-taverna whose terrace and en-suite balcony rooms have wonderful views. The rooms are a little run-down, but the warmth of the welcome and the chance to help out on the farm make up for that. Proprietor Lambros Papoutsakis has a wealth of knowledge on the area, and as well as leading walks (see box, p.211), he has a collection of books on the local area available for perusal, distils his own *rakí* (the distilling season begins in October, when you can visit his and other local stills to see the process, with a few samples thrown in) and has a small shop selling mountain herbs and home-made honey. There's also excellent home-made food in the taverna (mains €6–8). Taverna daily 9am–11pm. **€40**

Taverna Rooms Gerakari Main street, Yerakári ☎ 28330 51013. Simple rooms sharing bath above a bar-taverna. The proprietor's taverna kitchen is a veritable pickling and bottling factory for the fruits of the region – especially cherries, for which the village is famous – that are spread out to dry on every available rooftop during the picking season. **€25**

Windy Place Taverna and Rooms Fourfourás ☎ 28330 41366. The taverna on the northern edge of the village serves up hearty meals on an attractive terrace, while the en-suite rooms – in another building in the village proper – come with a/c and heating. The proprietors can describe a short cut (with your own vehicle) to the Psilorítis peak (see p.208) and advise on a 15km gorge walk along the Plátis river valley to Ayía Galíni; they can even collect you from there to return you to Fourfourás. Taverna daily 8am–11pm. **€30**

South from Réthymno

The main road south from Réthymno heads via Arméni and Spíli (see below) to Ayía Galíni (see p.217); for Plakiás (see p.221) and the western half of the south coast, you turn off a little over halfway across the island.

Arméni Minoan cemetery

Signed just before the village of Arméni, 10km south of Réthymno • Tues–Sun 8.30am–3pm • €2

The little-visited but fascinating **Minoan cemetery** at **ARMÉNI** (Αρμένοι) features more than two hundred rock-cut tombs dating from the Late Minoan period, after the fall of the great palaces. Most of the tombs, pleasantly sited today in a shady oak wood, are of the *drómos* (passage) and chamber type; each probably a family mausoleum. One large tomb under a cover on the south side of the site has a particularly spectacular *drómos* and finely cut chamber, and may well have belonged to a royal personage. Many others are almost as impressive, although at some only the *drómos* has been cut, and work seems for some reason to have been abandoned. A number of important discoveries have been made here, including many *lárnakes* (clay coffins) and rich grave goods – weapons, jewellery, vases and a rare helmet made from boar's tusks – now on display in the archeological museums at Réthymno and Iráklio. One mystery is still to be solved: the location of the sizeable settlement that provided this necropolis with its customers.

EATING   **ARMÉNI**

Goules Taverna Main square, Gouledhianá, about 4km east of the main road, south of Arméni vilage ☎ 28310 41001. An outstanding country taverna that uses local ingredients to create traditional Cretan cuisine, often with an inventive twist, with good meat, fish and vegetarian options; the pork in wine and honey (€8) is a perennial favourite. It also serves Brink's beers (see box below). Mon–Fri 2–10.30pm, Sat & Sun noon–10.30pm.

Spíli

The pleasant country town of **SPÍLI** (Σπίλι), tucked into the folds of the Mount Kédhros foothills 30km south of Réthymno, doesn't look much as you drive through, although the mountainside which towers over the houses is impressive. If you get off the main road, however, into the white-walled alleys that wind upwards towards the cliff, it can be very attractive. Plenty of people break their journey briefly here, but only a few stay,

---

GERMAN BEER COMES TO CRETE

When German Bernd Brink decided to build a **brewery** after marrying a local girl, many thought he had bitten off more than he could chew. But using tact, diplomacy, and not a little tenacity, he started work on what is now **Brink's Brewery** (☎ 28310 41243, ⊛ brinks-beer.gr) in 2001. Today this glittering stainless steel model of Teutonic efficiency receives orders from as far away as Cyprus and Denmark. He produces two very tasty brews, a blonde and a dark – both organic and made in accordance with sixteenth-century German beer purity laws. Unfiltered and unpasteurized, they are made only with water, hops, yeast and malt. You pass the brewery on the main road south of Arméni; sadly Greek bureaucracy means it's no longer open for visits, but the beer is widely available in bars and tavernas throughout Réthymno and Haniá provinces (often under the name Rethymnian Beer).

WALKS AROUND SPÍLI

Plenty of challenging **hikes** start in Spíli. Heracles at **Heracles Rooms** (see opposite) can advise on many of the local walking possibilities, has maps of some, and can help with route information. Both here and the nearby *Green Hotel* can book taxis back to Spíli (around €25 from either Yerakári or Moní Prevéli, for example). None of the available **maps** have enough detail to be really useful: best are the *Petrakis* or *Anavasi* 1:100,000 versions.

TO THE AMÁRI VALLEY VIA MOUNT KÉDHROS

The direct route to **Yerakári** in the Amári valley is on the paved road, but there's also a spectacular walk there on the E4 (which passes through Spíli). This heads south, initially along the road, to the village of Kissós and then up via the summit of Kédhros (1777m). A slightly easier route bypasses the summit, but this is still a tough, all-day, 19km trek with plenty of climbing.

SPÍLI CIRCULAR LOOP

An easy 2hr **loop walk** via the ancient chapel of Áyios Pnefma. This sets out from Spíli's health centre, up a side road on the left, 200m south of the centre (a road to the right just before the health centre leads 75m to the site of the Venetian fountain that once stood in Spíli's central platía), and meanders into the hills to meet the Spíli–Yerakári road, from where you can descend along narrow lanes to the central square; Heracles has details and a map.

NORTH FROM MIXÓRROUMA

West of Spíli, the E4 follows the road for 4km to the village of **Mixórrouma**, where you can loop back either north or south of the main road. The northern route is all on roads, initially signed for Karínes. This brings you to the pretty village of **Lambiní** and its domed Byzantine **church of the Panayía**, the scene of a terrible massacre in 1827 (marked by a plaque) when the Turks locked the congregation inside the church before setting fire to it. From here it's 5km to **Karínes**, another attractive village with a friendly *kafenío*, and 7km further to **Patsós**. A turn on the left 1km before Patsós leads for ten minutes to the **Áyios Andónios Cave**, which was a Minoan and later Dorian and Roman sanctuary, close to a beautiful gorge. From Patsós it's less than 10km to Thrónos in the Amári valley (see p.210), or about 7km back to Spíli.

SOUTH FROM MIXÓRROUMA

The southern route from Mixórrouma, via **Fratí** and **Mourné**, takes in some superb scenery and four ancient churches. It's probably easier tackled in the other direction – by road from Spíli to Mourné (4km), cross-country from there to Fratí (8km; you'll need directions), then an easy route above the Kíssanos river valley to Ayía Pelayía and Mixórrouma (4km).

TO MONÍ PRÉVELI

You can also walk the 15km southwest from Spíli to **Moní Préveli** and **Palm Beach** (see p.225). Head to Mourné, from where a track leads south towards **Dhrímiskos**; just before the village a cross-track heads west to the Megalopótamos River. Follow the river to reach the beach.

mostly ramblers and botanists: it's the trailhead for a series of attractive country **hikes**. It caters well for all these visitors, with ATMs and even foreign newspapers available along the main street.

A sharp curve in the road marks the centre of town, by a small platía overlooked by lofty plane trees. Just above this there's a prodigious 25-spouted **fountain**, a replacement for the elegant Venetian original, which has been removed to a less exalted position beside the health centre (see box above). Beyond the fountain begins a steep labyrinth of cobbled lanes and shady archways, full of flowered balconies, giant urns and whitewashed chimneypots. Spíli can become quite crowded – many of the bus tours passing along the road make a brief stop here, usually for lunch – but between times and in the evenings it is quiet and rural.

ARRIVAL AND DEPARTURE

By bus The main road passes right through the centre of Spíli, and the Réthymno–Ayía Galíni bus (5 daily each way; 1hr 30min) will drop you in the heart of town.

ACCOMMODATION AND EATING

Fabrika Fountain square ☎ 28320 22766. One of several places around the fountain, this modern bar-café is lively at night, and serves Brink's beers (see p.215). Daily 8am–1am.

Giannis Main road, 50m south of the square ☎ 28320 22707. Close to the heart of things, this is a decent, straightforward taverna for solid Cretan cooking (main dishes €6–8) served on a streetside terrace; they also offer breakfast. Daily 9am–11pm.

Green Hotel Main road, 100m north of the square ☎ 28320 22225, ⓦ maravelspili.gr. Lovely, newly refurbished rooms with a/c and TV; those at the back have fabulous views across the valley. The owners have a large herb garden outside town, and they organize herbal and botanical walks as well as other activities. Breakfast available. €30

★ Heracles Just off the main road, below the Green Hotel ☎ 28320 22111, ⓦ heracles-hotel.eu. Friendly pension with spotless a/c rooms with balcony, TV, fridge and an excellent breakfast (extra). The genial proprietor can advise on some superb walks in the surrounding hills, and rents out mountain bikes. He also has exceptionally well-equipped apartments, sleeping up to four, in his grandparents' newly converted house in the old part of town. Doubles €40, apartments €80

Platia Fountain square ☎ 28320 22555, ⓦ spilicafe platia.gr. Pleasant café with an elevated terrace above the fountain and a small but excellent selection of dishes, such as chicken in tomato sauce (€6) and home-made cheese or spinach pies (€4). Daily 8am–midnight.

Ayía Galíni

Forty years ago, **AYÍA GALÍNI** (Αγία Γαλήνη) must have been an idyllic spot: an isolated fishing community of some five hundred souls nestling in a convenient fold of the mountains which dominate this part of the **south coast**. Although this was the port of ancient **Syvritos** (see p.211), the modern village is barely a hundred years old, its inhabitants having moved down from the mountain villages of Mélambes and Saktoúria as the traditional threat of piracy along the coast receded.

Catch it out of season and the streets of white houses, crowded in on three sides by mountains and opening below to a small, busy **harbour**, can still appeal. But this is a face which is increasingly hard to find, especially given a surprising number of long-term expat residents. Crowded throughout the season, and confined by the limits of its narrow situation, the village has seen many of its older houses squeezed out by apartment buildings and uninspiring hotels. And for a place that bills itself as the province's major resort, the **beach** here is surprisingly small. If you're looking for strands with space to breathe you'll need to use the resort as a base for trips to nearby beaches or opt for a shorter stay. Nonetheless there's something about Ayía Galíni that attracts a loyal following, and there are certainly plenty of excellent restaurants and bars, well-priced rooms and a friendly atmosphere that survives and even thrives on all the visitors.

AYÍA GALÍNI ORIENTATION

Few of the streets in Ayía Galíni village are named and such names as there are seem rarely used. The streets which run steeply down to the harbour form the heart of the place: the first of these (**Venizélou**) is a continuation of the main road into town, ending at the harbour; along it you can take care of all the practicalities, from banks to car hire, English-language books and newspapers, laundry, pharmacies and even a doctor. Parallel to this to the east are a series of narrow, pedestrianized and sometimes stepped alleys; the first (known locally as "**Shopping Street**") is lined with stores, jewellery shops, bars and travel agencies; further in is "**Taverna Street**", named for obvious reasons – though the name actually applies to a number of alleys rather than a single street. All of this falls within a very small area where nothing is more than a couple of minutes' walk away.

The beach

The **beach** at Ayía Galíni lies to the east of the village, ten minutes' walk on a narrow path that tracks around the cliff from the harbour, or by a path that descends from the top of the town. You can also drive round and park behind the beach. Walking round by the cliffs, you'll pass **caves** that in World War II served as gun emplacements. The sandy beach is bisected by the River Platís (spanned by a footbridge) and backed by cafés, tavernas and rooms places; various **watersports**, from waterskiing to jet skis and pedaloes, are available.

ARRIVAL AND DEPARTURE   AYÍA GALÍNI

By bus Buses terminate at the platía on Venizélou, about 250m above the harbour.

Destinations Réthymno via Spíli (5 daily; 1hr 30min); Iráklio via Míres (8 daily, fewer at weekends; 2hr); Festós (5 daily, 25min).

By car Coming in by car, head for the large car park on the

harbour. Numerous travel agencies and car rental places line Venizélou; reliable operators include Alianthos (☎ 28320 32033, ⓦ alianthos-group.com), Auto Galini (☎ 28320 91241, ⓦ autogalini.com) and Motor Holidays (☎ 6972 094 190, ⓦ nick-holidays.gr).

ACTIVITIES

Boat trips Most people who stay here end up making regular excursions elsewhere. In season, the *Sactouris* (☎ 6976 693 729; €30 return) runs to Áyios Pávlos and Palm Beach at Préveli (see p.226); the *Elizabeth* (☎ 6936 848 445) offers a day-trip to Áyios Yeóryios (€15) and fishing day-trips (€30, including barbecue

lunch); and the *Agia Galini* goes to the Paximádhia islands, 12km offshore, which have wonderful fine-sand beaches but little shade (☎ 6930 979 864; €40 including on-board meal). All have booths open at the harbour in the evening and before departure; details can be found on ⓦ gogalini.com.

ACCOMMODATION

There are so many **rooms** in Ayía Galíni that you'll find exceptional bargains for much of the year – though perhaps not in August when many are pre-booked by tour operators. Dozens of places, including almost all of those that we review here, are represented on ⓦ agia-galini.com.

Camping No Problem Behind the beach, on the far side of the river ☎ 28320 91386. Big campsite with a pool, shop and restaurant, with sandy, tree-shaded pitches. April–Oct. Two people plus tent and car €16

Erofili High above the village, to the right off the entry road ☎ 28320 91319, ⓦ hotelerofili.com. This simple rooms place is wreathed in flowers and brightly painted in a Matala-hippy style. This high up, the views are tremendous from most rooms and from the communal area, where a substantial breakfast (included) is served; the height also means a very stiff walk in and out of town, however. €40

Hariklia Entry road from Réthymno on right just before the descent ☎ 28320 91257, ⓦ hotelhariklia.gr. Delightful, spotless *pension* with refurbished en-suite a/c rooms with fridge. The communal balconies have fine views and guests also have use of kitchen to prepare breakfasts and snacks. €35

★ **Minos** Entry road from Réthymno on left ☎ 28320 91292, ⓦ minos.agiagalini.com. Welcoming hotel with comfortable, modern a/c rooms with fridge and TV. Many enjoy the best sea views in town (cheaper rooms have partial views). Superb breakfast available. €40

Palazzo Greco Entry road from Réthymno on left ☎ 28320 91187, ⓦ palazzogreco.com. Immaculate boutique hotel done up in bright colours with marble floors, designer bathrooms and gorgeous sea views from many rooms; the suites (an extra €30) are fabulous, the standard rooms a little cramped for the price. It also squeezes in a small pool. €70

Romantika Behind the beach, on the far side of the river ☎ 28320 91388, ⓦ romantika-kreta.gr. Attractive modern rooms and apartments just 30m from the beach. Rooms come with a/c, fridge, satellite TV and balcony views; the apartments add an extra room and fully equipped kitchen. They also have a beachfront restaurant and bar (see opposite). Doubles €50, apartments €65

Tropica Club Behind the beach, far side of the river ☎ 28320 91351, ✉ tropica@otenet.gr. Good-value studios and apartments behind the beach with the added attraction of a big (seawater) pool. Studios have a/c, TV and kitchenette while the more spacious apartments also have a kitchen. There's a beachfront bar/taverna and poolside yoga sessions, too. Doubles €40, apartments €50

EATING AND DRINKING

Ayía Galíni's vast range of **food** and **drink** – one major and undeniable benefit of the resort's popularity – is often excellent and, thanks to the competition, not overpriced. There's a good bakery opposite the post office.

RESTAURANTS

Faros Shopping St ☎ 28930 91346. The resort's best and most unpretentious fish restaurant, with a small street terrace, where the friendly family who run it serve up what they catch themselves. The catch of the day is chalked up on a blackboard, and they also specialise in *astakomakaronada* (lobster with spaghetti); all priced per kilo, but a portion of fish is typically around €12. Daily 6pm–midnight.

La Strada Taverna St ☎ 28320 91053. Good pizza and decent pasta and risotto (all around €7.50) served on a street terrace, as well as all the usual Greek food; the brothers who run it are accomplished performers on the *lyra* and *laoúto* and often treat their customers to an impromptu concert. Daily 6pm–midnight.

Madame Hortense Overlooking the harbour, above Zorba's bar ☎ 28320 91215. Named after Zorba the Greek's floozy in the classic novel, *Madame Hortense* is a little pricier than the competition. Its upstairs timber-floored dining room offers arguably the town's best harbour view (worth booking for a ringside seat), and a slightly eccentric short menu with pasta and curry as well as Greek dishes; rabbit in a lemon and wine sauce and Thai chicken curry are both €9. Daily noon–3pm & 6pm–midnight.

Onar Bottom of Taverna St ☎ 28320 91288. Big, classic Greek taverna, serving all the standards at the heart of the action – charcoal-grilled fish and meat are a speciality. Good specials such as *soutzoukákia* (€7) or fresh dorado (€11), and several seating areas including a rooftop terrace. Daily noon–1am.

Platía On a small square slightly south of the bus stop ☎ 28320 91185. This café is famed for its breakfasts (€4–9; omelettes, fruit salads and muesli all feature), and later in the day also does snack meals and mezédhes (which it calls tapas; €4–5 each). Daily 8.30am–2pm & 6pm–1am.

Romantika Romantika Hotel, behind the beach, on the far side of the river ☎ 28320 91388. One of several enjoyable bar/tavernas behind the beach, with a mixed, international menu taking in breakfast (€6–9.50), omelettes (€3.50–6) and pizzas (around €8), as well as simple Greek dishes like chicken *souvláki* (€7.50). April–Nov daily noon–midnight.

★**To Petrino** Just off the bus stop platía ☎ 28320 91504. Friendly little gem of an ouzerí whose proprietor is an ex-sea captain. Serves breakfast and coffee plus excellent mezédhes later in the day (mixed plate €6.50 small, €13 large), and retains some of the flavour of the pre-tourist days. Daily 9am–2pm & 4.30pm–midnight.

CAFÉS AND BARS

Balloon Harbourfront ☎ 28320 91184. Modern bar serving breakfasts, snacks and salads by day and cocktails and juices by night, when it's often the liveliest place here. Pleasant seafront terrace with easy-on-the-ear rock and jazz music. Daily 8.30am–3am.

C'est la Vie Harbourfront ☎ 28320 91113. The best located of the harbourfront bars, serving breakfasts (€6–8.50), drinks and snacks, and stronger stuff as the day progresses. Daily 8am–2am.

Kafenío Elpida Shopping St ☎ 28320 91557. This good-value traditional *kafenío* has been given a modern makeover, but still attracts locals and serves bite-size mezédhes with every drink. Daily 9am–11pm.

Miro Music Café Taverna St, just above Onar. Bar/café with a rock soundtrack, catering to the local long-hairs and tourists reliving their youth. Daily 6pm–2am.

Zorba's Overlooking the harbour. A pleasant place for an early-evening drink, with a veranda overlooking the harbour, as well as a dartboard and a shrine to the Beatles. It changes character later, when the dancing starts around midnight. Daily 6pm–1am.

West of Ayía Galíni

In high summer visitors seeking breathing space tend to head west to the beaches of **Áyios Yeóryios**, **Áyios Pávlos** and beyond. Both of these first two have boat trips from Ayía Galini, and you can also walk to Áyios Yeóryios. If you're aiming for the more isolated beach settlements further west, at **Triópetra**, **Lígres** or **Ayía Fotiní**, you'll need your own transport. On clear days, the island of Gávdhos (see p.318) looms on the horizon.

Áyios Yeóryios

Less than 4km west of Ayía Galíni, the seaside hamlet of **ÁYIOS YEÓRYIOS** (Άγιος Γεώργιος) is fairly easily reached on foot, by a marked and well-trodden path that leaves town from the top of the main street, near the *Hotel Ostria*. The beach is almost two hours away, a shingle cove with a taverna. Daily boat trips from Ayía Galíni also visit, and you can drive here, on a paved road that turns off the Ayía Galíni–Mélambes road (accessed from the highway north of Ayía Galíni). When you get here, though the water is startlingly clear, the beach is not especially attractive, and has little shade (although parasols can be rented). If you have a car you're better off heading further west.

Áyios Pávlos

A driveable road, paved about half the distance, follows the coast 8km from Áyios Yeóryios to **ÁYIOS PÁVLOS** (Άγιος Πάυλος), though if you're coming direct from Ayía Galíni you're better off following the main highway north for about 10km before taking the road down via Saktoúria. It's an attractive spot, with some striking rock formations around a sheltered bay, and excellent snorkelling. The lovely **beach** can be subject to strong winds, which you can escape by climbing over the headland to the west, where you can scramble down a sandy slope to two fine-sand beaches, one very sheltered, one nudist. In addition to the visitors arriving by car from the surrounding hinterland, Áyios Pávlos is home to a colony of New Age practitioners who run **yoga** and related courses at their centre, Yoga Plus (bookable in advance only; ⊛yogaplus.co.uk).

West of Áyios Pávlos

West of Áyios Pávlos it's possible to drive all the way to Palm Beach (see p.226). Most of this is on paved roads, and though they can be steep, winding and narrow in places (and the route not always obvious), it's not an especially hard drive – by far the toughest section comes after you reach Palm Beach, where the road around the back of the beach is very rough, though this is also much the busiest part of the route. Along the way are a series of long beaches, with only the first stirrings of development. If you're coming from the north, they can also be reached by direct turnings off the Spíli road.

Triópetra

TRIÓPETRA (Τριόπετρα) – Three Rocks, named for the great crags offshore – is very close to Áyios Pávlos though the road winds around inland. If you just wanted to hole up for a couple of days in a tranquil haven, with a lovely small cove and a huge but exposed beach beyond it, this would be as good a choice as any. There's another excellent yoga retreat here (⊛yogaholidaysgreece.com) and a couple of good tavernas with rooms.

Lígres and around

To drive from Triópetra to **LÍGRES** (Λίγρες), 4km west, simply follow the beach; it's not obvious at first, but quickly becomes a paved road again. Another isolated grey-sand beach here seems to stretch for miles, with a couple of unexpectedly popular taverna-rooms places. Finally, a couple of kilometres beyond Lígres lies **Ayía Fotiní**, a still simpler place with a less attractive, pebbly beach. This is the last stop before the celebrated Palm Beach; the final section of coast road is unpaved.

ACCOMMODATION AND EATING	WEST OF AYÍA GALÍNI

There are relatively few rooms on these beaches, and they're popular, so you'll need to book ahead at pretty much any time of year.

ÁYIOS YEÓRYIOS

Nikos ☎ 28320 91001, ⊛aggeorgios.gr. Attractive a/c rooms with fridge and balcony. The eponymous proprietor serves his daily seafood catch, including langoustine and lobster (priced per kilo), on a beautifully sited terrace above the sea. Daily 9am–11pm. **€50**

ÁYIOS PÁVLOS

Ayios Pavlos Hotel ☎ 28320 71104, ⊛agiospavlos hotel.gr. A great place to stay, with lovely a/c sea-view rooms and some cheaper, more basic options; another complex in a slightly less perfect setting has modern, well-equipped apartments for up to four people. The café-restaurant boasts a terrace on the rocks directly above the sea. Daily 8am–midnight. Doubles €30, studios €45

TRIÓPETRA

Apanemia On the eastern cove ☎6972 122 186, Ⓦapanemiatriopetra.gr. A very good, chilled taverna, right on the beach with free loungers for patrons, serving breakfast and a standard Greek menu (*kléftiko* €9, *moussaká* €7.40) with an unexpectedly extensive wine list. Just a few simple a/c rooms with fridge and balcony. Daily 9am–11pm. €35

Pavlos' Place On the eastern cove ☎6945 998 101, Ⓦtriopetra.com.gr. Appealing a/c rooms with fridge and balcony above a little harbour; also a taverna, though this can be dominated by the yoga courses (mostly German-speaking) that the hotel also hosts. Daily 8.30am–11am, noon–4pm & 6.30–10.30pm. €35

★ **To Yiroyiali** Behind the western beach ☎6976 430 145, ✉galismar@yahoo.gr. Taverna with an attractive terrace overlooking the beach and a short menu of daily specials such as rabbit *stifádho* (€8.50). There are free loungers on the beach for clients and guests, and very pleasant a/c rooms with fridge and TV in a separate two-storey block overlooking a garden. Daily 9am–11pm. €35

LÍGRES

Ligres Beach ☎6974 234 509, Ⓦligres.gr. Simple a/c rooms with fridge, somewhat oddly decorated in an attempt to make them "designer", with sea-view balconies, above a reliable taverna serving fresh fish. Daily 9am–11pm. €35

Villa Maria ☎6949 477 081, Ⓦligres.eu. A slightly incongruous stone building beside a rushing stream houses simple but welcoming rooms and studios with a/c, TV and fridge as well as some great two-room apartments. The taverna offers good food (they catch their own fish) and icy spring water from the waterfall outside. Daily 7.30am–11pm. €35

AYÍA FOTINÍ

★ **Taverna Agia Fotia** ☎6937 124 600. A lovely, isolated and tranquil option that's a throwback to the Crete of thirty years ago; the excellent taverna, with a terrace out front, offers a range of traditional Cretan dishes as well as fresh fish – mains €7–9. Upstairs are four simple but spotless rooms overlooking the sea that come with a/c and a fridge. Breakfast included. €40

Plakiás and around

PLAKIÁS (Πλακιάς), 35km south of Réthymno, is a well-established resort, though it's a long way from the big league. Commercialized as it is, Plakiás has a very different feel to anywhere on the north coast, or even Ayía Galíni – the accommodation is simpler, less of it is booked up in advance, the beaches are infinitely better and it attracts a younger crowd. Don't come for sophisticated nightlife or for a picturesque white Greek island village: what you'll find is a lively, friendly place that makes a good base for **walks** in the beautiful surrounding countryside and trips to some great **beaches**.

The gorges

Approaching Plakiás from the main Réthymno–Ayía Galíni road you've a choice of routes, each of which passes through a spectacular gorge. The first turning, via the tiny settlement of **Kánevos** (where there's an excellent taverna) passes through the narrow **Kotsifóu Gorge**; the second approaches via the still more impressive **Kourtaliótiko Gorge**. Either way, it's worth pulling over to take time to appreciate the scenery and the wildlife, from snakes by the water to vast birds of prey soaring above. If you're coming from the south you can also turn off at Mixórrouma, from where you can join the Kourtaliótiko gorge route.

The beaches

Getting from town to the beach can involve no more than a two-minute walk. The town is set at the western end of the bay, and to the east the grey sand of the **town beach** curves around in an unbroken line to the headland a kilometre or more away, with an increasing amount of development behind it. This beach generally looks better from a distance than from close up, however – the long open sweep of the bay means it can be exposed and gusty, and the strong summer **winds** seem to affect Plakiás more than other places along this coast. There's plenty of space, especially towards the far end, but you'll find better sands beyond the headland – riddled with caves and wartime bunkers and gun emplacements – at Dhamnóni, or to the west at Soúdha Beach.

Soúdha Beach

Soúdha Beach is just over half an hour's walk west of Plakiás, with places to stop for a swim along the way and a couple of good tavernas when you get there. The sand may be a little gritty, but there's plenty of room and the water at the far end is sheltered by rocks; closer to town, where there are fewer people and less development, it's largely nudist.

Dhamnóni

To reach the beaches on foot, about a 40min walk, follow the main road east and turn right along a track which leads through the olive groves; by car, continue east towards Lefkóyia and turn down at the sign for Dhamnóni or, further on, for Amoúdhi

Just east of Plakiás lie some of the most tempting beaches in central Crete, albeit a very poorly kept secret. On arrival you'll find three splashes of yellow sand, divided by rocky promontories, that go by the general name of Dhamnóni. **Dhamnóni beach** itself is the first of them, and the only one that has so far really seen much development: the western half has been colonized by an ugly Swiss-owned holiday village, *Hapimag*, while the road down to the sand has an increasing number of **rooms** places. The **beach**, though, is a wonderful long strip of yellow sand and super-clear water with a couple of **tavernas** and seasonal *kantínas*. At the far end you're likely to find a few people who've dispensed with their clothes, at least out of season, and the little cove that shelters the middle of the three beaches (a scramble over the rocks, or a very rough track) is almost entirely **nudist**. This enclave can get very crowded, but they're a good-humoured bunch and, unusually, often include quite a few Greek naturists too. The water is beautiful and there are caves at the back of the beach and rocks to dive from, with some great snorkelling to be had. The third of the coves is **Amoúdhi beach**, where there's a rather more sedate atmosphere and another **taverna** attached to the *Ammoudi Hotel*.

Skhínaria

Skhínaria beach is almost adjacent to Amoúdhi, but to get there you have to drive several kilometres round, via Lefkóyia. Another fine, sandy cove, it's popular with Greek families at holiday times and weekends, and occasionally hosts groups learning to scuba dive, but is otherwise delightfully quiet. There's a taverna open during the day.

Mýrthios

The village of **MÝRTHIOS** (**Μύρθιος**) hangs high above Plakiás, with wonderful views over the bay exploited by some excellent tavernas and rooms places. There are few other facilities, though, so you really need transport if you're staying here. It's easy enough to walk to Plakiás, about twenty minutes steeply downhill, or to any of the nearby beaches, but the walk back up is considerably tougher.

ARRIVAL AND DEPARTURE	PLAKIÁS AND AROUND

By car If you've taken the Kourtaliótiko Gorge route you turn right for Plakiás, passing through Asómatos and Lefkóyia (continue straight and you'll follow the course of the Megalopótamos river all the way down to Préveli); the Kotsifóu Gorge route emerges on the main coast road west of Plakiás where you turn right for Selliá (see p.227), left for Mýrthios and Plakiás. Either way, the main road enters Plakiás from the east and heads straight into the heart of things along the seafront; virtually everything in Plakiás lies along or just off this main street, running beside the sea, or on one of the lanes

connecting it to the single parallel street that runs inland. Continuing through town, the coast road ends after 3km or so at Soúdha, though you can turn off to head up to Selliá and the road west via a vertiginous series of narrow hairpin bends.
By bus Buses arrive and depart from a stop just east of the little bridge, roughly halfway along the seafront opposite the big Forum supermarket; the timetable is usually pinned up and is also displayed at nearby travel agencies.
Destinations Réthymno (5 daily; 1hr), Préveli (June–Sept 6 daily; 30 min).

GETTING AROUND

Bike and car rental There are car rental outlets all along the seafront; Alianthos (☎ 28320 318510, ⓦ alianthos -group.com) is excellent, or try Anso Travel (☎ 28320 31444, ⓦ ansotravel.com), who also have mountain bikes.

By taxi There's a taxi office at the bottom of the street to the post office, or try Taxi4you (☎ 28320 31777, ⓦ taxi4you.gr).

INFORMATION AND ACTIVITIES

Travel agencies There are plenty of travel agencies on the seafront, including Anso Travel (☎ 28320 31444, ⓦ ansotravel.com). Elena Tours (☎ 28320 20465), in an alley up from the harbour, offers all the usual services plus interesting local small-group tours.

Boat trips and fishing In season, several boats a day head to Palm Beach (some via Dhamnóni), and at least once a week further afield to Triópetra and Áyios Pávlos, or west to Frangokástello and Loútro; you can buy tickets in advance at local travel agencies, or simply turn up at the harbour. They also offer fishing trips – for information on *Tassos* boat enquire at the *Tassomanolis* taverna (ⓦ plakiasboattours.gr);

for the *Finikas* at the *Smyrna* bar (☎ 6936 806 635).

Diving Some of Crete's best diving is near Plakiás, and there are also easy beaches for learners. Dive2gether is a Dutch company with an office on the front, east of the bridge (☎ 28320 32313, ⓦ dive2gether.com); Kalypso Rocks Dive Centre (☎ 28310 74687, ⓦ kalypsodivecenter.com) organizes dives at the nearby *Kalypso Cretan Village* resort (see below).

Horseriding The country around Plakiás is great to explore on horseback; the Horse Riding Center (☎ 28320 31196, ⓦ cretehorseriding.com) is out of town opposite the turning to Dhamnóni, with horses for every ability and also donkey rides; for information, ask at the *Alianthos Beach Hotel*.

ACCOMMODATION

While there are scores of **hotels** and **rooms** in Plakiás – indeed at times it seems there's little else – you may have difficulty finding a vacancy in high season. The places on the backstreets lack sea views but are quieter and usually the last to fill, and there are also lots of studio-apartment complexes on the road as you approach town and along the coast towards Soúdha Beach to the west. An excellent **list** of local accommodation can be found at ⓦ plakias-filoxenia.gr.

PLAKIÁS

Alianthos Beach At the start of the seafront road ☎ 28320 32033, ⓦ alianthosbeach-plakias.com. Friendly hotel above a good taverna. The comfortable rooms have a/c; those at the front have balconies overlooking the beach. Breakfast included. €55

★**Anna Plakias Apartments** Inland, towards the youth hostel ☎ 6974 078 308, ⓦ anna-plakias.gr. Classy modern apartments and studios with a/c, free wi-fi and kitchenettes, in a quiet spot shaded by palm trees. There's a roof terrace with tiny pool, bikes to hire and maps for hiking and cycling, plus a suite with a private plunge pool. €50

Gio-ma Western end of the seafront ☎ 28320 31942, ⓦ gioma.gr. In a prime position overlooking the harbour, these fabulously sited, if basic, rooms (with wi-fi, fridge and a/c) sit above the taverna of the same name, right on the water. Over the road are studios and two-room apartments, also with sea views. April–Oct. Doubles €35, apartments €45

Kalypso Cretan Village On the promontory south of town, 4km or so by road ☎ 28320 31296, ⓦ kalypsohotels .com. All-inclusive hotel in a stunning, rocky, seaside setting with its own tiny secret cove. It's good value considering the facilities – though rooms vary in quality. Breakfast included. Free wi-fi in public areas. There's also a good dive centre here, and other activities including mountain biking. €90

Limani Apartments Inland immediately behind the port ☎ 28320 32218, ⓦ plakiaslimani.gr. Modern two-room apartments on the height above the harbour, with good balcony views; all come with a/c, TV and wi-fi.

The same owners have two more apartment complexes a little further out. April–Nov. €40

★**Morpheas Apartments** On the seafront, above Plakías Market ☎ 28320 31583, ⓦ morpheas-apartments -plakias-crete-greece.com. Fine modern rooms, studios and duplex apartments with balconies overlooking the beach (although not all have sea view). They're double-glazed against the potentially noisy location, with a/c, TV, fridge and, in the larger apartments, even a washing machine. Doubles €38, studios €45

Phoenix Apartments 1.5km west, near Soúdha Beach ☎ 28320 32108, ⓦ phoenix-plakias.com. Tranquil complex with a good-sized pool in a great spot, high above the sea. Studios and three-room apartments are all a/c and well equipped. April–Oct. Studios €36, apartments €53

Skinos Apartments On the road to Soúdha Beach, 400m from town ☎ 28320 31737, ⓦ skinos-plakias .com. Prettily modernized a/c studios with large balconies looking out to sea, with cooking facilities. €45

★**Youth Hostel** Inland a little way behind town ☎ 28320 32118, ⓦ yhplakias.com. The best hostel on Crete – friendly, relaxed and well run, in an attractively rural setting, with a terrace for breakfast and evening drinks and a busy social scene. Hot showers included; wi-fi and internet. March–Nov. Dorms €10

DHAMNÓNI

Ammoudi Hotel Amoúdhi Beach ☎ 28320 31355, ⓦ ammoudi.gr. A fabulous place to get away from it all,

3

with a/c balcony rooms with fridge and TV plus apartments 100m from the shore. Breakfast (included) is served in their taverna. It also has a dive centre, and this is an ideal spot to learn. Doubles €45, 4-person apartments €60

Damnoni Paradise On the road to Dhamnóni Beach 28320 31480, damnoni-paradise.kreta-sun.com. Family-oriented place surrounded by a dense garden whose palms, jasmine and bougainvillea offer welcome shade; the rooms (with kitchenette) and two-room apartments are a bit dated, but it's a great location. Free wi-fi in lobby. Doubles €35, apartments €50

MÝRTHIOS

Anna Apartments Mýrthios 6973 324 775, anna view.com. These classy apartments, built with traditional stone and wood, are beautifully furnished and have fantastic views over Plakiás Bay. All come with kitchenette, balcony, a/c, satellite TV and wi-fi. €50

★**Village Apartments** 28320 31835, village -apartments.gr. Large apartments and maisonettes (the latter with two bedrooms, living room and washing machine; €20 extra) that are exceptional value for families and larger groups. Magnificent views. March–Nov. Apartments €40

EATING

Plakiás's seafront street is lined with **tavernas**, cafés and bars, but the prime spot is towards the harbour right at the centre of town, where a strip of places have tables next to the water. You'll pay a bit more here than at other places in the resort – but the setting is worth it. For breakfast, there are a number of **bakeries** along the seafront too, and many of the **cafés** open early. There are plenty of **supermarkets**, including a very large one on the edge of town by the *Alianthos Beach Hotel*, which has an excellent bakery and wonderful fruit shop, plus an organic mini-market, on an alley running inland from the harbour.

PLAKIÁS

Candia Bakery Between the hotels Livikon and Lamon on the seafront. A good place for breakfast, and throughout the day for coffee and juices; choose a pastry from the bakery at the back to have with your drink. Daily 8am–1am.

Christos Overlooking the harbour at west end of the seafront 28320 31261. The longest-established and arguably the best located of the seafront places, with a pleasant tamarisk-shaded terrace. The menu changes daily, with fresh fish prominent, and includes the likes of home-smoked sea-bass (€10.50), black spaghetti with calamari (€9.90) and lamb *tsigariasto* (€9.20). Service can be slow, though. Daily noon–11pm.

★**Kastro** High on the hill behind the town 28320 32246. This taverna's fine terrace with great views complements friendly service and some original and tasty dishes such as *kounéli lemonato* (rabbit with a lemon and garlic sauce; €8.20). It's signed by road, or on foot you can follow the path through the olive groves beside the *Alianthos Garden Hotel*, looking out for the taverna's crenellated roofline above you. Daily 11am–midnight.

Kri Kri Near the bridge on the seafront 28320 32223. Good pizza from a wood-fired oven (small from €6, large €12–15) as well as all the taverna standards such as *stifádho* and *kléftiko*. Daily noon–1am.

Medousa Inland, near the back of the Alianthos Garden hotel 28320 31521. The fanciest place in town, in both appearance and menu. Inventive dishes such as pork with leeks in white lemon sauce (€9) or calamari stuffed with chickpeas, herbs and citron feta (€13.50) don't always hit the mark, but can be excellent – and there's a decent wine list and a warm welcome. Daily noon–3pm & 6.30–10.30pm.

Sofia Seafront facing the harbour 28320 31226. The best of the tavernas right by the sea, with a slightly less touristy menu than some of its neighbours. Plenty of fish and seafood, including clam and shrimp spaghetti (€9.60) and cuttlefish in ink (€7.80). Daily noon–midnight.

★**Tassomanolis** Facing west along the shore beyond the harbour 28320 31229. One of three or four good places around this end of the beach. Seafood is king here, most of it caught by the proprietor from his own boat. Try the oven-baked *dorado* (bream; priced per kilo) or their three-fish *souvláki* (€12). Daily noon–midnight.

SOÚDHA BEACH

Taverna Galini Far end of the beach 28320 32103. On the beach is a beach bar with loungers for guests, while the taverna occupies a grassy space behind, serving all the standards plus some interesting daily specials, like rabbit in tomato sauce with walnuts and feta (€8.70). There's live Greek music every Wednesday night. Daily 9am–midnight.

MÝRTHIOS

Panorama Village square 28320 31450. A decent alternative to next-door *Plateia* if you can't get in there, with equally fine vistas from its terrace and a slightly simpler, cheaper menu (mains €7–9); it's also open for breakfast. Daily 9am–10.30pm.

★**Plateia** Village square 28320 31560. The village's oldest taverna, beautifully refurbished, although prices remain very reasonable and the view from its terrace has to be a candidate for the best in Crete. An outstanding kitchen produces tasty traditional Cretan cuisine with the odd creative twist; dishes include red lamb (€8.80), stuffed cabbage (€7.20) and rabbit in lemon sauce (€7.90). It can get busy, especially at Sunday lunchtimes, so turn up early if you don't want to wait (they don't accept bookings). Daily noon–11pm.

KÁNEVOS

Iliomanolis Kánevos, 7km north of Plakiás ☎ 28320 51053. An excellent and inexpensive rural taverna in a tiny settlement at the top of the Kotsifóu Gorge; there's no menu, so choose from the daily specials in the kitchen (typically around €7); they also have simple but beautifully-kept rooms.

DRINKING AND NIGHTLIFE

Frame Central seafront, above the Forum supermarket. ☎ 6976 972 927. Stylish café-bar with panoramic windows overlooking the water; coffee by day, cocktails at night. Daily 10am–3am.

Mes tin Ammo/Rich and Famous Behind the beach, 500m east of town ⓦ mestinammo-rf.com. *Mes tin Ammo* is a very cool beach bar towards the far end of the town beach, which hosts occasional beach parties; *Rich and Famous*, behind, is their nightclub, far enough out to be loud till late – they also host the odd live band. Daily 10am–4am.

On the Rocks Western end of town at the beginning of the Soúdha road ☎ 28320 31023. Café-bar serving good breakfasts and, later in the day, milkshakes, ice cream and snacks. At 6pm the kitchen closes and it becomes a laidback bar with a country/rock soundtrack. Daily 8.30am–1am.

Ostraco On the waterfront, close to the harbour ☎ 28320 32249. *Ostraco* has been here for ever, it seems, with a rock-based playlist and fun atmosphere. It's one of the best places in town, with two floors of bars and a balcony; the upstairs dancing bar opens at 9pm. Daily 9am–3am.

Paralia On the waterfront, close to the harbour ☎ 6976 718 706. A cooler version of its neighbour *Ostraco*, with an upstairs balcony and more club-oriented music; again there's a quieter café-bar downstairs, with music and dancing above. Daily noon–3am.

SHOPPING

Creta Earth Central seafront ☎ 6987 031 831. Two stores next to each other, one selling crafts, the other products such as oils and herbs, all extremely good quality.

Forum Central seafront ☎ 28320 31320. Supermarket that describes itself as a department store – which given that they stock everything you might conceivably need, from flip-flops to fishing gear, isn't far from the truth; also the best selection of maps, books and newspapers in town.

Savra Just inland from the harbour ☎ 6907 489 003. Quality handmade jewellery and other crafts.

DIRECTORY

Doctor A private doctor's surgery (☎ 28320 31770) and a pharmacy are in the street by the post office.

Laundry Laundromat, on the alley with Elena Tours and the organic minimarket (☎ 28320 32159); service wash €10.

Money There's no bank in Plakiás, but there are ATMs along the seafront street and you can change money at most travel agents and some supermarkets.

Post office On the street running inland near *Hotel Livikon* (Mon–Fri 7.30am–2pm).

Préveli and Palm Beach

Some 10km east of Plakiás a paved road descends into the fertile valley of the Megalopótamos River, which, unusually for Crete, flows throughout the year. Where it meets the river, the road turns south to climb past the fenced-off ruins of the **Monastery of Áyios Ioánnis**, also called Káto, or Lower, Préveli. This is the site of the original sixteenth-century monastery of Préveli, until it was left behind in the following century when the monks decided to move to the greater safety of the present site further uphill. Torched by the Turks in the nineteenth century and long abandoned, only the church now stands complete amid the broken walls, cattle mangers and derelict dwellings of the former monastic community.

Moní Préveli

April & May daily 9am–6pm; June–Oct Mon–Sat 9am–1.30pm & 3.30–9pm, Sun 8am–7pm; in winter, knock for admission • €3 • ⓦ www.preveli.org

The celebrated **MONÍ PRÉVELI** (Μονί Πρέβελη), perched high above the sea, is justifiably proud of its role in centuries of Cretan resistance and famed above all for the shelter provided to Allied troops, many of them Australian, stranded on the island after the Battle of Crete in World War II. The monks supported and fed many soldiers and helped organize them into groups to be taken off nearby beaches by submarine. There's a startling **monument** to these events, overlooking the sea just before the monastery, depicting a life-sized rifle-toting abbot and an Allied soldier cast in bronze. More commemorative plaques decorate the monastery interior, and alongside the icons in the church are a number of offerings from grateful individuals and governments. The church also houses a cross said to contain a fragment of the True Cross; there's a small **museum** with other relics and religious vestments; and a fountain in the courtyard with the palindromic Greek inscription *Nipson anomemata me monan opsin* "Wash your sins, not only your face". There are also fine views out to sea towards the distant and chunky-looking Paximádhia islands, which take their name from the tooth-cracking lumps of twice-baked bread served up with mezédhes in the *kafenía*.

Palm Beach

A sand-filled cove at the mouth of the Kourtaliótiko gorge, where a stream feeds a little oasis complete with palm grove and cluster of oleanders, **Palm Beach** certainly looks beautiful – but for much of the year it's overwhelmed by visitors, with loungers, sun umbrellas and pedaloes diminishing the natural charm of the place. Behind the beach, you can escape up the palm-lined riverbanks on foot or take a pedalo through the icy water. Further upstream, before the gorge becomes too steep to follow, are a couple of deep pools nice to swim in. On the beach, a small **bar-taverna** provides basic food and sells drinks, snacks and a few provisions. It's strange to think, as you bask on the crowded sands, that from here, in 1941, many of the Allied soldiers who sought refuge at Moní Préveli (see p.225) were evacuated by submarine.

ARRIVAL AND GETTING AROUND

By boat Boats from Plakiás and Ayía Galíni ply regularly to Palm Beach.

By bus In summer 4 buses a day run from Réthymno (1hr), and 6 from Plakiás (20min), to Préveli monastery.

By car Driving from Plakiás, after 9km the road bends right into the Megalopótamos river valley and shortly beyond this you'll pass an ancient-looking bridge across the river (actually a nineteenth-century copy of a Venetian original), where a sign indicates a left turn to Palm Beach. Immediately (across the river) you turn right, soon crossing another cobbled Venetian bridge, beyond which the track leads – in 5km, but 15min of tortuous, rough driving – to

PRÉVELI AND PALM BEACH

the *Dionysos Taverna*. From here, Palm Beach is a 5min climb around the cliff via a stairway carved into the rock – and your first view of it as you reach the crest is quite stunning. An alternative, easier, route is to head towards Moní Préveli and follow signs on the left to a car park (€2). From here a well-marked, stepped path with dramatic views heads steeply down over the rocks – a 10min descent to Palm Beach, and a sweaty, muscle-taxing 15–20min back up.

On foot If you arrive at the beach by boat, or the monastery by bus, you can easily walk between the two – 15–20min down, a strenuous 30min or so heading up.

ACCOMMODATION AND EATING

Dionysos Palm Beach ☎ 6977 230 931, ⓦ prevelicrete .com. The better of two places that offer food and rooms on the grey sand beach at the end of the road alongside Palm Beach. Rooms are simple but comfortable – only a couple have a/c (extra) – and the food served on the vine-shaded terrace is equally unfussy, but fresh and delicious (mains €7–9). They also have a shop for basic

supplies to take to the beach. **€25**

Taverna Gefyra By the "Venetian" bridge on the Préveli–Palm Beach road ☎ 6944 986 740. A pleasant taverna on the way to Palm Beach serving mezédhes, snacks and drinks on a shady terrace, plus more substantial daily specials (€7–8) chalked up on the blackboard, such as goat in tomato sauce. Daily 9am–10pm.

West of Plakiás

West of Plakiás the terrain becomes more mountainous as you approach Sfakiá and the foothills of the Lefká Óri. Leaving town, it's a stiff climb up towards Mýrthios and then round, hugging the mountainside, to **Selliá**. You can also approach Selliá direct by an alarmingly steep, winding road climbing from the coast west of Plakiás. Much of the road to Frangokástello (see p.290) runs high above the coast, with spectacular views, but below are some very attractive small beaches.

Selliá

Looking up from Plakiás or across from Mýrthios you would imagine that **SELLIÁ** (Σελλιά) had the best views of all across this area, but if you drive through you see nothing: only the backs of the houses that face out across the sea towards Africa. It's a pretty place, though, and if you want to stop and catch the view it's easy enough to find a path through; better still, pause for a drink or a bite to eat at the tiny taverna on the main street (see below). There are also several excellent shops featuring work by local potters and artists. You can walk from the centre of the village down to Plakiás, a steep thirty minutes below, or you could include Selliá in a long circular hike from Plakiás via Mýrthios.

Rodhákino

Beyond Selliá the country changes and there's a real feeling of the approach of western Crete. The road runs high above a series of capes and small coves, where the only village of any size is **RODHÁKINO** (Ροδάκινο), whose two halves are set on steep streets divided by a dramatic ravine. Below is the sand-and-shingle beach of **Koráka**, where General Kreipe was finally taken off the island after his kidnap in 1944 (see p.338). Some development has started on the coast around here, and if you want to get away from it all there are a few good **rooms** places.

Polyrízos and beyond

Immediately west of Koráka, in the next bay, is **POLYRÍZOS** (Πολυρίζος), where there are more rooms places and villas above a small sandy beach. Continuing west, the main road winds high above the coast, from where a number of beaches look tempting, though hardly any are accessible. Signs of development increase as you cross the provincial border into Haniá and approach Frangokástello, with villas, a few isolated rooms places and even the odd taverna. New tracks connecting these places pop up all the time, which makes things confusing; however, if you drive towards the coast you can often find a way through, though the last bit may be on foot. Some of the best are found by following the sign from the main road to **Lákki beach** – follow this road as it heads back east (it's paved till near the end, but avoid being seduced by new bits of tarmac or signs to tavernas) and you'll reach a headland from which you can easily walk down to a couple of beautiful patches of sand.

ACCOMMODATION AND EATING WEST OF PLAKIÁS

SELLIÁ

★**Elia** Main street ☎ 28320 36002. Excellent little ouzerí-taverna where the home-cooked food is every bit as good as the stunning terrace view; there are daily specials on the board, and often some offbeat choices alongside the traditional – orange, fennel and cheese salad (€6), for example, or simple *soutzoukákia* (€7.50). Daily noon–4pm & 6–10pm.

RODHÁKINO

Arokaria Set back behind the beach ☎ 28320 32177, ⓦ cleanthi-rooms.gr. A very good, friendly taverna with large, somewhat dated but quiet and comfy a/c rooms with TV, kitchenette and great views. The taverna serves mainly

grilled meat and fresh fish, or check out the kitchen for Sfakian specialities such as wild goat (€8.90); and don't miss their home-made orange liqueur. Daily 8am–11pm. **€30**

Sunrise A short way up the hill above the beach ☎ 28320 31787, ⓦ sunrise-hotel-crete.gr. Attractive rooms, studios and apartments with sea views, as well as a pool, bar and taverna. Rates include breakfast. Doubles **€40**, studios **€45**, apartments **€60**

POLYRÍZOS

Panorama Above the small sandy beach ☎ 28320 31788. Aptly named for its raised postion, *Panorama* has simple rooms (with TV, a/c and fridge), and a taverna

3

serving just a few home-made specials each day – delicious and inexpensive (€5–7). Daily 7am–11pm. €30

Polyrizos Hotel ☎ 28320 31334, ✉ polyrizo@otenet.gr.

A relatively large and fancy hotel complex, with a pool and good restaurant where any of the lamb dishes are worth a try. €40

West of Réthymno

Heading **west from Réthymno** the main road is easy and efficient, but offers little in the way of diversion. The E75 **highway** initially climbs above the coast before dropping back to sea level at **Yeráni**, 6km from Réthymno, with a rocky cove good for swimming. Beyond, after another brief flirtation with the hills, the road finally levels out beside the **Gulf of Almirós**, from where it traces the shore, flat and straight, all the way to Yeoryioúpolis (see p.259), alongside a long and windswept **sandy beach**. For the most part this beach, separated from the road by straggling bushes of oleander, is virtually deserted, but there can be dangerous currents so don't venture too far out; it gets more sheltered as you approach the development at Yeoryioúpolis.

The scenic **old road** is by comparison quite populous. To join it, you can either head west from Réthymno, turning inland shortly after you leave the city, or south past the Minoan cemetery at Arméni (see p.215), just after which you can cut west into the hills. Either way, you'll pass through half a dozen prosperous little villages before arriving, after some 20km, at **Episkopí**, a local market centre with narrow, twisting hilly streets at its heart. Here you're approaching the foothills of the White Mountains, which rise with increasing majesty ahead. Beyond Episkopí the road soon divides, the main way descending steadily towards Yeoryioúpolis, a secondary route climbing through the village of Kournás (see p.262) and then dropping steeply to the lake. Alternatively you can head **south** from Episkopí towards **Aryiroúpoli**, **Así Goniá** and a series of small mountain villages, a rarely travelled route where the old life continues, and where there are good opportunities for **hiking** in the surrounding hills.

Roústika

A diversion of 5km or so from the Episkopí road will take you to **ROÚSTIKA (Ρούστικα)**, whose **Church of Panayía and Sotíra** has some of the finest frescoes in Crete. Follow the signs to the left as you enter the village, and narrow streets lead to a square and the elegant, twin-aisled, Byzantine church. Inside (the key is kept at the café next door) are wonderfully preserved fourteenth-century frescoes, principally of scenes from the life of Christ.

Aryiroúpoli

ARYIROÚPOLI (Αργυρούπολη), 6km south of Episkopí, is a strikingly scenic village filled with rushing water, which historically was exploited by a series of watermills. Its **springs** made it a prosperous place throughout history: it was the site of the prestigious Greco-Roman city of **Lappa** and an important commercial centre through Byzantine

---

CROSSING THE ISLAND: SPECTACULAR DRIVES

If you enjoy driving on **Cretan mountain roads**, the trans-island routes west of Réthymno are among the finest on the island, though not for the faint-hearted.

There are a number of routes, paved all the way and emerging either at Plakiás or Frangokástello. The chief ones are: from Roústika or from Aryiroúpoli via Vilandhrédho to Kánevos at the head of the Kotsifoú Gorge (see p.221), and from there on to Plakiás; or from Aryiroúpoli via either Myriokéfala or Así Goniá (the latter in poor condition) to Kallikrátis, and thence a heart-stopping descent to Frangokástello.

ARYIROÚPOLI'S UPPER VILLAGE: A CIRCULAR TOUR

You can begin a **tour** of the upper village in the main square, opposite the church. Pass beneath a stone arch and keep straight ahead to find an elegant Venetian dwelling (perhaps part of the once extensive villa of the Clodio family) on the left, with a fine **portal** bearing the legend *Omnia Mundi Fumus et Umbra* (All Things in This World are Smoke and Shadow). The street eventually climbs and the houses become brilliant white. This is not a tourist village, however, and discreet glances inside open doorways will reveal the everyday work of the village women – rolling *bourekákia* pastries for the evening meal, peeling corncobs, or embroidering and repairing family clothing. The route will lead you past more crumbling Venetian houses, some being refurbished, to a superb **Roman mosaic floor** beneath a canopy on a street corner. Part of a third-century bathhouse, its quality is not only an indication of the wealth of the ancient town, but also of how much still lies buried beneath the modern village. Following the same street around the hill leads back to the arch and the main square.

and Venetian times. Today, with lovely views over the Mouséllas river valley and surrounded by some fine **walking** country in the foothills of the White Mountains, it attracts plenty of day-trippers and coach parties, but out of hours reverts to a peaceful backwater, a refreshing escape from the summer heat.

The springs

Below the village, down a right-hand fork as you come in, gushing **spring water** cascades in every direction. Vegetation is abundant in this fertile environment and the roar of water impressive; there's so much of it here that it supplies the whole of Réthymno town. Around the streams, shaded by great chestnut and plane trees, are half a dozen **tavernas** specializing in trout, kept in ponds, and barbecued meat. Also here are the remains of ancient **waterworks and mills**, some of the most obvious below the *Palios Mylos* taverna, accessed through its grounds. There's a restored Byzantine chapel fronted by a Roman pillar, and not far away by the stream a remarkable seventeenth-century **Venetian fulling mill** (used for shrinking, beating and preparing cloth), whose wooden machinery is rapidly crumbling away. Nearby are the scanty remains of the **Roman baths** of ancient Lappa.

The upper village

Aryiroúpoli itself lies around a tranquil square overlooked by the elegant seventeenth-century Venetian church of **Áyios Ioánnis**. This segment of the village is built over ancient **Lappa** (see below), parts of which can be seen near the church; archeologists have been busy over recent years excavating and documenting the city's ancient necropolis in the valley to the north, where they have unearthed a wealth of grave goods. Beyond the church, the village's **folk museum** is also worth a look (daily 10am–7pm; free).

Heading downhill from the west side of the square along narrow, stepped streets, you come to a smaller square (the old **marketplace**), with a couple of tiny churches en route. At the northern end of the village beyond the *Morfeas* guesthouse, a pleasant walk will bring you to the delightful chapel of **Áyios Nikólaos**, dating from the eleventh century, with fourteenth-century frescoes by Ioannis Pagomenos (John the Frozen). To get there, take the first track on the right off the road beyond the pension, heading down into the valley; then take the first track on the left and descend to the church (which is unlocked), some 300m further.

Ancient Lappa

Originally a Dorian settlement, **Lappa** was an ally of Lyttos (see p.79) in the latter's wars against Knossós. When it fiercely opposed the Roman invasion in 67 BC, the city was destroyed by the conquering legions. Later, when Lappa aided Octavian-Augustus in his struggle against Antony for the control of the Roman world, the victorious emperor permitted the Lappans to rebuild their town and gifted them a **water reservoir** in 27 BC which, incredibly, still supplies the village today. The city flourished for many centuries, even outlasting Roman rule, but was razed again by the Saracens in the ninth century. It recovered during the Venetian occupation and was an important centre, as is evident from the numerous villas left behind by Venetian landlords. Remnants of buildings from all periods of the village's history have been incorporated into most of the houses: you'll spot classical inscriptions, ancient columns and bits of Venetian stone carving in the most unlikely places.

The necropolis

Just over 1km north of Aryioúpoli • Access is by a signed footpath from the village

Ancient Lappa's **necropolis** is located at a site known as the Five Virgins, after a nearby chapel. Hundreds of **tombs** – currently being investigated by archeologists – have been cut into the rock cliffs here, many of them with elaborate interior and exterior decoration. One, opened only recently after its discovery by a goatherd, was found to contain a stunning gold diadem. The chapel takes its name from five young women put to death by the Romans in the third century for secretly practising Christianity in the tombs. Nearby, alongside yet another spring, stands a gigantic 2000-year-old **plane tree** (claimed by locals to be the oldest in Crete), with a path cut through it.

ARRIVAL AND INFORMATION

ARYIROÚPOLI

By bus Buses (Mon–Fri only) leave Réthymno at 6am and 2.45pm, and return at 6.45am and 3.30pm. There are also lots of tours from both Réthymno and Yeoryioúpolis.
Information Beneath the stone arch in the main square,

Lappa Avocado (✆ 28310 81070), a shop selling local wine, herbs and olive oil as well as various avocado products, is a helpful source of information when they're not busy. There are several other good craft shops nearby.

ACCOMMODATION

Maria M Cottages 2km south of the village ✆ 28310 81070, ✉ johanneg12@hotmail.com. New, fully equipped apartments in stone-built houses in a magnificent setting. The views are stunning and facilities include veranda or terrace balcony, a/c, heating, satellite TV, wi-fi and a shared pool. **€90**
Morfeas 1km along the Miriakéfala road off the main square ✆ 6977 258 343, ✉ valiaftilaki@gmail.com.

Good-value, a/c en-suite rooms with balcony, fridge and TV – rooms 1 and 2 are the ones to go for – with a fantastic view down the valley from its taverna terrace. May–Oct. **€28**
Taverna-Rooms Zografakis 50m along the Miriakéfala road just off the main square ✆ 28310 81269, ⊕ ezografakis.gr. Classic Greek-style rooms with fridge, TV and great views northwards from the balconies. above a decent taverna. Breakfast (extra) available. **€25**

EATING AND DRINKING

The village's main cluster of restaurants is at the **springs**, where tavernas have all incorporated water features into their terraces – walls of tumbling water, oriental wooden water bells, water wheels and the like. The whole scene is especially magical at night. The **upper village** can't really compete for ambience but there are a couple of places well worth a try.

Bar Maria Main square, upper village. The village's main bar, which serves breakfast and snacks. A speciality is their avocado and tuna salad prepared with organic village-grown avocados. Daily 9am–10pm.
★O Kipos tis Arkoudenas Just outside Episkopi on the Aryioúpoli road ✆ 28310 61607. Exceptional creative cooking in an unexpected setting, using local, organic ingredients in creative ways. There's a salad with 47 separate ingredients (home-grown or foraged) and mains such as pork stuffed with feta, and rabbit *stifádho* (mains €8–9). Daily 1–10pm.
Palios Mylos At the springs ✆ 28310 81209. Perhaps

the most atmospheric of the many good tavernas at the springs, with its tables arranged around a gushing spring. Specialities include mountain goat (€8.50), charcoal-roast lamb (€9.50) and fresh trout (sold by weight), and there are plenty of vegetarian options. April–June & Sept 11am–8pm; July & Aug daily 11am–11pm; Oct–March Sat & Sun 11am–8pm.
Taverna Arhea Lappa 200m along the Episkopí road below the village ✆ 28310 81004. Good, inexpensive local taverna with an outdoor terrace specializing, like most here, in grilled meat; try the *kontosoúvli* (spit-roast pork; €6) or *loukánika* (sausages; €6). April–Oct daily noon–midnight.

Myriokéfala

The road leading out of Aryiroúpoli's upper village beyond the church allows visits to more villages and interesting churches. After 7km – with possible stops en route to explore the hamlets of Marouloú and Arolíthi, just off the road to left and right – the road passes through **MYRIOKÉFALA** (**Μυριοκέφαλα**), whose former monastery church of the **Panayía Antifonitria** has ancient **Byzantine frescoes** depicting the Passion which are among the earliest examples on the island, dating from the eleventh and twelfth centuries. The tiny drum-domed edifice – in a courtyard at the bottom of the village (follow signs to the monastery) – also has an icon of the Virgin which is highly venerated locally.

Así Goniá

Beyond the springs at Aryiroúpoli, the road continues southwest for 6km through the verdant cleft of the Gipari Gorge, where trees thrust skywards from a riverbed flowing with water all winter, but which lies arid in the summer drought. This habitat breeds a profusion of **birdlife**: as well as blue rock thrushes, pipits and the ubiquitous tits, you may also spot griffon vultures and hawks hovering around the crags.

The road finally arrives in the broad platía of **ASÍ GONIÁ** (**Ασή Γωνιά**), an isolated and perpetually cloudy rustic settlement. You're now in Haniá province, and there is a real contrast here between the barren heights of the White Mountains to the west, and the softer green of the Aryiroúpoli side of the valley. The square is ringed by **busts** portraying Venizélou and associated village heroes, but curiously not its most celebrated recent son, **George Psychoundakis** (see p.353) who died in 2006 aged 85. From the square, the **main street** climbs uphill between simple stone dwellings, their yards piled with the firewood needed to stave off the bitterly cold winters here. A few of the men still wear the traditional *saríki* black headdress, baggy *vraka* trousers and high boots, and almost all still dress in black.

Haniá

BALOS BAY, GRAMVOÚSA

Haniá

Haniá, Crete's westernmost province, is still its least visited, which is a significant part of its attraction. Although tourist development is spreading fast, and has already covered much of the coast around the city of Haniá, the west is likely to remain one of the emptier parts of the island, partly because there are few beaches suited to large resort hotels, and partly because the great archeological sites are a long way from here. In their place are some of the island's most classic elements: scattered coves, unexploited rural villages, and a spectacular vista of mountains.

The city of **Haniá**, island capital until 1971, is unequivocally the most enjoyable of Crete's larger towns, littered with oddments from its Venetian and Turkish past, and bustling with harbourside life. To either side, along virtually the whole **north coast** of the province, spreads a line of sandy beach – at times exposed, and increasingly developed, but still with numerous stretches where you can escape the crowds. Three peninsulas punctuate this northern coastline: **Akrotíri**, enclosing the magnificent natural harbour of **Soúdha Bay**; **Rodhopoú**, a bare and roadless tract of mountain; and, at the western tip of the island, **Gramvoúsa**, uninhabited and entirely barren. Akrotíri, ringed with air bases and naval installations, is well worth a day-trip, with a couple of excellent beaches and two beautiful monasteries. Most tourists stay to the west, on the coast between Haniá and Rodhopoú, in one of a number of former villages now linked by an ever-expanding strip of low-rise development centred on **Ayía Marína** and **Plataniás**, with the villas and apartments thinning out as you head further from the city.

The south is overshadowed by the peaks of the **Lefká Óri** – the **White Mountains** – whose grey bulk, snow-capped from January through to June, dominates every view in western Crete. Although marginally less high than the Psilorítis range, they're far more rewarding for walking or climbing. Along the south coast the mountains drop straight to the Libyan Sea, and the few towns here lie in their shadow, clinging to what flat land can be found around the bays. Through the heart of the massif there's no road at all, nor is there any driveable route along the south coast: unless you want to travel back and forth across the island you'll have to rely on boats, or on walking. The hike through the National Park in the **Samariá Gorge**, Europe's longest, is stunning, despite the summer hordes. With a little spirit of adventure and preparation you can take scores of other, deserted **hiking** routes.

Highlights

❶ Haniá The island's second-largest city is also its most enjoyable, with a delightful Old Town, scenic harbour, and great food, drink and nightlife. **See p.237**

❷ Lefká Óri Haniá's White Mountains offer a huge range of hiking opportunities, from easy gorge walks to serious mountain expeditions. **See p.272**

❸ Loutró Accessible only on foot or by boat, the tiny village of Loutró epitomizes the isolated appeal of the southwest coast. **See p.279**

❹ Frangokástello A stunning seaside castle with a backdrop of stark mountains. **See p.290**

❺ West coast beaches Crete's little-known west coast boasts two of the island's finest beaches at Falásarna and Elafonísi. **See p.298**

❻ Byzantine churches Ancient churches, many of them with remains of original frescoes, are found throughout the region, particularly in Sélinos. **See p.306**

❼ Paleóhora The only real resort in the southwest, with a great beach, lively atmosphere and an enjoyable end-of-the-road feel. **See p.308**

❽ Gávdhos If you truly want to get away from it all, this island off Crete's south coast is about as far as you can go. **See p.318**

HIGHLIGHTS ARE MARKED ON THE MAP ON P.236

HANIÁ

The south-coast communities beneath the mountains see plenty of visitors, mostly gorge-trippers passing through, but none could really be described as a resort. **Ayía Rouméli**, the sometimes frenetic end-point of the Samariá Gorge walk, and serene **Loutró** can be reached only on foot or by boat. **Hóra Sfakíon**, the capital of the wild region known as **Sfakiá**, is a pleasant place to stay if you can handle the influx of day-trippers; more peace is to be found down the coast a little, at the superb beaches by the Venetian castle of **Frangokástello**.

The west end of the island, beyond Rodhopoú, is very sparsely populated. The port of **Kastélli** is the only town of any size, and there's a growing resort at **Paleóhora** in the south. **Soúyia** may be the next in line, but for the moment it seems in a rather charming state of limbo. The whole of the mountainous southwestern corner, an area known as **Sélinos**, is worth exploring, with rough roads leading to untouched mountain villages and little-known ruins and churches. On the west-facing coast – hard to get to but well worth the effort – are two of Crete's finest beaches, **Falásarna** and **Elafonísi**. Finally there's **Gávdhos**, an island some 30km off the south coast that is Europe's southernmost point, caught somewhere between the eighteenth and the twenty-first centuries.

Haniá town

HANIÁ (Χανιά), as any of its residents will tell you, is spiritually the capital of Crete, even if the formal political title was long ago passed back to Iráklio. With its shimmering waterfront, crumbling masonry and web of alleys, it is an extraordinarily attractive city, especially if you can catch it in spring when the Lefká Óri's snow-capped peaks seem to hover above the roofs. Although it is for the most part a modern place, whose permanent population – fast expanding into hill and coastal suburbs – always outnumbers the visitors, you might never know this as a tourist. Surrounding the harbour is a wonderful jumble of Venetian streets, a maze-like **old town** contained by ancient city walls and littered with **Ottoman**, **Byzantine** and **Minoan ruins**. Highlights include the **Venetian harbour** itself and a quartet of **museums**, but the greatest pleasure of all, perhaps, is to be had simply wandering the narrow streets and stepped alleyways. Add plentiful accommodation and tavernas, excellent **markets**, shopping and nightlife, and you'll almost certainly want to stay longer than you intended.

4

Brief history

Haniá is one of the longest continuously inhabited city sites in the world, though its convoluted and often violent history has left it with relatively little to show for it. Only recently has the arrival of **tourism**, amid a rare period of peace and prosperity, inspired the will – if not the resources – to save the city's crumbling architectural heritage.

Ancient Kydonia and La Canea

Ancient **Kydonia** was an apparently substantial **Minoan** community about which little is known: only scattered remnants have so far been brought to light, but many believe that there was a major palace here, probably beneath the modern buildings in Kastélli, overlooking the harbour. After the collapse of the Minoan palace culture, Kydonia grew into one of the island's most important cities – well enough known for its citizens to warrant a mention in Homer's *Odyssey* – and remained so through the Classical Greek era. When **Rome** came in search of conquest, the city mounted a stiff resistance prior to its eventual capitulation in 69 BC, after which it flourished once more. The Kastélli hill served as the Roman city's acropolis, but dwellings spread at least as far as the extent of the walled city that can be seen today: Roman mosaics have been discovered beneath Cathedral Square and up near the present-day market.

In early **Christian** times Kydonia was the seat of a bishop, and under the protection of Byzantium the city flourished along with the island. As the Byzantine Empire became

---

HANIÁ ORIENTATION

Haniá's **old city** clusters around the harbour, and most tourists confine themselves to this area or the fringes of the **new town** up towards the bus station. You may get lost wandering among the alleys, but it's never far to the sea, one of the main thoroughfares or some other landmark. The major junction at the top of Hálidhon marks the centre of town as well as anywhere. If you stand facing north at this junction, everything in front of and below you is basically the old, walled city; behind is Platía 1866 and the newer parts of town. To the east, **Odhós Yiánnari** leads past the market and on towards the Akrotíri peninsula and airport, or out to the main highway, while to the west, **Skalídhi** leads out of town towards the closest beaches, and eventually to the highway west and Kastélli Kissámou.

---

increasingly embattled however, so its further outposts, Kydonia included, suffered neglect. Not much is heard of the place again until the thirteenth century, when the **Genoese** seized the city from the Venetians and held it from 1263 to 1285.

When the **Venetians** finally won the city back they turned **La Canea** (as it was now known) into a formidable bulwark, as well as probably the island's most beautiful city. The city walls were built in two stages: in the fourteenth century Kastélli alone was fortified; in the sixteenth century, new walls were constructed as a defence against constant raids by pirate corsairs – in particular against the systematic ravages of Barbarossa. It is these defences, along with the Venetian harbour installations, that define the shape of Haniá's old town today.

Occupation and resistance

In 1645, after a two-month siege with terrible losses (the Turkish commander was executed on his return home for losing as many as forty thousand men), Haniá fell to the **Turks**. It was the first major Cretan stronghold to succumb, becoming the Turkish island capital. Churches were converted to mosques, the defences more or less maintained, and there must have been at least some new building, though today it is barely possible to distinguish Venetian from Turkish workmanship.

For the rest, it is a history of struggle. In the **independence** campaign, the city's most dramatic moment came in 1897, following the outbreak of war between Greece and the Ottoman Empire, when the Great Powers (Britain, France, Russia and Italy) imposed peace and stationed a joint force in the waters off Haniá. From here, they bombarded Cretan insurgents attempting prematurely to raise the flag of Greece on the hill of Profítis Elías (see p.250). When the Turks were finally forced to leave, Prince George, the high commissioner chosen by the powers, established his capital here for the brief period of his regency.

During **World War II**, with most of the German landings and the bulk of the fighting on the coast immediately west of the city, Haniá suffered severe bombardment, the destruction eventually compounded by a fire, which wiped out almost everything apart from the area around the harbour.

The harbour

The **harbour** area is at its busiest and most attractive at night, when the lights from bars and restaurants reflect in the water and the animated crowds – locals as much as tourists – parade in a ritualistic volta of apparently perpetual motion. Stalls sell everything from seashells to henna tattoos, and buskers serenade the passers-by. By day, especially in the hot, dozy mid-afternoon, it can be less appealing – often deserted and with the occasional whiff of decay from the rubbish washing up against the quayside. From waterfront Platía Sindriváni, almost always known simply as **Harbour Square**, Aktí Koundouriótou circles to the left around the outer harbour, crowded with outdoor cafés and tavernas, while straight ahead Aktí Tombázi heads past the mosque towards the inner harbour.

HANIÁ TOWN

▲ ⚪ (200m), Attikon Cinema (220m), ⚪ (300m), ⚪ (5km), Airport & Akrotiri

● CAFÉS

Alcanea	4
Iordanis Bougatsa	24
O Platanos tis Splantzias	12
Thea	13
To Kafenio	15

■ SHOPS

Canea	4, 5
Market	7
Mediterraneo Bookstore	1
Miden Agan	2
Saturday Street Market	3
See Crete	6

■ ACCOMMODATION

Alcanea	2
Amphora	10
Anastasia	14
Anemi Suites	17
Camping Hania	12
Casa Delfino	15
Casa Veneta	7
Chania Hostel	22
Doma	23
Ifigenia	8
Ionas	18
Kasteli	11
La Maison Ottomane	9
Lucia	16
Nora	6
Palazzo	3
Pandora Suites	13
Porto Veneziano	1
Splanzia	19
Stella	5
Thereza	4
To Dhiporto	21
Vilelmine	20

● RESTAURANTS

63° Mezedoskolion	22
Akrogiali	11
Amphora	10
Doloma	8
Enetikon	14
Faka	6
Glossitses	1
Kalderimi	9
Karnayio	7
Khrisostomos	2
Mihalis	5
Nykteridha	23
Pizzes Bié	21
Portes	20
Tamam	16
Tholos	19
To Maridhaki	17
To Stakhi	3
To Pigadi Tou Tourkiou	18

● BARS, CLUBS & LIVE MUSIC

Ababa	6
Fagotto	4
Ippopotamos	8
Miniatoura	1
Rakadhiko ta Halkina	5
Rudi's Bierhaus	7
Synagogi	3
Ta Duo Lux	9
To Monastiri tou Karolos	9

Mosque of the Janissaries

Aktí Tombázi

The curious, domed profile of the **Mosque of the Janissaries** (aka Hassan Pasha mosque) dominates the Harbour Square view. Built in 1645, the year Haniá fell to the Turks, it is the oldest Ottoman building on the island, and has been well restored – apart from the jarring concrete dome. Currently without a function, it occasionally hosts temporary exhibitions while a more long-term plan is considered, and one small room houses a part-time summer tourist booth. If you do get in, the most striking internal feature is the **mihrab** (a niche indicating the direction of Mecca) complete with Koranic inscription.

The Naval Museum

Aktí Koundouriótou • May–Oct Mon–Sat 9am–5pm, Sun 10am–6pm; Nov–April daily 9am–5pm • €3, joint ticket with Exhibition of Traditional Naval Architecture €4 • ☎ 28210 91875, ⓦ mar-mus-crete.gr

The hefty bastion at the western end of the outer harbour houses Crete's **Naval Museum**. Although largely of specialist interest, the enthusiasm here is infectious, and the model ships, maquettes of the town in Venetian times, old maps and working exhibits like the old harbour light are hard to resist.

Whether visiting the museum or not, it's worth going through the main gate (usually open in daylight hours) to see the compound of the small naval garrison. Here you can climb onto the renovated seaward fortifications of the **Firkás**, as this part of the city defences is known. It was on this spot that the modern Greek flag was first raised on Crete – in 1913 – and there are fine sea views.

The inner harbour

Around the sheltered **inner harbour** pleasure boats, private yachts and small fishing vessels are moored, while sixteenth-century Venetian arsenals look out towards the breakwater across a cluster of waterfront restaurants and bars. Many of the arched **Arsenali** are still in a ruinous state, but others have been sensitively restored: one, the sixteenth-century Great Arsenal, is occupied by the **Center for Mediterranean Architecture** (CMA), with offices, a café and a glitzy space for temporary exhibitions (times and prices vary).

At the eastern end of the inner harbour and in the tangled, atmospheric alleys behind there are more signs of regeneration and refurbishment; this is now a fashionable part of town. A pleasant stroll follows the outer sea wall around for some 600m as far as the minaret-style **lighthouse**, with excellent views back over the city.

The Exhibition of Traditional Naval Architecture

Inner harbour • May–Oct Mon–Sat 9am–5pm, Sun 10am–6pm • €2, joint ticket with Naval Museum €4 • ☎ 28210 91875, ⓦ mar-mus-crete.gr

One of the Arsenali, at the extreme eastern end of the harbour, houses the Naval Museum's **Exhibition of Traditional Naval Architecture**, the highlight of which is a reconstruction of a fifteenth-century BC **Minoan ship**, the *Minoa*. This was rowed to Athens for the start of the 2004 Olympics and, together with the vast boatshed itself, it easily outshines the rest of the exhibits.

Odhós Hálidhon and the old town

Odhós Hálidhon, climbing from the harbour to the new town, is perhaps the most commercially touristy street in Haniá, especially around its junction with animated **Odhós Skridhlóf** ("Leather Street"). Here, traditionally, leather-makers plied their trade and although many shops are now geared to tourists, prices for leather sandals, bags and the like remain some of the best in Crete. In this direction, east of Hálidhon and behind the cathedral, commercial streets blend into the new town and towards the market; to the west, behind the outer harbour, are some of the busiest alleys of the **old town**.

Platía Mitropóleos

Haniá's cathedral square, **Platía Mitropóleos**, opens off Hálidhon about halfway up. The **cathedral** itself is a modest 1860s structure with little architectural merit, but it's an attractive space, surrounded by outdoor cafés – more peaceful if you head round to the back of the building. There's a fine statue of Anagnostis Mandakas, a nineteenth-century insurgent who raised the first official Greek flag on Crete, in 1913.

The Archeological Museum

Hálidhon 21 • Tues–Sun 8.30am–3pm • €2, combined ticket with Byzantine Museum €3 • ☎ 28210 90334

Haniá's **Archeological Museum** is housed in the Venetian-built church of San Francesco. Though it doesn't look like much now, with its campanile gone and a crumbling facade, this building was once one of the island's grandest. Inside, you get a better sense of its former importance. The Turks converted the church into a mosque, from which a beautiful fountain and the base of a minaret have survived in the flowery garden.

The museum boasts a large collection of **Minoan metalwork and pottery**, including a few huge storage jars or *píthoi* and a collection of Minoan clay coffins (*lárnakes*), some wonderfully decorated, and one containing two small skeletons. For archeologists, the most significant items are the **inscribed tablets** excavated in Kastélli; this is the only place other than Knossós where examples of Linear A and Linear B script (see p.329) have been found together – more evidence supporting the existence of a major palace here. Another important find from the Kastélli excavations is the **"Master Impression" seal**. Dating from the Late Minoan period (1500–1450 BC), it is almost unique in depicting a townscape – a long-haired male figure in Minoan loincloth, holding a sceptre, is shown standing over a great complex of multi-storey buildings (the Kastélli hill?) with a rocky seaside landscape below.

Towards the back of the church, the collection is arranged chronologically, progressing through a large group of Classical **sculptures**, a case full of Greco-Roman **glassware** and some third-century Roman **mosaics**. The latter are truly lovely, particularly those of Dionysos and Ariadne, and of Poseidon and Anemone.

The museum is scheduled to move to a spectacular **new building** in the eastern suburb of Halepa in 2017. Designed by renowned Greek architect Theofanis Bobotis, the new edifice will have far more exhibition space and will provide library and laboratory facilities for researchers. Several previous opening dates have been and gone, though, so check with the tourist office (see p.245) for the latest.

The Cretan House Folklore Museum

Hálidhon 46B • Mon–Fri 9am–3pm & 6–9pm, Sat & Sun 9am–3pm • €2 • ☎ 28210 90816

The **Cretan House Folklore Museum** is a cluttered collection of artefacts, tapestries and traditional crafts equipment set out in a replica of a "traditional" house (though few can have been quite so packed). Embroidered cloths and tapestries made on site are for sale. On your way out, take a look at Haniá's elegant **Roman Catholic church** in the same courtyard, an interesting contrast to the city's Orthodox churches.

Evraïki

Between Hálidhon and the Renieri Gate (see p.242), the emphasis is on tavernas, bars and cafés. At the heart of this area, around busy **Kóndhilaki** street, was the medieval Jewish ghetto, a quarter still officially known as **Evraïki**.

Etz Hayyim Synagogue

Párados Kóndhilaki • Mon–Thurs 10am–5pm, Fri 10am–3pm • Suggested donation €2 • ☎ 28210 86286, ⓦ etz-hayyim-hania.org

Signed at the end of a small alley off the west side of Kóndhilaki is Haniá's fifteenth-century Etz Hayyim **synagogue**, renovated by a fraternity of local Christians, Muslims and Jews after falling into ruin. Virtually all of the city's Jews were rounded up by the Nazi occupation forces in 1944; they met their end (along with around seven hundred

Greek and Italian prisoners of war) when the transport ship taking them to Pireás (en route to Auschwitz) was torpedoed by a British submarine off the island of Mílos. The synagogue is entered through the original Venetian doorway, and its garden, *mikveh* (purification fountain), reconstructed interior and *bimah* (speakers' platform) have been sensitively restored. The names of the 276 Jews who perished in the ship are remembered on a plaque in a garden cemetery at the rear.

The city walls

Corralling the western edge of the Old Town lies much the best-preserved stretch of the **city walls**, impressive, weighty and threatening. On the outside, Odhós Pireós traces them all the way from the new town to the sea. Following them on the inside is rather trickier, but far more enjoyable. This is where you'll stumble on some of the most picturesque little alleyways and finest Venetian houses in Haniá, and also where the pace of renovation and gentrification is most rapid. The arch of the **Renieri Gate** is particularly elegant. There are also interesting art and craft stores around here, along Theotokopóulou and the many alleys that run off it down towards the harbour.

The Byzantine Museum

Theotokopóulou 78 • Tues–Sun 8.30am–3pm • €2, combined ticket with Archeological Museum €3 • ☎ 28210 96046

The **Byzantine Museum**, in the Venetian chapel of San Salvatore, has a tiny but beautifully displayed collection of mosaics, icons, jewellery, coins, sculpture and everyday objects, giving a fascinating insight into an era that's largely overlooked – the entire period from early Christian to the end of the Venetian occupation in the seventeenth century.

Kastélli

The bluff that rises behind the mosque and the inner harbour, known as **Kastélli**, was the site of the first habitation in Haniá. Favoured from earliest times for its defensive qualities, this little hill takes its name from a fortress that originally dated from the Byzantine era. Later it was the centre of the Venetian and of the Turkish towns. Little survived a heavy bombardment during World War II, though there are traces everywhere, with houses built against and from the ancient walls, a few surviving sections of which are being restored.

Walking up Kaneváro from Platía Sindriváni you'll pass various remains, including a couple of fenced-off sites where **Minoan Kydonia** is being excavated. The Swedish-Greek archeological team have traced the outline of substantial buildings engulfed by a violent fire about 1450 BC, similar to that which destroyed Knossós. Many believe that this could be the site of the **palace** long thought to have existed here – if so, it would complete a pattern across the island – but as yet no trace of a "Central Court", the defining feature of Minoan palaces in Crete, has come to light. Trial excavations in the nearby Odhós Dhaskaloyiánni at the end of Kaneváro revealed the whole area to be covered with Minoan remains, so there remains a real possibility that a Minoan palace could lie somewhere here. In the period following the Minoan demise it is also likely, given its proximity to the mainland, that this may well have been the focus of Mycenaean power on Crete.

Among pottery finds were some dating back to the Neolithic era, but the greatest prize uncovered was an archive of clay tablets bearing Minoan Linear A script (see p.329), the first to be found so far west in Crete. All around the Kastélli hill various other **trial excavations**, usually on vacant lots between existing houses, reveal further tantalizing glimpses of the substantial Minoan conurbation that lies beneath the modern town, and there are plans for much more extensive excavations once all the relevant property has been acquired. The alleys up to the left, onto the rise, end up going nowhere, but it's worth exploring up here for the traces of the old city that survive, and tantalizing glimpses of the views that the old buildings afford. Lithinón, for example, has various Venetian doorways and inscriptions and, at the top, a fine old archway, beyond which the rather derelict hilltop area allows fine **views** over the harbour and out to sea.

Splántzia

Inland from Kastélli, you can head through the backstreets towards the **market**. This area, still known by its Turkish name **Splántzia**, is full of unexpected architectural delights, with carved wooden balconies and houses arching across the street at first-floor level. Many of the streets between here and the inner harbour have recently been recobbled and refurbished, and they're among the most evocative in the old town.

Platía 1821 and around

The tranquil **Platía 1821** features the refurbished church of Áyios Nikólaos, whose **minaret** is missing its top. Built by the Venetians, the church was converted to a mosque under Sultan Ibrahim and reconverted after Crete's reversion to Greek authority. The square itself – whose name recalls the date of one of the larger rebellions against Turkish authority, following which an Orthodox bishop was hanged here – is a shady space set with café chairs. Nearby are two more old churches: San Rocco, at the square's northeast corner, is small and old-fashioned, while south of the square **Áyii Anáryiri**, which retained its Orthodox status throughout the Turkish occupation, has some very ancient icons.

4

The modern town

Modern Haniá sprawls in every direction, encircling the old town. The areas southwest of the **market**, on the way to **Platía 1866** and the bus station, have an attractively old-fashioned commercialism about them, full of stores stocking life's essentials.

HANIÁ'S BEACHES

Haniá's closest beaches lie west of town. The town beach can be reached on foot, while the others are accessible by bus #21 from Platía 1866.

Néa Hóra The city beach is about a 10min walk from the harbour, round past the Naval Museum and on by the city's open-air swimming pool and a small fishing-boat harbour. The beach has clean sand and sheltered water, showers, and usually crowds of people. Cafés and restaurants line the seafront, while offshore (a longer swim than it looks) is a tiny islet with a sandy beach large enough for about five people at a time.

Áyii Apóstoli Around 3km west of Néa Hora – about 20min on foot. A good long stretch of yellow sand, behind which is the city's campsite and a low-key cluster of development; the only drawback (as at most of these beaches) is the crashing breakers, which can become vicious.

Hrissí Aktí Some 2km beyond Áyii Apóstoli. Hrissí Aktí (Golden Beach) has more good sand, which has attracted the apartment-builders. But it's not yet overcrowded, has some good tavernas and is popular with locals.

Oasis beach and Kalamáki Beyond the Hrissí Aktí headland lies a tiny sand cove, another small promontory, and then the long curve of Oasis Beach running on round to Kalamáki. This is justly crowded – the swimming is probably the best in the area, with a gently shelving sandy bottom and a fossil-covered (and very sharp) rocky islet/reef that fends off the bigger waves. There's a string of cafés and tavernas, and other facilities including windsurf rental and lessons. Kalamáki is the furthest beach accessible by city bus, and it's right by the main road.

Further afield There are even finer beaches at Ayía Marína (see p.263) to the west, or Kalathás and Stavrós (see p.250) out on the Akrotíri peninsula, all of which can be reached by KTEL bus from the main station.

The public gardens

Between Odhós Tzanakáki and Odhós Papandhréou, southeast of the market

Laid out by a Turkish pasha in the nineteenth century, the **public gardens** include a few caged animals – Cretan wild goats, or *kri-kri*, ponies, loud monkeys and birds – a fine traditional café where you can sit under the trees and a children's play area. The open-air auditorium is often used as a cinema, and also hosts local ceremonies and folklore displays, including many events for the town's main annual **festival**, the commemoration of the Battle of Crete, around May 20.

Platía Eleftherías and around

At the end of Papandhréou, about 500m southeast of the public gardens, **Platía Eleftherías** has a statue of Venizélos in the centre and an imposing court building along the south side, which was originally the government building of Prince George's short-lived administration (see p.336). **Iróon Politehníou** runs due north from Platía Eleftherías down to the sea. A broad avenue divided by trees and lined with large houses, interspersed with several expensive garden restaurants and a number of fashionable café-bars, it makes for an interesting walk in a part of the city very different from that dominated by the tourist crowds around the harbour.

ARRIVAL AND DEPARTURE   HANIÁ TOWN

BY BUS

Bus station Odhós Kydhonías, within easy walking distance of the centre; there's a left-luggage office. Information and timetables at ☏ 28210 93052, ⓦ e-ktel .com.

Destinations Airport (at least one hourly, 5am–11pm; 30min); Almyrídha (4 daily; 40min); Ayía Marína (at least half hourly, hourly through the night; 15min); Balos (4 daily; 1hr 30min); Elafonísi (1 daily, 9am; 2hr 15min); Falásarna (7 daily; 2hr); Hóra Sfakíon (4 daily; 1hr 40min); Iráklio (18 daily; 2hr 45min); Kalýves (6 daily; 30min); Kastélli (15 daily; 1hr); Kolymbári (at least half hourly; 40min); Limnoupolis water park (4 daily; 30min); Máleme (at least half hourly; 30min); Omalós, for the Samariá Gorge (3 daily, 6.15am, 7.45am & 8.45am; 1hr 30min); Paleóhora (5 daily; 2hr); Plataniás (at least half hourly, hourly through the night; 20min); Réthymno (18 daily; 1hr); Soúyia (3 daily, 5.15am, 8.45am & 1.45pm; 1hr 45min); Stavrós (via Horafákia; 6 daily; 30min); Vámos (6 daily; 40min); Yeoryioúpoli (18 daily; 40min).

BY FERRY

Ferry dock At the port of Soúdha (see p.253), 10km east of Haniá. Frequent local buses (every 20min; 20min; €1.70) will drop you by the market on the fringes of the old town, or you can take a taxi (€9; prices to other destinations posted); KTEL buses to Réthymno and Kastélli also meet the ferries.

Ferry tickets Available from most travel agencies or the ANEK office, on Venizélou opposite the market; ☏ 28210 27500, ⓦ anek.gr.

Destinations Departures to and from Pireás (9hr) every evening year-round, plus daytime sailings at peak summer periods.

BY PLANE

Haniá airport About 15km northeast of the city, in the middle of the Akrotíri peninsula, the airport is served by frequent local buses (at least hourly; €2.30), and taxis (€18 to Haniá). The driving route into Haniá is pretty clear: for all destinations other than the city, it's quicker and easier to take the left turn signed to Soúdha at the roundabout some 7km from the airport; this will take you down past the head of Soúdha Bay and out onto the main E75 highway, bypassing Haniá's congestion.

Airlines Aegean (ⓦ aegeanair.com) and Ryanair (ⓦ ryanair.com) offer domestic flights; Easyjet, Ryanair and Thomson also have scheduled flights to the UK throughout the summer (see p.21).

Destinations Athens (4–8 daily with Aegean, 2–4 with Ryanair); Thessaloníki (1 each daily on Aegean and Ryanair).

BY CAR

Parking Driving can be a nightmare once you hit the harbour area and get tangled up in the one-way system and no-parking zones. As a car is near-useless inside the old walled city and distances are easily walkable anyway, the least stressful solution is to park outside the old town and walk in. Longer-term parking places can usually be found along Aktí Kanári to the west of the Naval Museum near the seafront, or on the side streets off Pireós leading down there, and to the north of the open-air theatre on the east side of the old town; there are also signposted pay car parks in the new town. Much of the old town is off-limits to vehicles, and parking within the walls is almost impossible in high season – get advice from your hotel if you are driving, as they may help you with your luggage, or have a temporary space where you can unload.

GETTING AROUND

By bus The terminus for most city buses, especially those heading west (including the beaches; bus #21), is at Platía 1866; for Soúdha and the eastern side of town you may find it easier to get on at one of the stops by the market. Timetables at ⓦ www.chaniabus.gr. Longer-distance buses, including those to the coastal resorts around Plataniás (see p.263), run from the main bus station (see opposite).

By car and bike For car rental try around the top of Hálidhon, where Tellus, Hálidhon 108 (☎ 28210 91500,

ⓦ rentacarchania.gr) is one of many. Alianthos is another reliable outlet (☎ 28320 32033, ⓦ alianthos-group.com), with offices at the airport and in Plataniás. Summertime, Dhaskaloyiánni 7 and other local branches (☎ 28210 45797, ⓦ strentals.gr), has a huge range, including cars, motorbikes and good bikes.

By taxi The main taxi rank is in Platía 1866, with smaller ones nearby at the bus station and on Venizélou near the market. For radio taxis call ☎ 18300 or ☎ 28210 94300.

INFORMATION AND ACTIVITIES

Tourist offices The helpful municipal tourist office is at Milonoyiánni 53, at the side of the *Dhimarhío* (town hall; Mon–Fri 8.30am–3pm; ☎ 28210 41665, ⓦ chaniatourism .com). They have timetables for buses, sites and museums, as well as details on excursions. In summer they also run two booths — one in the Mosque of the Jannisaries, the other in front of the market (July–Sept daily 10am–2pm). The Greek National Tourist Office is nearby at Kriári 40, just off Platía 1866 (Mon–Fri 9am–2pm; ☎ 28210 92943), and there's also an office at the airport in summer (July–Sept Mon–Sat 9am–9pm).

Travel agencies Concentrated around the top of Hálidhon and on Platía 1866, as well as around the bus station. Try Tellus Travel, Hálidhon 108 (☎ 28210 91500, ⓦ tellustravel.gr), or Kyriakakis, Yiánnari 78 (☎ 28210 27700, ⓦ kyriakakis.gr).

Boat trips A number of boats run trips from the outer harbour (typically €10–20), mainly to the nearby islands of Áyii Theódori and Lazarétta, for swimming and *kri-kri* (ibex) spotting: you're unlikely to escape the attentions of their touts around the harbour. Alternatives include sunset cruises and all-day trips to the Rodhopoú peninsula. On the inner harbour, smaller boats offer sailing and private charter excursions.

City tours There's a hop-on, hop-off city bus tour (€15)

that won't show you much of the old town, but does take in the town beach and new town, and heads out to Soúdha and the Venizélos Graves (see p.250); one way to see the old city is on a Segway with Chania Segway Tours, Khrysánthou Episkópou 25 (☎ 28210 08695, ⓦ chania segwaytours.com; from €39).

Climbing and walking The local EOS mountaineering club, Tzanakáki 90 (☎ 28210 44647, ⓦ eoshanion.gr), provides information about climbing in the Lefká Óri and takes reservations for the mountain refuge at Kallergi, near the Samariá Gorge (see p.275). They also maintain and mark a number of hiking trails, detailed on their website.

Cycling Hellas Bike (☎ 28210 60858, ⓦ hellasbike.net), in nearby Ayía Marína (see p.263), offers bike tours around the area (€38/half-day; €58/full day, including pick-up from your accommodation).

Diving There are numerous dive shops in Haniá; Chania Diving Center, Arholéon 1 (☎ 28210 58939, ⓦ chaniadiving .gr), is a quality outfit.

Water park The expansive Limnoupolis (adults €25/€17 after 3pm, kids €18/€14; ⓦ limnoupolis.gr) is near to the village of Varipetro, 8km southwest of the city; there four buses a day from the bus station.

ACCOMMODATION

In and around Haniá there's a huge range of accommodation, from simple **rooms for rent** to elegant **boutique hotels**. The popularity of the latter has led to anyone with a room near the harbour to tart it up, call it boutique, and attempt to rent it out at a ridiculously inflated price. Perhaps the most desirable rooms are those overlooking the **harbour**, which are sometimes available at reasonable rates: this is often because they're noisy at night. Most are approached from the streets behind; those further back are likely to be more peaceful. **Theotokopóulou** and the alleys off it make a good starting point. The best of the more expensive places are here, too, equally set back but often with views from the upper storeys. In the **addresses** below, Párodhos means side street, so 2 Párodhos Theotokopóulou, for example, is the second alley off Theotokopóulo.

HARBOUR AREA: WEST OF HÁLIDHON

★ **Alcanea** Angélou 2 ☎ 28210 75370, ⓦ alcanea.com. Gorgeous eight-room boutique hotel in a historic building beside the Naval Museum. Rooms come with all facilities including satellite TV and iPod docks, with Nespresso machines and traditional teas in the communal areas. The pricier rooms (at least twice the price of the most basic) have stunning views and balconies. Excellent breakfast included. March–Dec. **€75**

★ **Amphora** 2 Párodhos Theotokopóulou 20 ☎ 28210 93224, ⓦ amphora.gr. Set in a beautifully renovated fourteenth-century Venetian building, with spiral stair-cases and four-poster beds. Balcony rooms with harbour view are the best value; those without a view are cheaper. April–Oct. **€110**

Anastasia Theotokopóulou 21 ☎ 28210 88001, ⓦ anastasia-apartments.com. Attractive a/c en-suite rooms and fully equipped apartments in buildings on

4

each side of this atmospheric street. Doubles €45, apartments €55

Casa Delfino Theofánous 9 ☎ 28210 87400, ⊚ casa delfino.com. Over-the-top hotel offering big, deluxe suites with elegant decor, marble or polished-wood floors, satellite TV and jacuzzis; there's also a small spa. €190

Casa Veneta Theotokopóulou 57 ☎ 28210 90007, ⊚ casa-veneta.gr. Very well-equipped, comfortable studios and apartments run by a helpful, friendly proprietor, with kitchenette, TV and (some) balcony sea views behind a Venetian facade; the large duplex apartment is particularly attractive. Free wi-fi in reception area only. Studios €55, apartments €60

Ifigenia A. Gámba 23 ☎ 28210 94357, ⊚ ifigenia studios.gr. A small empire of rooms, studios and apartments at various prices, in old Venetian buildings scattered across the old town. Most have elegant, quirky decor (one has a jacuzzi bath right in the middle of the room), and there's free wi-fi in room or reception. Doubles €40, studios €70, apartments €100

Lucia Aktí Koundouriótou ☎ 28210 90302, ⊚ loukia hotel.gr. Harbourfront hotel with a/c balcony rooms with fridge; the furnishing is basic at best, hence much less expensive than you might expect for one of the best locations in town, and – thanks to double-glazing – reasonably soundproof. €60

Nora Theotokopóulou 60 ☎ 28210 72265, ⊚ pension -nora.com. Simple but charming a/c en-suite rooms in a refurbished wooden Venetian house. Also appealing studios (same price) in a building nearby. €40

Palazzo Theotokopóulou 54 ☎ 28210 93227, ⊚ palazzo hotel.gr. An old mansion conversion, with wood-beamed ceilings and old wooden floors. Good-sized, simple rooms, most with balconies, plus a roof terrace with harbour views and tasty breakfasts (included). Free wi-fi in reception. €70

Stella Angélou 10 ☎ 28210 73756, ⊚ rooms-stella -chania.weebly.com. Creaky, eccentric old house above an eclectic gift shop, with a wide variety of rooms equipped with a/c and fridge. The cheapest are very small; no.4 is airy, with a fine view, but more expensive. €35

Thereza Angélou 8 ☎ 28210 92798, ⊚ pensiontheresa .gr. Beautiful old *pension* in a great position with stunning views from its roof terrace and some rooms, characterful traditional decor and a kitchen (with breakfast ingredients supplied) for guests' use. They also have a 3-bedroom house round the corner. Very popular, so book ahead. €45

EAST OF HÁLIDHON

Anemi Suites Sarpáki 41 ☎ 28210 53001, ⊚ anemi suites.gr. Inviting, good-value one- and two-room apartments inside a Venetian house with a restored Turkish frontage; all are a/c with kitchen and TV. €70

Ionas Sarpáki, corner of Sórvolou ☎ 28210 55090, ⊚ ionashotel.gr. Small boutique hotel in a lovingly

restored Venetian mansion, with very comfortable rooms and beautiful architectural detail, though service is occasionally lacking. April–Oct. €85

★ **Kasteli** Kanęváro 39 ☎ 28210 57057, ⊚ kastelistudios .gr. Comfortable, modern, reasonably priced *pension*, very quiet at the back. All en-suite rooms come with a/c and fridge. The proprietor is very helpful and also has studios and a couple of beautiful apartments to rent nearby. Doubles €50, studios €80, apartments €125

★ **La Maison Ottomane** Párodhos Kanęváro ☎ 28210 08796, ⊚ lamaisonottomane.com. Stunning boutique hotel with just three luxurious apartments, opulently decorated in Ottoman pasha style. Facilities include free tablets for guests' use and Nespresso machines. €155

Pandora Suites Lithínon 29 ☎ 28210 43588, ⊚ pandora-hotel.com. Well set-up rooms and studios, plus a larger apartment at the back, some of which enjoy arguably the finest view in Haniá, from high above the harbour (for a small premium, well worth paying). All rooms have a/c and cooking facilities, and all guests can take in the view from the spectacular roof garden. €95

Porto Veneziano Overlooking the inner harbour ☎ 28210 27100, ⊚ portoveneziano.gr. The plushest hotel on the east side of the old town, with very comfortable rooms and all facilities, if a little business-class in atmosphere. The best rooms have balcony views (extra) over the harbour. Breakfast included. €115

★ **Splanzia** Dhaskaloyiánni 20 ☎ 28210 45313, ⊚ splanzia.com. Attractive and friendly boutique hotel in an elegantly refurbished Venetian mansion, with stylish rooms, each unique, some with four-posters, and extraordinary lighting. Breakfast (included) is served in a pretty courtyard. €115

To Dhiporto Betólo 41 ☎ 28210 40570, ⊚ todiporto.gr. The "Two Doors" runs between Betólo and pedestrian Skridhlóf: the balcony rooms over the latter, especially, are quiet. Friendly and good value, with a/c, TV, fridge and coffee machine in the rooms, which include singles and triples. €40

Vilelmine Betólo 32 ☎ 28210 46048, ⊚ www .vilelmine.gr. Boutique-style hotel in a *fin-de-siècle* building linking Betólo with the cathedral square. Lovingly furnished and reasonably soundproofed rooms and suites, and great service. €85

THE MODERN TOWN

Chania Hostel Venizélou 119 ☎ 28210 44955, ⊚ chaniahostel.gr. Exceptionally friendly new backpacker-style hostel, run by Cretan-Australian Angeliki. Great atmosphere and plenty of activities, though facilities, from rather crude hand-crafted wooden bunks to lack of a/c, are fairly basic. Dorms €17

★ **Doma** Venizélou 124 ☎ 28210 51772, ⊚ hotel-doma .gr. Elegant seafront hotel inside a late nineteenth-century building that served as the Austrian Embassy and later the British consulate until it was taken over by the Germans during World War II. There are fine sea views from some rooms and a serene patio garden. The comfortable rooms (and more expensive suites) are tastefully furnished, and the hotel is filled with fascinating photos of old Haniá. Breakfast included. Parking nearby. **€110**

CAMPSITE

Camping Hania Behind the beach in Áyii Apóstoli, 5km west of the city ☎ 28210 31138, ⓦ camping -chania.gr. A rather small site, hemmed in by new development, but with a pool and all the usual facilities, just a short walk from some of the better beaches. Also rents tents (€10). Two people plus tent and car **€22**

EATING

Evenings in Haniá for most visitors centre around the harbour, and you need not stray far from the waterfront to find a cocktail before **dinner**, a meal, a late-night **bar** and a **club**. These places tend to be pricey, however, and the quality at many leaves a lot to be desired. Away from the water, there are plenty of more interesting, attractive, and often slightly cheaper restaurants and tavernas. The abundant **cafés** round the harbour tend to serve cocktails and fresh juices at exorbitant prices, though breakfast can be good value. There are more traditional cafés by the cathedral, at the market – where you also find a couple of good *zaharoplastía* (one on Tsoudherón, the other, *Kronos*, on Mousoúron, down the steps from the side entrance of the market) – and along Dhaskaloyiánni, where Platía 1821 is a delightfully tranquil oasis. For **fast food**, head for the new town, especially Platía 1866.

CAFÉS

Alcanea Angélou 2 ☎ 28210 75377. Appealing terrace bar with a great harbour view beneath the hotel of the same name; it's good for breakfast, coffee and mezédhes and, after sunset, cocktails and Cretan wines. Occasional live acoustic music at night. March–Dec daily 8am–2am.
Iordanis Bougatsa Apokorónou 24 ☎ 28210 88855. Specializes in delicious traditional *bougátsa* (creamy cheese pie served warm and sprinkled with sugar and cinnamon), and nothing else, to eat in or take away. Mon–Sat 6am–2.30pm, Sun 6am–1.30pm.
O Platanos tis Splantzias Platía 1821 ☎ 28210 58930. Retro café-bar-ouzéri on a quiet square that serves interesting Asian food (mains around €6.50) and snacks alongside more traditional mezédhes. April–Oct daily 8am–2am.
Thea Platía Sindriváni ☎ 28210 73377. Café-bar overlooking the harbourside crowds from a first-floor terrace, for peaceful people-watching. Daily 9am–3am.
To Kafenío Platía 1821 ☎ 28210 43755. Perhaps the best of the relaxing cafés on this great old square, and the closest thing to a traditional *kafenío* in central Haniá; good prices, too. Daily 7.30am–3am.

TAVERNAS AND RESTAURANTS

63° Mezedoskolion Daliáni 63 ☎ 28213 05080. The "School of Meze" is a fashionable modern *mezedhopolío* (tick off what you want to order on a paper list; meze €6.50–7) with a literal old-school theme – you sit at old school desks, and chalky blackboards are everywhere. Packed with young locals late at night. Thurs–Tues 7pm–1am.
★ **Akrogiali** Aktí Papanikoli 19, Néa Hóra ☎ 28210 73110. Opposite the city beach, with a summer terrace, this excellent, reasonably priced fish and seafood taverna is well worth the 15min walk or short taxi ride. Always packed with locals, so may be worth booking – though

there are plenty of alternatives along the same street. Daily noon–midnight.
Amphora Aktí Koundouriótou 49, outer harbour ☎ 28210 71976. One of the more reliable places on the outer harbour, with good, simple Greek food and no hard sell. April–Oct daily 10am–midnight.
Doloma Kapsokalývon 5, behind the Arsenali ☎ 28213 01008. Fine little taverna set back off the street, with a shady terrace, serving well-prepared and economical Cretan dishes with good local wine. Mains such as pork with garlic or *païdhákia* cost around €6.50–7.50. Daily noon–11pm.
Enetikon Zambelíu 57 ☎ 28210 88270. A very good taverna whose proprietor is a wine buff: the house wine comes from the excellent Lyrarakis vineyard in Pezá. The food is also top-notch and lamb is recommended: try the *arní me stamnágathi* (lamb with chicory, €8.50). April–Oct daily noon–midnight.
Faka Arholéon 15 ☎ 28210 42341. Set back from the harbour, so significantly less touristy than many near neighbours, *Faka* serves good traditional local food, often with live Greek music. Check out the daily specials, made using seasonal ingredients, such as stuffed courgette flowers (€5.50) or *biftéki* (€8.50). April–Oct daily 11.30am–12.30am.
Glossitses Aktí Enóseos, inner harbour ☎ 28210 59074. Modern Greek restaurant on the waterfront serving classic dishes with a delicious twist; chicken in yoghurt sauce €9, *taş* kebab with mashed potatoes €8.50, plus good daily specials and fresh fish (tuna fillet €13). Daily noon–1am.
Kalderimi Theotokopoúlou 53 ☎ 28210 76741. A little gem of a place serving traditional Cretan dishes such as lamb *tsigariastó* with fried potatoes (€10.80), *moussaká* (€7.40) or local pasta with shrimps (€10). Occasional live traditional music too. Mon–Sat noon–1am.

4

Karnayio Platía Kateháki 8 **☎** 28210 53366. Not right on the water, but one of the better harbour restaurants nonetheless, with an inviting terrace. Its touristy looks belie good food, a friendly atmosphere and reasonable prices. House specials include oven-baked lamb (€10.50) and *bouréki* (€7.50), and there's an extensive wine list. April–Oct daily noon–midnight.

Khrisostomos Dhefkalíona and Ikárou **☎** 28210 57035. Sfakian restaurant – the original branch was an isolated taverna at Mármara beach (see p.281) – serving interesting and delicious Cretan food. The setting may not be the most attractive, but the fact that it's always full (booking recommended) attests to the quality; meat from Sfakiá is a speciality in dishes like goat *tsigariastó* (a rich stew, €9), wild pork *stifádho* (€11) and lamb with baked potatoes (€10.50). Daily 6pm–midnight.

Mihalis Aktí Tombázi **☎** 28210 58330. Arguably the best waterfront place on the outer harbour, with a varied menu (predominantly seafood; fish priced per kilo, octopus or mussels €9.50) and a good selection of Cretan specialities and *mezédhes*, the latter available as mixed platters. There's also a good wine selection at reasonable prices. April–Oct daily 9am–1am.

★Nykteridha 5km east of town off the Akrotíri road **☎** 28210 64215, **☎** nykterida.gr. Founded in 1933, this upmarket and stylish taverna is a Haniá institution, with a Greek/Mediterranean menu and stunning views over Soúdha Bay; expect to pay around €30 a head, more if you take advantage of the excellent wine cellar. It's a huge place, so can lack atmosphere when not full. April–Sept daily 7pm–1am; Oct–March Tues–Sat 7pm–midnight.

Pizzes Blé Daliáni 41 **☎** 28210 23102. Modern pizza joint that also serves salads, sandwiches and pasta on a street packed with bars and restaurants patronised by young locals; quiet by day but absolutely heaving at night. Pizzas €8–9.50. Daily 11am–1am.

★Portes Portoú 48 **☎** 28210 76261. A small group of restaurants nestles under the walls along Portoú. *Portes* is smarter than most, with an adventurous menu putting a modern twist on age-old dishes: starters include amazing stuffed courgettes with their flowers (€5.50), and mains

like rabbit with prunes, chicken with saffron and lemon, stuffed pork tenderloin and simple grilled octopus, all for around €9. See the blackboard for daily specials. April–Oct Mon–Sat 12.30pm–1am, Sun 5pm–1am.

★Tamam Zambelíou 49 **☎** 28210 96080. Popular place where the adventurous Greek menu includes much vegetarian food, with added spices giving an eastern flavour to dishes such as Smyrnian rabbit (€9.90) or Iranian rice (€7.60). The original restaurant is housed in an old Turkish baths, while opposite is a less atmospheric annexe. The tables squeezed into the alley between the two are very cramped, and you're likely to be jostled by the passing crowds. Daily noon–1am.

Tholos Ay. Dhéka 36 **☎** 28210 46725. A stone's throw north of the cathedral, *Tholos* is housed in a ruined Venetian mansion with tables romantically set in a courtyard and in the roofless interior. The food is good, too, with the likes of goat with wild greens (€11.90) or pork with halloumi (€12.60), and there are lots of seafood options. Daily 4pm–midnight.

To Maridhaki Dhaskaloyiánni 33 **☎** 28210 08880. Exceptional fish and seafood, keenly priced, at this on-trend place at the heart of a newly fashionable area, where young locals hang out at a series of bars, restaurants and ouzeri. Go for the catch of the day, or there's an excellent *psarósoupa* (fish soup, €5.50) or *okhtapódhi krasáto* (octopus in red wine €8.50). Mon–Sat noon–midnight.

To Pigadi Tou Tourkou Sarpáki 1 **☎** 28210 54547. The "Well of the Turk" is a Greco-Moroccan fusion restaurant with an interesting menu combining the two cuisines as well as adding a few dishes from the wider Middle East, with plenty of vegetarian choices. Expect the likes of lamb with preserved lemons (€12.50), aubergine meatballs (€10) or arab bread with spinach, *mizíthra*, nuts and raisins (€10). April–Oct Wed–Mon 6pm–12.30am.

To Stakhi Dhefkalíona 5 **☎** 28210 42589. Organic vegetarian diner serving a wide range of tasty daily specials including soups (€6.50), meze (around €5 each), and mains like *yemistá* (stuffed tomatoes and peppers) and *bouréki* (Cretan veggie and cheese bake) for €7–8. Also fresh juices, herbal teas, and organic beer and wine. Daily 1–11pm.

DRINKING, NIGHTLIFE AND ENTERTAINMENT

As you might expect, the harbour area contains plenty of beautifully set but touristy **bars**. Locals tend to congregate instead behind the inner harbour and up into Splántzia; here streets like Kalergón and Daliáni are boisterously jammed around midnight. In the early hours, the action may move on to the **clubs**, and where these are depends on the time of year. In summer, many of the downtown venues close and the action moves to the vibrant scene at **Plataniás** and **Ayía Marína** on the coast west of town (see p.265).

Ababa Isodhíon 12 **☎** 6937 965 936. Funky bar with childishly colourful decor, open all day, offering snacks, books and board games; chilled sounds and cocktails in the evening through to the early hours. Daily 10am–late.

Attikon Venizélou 118 **☎** 28210 40208, **☎** cineattikon

.gr. A great open-air cinema near the hostel and stadium; in winter showings move round the corner, where they have a couple of cosy indoor screens.

Fagotto Angélou 16 **☎** 28210 71877. Cosy, atmospheric backstreet jazz bar housed in an impressively restored

Venetian mansion. Great cocktails, and high-quality live performances in season. Daily 8pm–late.

Ippopotamos Sarpidhónos 6 ☎ 28210 44128. Popular bar-café in a street full of similar places that attract a slightly older crowd than most. Outdoor terrace and Mexican food, too. Daily 9am–3am.

Miniatoura Daliáni 4 ☎ 6979 526 340. Tiny bar, with cocktails and good music, set in an ancient, arched stone vault, at the heart of the nightlife. Daily 8pm–4am.

★**Rakadhiko ta Halkina** Aktí Tombázi 29–30 ☎ 28210 41570, ⓦ chalkina.com. Live Cretan music every evening, though the place doesn't really liven up till well after midnight, when the locals start to dance. There's also good meze (€5–7) and wine, but it's the traditional music everyone comes for. Hugely popular, but they can usually squeeze you in somewhere. Daily noon–late, music from 9pm.

Rudi's Bierhaus Kalergón 16 ☎ 28210 20319. Haniá's beer shrine: Austrian – and longtime Haniá resident – Rudi Riegler's bar stocks more than a hundred of Europe's finest brews, plus excellent mezédhes to accompany them. Other, more fashionable, bars crowd this street. Tues–Sat 8pm–3am.

Synagogi Párodhos Kondhiláki, between Kondhiláki and Skúfon ☎ 28210 95242. Taking its name from the restored Jewish synagogue next door, this is a beautiful bar set in the roofless, jasmine-scented remains of a bombed-out Venetian mansion. Good music, too, and salads and sandwiches. May–Sept daily 1pm–3am.

Ta Duo Lux Sarpidhónos 8 ☎ 28210 52515. Comfy café-bar in a street full of similar places, just off the inner harbour; regular DJs and club nights after midnight, and occasional live bands. Daily 10am–late.

To Monastíri tou Karolos Daliáni 22 ⓦ karolos.gr. Art and performance centre containing a gallery, a theatre, an exceptionally popular bar and a hairdressing school – founder Karolos Kambelopoulos is a celebrity artist and hairdresser whose works decorate the building, a restored sixteenth-century monastery. Mon–Sat noon–2am, Sun 8pm–2am; closed Nov.

SHOPPING

Stores aimed at tourists are mainly found in the old town, especially on Hálidhon and in the streets behind the outer harbour: Kanegáro, Zambelíou, Kondhiláki and Theotokopóulou. The **leather** goods on Skridhlóf are excellent value, while north of here along Sífaka the traditional shops of Haniá's cutlers will sell you fearsome **Cretan knives** with goat-horn handles or something less vicious for the kitchen. In the new town, around the junction of Hálidhon and Yiánnari and down towards the market you'll find pharmacies, newspaper stores, photographic shops and banks, and there's a sizeable **supermarket** at the top of Pireós. The major thoroughfares heading south off Yiánnari – Apokorónou, Tzanakáki and Papandreou – are full of clothes and furniture stores, car rental places and more banks, while the streets around Platía 1866, especially towards the town hall and market, have more interesting local shops, from food and fashion to pet shops and printers. English and other foreign-language **newspapers** are sold at a number of places, including a couple around the junction of Hálidhon and Yiánnari.

Canea Zambelíou 45 ☎ 28210 98639. Classy souvenirs, including T-shirts, bags, ceramics and more. There's another branch in Platía 1821 (open shorter hours). Daily 9.30am–11pm.

Haniá market Odhós Yiánnari, with another entrance on Tsoudherón. Haniá's market, an imposing and rather beautiful cross-shaped structure, dating from around 1900, is in full swing on weekday mornings, when it's a wonderful kaleidoscope of bustle and colour, and there are some good souvenirs to be had among the stalls of meat, fish and veg. Mon–Sat 8am–2pm.

Mediterraneo Bookstore Aktí Koundouriótou 57, near the Naval Museum ☎ 28210 86904. Impressively stocked book and magazine store with lots of English-language titles, maps and guides. Daily 8am–midnight.

Miden Agan Dhaskaloyiánni 70 ☎ 28210 27068. Deli with a big selection of Greek and Cretan wines, as well as elegantly packaged olive oils, spices and the like. Mon & Wed 10am–3pm, Tues, Thurs, Fri & Sat 10am–3pm & 6–10pm.

See Crete Khrysánthou Episkópou 52 ☎ 28210 46084. Gift shop and espresso bar, with a range of quality souvenirs, from oils and herbs to mugs and clothing. Daily 9am–11pm.

Street market Minóos. There's a fabulous weekly street market inside the eastern city wall, where local farmers sell their produce. Sat mornings.

DIRECTORY

Banks The main branch of the National Bank of Greece, with ATMs, is opposite the market. There's a cluster of banks with more ATMs around the top of Hálidhon, and lots of out-of-hours exchange places on Hálidhon, in the travel agencies.

Hospital For an ambulance, dial ☎ 166. The main hospital is in the village of Mourniés, 1.5km south of the centre (☎ 28210 22000).

Laundry Service washes are available at Oscar Laundry, Kanegáro 1 (Mon–Fri 7.30am–3pm & 6–9pm, Sat 8am–3pm); or there's cheap self-service at easywash, Dhaskaloyiánni 8 (daily 7am–midnight).

Pharmacies Several on Yiánnari between the market and Platía 1866; others up Tzanakáki.

Post office The main post office is on Odhós Péridhou just

4

off Kydhonías (Mon–Fri 7.30am–8pm, Sat 9am–1pm). **Tourist police** Iraklíou 23 (emergency ☏ 100, ☏ 28210 28750 or ☏ 28210 25931), some way south of the centre in the new town.

The Akrotíri peninsula

The hilly peninsula of **Akrotíri** loops round to the east of Haniá, protecting the magnificent anchorages of the **Bay of Soúdha**. It's a somewhat strange amalgam, with a couple of developing **resorts** along with burgeoning suburbs and a new university on the north coast, several ancient **monasteries** in the northeast, and military installations and the airport dominating the centre and south. This is very much apartment and villa country, geared to families and longer-term stays.

The Venizelos Graves

Off the main Akrotíri road at the top of the hill as you leave Haniá • Bus #11 and others from Haniá market (about 20min); the city tour bus also stops here

The **Venizelos Graves** are the simple stone-slab tombs of Eleftherios Venizelos, Crete's most famous statesman, and his son Sophocles. The immaculately tended garden setting, looking back over Haniá and the coast for miles beyond, is magnificent and also historic – the scene in 1897 of an illegal raising of the Greek flag by rebels led by Venizelos in defiance of the Turks and the European powers. The flagpole was smashed by a salvo from the European fleet, but the Cretans raised their standard by hand, keeping it flying even under fire. Two stories attach to this: one that the sailors were so impressed that they all stopped firing to applaud; the second that a shell fired from a Russian ship hit the little church of Profítis Elías, which still stands, and that divine revenge caused the offending ship itself to explode the next day.

EATING AND DRINKING	THE VENIZELOS GRAVES
Koukouvaya ☏ 28210 27449. Excellent, elegant café with a fabulous view over Haniá from its terrace. They specialize	in cakes and tarts (try the walnut cake, €4) as well as sandwiches, salads, teas and coffees. Daily 10am–2am.

The north-coast beaches

The road by the Venizelos Graves divides: straight ahead takes you east across the peninsula towards the **airport**, while the left fork heads north to Horafákia and the north-coast beaches, culminating at **Stavrós**.

Kalathás

Just beyond the village of **Kounoupidhianá**, the road suddenly plunges down and emerges by the **beach** at KALATHÁS (Καλαθάς), two little patches of sand divided by a rocky promontory, with a bar and taverna right on the sand. This makes a fine place to spend a lazy day, marred only slightly by the proximity of the road: there's an offshore island to which you can swim, and good snorkelling.

Horafákia and around

HORAFÁKIA (Χωραφάκια), inland, a little over 1km beyond Kalathás, has the bulk of the local facilities, including shops and car rental. From here a road leads down to the coast at **Tersanás** where there's a tiny cove beach, shallow and safe for small children, as well as a couple of tavernas.

Stavrós

Some 3km beyond Horafákia, you finally reach STAVRÓS (Σταυρός) and its near-perfect beach, an almost completely enclosed circular bay. The sea is dead calm with gently shelving sand underfoot, making it ideal for kids. It's an extraordinary-looking place, too, with a sheer, bare mountainside rising just 100m away from you on the far side of the bay. This is where the cataclysmic climax of *Zorba the Greek* was shot (the hill is known locally as Zorba's Mountain) and is also the site of a **cave**, whose entrance can just about be seen from the beach, in which there was an ancient sanctuary.

Stavrós beach is often crowded – sometimes unpleasantly so as it doesn't take many people to fill it up – but even so it's a great place to bask for a few hours. There's a far less visited patch of sand facing directly out to sea if you do find it oppressive.

ARRIVAL AND DEPARTURE

THE NORTH-COAST BEACHES

By bus There are services to Stavrós via Kalathás and Horafákia from Haniá's bus station (6 daily, fewer at weekends; 30min).

ACCOMMODATION AND EATING

Accommodation is widely scattered in the flat plain lining the coast between Stavrós and Tersanás, so you'll ideally need your own transport here, though all of the options below are within walking distance of town and beach. There are plenty of tavernas near the beaches, serving perfectly good standard Greek food, but few that stand out.

KALATHÁS

Giorgi's Blue Apartments Signed from the road, immediately west of Kalathás ☎ 28210 64080, ⓦ blueapts.gr. Very comfortable one- and two-bedroom apartments with pool and bar beautifully situated above a rocky coastline; steps lead down to what is in effect a private cove. Breakfast included. **€100**

Lena Beach Directly above the beach ☎ 28210 64750, ⓦ lenabeach.gr. Slightly old-fashioned hotel immediately above the beach; rooms have every facility and great views, and there's a pool and a path directly down to the sand. **€65**

Ta Skalakia Just above the beach ☎ 6981 685 494. Good taverna for Cretan classics and fresh fish (priced per kilo for the day's catch), with a terrace above the water. Try the *kontosoúvli* (spit roast pork €8.50) or *katsikáki yemistá* (stuffed goat €12). April–Oct daily 8am–midnight.

HORAFÁKIA

Bahar Outside Horafákia, on the road to Stavrós ☎ 28210 39410. One of the few restaurants on the peninsula with any pretensions, with a varied Cretan and Mediterranean menu served amid somewhat eccentric modern decor. Their "Aphrodisiac" plate – mussels, prawns and lobster bisque with pasta – is a bargain at €16.50 for two. There's also an excellent wine selection, and a house wine from noted Pezá grower Lyrarakis. The attached bar hosts live music (jazz, soul, Greek) on Saturday nights.

Mon–Sat 5pm–midnight, Sun noon–midnight; bar stays open later.

STAVRÓS AND AROUND

Almyriki Behind the beach ☎ 28210 29489. Attractive taverna with tables spread beneath the shady tamarisk tree that gives it its name, beside a windmill. Specialities include a range of mezédhes as well as Cretan dishes such as *bouréki* (veggie and cheese bake) and stuffed tomatoes; mains cost €7–9. May–Oct daily noon–11.30pm.

Blue Beach Apartments On the seafront at the western edge of Stavrós ☎ 28210 39404, ⓦ bluebeach .eu. Very large apartment complex with everything from studios to three-bedroom apartments with a tiny sand beach, small pool and a seaside terrace where meals are served. Free wi-fi in public areas, a/c €8/day. Studios **€65**, 2-room apartments **€120**

★ Georgia-Vicky Apartments About 1km west of Stavrós ☎ 6944 897 911, ⓦ georgia-vicky.com. Excellent-value, welcoming, well-equipped studios and apartments, all with stunning views from terraces and balconies over a rocky shore. There's also a large seawater pool and kids' playground too. Studios **€50**, apartments **€65**

Kavos Hotel About 1km west of Stavrós ☎ 28210 39255, ⓦ kavosbeach.gr. Attractive, modern apartment complex with a large pool, pool bar and well-equipped studios and split-level maisonettes. Breakfast included. Studios **€60**, maisonettes **€90**

Moní Ayía Triádha

5km east of Horafákia, 2km north of the airport • Daily: summer 8am–sunset; winter 8am–2pm & 4pm–sunset • €2

The monastery of **AYÍA TRIÁDHA (Μονή Αγίας Τριάδας)**, sometimes known as Moní Zangárolo after its founder, was established in the seventeenth century and built in Venetian style. Today, while not exactly thriving, it is one of the few Cretan monasteries to preserve real monastic life to any degree. Its imposing ochre frontage is approached through carefully tended fields of vines and olive groves – all the property of the monastery, which now bottles and markets its own wine and organic olive oil.

You can walk right through the complex and sit on benches shaded by orange trees in the patio. The **church**, which appears strangely foreshortened, contains a beautiful old gilded altarpiece and, around the walls, ancient wooden stalls; like most of the monastery it is built from stone that glows orange in the afternoon sun. By the entrance a small **museum** exhibits silver chalices, vestments, relics and manuscripts, mostly dating from the eighteenth or nineteenth centuries, and a few icons that are considerably older. In the courtyard there's a water cooler; in quieter times, if you're lucky, the traditional hospitality might extend to a glass of *rakí* and a piece of *loukoúm* (Turkish delight) in the hall where you sign the visitors' book.

Moní Gouvernétou

4km north of Ayía Triádha • Mon, Tues & Thurs 9am–noon & 5–7pm, Sat & Sun 9–11am & 5–8pm; Oct–Easter afternoon hours are 4–7pm • Free • The monastery is enclosed within a compound; leave any transport at the gate and approach via a path through a garden (around 100m)

The lonely road to **MONÍ GOUVERNÉTOU (Μονή Γουβερνέτου)** ascends through a biblical landscape of rocks and wild olives; the final section is paved but horribly rutted as it twists through a steep rocky gully. Older than Ayía Triádha (a Greek inscription above the entrance is dated 1573), the monastery is fortress-like from the outside, with two towers standing guard; inside there's the usual refreshingly shaded patio, ancient frescoes in the church and a tiny museum. Despite its more remote location, Gouvernétou feels like a thriving community: beautifully renovated and with carefully tended flowerbeds and chapel. Nevertheless, the stark surroundings help to give a real sense of the isolation that the remaining monks must face for most of the year, and their life is contemplative and strict; visitors are expected to respect this.

St John the Hermit's cave

500m beyond Gouvernétou monastery

Immediately above Gouvernétou is a simple marble war memorial. Beyond this, you can follow (on foot) a path that heads down towards the sea; after about ten minutes you reach the cave in which **St John the Hermit** is said to have lived and died. This large, low cavern – stark, dank and dripping – features hefty stalactites and stalagmites and a substantial bathing tank, probably for baptisms. Excavations revealed that this had been an important Minoan shrine too, and in the Greek period it became a sanctuary dedicated to the goddess Artemis.

Moní Katholikó

About 1km north of Gouvernétou monastery

Descending beyond St John the Hermit's cave the path deteriorates as the going gets steeper, rockier and sharper. After some 500m you reach the amazing **ruins** of **MONÍ KATHOLIKÓ (Μονή Καθολικού)**, built into the side of, and partly carved from, a craggy ravine of spectacular desolation. This older monastery, founded in the eleventh century and one of the oldest on the island, was abandoned more than three hundred years ago when the monks, driven by repeated pirate raids, moved up to the comparative safety of Gouvernétou. The valley sides are dotted with caves, which formed a centre of still-earlier Christian worship, at least one of which (just before the buildings) you can explore if you have a torch.

Spanning the ravine by the ruins is a vast **bridge** leading nowhere, evocatively captured by Edward Lear in one of his Cretan watercolours (see p.353). Cross it and you can scramble down to the bottom of the ravine and follow the stream bed for about another fifteen minutes to the sea. There's a tiny natural **harbour**, a fjord-like finger of water pushing up between the rocks, where remains of a port can still be made out. Hewn from the rock, and with part of its roof intact, is what appears to be an ancient boathouse or slipway. There's no beach, but it's easy enough to lower yourself from the rocks straight into the astonishingly clear green water. The walk back up takes perhaps an hour in all – and is much more strenuous than it might have seemed on the way down.

Soúdha Bay

Much of the **south side** of the Akrotíri peninsula, and the area round the airport, is a **military zone**, with naval installations in the bay and the air force on land. There are good beaches at **Maráthi**, beyond the airport to the south, extremely popular with locals at weekends and hence with some excellent tavernas, and a spectacular tiny cove at **Seitán**, on the peninsula's east coast, accessed via the village of Hordháki followed by a scary scramble down the cliff. Boat trips from resorts across the bay occasionally run to the little harbour at Maráthi, only adding to the crush for space on the beach; driving here affords some of the best views of **Soúdha Bay** and above all, of the fortified islet (**Néa Soúdha**) defending the entrance, bristling with Venetian and Turkish fortifications which, from a distance at least, appear miraculously well preserved. Ferries and some boat trips operate from the town of **SOÚDHA** (**Σούδα**), in the bay's innermost, southwest corner. If you are hanging around here you can find just about everything you need on the square right by the ferries, but it's not an attractive place.

The Allied war cemetery

1km northwest of Soúdha, signed off the main road towards the peninsula • The city tour bus (see p.245) stops here

Surrounded by eucalyptus trees and beautifully sited at the water's edge with Soúdha Bay stretching away beyond, **the Allied war cemetery** is a melancholy and moving spot. With its row upon row of immaculately tended headstones, many of them to unknown soldiers and very young men, the serene and dignified cemetery brings home with some force the scale of the calamity of the Battle of Crete in which most of them perished (see p.338). A grave in row 10E on the cemetery's northern side is that of the distinguished archeologist John Pendlebury, who took over at Knossós after Arthur Evans retired; he died fighting alongside Cretans during the German assault on Iráklio in 1941.

4

ARRIVAL AND DEPARTURE

SOÚDHA BAY

By bus Frequent local buses run between Soúdha and the market in Haniá (every 20min; 20min; €1.70), or you can take a taxi (€9; prices to other destinations posted); KTEL buses to Réthymno and Kastélli also meet the ferries.

Five buses a day run from Haniá's bus station to Maráthi (30min).

By ferry ANEK Line runs to Pireás (daily 9pm; peak summer also daytime sailing; 9hr; ⓦ anek.gr).

East from Haniá to Yeoryioúpoli

Heading east out of Haniá you can either make your way through the new town to pick up the main E75 road on the south side of town, or follow the buses and most of the other traffic along the old road to **Soúdha**, beyond which the routes merge. The new road is fast, but you'll see little through the screen of trees and flowering shrubs until you emerge on the coast at **Yeoryioúpoli**. If you're in no hurry, or you simply want an attractive circular drive, then the minor roads that head inland or out onto the **Dhrápano peninsula** have much more to offer.

Megála Horáfia

Some 6km east of Soúdha, and 1km (and a steep climb) inland, the village of **MEGÁLA HORÁFIA** (**Μεγάλα Χωράφια**) – which has officially changed its name to Áptera, though no one seems to pay this much attention – is a popular spot for villa holidays, with numerous houses and apartments (many with pool) offering spectacular hilltop views. Just 2km away, signed from the main square, is the archeological site of **Áptera**.

Áptera

Signed off the E75 highway, 2km above Megála Horáfia • Tues–Sun 8am–3pm • Free

The archeological site of **ÁPTERA** (**Άπτερα**) occupies the table top of a mesa-like hilltop, high above Soúdha Bay. This location appears in Linear B inscriptions, and therefore seems to have been **continuously occupied** from as early as the fourteenth century BC right up to 1964, when the monastery here was finally abandoned. From the fifth century BC into early Christian times Áptera was one of the island's most important cities. Work on the extensive remains is continuing, so new areas may be opened up, or others fenced off for excavation; the site has little shade and can be very hot in high summer – visit in the early morning if you can.

The main entrance is by the **Monastery of Áyios Ioánnis Theólogos**, the most obvious building at the site. Here the biggest of the fenced areas includes the monastery, the cisterns, a bath complex and, right by the entrance, a fifth-century BC Classical Greek **temple** marked by huge stone slabs. The Roman **cisterns**, brick-lined and mainly underground, must be among the largest surviving – an awesome, cavernous testament to Roman engineering genius. Below spreads an extensive **Roman bath** complex, all of which raises the question of just how enough water to fill the vast cisterns and feed the baths was collected on what is now a barren hilltop, although it could be that long-gone aqueducts were the source.

Numerous other remains are scattered around the immediate area, mostly signed but not all accessible. Check the map at the site entrance (or there may be a leaflet). Many are reached by a well-signed path on the opposite side of the car park from the monastery (and outside the fenced site). There are remains of a small **theatre** here, and of a **Roman villa** full of collapsed pillars. To reach the latter head along a path through the olives for 150m in a roughly southwest direction. When you reach them, the remains of the first- or second-century peristyle villa are impressive and the size of the collapsed stone columns show how grand it must once have been. You also pass a World War II machine-gun post, which, if it weren't signed, could easily be mistaken for another restored Roman ruin. The path continues down towards Megála Horáfia and ends, right on the edge of the village, by a substantial section of the ancient city **wall**, complete with defensive tower and gate. In the other direction, you can also take a paved road from the site entrance to a magnificent (but locked) **castle** on a point overlooking the defences at the entrance to the Bay of Soúdha.

ACCOMMODATION AND EATING	MEGÁLA HORÁFIA
Aptera Apartments On the road leading to the Áptera site ☎ 6946 654 426, ⊛ aptera-apartments.com. Attractive, fully equipped studios and apartments with a large pool and spectacular views over Soúdha Bay. Studios **€45**, apartments **€60** **Taverna Aptera** Centre of the village ☎ 28250 31313.	Very good taverna, one of several around the crossroads at the heart of Megála Horáfia, serving heartily traditional home-cooked daily specials; meat dishes generally cost €6.50–8.50, the likes of spinach with rice, or stuffed courgette flowers, around €4. Daily: April–Oct 10am–midnight; Nov–March 5–11pm.

Stýlos and around

South from Áptera you can follow minor roads inland to circle round via the Dhrápano peninsula, a very attractive drive. The first place of any size is **STÝLOS** (**Στύλος**), which is where the Australian and New Zealand rearguard made their final stand during the Battle of Crete (this was then the start of the main road south), enabling the majority of Allied troops to be evacuated while they themselves were mostly stranded on the island. Many found refuge in the villages in the foothills around here and were later smuggled off the island – some of these villages were destroyed in retribution. Today

Stýlos is an attractive old place on a rushing river, whose excellent tavernas are a popular outing for city-folk from Haniá. The local spring water is bottled under the Samariá brand (it comes in jugs in the restaurants here), and there's a very ancient church, Áyios Ioánnis Theológos, usually open, with damaged frescoes inside.

If you enjoy driving on Crete's **mountain roads**, head from Stýlos up towards **Samonás**, a twisting and turning ride of 4km, offering better views at every turn. Beyond, you can continue on a still more tortuous route via **Kámbi** (from where there's a good road back to Haniá) to **Dhrakóna** and **Thériso** (see p.269). At Samonás you can also take a diversion to visit the isolated Byzantine church of Áyios Nikólaos at **Kyriakosélia**.

Áyios Nikólaos

To fix a visit head for the *kafenío* in Samonás – preferably in late afternoon after the siesta – and they'll phone for a keyholder who'll accompany you to the church; they don't accept money for their time, but a contribution towards the upkeep of the church is unlikely to be refused

The beautiful restored church of **Áyios Nikólaos**, nestling in a valley outside the village of Kyriakosélia, boasts **medieval frescoes** as good as any on Crete. Painted in the thirteenth century, these have not been touched by the restorers – at least not recently – and are patchy and faded against their deep-blue background, but parts still seem as vivid as the day they were created. A *Madonna and Child*, at eye level on the left-hand side, and a dramatic *Christ Pantokrátor* in the drum dome stand out.

EATING AND DRINKING
STÝLOS AND AROUND

★ **Moustakia** Main road in Stýlos ☎ 28250 41190. The pick of the tavernas in Stýlos, with fountains, geese and ducks along the river, and terrace tables set beneath giant plane trees. Simple food, mainly grilled, but everything is as fresh as it can be; try the Greek salad topped with *mizíthra* sheep's cheese (a meal in itself) or the spit-roasted lamb – the chips, too, are gourmet standard. Meze are €2–5, mains €5–7. Daily 9am–11pm.

The Apokóronas

The **Apokóronas** region, east of Haniá, is rich agricultural land, a countryside of rolling green, wooded hills interrupted by immaculately whitewashed, and obviously wealthy, villages. The **Dhrápano** peninsula, on the coast, has a couple of popular resorts, though many once beautiful coastal villages here have been blighted by a real estate boom – prior to the economic crisis – which saw villas thrown up on any piece of land with a view. **Inland**, while there are few attractions to detain you long, there's a multitude of excellent roads criss-crossing the region, almost all of them scenic and well surfaced. Everywhere there are *kafenía* where you can sit and wonder at the rural tranquillity away from the main-road traffic, and there are a number of excellent restaurants too.

The Dhrápano coast

On the **north coast** of the Dhrápano peninsula are two sizeable resorts, **Kalýves** and **Almyrídha**, both with decent sandy beaches. Away from these, and especially on the peninsula's east-facing coast, low cliffs mean that there are few places where the water can be easily accessed, though there are glorious sea views from many of the villages – the more popular of which have been overrun by expats and unattractive villas.

Kalýves

KALÝVES (**Καλύβες**) is both a resort and an agricultural market centre of some size. As you approach, you pass a long sandy beach in the lee of Áptera's castle-topped bluff, which looks attractive but is hard to reach. The main **beach** stretches in both directions from the centre of the village, best at the eastern end where it curves round to a small harbour in the shelter of a headland. The village itself is not particularly attractive at first sight, a rather straggly development lining the main road for over 2km. It's very much a package resort, although the mainly low-rise apartments and studios keep it low-key; along with Almyrídha (see below), Kalýves has become a focus for the largely British villa-owning community in the surrounding hills and there are a number of businesses and bars with English names.

The centre of town is marked by a small square with a church, just to the east of which a river runs through to the sea. The most attractive parts are round here, especially if you cut down to the seafront just one block away. Just about everything you might need, from banks with ATMs to a launderette and travel agencies, can be found along the main street through town, within walking distance of the centre.

Almyrídha

ALMYRÍDHA (Αλμυρίδα), the next village along the coast from Kalýves, is smaller, marginally more of a resort, and considerably more attractive. The beach, lined with tavernas and cafés, is a popular spot for **windsurfing**, with a fairly reliable breeze once you're slightly offshore. It's worth looking at the remains of an **early Christian basilica** dating from the fifth century, with a wonderful mosaic floor. It lies beside the road as it enters the western end of the village close to the *Lagos* taverna.

Pláka and around

Beyond Almyrídha the coast becomes increasingly rocky, with cliffs almost all the way round to Yeoryioúpoli denying access to the sea. The roads and the signage also deteriorate if you go this way, but as you climb the views become increasingly worthwhile. The first place you reach, immediately east of Almyrídha and these days almost a suburb, is **PLÁKA (Πλάκα)**, a beautiful but overdeveloped hamlet, with tempting tavernas and cafés on a sleepy central platía; nearby *Sunset Taverna* has fabulous views back over Almyrídha and the coast.

Further around the coast, there are great views if you take the deserted coastal road via **Kefalás**, an absurdly pretty place perched above the sea with spectacular views towards Réthymno. Pretty much the only place to get down to the water, though, is at **Palelóni**, where a narrow road leads down to a rocky cove alongside a small naval base.

ARRIVAL AND GETTING AROUND   THE DHRÁPANO COAST

By bus There are regular buses connecting Haniá with both Kalýves (6 daily; 30min) and Almyrídha (4 daily; 40min), but no public transport around the region.
Car and bike rental Flisvos Travel (☎ 28250 31100, ⓦ flisvos.com), at the bottom of the inland road in

Almyrídha and on the main road west of the centre of Kalýves (☎ 28250 31337), has cars, scooters and bikes, and can also help with accommodation, money exchange and excursions; there's even an ATM in Almyrídha.

ACTIVITIES

Watersports UCPA (☎ 28250 31443), at the heart of the seafront in Almyrídha, rents out windsurfers (€10/hr), kayaks (€8/hr) and pedalos. Dream Adventures, with a desk under the tamarisks at the eastern end of the seafront (☎ 6944 357

383), runs speedboat and snorkelling trips to inaccessible parts of the nearby coast (both €22). Omega Divers (☎ 28250 31412, ⓦ omegadivers.com), on the seafront at the junction of the inland road, offers diving and dive courses.

ACCOMMODATION

KALÝVES

Blue Sea Apartments Eastern end of the seafront ☎ 28250 32159, ⓦ bluesea-kalyves.com. Almost the last building as you head east along the beach, *Blue Sea* has a great, quiet position and big roof terrace with wonderful views. All the apartments have a/c, cooking facilities and at least indirect sea views; a couple are directly above the beach. €40
Garifalo On the seafront east of the Kalyves Beach Hotel ☎ 28250 32718, ⓦ garifalohotel.com. Excellent-value

modern two-room apartments with kitchen and a/c, most with great sea views. Good for families, and they have their own loungers and umbrellas on the beach. €55
Kalyves Beach Hotel On the seafront in the centre of town, beside the river ☎ 28250 31285, ⓦ kalyvesbeach .com. Occupying the prime central beachfront position, the newly renovated *Kalyves Beach Hotel* is also much the largest in town, with facilities including indoor and outdoor pools, beach bar and a tiny gym. Only a few rooms have direct sea views, though. Breakfast included. €90

ALMYRÍDHA

Almyrida Resort In the centre ☎ 28250 32284, ⓦ almyridaresort.com. The centre of town is marked by two incongruous modern hotels: the four-star *Almyrida Residence* and slightly more downmarket and cheaper *Almyrida Beach* which, together with the suites and family rooms at beachfront *Almyrida Studios*, are all under the same management and share facilities, including several pools and a bowling alley. Rates include breakfast. **€70**

Rooms Pothoulakis Near the bottom of the Pláka road ☎ 28250 32132, ⓦ ypothoulakis.gr. Bright pink building in a lush garden with simply decorated studios

and apartments (all with flat-screen TV and kitchen). There can be a bit of traffic noise. Studios **€35**, apartments **€50**

PLÁKA

★ **Bicorna Rooms** Pláka ☎ 28250 32073, ⓦ bicorna .com. Family-run hotel that has been beautifully renovated in designer style – each room colourful and individual. There's a lush garden, a small pool and playground, and a bar/bistro, *Me Gusta Bicorna*. **€45**

Studios Koukouros Pláka ☎ 28250 31145, ⓦ studios koukouros.gr. Pleasant a/c rooms with balcony and fridge, and a stunning garden filled with palms, cacti and bougainvillea. **€35**

EATING AND DRINKING

KALÝVES

Cafe Arena y Mar Eastern end of the beach. Café-bar with TV sport, free wi-fi and free sunbeds on the beach for customers; one of the livelier places in town. April–Oct daily 9am–1am.

Elena Eastern end of the beach ☎ 28250 32544. The best of a bunch of traditional tavernas here, with well-priced local fish (mackerel €8.50, sea bass €9.50) and free sunbeds for customers. April–Oct daily 11am–midnight.

Il Forno Eastern end of the beach ☎ 28250 32520. Excellent pizza (€8.50–11) from a wood-fired oven, plus less tempting pasta and Greek dishes, and free sunbeds for customers. Daily 10am–midnight.

Kritiko In the centre of town, on the main road between the square and the river ☎ 28250 31096. Probably the fanciest place in town, with its own beach bar, garden and beachfront terrace. Pricier than most, too, but only marginally so, and worth it for dishes like roast lamb with lemon and aromatic herbs, smoked in a wood oven (€9.80) or rabbit in muscat wine with olives and cheese (€8.20). Daily 10am–midnight.

Potamos Overlooking the river close to the square. *Kafenío* serving snacks and drinks in an attractive waterside setting. Daily 8.30am–10pm.

Provlita Seafront promenade west of the centre ☎ 28250 31835. Almost the last taverna as you follow the seafront west from the centre, with an attractive seafront terrace and a reputation for perfectly cooked fish that makes it popular with locals. Go for whatever's fresh, such as black snapper or sea bass (each €11). Good wine list. April–Oct daily noon–midnight; Nov–March Sat & Sun noon–midnight.

ALMYRÍDHA

Café Françoise Towards the eastern end of the seafront ☎ 28250 32591. Vibrant little café-patisserie serving a wide range of tasty snacks including salads, sandwiches, omelettes and burgers. They also do a

mammoth "English breakfast" (€6.50), as well as pastries and ice cream, plus cocktails in the evening. April–Oct daily 7am–midnight.

Dimitri's In the centre of the seafront ☎ 28250 31303. Long-established, traditional taverna, open from breakfast to late at night. Good salads (tuna salad €6) and traditional Greek dishes including a tasty mixed meze (€8), *païdhákia* (lamb chops, €9) and *moussaká* (€7.50). March–Oct daily 8.30am–midnight.

Nikita's Place On the seafront next to Dimitri's ☎ 28250 31617. All-day café-bar with music and cocktails at night on a lovely waterfront terrace – their karaoke night is about as wild as the local nightlife ever gets. April–Oct daily 9am–1am.

O Lagos On the main road at the western edge of the village ☎ 28250 31654. "The Hare" taverna has an attractive garden setting and a meaty, traditional menu (*soutzoukákia* €7, rabbit *stifádho* €8.50), plus excellent *kalitsoúnia* (cheese pies) and stuffed peppers. May–Oct daily noon–midnight.

Psaros Central seafront ☎ 28250 32430. Busy place with a fancier than average international menu featuring the likes of chicken with caramelized onion and balsamic sauce (€10.80) or pork fillet with lemon, tarragon and mushrooms (€11.20); plainer fish dishes are also available. Daily 11.30am–midnight.

Thalami Central seafront ☎ 28250 31287. One of the most popular of the waterfront tavernas, with a slightly upmarket menu and atmosphere. There's a wide range of fish dishes (around €14), plus the usual meat and vegetable options (€7–12). April–Oct daily noon–midnight.

PLÁKA

Sunset Taverna At the entrance to the village coming from Almyrídha ☎ 28250 32047. It's really all about the views and – of course – sunsets at family-run *Sunset*, but the food is pretty good too, with a scattering of international items like spare ribs to attract the expats; mains €7–10. Daily 8am–midnight.

4

Inland Apokóronas

Good roads head inland from both Kalýves and Almyrídha, and this is lovely country to explore if you have a car, with interesting driving, plenty of alternative routes, and numerous villages worth a brief stop on the way. **Vámos** is the heart of the region and its main town – all roads seem to lead here in the end – while **Vrýsses** is the gateway to the road south into Sfakiá, and also to some far less visited villages on the south side of the E75 highway.

Aspró

Immediately inland from Almyrídha you pass below **ASPRÓ (Ασπρό)**, a tiny, ancient hamlet looking down over the coast. This is the old Greek village as you've always imagined it, with lots of bougainvillea-draped backstreets and dozing dogs stretched out in the road. A handful of foreigners have snapped up any empty houses and it seems only a matter of time before the remaining local residents decide to cash in, too.

Douliqná

DOULIANÁ (Ντουλιανά), a couple of kilometres southwest of Aspró as the crow flies but a few more along the back roads you're forced to take to reach it, is a delightful hamlet. Overflowing with plants and flowers and crisscrossed by winding lanes lined with fine old houses, it's yet another place where time seems to stand still.

Gavalohóri

The evidence that **GAVALOHÓRI (Γαβαλοχώρι)**, 2km south of Aspró, is an ancient settlement is scattered throughout the village's narrow, winding streets: there are Byzantine wells and Roman tombs on the outskirts, and on the corner by the museum you can see the cleverly preserved remains of a Turkish coffee shop. In a pedestrian area just off the main street, housed in a beautifully restored Venetian building with Turkish additions, Gavalohóri's small but excellent **folklore museum** (Mon–Sat 9am–7pm, Sun 11am–6pm; €2) documents the history and culture of the village. Of special interest are the examples of stone-cutting, woodcarving and *kopanéli* (silk lace made by bobbin-weaving), which is being revived in the village. The mulberry trees planted around here by the Turks still produce silk from the silkworms that feed on their leaves – although the worms themselves are now imported from Japan and China.

Vámos

The main agricultural centre of the peninsula and the capital of the Apokóronas district, **VÁMOS (Βάμος)** is hard to miss – from all over the region signs direct you to the local health centre. It's worth coming here, too, for a couple of excellent tavernas and for **Vámos Village** (see opposite), a co-operative founded to promote ecotourism and to rebuild and restore houses in the village. While you're here, make sure to see the upper part of the village, which is where most of the population lives; it's easy to get the idea that the co-operative's half is all there is. The upper village's main square has a number of quiet *kafenía* with street terraces.

Vrýsses

VRÝSSES (Βρύσες), on the south side of the E75 highway, was a major junction on the old road and is still at the crossroads for the route south to Hóra Sfakíon (if you're coming from Réthymno or anywhere else to the east, you usually have to **change buses** here), though nowadays bypassed by much of the traffic. Set on the banks of the Almirós River, Vrýsses is a wonderfully shady little town, its streets lined with huge old plane trees and busy with the life of a local agricultural centre. On the riverside are a number of inviting cafés and **tavernas**.

ARRIVAL AND ACTIVITIES

INLAND APOKÓRONAS

By bus There are regular buses connecting Haniá with Vámos (5 daily; 40min), while many (but not all) of the Haniá–Réthymno and Hóra Sfákion services call at Vrýsses, but there's no public transport between villages.

Vamos Village 75m from the Sterna Tou Bloumosifi tavern in Vámos, up a road alongside it (☎ 28250

22190, ⊚ vamosvillage.gr). Helpful tourist information as well as walking tours, cookery courses and all sorts of excursions and seasonal activities; they also sell an excellent local walking guide, *Discover Vamos On Foot*, detailing seven walks between 7 and 10km.

ACCOMMODATION AND EATING

DOULIANÁ

Iliopetra On the edge of the village by Ta Douliana ☎ 28250 22555, ⊚ iliopetra-milopetra.gr. Small complex of modern studios and one-bedroom apartments designed to blend into the village, well-equipped with a/c and washing machines; there's also a small pool. Studios €50, apartments €70

★ **Natalia's Houses** Signed in the heart of the village ☎ 28250 23356, ⊚ nataliashouses.gr. Four new but traditionally built houses, exceptionally thoughtfully fitted out and beautifully furnished, with an excellent taverna and welcoming hosts. €94

Ta Douliana Signed down a narrow track on the southern edge of the village ☎ 28250 23380. A friendly taverna with tables on a leafy terrace. Their fried chicken livers (€5) are a favourite, as are simple lamb (€8) or chicken (€6.50) casseroles, and they also make good pizza in a wood-fired oven, available for delivery to local villas. Daily noon–midnight.

GAVALOHÓRI

Arismari In pedestrian alley by the museum ☎ 28250 84066. A lovely spot, with tables outside under a venerable plane tree. Go for the freshly-made specials from the seasonal menu; there are lots of vegetarian choices such as home-made local pasta with cheese or stuffed courgette flowers (both €6). Occasional live Greek music. Daily noon–11.30pm.

VÁMOS

Marouvas On the main street ☎ 28250 22202. Good taverna with an attractive terrace serving well-prepared Cretan standards. Pork baked in a wood-fired oven (€8.50) and *marathópita* (fennel pie, €3.80) are popular specials. Daily noon–midnight.

★ **Sterna Tou Bloumosifi** Main road, near the centre of the lower village ☎ 28250 83220. Outstanding taverna with a tree-shaded terrace dedicated to traditional Cretan cuisine. The menu changes with the seasons; excellent salads and mezédhes are followed by the likes of chestnut stew with mushrooms (€8.90), goat with wild greens (€10.90) or pork with wine and goat buttermilk (€7.90). They have a decent wine list, and the *hýma* (barrelled house wine, red and white) is pretty good, too. Daily noon–midnight.

★ **Vamos Village** 75m from the Sterna Tou Bloumosifi taverna ☎ 28250 22190, ⊚ vamosvillage.gr. A range of carefully restored traditional cottages, mostly in Vámos, some in the surrounding countryside, all fully equipped with everything you might need. Some have pools. €75

VRÝSSES AND AROUND

O Progoulis Centre of town, on the north side of the river, Vrýsses ☎ 28250 51086. With a terrace overlooking the river and its pools filled with entertaining ducks and geese, *Progoulis* specializes in grilled meats, with a wood-fired barbecue; a mixed grill for two is €15, a portion of rotisserie chicken €6.50. Daily 9am–1am.

★ **Taverna Tsitsifias** In the tiny hamlet of Tsitsifés, off the road between Vrýsses and Frés ☎ 28250 71380. A wonderful rural taverna, rich with the smell of wood-smoke and with its own *rakí* still in the back yard. Locals from Haniá and Réthymno pack the place at weekends, lapping up the friendly, traditional atmosphere. There's a long menu from which only a few items are available on any given day, but on the whole it's the local meat barbecued over wood you should go for – village sausages (€6) or pork with marjoram (€8); if you call in advance they'll roast a whole joint for you. Getting here is part of the fun – though well-signed, Tsitsifés is down terrifyingly narrow roads in the middle of nowhere. Daily 2–10.30pm.

Yeoryioúpoli

YEORYIOÚPOLI (Γεωργιούπολη) – or Georgioupolis – lies at the base of Cape Dhrápano where the Almirós flows into the sea. It's named after the ill-starred Prince George, a son of the Greek king who was appointed High Commissioner to Crete in 1898 (see p.336). These days, the place has a distinctly split personality: on the one hand is a pretty **old town** by the river, its approaches shaded by ancient eucalyptus trees; on the other is a lively **package resort**, with development spreading further every year along the beach to the east of town. For the moment the two sides maintain a comfortable

> ## HIKING AROUND YEORYIOÚPOLI
> If you want to do some walking in the area around Yeoryioúpoli, pick up a copy of the excellent local walking guide, *Discover Kavros and Georgioupolis On Foot*, widely sold locally. As a taster, you could try hiking up the Almirós valley towards Vrýsses or tackling the steep climb to Exópoli, where there are some wonderfully sited tavernas with magnificent views. Hikes to and around Lake Kournás (see p.262) are another possibility.

balance and Yeoryioúpoli remains a pleasant place to spend a few days: small-scale, yet with plenty of action, and with the freshwater **Lake Kournás** an easy trip away.

Yeoryioúpoli beaches

The main course of the river runs into the sea on the northern edge of Yeoryioúpoli, by a small harbour protected by a long rocky breakwater, and there are numerous smaller streams crossing the **beach** all around, some of which have wooden bridges to let you cross without getting your feet wet. These can make swimming cold in places, and they also create little quicksands, mostly only ankle-deep. This area is also a favoured nesting ground of the loggerhead **sea turtle** (see p.351). Close to town it can be hard to find space between the sunloungers, but several **beach bars** offer these for free as long as you pay for the odd drink; the best of these is probably the *Tropicana Beach Club*, at the start of the long eastern stretch. Beyond *Tropicana* a large stream crosses the beach, and more beach bars and hotels stretch into the distance; you may find more space here, but you should swim close to a lifeguard as there are **dangerous currents** in places: don't venture too far out, and take heed of any warning notices.

A second, much more sheltered beach, **Kaliváki**, lies to the north of the river in a small bay. Swimming here is safer and there are generally fewer people, but the water can be extremely cold.

ARRIVAL AND INFORMATION YEORYIOÚPOLI

By bus All buses between Haniá and Réthymno call at Yeoryioúpoli, so there's an hourly service in each direction throughout the day. They drop you on the highway, just a couple of minutes' walk from the square and crossroads at the centre of town – a booth here sells tickets for onward buses.

Travel agencies Ethon Tours on the square (☎ 28250 61432, ⊕ ethon.gr) offers everything from car, mountain and motorbike rental to its own ATM.

TOURS AND ACTIVITIES

Boat trips Sofia Cruises (☎ 28250 61100) runs boat trips from the river just below the bridge, including a daily trip to Maráthi, at the mouth of Soúdha Bay (see p.253). Trips run from June to Sept and cost €39.

Horseriding Horseriding and tuition are offered by Zoraïda's (☎ 28250 61745, ⊕ zoraidas-horseriding.com); trips include beach rides and excursions up to Lake Kournás.

Train tours Two tourist trains transport visitors along the seafront and to various places of interest inland, including the lake, and even as far as Aryiroúpoli (see p.228).

Watersports There's usually at least one watersports operation on the main beach, offering banana rides, jet skis and the like, while Turtle River, at the mouth of the river on the Kaliváki side, rent pedalos and kayaks for trips upstream.

ACCOMMODATION

There are **rooms to rent** everywhere in Yeoryioúpoli, it seems, and only at the height of season are you likely to have any trouble finding a vacancy. The competition generally keeps prices low. **Mosquitoes** can be a problem if you're staying near the river, but the wildlife on the banks is some compensation and kingfishers are regular visitors. With your own transport, the hill village of nearby **Exópoli** becomes a viable alternative to staying in town. The big hotels are mostly out to the east, especially in and around the village of **Kavrós**. The best thing you can say about Kavrós, which is almost entirely purpose-built, is that it has plenty of nightlife, and there's a frequent tourist train into Yeoryioúpoli.

Andy's Rooms Near the church, on the road towards the beach from the south end of the square by the supermarket ☎ 28250 61394, ⊕ andymaliarakis @gmail.com. This friendly place shaded by trees has good-value a/c rooms, simple but spotless, with big balconies and fridge, plus a couple of well-equipped apartments. Doubles €30, apartments €50

Anna's House Just across the river from town, on the Exópoli road ☏ 28250 61556, ⓦ annashouse.gr. Lovely, newly-built studios and apartments with well-equipped kitchens and modern decor, around a full-size pool; a short walk to town or Kaliváki beach. Studios €70, apartments €100

Eligas On the first cross street below the square, heading towards the beach ☏ 28250 61541, ⓦ eligas.gr. Simply furnished but well-maintained a/c studios, plus one apartment, in a bougainvillea-draped building; upper floors have good views from the back. €35

Georgioupolis Beach Hotel On the seafront at the bottom of the road from the north corner of the square ☏ 28250 61056, ⓦ gbhotel.gr. Good value considering the enviable seafront location and excellent facilities – a/c rooms with beach views and satellite TV, plus a pool and tiny spa. Breakfast available. €70

★ Marika Apartments In the hill village of Exópoli, 3km northwest of town ☏ 28250 61500, ⓦ marika-apartments.com. Attractive place with lovingly tended a/c studios and apartments around a pool with a truly spectacular view; it's worth paying a little extra for the sea-view apartment, if it's available. Studios €40, sea-view apartment €50

Porto Kalivaki Behind Kaliváki beach on the far side of the river ☏ 28250 61316, ⓦ kalivaki.com. Inexpensive if rather basic studios (only those on the upper level have a/c) in a tranquil spot right behind a sandy beach, with a large pool and lovingly tended gardens with scale models of the Acropolis and Knossós, among others. €40

Sofia Seafront near the mouth of the river ☏ 28250 61325, ⓦ river-side.gr. Peach-coloured apartment complex with modern two-room a/c apartments with kitchen and TV, most with sea views. The same owners run the adjacent *Riverside Hotel*, with similar facilities but inland views (and some cheaper rooms), and have other places nearby and in the hills. €60

Sunlight Seafront, just east of the centre ☏ 28250 61396, ⓦ sunlight-geo.gr. Modern apartment complex that's ugly from the outside, but friendly and comfortable within, with good sea-view balconies and rooms for 2–6 people. €45

Zorba's Taverna Close to the square on the road towards the church ☏ 28250 61381, ⓔ zorbashotel @hotmail.com. Pleasant, modern a/c studios and apartments above a taverna, with a tiny courtyard swimming pool. Breakfast included. €45

EATING AND DRINKING

There are plenty of restaurants and tavernas in Yeoryioúpoli, mainly between the square and the river or along the waterfront; the square itself is ringed by cafés. There are a number of tavernas up in the hill village of **Exópoli** too, with stunning views over the coast. In terms of **nightlife**, Yeoryioúpoli itself is pretty quiet, though there are plenty of **bars** open late. There are regular Greek dance nights and other events at the *Tropicana Beach Club*, and look out for posters for weekend beach parties and the like.

Babis On the first cross street ☏ 28250 61819. Traditional taverna with good-value, simple Cretan food; *yemistá* (stuffed tomatoes and peppers) €5.50, rabbit *stifádho* €7.50. Daily 11am–11pm.

Blue Moon Overlooking the river, just upstream from the bridge ☏ 6972 705 310. Café-bar with a riverside terrace for breakfast (€5.50–7, made with produce from their own farm) or a sundowner, plus snacks and drinks all day. May–Oct daily 8am–9pm.

Corissia Park On the seafront in the centre of town ☏ 28250 83010. Pool-bar and restaurant. One of the best locations in town makes up for a somewhat bland menu, and customers can use the pool and loungers on the beach for free; there's a breakfast buffet (8–10am, €8), burgers and snacks by day, and a more formal atmosphere in the evening. Frequent live music. Daily 8am–midnight.

Efthimis On the road heading east out of town, parallel to the highway ☏ 28250 61886. Friendly little diner serving good wood-oven pizza (around €8, depending on size; also takeaway and delivery) and decent Greek dishes. March–Oct daily 5pm–midnight.

O Fanis Main street near the bridge ☏ 6998 795 979. Grill house offering the freshest catch from the quayside, 30m away, with fish dishes (mixed fish for two €22, sardines €6.50) and good meat dishes (lamb chops €9.50). April–Sept daily 11am–midnight.

Paradise Down by the river west of the square ☏ 28250 61313. Reliable taverna in an attractive garden setting. The Cretan kitchen turns out a range of popular standards from *biftéki* (€7.50) to *saganáki* shrimp (€9.50). May–Oct daily 6–11pm.

Poseidon Taverna Hidden away down a lane southwest of the square; look for the signs ☏ 28250 61026. In a lovely riverside setting and serving "every day fish from our own boat" at reasonable prices, this is definitely worth a try. There's no menu, and nothing but fish, seafood and chips; choose your fish carefully (it's sold by weight) to avoid a nasty surprise when the bill arrives. April–Oct daily 6–11pm.

Sirtaki Main street near the bridge ☏ 28250 61382. Excellent taverna-ouzerí with a raised terrace serving well-prepared *mezédhes* and delicious grilled meat and fish;

lamb's liver €7.50, mixed *souvláki* €10. April–Oct daily noon–midnight.

Sunlight Taverna Overlooking the beach, east of the centre ☎ 28250 83075. Fantastic seafront setting for

decent, plain Cretan food, with great-value daily specials, such as chicken in the oven with potatoes, €5.90, or sea bream and salad, €7.50. In the evening, tables are set up across the road by the water. April–Oct daily 8am–11pm.

Lake Kournás and around

Crete's only freshwater lake, **LAKE KOURNÁS**, shelters in a steep bowl of hills 4km inland from Yeoryioúpoli. As lakes go, it's small and shallow, but it nevertheless makes for an interesting excursion. Its appearance varies greatly according to when you visit: during the day its colours change remarkably as the sun shifts around the rim of the bowl, and its size alters over the course of a year. In late summer the level drops to reveal sand (or dried mud) beaches all around, and a number of popular camping spots. Earlier in the year, the water comes right up to the tidal ring of scrubby growth and it's much harder to find anywhere to camp or to swim from. The lake and the surrounding hills are also a good place to seek out some of the more unusual island wildlife. In summer it's possible to make a circuit of the lake using a path and the dried mud beaches where this runs out – about an hour's walk.

On the lakeshore where you arrive it can be extremely crowded, with **tavernas** competing for your custom and pedaloes and canoes for rent; a short stroll will usually find you a quieter spot. The nearby hamlet of **Mathés**, some 2km away on a back road to Yeoryioúpoli, is more peaceful still, with fine coastal views from an excellent taverna, and some lovely rooms.

Kournás

The village of **KOURNÁS** (**Κουρνάς**), a charming hill settlement fanning out around its inclined main street, is a stiff 4km climb beyond Lake Kournás. The church of **Áyios Yeóryios** here is a fine old Byzantine structure with Venetian additions and some impressive fresco fragments. If it's locked, ask around and someone should be able to produce a key.

ARRIVAL AND DEPARTURE   LAKE KOURNÁS

There's no public transport to the lake, but there are **tours** from many nearby resorts. To get to the lake from Yeoryioúpoli you could take the **tourist train** or rent a **bike**, or it's an easy **walk**. The best route is via the hamlet of Mathés (cross the highway at the crossroads in Yeoryioúpoli and a quiet road leads straight ahead). From here there's a waymarked rambling route to the lake's northern edge, linking in with the route around it – ask the villagers at **Mathés** to direct you to the path, should you have difficulty.

ACCOMMODATION AND EATING

LAKE KOURNÁS

Korissia North end of the lake ☎ 28250 61653, ⓦ kournas-lake-apartments.gr. Superbly sited place, away from the craziness at the end of the road, with simple a/c lake-view balcony rooms above a taverna; very comfortable so long as you have insect repellent. The taverna is one of the best lakeside options, too, with a giant charcoal grill. Daily 8am–11pm. €35

KOURNÁS

★ **Kali Kardia** Main street in the heart of the village ☎ 28250 96278. Great, inexpensive taverna with some of the best lamb (€8) and sausages (€6) in the province, together with tasty *souvláki* and super salads – and don't

miss their noted *galaktoboúreko* dessert, a lemony egg-custard pudding. Daily 9am–11pm.

MATHÉS

Taverna Mathes Centre of the village ☎ 28250 61514. Excellent food on a fine terrace with a stunning panoramic view. They specialize in charcoal-grilled and rotisserie meats, though there are also plenty of veggie dishes; try the *kalitsoúnia* (cheese pies, €4.50), or suckling pig (€8.80). April–Oct daily 10am–11pm.

★ **Villa Kapasa** ☎ 28250 61050, ⓦ villa-kapasas.com. Delightful old place with simple a/c rooms overlooking the leafy garden of an ancient restored house. It's high above the village so has fabulous views; they also do meals. €40

West of Haniá

West of Haniá, the E75 speeds you towards Kastélli with little to see along the way. The **old road**, meanwhile, also served by buses, follows the coastline more or less consistently, through a string of small towns and growing resorts, all the way to the **Rodhopoú peninsula**. Occasionally it runs right above the water, more often 100m or so inland, but never more than easy walking distance from the sea. As you drive along the coast everything may seem entirely modern, but in most cases there is a real village up in the hills behind, where traditional life survives to a remarkable degree. This area was also a crucial battlefield in the 1941 **Battle of Crete**, and the bridgehead from which the Germans established their domination.

The hotel zone

There are hotels and apartments the whole way from Haniá to Kolymbári at the base of the **Rodhopoú peninsula**, but the first real resort area starts at **Káto Stalós**, which runs into **Ayía Marína** and then into **Plataniás** without a break, creating the most built-up, touristy strip in the west of the island. This is better than it sounds: it's all fairly low-rise, there's a decent beach almost all the way along (with facilities including jet skis, windsurfers and parascending) and, by resort standards, it's pretty quiet. Beyond Plataniás development thins out, though there are still plenty of hotels and apartment complexes and one or two more concentrated resort clusters such as **Yeráni**. These on the whole are pleasantly low-key, but the beach is rarely that great, being very open to wind and waves and with rather gravelly, grey sand.

Ayía Marína

AYÍA MARÍNA (Αγία Μαρίνα) is distinguished by a beautiful beach, curving round a little promontory with a fine view of the sunset and of **Áyii Theódori**, an offshore islet that's a sanctuary for *kri-kri* or wild goats (you're not allowed to go ashore). From the west of the island a great cave gapes like the jaws of a beast; legend has Áyii Theódori as a sea-monster which, emerging from the depths to swallow Crete, was petrified by the gods. Remains found in the cave suggest that it was a place of Minoan worship in antiquity, while in more recent times the Venetians turned the island into a fortress. As for Ayía Marína itself, there's every facility and tour you could want on offer; uphill and inland the original village still retains some of its traditional character.

Plataniás

Seamlessly adjoining Ayía Marína to the west, **PLATANIÁS (Πλατανιάς)** is an even busier place boasting a delightful old quarter perched high on an almost sheer bluff above the road. At the top of this hill, under the church, a volunteer-run **World War II museum** (daily 5–8pm; €2) occupies tunnels dug by Cretan forced labour; the extensive tunnel system was used for weapons storage and as access to German defensive positions on the hillside.

Máleme

MÁLEME (Μάλεμε) is a place with significant historical resonance. This was the site of the **airfield** (still operational) that saw much of the early fighting in the Battle of Crete and where the German invasion began on May 20, 1941; the loss of this airfield in controversial circumstances was crucial to the German success (see p.338). There are also Minoan remains nearby.

German war cemetery

Signed up a narrow lane from the coast road just beyond Máleme

On a hillside below the ridge known as Hill 107, which played a pivotal role in the struggle for the nearby airfield, the **German war cemetery** overlooks the battleground where so many of the four and a half thousand remembered here lost their lives. The lines of flat headstones, each marking a double grave, lend a sombre aspect to an otherwise peaceful scene. In a piece of almost grotesque irony, the cemetery's keepers were for many years George Psychoundakis, author of *The Cretan Runner*, and Manoli Pateraki, who played a leading role in the capture of General Kreipe (see p.338).

Late Minoan tomb

Follow the lane down from the cemetery to the first left bend, where a track (signed) on the right leads 100m along a terraced hillside to the tomb on the right

The discovery in 1966 of a splendid **Late Minoan tomb** near Máleme demonstrated that this area had already been a graveyard for more than three thousand years. The *dhrómos* or entrance passage of the stone-built tomb and its enormous heavy lintel are well preserved.

ARRIVAL AND DEPARTURE   THE HOTEL ZONE

By bus There's an excellent bus service along the coast from Haniá, stopping frequently at all the resorts, with peak-season services at least half-hourly throughout the day, and hourly through the night as far as Plataniás.

ACTIVITIES

Bike tours Hellas Bike, in Ayía Marína (☏ 28210 60858, ⊕ hellasbike.net) offers bike rental and easy bike tours (€38/half-day; €58/full day, including pick-up from your accommodation) around this area and into the mountains.

Boat trips and watersports All sorts of boat trips depart from the little harbours in Ayía Marína and Plataniás, and there are watersports operators at regular intervals along the beach.

ACCOMMODATION

The best accommodation deals on the coast are invariably on **packages**; there are a few old-fashioned rooms places but, out of season at least, you'll be better off at one of the many modern, well-appointed apartment complexes (most have pools). Outside July or August there may well be bargains available. Any of the travel agencies along the main street should be able to arrange a deal.

AYÍA MARÍNA

Villa Life Upper village, beyond the highway ☏ 28210 95986, ⊕ villa-life.gr. Welcoming, purpose-built one- and two-bedroom balcony apartments around a nice pool, from where there's a great view down over the coast; some traffic noise from the nearby highway, however. **€55**

PLATANIÁS

Effi Apartments On the beach ☏ 6972 638 950, ✉ effi apartments@gmail.com. Lovely designer-style apartments with contemporary furnishings in a garden setting right on the beach, plus an exceptionally friendly welcome. **€85**

Ermis Suites On the beach ☏ 28210 60101,

⊕ ermis-suites.gr. Fairly simple studios and apartments, many with sea view and all with balcony or veranda. The larger apartments have two rooms and a fully equipped kitchen. Studios **€60**, apartments **€85**

Pelagos Holiday Apartments Halfway up the hill above the main square ☏ 28210 60075, ⊕ pelagos holidays.gr. Modern, exceptionally well-fitted-out duplex apartments – designed by the Finnish architect-husband of the owner – these are a step up in price and quality from most of the accommodation here. Designer furnishings (including Scandinavian beds) complete the picture, and all apartments come with balcony sea views, kitchenette and satellite TV. Five-night minimum stay. **€110**

EATING

A number of **tavernas** in Plataniás attract evening and weekend visitors from Haniá. The best views are from the eagles' eyries right at the top of the village, including the terraces of *Vigli* and *Astrea*. The best food, however, is down below.

AYÍA MARÍNA

Manolis Taverna In the heart of the upper village ☏ 28210 68311. Excellent little family taverna away from the seafront maelstrom, with a nice outdoor terrace. Solid Cretan cooking includes dishes like *bouréki* and *kounéli stifádho* (stewed rabbit, €8) and there's an outdoor charcoal grill and a decent selection of reasonably priced bottled

wines. April–Oct daily 6–11.30pm.

PLATANIÁS

★ 0 Milos tou Kerata Main road, just west of the centre ☏ 28210 68578. A restaurant of repute that opened its doors in 1960, *Milos* is dedicated to quality, and is expensive by Cretan standards, but worth it. Specialities include *kontosoúvli* – pork cooked on a spit over charcoal (€11) – and pricey steaks, plus a variety of salads (€8.50–10.50). You eat in a delightful walled garden with an old millstream running through it. April–Oct daily 6pm–12.30am.

★**Taverna Drakiana** Just outside the hamlet of Dhrakianá, 3km inland on the road beside O Milos ☎ 28210 61677. The food – organic and based on traditional recipes – may not be quite up to the same

standard as *Milos*, but the prices are more palatable (full Cretan menu for two €29.50; mains around €9) and the riverside setting, in wooded surroundings, couldn't be more romantic – especially at night. It's an easy walk inland, but they offer a free minibus from Plataniás or Ayía Marína that will also bring you home after you've eaten; simply call ahead. There's Cretan dancing every Wednesday evening. April–Oct daily 10am–midnight.

DRINKING AND NIGHTLIFE

PLATANIÁS

Mylos Main road, just west of the centre ☎ 28210 60449 or ☎ 6945 260 673, ✉ mylos-chania.com. For most young people in Haniá, Plataniás means clubs, and a great exodus from the city takes place in summer at around

midnight. This is the top place, with a beach bar by day and club at night, but there are plenty of other beach bars and bar-clubs open much of the day and most of the night. June–Sept: beach bar daily 11am–11pm, club Tues–Sat 11pm–early hours.

The Rodhopoú peninsula

Half a dozen villages cluster near the base of the **Rodhopoú peninsula**, and are beginning to be discovered by tourists. The peninsula itself is for the most part a barren, harsh landscape, with no roads penetrating northwards; if you want to explore towards the tip, you'll have to do so on foot or come by boat. **Inland**, a road heads south from Kolymbári through Spiliá, tracking the valley of the Spiliákos river and offering an opportunity to see an impressive **cave** and a trio of superb **churches**.

Kolymbári

KOLYMBÁRI (**Κολυμπάρι**), just off the main road, is much the most developed village on Rodhopoú, but still has far more appeal than anything that has preceded it along the north coast. If there were a sandy beach, it would be a perfect resort; as it is, there's a long strip of pebbles and clear water looking back along the coast towards Haniá in the distance. There's every facility you might need, including boat trips and car rental, but it's little spoiled, and from the narrow main street, where there are a couple of good tavernas, you can walk through to a seafront promenade lined with more restaurants and cafés. Nearby, a vast new concrete harbour is entirely deserted most of the time. Some villas and apartments are in the old village on the hill above, where the views compensate for the ten-minute walk up.

Moní Gonía

1km north of Kolymbári • April–Sept Mon–Fri & Sun 9am–2pm & 4–7pm, Sat 4–7pm; Nov–March Mon–Fri & Sun 8am–12.30pm & 3.30–5.30pm, Sat 3.30–5.30pm • €2 • Respectable dress required

A short walk from Kolymbári on the main road out onto the peninsula, the seventeenth-century **Moní Gonía** (**Μονή Γωνιάς**) occupies a prime site, with stupendous views and a scramble down to a sandy cove – rumoured to be the monks' private beach. Every monk in Crete can tell tales of a valiant heritage of resistance to invaders, but here the Turkish cannonballs are still lodged in the walls to prove it, a relic of which the good fathers seem far more proud than any of the icons. That said, the church has a splendid series of seventeenth- and eighteenth-century icons (plus a few modern examples); Áyios Nikólaos, in a side chapel, is particularly fine. More are kept in the small **museum**, along with assorted vestments and relics.

Afráta

A scenic road extends up the peninsula's east coast as far as **AFRÁTA** (**Άφράτα**), a tiny place with a couple of tavernas and the first stirrings of development. Keep right here, down an increasingly steep, narrow road, and after little more than 1km you'll reach a rocky **cove** at the far end of the gorge you can see from the village. There's a seasonal taverna here and the exceptionally clear water offers great swimming, although it's a tiny space and can get crowded.

Ravdoúha
RAVDOÚHA (Ραβδούχα) is the only place on the peninsula's west coast accessible by road, either directly from the highway or an attractive drive from Afráta on good roads via **Astrátigos** and **Áspra Nerá**, with a turn-off to the village of **Rodhopós**, all pleasant if unremarkable settlements with places to eat and drink. Much the same might be said of Ravdoúha itself, the difference being that from here you can head down to the shore, passing the ancient church of **Ayía Marína** with some fine fresco fragments and, next to it, an old communal washing place, evoking a Crete long gone. **Ravdoúha beach**, a dizzying drop below the village, is something of a misnomer, but there are patches of rocky foreshore to swim from, and an isolated taverna with rooms.

The tip of the peninsula
Towards the tip of the peninsula you'll find no easily driveable roads, although a rough track (for which you'll need a 4WD) heads north out of Rodhopós up the spine of the peninsula to Diktynna, 20km distant. There are, however, a couple of sites you might consider taking a major hike or a **boat trip** to reach. The latter is certainly the easier option – in summer the terrain is frighteningly hot, barren and shadeless.

Diktynna
There are regular boat trips to **Diktynna**, almost at the top of the peninsula above a little bay on the east side. An important Roman sanctuary to the goddess of the same name, this was probably built over more ancient centres of worship, and though it has never been properly excavated there's a surprising amount to be seen. The boats come here mainly because it's a sheltered spot to swim (when the sea is rough, fishing boats often shelter here too), but they allow plenty of time to explore.

Church of Áyios Ioánnis Giónis
If you've come to Diktynna by boat, there's a challenging 14km hike over to the isolated **Church of Áyios Ioánnis Giónis** on the western side of the peninsula, from where you could continue back to Rodhopós (7km) or Kolymbári (a further 7km); but let the boatmen know your plans to save them sending out a search party. On August 29, the church plays host to a major pilgrimage and a mass baptism of boys called Yiannis, marking one of the most important festivals of the Cretan religious calendar. At this time the two- to three-hour walk (each way) from Rodhopós among crowds of people is definitely worth it.

Spiliá and around
A little over 3km south of Kolymbári lies the rural village of **SPILIÁ (Σπηλιά)**. Signs from the southern edge of the village lead to the charming, finely restored fourteenth-century church of the **Panayía**, raised on the lower slope of a hill and ringed by junipers. Inside (the church is usually left open) the dark interior is decorated with fine fourteenth-century **frescoes**, though here the restoration of the building is rather crude. Several other fine churches can be found in the countryside surrounding Spiliá.

Cave of Áyios Ioánnis Ermítis
North of, and high above, Spiliá, close to the hamlet of Marathokefála • Usually open daylight hours • Free

The **Cave of Áyios Ioánnis Ermítis** (St John the Hermit) is a sizeable grotto with a church, dedicated to the eleventh-century evangelist, built inside it. There's a terrace with fine coastal views and a café and museum, open on weekends and holidays when this is a popular outing.

CLOCKWISE FROM TOP THE ARSENALI, HANIÁ (P.240); ASPRÓ (P.258); AYÍA TRIÁDHA (P.251) >

Áyios Stéfanos

Signed from the road just over 2km south of Spiliá, beyond the village of Dhrakóna • Usually open daylight hours • Free

The **chapel of Áyios Stéfanos** is an extraordinary, tiny, tenth-century white-walled chapel squatting in a grove of mature trees. Inside you'll find the hefty stone walls decorated with exquisite **frescoes** dating from the period following the Arab conquest, when the Christian faith was being triumphantly restored.

Miháil Arhángelos Episkopí

4km southwest of Spiliá on the outskirts of Episkopí • Mon–Sat 9am–1pm & 4–7pm • Free

The most impressive church in the area around Spiliá, and one of the oldest in Greece, is the remarkable **Miháil Arhángelos Episkopí**, whose concentric stepped **dome**, unique in Crete, gives the structure its local name, "The Rotunda". The church was, as its official name suggests, a bishop's seat during the Venetian period, but the edifice is much older than this. The core rotunda section dates to the first Byzantine period, completed perhaps as early as the sixth century, and originally stood alone; the rest of the building was added after the end of the Arab occupation in the tenth century. Recent excavations in the adjoining graveyard yielded evidence that the present church was built over the remains of a still earlier Christian basilica, with various layers of burials from all periods of the church's history. The exterior has arguably been over-restored – inside, fragmentary **frescoes** dating back to the tenth century include a poignant head and partial wing of Áyios Miháil, the church's patron. There are also impressive mosaic floor fragments (some thought to date to the earliest period), and a fine double-seated marble **font**.

Karavitakis Winery

Near Pondikianá, not far from Áno Voúves; extensively signed throughout the area • April–Oct daily 10am–6.30pm; booking recommended • Tour and tasting €4 • ☎ 28240 23381, ⓦ karavitakiswines.com

The **Karavitakis Winery** is an exemplar of the new wave of Cretan winemaking, a serious small boutique operation with 150 acres of vineyards growing both traditional and newly introduced grape varieties. There's an informative short tour of the process, including the attractive, traditional-looking modern buildings where the wine is made, followed by a tasting of some of their award-winning wines.

ARRIVAL AND DEPARTURE

THE RODHOPOÚ PENINSULA

By bus The Haniá hotel zone bus terminates at Kolymbári, with services along the coast at least half-hourly throughout the day; in addition, almost all buses between Haniá and Kastélli stop here (15 daily; 30min either way).

ACCOMMODATION AND EATING

KOLYMBÁRI

Aphea Village On the road to the upper village ☎ 28240 23344, ⓦ www.aphea-village.gr. Sizeable modern apartment complex with a big pool and great views. The two- and three-bedroom a/c apartments are large and have everything you need, but feel somewhat spartan. Simple breakfast and a home-cooked evening meal are available around the pool. **€50**

THE WORLD'S OLDEST OLIVE TREE

Áno Voúves, well-signed 4km east of Episkopí, has become famous throughout Greece as the location of one of the oldest olive trees in existence. Having seen the zenith of Minoan Crete and being seriously venerable at the time of Christ, the gnarled and contorted tree looks every one of the 4000-plus years attributed to it by experts from the University of Crete (the 3000 years quoted on information boards at the site is thought to be a conservative estimate). Still vigorously producing foliage and fruit, the ancient tree has become a source of huge pride for Áno Voúves, and there's a café and museum (ⓦ olivemuseumvouves.com) for visitors. In 2004 a branch from the tree was carried to Athens on a reconstructed Minoan boat (see p.240) and two victory wreaths fashioned from its leaves were used to honour the first and last winners of events in that year's Olympic Games.

★**Argentina** Main street, behind the harbour ☎ 28240 22243. One of the best tavernas in the village, with a sea-view terrace. There's generally a big variety of fresh fish to choose from (priced per kilo, around €12 per portion), plus the usual meat dishes and salads and very good house wine. April–Oct daily noon–11pm.

Diktina Main street, behind the harbour ☎ 6974 730 058. With a terrace at the rear overlooking the old harbour, this good taverna serves fresh fish (priced per kilo) and seafood (cuttlefish €8, shrimp spaghetti €10) along with the usual standards. April–Oct daily noon–11.30pm.

Grand Bay Beach Resort At the eastern end of the beach ☎ 28240 22690, ⓦ grandbay.gr. Classy adults-only hotel in a fabulous position right on the water. There are several pools and a swim-up bar; it's probably worth paying extra for the excellent sea view. €90

Palio Arkhontiko Overlooking the beach ☎ 28240 22124. Highly popular taverna with more pretensions to style than any of its neighbours and a few more elaborate dishes (Gruyère pies with fruit sauce €6.50; squid stuffed with cheese and peppers €14.80), as well as plenty of standard Greek fare and somewhat pricey fresh fish. Daily noon–11pm.

★**Villa Polichna** Upper village ☎ 6945 232 288, ⓦ villa-polichna.gr. Delightful two-storey a/c apartments, extremely well-equipped (most with washing machine) and thoughtfully furnished in traditional style. There's a tiny outdoor jacuzzi pool too. €45

AFRÁTA

Tis Litsas to Kamomata On the crossroads in the centre of the village ☎ 6976 228 778. Lovely place on a raised terrace serving coffees, snacks and drinks – including Brink's beer (see p.215) – throughout the day and delicious, simple home-made food at lunchtime and in the evenings. Lamb or goat dishes go for around €10, *yemistá* (stuffed tomatoes and peppers) €6.50. April–Oct daily 10am–10.30pm.

RAVDOÚHA

Ravdoucha Beach Studios Ravdoúha Beach ☎ 6939 995 465, ⓦ ravdouchabeachstudios.gr.Tucked away behind *Waves on the Rock* in a position that guarantees utter tranquillity, these modern two-room a/c studio apartments have great views from their balconies; meals are available at *Waves on the Rock*, run by the same family. €50

★**Waves on the Rock** Ravdoúha Beach ☎ 28240 23133, ⓦ wavesontherock.eu. An excellent, out-of-the-way taverna fronting a pebble beach shaded by tamarisks, serving up tasty Cretan dishes (mains around €8) and fresh fish (priced per kilo, around €15 a head). They also have five inexpensive, basic studio rooms, but the same family has newer apartments next door (see above). April–Oct daily 9am–midnight, Nov–March Fri–Sun only. €35

South of Haniá

The area immediately inland from Haniá, around **Thériso**, is one that's little explored by tourists, though plenty of local visitors head up here for the mountain air, rural tavernas, and associations with the revered Cretan statesman **Eleftherios Venizelos** who, as prime minister of Greece for most of the period from 1910 to 1932, finally brought Crete into the modern Greek nation. Further west, roads through **Alikianós** head south towards Omalós, the Samariá Gorge and the heart of the White Mountains, and also to Soúyia on the south coast. This is agricultural country, growing oranges above all, and paying little heed to tourism, though again there's a wealth of history here. Most recently this area was the scene of some of the fiercest fighting in the **Battle of Crete** (see p.338), though many of the villages also have a much longer history of resistance.

Thériso and around

One of the most attractive trips you can make around Haniá is the 14km drive up to the traditional country village of **THÉRISO** (Θέρισο), one of the cradles of Cretan independence and hometown of Eleftherios Venizelos's mother. Here in 1905 the Revolutionary Assembly was held (all baggy black shirts and drooping moustaches, as depicted in so many Cretan museums) that ousted Prince George and did much to precipitate union with Greece. Venizelos's family home is now a tiny **folklore museum** (signed off the main street; July & Aug Mon–Fri noon–1.30pm & 7–8.30pm, Sat & Sun 11.30am–1.30pm; Sept–June Mon, Wed–Fri & Sun 10.30am–1.30pm; €1; ☎ 6945 770 235) and, with its plaque commemorating the famous son, is all but obligatory for Cretans – the village is frequently crowded with busloads of schoolkids.

There's also a newly refurbished **Museum of National Resistance 1941–45** (signed off the main street; irregular hours; €1; ☎ 28210 78780) and numerous **tavernas**, some of them huge, mostly empty except at weekends and holidays.

Thériso Gorge

The route up to Thériso passes through the **Thériso Gorge**. In terms of spectacle it can't, of course, compare with Samariá and, in any case, the bed of the ravine is given over to the road. But it is exceedingly pretty in the lower reaches, gentle and winding with the stream crossed and recrossed on concrete bridges, and surprisingly craggy towards the top where the walls are cracked and pocked with caves. There are plenty of opportunities to pull over and explore.

South of Thériso

South of Thériso, spectacularly heady mountain roads skirt the foothills of the White Mountains in two directions. East, you can head through the hamlet of **Dhrakóna**, where there are a couple of excellent places to eat, and then circle back to Haniá or continue east on still narrower byways towards Stýlos (see p.254). To the west you climb over what feels like an impressively lofty ridge to **Zoúrva**, a cluster of whitewashed houses with a lovely taverna and stupendous views over the surrounding valleys, and from there can continue down via Mesklá to the Alikianós road. This route makes a wonderful long **hike**, occasionally traversed by rambling groups but quite possible on your own if you arrange for a taxi pick-up at the other end.

Mesklá

MESKLÁ (Μεσκλά) is another beautiful village, set on a swift-flowing brook and surrounded by lush agricultural land and orange groves. Under the Venetians, Mesklá was a place of considerably more importance than it is now, as indicated by the tiny chapel of **Metamórphosis Sotírou** (Transfiguration of the Saviour), which lies at the bottom of the village – cross the bridge and it's signed up a track. The freshly restored, barrel-vaulted church preserves some truly impressive fourteenth-century **frescoes**, many of which are also newly restored; there are some particularly striking scenes of the Last Judgement. At the top of the village there's another chapel dedicated to the **Panayía** (next to a large modern church of the same name), which was constructed in the fourteenth century over a fifth-century basilica which had, in its turn, been raised over a Roman temple to Aphrodite.

Alikianós and around

ALIKIANÓS (Αλικιανός) is a historically important village astride the main road south into the mountains. Here – nowadays just outside town, as the main roads bypass it – is a junction where you can head directly south towards Omalós and the heart of the mountains, or southwest towards Soúyia and the south coast. Beside this turning there's a large **war memorial**, commemorating local members of the irregular forces that defended this area, known as "Prison Valley", in the Battle of Crete (you can't miss the prison; it's the big white building bristling with aerials). Cut off from any other Allied units – who believed that resistance here collapsed on the first day of the battle – the Greeks fought on even as everyone else was in full retreat. By doing so they prevented the Germans getting around the mountains to cut the road and guaranteed that the evacuation from Hóra Sfakíon could go ahead. In much earlier history, Alikianós was also the site of the wedding massacre that ended the Kandanoleon revolt (see box opposite).

The village itself has a couple of churches worth a look. Follow the lane signed to Koufós and you'll reach the small fourteenth-century church of **Áyios Yeóryios**, on the northern edge of the village, whose frescoes were destroyed during World War II. Continue along the same road, out of the village, for 1km for **Áyios Ioánnis** (also signed

THE KANDANOLEON REVOLT

The village of Mesklá (see opposite) was the centre of one of the great legends of Cretan resistance, the **Kandanoleon revolt**. According to the story (which is certainly not historically accurate, though probably has some basis in fact), much of western Crete rose against the Venetians early in the sixteenth century. They elected as their leader one George Kandanoleon, who established a base in Mesklá and from here ran a rebel administration, controlling much of the west. In order to legitimize his authority, Kandanoleon arranged for his son to marry the daughter of a Venetian aristocrat, Francesco Molini. During the wedding celebrations Kandanoleon and several hundred of his supporters ate and drank themselves into a stupor – at which point, by pre-arranged signal, a Venetian army arrived and captured the Cretans as they slept. Their leaders were hanged at villages around the countryside, and the revolt was over.

You can visit the alleged scene of the massacre in Alikianós. Ask directions to the ruins of the **Da Molini castle**, in an orange grove over the road from the church of Áyios Yeóryios. To reach the castle, with your back to the church gate turn right to a new porticoed building on the left. Follow a narrow alley to the left of this for 50m: the castle ruins lie in an orange grove off to the right. Impressive walls still stand, festooned with weeds, and the overgrown entrance lintel carries the inscription *Omnia Mundi Fumus et Umbra* ("All in the World is Smoke and Shadow"), a sentiment to which the Venetians were particularly attached, and which ultimately turned out to be grimly accurate regarding their Cretan possessions.

as Zoödóhos Píyi), down a track into orange groves on the right. An impressively large fourteenth-century building on the site of at least two previous churches dating back to the sixth century, the domed church employs parts of the previous basilica in the construction of its apse. Inside, surviving **frescoes** depict the Ascension as well as a number of saints.

Galatás

About 5km out of Hanía on the Alikianós road, a turn-off to the right is signed to the hilltop village of **GALATÁS (Γαλατάς)** one of the major battlegrounds in the Battle of Crete, when poorly armed villagers and a contingent of New Zealand soldiers stood between Hanía and the might of the German army. Heroically, and against all odds, they held back the German army for almost a week with huge loss of life. The village today is a pleasant and fair-sized place, with a tiny, one-room **Battle of Crete museum** dedicated to the events of 1941 (usually daily 9am–2pm; free). Sited on the main square, it's basically a collection of rusty guns, helmets, photos and newspaper cuttings, but fascinating nevertheless. Outside is a memorial to those who died here, including 145 New Zealand soldiers. If the museum is closed, enquiries at any of the nearby *kafenía* should soon produce the key (and possibly a guided tour).

The Ayiá Reservoir

On the edge of the village of Ayiá

The **Ayiá Reservoir** is arguably the best **bird-watching** spot on Crete. This watery marshland is home to a rich variety of species, including crakes, avocet, marsh harrier, spotted flycatcher and squacco heron in season. The kingfishers are a particular delight and not at all put off their diving tricks by human visitors. Terrapins too, are residents here and when not squelching around in the marshy pools they can often be spotted sunning themselves on a raised mud bank. The best sightings should be in the early morning or a couple of hours before dusk, though there's plenty of birdlife year-round, at almost any time of day; binoculars are helpful. There are a number of walkways around the lake, and a couple of upmarket and rather incongruous cafés on the banks. The *Limni* café is signed off the main road, and has a terrace with views over the water, but for the best access to the lake you are better off continuing into the village, where a swan-shaped sign will take you to the *Erasma* café and lakeside walkways.

ARRIVAL AND DEPARTURE

By bus Although there are a couple of daily buses from Haniá to Thériso, and a single daily bus to some of the other villages, it's not really practical to explore this area by bus. The one place that has a regular service is Alikianós, with seven buses a day from Haniá (4 at weekends; 20min).

SOUTH OF HANIÁ

By car There are some lovely drives in this region, and several circular routes; most obviously up to Thériso, returning via Mesklá and Alikianós. From Mesklá there's also a short cut directly up to the Omalós road, for those heading for the mountains.

ACCOMMODATION AND EATING

THÉRISO

Andartes Main street, near the village centre ☎ 28210 78833. Huge taverna set up for feasting, with Cretan dishes including spit-roasted lamb, *singlino* (cured pork), *stifádho* and *sfakianó* (lamb casserole); mains €8–10. Daily: July & Aug 11am–10.30pm; Sept–June 11am–6pm.

Madares Taverna-Rooms Main street, near the village centre ☎ 28210 92127. These rustic rooms are more like mini-apartments, with beds in a gallery under the eaves, a fireplace as well as a/c (this is also a winter destination, when rooms cost more to cover the cost of firewood), and kitchenette. The speciality in the inexpensive taverna below is tasty charcoal-grilled *arní* (lamb; €7). Taverna and rooms daily April–Sept 11.30am–10pm; Oct–March Fri–Sun only. **€40**

DHRAKÓNA

★**Dounias** Right at the top of the village ☎ 28210 65083. *Dounias* slow-food taverna is an exceptional place set up by a professional chef who decided to move home to his village. Everything is sourced locally and cooked in the traditional manner on wood-burning stoves or in wood-fired ovens, down to the home-made bread. Don't expect glamour – you eat at rickety wooden tables on an earth-floored outdoor terrace and choose your food from burnt pots in the

smoky kitchen – but the daily specials (such as pork with orange, or lentil stew) are authentic, delicious and inexpensive (€6–8). Best to come at lunchtime as when the food is gone, it's gone. Fabulous views too. Daily noon–8pm.

ZOÚRVA

Apirathes Houses Centre of the village ☎ 6944 414 710, ⊚ apirathes-zourva.gr. Impressive traditional-looking modern stone building offering superbly equipped and furnished maisonettes (sleeping 2–6), all with tremendous views. **€90**

Emilia Entrance to village ☎ 28210 67470. Very appealing, good-value taverna with a terrace. Much of the food is home-grown or raised; specials might include *tsigariastó* (goat in rich sauce) or charcoal-grilled lamb, for around €8 each. April–Oct daily 9am–midnight.

MESKLÁ

Taverna Halari At the top of the village beyond the modern church ☎ 28210 67480. A fine little taverna in a woodland setting with tables shaded by plane trees. The traditional cooking uses many home-grown ingredients, with specialities including *bouréki*, *stifádho* and – according to proprietor Manolis – the best *païdhákia* in the province (€9 a portion). Daily 9am–midnight.

Sfakiá and the Lefká Óri

Just a couple of metres short of the highest point of the Psilorítis range, the **Lefká Óri** (White Mountains) are in every other way more impressive mountains: barer, craggier and far less tamed. Along with the coast to the south and east they form the heart of **Sfakiá** – a region that for all its desolation and depopulation is perhaps the most famous, and certainly the most written about, in Crete. It is an area notorious for its fierceness: harsh living conditions, unrelenting weather and warlike people. Historically the region was cut off and barbaric, almost a nation apart which, as occupying armies came and went, carried on with life – feuding, rustling, rearing sheep – pretty much regardless. Many of the great tales of Cretan resistance, of *pallikári* fighters and mountain guerrillas, originate in Sfakiá.

Stealing was a way of life and so was feuding and revenge – with vendettas on a Sicilian scale continuing well into the twentieth century, and occasionally rumoured even now. The Venetians had plans to pacify the region, but their castle on the coast at **Frangokástello** was rarely more than an isolated outpost. The Turks did more, imposing taxation for example, but they also provoked more violent revenge, notably in the revolt of Dhaskaloyiannis (see box, p.284) and many that succeeded it. The mountains were always a safe refuge in which bandits and rebels could conceal themselves while armies took revenge on the lowlands. In World War II Sfakiá resumed this traditional role: when the Germans invaded, King George of Greece was rushed across the island and down the Samariá Gorge to be evacuated, and it was from the region's tiny capital, **Hóra Sfakíon**, that the bulk of the Allied forces were evacuated. Throughout the war, the mountain heights remained the realm of the resistance.

Nowadays all of this seems romantically distant. There are frequent **buses** to Hóra Sfakíon and Omalós and a constant stream of people trekking between the two, but you don't have to get far off this path to realize how the reputation grew, and why it still holds such sway. Anyone who spends any time at all here is eventually taken with the urge to explore, whether it's an arduous mountain trek, or simply getting a boat to a nearby beach. And even now there is just one road into the heart of the area, climbing up to the cold, enclosed plateau of **Omalós** in the heart of the mountains. From here the most spectacular, and spectacularly popular, way to the south coast is on foot, through the great cleft of the **Samariá Gorge**. Famous as it is, this is just the largest of a series of ravines by which streams make their escape to the coast. Far less beaten tracks lead, for example, down the **Ímbros Gorge** towards Hóra Sfakíon, or from **Ayía Iríni** to Soúyia. With more preparation you could also go climbing among the peaks or undertake an expedition right across the range, though bear in mind that this is a genuinely wild mountain zone – venture nowhere alone or without adequate equipment. In the south, the mountains drop steeply to a **coastline** dotted with hard-to-reach **coves and beaches**, with further enticing opportunities to **walk** between them.

The Omalós plateau

From Hanía the road up to Omalós forks at Alikianós (see p.270) and then, beyond the substantial and prosperous village of **FOURNÉS (Φουρνές)**, begins to climb in earnest to the Lefká Óri through a series of sweeping great loops with increasingly alarming drops. After eighteen steeply ascending kilometres you eventually reach the the **Omalós plateau** at more than 1000m – a cold, flat expanse dotted with stunted vegetation, and with the enclosing ring of stone peaks clearly visible all around.

Fournés Botanical Park

4km south of Fournés on the Omalós road • April–Oct daily 9am–sunset • €6 • ☎ 6976 860 573, ⓦ botanical-park.com

When the four Marinakis brothers lost their olive groves in a disastrous fire in 2003, instead of replanting the olives they decided to create a **botanical park** on the land to enable Cretans to understand and learn to care for the natural environment. Making use of the steep site's unique set of microclimates they imported plants and trees from all over the world; there are separate areas for fruits, vegetables, cacti and many more, as well as a lake and mini-zoo. You can race round in as little as an hour, or linger and spend half a day here. There's an excellent **taverna-café** using produce from the gardens, and they also sell honey and other farm goods.

Lákki

LÁKKI (Λάκκι), the only village of any size on the climb up towards the plateau, has stupendous views from its leafy churchyard, to the rear of a small platía. A bracingly exposed place, it makes an ideal base for walking in the surrounding hills, especially in spring when wildflowers abound.

Omalós

OMALÓS (Ομαλός), at the heart of the Omalós plateau, is largely unaffected by the daily dawn procession in summer when up to fifty buses pass through, transporting walkers from all over the island to the Samariá Gorge entrance. Once the hordes have gone it settles back into the tranquil rustic settlement it remains for most of the year. Walk out into the plain in almost any direction and within five minutes you'll have left all traces of

HIKING AROUND OMALÓS

The area around Omalós is excellent for **walking**. The paths into the hills surrounding the plateau (a branch of the E4 Pan-European footpath crosses the southern edge of the village) are strewn with wildflowers in season, birdlife is profuse year-round and temperatures even in high summer are refreshingly cool. Despite this, as so often in places like this in Crete, you'll usually find that most of the excellent, good-value accommodation is empty throughout the season.

If you are not planning to walk from Omalós to the Samariá Gorge (see opposite), you can take a spectacular surfaced road that cuts west through the mountains to link up with the Soúyia–Haniá road just north of Dimitrianá and Ayía Iríni. You can also walk **to Soúyia**, starting either from the top of the gorge or from Omalós and descending via the Ayía Iríni Gorge (see p.316) or on a slightly tougher, higher route through Koustoyérako (see p.316). These are alternative branches of the E4, so reasonably well signed – though take care not to miss the point where you turn off the road. Either route is a full day's walk and both are detailed on the excellent *Anavasi* 1:25,000 Lefká Óri (White Mountains) maps (see p.41).

SCALING THE PEAKS

The **Kallergi Refuge** (see box opposite) acts as the base for climbing into the highest peaks, and the staff here are the best source of information on doing so. As well as the high-mountain treks from the hut, there are also walks to the west of the Samariá Gorge. Most impressively, you can tackle the climb to the peak of **Mount Gíngilos** (2080m), beginning from the top of the gorge. Its north face, the one everyone sees, is a near-vertical slope of solid rock; round the back, though, you can reach the summit with only a little scrambling. It's hard work and you need confidence with heights, especially if it's windy, but no special mountaineering skills are necessary. A large yellow sign points the way from the back of the *Tourist Lodge* and the path should be easy enough to follow for the two and a half hours to the top. The final ascent is signalled with red paint – stick to the path as there are hidden hazards and even the official route needs hands as well as feet. The rewards are an all-round panorama from the summit and, with luck, the chance to spot some of the rarer animal life that the crowds have driven from the gorge itself.

modern life behind, with only the jingling of the occasional goat's bell or the deliberate piling of stones to remind you of human presence. Few people live here year-round: in winter everything is deep in snow and deserted. In spring the land is marshy and waterlogged – almost becoming a lake if there's a sudden melt. Only in summer do most residents move here full-time, coming up from Lákki and other villages on the lower slopes to pasture sheep and goats or to cultivate, on a small scale, cereals and potatoes.

ARRIVAL AND DEPARTURE   THE OMALÓS PLATEAU

By bus There are two daily buses from Haniá to the Botanical Park (30min), and three early-morning services (the ones that continue to the gorge) to Omalós (1hr 10min).

ACCOMMODATION AND EATING

FOURNÉS

Botanical Park taverna Entrance to the Botanical Park ☎6976 860 573. You don't need to pay the entry fee to visit the Botanical Park's taverna, where much of the food is sourced from the park's plants and the rest is mainly local and organic. Interesting salads (€6.50), plenty of vegetarian options and excellent fresh lemonade; meatier mains are €10–13. April–Oct daily 9am–sunset.

LÁKKI

Taverna-Rooms Nikolas Main square ☎28210 67232. The village taverna serves hearty food, including great breakfasts, catering for appetites generated by mountain

air and whetted with the prospect of strenuous activity. The en-suite a/c rooms are less impressive than the food, but they are clean, and come with wonderful views. Taverna daily 7am–11pm. **€30**

OMALÓS

Hotel Exari Omalós village ☎28210 67180, ⓦexari.gr. Impressive new, stone-built hotel with comfortable balcony rooms with TV and a decent restaurant. Free wi-fi in bar. April–Oct. Daily 6am–midnight. **€30**

Hotel Neos Omalos Omalós village ☎28210 67269, ⓦneos-omalos.gr. Perhaps the pick of the hotels in Omalós, and certainly the busiest taverna, this has pleasant

balcony rooms with central heating and satellite TV. April–Oct. Daily 7am–10pm. **€35**
Taverna Xyloskalo Gorge entrance ☎ 28210 52122, ⓦ omalos.com. Perched above the gorge entrance, with magnificent mountain views from its terrace, this is a good place to take breakfast or lunch before heading down the gorge (though not open for early starters). They also have comfortable modern stone-built apartments on the road approaching the gorge. April–Oct. Taverna daily 10am–8pm. **€50**

The Samariá Gorge

May–Oct 6am–sunset, weather conditions permitting; last entry to hike through 4pm • €5 • ☎ 28210 67179, ⓦ samaria.gr

The one trip that every visitor to Crete – even those eminently unsuited to it – feels compelled to make is the hike down the **SAMARIÁ GORGE** (**Φαράγγι Σαμαριάς**) which, at 16km, is claimed to be the **longest in Europe**. Protected as a National Park since 1962, this natural wonder was formed by a river flowing between Mount Volakiás to the west and the towering bulk of the heart of the Lefká Óri to the east. In summer the violent winter torrent reduces to a meek trickle and this is when the multitudes descend. If you're expecting a wilderness experience, think again; Friday and Saturday are the days attracting fewest visitors. Bear in mind that this is not a gentle stroll to be lightly undertaken; especially in spring when the river is roaring, or on a hot midsummer day, it can be a thoroughly gruelling test of fitness and stamina. The mules and helicopter standing by to rescue the injured are not mere show: anyone who regularly leads tours through the gorge has a stack of horror stories to regale you with – broken legs and heart attacks feature most frequently. To undertake the walk you need to be reasonably fit and/or used to lengthy walks, and you should have walking boots or sturdy trainers that will stand up to hot, sharp rocks.

The gorge hike itself is some **18km long** (the final 2km to reach the sea from the mouth of the gorge) and the **walk** down takes between four and seven hours, depending on your level of fitness and how often you stop to admire the scenery, bathe your feet and take refreshment. Be wary of the kilometre markers – these mark only distances within the park, not the full extent of the walk.

THE KALLERGI REFUGE

If you are staying on the Omalós plateau for a couple of days a hike to the wonderful **Kallergi Refuge** (April–Oct daily; Nov–March Sat & Sun; April–Oct ☎ 6976 585 849, Nov–March ☎ 6973 400 077, ⓦ kallergi.com; €12) is a bracing introduction to the high mountains. Perched high over the eastern edge of the Samariá Gorge at 1680m, it's a fairly easy (if unrelenting) ascent for 5km from the Omalós plain and once you're there makes an excellent base for many other mountain treks.

To get to the hut from Omalós, follow the road towards the gorge entrance for 3km, then turn left onto the dirt track signed to the hut, a 90min climb (with a 4WD vehicle you can also drive this, along – in the early stages – a badly rutted dirt road); alternatively, from the top of the Samariá Gorge a signed path leads up, also in about 90min. From Kallergi you can peer down into the gorge, looking exceptionally impressive from the isolation of the bare stone peaks up here, a slash of rich green in an otherwise remorseless landscape of grey and brown. On clearer days both the Libyan and Aegean seas can also be seen from the hut, while the nights are spectacular, with the whole dome of the starry heavens arranged above you.

There's usually no problem finding a bed at the refuge (although it's best to ring ahead) and the hut is comfortably equipped with wood-burning stoves and space for fifty in cosy two- and four-bed dorms. There's also an excellent **taverna**. With advance warning they can also collect you from the plateau and arrange guided climbs and **hikes**. Walking routes include the 6hr circular waymarked route to **Melindaoú** (2133m) via Mount Psarí (1817m), or the 16hr hike to Anópoli via **Mount Páhnes** (at 2453m, just 3m short of Psilorítis for the title of loftiest in Crete: Haniot mountaineers regularly add stones to the cairn on the peak in an attempt to catch up) with an overnight stop at a refuge en route. Both follow the E4 much of the way.

4

FLORA AND FAUNA IN THE SAMARIÁ GORGE

Gorge **wildlife** means most famously the **kri-kri** (variously the *agrimi*, *Capra aegagrus*, the Cretan wild goat or ibex), for whose protection the park was primarily created. You are unlikely to see one of these large, nimble animals with their long backswept horns, though you may well see ordinary mountain goats defying death on the cliff faces. In addition, almost four hundred varieties of **birds** are claimed to have been seen here, including owls, eagles, falcons and vultures; birdwatchers after a coup should look out for the endangered lammergeier (or bearded vulture). On the ground lizards abound, there's also the odd snake and you may just spot a beech marten, spiny mouse or weasel.

The multifarious **trees** – Cretan maple, pine and cypress – provide the backdrop to an often dazzling array of **wildflowers**; the purple *Tulipa saxatilis* and rock plants such as aubretias, saxifrages and anemones stand out, and there are wild irises and orchids too. **Herbs** are also in abundance; besides the aromatic thyme and rosemary, common sage and oregano, there are half a dozen species that exist exclusively here. Also to be found – and usually growing in the most inaccessible places – is **Cretan dittany**, a celebrated medicinal herb referred to by Aristotle and Hippocrates and taken by women in ancient times as a method of abortion.

Two **books** on the gorge can prove useful and are portable enough to take along. *The Samariá Gorge Yesterday and Today* (Toubis, Athens) documents the history of the gorge and includes an illustrated guide to its flora and fauna, while *The Gorge of Samariá and its Plants* by Albertis Atonis (Albertis, Iráklio) provides a step-by-step description of the flora. Both are widely available from bookshops on the island.

The Samariá Gorge hike

4

The gorge begins, with startling suddenness, on the far side of the Omalós plateau. After the dull tranquillity of the plain you are faced with this great cleft opening beneath your feet and, across it – close enough to bounce stones off, it seems – the gaunt limestone face of Mount Gíngilos. The descent starts on the **Xilóskalon** ("wooden stairway"), a stepped path cut from the rock and augmented by log stairs and wooden handrails, which zigzags rapidly down to the base of the gorge, plunging 350m in the first 2km or so of the walk. Near the bottom the chapel of Áyios Nikólaos stands on a little terrace of coniferous trees where there are benches from which to enjoy the view, and fresh water. Beyond, the path begins gradually to level out, following the stream bed amid softer vegetation which reflects the milder climate down here. In late spring it's magnificent, but at any time of year there should be wildflowers and rare plants (no picking allowed), including the endangered large white peony, *Paeonia clusii*. The stream itself is less reliable: there are places where you can be sure of icy fresh water and pools to bathe sore feet all year round (particularly in the middle sections), but what starts in spring as a fierce, even dangerous torrent has dwindled by autumn to a trickle between hot, dry boulders, disappearing beneath the surface for long stretches.

The abandoned village of **Samariá** lies a little under midway through the walk, shortly before the 7km marker. One of the buildings here has been converted to house the wardens' office, another has been pressed into (inadequate) service as a public toilet, but for the most part the remains of the village are quietly crumbling away. Its inhabitants, until they were relocated to make way for the park in 1962, were predominantly members of the Viglis family, who claimed direct descent from one of the twelve aristocratic clans implanted from Byzantium. Certainly this settlement, as isolated as any in Crete and cut off by floodwater for much of the year, is a very ancient one – the church of **Óssia María**, from which both gorge and village take their name, was founded in the early fourteenth century.

After Samariá the ground is more level, the walls of the gorge begin to close in and the path is often forced to cross from one side of the stream to the other, on **stepping stones** which at times may be submerged and slippery. Beside you, the contorted striations of the cliffs are increasingly spectacular, but the highlight comes shortly after the Christós resting point with the **Sidherespórtes** (Iron Gates) where two rock walls rise sheer to within a whisker of a thousand feet: standing at the bottom, one can almost touch both at once. For this short stretch, there's a wooden walkway raised above the stream, whose swirling waters fill the whole of the narrow passage. Almost as suddenly as you entered this mighty crack in the mountain you leave it again, the valley broadens, its sides fall away, and you're in a parched wilderness of rubble deposited here by the spring thaw.

Before long you reach the fringes of **Ayía Rouméli**, where there's a gate by which you leave the park and a couple of stalls selling cool drinks at crippling prices. Frustratingly, however, this is not the end of the walk: old Ayía Rouméli has been all but deserted in favour of the new beachside community, a further excruciatingly hot, dull twenty minutes away. A **shuttle bus service** (€1.50) means that you can now avoid this final rather tedious stretch; the bus drops you in the coastal settlement.

Ascending the gorge

Starting from the bottom, the hike **up the gorge** to **Omalós** is not as hard as some imagine, though it will take rather longer – six to seven hours at a reasonable, steady pace. Few people do it all the way, which means that at the top you may well find the gorge almost empty; on the way up, however, you'll have had to pass the hordes charging down. You could also walk a short way up and come back – an outing offered as a day-trip known as "Samariá the Lazy Way". This will show you the Iron Gates, the most spectacular individual section, but none of the almost alpine scenes nearer the top.

ARRIVAL AND DEPARTURE   **THE SAMARIÁ GORGE**

4

WITH A TOUR

The vast majority of people who walk through the gorge do so as part of a day-trip: a very early bus to the top, walk down by early afternoon, boat from Ayía Rouméli to Hóra Sfakíon or Soúyia and bus from there back home. Most go with one of the guided tours offered by every travel agent on the island – certainly if you're staying in a hotel anywhere in the east of Crete this is much the simplest method, and probably the only way of doing it in a single day. Most tours will include all bus and ferry connections, but not food or the park entrance fee. They can be very good value, adding only €5–10 to the cost of doing it yourself (from Haniá, the cost of bus, ferry and entry tickets adds up to about €30). If you're planning to stay on the south coast, the tour bus can save you the effort of carrying your bags; simply stow them underneath and retrieve them in Hóra Sfakíon. Do let them know your plan, though, both to guard against an unexpected switch of bus and to prevent search parties being sent out.

BY PUBLIC TRANSPORT

Buses to the gorge from Haniá From Haniá there are three departures a day (6.15am, 7.45am & 8.45am), arriving at the top about 1hr 15min later. You'll normally be sold a return ticket, including the return leg from Hóra Sfakíon (which needn't necessarily be used the same day), so if you don't want this you'll have to make your intentions very clear; the bus station is chaotic when the first buses leave. There's a lot to be said for taking the earliest bus: more of the walk can be completed while it's still relatively cool, there's no need to force your pace, and if you're

planning to stop over anywhere at the bottom you've more chance of being among the first to arrive. On the other hand, everyone does this – there's often a procession of as many as four full buses leaving Haniá before dawn, there are queues and confusion when you arrive, and you're unlikely to escape from crowds the whole way down. It may be hotter, but it's also quieter if you set out later.

Buses from other destinations The first couple of buses of the day from Iráklio and Réthymno allow you to connect in Haniá for the journey to Omalós. There are also services from Paleóhora (6.15am) and Soúyia (7am); these meet in Ayía Iríni from where one continues to the gorge and the other direct to Haniá, so you may have to change.

Ferries from Ayía Rouméli Having reached the south coast you can continue to walk in either direction, but it's a great deal easier to get around by boat. There's a kiosk selling tickets just above the end of the jetty, in the centre of the village; ferries (Ⓦ anendyk.gr) run to Loutró/Hóra Sfakíon (May–Oct at least 3 daily; 40min–1hr) and Soúyia/Paleóhora (April–Oct daily at 5.30pm; 45min–1hr 20min). Return bus journeys from Hóra Sfakíon and Soúyia (both at 6.30pm) are timed to coincide with the ferries and will wait for them – theoretically, no one gets left behind, but it makes sense to hurry off the ferry and grab a seat.

INDEPENDENT TRAVEL

If you want to see the gorge using your own transport, or while staying in Omalós, it's possible to walk down (the hotels will take you to the gorge entrance for free if you're a guest), take the boat to Soúyia, and then get a taxi back up to Omalós or the gorge parking area from there – Soúyia

SAMARIÁ GORGE PRACTICALITIES

Be aware that the gorge is **regularly closed** for safety reasons; generally in spring and autumn if there's a risk of flash floods, or in extremely hot weather in mid-summer. If in any doubt check in advance to save a wasted journey.

PARK REGULATIONS

There is a whole series of national park **rules** (posted at the entrance), of which the most important are: no camping, no fires (or smoking outside the designated areas), no alcohol, no hunting and no interfering with the wildlife or collecting plants. Wardens patrol to ensure these rules are obeyed, that no one wanders too far from the main path, and that no stragglers are overtaken by nightfall. At the entrance, you'll be given a **date-stamped ticket** in return for your entrance fee, which you should hand in at the gate when you leave; this, too, is partly to check that nobody is lost inside, and partly to make sure no one tries camping.

SUPPLIES

Carry the minimum possible. A **water bottle** is essential (there are springs at regular intervals and ice-cold water in the stream, but for long periods you'll find neither – especially over the last, hottest hour) and something to munch on the way definitely worthwhile, as is some means of carrying clothes you discard en route (7am at the top feels close to freezing; 1pm at the bottom may hover around 38°C/100°F).

FACILITIES

Near the gorge entrance there's a **café** and stalls for hot drinks, bottled water and snacks (all open early), as well as the *Taverna Xyloskalo* (see p.275), while Ayía Rouméli is more than equipped to feed everyone arriving at the bottom; there are **toilets** at regular intervals along the walk. The nearest **bed** you can get to the entrance is in Omalós (see p.274) or at the excellent *Kallergi Refuge* (see box, p.275). Even here you'd have to be up very early to steal a march on the first arrivals from Haniá. Nonetheless, it does make quite a change to stay up here and freeze for a night, and of course it gives you the opportunity to explore more than just the gorge. Staying on the south coast for a night or more after your exertions makes more sense: in addition to Ayía Rouméli (see below), there are rooms at Loutró (see opposite) and Hóra Sfakíon (see p.286) or westwards in Soúyia (see p.315) and Paleóhora (see p.308).

taxis generally charge about €60 for this; there should also be an evening bus from Soúyia to Omalós, but check the schedule. Should you plan to stay longer on the coast, the Omalós hotels can also (by prior arrangement and for a fee) put your luggage on the morning ferry in Soúyia, so that it's waiting for you at the bottom of the gorge.

Ayía Rouméli

For most people **AYÍA ROUMÉLI (Αγία Ρουμέλη)** is nothing more than the end of the Samariá Gorge walk, a place to eat and drink your fill, then rest up on the beach before leaving on one of the afternoon ferries. If you have walked here, the place at first has an almost mirage-like quality, where you face an agonizing choice between plunging into the sea or diving into a taverna for an iced drink, likely to live in the memory as the most refreshing ever. Once your senses adjust, you'll find that the village isn't all that appealing, but while it's far from the most attractive place on this coast, it is wonderfully peaceful at night, and locals are making strenuous efforts to develop alternative attractions to persuade people to stay longer. Most obviously this involves other **hikes** – there are smaller but more challenging gorges to both east and west, as well as coastal paths to various beaches – but there are also boat trips and kayaks for hire. You can find details of many of these, and a walking map, at the *Calypso* taverna (see opposite)

There was an ancient settlement on this site – **Tarra**, inhabited probably from the fifth century BC through to the fifth AD – and more or less constant later habitation, though very little remains to be seen. Tarra straddled the stream where it ran into the sea, just to the east of the present village – the only obvious remains are the foundations of an early

Christian basilica by the present **church of Panayía**, around which you ma·few tiny fragments of mosaic. This, supposedly, was the site of a much ear of Apollo.

ARRIVAL AND DEPARTURE

By ferry Ferries run east to Loutró and Hóra Sfakíon (May–Oct at least 3 daily; 40min–1hr) and west to Soúyia and Paleóhora (April–Oct daily at 5.30pm; 45min–1hr 20min). In peak season there are also a couple of weekly departures to Gávdhos (3hr). A kiosk selling tickets is just above the end of the jetty, in the centre of the village; timetables at ⓦanendyk.gr.

On foot The majority of people who get to Ayía Roumen have done so on foot, down the Samariá Gorge. You can also get here, or leave, along the coastal path, part of the E4. East to Loutró or Anópoli is challenging but relatively straightforward (see p.281); west to Soúyia is a very tough two-day hike – don't attempt it without checking conditions locally, as the path can be blocked by rockfalls.

ACCOMMODATION AND EATING

There are often people camping on the beach east of the village, where there are showers and toilets, or in the caves nearby. The bigger beachfront tavernas often offer free loungers to clients, and a couple have bars on the beach, but these tend to be packed with huge tour groups.

Hotel Calypso Western side of the village, not far from the jetty ☎28250 91314, ⓦcalypso.agiaroumeli.gr. Friendly, family-run taverna and rooms place. The taverna has good fresh seafood from their own boat (swordfish €11) as well as local goat and all the usuals (meat mains €6–8). They rent kayaks on the beach and have a wall map of local kayaking and walking routes. The comfortable a/c rooms have fridge, balcony and sea view. Daily 8am–11pm. €35
Pachnes Bed & Breakfast 200m inland, off the path from the gorge ☎28250 91312, ⓦagiaroumelihotel

.com. Great value, rustically furnished a/c rooms in a quiet position just outside the main village, popular with serious hikers – they can advise on local walks. Breakfast included. €35
Taverna Tarra Seafront by the jetty ☎28250 91231, ⓦtarra.agiaroumeli.gr. Some of the best views in town from both the taverna and rooms above, situated directly above the water. Fine local meat dishes, such as lamb in the oven for €8, and home-grown veg. The a/c rooms are simple, but more than adequate. Daily 8am–11pm. €30

4

Loutró and around

Of all the south coast villages, **LOUTRÓ** (Λουτρó) perhaps best sums up what this coast ought to be all about. It's a soporific place, where there's nothing to do but eat, drink and laze – and where you fast lose any desire to do anything else. There are few facilities and no ATM, so you should bring sufficient cash to see you through your stay (though at a pinch your hotel or rooms place may give you cash on a credit card or change money). The big excitements of the day are the occasional arrivals and departures of the ferries. Little happens all summer long to interrupt this easy-going idyll, but if you're here for the great **feast of the Panayía** on August 15 the small church is the place to head for. From early dawn the formidable local priest conducts the service, which lasts until after midday. The small churchyard then fills up with all those who had intended to come earlier – and each of whom receives a disapproving glare from the *papás* – as biblical quantities of *arní*, *psomí* and *krasí* (lamb, bread and wine) are doled out and everyone enjoys a great feast.

HIKING IN SFÁKIA

Sfákia can boast some of the finest walking country in Crete. Along the **coast**, a series of paths link Ayía Rouméli in the west with Hóra Sfakíon in the east; **Loutró**, accessible only on foot or by boat, lies close to the heart of this network. **Inland**, ancient paths and trails survive to give a variety of marvellous hikes, even the easiest of which can be demanding in the heat of high summer. You'll need, at the very least, decent boots or shoes to cope with rough, rocky terrain and a water bottle, which you should fill at every opportunity. You should also have a companion, since some of these paths are pretty isolated, and outside help cannot be relied upon.

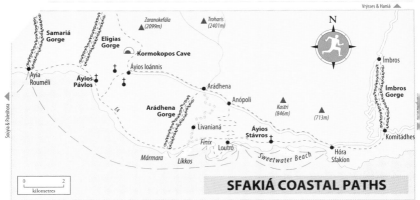

SFAKIÁ COASTAL PATHS

The waterfront

The short **waterfront** arching around a beautiful little bay consists of a row of perhaps a dozen tavernas and cafés and a similar number of rooms places and small hotels; the mountains rise immediately behind. There's no road in – everyone here has either come on the boat or walked, which helps to keep things very low-key, prices reasonable, big groups rare and the people genuinely friendly. Although the transparent blue water is always inviting, perhaps Loutró's main drawback is its lack of a real **beach**. There's an overcrowded stretch of pebbles in front of the tavernas and a much smaller, more private beach immediately beyond the last of the buildings. But the sheltered bay is otherwise ideal for **swimming**, clear and warm, and people bask nude on the rocks around the point, far enough out to avoid offence. Other excellent beaches are within walking distance, with small boats or rented canoes ferrying visitors to the best, at **Sweetwater** to the east (see below), and **Mármara** to the west (see opposite).

Sweetwater Beach

East of Loutró, **Sweetwater Beach** lies in the middle of a barren coastline, approximately halfway to Hóra Sfakíon. From the sea, as you pass on one of the coastal boats, it appears as a long, extremely narrow slice of grey between sheer ochre cliffs and a dark, deep sea. Closer up, the beach seems much larger, but there's still a frightening sense of being isolated between unscaleable mountains and an endless stretch of water.

The beach takes its name from the small springs that bubble up beneath the pebbles to provide fresh, cool drinking water. You can dig a hole almost anywhere to find water, but take care not to pollute the groundwater with soap. Daily boat services bring in quite a few people, but so far these have not spoilt the place – the beach is easily big enough to absorb everyone – and the nudist campers who once had Sweetwater practically to themselves remain, doing a good job of keeping things pristine: signs warn against leaving rubbish, and people make an effort to pick up any junk that is left behind.

The long-term residents (including local goats) tend to monopolize the only shade, in the **caves** at the back of the beach, but you can always escape the sun at the small **bar-taverna**, which also rents out sun umbrellas.

Fínix

In the beautiful little bay immediately west of Loutró stood **ancient Fínikas**, now known as **Fínix** or Phoenix. This was a major town during the Roman and Byzantine periods, and a significant port long after that: it was the harbour at Fínix, a more comfortable place to wait out the winter storms than Kalí Liménes, which St Paul's ship was hoping to reach when it was swept away. A local story has the saint actually landing here and being beaten up by the locals he tried to convert. Today there is very little to be seen and, with nothing beyond a popular taverna and a small rooms place, it's hard to believe there could ever have been a population of any size here. Up on the headland, though, there's certainly evidence of later occupation, principally in the form of the **Venetian fortification** on the point. Nearby are traces of a Byzantine basilica and other scattered remains.

Líkkos

West of Fínix, the path continues over cliffs to another, much longer bay, **Líkkos**. Again there's very little here beyond a couple of very simple **taverna-rooms** places, and far fewer people get this far, making it an escapist's paradise. One thing that is in bountiful supply is fresh, cool spring water, proudly served up (often with a home-made *rakí*) in the tavernas. The **beach** itself is rocks and pebbles, awkward to swim from unless you wear shoes, but with plenty of room to spread out. Behind, you can look up and see the village of Livanianá, perched on the eastern flank of the Arádhena Gorge (see p.284); there's a rough dirt road down from there, a scary drive, but one which any vehicle should be able to manage, with care.

Mármara Beach

The Arádhena Gorge (see p.284) emerges at the sea in the next bay west of Líkkos, **MÁRMARA BEACH**, which takes its name from marble deposits visible near the jetty where you land. The small cove, with a sandy beach surrounded by interesting rock

4

WALKING THE COASTAL PATH FROM LOUTRÓ

The **coastal path** – now part of the E4 Pan-European Footpath – is the most obvious hike from Loutró, the most frequently used by tourists and, in terms of not getting lost, the simplest to follow. There's not a great deal to see en route, however, nor is it an easy walk – the path is often frighteningly narrow and uneven as it clings to the cliff face, and in summer it is very, very hot, offering no shelter at all from the sun. In Loutró the path runs inland, behind most of the houses; to find it, climb up until you see the signs.

LOUTRÓ TO HÓRA SFAKÍON

Heading east from **Loutró to Hóra Sfakíon** is barely a problem: it's the most heavily travelled part, the whole walk takes less than two hours (8km), and there's a rest stop at Sweetwater Beach (see opposite) halfway. Loutró to Sweetwater is straightforward and fairly well beaten: beyond here the path clambers over a massive rockfall and then follows the cliffs until it eventually emerges on the Hóra Sfakíon–Anópoli road about thirty minutes' walk above Hóra. This is easy to find from the other direction too, the path (to the left) leaving the road at the first hairpin bend.

LOUTRÓ TO AYÍA ROUMÉLI

Heading west, **Loutró to Ayía Rouméli** is an altogether tougher proposition. You can expect to be walking for at least four hours solid, a real sweat in high summer, and after the tavernas at Líkkos and Mármara the only chance of refreshment is at Áyios Pávlos (see below). After Mármara (see above) you climb again to track along the exposed cliff face for around an hour before reaching the first sign of civilization, a solitary cottage and a few trees. In about another hour, you'll arrive at the eleventh-century cruciform chapel of **Áyios Pávlos**, yet another site where St Paul is supposed to have landed. Here he allegedly christened locals in a spring close to the church (now only a trickle). The chapel itself is ancient and rather beautiful, set on a ledge above the water, and surrounded by dunes; inside are fresco fragments dated to the thirteenth century. You could cool off in the sea here before setting out on the final hour to Ayía Rouméli, and there is a simple **taverna** (June–Sept only), which also rents out tents for nearby camping.

Returning from Ayía Rouméli this path is well marked, heading east out of the village. Ten to fifteen minutes after Áyios Pávlos it splits, heading left to climb inland to Áyios Ioánnis and Anópoli, or right to continue along the coast to Mármara.

formations full of caves and slabs to dive from or sunbathe on, can get uncomfortably busy in summer, what with boats from Loutró and people walking down the gorge, but even when busy it's charming, with a simple **taverna-rooms place** to give the place focus, as well as providing sun umbrellas, loungers and tempting cool drinks.

ARRIVAL AND GETTING AROUND

LOUTRÓ

By boat Ferry tickets are sold from a kiosk behind the dock at the western end of the seafront, which opens only for a few minutes before each departure. The timetable is highly seasonal, so check locally or online (ⓦanendyk.gr), but from May to October there are at least 4 daily departures to Hóra Sfakíon (20min) and 3 to Ayía Roúmeli (35min). In summer there are also three crossings a week to Gávdhos (see p.318), taking 3hr. A taxi-boat from Hóra Sfakíon costs around €35 and can be arranged by any of the seafront tavernas in either village.

SWEETWATER BEACH

By boat Boats from Loutró and Hóra Sfakíon arrive once in the morning and again at 5pm; more frequently in peak season. A taxi-boat (one way) from Loutró costs around €15. Kayaking to the beach is also possible.

On foot It's a very hot and shadeless 45min walk from Loutró, an hour from Hóra Sfakíon – boats back to each leave at 5.30pm in summer. In Loutró the path runs behind the houses – climb the hill to find it.

FÍNIX

By boat A taxi-boat will cost about €10 one way (ask at tavernas in Loutró), or you can kayak round. The boat from the *Old Phoenix* (see opposite) regularly collects groups for lunch, so you may be able to hitch a ride with them.

LOUTRÓ AND AROUND

On foot To walk to Fínix by the most direct route, join the well-signed path – part of the E4 – that runs behind Loutró (head up behind the beachside kiosk, past *Taverna Stratis*). This will lead you straight up, past the castle and directly over the headland, in around 20min. It's also possible to get there by walking out past the last house in Loutró and simply following the rocky coast around. This is twice as far but it does pass plenty of good rocks to swim from, and extensive remains of old buildings which you can imagine are, and may indeed be, ancient Fínikas.

By car It's just about possible to drive here, on a hair-raising barrierless dirt road that descends via Livanianá and Líkkos.

LÍKKOS

By boat A taxi-boat from Loútro will cost about €15, or you may get a better deal by calling one of the Líkkos tavernas, assuming you plan to eat there.

On foot From Fínix the path heads up and over the headland to Líkkos in about 20 minutes.

MÁRMARA BEACH

By boat A boat runs between Loutró and Mármara twice a day in summer; if you walk there, the return is at 5pm. A taxi-boat (one way) to or from Loutró costs around €15.

On foot From Líkkos to Mármara takes around 25 minutes, a steep and occasionally scary clamber over the rocks and close to the cliff edge.

ACTIVITIES

Boat trips Small boats depart from Loutró's jetty daily at 11am (after the arrival of the ferry) to Sweetwater and Mármara beaches, returning at 5pm.

Kayak and boat rental You can rent kayaks in Loutró for

expeditions to the nearby coves and beaches, and there are also pedalos (which can't leave the bay) and motor boats for hire. Taxi-boat numbers are widely advertised, or ask at the tavernas.

ACCOMMODATION

There's a huge amount of choice in Loutró, where the vast majority of the rooms are simple and traditional; a sea view is the one significant difference. The quietest places are generally the furthest round to the east, but nowhere is exactly loud or stays open late. If you're staying anywhere outside Loutró, the proprietors will pick you up by boat if you let them know when you're arriving. Almost everything here closes from November to March.

LOUTRÓ

★**Blue House** ☎ 28250 91035, ⓦbluehouse.loutro.gr. One of the original places here, and still one of the friendliest and best. Good-value a/c, sea-view rooms with fridge and TV, plus superior rooms in a wonderful (more expensive) top-floor extension. **€35**

Hotel Porto Loutro In the middle of the village above the beach ☎28250 91433, ⓦhotelportoloutro.com.

Run by Anglo-Greek proprietors, this hotel – one of the few with any pretensions at all – is a lovely place whose white cubes fit in surprisingly well with the surroundings; as the a/c rooms are pretty accurate reproductions of a simple Greek room you may question whether it's worth paying the extra. Breakfast included. Free wi-fi in bar. **€65**

★**Nikolas** Eastern end of the seafront ☎ 28250 91352. Virtually the last building in Loutró and probably the quietest you'll find; simple but comfortable a/c rooms all with fridge and great views. Top-floor rooms cost more but are bigger, with large balconies and even finer views. **€35**

Protopapas Inland, eastern end behind Taverna Limani ☎ 28250 91400, ✉ geoprotop@hotmail.com. Simple, good-sized rooms with a/c and fridge, some triples and quads; it's not right on the water, which keeps the prices down, and often has vacancies when others are full. Partial sea views from some rooms. **€35**

★ **Villa Niki** High above the centre of the village ☎ 28250 91213, 🌐 loutro-accommodation.com. The classiest accommodation in town, with a beautiful 3-bedroom apartment (the "villa") and some rather simpler two-bedroom apartments and studios. The smallest studios have no view. Studios **€45**, apartments **€65**, villa **€110**

FÍNIX

Rooms Manousoudakis ☎ 28250 91482. Very simple rooms with fan and fridge, but an absolutely lovely, tranquil location on the side of the bay, not too close to the sometimes crowded *Old Phoenix*. **€35**

LÍKKOS

★ **Akrogiali** ☎ 28250 91446, 🌐 akrogiali-lykos.gr. For an absolute away-from-it-all experience you'd struggle to find a quieter spot than Líkkos, and these are the more comfortable rooms here, purpose-built, with a/c and sea-view balconies. Also great food and an enthusiastic welcome. **€35**

Small Paradise ☎ 28250 91125, 🌐 thesmallparadise .com. Run by a friendly Irish-Cretan couple, *Small Paradise* offers simple en-suite balcony rooms above an excellent taverna with wood-burning oven. Only a couple of rooms have a/c. **€25**

MÁRMARA BEACH

Chrisostomos ☎ 6942 201 456. Simple cabins on the headland above the beach, with a generator providing power for lighting, water and fans. There's also an excellent taverna. **€25**

EATING AND DRINKING

LOUTRÓ

Café Bistro Seafront at the western end of Loutró, beneath Sifis hotel ☎ 28250 91346. Monopolizing most of the waterfront near the jetty, *Café Bistro* (aka *Christina's*), serves breakfast, juices and coffee, and beer and cocktails in the evening. Busy throughout the day. April–Oct daily 7am–midnight.

Blue House Central seafront ☎ 28250 91035. Arguably the best traditional taverna in Loutró, serving an array of Cretan specialities (mains €6–8), plus fresh fish and plenty of vegetarian options; the owners, brothers Vangelis and Yiorgos, are among the village's friendliest characters. April–Oct daily 8am–10.30pm.

Ilios Eastern end of the seafront ☎ 28250 91160. Good fresh fish caught from their own boat (priced per kilo) as well as a range of taverna standards (€6–8) served on a waterfront terrace. It's also a good breakfast stop, with overhead fans keeping temperatures down. Daily 7.30am–11.30pm.

Notos Central seafront ☎ 28250 91501. Excellent range of mezédhes including plenty of vegetarian possibilities (€3.50–5), plus some more unusual mains such as shrimp curry (€9) or chicken in mustard sauce (€6), served on an attractive raised terrace. April–Oct daily 7am–11pm.

Oasis Above the east end of town, where the E4 path arrives ☎ 28250 91017. Pretty rooftop bar/café with fine views, which can be breezy when the waterfront is baking. They lure walkers with chilled fresh lemonade. April–Oct daily 8am–11pm.

Stratis Inland from the centre of the seafront ☎ 28250 91348. Superb charcoal-grilled meats from the mountains (go for whatever is on the outdoor grill), as well as traditional specialities including snails (€6). April–Oct daily 7am–10pm.

FÍNIX

Old Phoenix ☎ 28250 91257. Big hotel-taverna that can be too popular for its own good – there are often large tour groups shipped in, and the place can barely cope. At quiet times, though, it's lovely, with a waterfront terrace serving fine traditional Greek food (mains €7–11). April–Oct daily 9am–10.30pm.

LÍKKOS

★ **Akrogiali** ☎ 28250 91446. Shaded seafront terrace where excellent traditional Cretan food (daily specials such as meatballs in tomato sauce or oven-baked chicken with potatoes for €6–8) is washed down by jugs of fresh spring water (though there's plenty of good house wine and *rakí* too). April–Oct daily 9am–10.30pm.

Anópoli and around

ANÓPOLI (Ανώπολη), high above Loutró, is a quiet country village dominating a small upland plain with a few rare vestiges of forest. If you're hiking for its own sake, or for that matter if you want to take the easiest route from Ayía Rouméli to Hóra Sfakíon without necessarily calling at Loutró, then the inland trails centring on Anópoli have a

DHASKALOYIANNIS

Anópoli was the home of the first of the great Cretan rebels against the Turks, **Dhaskaloyiannis** – the subject of a celebrated epic ballad. To cut a very long story extremely short, Dhaskaloyiannis, a wealthy ship-owner, was promised support by Russian agents if he raised a rebellion in Sfakiá, support which in the event never materialized. (The Russians hoped only to divert attention from their campaigns against the Ottoman Empire elsewhere.) The revolt, in 1770, was short-lived and disastrous for Sfakiá, which for the first time was brought well and truly under the Turkish heel. Dhaskaloyiannis went to the Turks in an attempt to negotiate acceptable surrender terms; instead the Turkish authorities seized him and took him to Iráklio, where he was publicly tortured, skinned alive and executed. There's a statue honouring him in the square at Anópoli.

great deal to be said for them: it also makes a good base for an exploration of the **Arádhena Gorge** and for walks into the heart of the White Mountains. The village itself, which straggles for some distance along the road, is a wonderful location to sample the simple delights of rural Crete, and except at the busiest local holiday periods you should have no problem finding somewhere to stay, away from the hustle of the coast.

Arádhena

West of Anópoli, a paved road continues northwest to the virtually abandoned hamlet of **ARÁDHENA (Αράδαινα)**, some 3km away. This also makes a pleasant forty-minute walk, with plenty of obvious short cuts close to the little-travelled road. With the coming of the paved road, one or two people have moved back and started to restore some of the settlement's crumbling buildings.

The bridge

The first thing to grab your attention in Arádhena is a steel **bridge** across a dramatic gorge – a remarkable construction, all the more so when you discover that it's a bridge to nowhere, as the road on the far side soon peters out at nearby Áyios Ioánnis (see opposite). Built in 1986 by the local Vardinoyiannis family, controllers of an international business empire, the bridge was a gift to provide a lifeline to the outside world without which their home village, Áyios Ioánnis, would probably have died. Rumble across it in a car and the terrifying crack of the wooden boards against metal thunders around the gorge below. The **views** from the bridge down into the gorge – one of Crete's most precipitous – are vertiginously spectacular, and you can even take a **bungee jump** (July & Aug Sat & Sun noon–6pm, June & Sept only with booking; €100, including video; ⓦbungy.gr), plunging 138m into the ravine.

Miháïl Arhángelos

Right on the rim of the Arádhena Gorge • The church is locked following a number of thefts; ask about access at the *kantína* at the bridge's northern end

The romantically picturesque Byzantine church of **Miháïl Arhángelos**, with its curious "pepper-pot" dome, stands proud above the gorge with the Lefká Óri's heights as a backdrop. The white-walled church dates from the fourteenth or fifteenth century and was constructed on the ruins of a much earlier basilica. Inside, outstanding **frescoes** depict the life and crucifixion of Christ as well as the church's patron saint. Scattered round about, beyond the nearly deserted village, are a few traces of ancient Araden, a still unexcavated Greco-Roman town from whose stones the church is said to have been built.

The Arádhena Gorge

Standing on the Arádhena bridge you can see the old path, negotiable only on foot or by pack animals, zigzagging down to the bottom of the **ARÁDHENA GORGE** and back

LOUTRÓ TO THE ARÁDHENA GORGE: THE CIRCUIT

The **circuit from Loutró**, up to Anópoli, through the gorge and down to Mármara beach (see p.281), from where you can get a boat back to Loutró, is about 11km in total and will realistically take at least 6hr; significantly more if you make many stops along the way. Add an extra 3km (or 1hr 30min) if you walk back to Loutró from Mármara. You can cut out the hardest part (the initial climb), by taking a boat to Hóra Sfakíon and a taxi from there to Anópoli or Arádhena. A shorter but less spectacular route from Loutró would be to head out past Fínix and follow the road to Livaniiná (see below), clearly visible above you; from there a path descends into the lower reaches of the gorge.

The start of the **descent** into the gorge at Arádhena is not obvious: you need to turn right off the road just after you catch your first glimpse of the bridge, about 200m before the turn-off to Livaniíná, following a narrow trail below a pine coppice. This will lead you to the unmistakable monopáti, the ancient stone path down to the bottom (this side should be used rather than the track on the far side, which is in much worse condition). The impressive stepped stone path and the relatively flat section as you head under the bridge conspire to lull you into a false sense of security: as it gets steeper further down, you find yourself jumping from rock to rock or taking narrow steps around dry cascades. Look out as you go for the paint marks indicating the route – these often seem to take you over unnecessarily tricky terrain, but you usually discover the reason further on when you reach an impassable portion. Fill up with water at every opportunity, as there's none towards the end of the gorge.

up the other side. For well over two millennia this was the only way across the gorge, and it's still the path you take to follow the gorge down to the sea, a walk of around two and a half hours. This is a superb hike, and though it has been tamed in recent years and is fairly well trodden, it's still reasonably tough, with steep staircases and scrambles over rocks in places. Parts can be scary too, not helped by the ominous presence of picked-clean skeletons of goats, which presumably have either fallen from the top or been washed away in spring floods. The sense of achievement, however, is immense, and the gorge, though far smaller than that of Samariá, is in physical terms almost as impressive. There isn't much in the way of wildlife, but the rocky riverbed is forced into an extremely narrow gap between sheer walls almost all the way down – and there'll be hardly anyone else around.

Livanianá

Just before the bridge in Arádhena, a signed, mostly asphalted road on the left heads for **LIVANIANÁ (Λιβανιανά)**, a hamlet perched above the lower reaches of the Arádhena Gorge, some 4km away. There are a few potholed patches, but the road is easily driveable as far as Livaniiná. Beyond, a rough dirt road continues to Líkkos (see p.281) and Fínix (see p.280). In the village there's a path (signed "Mármara") down into the gorge. It starts beyond a gate just above the church and emerges fairly near the bottom of the gorge, having bypassed all the hardest bits. The red markings show you the best path down and you'll reach the beach after about 45 minutes.

Áyios Ioánnis

Beyond Arádhena, the paved road from the bridge climbs westward for about an hour on foot (5km) to **ÁYIOS IOÁNNIS (Άγιος Ιωάννης)**, beneath the massed peaks of Páhnes, Troharís and Zaranokefála. The village has a good rooms place, the *Alonia* hostel, and a couple of **Byzantine churches** with fourteenth-century frescoes; enquire at the hostel (see p.286) for information on getting in. There are also several impressively large **caves** nearby: a signed track leads up to the Kormokopos Cave, about an hour's climb above the village.

The onward path to Ayía Rouméli (see p.278) is also signed, at least initially, though it becomes hard to follow for a while until it emerges on top of the cliffs. From here it loops down as a rough but obvious path to join the coastal trail before the chapel of

Áyios Pávlos. You should be able to complete the approximately 17km walk from Anópoli to Ayía Rouméli in about four hours, though with rest stops and wrong turnings it could well take much longer; leave plenty of leeway if you need to catch a boat back. If you are undertaking this walk in reverse, start early so as to complete the climb of the cliffs before it gets too hot.

ARRIVAL AND DEPARTURE
ANÓPOLI AND AROUND

By bus A bus from Hóra Sfakíon heads up to Anópoli (15min) and Arádhena (25min) daily at 9am.

On foot from Hóra Sfakíon There's a good road from Hóra Sfakíon to Anópoli, 12km away, but it's still a very steep climb; having to follow the road means it's not a very attractive walk, but there's no real alternative.

On foot from Loutró The climb up from Loutró looks terrifying – you can see the path tracking back and forth across an almost vertical cliff – but is not as bad as it appears, though it will take about 2hr, climbing steeply

most of the way. This is best done very early, before the sun gets too hot. The path diverges from the coastal route immediately outside Loutró, by the gate at the edge of the village; near the top the old path has been disrupted by fencing and a farmers' track – the easiest course is to follow the latter to the paved road (the Hóra Sfakíon–Anópoli road), and turn left on that into the village. If you continue to climb you'll go right over the top of the ridge and into Anópoli from above.

By taxi A taxi from Hóra Sfakíon to Anópoli will cost around €25.

ACCOMMODATION AND EATING
ANÓPOLI

Taverna Plátanos On the main square ☎28250 91169, ✉anopoli-sfakia.com. You'll get a warm Sfakiá welcome here, along with comfortable rooms with a/c, heating, fridge and a wonderful mountain view. The busy taverna below, serving excellent breakfasts and hearty local food (mains €6–9), is right at the heart of village life. Taverna daily 8am–11pm. **€30**

Xenonas Main road, east of the square ☎28250 91189. Very pleasant purpose-built modern studios and apartments, all with kitchen, heating, a/c and TV. The same family runs the superb bakery nearby (enquire there if there's no one around) – try their sweet sesame bread or Sfakian pie topped with honey. Bakery Mon–Sat 8am–8pm. **€35**

LIVANIANÁ

Taverna Livanianá Centre of village. The old village taverna has recently been reopened; the German owner has great plans, but in the early days just cold drinks and snacks are available. There are lovely views, though, and it's a welcome break for hikers. Daily 9am–10pm.

ÁYIOS IOÁNNIS

★**Alonia Mountain Hostel** Turn left as you enter the village, then left again ☎6938 792 695, ✉alonia.gr Appealing hostel with an "end of the world" feel, bigger than it first appears – it's tricky to find, so you may need to ask. The stone-built rooms are simply furnished with rustic wooden furniture handmade by the owner, who is also a good source of information on local walking and climbing. Meals are available, at €10–15 a head for dinner and breakfast. **€30**

Hóra Sfakíon

Squeezed between the sea and the mountains, **HÓRA SFAKÍON** (Χώρα Σφακίων) – often known simply as Hóra, meaning "chief town" – couldn't grow even if it wanted to. Nevertheless it's a surprise to find the capital of Sfakiá quite so small. It is, though, a thoroughly commercial place: there's a post office and a couple of ATMs on the main square; restaurants cram the seafront promenade; and half the houses in town seem to display a large "Rooms" sign. That said, it's inexpensive and pleasant, relatively quiet by the end of the day, and a good base for local hikes and boat trips. The **beach** facing the harbour in front of town is rather pebbly; there's better swimming at Vríssi beach, just round the corner to the west.

There are just two pedestrian streets leading into town off the square: one along the waterfront, with an unbroken row of tavernas leading round to the old fishing harbour, the other just inland, lined with shops and rooms places. In the other direction from the square, more restaurants and snack bars line the road to the ferry jetty and the new harbour. For all the town's and region's history there's not a lot to show; several ancient-looking but locked **churches**, a **war memorial** on the eastern side of the bay commemorating the evacuation of some ten thousand Allied troops in 1941, and the **Cave of Dhaskaloyiannis**, one of several large caves in the cliffs west of Hóra. Always a hideout in times of trouble, this was where the rebel leader (see p.284) set up a mint to produce revolutionary coinage.

ARRIVAL AND DEPARTURE

HÓRA SFAKÍON

By car The road into Hóra Sfakíon ends at a small square just above the water. You have to pay to park here (€1/hr or €3/day), or anywhere on the road down towards the new harbour. You can park for free higher up, most obviously at the beginning of the Anópoli road; if you're staying, your hotel should also be able to find you a free space.

By bus Buses stop immediately above the square and there's a ticket booth on the square, which should be open before departures. Anyone who has walked the gorge and already has a ticket should get on the bus and secure a seat; the last bus waits for the ferry.

Destinations Anópoli (1 daily at 9am; 15min); Arádhena (1 daily at 9am; 25min); Frangokástello (4 daily; 10min); Haniá (4 daily; 1hr 40min).

By ferry and boat Large ferries leave from the concrete jetty on the east side of the harbour, not far from the square; smaller vessels (including the *Neptune* to Loutró, operated by the Anendyk ferry company) and taxi-boats go from the new harbour beyond, a good ten-minute walk from most hotels. The ferry ticket booth at the top of the jetty opens about 1hr before departure; schedules are posted but are highly seasonal, so check in advance (☎ 28250 91221, ⓦ anendyk.gr; summer schedules are quoted below, there are more at peak times and a reduced service runs year-round). Early departures generally wait for the arrival of the first bus. Taxi boats and day-trips have ticket booths at the new harbour, and advertise widely in town.

Destinations Loutró (May–Oct at least 5 daily; 20 min) Ayía Rouméli (May–Oct 3 daily; 1hr); Gávdhos (June & Sept Tues & Fri 10.30am, July & Aug Tues, Fri & Sun 8.30am; 2hr 30min); Sweetwater Beach (summer daily 10.15am, after the bus arrives; return 5.30pm).

By taxi There's a taxi office on the main square, also good for long-distance transfers (☎ 28250 91269, ⓦ taxi-sfakia .com).

INFORMATION AND ACTIVITIES

Tourist information The bus ticket kiosk on the main square (erratic hours) can also provide information on ferries (but not tickets) and taxi-boats along with general information about the town and surroundings.

Travel agencies Sfakiá Tours (April–Sept daily 9am–10pm; ☎ 28250 91272, ⓦ www.sfakia-tours .com), on the main square, is a useful source of local information, offering car rental and help with finding accommodation.

Diving Notos Mare is a good dive place at the new harbour (☎ 6947 270 106, ⓦ notosmare.com). They also run boat trips and a 24hr taxi-boat service.

Kayaking There's kayak rental on Vríssi beach (☎ 6972 690 139).

ACCOMMODATION

Hotel Stavris Follow the inland street around, or climb the steps behind the waterfront tavernas ☎ 28250 91220, ⓦ stavris.com. A variety of rooms and studios, all with balconies, increasing in price as you add a/c, kitchenette, or sea views. The Perrakis brothers, who own and run the place, have more rooms elsewhere in town, and at Frangokástello. Doubles **€35**, studios **€40**

★ Hotel Xenia At the far end of the seafront promenade, just above the harbour ☎ 28250 91490, ⓦ xeniacrete.com. This former state-owned hotel, now refurbished, has the best location in town with amazing views across the Libyan Sea. All rooms have a/c, fridge, satellite TV and balcony with sea view; some are huge, though as a result rather sparsely furnished. Steps at the rear let you swim off the rocks, and the bar-taverna terrace is a great place to watch the harbour activity. There's a car park, and breakfast is included. **€56**

Tria Adelfia Top of the inland street, above Vríssi beach ☎ 28250 91450, ⓦ three-brothers-chora-sfakion-crete .com. Another place with a big variety of comfortable, a/c en-suite rooms and apartments, many of them overlooking Vríssi beach. Doubles **€37**, apartments **€50**

EATING AND DRINKING

Finding food is never a problem in Hóra Sfakíon, and the excellent **seafront tavernas** have a good array of vegetarian options; almost everywhere here serves breakfast, too. There's little to choose between them, though you'll find cheaper **cafés** and takeaway places on the east side of the bay, towards the ferry jetty. The **supermarket** just above *Niki's Bakery* has better prices than those on the front.

Lefka Ori Corner of the harbour ☎ 28250 91209. Probably the best of the waterfront tavernas for seafood, with a decent terrace by the water. Like everywhere on the seafront they have a tempting display of traditional dishes like *moussaká* (€6.90) or fish casserole (€7.50), and also the hearty local speciality *kreatópita* (lamb and cheese pie; €11.50). April–Oct daily 9am–11pm.

Niki's Bakery On the inland street ☎ 28250 91268. A Hóra institution, offering a superb range of breads, cookies and other sweet temptations. Daily 3am–midnight.

★**Tria Adelfia** Overlooking Vríssi beach ☎ 28250 91040. In a quiet spot, with a lovely terrace above the sea, this taverna serves good food with a wide range of salads, pasta and vegetarian dishes. Mezédhes (€7.50) include a tasty *melitzánes tiganites* (fried aubergine), while *kounéli stifádho* (rabbit stew, €8.40) is just one of many Cretan specials. If you like smoked fish, don't miss their home-smoked local dorado. Daily 9am–11pm.

Xenia At the far end of the seafront promenade, under the Hotel Xenia ☎ 28250 91490. The hotel's taverna has a limited but well-prepared menu supervised by hotel manager and all-round good guy Yiorgos Lykoyiannakis. House specials include charcoal-grilled lamb, goat and pork, and the grilled fresh fish is excellent. Mains €6–9 Daily 8.30am–11.30pm.

From Vrýsses to Sfakiá

The easy way **into Sfakiá** from the north coast is by a good road that cuts south from Vrýsses (see p.258), almost immediately beginning to spiral up into the mountains towards the **plateau of Askífou**. The climb seems straightforward from a vehicle, but the country has a history as bloody as any in Crete: you pass first through a little ravine where two Turkish armies were massacred, the first during the 1821 uprising, the second in 1866 after the heroic events at Arkádhi (see p.202); while the road itself is the one along which the Allied troops retreated at such cost in the final stages of the Battle of Crete. This chaotic flight has been described in detail in just about all the books covering the battle (and also in Evelyn Waugh's *Officers and Gentlemen*).

The final descent to the coast is stunning, running high above the **Ímbros Gorge** until the road breaks out of its confinement, way above the sea, and plunges down through a series of hairpin bends. Frangokástello can be made out on the broad plain to the east and ahead are immense vistas out towards Africa, with Gávdhos hazy on the horizon.

Dourakis Winery

Between Vrýsses and Alíkambos • Mon–Sat 11am–7pm; booking advised for wine tasting • Free; tasting from €6 • ☎ 28250 51761, ⓦ dourakiswinery.gr

Part of the Cretan wine "revolution" which has seen the emergence of many prize-winning vineyards on the island in recent years, the **Dourakis Winery** was founded in the 1980s and produces red, white and organic wines. The visit (often guided by amiable owner Andreas Dourakis, or by the next generation of the family, who are gradually taking over the business) includes the impressive cellars and an explanation of the entire production process.

Alíkambos

About 4km south of Vrýsses there's a turn-off to the ancient village of **ALÍKAMBOS** (Αλίκαμπος), which has a couple of *kafenía*. Just before the village, the **church of the Panayía** (signed "Kimisis tis Theotokou") is beautifully set in a steep valley. In its nave are outstanding, remarkably well-preserved **frescoes** by the fourteenth-century master, Ioannis Pagomenos; they depict the Virgin and Child, Áyios Yeóryios and Áyios Dimítrios. The paintings around the altar are by a later artist. You can just about make the frescoes out even if the church is locked; if it is, the key should be available in the village.

Askífou plateau

The **Askífou plateau** is dominated by a ruined Turkish castle on a hill – a hill so small and perfectly conical it almost looks fake, put there expressly to raise the castle above its surroundings. Chief among the several small villages up here, all bypassed by the main road, is **AMMOUDHÁRI**, with a couple of small tavernas. There are more tavernas

HIKING ON THE ASKÍFOU PLATEAU

For keen **walkers**, the most obvious hike from the plateau is the Ímbros Gorge (see below), but there are also a couple of more serious treks into the Lefká Óri, most obviously on the E4 Pan-European footpath, which passes through Ammoudhári. To the west the E4 climbs into the foothills – initially easy walking with good opportunities for bird-spotting – before beginning to ascend seriously into the heart of the mountains. This little-travelled section eventually reaches the Kallergi Refuge (see box, p.275): a two-day trek with a possible overnight stop at the Katsiveli or Svourihti refuge (if open). In the other direction the E4 follows the road south across the plain to Ímbros, where one branch heads down the gorge to meet the coastal path while another climbs east to Asféndou (see p.291) and from there to Así Goniá (see p.231).

Alternative routes include a short-cut from Ammoudhári, via the nearby village of **Goní**, to Así Goniá, some 12km in all, or a long day's hike west to Anópoli (see p.283). For the latter you can either follow a track from Ímbros via Trikoukiá to the hamlet of **Kalí Láki** (abandoned but for the odd shepherd in summer) and thence south to Anópoli, or take a path from the village of Petrés, immediately south of Ammoudhári, to join this route at Trikoukiá. Though detailed on the *Anavasi* Lefká Óri map (see p.41), it's not an easy route to follow and you should get thorough directions locally before setting off.

in nearby **KARÉS**, along with home-made signs to an equally home-made Battle of Crete **museum** (usually open 9am–dusk; "voluntary" donation; ☏6979 149 719, ⊕warmuseumaskifou.com). Gathered in the home of the late Yiorgos Hatzidakis, who witnessed the German invasion as a child, this is a fascinating jumble of weapons, helmets, badges and photos, much of it picked up in the immediate area. Yiorgos' children seem a lot less keen on his collection than he was, however, and their tours can be perfunctory at best, at least until it comes to collecting your money.

The Ímbros Gorge

April–Oct 8am–sunset; Nov–March unmanned • April–Oct €2; Nov–March free

On the far side of the Askífou plateau lies **ÍMBROS** ('Ιμπρος), the entry point for the Ímbros Gorge. Barely even a village, it consists primarily of a clutch of tavernas and rooms places strung out along the road. The **gorge walk** is clearly signed from here, and there are several ways down into it. Once in the gorge, you are following a **track** that was once the district's main thoroughfare; this well-trodden trail soon passes a booth where you will be charged the entry fee. The hike is easily enough done in less than three hours and provided you don't coincide with a tour bus (set out early), it can be wonderfully peaceful, certainly in contrast to the crowds at Samariá. In its own way the gorge is as interesting as its better-known rival, albeit on a smaller scale: narrow and stiflingly confined in places, speckled with caves in others and at one point passing under a monumental, natural stone archway. Through the ravine you simply follow the stream until, emerging at the lower end, an obvious track leads away again towards the village of **Komitádhes**, full of huge, usually empty, tavernas waiting for the occasional tour party to arrive.

ARRIVAL AND DEPARTURE   **THE ÍMBROS GORGE**

There are numerous entry points to the gorge in Ímbros, where many of the tavernas offer parking and a service to pick you up from the bottom (around €20); the lowest of these is the *Taverna Porofarago* (see p.290).

By bus It's possible to walk the gorge as a half-day trip from Hóra Sfakíon (or Loutró, by getting the first boat from there): simply take the early bus to Haniá, and get off at Ímbros.

By taxi A taxi to the top from Hóra Sfakíon will cost around €20; if you don't have a number to call for a pick-up at the bottom, the tavernas in Komitádhes can order one for you – about €20 back to the top, €10 to Hóra Sfakíon.

On foot From the bottom of the gorge you can walk to Hóra Sfakíon easily enough, though this final 5km makes a hot, boring anticlimax to what has gone before.

ACCOMMODATION AND EATING

Tavern-Apartments Kalinorisma Ímbros ☎ 6944 799 859. Lovely, large modern apartments with separate sitting area and full kitchen, above a taverna serving quality food on a terrace looking out towards the gorge. Parking and transfers available for walkers; hearty breakfast included for guests. April–Oct daily 9am–10pm. **€40**

Taverna Porofarago Ímbros ☎ 28250 95450. A very good, friendly taverna with an attractive shady terrace overlooking the gorge. Sfakian specialities include goat stew (€9) and meat pie (€4.50), and they're also open for breakfast. Parking and transfers available for walkers. April–Oct daily 7am–11pm.

Frangokástello

FRANGOKÁSTELLO (Φραγκοκάστελλο) lies 14km east of Hóra Sfakíon, about 3km south of the road heading east towards Plakiás (see p.221). A series of isolated dwellings dotted across a plain between the mountains and the Libyan Sea, it's a curious place, with a fabulous **beach** but no real centre, leaving you with little option but to head for the **castle** – the imposing silhouette of which comes into view long before anything else.

The castle

Centre of the village fronting the sea • May–Oct daily 9am–7pm • €1.50

The **castle**, so impressively four-square from a distance, turns out close-up to be a mere shell. Nothing but the bare walls survives, with a tower in each corner and, over the seaward entrance, an escutcheon which can just be made out as the Venetian lion of St Mark. Still, it's some shell. The fortress was originally built in 1371 to deter pirates and in an attempt to impose some order on Sfakiá: a garrison was maintained here throughout the Venetian and Turkish occupations, controlling the plain as surely as it failed to tame the mountains – even today, the orange-pink walls look puny when you see them with the grey bulk of the mountains towering behind. In 1828, Frangokástello was occupied by **Hadzimihali Daliani**, a Greek adventurer attempting to spread the War of Independence from the mainland to Crete. Instead of taking to the hills as all sensible rebels before and since have done, he and his tiny force attempted to make a stand in the castle. Predictably, they were massacred and their martyrdom became fuel for yet more heroic legends of the *pallikári*. Locals claim that to this day, around May 17, the ghosts of Daliani and his army march from the castle: they are known as *dhrossoulítes*, or dewy ones, because they appear in the mists around dawn.

The beach

For peaceful lassitude the **beach** at Frangokástello is among the best spots in Crete, with fine sand, crystal-clear water (with good snorkelling opportunities), and very little effort required either to get here or to find food and drink once you've arrived. If you want company you'll find it around the castle, where the best part of the sand is almost lagoon-like, sheltered and slowly shelving. For solitude, head west along the shoreline, where it's windier and the sand is less soft, but it's still very pleasant. There are beaches to the east too: follow the coastal path for ten to fifteen minutes and you'll arrive at the top of a low cliff overlooking perhaps 1km of beautiful, deserted sand and rocks.

ARRIVAL AND GETTING AROUND   FRANGOKÁSTELLO

By bus In summer there are four buses a day from Hóra Sfakíon (10min).

Vehicle rental You can rent cars, scooters and mountain

bikes from Drive Kreta (☎ 28250 92095, ⑩ drivekreta.com) based at *Blue Sky* apartments, and cars from Tracer (☎ 6979 091 339, ⑩ tracercarrentals.com), based at *Paradisos*.

ACCOMMODATION

Most of the **places to stay** and other facilities are strung out for some distance along the road that heads in from Hóra Sfakíon: a turn-off immediately before the castle leads to another little group of seaside rooms places and tavernas; and there are a couple more east of the castle. Wherever you stay, come prepared for **mosquitoes**. Pretty much everything here closes in winter, from November to March.

Babis & Popi Main road west of the castle ☎ 28250 92092, ⓦ babis-popi.com. A range of accommodation from simple, old-fashioned rooms (most but not all a/c) above the popular taverna and mini-market, to very comfy, well-equipped studios and apartments in a purpose-built block a short walk from the beach, most with great sea views. Rooms €25, studios €45, apartments €65

Blue Sky Apartments Signed inland off the main road, west of the castle ☎ 28250 92095, ⓦ blue-sky-kreta.de. Very attractive modern two-room apartments (sleeping five) with a/c, kitchen and TV in a tranquil location; there's a large pool and a decent café/tavern too. €60

Oasis Main road west of the castle ☎ 28250 92136, ⓦ oasisrooms.com. A good taverna with very pleasant,

generously-sized a/c studios and ap_____ by flowers, with a path to what is in effect a ___ where they have their own umbrellas and sunb___ two-room apartments with full kitchen are particular___ good value. Daily 8am–11pm. Studios €45, apartments €50

Paradisos Signed off the road east of the castle ☎ 28250 92078, ⓦ paradisos.gr. Large studio and apartment complex in a tranquil setting amid olive groves very near the sandy eastern beach; well-equipped accommodation with kitchen, a/c and TV, plus a tennis court, free bikes and communal washing machine for guests (some larger apartments have their own). Studios €50, apartments €65

EATING AND DRINKING

Babis & Popi Main road west of the castle ☎ 28250 92093. Much the most popular place here, which means they have a wider choice than many, though also slightly higher prices than elsewhere (mains and excellent daily specials still only €8–10). *Astakomakoronáda* (lobster with spaghetti) is a house special, while Saturday, barbecue night, offers charcoal-grilled fish, meat and sausage. All served on a raised terrace with views out to sea. March–Oct daily 7am–11pm.

Kali Kardia Main road, almost next to the castle ☎ 28250 92311. The "Good Heart" started life as the village's *kafenío*, and is still the place you're most likely to see locals. Although they have a menu there's normally a limited selection available, so go with what they recommend; local goat (€7) is a favourite, and they also make a mean tomato soup. This is also a good stop for

breakfast, drinks and snacks, including takeaway pizza. March–Nov daily 8am–midnight.

Milos Side road by the castle ☎ 28250 92162, ⓦ milos -sfakia.com. Enjoying probably the best position in town, right on the waterfront between the beach and tiny fishing harbour, this is a reliable place for fresh fish (sardines €7) and solid Greek cooking (mains around €8.50, lamb pilaf €10). Good wine list too. April–Oct daily 8am–11pm.

Sunrise Taverna On the clifftop east of the castle ☎ 28250 92041. Great views from a position hanging above the shore (with steps down to a little-used part of the beach), and good food; all the meat (goat and lamb) comes from its own herds (try the tasty Sfakian lamb casserole, €8). The mezédhes are recommended, too, and there are many vegetarian possibilities. April–Oct daily 8.30am–11pm.

4

Kallikrátis and around

The road from Frangokástello to **KALLIKRÁTIS** (**Καλλικράτης**), in the mountains directly above, is among the steepest, most winding and spectacular in Crete, which is saying something. It ascends beside the Kallikrátis Gorge to emerge on a rocky, high plateau – often ten degrees or more cooler than the coast, and a blessed relief in summer. There's a great café here as well as a couple of more traditional tavernas, and **onward roads** head west via the village of **Asféndou** to join the main trans-island route just above Ímbros (see p.289), or northeast via either Myriokéfala or (a much worse road) Así Goniá towards Aryiroúpoli (see p.228) and the north coast. There are also a couple of reasonably easy gorge walks that can be combined into a 17km all-day loop. The **Kallikrátis Gorge** is a branch of the E4, so reasonably well marked; the path cuts off near the bottom of the road up to Kallikrátis and the climb takes around two hours, though from the top of the gorge it's a good half-hour more to the village. The **Asféndou Gorge**, west of here, descends from Asféndou (where there's another café) to Áyios Nektários, on the coast road. Again, it's about two hours up or down, much of it on the remains of an ancient *kalderími* (cobbled path) that was once a major thoroughfare. To combine the two there are short-cuts that cross the plateau from near the top of the Kallikrátis Gorge to Asféndou, but these are poorly marked and they also mean missing the village of Kallikrátis; it's a great deal easier to do this section on the road.

as you come in to
☎ 6949 092 073,
...l-bedecked rustic café run
...artner Janina. It's a very basic
..., but wonderful Greek coffee,
(sipped through a literal straw,

picked from the fields) and cold beers. They also collect and distil local herbs into essential oils, and these are on sale along with home-made preserves and excellent honey. Walkers in need of a place to stay can usually be catered for, and they can also help with hiking directions. Tues–Sun 11am–8pm.

Kastel.í and the far west

Crete's **far west** has, to date, attracted surprisingly little attention from tourists or developers, and though that is beginning to change, such development as there is consists of mostly low-key apartments and rooms rather than big hotels. The one town of any size west of Haniá is **Kastélli Kissámou**, a port with a ferry service to the Peloponnese, very regular buses to Haniá and a fine museum. To the northwest of Kastélli the long, slender finger of the **Gramvoúsa peninsula** reaches out into the Aegean with, on its western flank, the fabulous white-sand beach of **Bálos Bay**. Extending to the south of this peninsula, Crete's west-facing coast remains remote: there's little public transport and virtually nothing in the way of luxurious facilities. However, here you'll find two of the finest **beaches** on the island – **Falásarna** and **Elafonísi** – both of them, sadly, all too well known.

4

The Gulf of Kissámou

Kastélli lies some 20km beyond the crossroads at Kolymbári (see p.265) on the coast of the **Gulf of Kissámou**. If you're in a hurry to head west, the new highway is fast and efficient, taking you right to the edge of Kastélli, where it finally ends. The **old road** – always a beautiful drive – has been left behind as a little-travelled, delightful backwater. Going this way you wind steeply up a rocky spur thrown back by the peninsula and emerge through a cleft in the hills to a magnificent view of the Gulf of Kissámou, with Kastélli in the middle distance. Caught with the sun setting behind the craggy heights of **Cape Voúxa** at the far west of Crete, this is a memorable panorama.

Leaving the hills behind, both roads run parallel across the fertile **plain of Kastélli**. Almost as soon as you hit level ground you'll see turnings to the beach, a long stretch of grey sand which, while not the best in Crete, is at least clean and uncrowded. The old road, further inland, passes through a number of quite large, entirely unvisited villages, such as Nochiá, Koléni or Kaloudhianá, where you could stop for a drink or a bite to eat at a number of inviting tavernas. **Kaloudhianá** marks the turn-off for the inland route to Topólia and Elafonísi (see p.304).

ACCOMMODATION
GULF OF KISSÁMOU

There are scattered rooms places on the plain of Kastélli, and two good **campsites**, right on the beach about 1km from the road. There's a regular bus service to and from Kastélli, and though the sites are popular with people arriving in Kastélli on the ferry, there should always be space.

Camping Mithimna Between Nopíyia and Dhrapaniás ☎ 28220 31444, �🌐 campingmithimna .com. Much the larger of the two sites, *Mithimna* takes its name from the ancient Minoan town of Mithymna, thought to have stood nearby. There's a taverna and mini-market, and they also have studios and apartments (sleeping 4) to rent nearby. April–Oct. Two adults plus tent and vehicle €19, studios €45

Camping Nopigia Near Nopíyia village, at the eastern extremity of the beach ☎ 28220 31111, ⍵ camping nopigia.gr. Attractive site in a tranquil spot close to the Ródhopou peninsula, with a pool and taverna; you can also rent a tent here (2-person tent €24). April–Oct. Two adults plus tent and vehicle €19

4

Kastélli Kissámou

KASTÉLLI KISSÁMOU (Καστέλλι Κισσάμου; the Castle of Kíssamos) rarely goes by its full name – it's either **Kastélli** or **Kíssamos**, which officially is the name of the region but more readily distinguishes it from the many other Kastéllis across Greece. It's a busy little town and port with a long seafront, a rather rocky strand to the east and a small sandy beach to the west. This very ordinariness has real charm: it's a working town full of stores used by locals and cafés not entirely geared to outsiders. **Kísamos** was the Greco-Roman city-state that stood here in ancient times, and ongoing excavations in the town centre – whose finds are displayed in an outstanding **museum** – are revealing just how important the ancient city was.

The Archeological Museum

Platía Tzanakáki • Tues–Sun 8.30am–3pm • €3 • ☎ 28220 83308

Housed in the former Venetian governor's palace on the main square, the fine **Archeological Museum** is Kastélli's major attraction. The lower floor exhibits finds from the prehistoric and Minoan periods, many of them from Polyrínia (see p.296) and Falásarna (see p.298), but the second floor – devoted to the Roman town – holds the highlights of the collection.

During the first and second centuries, when Kísamos thrived as an important municipality in the Roman Empire, many wealthy aristocrats embellished their luxurious villas here with sculptures, frescoes, inlaid marble floors (*opus sectilis*) and fine mosaics. Many of these arts and crafts are exhibited in the museum, but it is the **Roman mosaics** that steal the show. Kísamos was a key centre of mosaic production, and at least a dozen other, equally splendid, mosaics have been discovered in excavations across the town, but the museum has no space to exhibit them. There are plans to open an extension on the Villa of Phidias excavation site nearby (see p.294); if this ever

> ## KASTÉLLI ORIENTATION
> On the eastern outskirts the old and new roads merge to head straight through town as Iróon Politehníou, south of the centre. This is lined with stores and supermarkets, and there are cafés and banks on **Platía Venizélou**, where it passes through the centre of town. The heart of Kastélli's life, however, lies a couple of blocks towards the sea from here, around **Platía Tzanakáki** and the main street that runs through it, **Odhós Skalídhi**. There's a further cluster of development along the **waterfront**, directly down from the main squares, with an attractive promenade separating the town's **beaches** to the east and west.

happens the display would become one of Greece's most important museums of Greco-Roman mosaics.

Roman mosaics

The huge, polychromatic **Dyonysiac mosaic** covers most of Room 4 and depicts various scenes in a Dyonysiac ritual. Interestingly, the mosaic had been restored many times by the various owners of the villa that housed it. The museum's star exhibit, however, is **Horae and the Seasons**, displayed beside it. A brilliant work, its colours still remarkably vivid, the almost perfectly complete mosaic depicts a trio of dancing *horae* (goddesses of the seasons). There were only three seasons (spring, summer and winter) in the old Hellenic calendar but at the four corners the mosaicist has added depictions of the four seasons of later antiquity.

Archeological excavations
Originally the port of nearby Polyrínia, Kísamos grew to become the more powerful city; various **archeological excavations** have revealed substantial remains of the ancient town (and more mosaics). However, as the mosaics have been covered in sand and gravel to protect them until they are removed for display in the museum, all you can do is stare at the dirt, a few foundation walls and the odd stretch of ancient roadway, through a chain-link fence. One villa that should be opened to the public at some stage (economic crisis permitting) is the **Villa of Phidias**, so named from the owner whose name has been found on a mosaic. An enormous place, now partly covered by the town's health centre, it has six fine mosaics that will be viewed from a walkway.

The Venetian and Ottoman town
Immediately north of Platía Tzanakáki, where the ground falls sharply away towards the coast, are substantial **defensive bastions** connected with a Venetian castle here (which gave the town its name) and which was largely destroyed by Turkish pirates in the early sixteenth century. In the streets surrounding the square, particularly to the west, surviving sections of city wall from the same period can still be seen. There's also a beautiful old **Venetian fountain**, inscribed with the date 1520, about 100m east of the main square in a small courtyard to the left off Kampoúri.

ARRIVAL AND GETTING AROUND KASTÉLLI KISSÁMOU

By bus The bus station is west of the centre, accessed from the main road via the car park at Carrefour; most buses make a stop in Platía Venizélou as they pass through.

Destinations Bálos (May–Sept 4 daily; 1hr); Elafonísi (May–Sept daily at 10am, returning 5pm; 1hr 20min); Falásarna (May–Sept 6 daily; 40min); Haniá (14 daily; 1hr); Soúdha (daily to meet the ferries; 1hr 15min).

By ferry The ferry harbour, for ferries to the Peloponnese, is 3km west of town – a cheap taxi ride; tickets are available from travel agencies in town, or

before departure from a booth on the quayside. Check detailed timetables for the complex schedule at ⊕ lane .gr. Day-trips to the island of Gramvoúsa and Balos Bay (see p.297) also depart from here.

Destinations Andikýthira (2 weekly; 2hr 15min), Kýthira (3–4 weekly; 4hr), Yíthio (1 a week; 7hr) Kalamáta (1 a week; 9hr 30min), Pireás (1 a week; 24hr).

By taxi The main rank is on Platía Venizélou, or try ⊕ 28220 22324 or ⊕ 28220 22069.

Bike and car rental For cars, motorbikes, scooters and

mountain bikes try the longstanding and helpful Motofun/Autofun (☎ 28220 23440, ⓦ auto-motofun.info) on Platía Tzanakáki; they offer remarkably cheap deals for a week's rental, and will also deliver to Haniá airport. Horeftakis Tours (see below) and others on Skalídhi also rent cars, while Balos Travel (see below) hire bikes.

INFORMATION AND TOURS

Boat trips Daily boat trips run from Kastélli port to the beautiful beaches at Gramvoúsa and Bálos Bay (see p.297). A public bus runs to the port before departure.

Hiking, cycling and other tours Strata Tours, opposite the archeological museum (☎ 28220 24249, ⓦ stratatours .com), offers walking and wildlife tours of the beautiful country around Kastélli (spring and autumn only), as well as other special-interest activities. Balos Travel, Iróon

Politehníou 131, opposite Platía Venizélou (☎ 28220 22900, ⓦ balos-travel.com), runs cycling tours to Falásarna, Polyrínia and other areas, with picnic lunch and guide included. They can also organize Cretan cooking lessons and many other tours and activities.

Travel agencies Several along Skalídhi: Horeftakis Tours at no. 33 (☎ 28220 23250, ⓦ horeftakistours.com) sells LANE ferry tickets and offers car rental.

ACCOMMODATION

Argo Central seafront ☎ 28220 23322, ⓦ papadakisargo .gr. Given their great location and low prices, these rather plain, old-fashioned, marble-floored a/c balcony rooms, with fridge and TV, are a real bargain. **€30**

★ **Galini Beach Hotel** On the eastern beach, just past the football pitch ☎ 28220 23288, ⓦ galinibeach.com. Friendly, good-value hotel with light and airy a/c rooms with TV and balcony, some with fabulous sea views. It also offers an excellent breakfast (extra) served on its seafront terrace, in front of which is what is virtually a private beach, with sunbeds and umbrellas. The friendly proprietor has lots of information on hiking in the area. April–Oct. **€45**

Maria Beach On the western beach ☎ 28220 22610, ⓦ mariabeach.gr. Right on the sandy beach, family-run *Maria's* consists of two separate buildings housing

some fairly plain rooms (some with fridge) as well as new, fully equipped sea-view studios (with kitchenette) and apartments (sleeping 5) with kitchen; breakfast is included in the rates for rooms, not for studios or apartments. April–Nov. Doubles and studios **€60**, apartments **€65**

Mirtilos Platía Tzanakáki ☎ 28220 23079, ⓦ mirtilos .com. Modern, stylish and well-equipped studio-apartment complex round a large pool, right off the main square. Studios can sleep up to 4, and there are a couple of larger apartments, plus a roof terrace with great views; breakfast is available. May–Oct. **€55**

Revekka A block back from the seafront ☎ 28220 22092. Bright pink building housing simple, spacious, stone-floored a/c balcony rooms with fridge and TV, plus a couple of larger apartments. Breakfast included. **€40**

EATING AND DRINKING

There's no shortage of **places to eat** in Kastélli: in the evening the seafront promenade, which can have a listless, end-of-season air by day, comes to life. As well as the tavernas here, there are a few **café-bars** that carry on late into the night: *Babel* and *Aqua* are among the most popular. By day, for light meals and breakfasts, the area around Platía Tzanakáki is a better bet; there's also a good **bakery**, *Hairetakis*, nearby at the corner of Ameríkis and Skalídhi. Wherever you eat, you'll probably be offered the local **red wine**. Made from the *roméïko* grape, believed to have been brought to the island by the Venetians, it is as good as any produced on Crete, and there are a number of new wineries in the area.

★ **Aéras** Skalídhi 85, at the top of Platía Tzanakáki ☎ 28220 22913. "Winds" is the town's oldest *kafenío* and meeting place, serving customers for over a century. Remarkably, it's still in the hands of the same family and remains a great place for a breakfast coffee in the atmospheric bar (with photos of old Kastélli) or a sundowner on its terrace on the square, beneath the spreading rubber tree. They also serve a full menu throughout the day, including a Cretan breakfast (with wine) for €7. Daily 6.30am–1am.

★ **Akrogiali** Korfalónas Beach, about 4km east of town ☎ 28220 31410. *Akrogiali* is the real deal, serving fresh seafood caught daily by the friendly proprietor from

his own boat, accompanied by home-made bread, veg from their garden and wine from the family vineyards. It's not attractive as you approach (immediately east of a seafront soap factory whose chimney stacks are visible from some distance), but food is served on a terrace with the waves almost lapping the table legs. Apart from the fish (priced by weight), try the likes of fresh squid (€10.50), or *yemistá* (€6.50). They also have rooms. April–Oct daily 11am–midnight.

Aretousa Eastern end of the seafront promenade ☎ 28220 23569. A family taverna with mum in the kitchen, dad on the grill and the younger generation serving, this is a good bet for simple, traditional dishes like

4

pork *souvláki* (€7) or stuffed squid (€10). Also has good mezédhes, a decent wine list and a nice terrace. Daily 9am–midnight.

Captain At the small-boat and fishing harbour, about halfway to the ferry port ☎ 28220 22857. Along with *Akrogiali* (see p.295) this place, a short drive or taxi ride west of town, probably has the freshest (if not the cheapest) fish in town – the catch is landed on the quayside, 10m from the taverna's terrace tables. Fish is priced per kilo; fresh *kalamari* €9, shrimp spaghetti €10. Daily 9am–11pm.

Kastello Skalidhi 96, immediately west of Platía Tzanakáki, behind the museum ☎ 28220 24083. Highly popular place with cost-conscious locals who queue for tasty takeaway *souvláki* and *yíros* (€2.50); there are also tables in a small garden for sit-down meals (mixed grill €8). Daily 10am–1am.

Papadakis Western end of the seafront promenade ☎ 28220 22340. The best choice at this end of the seafront, an old-fashioned place where you can check out the day's offerings in the kitchen (mains €7–8); also reasonably priced seafood and courteous service. April–Nov daily noon–midnight.

Petra Platía Tzanakáki ☎ 28220 24387. Simple, inexpensive traditional taverna serving hearty meals and grills at tables out on the square; *moussaká* €7 or lamb with potatoes €8. Daily 10am–midnight.

To Kelari Eastern end of the seafront promenade ☎ 28220 23700. One of the most popular places on the seafront, with a more adventurous menu than most. Try the likes of fish fillet cooked in paper with onions and tomato (€12), *yogurtlu* (Turkish-style kebab with tomato and yoghurt sauce; €8.50) or goat in white wine sauce (€8). Daily 9am–midnight.

SHOPPING

Fountoulakis Skalidhi 53 ☎ 28220 22361. You can buy foreign-language newspapers at several of the super-markets, but the best selection, along with some books in

English, is at Fountoulakis, just off the square. Mon–Sat 9am–2pm & 6–9pm.

DIRECTORY

Banks There are several with ATMs on Platía Venizélou, and a couple more along Skalídhi.
Laundry Kissamos Laundry, Papayiannakis 45 between

the two squares (☎ 28220 24066; Mon–Sat 8am–2.30pm & 5–9.30pm); service washes and dry cleaning.
Post office Iróon Politehníou (Mon–Fri 7.30am–2pm).

Polyrínia

7km south of Kastélli above Polyrínia village • Open daylight hours • Free

Substantial vestiges of the ancient city of **POLYRÍNIA** (Πολυρρήνια) can be seen in and around the village of the same name, inland from Kastélli. **Polyrínia village** is a beautiful place, scattered with ancient remains including an aqueduct. From here it's a hot climb to the **hilltop site**, where ruins are scattered across two horns of high ground that seem to reach out to enclose the Gulf of Kissámou. Originally an eighth-century BC Dorian colony occupied by settlers from the Peloponnese, Polyrínia – a name meaning "rich in lambs" – remained a prosperous city down to Roman times and beyond. One of its main claims to fame, however, would not endear it to most Cretans: an inscription found here and dated to 69 BC tells of how the Polyrinians created a statue in honour of the Roman conqueror of Crete, Quintus Metellus, referring to him as the "saviour and benefactor of the city". It seems that Polyrínia did not join in the resistance put up by Haniá and other cities to the Roman invasion, and as a result was spared destruction.

The most obvious feature, right at the summit, is the **Acropolis**, reached via a circuitous track starting east of the church. There are stunning **views** of the coast from here, and though much of what you see is in fact a Venetian defensive structure, the site is dotted with ancient remains including Roman **cisterns** and the vestiges of an **aqueduct**. Miscellaneous Roman and Greek masonry is incorporated into the **church** that now stands below the Acropolis. The church is itself constructed on the base of what must have been an enormously impressive Hellenistic building, possibly a fourth-century BC temple. The sheer amount of work involved in cutting and dressing these stone blocks and transporting them to places as inaccessible as this makes you wonder at the phenomenal scale of manpower at the service of these towns in antiquity.

SOUTH OF KASTÉLLI: A WEST COAST CIRCUIT

Beyond Kastélli you've a choice of two roads. To the west, you cut through hills across the base of the Gramvoúsa peninsula (see below) to emerge high above the west coast (see p.298) and a spectacular **coast road** that heads all the way down to Elafonísi, where it ends; here you must either turn round to return the way you came or complete a circuit via the inland route. This **inland road** starts a couple of kilometres east of Kastélli at Kaloudhianá, heading down through the Topólia Gorge (see p.304). Further on you've a choice; fork left towards Paleóhora (see p.308) and the south coast, or continue round to join the coast road outside the village of Kefáli (see p.302). The two routes make a fascinating **contrast**: the coast harsh, sparsely populated and occasionally nerve-wracking to drive; the inland route passing dozens of villages, lush and beautiful in a far softer way.

Just below the church are the remains of Hellenistic **dwellings** with cisterns and cave-like storage cellars. The site is extensive and widely scattered across a steep hillside; to explore properly you'll need a couple of hours at least.

ARRIVAL AND DEPARTURE
POLYRÍNIA

By taxi There's no public transport; you could taxi up from Kastélli (around €8) and walk back down.

By car Drivers wanting to go straight to the main site should follow signs to the *Acropolis Taverna*.

On a tour Walking, cycling and bus tours from Kastélli (see p.295) and elsewhere come here.

EATING AND DRINKING

Acropolis Taverna Above the village close to the site ☎ 28220 23340. A good lunch stop, serving simple but tasty food on a shady terrace; omelettes €3.50, chicken in red sauce €5.50, local veg dishes €5. They can also arrange a taxi back to Kastélli. May–Sept daily noon–10pm.

Old Kafeníon Polyrínia village, on the way up to the site ☎ 6975 719 342. Quaint small café serving snacks and drinks; they have information on the site, local walks and more. April–Oct daily 9am–6pm.

4

The Gramvoúsa peninsula

Leaving Kastélli Kissámou for the west, the main road follows the coast as far as the base of the **Gramvoúsa peninsula**, where it turns inland, cutting southwest into the hills. Along this first stretch there are plenty of signs of development, with new apartment blocks and small hotels. To get to **Bálos Bay**, you need to turn off towards **Kalyvianí**. This marks the start of a 10km road (only the first kilometre of which is paved) up the east coast of the peninsula. It's a slow, 25-minute drive, ending at a car park high up on the spine of the peninsula (with a seasonal drinks stall). From here a well-marked path leads across to west-facing **Bálos** (twenty minutes' walk down, thirty or more back up), where there's a really spectacular white-sand **beach** more or less opposite Gramvoúsa island. There are a couple of seasonal tavernas here, and sunbeds and umbrellas, though these soon run out once the boat trips arrive.

Hiking on Gramvoúsa

Walking on the extraordinarily barren and quite unpopulated peninsula is great – but lonely, so take plenty of water and all the other provisions you're going to need. Apart from the car park stall and a spring near the chapel of Ayía Iríni, about 6km out (neither of which it's safe to rely on), there's nothing to be had beyond Kalyvianí.

On the **eastern side**, the walk as far as the car park will take around three hours. From there you can drop down to the beach or continue to **Cape Voúxa** at the tip of the peninsula, on a reasonably well-marked trail. It's also possible to hike up the peninsula's **western side** from Falásarna, but this is a much tougher route and you'll need a head for heights. Head out past the Falásarna archeological site and the bay beyond it (see p.299) and you'll find yourself on an occasionally scary path above the coast, marked by blue paint and cairns. After about four and a half hours you reach a crest, the highest point on the walk, with breathtaking views over the islands. If you do try this, don't do it alone, and take plenty of water.

Gramvoúsa Island

Along with the fortified islands of Néa Sóudha and Spinalónga, the formidable **castle** on **Gramvoúsa Island** was one of the points that held out against the Turks long after the Cretan mainland had fallen. When the Venetians left, the fort was allowed to fall into disrepair until it was taken over by Greek refugees from other Turkish-occupied islands (notably Kássos), who used it as a base for piracy. It took a major Turkish campaign to wrest the fortress back, and thereafter they maintained a garrison here. In the War of Independence it became a base for the Turkish ships attempting to maintain a blockade of the coastline.

Today boat trips call daily in summer, and the island is briefly overrun; there's a small seasonal café, and a beach with very little shelter. You can climb up to the fort (a gruelling fifteen- to twenty-minute ascent in high summer), walk around its well-preserved ramparts with stunning **views**, and examine the huge water cisterns and chapel. There are lovely wildflowers in season.

ARRIVAL AND DEPARTURE   THE GRAMVOÚSA PENINSULA

By boat Boat trips to Gramvoúsa Island and Bálos operate daily throughout the summer from the ferry harbour at Kastélli (May, June, Sept & Oct 10.20am & 10.40am; July & Aug 10.20am, 10.40am & 12.30pm; returning at 4.30pm, 5.45pm and, in July & Aug, 7.30pm; €25; ☎ 28220 22888, ⊛ cretandailycruises.com). The boat trip takes about an hour. Coach trips from around the island connect with these boats.

By bus In summer, four buses a day (the first at 9.30am)

head from Kastélli up the track to the car park above Bálos (45min).

On foot If you're walking it's worth setting out early to get to Bálos before the boats arrive. If you got a taxi to Kalyviani, you could walk up and get the boat back to Kastélli, though it's worth checking in advance that there will be space. Alternatively the Bálos bus could drop you off en route, or a main-road bus could drop you at the turn-off, about 1.5km from Kalyviani.

ACCOMMODATION AND EATING

Balos Beach Hotel 6km west of Kastélli ☎ 28220 24106, ⊛ balosbeach.gr. An attractive hotel in an isolated spot above the sea at the bottom of the peninsula, offering well-equipped studios and apartments (sleeping 4) with balconies and fabulous sea views back towards Kastélli. Also has a bar, restaurant, pool and children's pool. May–Oct. Studios €60, apartments €75

Kaliviani Traditional Hotel Kalyviani ☎ 28220 23204, ⊛ kaliviani.com. Hotel-restaurant on a raised terrace in the centre of the village. The thoughtfully refurbished a/c rooms come with fridge, TV and queen-size

beds, plus balconies with good views out towards the bay. Breakfast available. €60

Mama's Dinner Kalyviani ☎ 28220 23204, ⊛ mamasdinnerkaliviani.com. The restaurant of the Kaliviani Hotel, open for breakfast and dinner, is far more cosmopolitan than you might expect in this out-of-the-way spot. The modern Greek/Mediterranean menu features excellent salads for around €8, risottos and pastas (risotto with shrimps and fresh pesto €9.50) and adventurous meat and fish mains for €12–16. Daily 8.30am–11am & 6pm–midnight.

Falásarna and the west coast

The road along **Crete's west coast** is spectacularly scenic, winding for the most part high above the sea with magnificent coastal views. The further south you go, the finer the vistas, until eventually you begin to see the distant beaches of **Elafonísi** shimmering mirage-like in a turquoise sea. Around you, olives ripen on the terraced hillsides and the few villages seem to cling desperately to the high mountainsides, as if miraculously saved from some calamitous slide to the water, glittering far below. The great beaches at **Falásarna** and **Elafonísi** apart, there are few places to stop, though **Sfinári** and **Kámbos** do offer accommodation and food, and access to far less frequented sand.

Falásarna

The descent from Plátanos, 10km southwest of Kastélli, to the beautiful beach at **FALÁSARNA** (**Φαλάσαρνα**) is via a hair-raising series of hairpin bends above a narrow coastal plain where farmers grow tomatoes, melons and the like in plastic greenhouses. Below, you can see two main **beaches**, with several smaller patches of sand between – the southern one (enterprisingly named "Big Beach") is much bigger, but the best and most sheltered spot is reached by continuing to the end of the asphalt, where there's a car park, the bus stop and a couple of taverna/rooms places above a broad crescent of yellow sand lapped by turquoise waters. You can either head straight down to the sand here, or walk a bit further north, past the *Orange & Blue* bar. Although the beach can occasionally be afflicted by washed-up oil, tar and discarded rubbish, this doesn't detract from the overall beauty of the place. When it gets too crowded (and on Sundays in summer it will, as half of Haniá seems to head here) you can find other patches of sand within easy walking distance in either direction.

Ancient Falásarna

1km north of the car park • Officially Tues–Fri 9am–3pm, but in practice always open and unattended

The **ancient city** and port of Falásarna lies to the north of the beaches. Following the (driveable) dirt track through olive groves you will pass a large stone "**throne**", at the edge of the archeological site, that has puzzled experts for a century – there is still no satisfactory explanation for its function. There's evidence of habitation here in the Minoan era but what you see now, the remains of the westernmost of the cities of ancient Crete, was founded around the seventh or eighth century BC. The scattered remnants of the city are built around a large depression – its inner **harbour** – and the bed of a canal that once joined this to the sea. The harbour was defended by part of the city wall linked by a number of towers to a harbour mole, with the **South Tower**, the nearest to the sea, a formidable bastion built of huge sandstone blocks. More ruined structures can be seen ascending the acropolis hill behind, and near the chapel of Áyios Yeóryios a recently excavated building (beneath a canopy) revealed a number of well-preserved **terracotta baths**.

The entire site is now high and dry, offering conclusive proof that Crete's western extremities have risen at least 8m over the last 24 centuries or so. Excavators discovered large stone blocks thrown across the entrance to the old harbour; current thinking suggests that this was carried out in the first century BC by the Romans to prevent pirates using the port as a base. On the southwest side of the site (after scrambling over rocks) you can see the impressive remains of the **Roman quarries** where the stone was hewn to build the harbour and surrounding town. Nearer the sea here you can also view huge **fish tanks** carved in the rock where captive fish were maintained alive until they were required.

If you continue on the best of the tracks past the archeological site, you pass under Cyclopean walls to emerge above a small bay. Tempting as it is, this is too sharp and rocky to be able to get to the sea, but it does give you **views** to the north, over Cape Voúxa, which are shielded from Falásarna itself. Towards the top you can see the island of Gramvoúsa (not to be confused with the uninhabitable rock of Pontikonísi, a more distant islet that can sometimes be seen from the beach at Falásarna).

ARRIVAL AND DEPARTURE   FALÁSARNA

By bus In summer there are direct services to and from Haniá via Kastélli (7 daily; 2hr 40min); they make stops at various points along the beach.

ACCOMMODATION

An increasing number of **rooms** places are scattered along the road behind Falásarna, many of them very comfortable; all of the following are well signed, on or just off this road. Quite a few people also **camp** at the back of the beach, either in a couple of small caves or beneath makeshift shelters slung between a few stumpy trees. Pretty much everything here closes from November to March.

Golden Sun Near the end of the road ☎ 28220 41485, 🌐 hotelgoldensun.net. Charming, relatively new place where simple a/c rooms, studios and apartments come with balconies or terraces, many with fine views over the coast. The friendly proprietors can also provide food, and there's a garden and a washing machine for guests' use. Rooms €35, studios €45, apartments €60

Magnolia Apartments Overlooking Big Beach, opposite Plakures ☎ 28220 41407, 🌐 magnolia -apartments.gr. Modern studio and apartment complex with some of the area's finest views from the surrounding gardens and from many of the balconies; well-equipped and comfortable. Rooms €45, apartments €60

Plakures Near the end of the road ☎ 28220 41581, 🌐 plakures.de. The fanciest of the local accommodation with well-appointed balcony rooms and apartments, run

by Greek-German proprietors; can be a bargain out of season. Facilities include minibar, pool, tennis court, bar and restaurant. Breakfast included. €75

Stathis & Anastasia Just off the road, above Golden Sun ☎ 28220 41480, 🌐 anastasiastathis.com. A simple, family-run rooms place in a quiet spot. Rooms (some with sea views) come with a/c, fridge, balcony and an exceptionally warm welcome. €40

Sunset By the car park ☎ 28220 41204, 🌐 sunset.com .gr. With an enviable location, right above the beach, and a good taverna, the long-established *Sunset* has a lot going for it, though some of its rooms (a/c, with balcony) could do with modernization. They also have very basic seafront apartments and, nearby, luxurious two-storey stone villas, sleeping up to six, overlooking the sea. Doubles and apartments €40, villas €150

EATING AND DRINKING

There are seasonal drinks stands and beach bars on the busier stretches of beach. For something more substantial to eat, the places immediately above the beaches are as good as any – all simple, and somewhat overwhelmed on busy weekends. There's an excellent, if rather pricey minimarket – with all the necessities and more – on the road by the junction to Big Beach. A couple of slightly bigger supermarkets and other facilities can be found in Plátanos.

Orange and Blue Bar Signed from the car park near the Sunset hotel ☎ 6943 627 803. A lovely, chilled-out spot above the water, with sandwiches, burgers and snacks by day, cocktails and a widely varied soundtrack at night; there's often live music at weekends and occasional bigger events. April–Oct daily 10am–5am.

Sunset By the car park ☎ 28220 41204. Simple food served on a terrace above the beach with views to die for, though the premium position does mean it can get crazily busy at weekends. The Sunset salad (€7), with

pomegranate, pistachio, figs and avocado, is excellent. April–Oct daily noon–11pm.

Taverna Mouraki Outside Plátanos, right at the top of the road before it heads down to Falásarna ☎ 28220 41666. Welcoming, excellent taverna with spectacular views over the whole coast. Lamb dishes are recommended (€8.50), and house specials include stuffed cuttlefish (€9); there are also mixed meze plates for €11 or €16. Daily 9am–midnight.

Sfinári

Some 9km south of Plátanos the road descends towards the sea at the village of **SFINÁRI** (Σφηνάρι), where a turnoff leads to its beachfront extension a kilometre away. This consists of a quiet pebble beach somewhat spoiled by greenhouses and derelict buildings too close to the water for comfort. It is, however, a very friendly place, with plenty of places to eat by the strand. The southern end of the beach is marginally less cluttered and here a cluster of **tavernas** gather beneath shady tamarisks; they positively encourage **camping**, and there are showers on the beach and free loungers for customers at the tavernas.

ACCOMMODATION AND EATING   SFINÁRI

Captain Fidias Southern end of the waterfront ☎ 28220 41107. The first taverna in line, this is a friendly place where you'll usually see octopus – the house speciality – hanging out to dry by the entrance. All the fish is caught from their own boat, and other tasty dishes include *kakaviá* (fish soup); all of this is priced by weight, or a mixed fish plate will cost you €11, goat in tomato sauce

€8.50. They also have a couple of pleasant, fully equipped apartments in the upper village. March–Oct; taverna daily 9am–midnight. €65

Sunset Southern end of the waterfront ☎ 28220 41627. Good taverna offering fresh fish – stuffed cuttlefish is a house special (€8) – along with locally sourced meat and veg. April–Oct daily 9am–midnight.

Kámbos

Beyond Sfinári the road climbs again for a sinuous 10km to **KÁMBOS (Κάμπος)**. Less developed than its neighbour, there's a **beach** accessible below the village, albeit an hour's hike down a gorge inhabited by colonies of doves. The path, waymarked with yellow and blue dots, sets off from the church by the village square; alternatively there's a steep but driveable track down, apshalted until the last 100m or so. Isolation is the main attraction of the beach, which, close up, is rather stony.

ACCOMMODATION AND EATING   **KÁMBOS**

Taverna Hartzoulakis Main road ☎ 28220 41445. Taverna with an attractive terrace hanging over a little gorge. Much of the produce, including the meat, is home-produced and organic (mains around €8). They also have simple a/c rooms and a rather faded wall-map detailing walking trails around this coast. Daily 9am–11pm. **€35**

Kefáli

Shortly before **KEFÁLI (Κεφάλι)** the road turns inland and just beyond the village the road splits; south to Elafonísi or east towards Élos. Kefáli itself is a charming village, with a wonderful setting perched on a hill looking down the Tiflós valley towards the distant sea, closely linked to villages further inland – it is one of the so-called Innachorí, or "Nine Villages" (see p.305). There's a fine fourteenth-century frescoed **church**, Metamórphosis tou Sotirís (Transfiguration of Christ), signed down a track off the Elafonísi road; it's not easy to find, so ask at one of the roadside tavernas. Inside, the fine **frescoes** depict the betrayal by Judas (whose face has been gouged) and the lowering of Christ from the cross. There is also some interesting and apparently genuine early graffiti, scratched across the paintings. An Englishman, Francis Lerfordes, has marked his contribution with the date 1553, while Turks later inscribed their blasphemous thoughts along with the crescent symbol.

ACCOMMODATION AND EATING   **KEFÁLI**

Taverna-Rooms Panorama Main street ☎ 28220 61198. The best of several tavernas along the main road, this aptly named, welcoming place has a fantastic view from its terrace, where they serve reliable standards (pork *souvláki* €5.50; *soutzoukákia* €6.50) and changing daily specials. Just two well-appointed little rooms in an attractive stone-built house in the old village, with balconies and roof terrace. Daily 8am–11pm. **€40**

Váthi

One kilometre south of Kefáli on the Elafonísi road, **VÁTHI (Βάθη)** has two ancient frescoed **churches**: thirteenth-century Áyios Yeóryios off the central square, and the century-older Mihaíl Arhángelos, just to the south. To reach the former take a track uphill facing the plane tree in the central platía to the left of a drinking fountain. Follow the track uphill for 200m, where it turns into a narrow *kalderími* (ancient footpath) that leads you to the sturdy, overgrown church. Inside, the frescoes are in good condition, with a sensitive portrayal of the Archangel Gabriel and an unusual image of the Virgin and Child in the apse. Mihaíl Arhángelos, at the southern end of the village, has wonderfully preserved early fourteenth-century **frescoes** depicting the Emperor Constantine and his mother Helena, the Fall of Jericho, Christ entering Jerusalem, and a moving portrayal of the betrayal by Judas. Keys for both are kept at the wonderfully old-school *kafenío/pantopolío Kouneni*, just off the square; this generally closes for a siesta from 2–5pm.

Moní Khrysoskalítissa

10km southwest of Kefáli • Daily 7.30am–7.30pm • Museum €2 • ☎ 28220 61261

MONÍ KHRYSOSKALÍTISSA (Μονή Χρυσοσκαλίτισσας; the Monastery of the Virgin of the Golden Step) is a weathered, white-walled nunnery beautifully sited on a rocky promontory above the waves. Today barely functioning, it has reduced from some two hundred residents to a solitary nun and one monk, whose main task seems to be keeping the place acceptable for tourists. The present church – containing a much venerated thousand-year-old icon of the Virgin – dates only from the nineteenth century, but this is an ancient foundation: the first church was built in a cave here in the thirteenth century and recent investigations have turned up evidence of a much earlier Minoan settlement (or shrine) as well. A small **museum** has a few icons along with assorted religious paraphernalia. Look out for the ninety steps that lead to the top of the crag around which the place is built: one of them appears golden (*hrissí skála*) to those who are pure in spirit – a fact that the authors of this guide are unable to verify.

ACCOMMODATION AND EATING
KHRYSOSKALÍTISSA

Glykeria Immediately north of Moní Khrysoskalítissa. 📞 28220 61292, 🌐 glykeria.com. An excellent taverna (mains €7–8) with fine views from its terrace, plus a nearby modern block of tranquil a/c rooms whose balconies have if anything even better sea views. There's also a good-sized pool and gardens. April–Oct; taverna daily 8am–11pm. €55

Elafonísi

Just over 5km south of Moní Khrysoskalítissa, the tiny uninhabited islet of **ELAFONÍSI** (Ελαφονήσι) lies marooned on the edge of a gloriously scenic turquoise lagoon. The almost tropical waters sheltered by the islet boast white sand tinged pink by coral, aquamarine waters, salt-encrusted rock pools and bright-red starfish. The water is incredibly warm, calm and shallow and the islet itself is a short wade across the sand bar. There are more beaches on its far side (with waves), along with the odd ruined wall and a monument to Australian sailors shipwrecked here in 1907.

It's all too easy to get here, a fact reflected in the huge number of visitors who do so, and at peak times Elafonísi can be unbearably jammed. While the arrival of crowds has brought lines of sun umbrellas and loungers to the **beach**, there's little else in the way of infrastructure; the area is a national park, so no permanent structures can be erected. There are stalls selling cold drinks and basic food, and there are portable toilets and an incongruous phone box, but if you're here on a day-trip, the best option is to bring your own picnic.

ARRIVAL AND DEPARTURE
ELAFONÍSI

By bus In summer there are daily buses from Haniá (9am; 2hr 15min), Kastélli (10am; 1hr 20min) and Paleóhora (10am; 1hr), with a return at the end of the day. There are also coach tours from all over the west of the island.
By boat In summer there's a daily boat trip from Paleóhora

(10am, returning 4.30pm; 1hr).
By car For drivers the inland route is faster and easier, but a visit also gives you the chance to complete a circuit of the west (see p.297). Beware the well-signed route to Sklavopoúla, which is exceptionally tough going (see p.313).

ACCOMMODATION AND EATING

Elafonisi Resort On the approach road to the beach 📞 28220 61274, 🌐 elafonisi-resort.com. Probably the best choice here, with a good taverna (meat mains €8.80, also pricey fresh fish, around €14, and cheaper veg dishes) and a/c balcony rooms and studios, many with sea views, dispersed across an extensive site. April–Oct; taverna daily 8am–midnight. Doubles €40, studios €55

Panorama On the approach road to the beach 📞 28220 61548, 🌐 elafonisi-village.gr. The closest place to the beach, which means the taverna terrace has much the best views here – looking out over the beach – though the range of food is limited to salads, grills (chicken €7.50) and frozen pizza. The a/c rooms too, known as *Elafonisi Village*, are less enticing than they first appear. April–Oct; taverna daily 8.30am–10.30pm. €50

WALKS FROM ELAFONÍSI

Continuing south from Elafonísi, the E4 **coastal path** to Paleóhora (about 17km away) is reasonably well marked, but it's a tough walk, especially in the early stages, with one hair-raising section above a sheer drop near the hill of Ktista (6km out), which is definitely not for the faint-hearted. Check the route before you set out, and don't venture this way alone, or without plentiful water. You could also hike up the track heading inland to **Sklavopoúla**, 13km away (see p.313), from where paved roads head on towards Paleóhora.

4

Kastélli

...south of Kastélli Kissámou passes through some of the most fertile
...island. Here, lush **woodland** watered by tumbling streams is a haven for
...flora and fauna, and in the sturdy farming villages there are plenty of
...o take in the local wildlife, or to do some walking in the oleander- and
...d hills and along numerous gorges.

Voulgáro and around

VOULGÁRO (Βουλγάρω) is a large village astride the main road south, with an
exceptional number of cafés, restaurants and stalls selling honey and olive oil. A minor
diversion here allows you to stretch your legs in search of the ancient church of Áyios
Nikólaos at **MOURÍ** (Μουρί), a hilltop village about 5km away, signed from the centre
of Voulgáro. The chapel is further signed up a track as you enter the village; follow this
for 500m and you crest a ridge, suddenly revealing fine views northwards over the Gulf
of Kissámou. The whitewashed **church** (normally unlocked) sits alone in an entirely
rural setting, surrounded by olive groves and vineyards, often with birds of prey soaring
overhead. Inside, the **fresco fragments** – especially those of Áyios Pandeleímon and the
scenes from the Bible – are extremely fine.

Topólia Gorge

As you pass through **TOPÓLIA** (Τοπόλια), 3km beyond Voulgháro, it seems just another
large village strung along the road. Pull over, however, and follow one of the many
signs to the upper village, and in a few paces you feel as if you've stepped back fifty
years; there's a dramatic change of pace as you suddenly find yourself in streets designed
for pack-animals rather than cars, and surrounded by the little-changed life of rural
Crete. One thing to seek out here is the twin-aisled **church of Ayía Paraskeví**, with
frescoes from the late Byzantine period.

Beyond the village the road enters the dramatic **Topólia Gorge**, short, but in its way
among the most imposing on the island. The road sticks high to the western edge, at
one point passing through a single-file tunnel, controlled by lights. Far below, it's a
relatively easy **walk** through the gorge, just an hour or so from Topólia to
Katsomatádhos; black-and-yellow waymarks in Topólia village will lead you down into
the valley and through the gorge. Keep an eye out for the vultures that nest in the
surrounding cliffs.

Katsomatádhos

The hamlet of **KATSOMATÁDHOS** (Κατσοματάδος) marks the bottom end of the Topólia
Gorge, with a couple of excellent tavernas (and even rooms) that make an enjoyable
spot to break the journey. If you stay longer there are a number of potential hikes in
addition to the gorge walk, many of which are signed. The most obvious is the
ten-minute path to the **Cave of Ayía Sofía** (daily 8am–8.30pm; free). You can also get
here from the road through the gorge, where a well-signed stairway cut into the rock
offers a muscle-taxing short climb to the cave, one of the largest on Crete. Remains
found here date its usage back to Neolithic times, and it now shelters a small chapel,
along with stalactites, stalagmites and its present residents, a colony of bats. Other local
walks include a path to Miliá (see below), about an hour's climb, and the ascent of
Koproúla, the highest peak hereabouts.

Miliá

A couple of kilometres south of Katsomatádhos, a beautifully scenic diversion would
take you on backroads, through leafy hills and farming villages, along the western flank
of the Tiflós valley via **Vlátos**, to rejoin the main road at Élos. Not far up here, a road is
signed to the remarkable "eco-tourist" village of **MILIÁ** (Μηλιά). The precipitous track,
only the first half of which is surfaced, climbs dizzily along the shoulder of Mount

4

Kefáli for 5km, offering magnificent views over the chestnut- and olive-clad valley below. This eventually arrives at a car park, from where a path leads into a stunningly picturesque hamlet of stone houses, once occupied by farmers and shepherds. The isolation of the village eventually led to its abandonment around a century ago until, in the early 1980s, a relative of a former inhabitant proposed to restore the whole place as a working village, welcoming visitors. Other families who owned ruined houses joined in and a co-operative was formed, backed by EU money. Stonemasons skilled in building traditional dwellings were brought over from the Peloponnese and helped to recreate what you now see: an almost too perfect village with solid stone houses on many levels overlooking a verdant cleft.

You should soon locate the house that serves as the community centre and **bar-taverna** (see p.306). Visitors are welcome to get involved in the farming activities, including planting and sowing as well as chestnut-, olive- and apple-harvesting (Miliá means "apple tree" in Greek), and there are occasionally cookery courses and other activities – you can even help make *rakí* at the village's still. Otherwise you can **walk** in the nearby hills – the easier paths are signed – or simply contemplate the natural surroundings; nights up here are truly magical.

Élos

A kilometre beyond the turn-off for Vlátos and Miliá there's a turn on the left for Strovlés and Voutás, leading to the south coast resort of Paleóhora (see p.308). The main route continues southwest past slopes covered with magnificent stands of chestnut, plane and other deciduous trees. Chestnuts are a major local crop, and the picturesque village of **ÉLOS** ('Ελος), 4km along, is the chief village of the **Innachorí** – the "Nine Villages" – at the centre of the **chestnut-growing** region. Even at the height of summer, this is a wonderfully refreshing place, and it's easy to forget just how high you are here – the mountains to the south rise to about 1200m. Behind the village's *Kastanofolia* taverna (see p.306) there is an impressive section of aqueduct, claimed to be Roman (though perhaps more likely Turkish). A path leads up the stream here to the fourteenth-century Byzantine **chapel of Áyios Yeóryios**, whose damaged frescoes include an impressive *Pantokrátor* in the apse; if it's closed, the key should be available from the taverna. The great event in Élos's year is the annual **chestnut festival** in late October.

Perivólia

Some 5km southwest of Élos, a turn on the left indicates a sharp descent to the picturesque hamlet of **PERIVÓLIA** (Περιβόλια), tucked into the folds of a high gorge beneath the northern flank of Mount Áyios Díkeos Ióv (Job the Just). The village is a verdant oasis with charming narrow streets punctuated by simple white-walled dwellings and smallholdings overflowing with vigorously sprouting vegetables. Park any vehicle where you cross a bridge at the foot of the descent and, turning right, continue on foot to the bottom of the village and a fountain, near a bust to one of the noted local *pallikári* (guerrilla fighters) of the nineteenth century, Anagnostis Skalidis.

Anagnostis Skalidis Museum

Near the fountain, Perivólia • Daily 10am–1pm & 5–8pm • €1 • ☎ 28220 61544

The small **museum** was assembled by one of Anagnostis Skalidis' descendants, Zacharia Skalidis. An amiable man who speaks only Greek, he will be delighted to show you around his collection, which includes lots of atmospheric photos from a Crete long gone, as well as old guns, letters and coins.

ACCOMMODATION AND EATING	INLAND FROM KASTÉLLI

KATSOMATÁDHOS

★**Arhondas** Just below the main road, at the gorge entry ☎ 28220 51531. Like many of the best Cretan tavernas, *Arhondas* doesn't look special at all, with rickety wooden tables haphazardly spread over a concrete terrace and under trees in the garden. But the food, almost all of which is organic and from their or their neighbours' farms, bursts with flavour; a simple meal of grilled pork chops, accompanied by fried courgettes, Greek salad (with home-made *mizíthra* cheese), hand-cut chips and freshly baked bread, is a revelation. Meat dishes cost €7–8. They also have clean and comfy rooms in an utterly rural setting, with use of a communal kitchen and washing machine; and they sell their own olives, olive oil and preserves. Daily 10am–midnight. **€30**

Taverna Oasis On the main road ☎ 6945 082 619. Pleasant a/c en-suite rooms with views over the gorge. The taverna is good, too, offering local food including quite a few vegetarian possibilities; mains €8. The proprietors can advise on walking routes in the area, and there's a track down into the gorge next to the taverna. March–Oct daily 9am–11pm. **€25**

VLÁTOS

Taverna Platania Down a track off the Vlátos road, about 1km from the turn-off ☎ 28220 51406. A rural taverna, surrounded by venerable olive and vast monumental plane trees. With tables spread out beneath the planes, this friendly hideaway serves up good meat and mezédhes – the grilled lamb dishes (around €8) are recommended – though at times it can feel very empty, as much of its business comes from mammoth wedding feasts. March–Oct daily 9am–midnight.

MILIÁ

★ **Miliá Eco Village** 3km above Vlátos village ☎ 28210 46774, ⊛ milia.gr. The rustic accommodation in Miliá varies from small "semi-detached" cottages to houses for four, but all are delightful, with huge fireplaces (wood provided in winter) and stone ovens. There's solar hot water but no mains electricity – candles illuminate the rooms and the restaurant in the evening – and the only concession to modernity is a satellite internet connection in the bar. Everything served in the taverna (booking advised) is local, and much of it produced in the village; there are excellent traditional soups, stews and salads (meat dishes €8.50–11, veg €6.50–7.50). Buffet breakfast included, featuring freshly baked bread with their own fruit, cheese and preserves. Daily noon–9.30pm. **€75**

ÉLOS

Taverna Kamares In the centre of the village ☎ 28220 61332. The *Kastanofolia* across the road tends to grab all the attention, but this is a very friendly alternative for traditional Cretan cooking, with valley views from the terrace; the lamb chops (€8) and goat dishes are recommended (with potatoes and chestnuts, €8.50). Daily 7am–midnight.

Taverna-Rooms Kastanofolia In the centre of the village ☎ 28220 61258. Shaded by plane, eucalyptus and, of course, chestnut trees, *Kastanofolia* ("Chestnut Den") is a lovely-looking place, with a terrace above the brook and ducks swimming by. However, it is often overrun by coach parties, when service can suffer badly; at quieter times the simple food is pretty good (*papoutsákia*, stuffed aubergine, €8; chicken *souvláki* €7). They also have some fairly basic rooms. Daily 7am–midnight. **€35**

Sélinos

Despite its isolation from the north and centre of the island, the eparchy (province) of **SÉLINOS** (Σέλινο), stretching roughly from the village of Flória to the south coast, has played a significant role in the island's history since ancient times. As early as the third century BC several of the communities here were important enough to form a confederation with Górtys (see p.100) and Cyrenaica, in Libya, and under the Romans, cities such as **Lissos**, **Elyros** and **Syia** (modern Sóuyia) prospered greatly. This distinguished past laid the foundations for the communal pride that created the scores of frescoed **Byzantine churches** here, perhaps the main reason to visit inland Sélinos today. One of the glories of Crete, every village seems to offer at least one example, while some have as many as three or more. We have detailed some wonderful examples in this account, but many more small churches can be found throughout the whole area, particularly if you get off the road into the

---

ROUTES TO THE SOUTHWEST COAST

Though you can approach from Kastélli, the fastest and most direct routes into Sélinos and to the south coast resorts start further east. For **Sóuyia**, the direct approach is via Alikianós (see p.270), on a road that diverges from the north-coast highway immediately west of Haniá. For **Paleóhora** the main road turns off about 20km further west, outside Tavronítis, heading south via Voukoliés.

smaller villages. Few, if any, of them will be open when you arrive – but express an interest at the nearest *kafenío* or to a local passer-by and it rarely takes long to hunt out the priest or someone else with a key.

Flória

FLÓRIA (**Φλώρια**), roughly halfway across the island on the Paleóhora road, is divided into two halves: Káto (lower) Flória, straddling the road, and Apáno (upper) Flório above it. The upper village has the church of Áyii Patéres (the Holy Fathers), although here only fresco fragments remain. In the lower village, **Áyios Yeóryios** preserves thirteen panels of fine fifteenth-century frescoes. To reach it, entering from the north end of the village, go down a lane to the right of the second taverna you pass on the right. After about 600m you'll come to a small footbridge over a dry stream bed; cross this and after 50m veer left at a fork to follow the path leading to the church. Near the first taverna (the better of the pair), two war memorials – one German, one Greek – face each other across the road, serving as grim reminders of the terrible atrocities that happened here during World War II.

Kándanos and around

KÁNDANOS (**Κάντανος**), 9km south of Flória and approached along a verdant valley planted with olives, is the chief village of Sélinos (though it's a great deal smaller than Paleóhora), and makes an appealing, quiet place to stop for coffee or a meal. Despite an ancient name that goes back to Dorian times and the existence of twenty or more Byzantine **churches** in the immediate vicinity (it was the seat of a bishop throughout the Byzantine and Venetian periods), the village buildings are almost entirely new, for the place was razed to the ground by the Germans for its role in the **wartime resistance**. In 1941, after the German army had taken Máleme (see p.263), troops were dispatched urgently along this road to prevent the Allies landing reinforcements at Paleóhora. The resistance fighters of Kándanos determined to stop them, and despite a ferocious pitched battle the Germans could not break through for two crucial days. In retribution the Germans utterly destroyed the village. The original sign erected at the time is today preserved in the museum (currently closed) but a copy stands on a war memorial in the square – in German and Greek it reads: "Here stood Kándanos, destroyed in retribution for the murder of 25 German soldiers, and never to be rebuilt again."

The village that arose defiantly from the ashes after World War II is today an easygoing place, with attractive cafés and tavernas around its main square. Here you may be able to pick up a copy of a free **map**, detailing local sights including all the churches in the surrounding area. On the outskirts is a waterworks, given to the village by the Germans after the war as an act of reconciliation. Many of the German military who served here have since returned to forge friendships with their erstwhile adversaries.

The Kándanos churches

Four Byzantine **churches** are within a couple of minutes' stroll of the main road through Kándanos. Approaching from the north there are good but damaged frescoes at the restored **Mihaíl Arhángelos**, signed to the east up a lane on the northern edge of the village, and in the charming small white chapel of **Áyios Mámas**, 1km away through the olive groves, signed down a road by the petrol station, opposite the village's main road junction. **Ayía Ekateríni**, signed off the main street near the central platía, is a beautiful old building with faded fresco fragments. The best of all, though, is **Áyios Ioánnis**, another small white church with superb fresco fragments, signed downhill off the Paleóhora road on the southern edge of the village, around 1km from the road.

Anisaráki

A short detour from Kándanos climbs a couple of kilometres east to **ANISARÁKI** (**Ανισαράκι**), on a minor mountain road which is also a short-cut to Soúyia via Teménia (see p.314). Halfway up to Anisaráki, in the hamlet of **Koufalotós**, the chapel of **Áyios Mihaíl Arhángelos** has fourteenth-century paintings by the Cretan master Ioannis Pagomenos. The chapel is located down a track on the left, across a stream. Anisaráki itself has more fine frescoes in the fifteenth-century churches of **Ayía Ánna** (signed on the left in an olive grove as you enter), with a rare stone iconostasis, **Panayía** and **Ayía Paraskeví** (both signed from the centre).

South of Kándanos

Beyond Kándanos the main road south bypasses several more villages with frescoed churches: Áyios Yeóryios, in **Plemenianá**, has paintings dating from the fifteenth century, while **Kakodhíki**, known for its curative springs, has several churches nearby. These include the very ancient chapel of **Mihaíl Arhángelos**, probably early thirteenth-century, beside the modern church of Ayía Triádha, and the hilltop Áyios Isidhóros, with magnificent views and frescoes defaced by the Turks. **Kádhros**, some 9km south of Kándanos, has the churches of Ioánnis Chrysóstomos and the **Panayía** (reached via a downhill path beside a gaily decorated *kafenío*; key from the house near the church), whose fine frescoes are almost complete.

Paleóhora

PALEÓHORA (**Παλαιόχωρα**) was known originally as Kastél Selínou – the castle of Sélinos – and for much of its history was no more than that, a castle. Built by the Venetians in 1279, the fort was destroyed by Barbarossa in 1539 and never properly reconstructed even when the small port grew up beneath it. The ruins are still perched at the bulbous end of the headland now occupied by the settlement of Paleóhora – at its narrowest a bare four blocks across from the harbour on one side to the beach on the other.

Today, the village has become a small town and an enjoyably laidback, end-of-the-line resort, helped by superb and extensive sands and by the fact that there are no big hotels, and almost all the rooms and restaurants are still owned and run by local families. Warm right through the winter, this out-of-season backwater makes an excellent place to rent an inexpensive apartment long-term. Other than head for the beach, eat and drink, there's not a great deal to see or do here, which of course is a major part of its attraction. However, there are plenty of trips on offer (see p.310), as well as attractive **walks** inland, to charming villages like Ánidhri and Azoyirés (see p.313), or along the coast in either direction.

PALEÓHORA ORIENTATION

The main road from Kándanos leads you into a eucalyptus-lined avenue that becomes Paleóhora's single main street, **Odhós Venizélos**, lined with taverna after café after bar. If you come from the west, on the roads via Voutás or Sarakína, you'll emerge on the road behind the sandy western beach, by the post office. Bisecting the village north to south, **Venizélos** is Paleóhora's vibrant soul, and on summer evenings its central stretch is closed to traffic, brightly illuminated and filled to overflowing as the bar and restaurant tables spill across the pavement and encroach onto the road. From the main street, nothing is further than a five-minute walk away: straight ahead (south) lies the **castle** with a virtually empty marina beyond it; to the left (east) is the aptly named **Pebble Beach**, with its harbour from where boats to Soúyia and Gávdhos depart; to the right (west) are the broad sands of the fabulous **Sandy Beach**, where you'll find quite a few hotels.

CAFÉS & RESTAURANTS

Akrogiali	8
Caravella	3
Methexis	1
Oriental Bay	9
Pizzeria Niki	5
Samariá	7
Taverna Grameno	10
The Third Eye	4
Vakakis Bakery	6
Water's Edge Café	2

SHOP

To Delfini	1

ACCOMMODATION

Anonymous Homestay	5
Aris	2
Camping Grammeno	9
Camping Paleohora	7
Caravella Luxury Apartments	8
Castello Rooms	3
Haris Studios	1
Third Eye Rooms	4
Villa Anna	6

BARS & CLUBS

Ayios Music Café	2
Jetée	6
Monica's Kafenio	5
Nostos Bar	3
Pearl Cavo	7
Skala	1
Yianni's Place	4

OLD TOWN

Castle

Jetty

KONTEKAKI

Sandy Beach

Pebble Beach

Old Dhimarhio

VENIZELOS

Bus Station

Cinema

PALEÓHORA

Paleóhora castle

In town you can check out the **castle**, for the views back over town, or walk right around the end of the promontory to return to the beach on the other side. Neither of these options is as appealing as it might be, since the fortress itself is little more than a hillock ringed with broken walls, while a new concrete marina and some unsightly harbour buildings dominate the point. Heading up towards the castle, where steps lead up from the church, you'll see the oldest parts of town, to the south of the harbour.

The beaches

Of the beaches, the western **Sandy Beach** is more impressive: magnificently broad and sandy, lined with tamarisks and supplied with showers, on a bay with excellent, easy windsurfing. **Pebble Beach**, facing east, is at first sight a much less attractive proposition. However, this eastern side is far livelier at night, when the beachfront promenade rivals the main street for action and choice of eating; the cafés and restaurants over here have a stunning view of the moon rising over the mountains. The beach is also more sheltered when the wind is blowing, and if you venture far enough north, away from town, you'll even find some sand.

ARRIVAL AND GETTING AROUND

PALEÓHORA

By bus The bus terminus is at the northern end of Venizélos. The Omalós bus takes you to both the Ayía Iríni and Samariá gorges, and connects in Ayía Iríni with buses to Soúyia.

Destinations Elafonísi (daily at 10am; 1hr); Haniá (4 daily; 2hr); Koundoúra (for local beaches to the west; 4 daily; 20min); Omalós (3 daily, first at 6.15am; 1hr 45min).

By boat or ferry Ferries dock on the east side of town, at the jetty at the bottom of Pebble Beach, as does the smaller boat to Elafonísi and any tour boats. Summer schedules are below, but confirm times with any of the local travel agencies, or online (ⓦanendyk.gr); the ferries run a restricted schedule year-round. From Ayía Rouméli there

are onward ferries to Loutró and Hóra Sfákion.

Destinations Ayía Rouméli (April–Oct daily 8.30am; 1hr 20min) via Soúyia (30min); Elafonísi (April–Oct daily 10am, returning 4.30pm; 1hr); Gávdhos (April–Oct Mon & Wed 8.30am; 4hr).

By taxi There's a taxi office just by the ferry dock (☎ 28230 41128, ⓦpaleochora-taxi.com), and another at the top of Venizélos near the bus station (☎ 28230 41368).

Bike rental Nikos (daily 9am–3pm & 6–10pm; ☎ 6988 480 414), towards the northern end of Venizélos, has good mountain bikes, though you can also rent them from the Notos and Sabine travel agencies (see below).

Car rental You can rent a car or motorbike at the Notos and Sabine travel agencies (see below).

INFORMATION AND ACTIVITIES

Tourist information The helpful municipal tourist office (June–Sept Mon & Wed–Sun 8am–2pm; ☎ 28230 41507) is in a cabin fronting Pebble Beach.

Travel agencies Notos Travel (☎ 28230 42005, ⓦnotoscar .com), on Venizélos opposite the old town hall, has a finger in every pie, with a laundry and internet access as well as exchange, vehicle rental, tours and more. Sabine Travel (☎ 28230 42105, ⓦhermescar.gr), virtually next door, also has trips, exchange and vehicle rental. Selino Travel (☎ 28230 42272), on Kontekáki just up from the harbour, is a little less frenetic and good for the latest ferry updates.

Boat trips Local boat trips include dolphin-spotting cruises (though despite claims of 70 percent likelihood,

these don't seem to have a very high success rate), plus excursions to Lissós, Elafonísi, Samariá and Gramvoúsa. Contact any of the travel agents.

Diving and adventure sports Nireas Adventures (☎ 6940 111 165, ⓦnireasadventures.com) can take you scuba diving or snorkelling, and also organize canyoning and hiking trips.

Walking There are organized gorge walks of Samariá and Ayía Iríni; enquire at one of the travel agencies. It's possible to do these yourself by bus, with a service heading for Omalós via Ayía Iríni daily at 6.15am throughout the summer. You can then get the boat back from Ayía Rouméli or Soúyia in the late afternoon.

ACCOMMODATION

Anonymous Homestay In a backstreet off Venizélos ☎ 28230 41509, ⓦcityofpaleochora.gr. Among the least expensive places in town, and something of a travellers' meeting place. Simple rooms, with use of a communal kitchen, off a charming garden courtyard, plus two two-bedroom apartments. A/c €5 extra. Doubles €25, apartments €50

★**Aris** Last place on the upper road at the south end of the peninsula, beneath the castle ☎ 28230 41502, ⓦarishotel.gr. Charming, welcoming and peaceful hotel, newly and artistically renovated with particularly lovely handmade wooden headboards. A/c rooms have balconies, many with sea views, others over the lush gardens, along with fridge and tea- and coffee-making facilities (but no TV), and there's an excellent breakfast available. €50

Camping Grammeno 4km along the coast to the west ☎ 6979 228 601, ⓦgrammenocamping.gr. Friendly campsite with youthful management, close to a truly beautiful beach and some good tavernas. Two people plus tent and car €21

Camping Paleohora 2km northeast of the centre, reached along the road behind Pebble Beach ☎ 28230

41120, ⓦcampingpaleochora.eu.ki. Attractively sited in an olive grove close to the beach, with plenty of shade. The only drawback here is the bone-hard terrain. Two people plus tent and car €16

Caravella Luxury Apartments Reached via the turn-off for Voutás at the northwest end of town ☎ 28230 41131, ⓦcaravella.gr. On a rise above the resort, these ultramodern luxury apartments have large terraces or balconies with stunning views and come with marble floors, lounge (some with wood-burning stove) and satellite TV, plus a fully equipped kitchen. €88

★**Castello Rooms** Overlooking the southern end of Sandy Beach ☎ 28230 41143. Exceptionally friendly place, most of whose simple rooms come with a/c and fridge and have balconies overlooking the beach; a few rooms at the back without view are less expensive (singles available too), and you can still enjoy the views from the terrace taverna. €37

Haris Studios On the seafront below the east side of the castle ☎ 28230 42438, ⓦpaleochora-holidays .com. A friendly Cretan-Scottish-run place with some fairly simple a/c studios close to the water, most with great sea views, and a new block (*Yiorgos Studios*) of excellent,

well-equipped modern studios and apartments with a garden, roof terrace and small pool (which all guests can use) set further back. Studios €45, apartments €50
Third Eye Rooms Inland from Sandy Beach ☏ 28230 41234, ⊚thethirdeye-paleochora.com. Budget a/c rooms and apartments attached to and directly behind the restaurant of the same name, with fridge and balcony, some with sea view. Larger family apartments (sleeping 5) come with kitchen. Doubles €25, apartments €40
Villa Anna In a broad side street off Sandy Beach near the post office ☏ 28103 46428, ⊚villaanna-paleochora .com. Somewhat pricey but very pleasant apartments for four to six people – large, nicely furnished, all with kitchen and a/c, and surrounded by lush gardens. €60

EATING

Akrogiali Pebble Beach ☏ 28230 41312. Attractively old-fashioned taverna among the glossier places on Pebble Beach, with a solidly traditional menu of Greek standards; *briám* €5, lamb €7, beef *stifádho* €8. April–Oct daily noon–11pm.

★**Caravella** Old town seafront, just south of the ferry jetty ☏ 28230 41131. Paleóhora's best seafood restaurant, with a waterfront terrace. All the fish is caught locally (and sold by weight; typically around €12 a portion), and both cooking and service are excellent, as are their house wines, including a very tasty French-style muscatel dessert wine from the Sélinos village of Máza. They also serve some meat (mains €7.50–8.50), plus a daily selection of *mayireftá* (pre-cooked dishes). April–Nov daily 9am–11.30pm.

Methexis Far southern end of the eastern seafront ☏ 28230 41431. Hugely popular new taverna above a tiny pebbly beach, where it has its own beach bar. Food is served on a terrace higher up and is traditional with a twist; daily specials (€7–8) might be goat with green beans, or rabbit with chestnuts and olives. Also good salads, inexpensive house wine and a decent wine list. April–Oct daily 1–11.30pm.

★**Oriental Bay** Northern end of Pebble Beach ☏ 28230 41322. With an inviting, tamarisk-shaded terrace fronting the sea, *Oriental Bay* serves some of the best traditional food in town, with daily specials such as *arnáki kokkinistó* (lamb stewed with tomatoes, onion and garlic, €7) stuffed courgette flowers (€5) or "granny's meatballs" €9. There's occasional live music and also fresh juices and breakfasts. April–Oct daily noon–11pm.

Pizzeria Niki Off the south side of Kontekáki ☏ 28230 41532. An attractive, bougainvillea-filled courtyard setting for excellent wood-fired pizzas (€6.50–7.50), as well as pasta and salads. May–Oct daily noon–midnight.

Samariá Behind the old Dhimarhio building ☏ 28230 41572. Elegant taverna in an atmospheric roofless ruin; in winter a canvas roof is unfurled and they light the fires. The traditional Cretan cuisine is excellent; visit the kitchen to see what's cooking, which might include specials such as *arní tsighariasto* (lamb in olive oil casserole) or goat *stifádho* (stewed with onions) for around €9 each. Daily 6–11pm.

★**Taverna Grameno** 3km west towards Koundourá along the coast road, near Graméno beach ☏ 28230 41505. Perhaps the area's most authentic Cretan restaurant, this is a friendly garden taverna with a play area for kids, and the cooking is outstanding – take a look in the kitchen for what is seasonal and fresh. Mains are €7–8, or try the excellent mixed meze for two (though it would easily feed three; meat €28, fish €30). April–Oct daily noon–midnight.

The Third Eye Inland from Sandy Beach ☏ 28230 42223, ⊚thethirdeye-paleochora.com. Excellent vegetarian restaurant run by a Greek-New Zealand couple. It's worth putting up with the sometimes brusque service for great food and spices rarely seen on Crete, from curries to *gado-gado* and bean salads, as well as more conventional Greek dishes; mains around €7 and healthy breakfasts for €4–5. The world music background sounds go well with the cuisine, and there are regular concerts of *lyra*, Greek and Asian music in summer. April–Oct daily 8am–3pm & 6–11pm.

Vakakis Bakery Bottom of Kontekáki, facing the jetty ☏ 28230 41850. This long-established bakery has now opened a café where you can enjoy their cakes, pies and pastries, as well as sandwiches, coffee and ice cream. Also a handy place to grab some breakfast if you're leaving on the ferry. Daily 7am–11pm.

Water's Edge Café On the seafront below the east side of the castle, at Haris Studios ☏ 28230 42438. As well as having a lovely sea-view terrace for breakfasts, snacks and drinks, the *Water's Edge* serves dinner on Saturdays (booking recommended, around €18–20 for 3 courses) with a limited range of freshly made, excellent dishes. Daily 8am–midnight.

DRINKING, NIGHTLIFE AND ENTERTAINMENT

Paleóhora clings to its village origins, and has no pretensions to be anything other than a tranquil seaside resort with family appeal: if you're looking for all-night clubs and raucous bars you've come to the wrong place. Most **bars** keep their volume well down after dark; many of the most popular of these are shoehorned into the area around the Venizélos–Kontekáki junction and down towards the harbour. Nightly showings at the open-air **cinema**, Cine Attikon, tucked away in the northern backstreets, are wonderfully atmospheric; most of their recent-release films are in English and programmes (advertised on billboards outside the cinema and along Venizélos; tickets €5) change daily.

4

Ayios Music Café Corner of Venizélos and Kontekáki ☎ 28230 41258, 🌐 agiosbar.gr. Café and central meeting place by day, cocktail bar at night, when there's decent music too. April–Oct daily noon–2am.

Jetée Sandy Beach, right on the sand near the post office ☎ 28230 83018. A classy, quiet spot to linger over a sundowner, with cocktails and a jazzy soundtrack, and often lively later on; occasional "beach party" events in high summer. Also open all day with a breakfast buffet (8–11am, €7) and snacks. April–Oct daily 8am–3am.

★**Monica's Kafenío** Venizélos 39, slightly north of the old Town Hall. Opening at dawn to give the fishermen their morning coffee, this is a plain and simple traditional *kafenío* where the (Greek) coffee is excellent and an ouzo (and other drinks) comes with a free meze. Daily 6am–1am.

Nostos Bar Pebble Beach ☎ 28230 42145. The liveliest late-night joint in town, with a chilled club atmosphere and outside courtyard bar; doesn't really get lively until near midnight. June–Oct daily 6.30pm–5am.

Pearl Cavo 1km or so from the north end of Pebble Beach ☎ 28230 43127. Beach bar by day, with chilled sounds, but comes into its own by night, when it's far enough from town to be able to make some noise; occasional live music and DJ sets. In the evenings a beaten-up shuttle bus runs from the ferry jetty. May–Sept daily 11am–4am.

Skala By the ferry jetty ☎ 28230 41671. In the morning this is one of the town's best spots for breakfast; later the drinks get stronger and there's live music on Monday nights. April–Oct daily 8am–3am.

Yianni's Place Venizélos near the old Town Hall ☎ 28230 41396. Café/ouzerí with tables spread across the main street (good for people-watching) and whose eponymous proprietor is one of the town's characters. Daily 10am–1am.

SHOPPING

Supermarkets There are a couple of large supermarkets behind Sandy Beach.

To Delfíni Kontekáki. This bookshop sells foreign newspapers, also available at the well-stocked *períptero* on Venizélos. To Delfíni also has a good selection of books in English, including local walking guides.

DIRECTORY

Banks There are several banks with ATMs on Kontekáki west of Venizélos and on Venizélos itself, north of the town hall.

Laundry At Notos Travel (see p.310).

Post office On the road behind Sandy Beach (Mon–Fri 7.30am–2pm).

West of Paleóhora

The coastline **west of Paleóhora**, where you can get a bus as far as the farming centre of **Koundourá**, is an uneasy mix of tourist development and polytunnel agriculture, rarely very attractive but with a number of worthwhile little coves and beaches along the way. Much the best of the beaches is **Graméno**, after about 5km, where a small peninsula shelters lagoon-like water and there's a glorious sandy beach with trees for shade. There are a couple of rooms places here, as well as *Taverna Grameno* and the campsite (see p.310). Beyond Koundourá, a driveable track continues, petering out shortly after aptly named, pebbly **Kríos** beach ("cold", which the water here generally is, thanks to underwater springs). The E4 path to Elafonísi (see p.303) leads onward from here.

The Pelekaniotikós valley

Northwest from Paleóhora a lovely, deserted drive tracks the valley of the River Pelekaniotikós through a string of charming Sélinos hamlets. At **Voutás**, 12km northwest of Paleóhora, you can choose one of two routes to circle back to the coast. A left turn will take you to the isolated village of Sklavopoúla and its wonderful frescoed **churches** (see opposite), from where you can drop directly down to the coast at Koundourá. Straight ahead, the road winds northwards through dramatic mountain scenery to join the route that cuts across from the far west to Paleóhora, a couple of kilometres south of **Stróvles**. Keep going north here and you'll reach the Élos road (see p.305); south takes you back towards Paleóhora and the main road from Haniá.

On the Sklavopoúla route, 1km before the village of Kítiros, the small fourteenth-century church of **Ayía Paraskeví** is worth a stop to see some faded frescoes on its rear

THE SKLAVOPOÚLA CHURCHES

As you come in to the village of Sklavopoúla from the east you pass the church of **Áyios Yeóryios**, next to a school playground on the left, with some fine frescoes dating from the thirteenth century. To get the key go to the second house below the school, the home of Petros, the guardian. Continuing into the village, two other notable churches (usually open) are reached down a path next to the primitive **kafenío/village shop** – itself something not to be missed. Head downhill along a very rough ancient *kalderími* (cobbled track), running the gamut of chained dogs, for 200m or so, through a farm where if anyone is around you could ask further directions. The church of the **Panayía** is obvious, just beyond the farm, with frescoes including superb gospel scenes and a portrait of the donor. **Sotíros Christós** is less easy to find, hidden away in the fields.

wall; one has a remarkably lurid portrayal of hell with devils putting sinners into the flames while others are being crushed by serpents.

Sklavopoúla

SKLAVOPOÚLA (Σκλαβοπούλα), one of the remotest communities in the Sélinos at an altitude of 640m, is, unexpectedly, a place with a considerable history. The nineteenth-century English traveller Robert Pashley visited and identified Sklavopoúla as the site of Doulópolis, a Dorian city renowned for its military prowess. The village's present name ("Village of the Slavs") may stem from a resettlement of Slavs here by Nikiforos Fokas (see p.333) following his reconquest of Crete from the Saracens in 961. There are no less than seven **churches** in the vicinity, all with wall paintings (see box above). Beware the enticing road **signs to Elafonísi** near the southern edge of the village; a route also marked on many maps. It is just about possible to drive this in a regular car but it requires great care, and will take around 45 minutes to cover 13km.

East of Paleóhora

East of Paleóhora several routes head towards Soúyia, though if you want to follow the **coast** you'll have to do so on foot. Here a driveable dirt road continues beyond the *Camping Paleohora* campsite for a couple of kilometres to **Yialaskári** beach, an attractive spot with sunloungers and a seasonal *kantína*. Beyond, the **E4 path** (see p.314) traces the shore, passing a succession of grey pebble strips with fewer people clad in fewer clothes the further you venture.

Ánidhri

Some 6km east of Paleóhora, on the paved road that climbs beyond the campsite, **ÁNIDHRI (Άνιδρι)** is a particularly beautiful village, with a popular taverna. Just below this you'll find the fourteenth-century church of **Áyios Yeóryios**, which has an unusual double altar and fine **frescoes** depicting the lives of Christ and Áyios Yeóryios by Ioannis Pagomenos (John the Frozen), the most prolific of several painters whose signatures appear frequently around Sélinos. Beyond Ánidhri the road deteriorates beyond **Prodhrómi**, from where it's a tortuous drive round to Azoyirés; alternatively it's an easy walk from Ánidhri (see box, p.314).

Azoyirés

Heading north out of Paleóhora on the main road, you'll soon see signs to **AZOYIRÉS (Αζογυρές)**, "Paradise Village". The road up to the village is set amid woods of cypress and pine, a lovely drive on good roads, and Azoyirés itself is set in a beautiful wooded valley above a rushing brook. Several short **walks** in the valley are well signed, taking you past plenty of evidence that this was once a much bigger place; there's an ancient bridge, a monastery (still just about functioning), an abandoned school, an olive oil

WALKS EAST OF PALEÓHORA

If you take a taxi up to Azoyirés (or the early-morning Omalós bus), you could easily hike back to Paleóhora or, more strenuously, on to Soúyia; taxis to Ánidhri or Yialaskári offer shorter versions of the same. It's a relatively easy, well-marked walk down the valley from **Azoyirés to Ánidhri** (1hr 30min or less) and from there down the verdant **Ánidhri Gorge** to the beach at Yialaskári, about an hour below. From Yialaskári you could head back into Paleóhora or follow the E4 towards **Lissós** and **Soúyia** (see opposite). Walking from Paleóhora to Yialaskári will take around 1hr 30min; it's a further 3 hours to Lissós, and 1hr 30min more to Soúyia; if you time it right you can return to Paleóhora on the evening boat from Soúyia. The **E4** is waymarked, but it doesn't simply follow the coast all the way, and there are one or two steep scrambles. Since the most scenic section is through the gorge between Lissós and Soúyia (see box opposite), it might be easier to head to Soúyia and do the shorter walk from there.

factory and more. All of this is recorded on a map which you can find on the back of the menu at the *Alpha* taverna (see below) – handily printed on paper so you can take it with you – and there's also a tiny one-room **museum** (officially Sat & Sun 9am–2pm; when closed enquire at the *Alpha*), delightfully located in the valley at the bottom of the village.

The Azoyirés cave

The biggest of several local **caves** is on an easy-to-miss road which (approaching from Paleóhora) sets off left just before the *Alpha* taverna, and winds steeply upwards for nearly 2km (keep climbing and turning where there's any doubt about the way). At the top you'll need to park any transport. From here there's an obvious path leading on – look up and you'll see a cross, some 200m above, which marks your destination. Approaching the cave you may disturb quail; the eerie sounds in the cave itself emanate from more birds, mostly pigeons, amplified by the acoustics. A steep metal stairway and rock-cut steps descend 50m or so to a little shrine lit from above by dim, reflected light. If you have a powerful torch you can continue a fair way, although there's no proper path.

Teménia

Beyond Azoyirés it's 10km or so to **TEMÉNIA** (Τεμένια), source of the drinks of that brand name sold throughout western Crete. Turn right at the edge of the village, downhill along the Rodováni road, and you'll pass a stone chapel atop a low hill to the left and see, about 200m further on, a sign on the right to **ancient Hyrtakína**. Head down this narrow track, and on your right you will soon see the charming, tumble-down church of **Sotíros Christós**. Inside, a number of damaged **frescoes** include a stirring image of a mounted Áyios Yeóryios slaying the dragon. Of the ancient Doric city, on the hilltop high above, there's almost no trace, but there are fine views and it's a bracing walk, or teeth-rattling drive, up there.

ACCOMMODATION AND EATING

Alpha Azoyirés ☎ 28230 41620, ⦿ azogires-alpha .blogspot.com. Exceptionally friendly and helpful café-taverna with a limited menu (fried chicken and potatoes €6.50, pie €4, burger €4.50) and economical balcony rooms nearby, some with a/c and fridge. Free wi-fi in taverna. Daily 9am–11pm. **€25**

Kafenío Sto Scolio Ánidhri ☎ 28230 83001. "The Old School", tastefully converted, makes a good place to pause for a drink or a bite to eat. The cooking is good, with a range of mezédhes and specials chalked up on the blackboard

(such as tomato fritters €5.50, pork leg with rosemary €8.50, lamb's liver with sage and Metaxa €6), and there's an inviting, shady terrace with views. Daily 9am–11pm; closed Oct.

Ta Tamenia Taverna Teménia ☎ 28230 51590. Welcoming taverna serving delicious Cretan traditional cuisine. All of the dishes are recommended, especially the home-reared lamb, village chicken and very tasty *loukánika* sausages (mains €6–8). Daily 8am–11pm.

Soúyia and around

The south coast settlement of **SOÚYIA** (Σούγια) is a small village gradually on its way to becoming a resort. There are no big hotels, no major tour operators (and no bank or ATM, so bring cash), just lots of rooms, simple restaurants and bars, added to a couple of general stores which double as travel agencies. A rather unkempt little place – not particularly attractive at first sight – Soúyia tends to grow on you. Its best feature lies right at the end of the road: an enormous swathe of bay with sparklingly clean, clear sea and a long, pebbly **beach**. There's plenty of room to spread out here – even on summer weekends when it's popular with locals – there are beachfront cafés and restaurants, and you could **camp** under the few scraggly trees if you wanted, although you'd be advised to get as far away from the central beach as possible to be left in peace. Around at the east end of the bay there's something of a nudist camping community – known locally as the **Bay of Pigs**.

Lissós

4km west of Soúyia • You can walk (see box below), or book a taxi-boat from Soúyia (about €20 for up to five people)

The archeological site of **Lissós** is a great deal more rewarding than anything you'll see in Soúyia itself. Originally a Dorian city, Lissós grew through the Hellenistic and Roman eras and continued to thrive, along with its neighbours Syia and Elyrós, right up to the Saracen invasion in the ninth century, when they were all abandoned. Little is known of these places' history, although they did join together around 300 BC – along with Hyrtakína in the hills behind, Pikilássos on the inaccessible coast between here and Ayía Rouméli, and Tarra, at modern Ayía Rouméli – to form the **Confederation of Oreioi**, later to be joined by Górtys and Cyrenaica (the latter in North Africa).

The ideal way to visit is either to walk over early and get the boat to pick you up in the middle of the day (precarious embarkation), or have them drop you here late in the afternoon, leaving time for a look around the site (you'll very likely have it all to

WALKS FROM SOÚYIA: LISSÓS AND OMALÓS

The walk from **Soúyia to Lissós**, a little over an hour (3km), is part of the pleasure of a visit to the ancient site: you set out on the road which heads west, behind the beach, and at the harbour turn right onto a track leading slightly inland. The route – also the path trodden by ancient pilgrims – is part of the E4 coastal path, so it's well marked with black and yellow splodges. It leads up a beautiful echoing gorge, which you follow for about thirty minutes, and then climb steeply out of towards the coast. After a short level stretch the sea comes into view, followed almost immediately by Lissós, below you at the back of a delightful little bay. If you're continuing the walk **west towards Paleóhora** (see p.308), the path is again pretty obvious; there may be a guard in the hut at the site who can help, but don't rely on it. The path back to Soúyia from the beach is fairly obvious, as it climbs the steep hill on the east side of the archeological site.

Hiking from **Soúyia to Omalós** (or vice versa, which is slightly easier) is a far more arduous proposition, not to be undertaken alone or without proper preparation: although Omalós is only some 12km away, the country in between is mountainous, remote and almost entirely uninhabited; it's a very full day's climb. If you head east along the beach in Soúyia, you'll see signs for the trail to the **Polifimos Cave** and Koustoyérako (see p.316). This part (4–5hr) is generally well marked (it's yet another E4 branch), with the cave, a little under halfway, to add interest (Polifimos was the Cyclops who imprisoned Odysseus in this cave, and was blinded by him) and a handy picnic spot. An easier way to do this would be to get a taxi up to Koustoyérako and walk down. **Beyond Koustoyérako** the terrain is marginally less steep but the path generally harder to follow. There are two alternative routes: more or less due north, to meet the road out of the plateau; or a turning to the east, heading for Mt Gíngilos and the top of the Samariá Gorge. You can also get to Omalós from the top of the **Ayía Iríni Gorge** (see p.316) on a path which heads east, cutting off a huge loop of the road.

4

yourself and it's just the place to open a chilled bottle of wine) before the walk back to Soúyia in the cool of the evening. There's a small pebble **beach** for a refreshing swim after your explorations.

The site

The remains at Lissós are mostly Classical Greek and Roman, the most important survival being an **Asklepion**, or temple of healing, built beside a curative spring against the cliffs on the east side of the site. The temple probably dates from the third century BC, although the **mosaic floor** (protected by a broken-down fence) that is its most obvious feature was added later, in the first century AD; it's a poignant ancient relic, depicting images of polychrome birds in its central section (including a quail) and elaborate and beautifully crafted geometric patterns on its outer borders. Notice also the marble altar-base that would have supported a statue, and the "snake pit" (or hole to place sacrifices) next to it. On the gentler, western slope of the valley, opposite, are a group of tombs that look like small stone huts, with barrel-vaulted roofs – hardly the best advertisement for the healing temple. You'll also find a small ruined theatre and two thirteenth-century churches, Áyios Kiriákos – with a nearby **spring** – and Panayía, which reused older material from the site.

Koustoyérako

About 5km northeast of Soúyia, a road cuts off from the main Hanía highway to the villages of Livadás and **KOUSTOYÉRAKO** (**Κουστογέρακο**). The latter is a very ancient village that is still the home of the Paterákis family, famed in the annals of resistance to German occupation. Manoli Paterákis was one of those who took part in the capture of General Kreipe (see p.338); he died some years ago at the age of 73, when he fell while chasing a wild goat through the mountains. Today the village seems to be in steep decline, with the *kafenía* and school closed, though it does see a few passing **walkers**, with a branch of the E4 path passing through between Soúyia and the Omalós plateau (see box, p.315). At the top of the village, behind a pristine restored house, the tiny Byzantine chapel of **Áyios Yeóryios** contains some beautiful remains of frescoes, with sixteenth-century graffiti carved into them; the chapel itself may be as early as the tenth century in origin.

The Ayía Iríni Gorge

€2, though often unattended • The gorge is an easy day-trip from Paleóhora (the early-morning Omalós bus passes through Ayía Iríni, and you can get the afternoon ferry back from Soúyia) or Soúyia (again, take the early Hanía/Omalós bus); you could also get a taxi to the top from either of these places

The **AYÍA IRÍNI GORGE** descends from the village of **Ayía Iríni**, a green place, shaded by venerable chestnut trees, to the coast at Soúyia, roughly 12km in all, though the last five are along the road – about a four-hour trek. It's an attractive hike, not too taxing and usually very quiet unless you're unlucky enough to coincide with one of the occasional tours (mainly from Paleóhora). The well-marked route down into the gorge can be picked up on the south edge of the village; for the first few kilometres it's easy walking, with plenty of water, shade and picnic spots, but it gradually becomes drier, tougher and hotter as you descend. There are places to eat and drink at the top, and the aptly named *Oasis* café at the bottom end of the gorge; from here, you could summon up a taxi to collect you from Soúyia, or you might well be able to beg a lift from a fellow traveller.

| ARRIVAL AND INFORMATION | SOÚYIA AND AROUND |

By bus There's no bus station: buses drive down the main road and drop passengers on the seafront, then park up halfway to the harbour. The early Hanía bus offers the opportunity to walk either the Ayía Iríni or the Samariá Gorge – it meets the early bus from Paleóhora in Ayía Iríni and from there one continues to Omalós and the other to Hanía, so you may have to change. Tickets are sold at *Roxana's*, at the bottom of the main road.

Destinations Haniá/Omalós (3 daily, first at 7am; 2hr/1hr), Paleóhora (connecting to Elafonísi; daily at 9am; 45min).

By ferry The harbour is right at the western end of the seafront, a 5min walk from the centre. Ferry tickets are sold from a booth here, which opens 1hr before each departure. Timetables are generally posted up locally, or check online (ⓦ anendyk.gr); the ferries run a restricted schedule year-round.

Destinations Ayía Rouméli (April–Oct daily 9am; 45min); Gávdhos (April–Oct Mon & Wed 9am; 3hr 30min); Paleóhora (April–Oct daily 6.10pm; 30 min).

By taxi or taxi-boat Taxi-boats can be arranged from the Pelican supermarket (see below) or from *Captain George* (ⓣ 6947 605 802). These are handy for getting to isolated

beaches along the coast or ancient Lissós (€20 one way). Almost opposite the seafront *Santa Irene* hotel a taxi kiosk (ⓣ 6977 745 160 or ⓣ 6972 370 480) can arrange taxis to various destinations, including the Ayía Iríni Gorge (€30 one way).

Tourist information Soúyia has virtually no formal tourist infrastructure – boat trips, tours, car rental and the like are arranged through the shops, restaurants or hotels. The seafront taxi booth (see above) is a good source for general and travel information, as is ⓦ sougia.info, but the most useful sources of local information are the two minimarkets: Idomeneas, halfway down the main street, and Pelican near the bottom. The latter also has newspapers and books in English.

ACCOMMODATION

Almost every building in Soúyia seems to offer **rooms**. Some of the best are off the main road at the top of the hill as it enters town; others, more expensive, are right on the seafront (mostly to the right from the seafront junction); while another cluster of cheaper rooms can be found by turning left along the seafront and left again before the stream. Details of many of the following (and more) can be found on ⓦ sougia.info.

Captain George To the west of the main street, near the top ⓣ 28230 51133, ⓦ sougia.info/hotels/captain _george. Simple a/c balcony rooms with fridge, TV and kettle, plus slightly pricier studios and apartments with kitchenette, in a garden setting. March–Nov. Doubles €40, studios €45

Idomeneas Apartments Main road, at the top of the hill ⓣ 28230 51540, ⓦ idomeneas-sougia.gr. Bright, modern a/c studios and spacious apartments with kitchens, TV and balcony; comfortable, but not the best value in town. Studios €60, apartments €70

Paradisos On the lane by the stream, left and left again at the seafront junction ⓣ 28230 51486, ⓦ sougia.info/hotels/paradisos. Old-fashioned but clean and very cheap rooms with fridge and kettle; most with a/c and balcony. April–Oct. €25

Pension El Greco To the west of the main street, near the top ⓣ 28230 51186, ⓦ sougia.info/hotels/elgreco. Upper-floor rooms place with simple a/c rooms with

balcony, fridge and kettle, plus a couple of ground-floor studios. Set back from the road in a quiet, semi-rural setting. April–Oct. Doubles €40, studios €45

Santa Irene On the seafront ⓣ 28230 51342, ⓦ santa -irene.gr. Smart, modern studios and apartments around a courtyard in a great waterfront location (though only a few have sea views), all with a/c, TV, kitchenette and balcony. March–Oct. Studios €60, apartments €80

Syia Main street, near the top ⓣ 28230 51174, ⓦ syia hotel.com. Incongruously chic, boutique-style hotel; the most comfortable studios and apartments in town, if not the most beautiful surroundings. Breakfast included. April–Oct. Studios €70, apartments €90

Villa Galini Main road, at the top of the hill ⓣ 28230 51488, ⓦ galinisougia.com. Run by a friendly proprietor, *Villa Galini* offers big, comfortable and good-value modern studios and apartments with balconies and satellite TV – one apartment has a hidden upper level, perfect for kids. March–Dec. Studios €50, apartments €70

EATING, DRINKING AND NIGHTLIFE

SOÚYIA

Fortuna On the main road north of town ⓣ 6977 423 023. Open-air club with frequent live music and party events; a great deal busier and wilder than you might expect down here. Look out for posters promoting special events. April–Oct Tues–Sat 11pm–4am.

Liviko At the western end of the seafront ⓣ 28230 51414. A good bet for traditional Cretan standards (lamb in the oven €7.80) as well as grills and fresh fish, often with live music in the evening. April–Oct daily 8am–midnight.

Lotos Seafront, at the corner of the main road ⓣ 28230 51191. Big breakfasts, followed by coffees and juices,

crêpes and snacks by day, and drinks and music in the evening; there are numerous similar café-bars on the seafront. April–Oct daily 7am–3am.

Omikron On the seafront east of the main road ⓣ 28230 51492. German-run restaurant with a more north European ambience; international menu – including pastas and risottos (€7–8) and numerous vegetarian choices (around €7). April–Sept daily 8am–11pm.

Polifimos Set back from the main street, halfway up ⓣ 28230 51343. Long-standing Soúyia favourite run by Yiannis, one of the village's characters. He serves his own wine and cooks with home-grown (and pressed) olive oil.

Tasty dishes include interesting salads, *kontosoúvli* (spit-roast pork €8.60), rabbit *stifádho* (€7.80) and shrimp spaghetti (€9.50). There's live Greek music on Thursdays. April–Oct daily 1pm–midnight.

★**Rebetiko** Halfway up the main street 📞 28230 51510. Cretan/Dutch-owned taverna offering well-prepared traditional dishes – including plenty of vegetarian options – on a delightful garden terrace. House specials include *bouréki* (€6.50), stuffed aubergine (€6.20) and good lamb and chicken dishes (€7–8) made with produce from their own farm; there's also excellent *hýma* (barrelled) wine, both red and white. April–Oct daily 1pm–midnight.

Roxana's Bakery Bottom of the main street 📞 28230 51362. Great little bakery for breakfast, cakes and savouries like *tirópita* and *spanakópita*, plus sandwiches and cold drinks to eat in or take away; they're open early for snacks for the bus (and to sell bus tickets). Daily 5am–midnight.

AYÍA IRÍNI

Kri-Kri 50m down the access track to the gorge 📞 28230 51550. Ramshackle but very welcoming family-run café with tables spread under the trees near the gorge entrance. There's rarely much choice (they'll cook a couple of dishes a day; there's often a lamb or goat stew for around €7), but they're open for breakfast (with their own eggs), and have salad with home-made cheese and plentiful cold drinks too. April–Oct daily 8am–8pm.

Gávdhos

GÁVDHOS (Γαύδος), the southernmost landmass in Europe, is the largest of Crete's offshore islands and the only one with any significant population. Gávdhos is small (about 9km by 7km) and barren, but it has one major attraction: the enduring **isolation** which its inaccessible position has helped preserve. The 50km of rough sea – more than 3000m deep – separating it from the coast of Crete frequently proves too much for the small ferries, which can leave visitors stranded for days when sailings are suspended.

If all you want is a **beach** and a taverna to grill your fish, this remains the place for you. Just don't expect luxury. There's a semi-permanent community of campers and would-be "Robinson Crusoes" on the island year-round, swelling to thousands in August – but just six indigenous families. **Water** is in short supply, and although most rooms on the island have showers and relatively modern plumbing, much of it is not drinkable. Few places have 24hr **electricity** either – most rely on candles, solar power or part-time generators, and even where there's enough power for lights, there's rarely air-conditioning. One huge benefit of this is an amazing **night sky**, when the few lights twinkling from the mainland are overwhelmed by the extraordinary brightness and density of the stars.

Brief history

Little is known of the island's early history and although evidence has been found of **Neolithic** and **Minoan** activity, it was most probably not settled until **Classical Greek** times when it was a dependency of Górtys (see p.100) and famous for its juniper berries. Despite Gávdhos's claim to be Calypso's island (visited by Odysseus in Homer's *Odyssey*), it only appears in verifiable record later as a place well known to the **Romans**, who christened it Clauda or Kaudos: the New Testament relates how St Paul was blown past Clauda in the storm which carried

HIKING ON GÁVDHOS

It may be fiercely hot in summer, but Gávdhos is also small, so **hiking** from place to place is a realistic endeavour, especially as the roads are awful and there are few other transport options. Numerous trails have been well marked out across the island, and you'll find shelters with maps and information at the beginning of most of them. The maps pinpoint a number of **archeological sites** en route, though none with a great deal to see.

Lavrakás

Pírgos

Áyios Ioánnis

Áyios Ioánnis †

Heliport (H)

Padhouráki

Bo

Potamós

Sarakíniko

▲ (165m)

● **Sarakíniko**

▲ (313m)

▲ (140m)

Áyios Yeóryios †

Áyios Pávlos †

● **Karavé**

Ámbelos ●

▲ (381m)

Archeological Site

† **Panayía**

† **Áyii Patéres**

Kastrí ●

DEH Solar Energy Farm ✦

† **Áyios Mihailis**

Kórfos

Áyios Harálambos †

▲ (400m)

● **Metóhi**

Vatsianá

N

▲ (339m)

Fokiás

GÁVDHOS

0   1
kilometre

Kamaréles

Trypití

him off from Kalí Liménes (see p.115). During the Middle Ages, Gávdhos is said to have had eight thousand residents and a bishop of its own; it was also notorious as a **pirates**' lair. In more modern history the island was used by dictatorial governments as a place of **exile** for political opponents, and later was a hideout for members of the notorious November 17 terrorist group (which was broken up in 2003). Publicity generated by this is at least one of the reasons for a recent upsurge in visitors, but it's still a harsh place to live, and many locals leave to spend the winter on the mainland.

Karavé

As you approach Gávdhos, the harbour at **KARAVÉ** (**Καραβέ**) is hidden behind a headland, and the island looks totally uninhabited – only with binoculars might you pick out one or two isolated homes. For an hour or so either side of the ferry's arrival, Karavé is crowded and chaotic and the couple of cafés busy; the rest of the time, there's hardly anyone here at all. In front of the concrete harbour is an open space where everyone mills about as the ferry loads and unloads: somewhere here will be the buses to Sarakíniko and Áyios Ioánnis, and any other accommodation transport. On the heights behind the harbour squat a few dwellings and a small white church, alongside the modern municipal buildings.

Sarakíniko

SARAKÍNIKO (Σαρακίνικο) is Gávdhos's principal resort, with one of the best of the island's beaches, shaded by scattered juniper and tamarisk trees, half a dozen fairly basic tavernas and cafés, and a similar number of rooms places. Even here the broad strip of golden sand has a community of nudist campers settled at each end, often outnumbering those staying in the rooms. The largely ugly, unplanned architecture aside, this is a beautiful spot, with giant dunes sheltering the eastern end of the beach: each evening the setting sun illuminates and silhouettes Crete and the Lefká Óri on the horizon against a crimson sky.

Áyios Ioánnis

A 3km hike to the west of Sarakíniko (or a ten-minute bus ride) brings you to the fine beach of **ÁYIOS IOÁNNIS (Άγιος Ιωάννης)**. There are high dunes here, and a forest of miniature cedars that provide shade for an army of tents. This is the prime destination for campers, and the summer hangout of a substantial alternative nudist community, despite (or because of) the fact that there are few facilities and little fresh water. The road ends by a couple of **tavernas**, from where the beach itself is ten minutes' walk further west; there are usually stalls offering massage, handmade jewellery and hippy accoutrements.

Kastrí

KASTRÍ (Καστρί), the island "capital", is an hour's walk along a steadily climbing, paved road from Karavé. When you get there it turns out to be a ghostly sort of place with only a handful of dwellings, mangers, stables and barns clustering around the old police station and *dhimarhío*, both rehoused to Karavé, while in the surrounding parched and arid fields older dwellings gradually crumble away to become one with the weathered and fissured rock on which they stand. Signs of life are beginning to return, however: some of the dwellings are being refurbished and there's a tiny school and health centre, as well as the incongruously snazzy *Gavdos Princess Apartments* (see p.322). There are fine views from up here, too.

Ámbelos and around

Climbing out of Kastrí the track heading west across the island reaches the ridgeline and divides. The right branch leads to the sparse hamlet of **ÁMBELOS (Άμβελος)**, 3km north, from where there's a particularly fine view towards North Africa, a sea lane ploughed constantly by enormous supertankers. On the way there you'll pass the impressive nineteenth-century **lighthouse,** bombed by the Germans in 1941 but fully restored with a café and **museum** depicting images, plans and sketches of other lighthouses throughout Greece (both have been closed for family reasons; check locally to see if they have reopened). A track north from Ámbelos leads to the scenic isolated beaches of **Potamós**, **Pírgos** and, further east, **Lavrakás**; you are totally on your own here, there are no facilities, and you'll need to take along plenty of drinking water.

Vatsianá

Turning left at the junction beyond Kastrí leads, after 3km, to **VATSIANÁ (Βατσιανά)**, a hamlet marooned in a rocky, almost lunar landscape. There's a chapel here, and half a dozen dwellings, one of which is a ramshackle **kafenío**, the last in Europe before you reach Africa. From Vatsianá you are in easy walking distance of Kórfos and its beach, to the east. Striking out more adventurously, there's also a path to the southernmost tip of the continent at Trypití, 3km to the south.

Kórfos

You can walk pretty much directly down from Vatsianá to **KÓRFOS** (Κόρφος), 2km away, where there's a good (but shadeless) sand and shingle beach and a couple of excellent places to stay. With a vehicle you'll have to head some way back for the track via Metóhi, or there's a paved road from Karavé.

Metóhi

The rooms place at **METÓHI** (Μετόχι) – see p.322 – is also host to a tiny **museum**. This two-room family collection won't take long to see, but it's a fascinating glimpse into traditional island life (or a pile of domestic junk, depending on your viewpoint): most was collected by the grandfather, Manolis Bikoyiannakis, who was the island's priest for many years; his son Stefanos now runs the island's car and bike rental from here, while his wife and children look after the rooms and taverna.

Trypití

TRYPITÍ (Τρυπητή), the most southerly point of Europe, can be reached in little over an hour on a well-marked path downhill from Vatsianá (a steep slog back up), or on a slightly longer trail from Kórfos. The beach here, **Kamaréles**, is pebbly with little shade but the water is brilliantly clear and a snorkeller's paradise, with plenty of aquatic life. When you need a break, you can do what everyone else comes here to do: climb the famous **three-holed rock**, sit in the **giant chair**, and dangle your feet off the edge of a continent.

4

ARRIVAL AND DEPARTURE

GÁVDHOS

By ferry There are ferries to Gávdhos from Hóra Sfakíon year-round, and from Paleóhora from April to October; in summer many of them call at Ayía Rouméli, Loutró and Soúyia. All, however, are dependent on the weather, which is unpredictable even in high summer; the high-sided, shallow-draft *Samariá* cannot handle even moderate winds and seas, while August is particularly dodgy given the frequency with which the *meltémi* blows. Be aware that you may be stranded on the island longer than you expect,

and plan accordingly. Schedules change throughout the year, and at short notice if there are weather disruptions: details can be found online (ⓦ anendyk.gr) and are posted at the harbour in Karavé and at Sarakíniko. The following timings refer to the main summer season.
Destinations Hóra Sfakíon (June–Sept Tues & Fri 2.30pm; July & Aug also on Sun; 2hr 30min–3hr); Paleóhora (May–Oct Mon & Wed 2.30pm; 3–4hr).

GETTING AROUND

By bus There are two buses, one run by KTEL, the other by Gavdos Tours (ⓣ 6942 480 815), at least one of which will meet every ferry and make the trip to Sarakíniko, Áyios Ioánnis and Kastrí (€2); there's a return trip from the beaches about 1hr before the ferry departs. Timetables are posted at Karavé, Sarakíniko and elsewhere; the schedule changes daily, but there's an evening round-island trip most days in summer (€5), starting from Sarakíniko, and often a lunchtime journey between the major centres. If you're staying anywhere other than Sarakíniko or Áyios Ioánnis, and have booked

in advance, you should be met at the ferry by a minibus from your accommodation.
Vehicle rental Gavdos Travel (ⓣ 6940 813 613, ⓦ metoxigavdos@gmail.com; cash only), based at *Metoxi Rooms*, rents battered cars (around €35–40/day plus petrol) and elderly mopeds (around €15–20/day including petrol); Odyssey (ⓣ 6948 635 685, ⓔ nikoskaramarkos @gmail.com), based at *Gavdos Princess*, has reasonably new mountain bikes for around €10 a day. Both will deliver the vehicle to you, which is a great deal easier than seeking them out.

ACCOMMODATION AND EATING

Many visitors to Gávdhos (the vast majority in peak season) still camp out by the beach, so most of the time there's no shortage of **rooms**. In August, however, the island is packed and prices are far higher; July and September are becoming increasingly busy too. Whenever you come, it would be foolish to turn up without having booked (unless you're happy to sleep under the stars), and there's the added advantage that many places will pick you up from the ferry; travel agencies in

Paleóhora (see p.308) or Hóra Sfakíon (see p.286) can help if necessary. Very few places have effective **air-conditioning**; plenty of others have a/c units they can't use, because promised mains electricity never materialized. As for **food**, there are minimarkets in Karavé, Sarakíniko and Áyios Ioánnis, but they're pricey (almost everything is brought over on the ferry) and none is very well stocked – in particular there's little in the way of fresh fruit or vegetables. There's also an excellent **bakery**, on the road below Kastrí. Nonetheless it makes sense to bring some supplies with you, especially if you plan to camp out.

SARAKÍNIKO

Consolas Gavdos Studios By the road above the beach to the west ☎28230 42182, ⓦgavdostudios.gr. A breezy hillside setting for the island's largest apartment complex, which offers rooms, studios and "villas" (basically a single, huge room, with kitchenette and multiple beds); there are some very pleasant rooms, with terraces and views (plus fridge and something to cook on), but others are not so good, and there's a slightly regimented atmosphere. Wi-fi in the café, where they also serve breakfast (extra). A bus collects from the ferry. Doubles €40, studios €50, villas €60

Haroto On the approach road. Describing itself as a café/bar/party space, *Haroto* is a makeshift place hidden away in the dunes that hosts party nights a couple of times a week: open-air affairs with fairy lights strung between trees and sand underfoot. Look out for posters and local publicity. Also open in the evening for cocktails. April–Sept daily 6pm–3am.

Nikterida Taverna-Rooms Beachfront ☎28230 42120. Very pleasant, simple rooms right by the beach with power from a generator at night and a bottled gas cooker. They also have one of the better beachfront tavernas (with wi-fi) and the local minimarket (daily 9.30am–3pm & 6.30–9.30pm), stocking basic items and essentials. €35

★**Vailakakis (aka Gerti & Manolis)** Behind the beach, where the bus stops ☎28230 41103, ⓦgavdos-crete.com. Simple rooms (with 24hr generator power) and rather fancier stone-built houses, with full kitchen, for four to six people. It also has probably the best food on the beach, with excellent, good-value seafood caught daily by Manolis himself. €40

ÁYIOS IOÁNNIS

Sofia Just above the car park ☎28230 41418 ⓦsofiaroomsgavdos.com. Lovely modern rooms with huge picture windows and spectacular terraces looking towards Crete. There's a/c but only solar power, so it can only be used during the day. Also a friendly family bar-taverna. May–Oct. €45

Taverna Ai Giannis At the end of the road, by the car park ☎28230 41418. The closest place to the beach (there's another taverna and a minimarket almost next door), *Ai Giannis* serves excellent, simple food from a short menu (starters €3–5, mains €6–8.50), with daily specials and good breakfasts. April–Oct daily 9am–10pm.

KASTRÍ

Gavdos Princess Apartments Beside the road on the way into the village ☎28230 41181, ⓦgavdos-princess.com. Some of the fanciest accommodation on Gávdhos – though that isn't saying a great deal and it's far from the best location – these modern-built studios and two-room apartments have a/c (Kastrí is one of the few places supplied by the island's solar power plant), terraces and kitchenettes. There's also a decent taverna, and a minibus to collect guests from the harbour. €50

Stella's bakery On the road approaching Kastrí ☎28320 41411. Super bakery with all sorts of delicious treats, from croissants to chocolate cake to home-made ice cream, as well as a range of traditional breads, biscuits and savoury pies. There's also a terrace to enjoy them all with a coffee or juice. Daily 8am–7pm.

To Steki tis Gogos Across the road from Gavdos Princess ☎28320 41932. Simple taverna where Gogo, with her sister and daughter, prepares a limited range of local dishes every day, full of earthy rural flavour. Goat, rabbit or pork mains go for €8–9, and there's a little terrace with lovely views. April–Oct daily 9am–10pm.

KÓRFOS

★**Akroyiali** On the beach ☎28230 42384, ⓦgavdoshotel.com. Plain but comfortable rooms directly above the beach, so you're lulled to sleep by the sound of the sea; 24hr power from the island's solar plant means effective a/c and hot water, and the taverna serves good food on a seafront terrace. There's a minibus to pick guests up from the ferry, and which also does occasional tours of the island. April–Sept; taverna daily 9am–10pm. €25

Panorama On the hill down to the beach ☎28230 42166, ⓦgavdos-panorama.gr. Appropriately named place with stunning views from rooms and taverna. Rooms are simple but spotless, with 24hr power, and they'll collect you from the harbour if you ring ahead. The taverna serves excellent fresh fish (priced by weight) and other local dishes on a terrace overlooking the beach. April–Sept taverna daily 9am–11pm. €30

METÓHI

Rooms Metoxi ☎28230 41220, ✉metoxigavdos@gmail.com. Friendly family atmosphere and a good taverna with views. The rooms are rather run-down, with solar power for ceiling fans and fridge, and camping gas stoves. There's a small pool, but water shortages mean it's often empty. A minibus collects guests from the harbour.

Free wi-fi in the taverna only. May–Sept; taverna daily 9am–10pm. €35

DIRECTORY

Doctor The health centre in Kastrí (☎ 28230 42195) is usually staffed by an intern opting out of military service.

Money There is no bank or official place to change money on the island: bring sufficient cash with you, remembering that, though life is simple, supplies are relatively expensive and you may be stuck here longer than expected should ferries be cancelled.

Police There is a police station (☎ 28230 41019) attached to the new *dhimarhío* (town hall) above the harbour at Karavé.

BYZANTINE CHAPEL, PANAYÍA GOUVERNIÓTISSA

Contexts

History

The people of Crete unfortunately make more history than they can consume locally.

Saki

The discovery of the Minoan civilization has tended to overshadow every other aspect of Cretan history; indeed it would be hard for any other period to rival what was, in effect, the first truly European civilization. It was in Crete that the developed societies of the East met influences from the West and North, and here that "Western culture", as synthesized in Classical Greece and Rome, first developed.

Yet this was no accident or freak one-off: Crete's position as a meeting place of East and West, and its strategic setting in the middle of the Mediterranean, has thrust the island to the centre stage of world history more often than seems comfortable. Long before Arthur Evans arrived to unearth Knossós, and for some time after, the island's struggle for freedom, and the Great Powers' inactivity, was the subject of Europe-wide scandal. The battle for the island when the Turks arrived had similarly aroused worldwide interest, and represented at the time a significant change in the balance of power between Islam and Christianity. In fact from Minoan times to World War II, there was rarely a sustained period when Crete didn't have some role to play in world affairs.

The Stone Age

Crete's first inhabitants, **Neolithic cave dwellers**, apparently reached the island around 7000 BC. They came, most probably, from Asia Minor (see box, p.145), or less likely from Syria, Palestine or North Africa, bringing with them the basics of Stone Age culture – tools of wood, stone and bone, crude pottery and simple cloth.

Development over the next three thousand years was almost imperceptibly slow, but gradually, whether through new migrations and influences or internal dynamics, advances were made. Elementary agriculture was practised, with domestic animals and basic crops. **Pottery** (the oldest samples of which were found beneath the palace at Knossós) became more sophisticated, with better-made domestic utensils and clay figurines of humans, animals and, especially, a fat mother goddess or fertility figure. Obsidian imported from the island of Mílos was used too. And though caves continued to be inhabited, simple rectangular huts of mud bricks were also built, with increasing skill and complexity as the era wore on. One of the most important of the Neolithic settlements was at Knossós, where two remarkable dwellings have been revealed below the West Court, and there is abundant evidence that many other sites of later habitation were used at this time – Mália, Festós, Ayía Triádha, the Haniá area – as were most of the caves that later came to assume religious significance.

6000–2600 BC	2600–2000 BC
Crete's first inhabitants arrive during the Stone Age when habitation starts in caves. Settlements grow at Knossós and elsewhere.	New migration by the "first Minoans" brings more sophisticated culture and settlements: Vasilikí, Mókhlos and Mýrtos are among the best known.

The Bronze Age: Minoan Crete

Minoan Crete has been the subject of intense and constant study since its emergence from myth to archeological reality at the beginning of the twentieth century. Yet there is still enormous controversy even over such fundamental details as who the Minoans were and what language they spoke. No written historical records from the time survive

THE DISCOVERY OF BRONZE AGE CRETE

So ancient is **Minoan civilization** that even by Classical Greek times it had long disappeared into the mists of mythology and Homeric legend. The story of its rediscovery at the beginning of the twentieth century – dominated by two larger-than-life characters in **Heinrich Schliemann** and **Arthur Evans** – is almost as fascinating as that of the Minoans themselves.

HEINRICH SCHLIEMANN

Heinrich Schliemann, a wealthy, self-made, self-educated German, was determined to prove that Homer's stirring tales of prehistoric cities and heroes were true. In the 1870s and 80s, in the face of unremitting hostility from the archeological establishment, he discovered and excavated both Troy and Mycenae, revolutionizing our knowledge of the pre-Classical era. In 1887 he arrived in Crete, made a visit to the site at Knossós, and became convinced that a substantial palace lay waiting to be unearthed. But Crete was still under the subjection of Turkey, and Schliemann never succeeded in getting permission to excavate the site.

ARTHUR EVANS AND KNOSSÓS

Arthur Evans, an independently wealthy British scholar who had been inspired by Schliemann, arrived in Crete for the first time on March 15, 1894. With the assistance of Joseph Hatzidhákis, president of the Cretan Archeological Society, Evans began to negotiate for the purchase of the land at Knossós with its Turkish owners. As the Ottoman Empire crumbled, Evans succeeded in buying the site and excavation began in March, 1900. Within days, evidence of a vast and complex building had been revealed – elegant courtyards with sublime frescoes, pottery, jewellery and tablets bearing an undeciphered ancient script.

Evans was an autocrat whose personal ownership and financing of one of the major sites of antiquity – something that would be unthinkable today – allowed him extraordinary latitude. It was he who named the new civilization **Minoan** after the legendary Cretan king. Far more controversially, he determined that he would not only reveal the palace of Minos but would also restore large parts of it to its original splendour. With the assistance of architects Theodore Fyfe and Piet de Jong, he roofed the Throne Room and reconstructed the grand staircase, replacing the tapered columns with his speculative concrete reconstructions (none of the wooden originals was ever found). Two Swiss artists then began to repaint the reconstructed walls with copies of the frescoes. An almost entirely conjectural upper storey, the Piano Nobile, was added using reinforced concrete, and the Central Court was extensively restored as the archeological dig became a building site. Evans argued that he wanted to recreate the "spirit" of the palace structure and decor rather than undertake a literal reconstruction. Few professional archeologists now would defend him, and certainly none would be allowed to carry out such work again, but there can be no doubt that it was the publicity Evans generated that brought Minoan culture to a worldwide audience.

In 1924 Evans donated the Knossós site and the Villa Ariadne, where he lived in style throughout the excavation, to the British School at Athens – it was only in 1952 that it was to become the property of the Greek government. His successor at Knossós – a young English archeologist, John Pendlebury – was killed in the early years of World War II, fighting alongside the Cretans during the German attack on Iráklio in 1941.

2000–1700 BC	c.1700 BC	c.1700–1450 BC	c.1450 BC
Evidence of a more formally structured society. First palaces built at most of the famous sites.	Earthquake destroys the palaces.	The Minoan Golden Age. Great palaces at Knossós, Festós, Mália and Zákros; thriving towns at Gourniá and Palékastro.	Final destruction of the palaces.

(or if they do, they have not yet been deciphered), so almost everything we know is deduced from physical remains, fleshed out somewhat by writings from Classical Greece, almost one thousand years after the destruction of Knossós. Nevertheless it is not hard to forge some kind of consensus from the theories about the Minoans, and this is what is set out below. Fresh discoveries may yet radically change this view.

One of the central arguments is over **dating**. The original system, conceived by Sir Arthur Evans, divided the period into Early, Middle and Late Minoan, with each of these again divided into three sub-periods – a sequence that has become extremely complicated and cumbersome as it has been further qualified and subdivided. Arcane distinctions between the pottery styles of Early Minoan IIa and IIb have no place in a brief history and a simpler system is used here (following the archeologist Nikolaos Platon) of four periods: **Prepalatial**, **Protopalatial** or First Palace, **Neopalatial** or New Palace, and **Postpalatial**.

However, as many archeological texts and guides, as well as numerous museums on the island use the Evans system, the approximate corresponding periods – Early Minoan (**E.M.**), Middle Minoan (**M.M.**) and Late Minoan (**L.M.**) – are given in brackets.

Prepalatial: 3500–1900 BC (E.M.–M.M.I.)

Among the more important puzzles of Minoan society is its comparatively **sudden emergence**. During the centuries before 2600 BC, there were important changes on the island, and thereafter very rapid progress in almost every area of life. Villages and towns grew up where previously there had been only isolated settlements, and with them came craft specialists: potters, stonecutters, metalworkers, jewellers and weavers.

It seems safe to assume that these changes were wrought by a new **migration** of people from the east, who brought with them new technologies, methods of agriculture and styles of pottery, but most importantly perhaps, a knowledge of seafaring and trade. The olive and the vine – which need little tending and therefore help free a labour force – began to be produced alongside cereal crops. Copper tools replaced stone ones and were themselves later refined with the introduction of bronze. Art developed rapidly, with characteristic **Vasilikí ware** and other pottery styles, as well as gold jewellery, and stone jars of exceptional quality, based originally on Egyptian styles. Significantly, large quantities of seal stones have been found too, almost certainly the mark of a mercantile people. They were used to sign letters and documents, but especially to seal packets, boxes or doors as proof that they had not been opened: the designs – scorpions or poisonous spiders – were often meant as a further deterrent to robbery.

At the same time new methods of burial appear – tholos and chamber tombs in which riches were buried with the dead. These appear to have been communal, as, probably, was daily life, based perhaps on clan or kinship groupings.

Protopalatial (The first palaces): 1900–1700 BC (M.M.I–M.M.II)

Shortly before 1900 BC, the first of the palaces were built, at **Knossós**, **Festós**, **Mália** and **Zákros**. They represent another significant and apparently abrupt change: a shift of power back to the centre of the island and the emergence of a much more hierarchical, ordered society. The sites of these palaces were also no accident: Festós and Mália both dominate fertile plains, while Zákros had a superbly sited harbour for trade with the east. Knossós, occupying a strategic position above another plain to the south and west of Iráklio, was perhaps originally as much a religious centre as a base of secular power. Certainly at this

c.1450–1100 BC	**c.1100–67 BC**
Gradual revival under Mycenaean influence. Earlier sites reoccupied, with Kydonia the island's chief city. Eteo-Cretans keep Minoan culture alive at Présos and Karfí. Mycenaean control yields to Dorian.	Island divided into rival groupings, gradually emerging as constantly warring city-states. The most powerful included Láto, Kydonia, Knossós, Górtys and Ierápytna.

THE MINOAN ECONOMY

The extent and grandeur of the Minoan palaces themselves in this Protopalatial era are proof of the island's great prosperity at this time, and the artefacts found within offer further evidence. Advances were made in almost every field of artistic and craft endeavour. From this era came the famous **Kamáres** ware pottery – actually two distinct styles, one eggshell-thin and delicate, the other sturdier with bold-coloured designs. These remarkable works were enabled by the true potter's wheel (as against the turntable) now introduced for the first time, along with a simple form of hieroglyphic writing. Elaborate jewellery, seals and bronzework were also being produced.

Cretan bronze was used throughout the Mediterranean, and its production and distribution were dependent on a wide-ranging **maritime economy**. For though Crete may have produced some copper at this time, it never yielded tin, the nearest significant sources of which were as distant as modern Iran to the east, Central Europe in the north, Italy, Spain, Brittany and even Britain in the west. Nevertheless, Crete controlled the trade routes in the Mediterranean, importing tin, copper, ivory, gold, silver and precious stones of every kind, exporting timber from its rich cypress forests, olive oil, wine, bronze goods and its fine pottery, especially to Egypt. Minoan colonies or trading posts were established on many Cycladic islands as well as the island of Kýthira off the Peloponnese, Rhodes and the coast of Asia Minor; a fleet of merchant vessels maintained regular trade links between these centres and, above all, with Egypt and the east.

time religion took on a new importance, with the widespread use of mountain-top sanctuaries and caves as **cult centres**. At the same time much larger towns were growing up, especially around the palaces, and in the countryside substantial "villas" appeared. Around 1700 BC, the palaces were destroyed for the first time, probably by earthquake, although raiders from the early Mycenaean Greek mainland may also have seized this opportunity to raid the island while it was temporarily defenceless; this may well account for the wealth of gold and other treasure – much of it obviously Cretan – found in the later royal shaft graves at Mycenae.

The Neopalatial Period: 1700–1400 BC (M.M.II–L.M.I)

Though the destruction must have been a setback, Minoan culture continued to flourish, and with the palaces reconstructed on a still grander scale the society entered its golden age. It is the new palaces that provide most of our picture of Minoan life, and most of what is seen at the great sites – Knossós, Festós, Mália, Zákros – dates from this period.

The **architecture** of the new palaces was of an unprecedented sophistication: complex, multistorey structures in which the use of space and light was as luxurious as the construction materials. Grand stairways, colonnaded porticoes and courtyards, brightly frescoed walls, elaborate plumbing and drainage, and great magazines in which to store the society's accumulation of wealth, were all integral, as were workshops for the technicians and craftsmen, and areas set aside for ritual and worship.

Obviously it was only an elite that enjoyed these comforts, but conditions for the ordinary people who kept Minos and his attendants in such style appear to have improved too: towns around the palaces and at sites such as Gourniá and Palékastro were growing as well.

Very little is known of how the society was organized, or indeed whether it was a single entity ruled from Knossós or simply several city-states with a common cultural heritage. However, in an intriguing reference to Crete in his *Politics*, Aristotle implied

c.300 BC	71 BC	69–67 BC
Cities on south coast form Confederation of Oreoi.	Failed Roman invasion.	Romans invade again and subjugate the island.

that a caste system had operated in the time of Minos. Clearly, though, it was a society in which **religion** played an important part. The great Corridor of the Procession fresco at Knossós depicted an annual delivery of tribute, apparently to a mother goddess; bull-leaping had a religious significance too; and in all the palaces substantial chambers were set aside for ritual purposes. Secular leaders were also religious leaders.

That Minoan society was a very open one is apparent too. There are virtually no **defences**, internal or external, at any Minoan site, and apparently the rulers felt no threat either from within or without, which has led scholars to emphasize a military strength based on sea power. As far as internal dissent goes, it seems safe to assume that the wealth of the island filtered down, to some extent at least, to all its inhabitants: the lot of a Minoan peasant may have been little different from that of a Cretan villager as little as fifty years ago.

Externally, **maritime supremacy** was further extended: objects of Cretan manufacture turn up all over the Mediterranean and have even been claimed as far afield as Britain and Scandinavia (amber from the Baltic certainly found its way to Crete). Behind their sea power the Minoans clearly felt safe, and the threat of attack or piracy was further reduced by the network of colonies or close allies throughout the Cycladic islands – Thíra most famously but also at Mílos, Náxos, Páros, Mikonós, Ándhros and Dílos – and in Rhodes, Cyprus, Syria and North Africa. Nevertheless, this appears to have remained a trading empire rather than a military one.

CULTURAL ADVANCES IN THE NEOPALATIAL PERIOD

If the Neopalatial period was a high point of Minoan power, it also marked the apogee of arts and crafts in the island: again, the bulk of the objects you'll admire in the museums date from this era. The **frescoes** – startling in their freshness and vitality – are the most famous and obviously visible demonstration of this florescence. But they were just the highly visible tip of an artistic iceberg. It was in intricate small-scale work that the Minoans excelled above all. Naturalistic sculpted figures of humans and animals include the superb ivory bull-leaper, the leopard-head axe and the famous snake goddesses or priestesses, all of them on show in the Iráklio Archeological Museum. The carvings on seal stones of this era are of exceptional delicacy – a skill carried over into beautifully delicate gold jewellery. Examples of stone vessels include the bull's head rhyton from Knossós and the three black vases from Ayía Triádha, which are among the museum's most valuable possessions. And pottery broke out into an enormous variety of new shapes and design motifs, drawing inspiration especially from scenes of nature and marine life.

The other great advance was in writing. A new form of script, **Linear A**, had appeared at the end of the Prepalatial period, but in the new palaces its use became widespread. Still undeciphered, Linear A must record the original, unknown language of the Minoans: it seems to have been used in written form almost exclusively for administrative records – stock lists, records of transactions and tax payments. Even were it understood, therefore, it seems unlikely that the language would reveal much. The pieces that have survived were never intended as permanent records, and have been found intact only where the clay tablets used were baked solid in the fires that destroyed the palaces. It is probable that a more formal record, an abstract of the annual accounts, was kept on a more valuable but also more perishable material such as imported papyrus (the Minoans had strong trading links with Egypt) or even a paper produced from native date-palm leaves. There is evidence in the Iráklio museum of the use of ink to inscribe text on ceramic drinking cups that lends support to this proposition.

67 BC–395 AD	67 BC	395 AD
Roman rule with Górtys the chief city. Others include Lýttos, Áptera and Knossós. Public works constructed across the island.	Crete merges with the Libyan kingdom of Cyrenaica to form a new province.	Roman Empire splits; Crete falls under Byzantium.

Destruction

Around 1600 BC the island again saw minor earthquake damage, though this was swiftly repaired. But in about 1450 BC came destruction on a calamitous scale: the palaces were smashed and (with the exception of Knossós itself) burned, and smaller settlements across the island were devastated. The cause of this disaster is still the most controversial of all Minoan riddles, and until recently the most convincing theory linked it with the explosion of the volcano of **Thíra** in about 1500 BC – a blast that may have been five times as powerful as that of Krakatoa. The explosion threw up great clouds of black ash and a huge tidal wave, or waves. Coastal settlements would have been directly smashed by the wave, and perhaps further burnt by the overturn of lamps lighted on a day made unnaturally dark by the clouds of ash. Blast, panic and accompanying earth tremors would have contributed to the wreck. And then, as the ash fell, it apparently coated the centre and east of the island in a poisonous blanket under which nothing could grow, or would grow again, for as much as fifty years. Recent surveys by vulcanologists have traced ash from the explosion as far away as Greenland, the Black Sea and Egypt, suggesting that the thousands of tons of ash and pumice thrown into the atmosphere by the blast created a "nuclear winter" across much of Europe and beyond.

Only at Knossós was there any real continuity of habitation, and here it was with **Mycenaean Greeks** in control, bringing with them new styles of art, a greater number of weapons and, above all, keeping records in a form of writing known as **Linear B**, an adaptation of Linear A used to write in an early Greek dialect. In about 1370 BC, Knossós was itself burnt, whether by rebellious Cretans, a new wave of Mycenaeans or perhaps as a result of another natural disaster on a smaller scale.

Such at least is the prevailing theory. But it has its problems – why, for example, should Festós have been burnt when it was safe from waves and blast on the south side of the island? And why should the eruption that vulcanologists dated to 1500 BC have had such a dramatic effect only fifty years later – indeed there are signs that away from the worst effects of the devastation many areas on Crete experienced comparative prosperity after it. As the debate continues, the best that can be said currently is that the volcano theory fits

THE RIDDLE OF THE OLIVE BRANCH

The confusion surrounding theories about the end of the Neopalatial period was dramatically added to in 2005 when Danish vulcanologists working on Thíra discovered an **olive tree branch** buried inside a rock face formed from volcanic debris. The researchers are convinced that the tree was alive when buried in the cataclysmic eruption. The branch's growth rings were intact and using radio-carbon dating the researchers were able to date the tree's death to between 1627 and 1600 BC. If this dating is correct it suggests that the eruption occurred at least 100 years earlier than previously thought. It has also plunged ancient Aegean chronology into confusion. Historians tend to rely on the Egyptian chronology (with its long history, king lists and 365-day years) for setting Minoan dates. Accepted thinking thus far is that Minoan civilization was contemporary with that of the Egyptian New Kingdom (dated c.1550–1050 BC). If the vulcanolgists' new dating is correct and Minoan civilization effectively collapsed c.1600 then this is wildly out of sync. As one Cretan archeologist put it: "We now have absolute chaos as far as giving years to events is concerned and something must give – this is likely to be Egyptian dates which are now out by up to two centuries."

395–824	824–961	961
Crete ruled from Byzantium. Traces of early churches at Górtys, Soúyia and Thrónos.	Arab invasion and rule. Górtys sacked with al-Khandak, later Iráklio, the Arab base.	Liberation by Byzantine general Nikíforos Fokás.

the available evidence better than most of its rivals. But many scholars still claim that the facts are more consistent with destruction by human rather than natural causes.

The main counter-theory assumes an invasion by the Mycenaeans, and points to some evidence that Linear B was in use at Knossós before 1450 BC. But if the Mycenaeans came to conquer, they would have gained nothing by destroying the society already flourishing on Crete; nor would they have subsequently left the former population centres deserted for a generation or more.

A third theory attempts to answer these inconsistencies, suggesting that an **internal revolt** by the populace against its rulers (possibly in the wake of the chaos caused by the Thíra eruption) could provide an explanation. This theory would fit the evidence from sites such as Pýrgos near Mýrtos on the south coast, where a villa dominating the site was burned down while the surrounding settlement remained untouched. Needless to say this theory does not find favour with those who see Minoan civilization as a haven of tranquil splendour, but it does fit with the later Greek tradition of a tyrannical Minos oppressing not only his own people but those abroad as well.

Post-Palatial: 1450–1100 BC (L.M.II–L.M.III)

From their bridgehead at Knossós, the Mycenaeans gradually spread their influence across the island as it became habitable again. By the early fourteenth century BC they controlled much of Crete, and some of the earlier sites, including Gourniá, Ayía Triádha, Týlissos and Palékastro, were **reoccupied**. It is a period that is still little known and that was written off by the early Minoan scholars almost entirely. However more recent excavations are revealing that the island remained productive, albeit in a role peripheral to the mainland.

In particular **western Crete** now came into its own, as the area least affected by the volcano. **Kydonia** – the nearest port to the Mycenean heartland – became the chief city of the island, still with a considerable international trade and continuing, in its art and architecture, very much in the Minoan style. But Kydonia lies beneath modern Haniá and has never been (nor is ever likely to be) properly excavated – another reason that far less is known about this period than those that preceded it. In **central Crete** the main change was in retreat from the coasts, a sign of the island's decline in international affairs and trade, and perhaps of an increase in piracy. Even here, however, despite the presence of new influences, much of the art is recognizably Minoan. Most of the famous clay and stone *lárnakes* (sarcophagi) – which were a distinctly new method of burial – date from this final Minoan era.

More direct evidence of the survival of Crete comes in Homer's account of the **Trojan War**, when he talks of a Cretan contingent taking part under King Idomeneus (according to him, the grandson of Minos). The war and its aftermath – a period of widespread change – also affected Crete. In the north of Greece the Mycenaeans were being overrun by peoples moving down from the Balkans, in particular the **Dorians**. Around 1200 BC the relative peace was disrupted again: many sites were abandoned for the last time, others burnt. Briefly, Mycenaean influence became yet more widespread, as refugees arrived on the island. But by the end of the twelfth century BC, Minoan culture was in terminal decline, and Crete was entering into the period of confusion that engulfed most of the Greek world. Some of the original population of the island, later known as **Eteo-Cretans** (true Cretans), retreated at this time to mountain fastnesses at sites such as Présos and Karfí, where they survived, along with elements of Minoan culture and language, for almost another millennium.

961–1204	1204	1204–1669
Byzantine rule returns. Small frescoed churches built throughout Crete.	Fourth Crusade. Byzantium sacked; Crete sold to Venice.	Venetian rule. Extensive early building includes churches and monasteries; later, major defence works at Iráklio, Réthymno and Haniá and castles at Frangokástello and on the fortified islets.

Dorian and Classical Crete

By the end of the twelfth century, the bulk of the island had been taken over by the **Dorians**: there may have been an invasion, but it seems more probable that the process was a gradual one, by settlement. At any event, over the succeeding centuries the Dorians came to dominate the central lowlands, with substantial new cities such as Láto near modern Áyios Nikólaos.

Dorian Crete was not in any real sense a unified society: its cities warred with each other and there may, as well as the Dorians and Eteo-Cretans, have been other cultural groupings in the west, at Kydonia and sites such as Falásarna and Polyrínia. Nevertheless the island saw another minor **artistic renaissance**, with styles now mostly shared with the rest of the Greek world; in the making of tools and weapons, **iron** gradually came to replace bronze.

Much the most important survival of this period, however, is the celebrated **law code** from Górtys. The code (see p.102) was set down around 450 BC, but it reflects laws that had already been in force for hundreds of years: the society described is a strictly hierarchical one, clearly divided into a ruling class, free men, serfs and slaves. For the rulers, life followed a harsh, militaristic regime similar to that of Sparta – the original population, presumably, had been reduced to the level of serfs.

As mainland Greece approached its **Classical Age**, Crete advanced little. It remained a populous island, but one where a multitude of small city-states were constantly vying for power. Towns of this period are characterized by their heavy defences, and most reflected the Górtys laws (Górtys remained among the most powerful of them) in tough oligarchical or aristocratic regimes. At best, Crete was a minor player in Greek affairs, increasingly known as the den of pirates and as a valuable source of mercenaries unrivalled in guerrilla tactics. The island must have retained influence though, for it was still regarded by Classical Athenians as the source of much of their culture, and its strict institutions were admired by many philosophers. In addition, many Cretan shrines and caves show unbroken use from Minoan through to Roman times, and those associated with the birth and early life of Zeus (the Dhiktean and Idean caves especially) were important centres of pilgrimage.

The multitude of small, independent **city-states** is well illustrated by the Confederation of Oreoi, an accord formed around 300 BC between Elyros, Lissós, Hyrtakina, Tarra, Syia (modern Soúyia) and Pikílassos, six towns in a now barely populated area of the southwest. They were later joined in the Confederation by Górtys and Cyrenaica (in North Africa). Meanwhile Roman power was growing in the Mediterranean, and Crete's strategic position and turbulent reputation drew her inexorably into the struggle.

Conquest by Rome

From the second century BC onwards, **Rome** was drawn into wars in mainland Greece, and the involvement of Cretan troops on one or often both sides became an increasing irritation. The island was also a notorious haven for pirates that frequently preyed upon Roman merchant vessels. Hannibal was staying at Górtys at the time of one Roman attempt to pacify the island, around 188 BC. More than a century passed with only minor interventions, however, before Rome could turn its full attention to Crete – the last important part of the Greek world not under its sway.

1453	1541	1587
Fall of Constantinople; renaissance of Byzantine art on Crete.	The artist El Greco (Domenico Theotokópoulos) born in Crete; in 1577 moves to Toledo, Spain where he makes his name.	Vitzéntzos Kornáros, Crete's greatest poet and creator of the epic poem *Erotókritos*, born near Sitía.

In 74 BC Marcus Antonius (father of Mark Antony) attempted an invasion mainly aimed at chastising the pirates, but was heavily defeated by the Kydonians. A fresh attempt was made under **Quintus Metellus** (afterwards called Creticus) in 69 BC. This time a bridgehead was successfully established by exploiting divisions among the Cretans: Metellus was supported in his initial campaign against Kydonia by its rivals at Polyrínia. The tactic of setting Cretan against Cretan served him well, but even so it took almost three years of bitter and brutal warfare before the island was subdued in 67 BC. It was a campaign marked by infighting not only among the Cretans – Górtys was among those to take Metellus's side – but also between Romans, with further forces sent from Rome in an unsuccessful bid to curb Metellus's excesses and his growing power.

With the conquest complete, Crete was combined with Cyrenaica (in North Africa) as a single province whose capital was at **Górtys**, and though there was little contact between the two halves of the province, both were important sources of grain and agricultural produce for Rome.

Through the first and second centuries AD, important public works were undertaken throughout Crete: roads, aqueducts and irrigation systems, important cities at Knossós, Áptera, Lýttos and others, as well as considerable grandeur at Górtys. **Christianity** arrived with St Paul's visit around 60 AD; soon after, he appointed Titus as the island's first bishop to begin the conversion in earnest. Around 250 AD, the Holy Ten – Áyii Dhéka – were martyred at Górtys, probably during the first great persecution of the Christians initiated by the Emperor Decius.

The Byzantine Age

With the split of the Roman Empire at the end of the fourth century, Crete found itself part of the Eastern Empire under **Byzantium**. The island continued to prosper – as the churches that were built everywhere testify – but in international terms it was not important. Byzantine rule, here as everywhere, imposed a stiflingly ordered society, hierarchical and bureaucratic in the extreme. Of the earliest churches only traces survive, in particular of mosaic floors like those at Soúyia or Thrónos, though there are more substantial remains at Górtys, of the basilica of Áyios Títos.

Then in 824 Crete was invaded by a band of **Arabs** under Abu Hafs Omar. Essentially a piratical group who had been driven first from Spain and then Alexandria, they nevertheless managed to keep control of the island for well over a century. There was not much in the way of progress at this time but there was a fortress founded at al-Khandak, a site that later developed into Iráklio. At the same time Górtys and other Byzantine cities were sacked and destroyed.

After several failed attempts, the Byzantine general **Nikiforos** reconquered Crete in 961, following a siege at Khandak in which he catapulted the heads of his Arab prisoners over the walls. For a while the island revived, boosted by an influx of colonists from the mainland and from Constantinople, including a number of aristocratic families (the Arhontopouli) whose power survived throughout the medieval era. By now, however, the entire empire was embattled by Islam and losing out in trade to the Venetians and Genoese. Frescoed churches continued to be built, but most were small and parochial.

Ironically enough it was not Muslims who brought about the final end of Byzantine rule, but Crusaders. The **Fourth Crusade** turned on Constantinople in 1204 (at the

1645	1669	1669–1898	1770
Turks capture Haniá.	Iráklio surrenders.	Turkish rule. Mosques and fountains constructed in the cities, especially Haniá, Réthymno and Ierápetra, but few public works undertaken elsewhere.	Revolt against Turkish rule by rebel leader Dhaskaloyiannis in Sfakiá; he is defeated and executed at Iráklio.

instigation of the Venetians), sacking and burning the city. The leader of the Crusade, Prince Boniface of Montferrat, ceded Crete to the Venetians for a nominal sum.

Venetian Crete

Before Venice could claim its new territory, it had to drive out its chief commercial rivals, the **Genoese**, who had taken control in 1206 with considerable local support. By 1210 the island had been secured, though for more than a century thereafter the Genoese pursued their claim, repeatedly siding with local rebels when it looked like there was a chance of establishing a presence on the island.

The Venetians, however, were not going to surrender the prize lightly. Crete for them was a vital resource, both for the control of eastern Mediterranean trade routes that the island's ports commanded, and for the natural wealth of the agricultural land and the timber for shipbuilding. The Venetian system was rapidly and stringently imposed, with Venetian overlords, directly appointed from Venice, administering what were effectively a series of feudal fiefdoms.

It was a system designed to exploit Crete's resources as efficiently as possible, and not surprisingly it stirred up deep resentment from the beginning. There were constant **rebellions** throughout the thirteenth century, led as often as not by one or other of the aristocratic Byzantine families from an earlier wave of colonization. Certainly the wealthy had most to lose: it was their land that was confiscated to be granted to military colonists from Venice (along with the service of the people who lived on it), and their rights and privileges that were taken over by the new overlords. The rebellions were in general strictly noble affairs, ended by concessions of land or power to their Cretan leaders. But there were more fundamental resentments too. Heavy taxes and demands for feudal service were widely opposed – by the established colonists almost as much as by the natives. And the **Orthodox Church** was replaced by the Roman as the "official" religion, the senior clergy expelled and much Church property seized. Local priests and monasteries that survived helped fuel antagonism: even from this early date the monasteries were becoming known as centres of dissent.

The **Middle Ages** were perhaps the most productive years in Crete's history, with exports of corn, wine, oil and salt, the ports busy with trans-shipment business and the wooded hillsides being stripped for timber.

After 1453, and the final fall of Constantinople, Crete saw a spectacular cultural renaissance as a stream of refugees arrived from the east. **Candia** – as the island and its capital were known to the Venetians – became the centre of Byzantine art and scholarship. From this later period, and the meeting of the traditions of Byzantium and the Italian Renaissance, come the vast majority of the works of art and architecture now associated with the Venetian era. The great icon painter Dhamaskinos studied alongside El Greco in the school of Ayía Ekateríni in Iráklio; the Orthodox monasteries flourished; and in literature the island produced, among others, what is now regarded as its greatest work – the *Erotókritos* (see p.354).

But it was the growing **external threat** that stimulated the most enduring of the Venetian public works – the island defences. Venice's bastions in the mainland Middle East had fallen alongside Constantinople, and in 1573 Cyprus too was taken by the Turks, leaving Crete well and truly in the front line. Large-scale pirate raids had already been common: in

1821	**1828**
Greek War of Independence declared. Island repressed by Turkish and Egyptian troops with much bloodshed.	Major battle between Cretans and Turkish forces at Frangokástello fort; more than a thousand killed.

1538 Barbarossa had destroyed Réthymno and almost taken Haniá, and in the 1560s there were further attacks. Across the island, cities were strengthened and the fortified islets defending the seaways were repaired and rebuilt. As the seventeenth century wore on, however, Venice itself was in severe decline: Mediterranean trade was overshadowed by the New World, a business dominated by the Spanish, English and Dutch.

Finally, in 1645 an attack on an Ottoman convoy provided the excuse for an all-out **Turkish assault** on Crete. Haniá fell after a siege that cost forty thousand Turkish lives, and Réthymno rapidly followed. By 1648 the Turks controlled the whole island except **Iráklio** and here they dug in for the long haul. For 23 years of war and siege the city resisted, supplied from the sea and with moral support at least from most of Europe. The end was inevitable, though, and from the Turkish point of view there was no hurry: they controlled the island's produce, they were well supplied, and they enjoyed a fair degree of local support, having relaxed the Venetian rules – for example, they allowed Orthodox bishops back into Crete. By 1669 the city was virtually reduced, and in a final effort the pope managed to persuade the French to send a small army. After a couple of fruitless sorties involving heavy losses, the French withdrew in an argument over the command. On September 5, when Iráklio finally surrendered, close to 140,000 Turks, Cretans and Venetians had perished in the struggle for control of the city. Iráklio's fall left only the three fortified islets of Soúdha, Spinalónga and Gramvoúsa in Venetian hands, where they remained until surrendered by treaty in 1715.

Turkish Crete

It is arguable whether the **Turkish occupation** was ever as stringent or arduous as the Venetian had been, but its reputation is far worse. In part this may simply be that its memory is more recent, but Turkish rule was complicated too by the religious differences involved, and by the fact that it survived into the era of resurgent Greek nationalism and Great Power politics.

If on their arrival the Turks had been welcomed, it was not a long-lived honeymoon. Once again Crete was divided, now between powerful pashas, and once again it was regarded merely as a resource to be exploited. The Ottoman Empire was less strictly ordered than the Venetian, but it demanded no less: rather than attempt to take control of trade themselves, the Turks simply imposed crippling taxes. Imposition of local administration was left to local landlords and the mercenary **Janissaries** they controlled. At the local level, then, there was a further level of exploitation as these men too took their cut. Stultified by heavy taxes and tariffs, slowed by neglect, the island economy stagnated.

One way to avoid the worst of the burden was to become a Muslim and, gradually, the majority of the Christian population was converted to **Islam** – at least nominally. Conversion brought with it substantial material advantages in taxation and rights to own property, and it helped avoid the worst of the repression that inevitably followed any Christian rebellion. These Greek Muslims were not particularly religious: even among the Turks on the island, Islamic law seems to have been loosely interpreted, and many continued to worship as Christians in secret, but the mass apostasies served to further divide the island. For those who remained openly Christian the burden became increasingly heavy as there were fewer to bear it. Many took to the mountains, where Turkish authority barely reached.

1864	1866	1883
Elefthérios Venizélos, Cretan revolutionary and statesman, born at Mournies, near Haniá.	Explosion at Arkádhi, a Cretan guerrilla stronghold. Hundreds die in blast and international sympathy for Crete is aroused.	Nikos Kazantzákis, Crete's most famous writer and creator of *Zorba the Greek*, born in Iráklio.

As the occupation continued, the Turks strengthened their hold on the cities and the fertile plains around them, while the mountains became the stronghold of the Christian *pallikáres*. The first major **rebellion** came in 1770, and inevitably it was centred in the recalcitrant region of Sfakiá. Under **Dhaskaloyiannis** (see box, p.284) the Cretans had been drawn into Great Power politics – drawn in and abandoned, for the promised aid from Russia never came. With the failure of this struggle, Sfakiá was itself brought under Turkish control for a while. But a pattern had been set, and the nineteenth century saw an almost constant struggle for independence.

The War of Independence

At the beginning of the nineteenth century the Ottoman Empire was under severe pressure on the Greek mainland, and in 1821 full-scale revolution, the **Greek War of Independence**, broke out. Part of the Turkish response was to call on the pasha of Egypt, **Mehmet Ali**, for assistance: his price was control of Crete. By 1824, in a campaign that even by Cretan standards was brutal on both sides, he had crushed the island's resistance. When in 1832 an independent Greek state was finally established with the support of Britain, France and Russia, Crete was left in the hands of the Egyptians, reverting to Turkish control within ten years.

From now on guerrilla warfare in support of union with Greece – **énosis** – was almost constant, flaring occasionally into wider revolts but mostly taking the form of incessant raids and irritations. The Cretans enjoyed widespread support, not only on the Greek mainland but throughout western Europe, and especially among expatriate Greek communities. But the Greeks alone were no match for the Ottoman armies, and the Great Powers, wary more than anything of each other, consistently failed to intervene. There was a major rising in 1841, bloodily suppressed, and in 1858 another which ended relatively peacefully in the recall of the Turkish governor and some minor concessions to the Christian population.

In 1866 a Cretan Assembly meeting in Sfakiá declared independence and union with Greece, and Egyptian troops were recalled to put down a further wave of revolts bolstered by Greek volunteers. Again the Egyptians proved ruthlessly effective, but this campaign ended in the explosion at **Arkádhi** (see p.202), an act of defiance that aroused Europe-wide sympathy. The Great Powers – Britain above all – still refused to involve themselves, but privately the supply of arms and volunteers to the insurgents was redoubled. From now on some kind of solution seemed inevitable, but even in 1878 the Congress of Berlin left Crete under Turkish dominion, demanding only further reforms in the government. In 1889 and 1896 there were further violent encounters, and in 1897 a Greek force landed to annex the island. Finally, the Great Powers were forced into action, occupying Crete with an international force and dividing the island into areas controlled by the British, French, Russians and Italians.

Independence and union with Greece

The outrage that finally brought about the expulsion of Turkish troops from Crete in 1898 was a minor skirmish in Iráklio (see p.57) that led to the death of the British vice-consul. A **national government** was set up, still nominally under Ottoman suzerainty, with Prince George, younger son of King George of Greece,

1894	1897
British archeologist Arthur Evans arrives in Crete and visits the site of Knossós, which would later bring him worldwide fame.	Great Powers occupy Crete after more uprisings; island divided into British, French, Russian and Italian sectors.

as high commissioner; under him was a joint Muslim-Christian assembly, part elected, part appointed.

Euphoria at independence was muted, however, for full union with Greece remained the goal of most Cretans. A new leader of this movement rapidly emerged – **Eleftherios Venizélos**. Born at Mourniés, outside Haniá, Venizélos had fought in the earlier independence struggles, and become a member of the Cretan Assembly and minister of justice to Prince George. Politically, however, he had little in common with his new master, and in 1905 he summoned an illegal Revolutionary Assembly at Thériso. Though the attempt to take up arms was summarily crushed, the strength of support for Venizélos was enough to force the resignation of Prince George. In 1908, the Cretan Assembly unilaterally declared *énosis* – much to the embarrassment of the Greek government. For, in the meantime, the "Young Turk" revolution looked set to revitalize the Ottoman Empire, and the Great Powers remained solidly opposed to anything that might upset the delicate balance of power in the Balkans.

The failure of the Greek government to act decisively in favour of Crete was one of the factors that led to the Military League of young officers forcing political reform on the mainland. With their backing, Venizélos became premier of Greece in 1910. In 1912 Greece, Serbia and Bulgaria declared war on the Ottoman Empire, making spectacular advances into Turkish territory. By the peace of 1913, Crete finally and officially became part of the Greek nation.

Though Greece was politically riven by **World War I**, and succeeding decades saw frequent, sometimes violent changes of power between Venizelist and Royalist forces, Crete was little affected. On just one further occasion did the island play a significant role in Greek affairs before the outbreak of war in 1940: in July 1938 there was a popular uprising against the dictator Metaxas and in favour of Venizélos, but it was swiftly put down.

The island was, however, hit hard by the aftermath of the disastrous Greek attempt to conquer Istanbul in pursuit of the "Great Idea" of rebuilding the Byzantine Empire. As part of the peace settlement that followed this military debacle, there was a forced **exchange of populations** in 1923: Muslims were expelled from Greece and Orthodox Christians from Turkey. In Crete many of these "Turks" were in fact Muslim Cretans, descendants of the mass apostasies of the eighteenth century. Nevertheless they left – some thirty thousand in all – and a similar number of Christian refugees from Turkey took their place.

World War II and occupation

In the winter of 1940 Italian troops invaded northern Greece, only to be thrown back across the Albanian border by the Greek army. Mussolini's humiliation, however, only served to draw the Germans into the fight, and although an Allied army was sent to Greece, the **mainland** was rapidly overrun.

The Allied campaign was marked from the start by suspicion, confusion and lack of communication between the two commands. On the Greek side Metaxas had died in January, and his successor as premier committed suicide, leaving a Cretan – **Emanuel Tsouderos** – to organize the retreat of king and government to his native island. They were rapidly followed by thousands of evacuees, including the bulk of the Allied army, a force made up in large part of Australian and New Zealand soldiers. Most of the native Cretan troops, a division of the Greek army, had been wiped out in defence of the mainland.

1898	1898–1913	1905
Riot in Iráklio precipitates the end of Turkish rule. Independence follows, with Prince George acting under Ottoman suzerainty.	Independence and emergence of Venizélos, who summons a Revolutionary Assembly at Thériso urging full union (*énosis*) with Greece.	The unpopular Prince George resigns.

THE KIDNAP OF GENERAL KREIPE

The Cretan resistance to the Nazi occupation had one spectacular success in 1944 when they kidnapped the German commander **General Kreipe** outside Iráklio, and succeeded in smuggling him over the mountains to the south coast and off the island to Egypt. Among this group were the author Patrick Leigh Fermor and Stanley Moss (whose *Ill Met by Moonlight* describes the incident in detail). The immediate result of this propaganda coup, however, was a terrible vengeance against the Cretan population, in which a string of villages around the Amári valley were destroyed and such menfolk as could be found were slaughtered. Harsh **retribution** against Cretan civilians, indeed, was the standard reaction by the German army to any success the resistance had.

According to the Allied plan, Crete should by now have been an impregnable fortress. In practice, though, virtually nothing had been done to improve the island defences, there were hardly any serviceable planes or other heavy equipment, and the arriving troops found little in the way of a plan for their deployment.

On May 20, 1941 the **invasion** of the island began, as German troops poured in by glider and parachute. It was at first a horrible slaughter, with the invaders easily picked off as they drifted slowly down. Few of the first wave of parachutists reached the ground alive and many of the gliders crashed, while the main German force was smashed before it ever reached the ground. In the far west, however, beyond the main battle zone, they succeeded in taking the airfield at Máleme. Whether through incompetence (as much of the literature on the Battle of Crete suggests) or breakdown of communications, no attempt to recapture the field was made until the Germans had had time to defend it and, with a secure landing site, reinforcements and equipment began to pour in. Not long before the battle, the German codes had been cracked, and the Allied commander in Crete, General Freyberg, therefore knew in detail exactly where and how the attacks would come. However, because he was not allowed to divulge secret intelligence findings to his junior officers (who were not cleared to receive them), a fatal misunderstanding by the commander regarding the enemy's intentions contained in the intelligence led him to reduce the forces at Máleme. From now on the battle, which had seemed won, was lost, and the Allied troops, already under constant air attack, found themselves outgunned on land too.

Casualties of the **Battle of Crete** were horrendous on both sides – the cemeteries are reminiscent of the burial grounds of World War I victims in northern France – and the crack German airborne division was effectively wiped out, causing a devastated Hitler to erect the monument to it which still stands outside Haniá (although recently damaged by protesters). No one ever attempted a similar assault again. But once they were established with a secure bridgehead, the Germans advanced rapidly, and a week after the first landings the Allied army was in full retreat across the mountains towards Hóra Sfakíon, from where most were evacuated by ship to Egypt. On May 30, the battle was over, leaving behind several thousand Allied soldiers (and all the Cretans who had fought alongside them) to surrender or take to the mountains.

The resistance

One of the first tasks of **the resistance** was to get these stranded soldiers off the island, and in this they had remarkable success, organizing the fugitives into groups and

1908	**1913**	**1923**
Crete unilaterally declares *énosis*, which is opposed by the Great Powers.	Following the First Balkan war by Greece and its allies against Ottoman Turkey, union of Greece and Crete is formally declared.	Forced exchange of populations between Greece and Turkey following Greek military debacle in the Greco-Turkish war; 30,000 Cretan Muslims expelled.

arranging their collection by ship or submarine from isolated beaches on the south coast. Many were hidden and fed by monks while they waited to escape, most famously at the monastery of Préveli. In this and many other ways the German occupation closely mirrored earlier ones; opposition was constant and reprisals brutal. The north coast and the lowlands were, as in the past, easily and firmly controlled, but the mountains, and Sfakiá above all, remained the haunt of rebel and resistance groups throughout the war.

With the boats that took the battle survivors away from Crete came intelligence officers whose job it was to organize and arm the resistance; throughout the war there were a dozen or so on the island, living in mountain shelters or caves, attempting to organize parachute drops of arms and reporting on troop movements on and around the island. How effective the sporadic efforts of the resistance were in wartime Crete is hard to gauge and it is questionable whether stunts such as the kidnapping of General Kreipe (see box opposite) brought the end of the war any nearer.

At the end of 1944, the German forces withdrew to a heavily fortified perimeter around Haniá, where they held out for a final seven months before surrendering. In the rest of the island, this left a **power vacuum** that several of the resistance groups rushed to fill. Allied intelligence would no doubt claim that one of the achievements of their agents in Crete was the near-avoidance of the civil war that wracked the rest of Greece. On the mainland the organization of the resistance had been very largely the work of Greek Communists, who emerged at the end of the war as much the best organized and armed group. On Crete, groups in favour with the Allies had been the best armed and organized, and certainly in the latter stages of the war, Communist-dominated organizations had been deliberately starved of equipment.

Postwar and modern Crete

In avoiding the civil war, Crete was able to set about **reconstruction** some way in advance of the rest of Greece, and after 1945 it grew to become one of the most prosperous and productive regions of the nation. Politically, postwar Crete was deeply mistrustful of outside control, even from Athens, a situation that persists today. At the local level above all, loyalties are divided along clan and patronage lines rather than party political ones, and leaders are judged on how well they provide for their areas and their followers.

Cretan politicians at the local level (there is no overall island government, only a regional **administration** controlled by appointees from Athens) continue to take an almost universal joy in standing up to central authority. **Rivalries** within Crete are fierce, too, most notably between Haniá, which was nominated as capital for a short period at the beginning of the century, and Iráklio, the traditional and present capital and nowadays the richer and politically more important city. This factionalism results in all sorts of anomalies and compromises: symptomatic was the rather impractical decision to spread the University of Crete across three campuses, at Iráklio, Réthymno (which has always considered itself the most cultured town in Crete) and the autonomous polytechnic of Haniá.

In **national politics**, the island presents a more unified front as the upholder of the liberal tradition of Venizélos. The 1967 anti-left coup in Athens that brought the junta of the Colonels to power was passionately opposed in Crete – one of the few areas of Greece to offer overt resistance to the regime. There followed seven years of repression during which all political activity was banned, the press heavily censored and

1941	1944
German invasion of Crete. A fatal blunder allows invaders to take the airport at Máleme and establish a bridgehead.	The island's German commander, Kreipe, is kidnapped by the resistance. The German army carries out brutal reprisals against the islanders.

communists arrested, imprisoned and tortured. In a referendum following the overthrow of the Colonels in 1974, Crete voted heavily against a restoration of the monarchy (the king had been implicated in the coup) and for a republican system. Then, in the succeeding presidential election, support for the right-winger Karamanlis (the winner) was less than half as strong on Crete as it was in the rest of Greece. Prior to the new millennium this was an abiding pattern: the socialist PASOK party consistently polled twice as many Cretan votes as the conservative ND.

Into the new millennium

The dominant parties of the restored democracy, the conservative **Néa Dhimokratía** (New Democracy; ND) and socialist **Panhellenic Socialist Movement (PASOK)**, had both been founded in the aftermath of the dictatorship and alternated in power for four decades until the end of 2014. The dominant figures in both parties were the respective founders, **Konstantinos Karamanlis** of ND and **Andreas Papandreou** of PASOK. The cause of many of Greece's current problems can be traced back to the first Papandreou administration, which came to power following an election victory in 1981, the same year that Greece entered the European Community. Promising "*allaghí*", the great change, he overturned the relatively cautious economic policies of the previous ND governments and introduced sharp pay rises and an unprecedented increase of jobs in the public sector. These measures were supplemented by the introduction of universal health care and state pensions. How this was all going to be financed was never seriously addressed. This free-spending populist policy enabled PASOK to maintain power for most of the 1990s and early 2000s while the debts mounted. Following Papandreou's death in 1996 there was no change of direction by PASOK and the new leader, **Costas Simitis**, broadly followed the spendthrift policies of the Papandreou years. Simitis's major achievement was to steer Greece into the eurozone, although it later emerged that the accession criteria had not only not been met, but that the Greek government had falsified the figures relating to public debt and inflation to enable entry to go ahead.

The new ND leader, Konstantinos Karamanlis, namesake and nephew of the party's founder, did not oppose the policies of PASOK, but adopted an even more populist stance which enabled him to win the election of 2004. Ironically his victory was over the new leader of PASOK, **Yiorgos (George) Papandreou**, the son of PASOK's founder. However, the Karamanlis government proved little more successful than its predecessors in dealing with an ailing economy and rising unemployment. Still, despite industrial action by unions throughout much of 2006 and 2007 opposing labour and pension reforms, in the autumn of 2007 Karamanlis called and won a snap general election. However, his party gained only a perilously slim two-seat majority over PASOK and it was clearly going to be difficult to impose the government's authority.

And so it proved as the ND administration reeled from one crisis to another. A string of corruption scandals linked to the government rocked the administration, and in late 2008 riots broke out across the country, ostensibly against a police shooting, but which flared into a nationwide protest against the effects of the world economic downturn and frustration at the severely limited prospects for young people.

In September 2009, with the government barely clinging to power, Karamanlis called another election. Voters turned out to eject ND and **hand victory to PASOK** and its

1945	1960s	1967–74
Liberation. A war-shattered island begins the slow task of reconstruction.	Tourist boom begins.	Dictatorship of the Colonels. Following their overthrow, in a referendum Crete votes heavily against a restoration of the monarchy.

A GREEK TRAGEDY

The **debt crisis**, which began in 2009, has seen Greece's economy nosedive. GDP has shrunk by 25 percent since 2010, almost 28 percent of the workforce are unemployed (most of whom do not receive benefits) and the nation's public health and education budgets have been decimated. In the prolonged recession wages and pensions have been slashed and a fifth of the nation cannot meet their food needs, while a third live below the poverty line. Since most of the bailout funds have gone to pay off creditors, almost nothing has been invested in economic recovery. To top it all, Greece's debt mountain is now almost twice the country's annual economic output.

Despite what seems to be a desperately bleak outlook, Greece does have the potential to be a successful economy. But to even start to get itself on a sound financial footing it will have to deal effectively with key issues such as **tax evasion** and **corruption** – often two sides of the same coin. The Greek debt crisis is, in short, the product of thirty years of budget deficits – racked up by the corrupt political dynasties of PASOK and Néa Dhimokratía – abetted by cripplingly low tax receipts. A survey by the Chicago Business School in 2012 estimated that self-employed workers (Greece has proportionally more than any other EU country) had failed to report around €28 billion in taxable income in 2009 alone.

One of the success stories of the Greek economy is **shipping**: one in every four tankers on the world's seas is Greek-owned, and a whopping 42 percent of the EU's merchant fleet is in Greek hands. But Greek shipping companies operate in a largely tax-free zone. Indeed, when embarrassed by criticism of their tax evasion, they made a one-off donation to the state of €417 million to cover the period 2014–17. Greece's new accord with its creditors to secure the third bailout insists on taxes – such as those of the shipping companies – being collected. However, the shipping companies' loyalty to their motherland is not unconditional and they have threatened – should the tax authorities come after them – to up sticks and move to Cyprus or other havens with a laxer fiscal regime.

leader George Papandreou. The electorate seemed more intent on punishing Karamanlis – whose party suffered its worst-ever showing at the polls – than being persuaded by the vague promises offered by Papandreou.

The worst of times

Any chance the new government had of dealing with Greece's ongoing problems was capsized by the financial tsunami of the **government debt crisis** that overwhelmed the country at the end of 2009. Reports that Greece had been using dubious accounting practices to hide the scale of its borrowing triggered panic among overseas investors concerned that the country would be unable to meet its debt obligations. Following numerous revisions of the debt figures, in May 2010 the Greek deficit was again revised upwards to an estimated fifteen percent of GDP (against a eurozone limit of three percent), one of the highest in the world. Credit ratings agencies then downgraded Greek government bonds to junk status creating further alarm in financial markets. In order to avert a default by the Greek government, in May 2010 the IMF, ECB (European Central Bank) and the European Commission constructed an urgent €45 billion **rescue package**, with a further €65 billion to follow. The price of this funding was a harsh series of **austerity measures** intended to bring the government's deficit under control. These measures – consisting of public sector workforce cuts and salary reductions, as well as labour and pension reforms – were opposed by large segments of

1986	1999	2001
Greece becomes a full member of the EU.	Greece joins eleven other EU states in creating the European Economic and Monetary Union (EMU) and a single currency, the euro.	The drachma is replaced by the euro as Greece's official currency.

the Greek populace, and a wave of **social unrest** swept across the country, with strikes and riots occurring in Athens and other cities.

Throughout 2011 Papandreou's government continued to grapple with the crisis, implementing more austerity measures as its popularity plummeted. In November, after failing to enlist the support of the other major parties to form a coalition administration, Papandreou **resigned as prime minister**. The PASOK and Néa Dhimokratía parties agreed to form an emergency government headed by former vice president of the European Central Bank, **Lucas Papademos**, until new elections could be held. In May 2012 the country went to the polls but the outcome was a stalemate in which no party was able to form a government. On June 17 new polls were held, with politicians urging electors to vote responsibly to save the country. The ND under its new leader, **Antonis Samaras**, gained the most seats and on June 20 formed a coalition with PASOK under its new leader, Evangelos Venizélos. The new coalition government had a workable majority over the other parties but, worryingly for the future, these included extreme left and neo-Nazi groups opposed to the financial strictures "imposed by foreigners".

The arrival of Syriza

In November 2012 the coalition government voted through a further round of severe austerity measures to receive the country's **second economic bailout** from the EU and IMF. The measures included pension cuts, increases in retirement age and wage cuts of up to thirty percent for civil servants and government employees. In the succeeding two years more cuts followed, plunging the country into deep economic distress as unemployment hit 28 percent (the EU's highest) and youth unemployment topped sixty percent. Now highly unpopular, the government – unable to set in place its candidate for the presidency – fell, and new elections were announced for January 2015.

In the poll held on January 25 an electorate, weary of the incompetent and corrupt dynastic parties PASOK and ND, handed a historic victory to the leftwing coalition **Syriza** that sent shockwaves through European capitals. Its young and charismatic leader, 41-year old **Alexis Tsipras**, vowed not only to end the old order but also "Greece's five years of humiliation and pain" by ditching austerity and renegotiating the country's €240 billion bailout. In a policy statement that harked back to the Papandreou governments of the 1980s he pledged to create 300,000 new jobs in the private, public and social sectors as well as promising substantial wage increases, and free electrical power and food subsidies to poor households. In order to gain breathing space, Tsipras then negotiated a four-month extension to the current bailout and embarked on a public relations campaign to attempt to pressure Greece's creditors into watering down their austerity demands. However, the other members of the eurozone did not accept Greece's arguments and insisted that it must "pay its own way". At the end of this period, in June, a meeting of EU finance ministers rejected a further extension of the bailout, effectively cutting Greece adrift. To prevent a flight of capital the Greek government **closed the banks** and imposed capital controls. Tsipras then declared that the bailout terms would be put to the people in a nationwide **referendum** on July 5. The predictable result was an overwhelming rejection of the creditors' terms by over sixty percent of voters.

Despite having recommended a "No" vote, after the result Tsipras was again faced with the same situation as before and a real danger that Greece would be forced out of the eurozone. Following several days of tense negotiations with Greece's creditors, he

2004	2008	2009–12
Athens stages the Olympic Games, with some events held in Crete.	Crete is badly hit by the worldwide recession.	Greek government debt crisis and a possible default threatens the stability of the world's monetary system. Crete shares in severe austerity measures to cut the nation's deficit.

finally climbed down and backtracked on almost all of the reforms he had announced in his victory speech in January. A new agreement with harsher terms than had been on offer then was the price to secure a **third bailout** of €85 billion over three years. This was put in place on July 13 but Tsipras's party split, with over forty deputies voting against the deal – which they condemned as "capitulation and treason" – in the Greek parliament. Tsipras replied by stating that for the nation it was a question of "staying alive or suicide", and got the vote through only with the support of pro-European opposition deputies.

No longer able to command a majority in the Greek parliament, on August 20 Tsipras resigned as prime minister and announced that the country would again go to the polls on September 20. In a historically low turnout of just over fifty percent, Syriza won the election and Tsipras was able to form a new government with the aid of a small nationalist party, **ANEL**. The second Tsipras administration inside a year embarked on implementing another round of draconian reforms demanded by the international creditors in return for the third bailout. Should he fail, a Greek default and ejection from the eurozone are the likely consequences.

TOURISM: THE ISLAND'S FUTURE?

As falling prices for Crete's major agricultural products – olive oil, raisins and citrus fruits – contribute less to the island's prosperity, a greater dependence on **tourism** has come to the fore. But the age of mass-market tourism is beginning to pall as the attractions of sun, beach and cheap booze along much of the coast attract mainly younger holidaymakers, who tend to move on when prices rise – as they have done as a consequence of the current financial calamity. The fallout from the global economic recession and the country's debt crisis has also taken its toll, and tourism is forecast to fall by at least twenty percent over the next few years as a result of this.

Efforts to build a market in **green tourism** are in their infancy, held back by an indifference to environmental concerns by politicians, farmers and a populace that has yet to realize that environmentally organized tourism – for which the island, with its extended season, picturesque landscape and rich variety of flora and fauna is an ideal location – can be enormously profitable. The creation of an autonomous Cretan tourist authority in 2000, with a brief to promote the island, should also have been a force for change, but a lack of funding by Athens has left it hamstrung.

The island has faced up to several invaders throughout its history, but the tourist invasion presents it with a new dilemma: to submerge its traditional ways in the pursuit of ever greater numbers or to try to raise the quality of its tourism and at the same time preserve Crete's unique character. The government in Athens has sent conflicting messages in recent years: on the one hand encouraging the Cretan authorities to do more to cater to ramblers, birdwatchers, naturalists and those interested in the island's archeology and history, on the other stating that funds would be available to support the development of conference centres (with golf courses attached), luxury hotels and casinos. The proposed Cape Sídheros project in eastern Crete (see box, p.162), where a wild and rugged coastal peninsula has been threatened with a resort complex, is a prime example of this confusion.

Given the island's serious economic plight, any ventures offering jobs are often keenly supported by local politicians, often with little regard for the potential environmental consequences. It's to be hoped that the current economic hurricane faced by Crete and Greece will not lay waste to much good work in the area of sustainable tourist development done over previous decades.

2012

Reopening of the Iráklio Archeological Museum, following a seven-year closure for reconstruction.

2015

Left-wing Syriza party wins election victory and rejects EU's bailout terms; threat of ejection from the eurozone forces government to call another election to enable it to reverse its previous policy.

Crete in myth

Crete is intimately associated with much of ancient Greek mythology, and in particular with Zeus, who was not only brought up on the island, but according to some ancient Cretans was buried here as well. The Dhiktean Cave, a gash on the face of Mount Dhíkti, which soars above the Lasíthi plateau, has most claims to be the birthplace of the greatest god in the Greek pantheon, and symbolizes the potent influence of Minoan Crete on the land to the north.

The birth of Zeus

According to the earliest accounts of the myth, **Zeus** was the third generation of rulers of the gods. The original ruler, Uranus, was overthrown by his youngest son Kronos. In order to prevent such a fate overtaking him, too, Kronos ate his first five children at birth. When she was bearing the sixth child, his wife, Rhea, took refuge in a Cretan cavern – a site much argued over, but most commonly assigned to the Dhiktean Cave (see p.143). Here Zeus was born, and in his place Rhea presented Kronos with a rock wrapped in blankets, which he duly devoured. Zeus was brought up secretly in the cave, his cries drowned by the **Kouretes**, who kept up a noisy dance with continuous clashing of shields and spears outside. The Kouretes, believed by Cretans to be the sons of the Earth Mother, were especially revered on the island as the inventors of beekeeping and honey as well as the hunting bow, and an inscription found at Palékastro suggests that they may well have a Minoan origin. The baby fed on milk from a mountain goat-nymph, Amalthea, one of whose horns he later made into a miraculous gift that a wish would fill with whatever was desired (hence the horn of plenty).

Having grown to manhood on Crete, Zeus declared war on Kronos and the Titans, a struggle that lasted ten years. Eventually, however, Zeus emerged as supreme ruler of the gods on **Mount Olympus**, and Kronos was banished to the Underworld. This myth has a precedent in Hittite texts of the second millennium BC that themselves had taken it over from the earlier Hurrians, a people who had settled in Syria and northern Mesopotamia. The Minoans passed it on to the Greeks.

The origin of the Cretans

The sexual prowess of Zeus led him into a bewildering number of affairs, one of which led to his best-known return to the island of his birth – with Europa – and the founding of the Cretan race. **Europa** was a princess, the daughter of King Phoenix (after whom Phoenicia was named), and Zeus lusted after her mightily. Approaching the shore of Phoenicia, Zeus saw her gathering flowers, and came to her in the guise of a **white bull**. Fascinated by the creature's docility Europa climbed onto its back, at which he leapt into the sea and carried her off across the sea to Crete. They landed at Mátala, travelled to Górtys (where one version has it Zeus ravished her beneath a plane tree that has never lost its leaves since) and were married at the Dhiktean Cave. One of the presents Zeus gave to his bride was **Talos**, a bronze giant who strode round the island hurling boulders at approaching strangers. Jason and the Argonauts were greeted by a hail of stones from Talos when they approached Crete. Aided by their companion, the sorceress Medea, they brought about the giant's fall by piercing a vein on his ankle – his single vulnerable spot – thus allowing the *ichor*, a divine fluid that served as blood, to drain from his body.

Minos and the Minotaur

The Zeus of the Europa tale, taking the form of a **bull**, is almost certainly mixed up with earlier, native Cretan gods. The sun god of Crete also took the form of a bull, and the animal is a recurrent motif in the island's mythology.

In the story of **Minos**, a bull once again has a prominent role. Europa bore Zeus three sons – Minos, Rhadamanthys and Sarpedon – before eventually being abandoned. Later she married the king of Crete, Asterios, who adopted her children. Upon reaching manhood the three brothers quarrelled for the love of a beautiful boy named Miletos (a reflection of the mores and customs of the time). When Miletos chose Sarpedon, an enraged Minos drove him from the island. However, before boarding a ship to Asia Minor, Miletos killed King Asterios. Legend associates both Miletos and Sarpedon – who joined him in Asia Minor – with the founding of Miletus (see p.140), later an important city in Greek and Roman times.

With Sarpedon removed, Minos claimed the throne and settled upon Rhadamanthys a third of Asterios' dominions. Rhadamanthys became renowned as a law-maker, appears in some tales as ruler at Festós, and every ninth year visited Zeus's cave on Mount Dhíkti to bring back a new set of laws. So great was Rhadamanthys's fame as a law-giver that Homer tells of how Zeus appointed him one of the three judges of the dead along with Minos and Aeachus.

Minos, meanwhile, was another ruler driven by lustful passions. He liaised with a succession of lovers including the Minoan goddess **Britomartis**, whom he chased relentlessly around the island for nine months until she threw herself into the sea off the end of the Rodhopoú peninsula to escape his attentions. Rescued from drowning by the net of a fisherman, she became known as Diktynna ("of the net"), and a great temple to her was erected on the site (see p.266). Minos's wife and queen, **Pasiphae**, incensed by her rakish husband's infidelities, put a spell on the king: whenever he lay with another woman he discharged not seed but a swarm of poisonous serpents, scorpions and insects that devoured the woman's vitals. News of his affliction (which bears a striking resemblance to venereal disease) apparently got around, and one of his bedmates Prokris, daughter of the Athenian king Erechtheus, insisted that he should take a prophylactic draught before their tryst which apparently prevented her invasion by serpents and scorpions.

Earlier, when he had gained the throne of his father, Minos prayed to Poseidon (or perhaps his father Zeus) to send a bull from the sea that he could offer as a sacrifice, thus signifying the god's recognition of the justice of his claim to the throne. When the radiant bull emerged from the sea, Minos was so taken by its beauty that he determined to keep it, sacrificing in its place another from his herds. Punishment for such hubris was inevitable, and in this case the gods chose to inflame Minos's wife, Pasiphae (a moon goddess in her own right – again the bull symbolizes the sun), with intense desire for the animal. She had the brilliant inventor and craftsman **Daedalus** construct her an artificial cow, in which she hid and induced the bull to couple with her: the result was the **Minotaur**, a beast half man and half bull (probably human with a bull's head). To hide his shame, Minos had Daedalus construct the **labyrinth** in which to imprison the monster.

Theseus and Ariadne

The myth goes on to relate how Minos waged war on Athens after Androgeous, one of his sons by Pasiphae, had gone off to that city and won every event in the Panathenaic games, only to be slain on the orders of the outraged Athenian king, Aegeus. Part of the settlement demanded by the victorious Minos was that an annual tribute of seven young men and women be provided as sport or sacrifice for the imprisoned Minotaur. The third time the tribute was due, **Theseus**, the son of King Aegeus, resolved to end the slaughter and himself went as one of the victims. In Crete he met Minos's daughter

THE DEATH OF ZEUS

The postscript to these Greek myths concerns **Zeus's death**. According to the Cretans, and reflecting the older Minoan idea of a fertility god who annually died and was reborn, Zeus was buried beneath Mount Yioúhtas near Knossós, in whose outline his recumbent profile can still be seen from the palace site. It was a purely local claim, however, and clashed with the northern Greek concept of Zeus as an immortal and all-powerful sky-god. The northern Greeks regarded the islanders' belief in a dying Zeus as blasphemy, and their contempt for the Cretan heresy may have given rise to the saying "all Cretans are liars".

Ariadne, who fell in love with him and resolved to help him in his task. At the instigation of the sympathetic Daedalus, she provided Theseus with a ball of thread that he could unwind and, if he succeeded in killing the Minotaur, follow to find his way out of the labyrinth.

At first everything went to plan, and Theseus killed the beast and escaped from the island with Ariadne and the others. On the way home though, things were less successful. Ariadne was abandoned on a beach in Náxos (where she was later found by the god Dionysos and carried off to Olympus). Approaching Athens, Theseus forgot to change his black sails for white – the pre-arranged signal that his mission had succeeded. Thinking his son dead, King Aegeus threw himself into the sea and drowned.

Back on Crete, Minos imprisoned Daedalus in his own labyrinth, furious at Ariadne's desertion and his part in it, and at the failure of the maze. Locked up with Daedalus was his son, **Ikarus**. They escaped by making wings of feathers – from birds devoured by the Minotaur – held together with wax. Daedalus finally reached Sicily and the protection of King Kokalos: Ikarus, though, flew too close to the sun, the wax melted and he plunged to his death in the sea. Still set on revenge, Minos tracked Daedalus down by setting a puzzle so fiendishly difficult that only he could have solved it: a large reward was promised to the first person who could pass a thread through a triton shell. When Minos eventually arrived in Sicily he posed the problem to Kokalos who said it would be easy. He then consulted secretly with Daedalus who drilled the shell at its point and tied a thread to the leg of an ant that was sent into the shell. When the insect emerged through the hole, Kokalos took the shell to show Minos. Now certain that Daedalus was hidden in the palace, Minos demanded that Kokalos hand him over. Kokalos appeared to agree to the request and offered Minos hospitality in the palace. There Minos met an undignified end when he was scalded to death in his bath by the daughters of the king, urged on by Daedalus.

Wildlife

Although the south coast of Crete is closer to Libya than it is to Athens, the island's wildlife owes much more to mainland Greece than it does to Africa. This is because Crete lies at the end of the long range of drowned limestone mountains called the Hellenic arc which make up most of the Balkan peninsula, and you need to go a long way south into the Sahara before you again find mountains as high as the Cretan ones. Crete, then, has northern Mediterranean fauna and flora across a range of habitats.

Islands tend to be short on wildlife because of their isolation from the main bulk of species on the mainland. Not so Crete – it's rich in flora and fauna, and provides the full range of Mediterranean habitats. In fact, there are over two thousand species of **plants** in Crete, of which over 180 are endemic to the island, making up nearly a third of the Greek flora, and about as many as in the whole of Britain. With the wealth of plant life come far more **insects** than you get further north. The survival of Cretan wildlife in all its richness and diversity has been facilitated by the fact that agriculture remains fairly "undeveloped", although the pressures are mounting, in the form of widespread use of chemicals, increased water abstraction, road construction and tourist development. You won't find many birds or wildflowers among the hectares of polytunnels around Timbáki, but you will in the mountains where such methods remain uneconomic.

The only feature really lacking, as elsewhere in Greece, is **trees**. The Minoan civilization was a seafaring one, so as early as the Bronze Age there was a high demand for timber for shipbuilding. Some of the lower hills were perhaps deforested four thousand years ago, a process completed by the Venetians. Today, native forests exist only in remote uplands and gorges.

Crete's chief drawback, at least if you hope to combine nature with the rest of the island's sights and life, is the pattern of its **climate**. Because it's so far south, the summers are long and dry, and that period equates to our northern winters, when many plants shut down or die, with a corresponding decline in activity from all other wildlife. Trying to see wildflowers or birds in lowland Crete in August is a bit like going out for a nature ramble in Britain or Massachusetts in January.

Habitats

Rarely in Europe do you find such a wide range of habitats so tightly packed, or real "wilderness" areas so close to modern towns and resorts, as in Crete. Broadly speaking, you can divide the island into four major **habitats**: the coast; cultivated land; low hillsides less than 1000m; and mountains above 1000m. Crete is the only Greek island that is mountainous enough to have all four of these habitats.

Along the coast, sandy beaches and low rocky cliffs are the norm. Marshy river deltas or estuaries are rare (simply because Crete is a dry country and there aren't many rivers), but where you can find them, these wetland habitats are among the best places to look for birds.

Cultivated land is very variable in its wildlife interest, though look out for small market gardens – *perivólia* – often found on the edges of towns and villages, which are particularly good for small birds. Small hayfields can be a colourful mass of annual flowers and attendant insects in spring and early summer.

Low hillsides up to 1000m comprise much of Crete. Scrubby hillsides, loosely grazed by goats and sometimes sheep, are the most typical Mediterranean habitat, extremely rich in flowers, insects and reptiles. Botanically, they divide into two distinct types: the first is *phrígana*, and consists of scattered scrubby bushes, always on limestone, especially rich in aromatic herbs and wildflowers. You can often find *phrígana* by looking for beehives: Cretan beekeepers know where to find the thyme and rosemary that gives the local honey its wonderful flavour. The other hillside habitat is maquis, a dense, very prickly scrub with scattered trees. Of these two hillside habitats, *phrígana* is better for flowers, maquis for birds.

Mountains over 1000m are surprisingly common: three separate ranges go over 2000m, and they are responsible for much of the climate, creating rain and retaining it as snow for a large part of the year. The small upland plateaux among the mountains – Omalós or Lasíthi most famously – are a very special feature, with their own distinctive flora and fauna. Although the Cretan mountains don't as a rule have the exciting mammals of the mainland, they are very good for large and spectacular birds of prey.

Flowers

What you will see, obviously, depends on where and when you go. The best time is **spring**, which is heralded as early as January when the almond tree flowers, its petals falling like snow and carpeting the streets of small mountain villages. The season seriously gets under way in mid-February, however, in the southeast corner of the island, is at its peak during March over most of the lowlands (but continues well into April), and in the mountains comes later, starting in late April and going on through to June. In **early summer**, the spring anemones, orchids and rockroses are replaced by plants like broom and chrysanthemum; this ranges from mid-April in southern Crete to late July in the high mountains, though these timings can vary – exceptionally by as much as a month.

Things are pretty much burnt out over all the lowlands from July to the end of September, though there are still some flowers in the mountains. Once the hot summer is over, blooming starts all over again. Some of the **autumn-flowering** species, such as cyclamens and autumn crocus, flower from October in the mountains to December in the south. And by then you might as well stay on for the first of the spring bulbs in January.

Year-round, the best insurance policy is to be prepared to move up and down the hills until you find flowers – from the beginning of March to the end of June you are almost guaranteed to find classic displays somewhere on the island, and you'll see the less spectacular but still worthwhile autumn-flowering species from October to early December. If you have to go in July, August or September, then be prepared to see a restricted range, and also to go high up the mountains. The four habitats all have their own flowers, though some, of course, overlap.

Flower species

On the **coast** you might find the spectacular **yellow horned poppy** growing on shingled banks, and **sea stocks** and **Virginia stocks** growing among the rocks behind the beach. Sand dunes are rare but sometimes there is a flat grazed area behind the beach; these are often good for **orchids**. In the autumn, look for the very large white flowers of the **sea daffodil**, as well as **autumn crocuses** on the banks behind the shore.

The trees and shrubs on **low hillsides** are varied and beautiful, with colourful brooms flowering in early summer, preceded by bushy **rockroses** – *Cistaceae* – which are a mass of pink or white flowers in spring. Dotted among the shrubs is the occasional tree; the **non-deciduous plane tree** is an endemic variety, and the **Judas tree** flowers on bare wood in spring, making a blaze of pink against green hillsides that stands out for miles. Lower than the shrubs are the **aromatic herbs** – sage, rosemary, thyme and lavender – with perhaps some spiny species of **Euphorbia**. Because Crete is dry and hot for much of the year, you also get a high proportion of **xerophytes** – plants that are adapted to drought by having fleshy leaves and thick skins.

Below the herbs is the ground layer; peer around the edges and between the shrubs and you'll find a wealth of **orchids**, **anemones**, **grape hyacinths**, **irises**, and perhaps

fritillaries if you're lucky. The orchids are extraordinary; some kinds – the *Ophrys* species – have especially fascinating and unusual flowers.

Once spring is over, these plants give way to the early summer flowering of the brooms and aromatic herbs, as well as a final fling from the annuals that sense the coming of the heat and their own death. When the heat of the summer is over, the autumn bulbs appear, with species of **crocus** and their relatives, the **colchicums** and the **sternbergias**, and finally the **autumn cyclamens** through into early December.

Mountains are good to visit later in the year. The rocky mountain **gorges** are considered to be the elite environments for plants, and house the greatest biodiversity; this is because most gorges are generally left ungrazed and undisturbed and it's often possible to find at least ten Cretan endemics without too much difficulty. The gorges are the home of many familiar garden rock plants, such as the **aubretias**, **saxifrages** and **alyssums**, as well as **dwarf bellflowers** and **anemones**. Look for dwarf **tulips** in fields on the upland plateaux in spring. The mountains are also the place to see the remaining Greek native pine **forests**, and in the woodland glades you will find **gentians**, **cyclamens** and **violets**. Above 1500m or so the forests begin to thin out, and in these upland meadows glorious **crocuses** flower almost before the snow has melted in spring – a very fine form of *Crocus seiberi* is a particularly early one. Autumn-flowering species of crocus and cyclamen should reward a visit later in the year.

Birds

More than 330 species of **birds** have been reported in Crete to date. Greece has a good range of Mediterranean species plus a few very rare ones such as the **Eleonora's falcon** and the **Ruppell's warbler**, which have their European breeding strongholds in Greece, particularly on Crete. The great thing about bird-watching in Crete is that, if you pick your time right, you can see both resident and migratory species. Crete is on one of the main fly-past routes for species that have wintered in East Africa, but breed in eastern and northern Europe. They migrate every spring up the Nile valley, and then move across the eastern Mediterranean, often in huge numbers. This happens from mid-March to mid-May, depending on the species, the weather, and where you are. The return migration in autumn is less spectacular because it is less concentrated in time, but still worth watching out for.

On the outskirts of towns and in the fields there are some colourful residents. Small predatory birds such as **woodchat shrikes**, **blackeared wheatears**, **kestrels** and migrating **red-footed falcons** can be seen perched on telegraph wires. The dramatic pink, black and white **hoopoe** and the striking yellow and black **golden oriole** are sometimes to be found in woodland and olive groves, and **Scops owls** (Europe's smallest owl) can often be heard calling around towns at night. They monotonously repeat a single "poo", sometimes in mournful vocal duets.

Look closely at the **swifts** and **swallows**, and you will find a few species not found in northern Europe: **crag martins** replace house martins in the **mountain gorges**, for example, and you may see the large **alpine swift**, which has a white belly. The **Sardinian warbler** dominates the rough scrubby **hillsides** – the male with a glossy black cap and an obvious red eye. These hillsides are also the home of the **chukar**, a species of partridge similar to the red-legged partridge found in Britain.

Wetlands and **coastal lagoons** are excellent for bird-spotting, especially at spring and autumn migration, although this habitat is hard to find. There's a wide variety of **herons** and **egrets**, as well as smaller waders such as the rare **avocet** and **marsh sandpiper** and **black-winged stilt**, which has ridiculously long pink legs. **Marsh harriers** are common too, drifting over the reedbeds on characteristic raised wings. Scrubby woodland around coastal wetlands is a good place to see migrating smaller birds such as **warblers**, **wagtails** and the like.

The mountains hold some of the most exciting birds in Crete. Smaller birds like the **blue rock thrush**, **cirl bunting** and **alpine chough** are common, and there is a good chance of seeing large and dramatic birds of prey. The **buzzards** and smaller eagles are confusingly similar, but there are also **golden eagles**, **Bonelli's eagles** and **vultures**. One very rare species of vulture, the **lammergeier** (or bearded vulture), is currently on the dramatically endangered list, although it used to be more common in Crete than anywhere else in Europe; you may be lucky enough to spot one of the island's thirty-five remaining birds (only seven breeding pairs) soaring above the Lasíthi or Omalós plateaux. It's a huge bird, with a wingspan of nearly 3m, and with narrower wings and a longer wedge-shaped tail than the other vulture you are likely to see, the **griffon vulture**.

Mammals

Cretan **mammals** are elusive, generally nocturnal, and very hard to see. Islands tend to have fewer species than the mainland and in this Crete is no exception, with about half the species that you could expect to see on mainland Greece. Even such common animals as the red squirrel and fox have never made it across the water, nor will you find large exciting mammals like wolves or lynxes in the mountains, as you might (rarely) on the mainland.

However, there are some compensations. Islands often have their own endemic species, and one in Crete is the **Cretan spiny mouse**, which is found nowhere else; if you happen to be on a rocky hillside at dusk you may see this largish mouse with very big ears and a spiny back fossicking around. The other compensation in Crete is the ancestral **wild goat** or *kri-kri*; a small population still exists in the White Mountains around the Samariá Gorge, and also on some offshore islands – but you'll be lucky if you see one outside the zoos. Apart from those, Crete has fourteen bat species, as well as **weasels**, **badgers**, **hares**, **hedgehogs**, **field mice**, **shrews** and **beech martens**.

One relatively recent addition to the zoological record was the rediscovery in 1996 of the **Cretan wildcat** – *fourógatos* (see p.210) – long thought to be either extinct or a folktale. Only a single specimen has ever been captured alive (in the Amári valley) and the population status of the animal is still unknown. A few years after the find an Amári valley shepherd claimed to have discovered a den containing five kittens.

There are several marine mammals that can occasionally be seen in offshore waters. The critically endangered and extremely rare **Mediterranean monk seal** breeds in a few sea caves around the island. The deep waters off the south coast of Haniá have recently become well known for a resident population of **sperm whales**. **Dolphins** – which so delighted the Minoans – can be seen all round the island but you'll be most likely to see them while on a boat or ferry.

Reptiles and amphibians

The hot, rocky terrain of Crete suits **reptiles** well, with plenty of sun to bask in and plenty of rocks to hide under, but the island's isolation has severely restricted the number of species occurring: fewer than a third of those that are found on the mainland. Identification is therefore rather easy. If you sit and watch a dry stone wall almost anywhere in the western half of the island you're bound to see the small local wall lizard, **Erhard's wall lizard**. A rustle in the rocks by the side of the road might be an **ocellated skink** – a bit like a lizard, but with a thicker body and a stubbier neck. In the bushes of the maquis and *phrígana* you may see the **Balkan green lizard**, a truly splendid bright-green animal up to 50cm long, most of which is tail – usually seen as it runs frantically on its hind legs from one bush to another.

At night, **geckoes** replace the lizards. Geckoes are small (less than 10cm), have big eyes and round adhesive pads on their toes that enable them to walk upside down on the ceiling. Sometimes they come into houses – in which case welcome them, for they will keep down the mosquitoes and other biting insects. Crete has three out of four European species. The island is also one of only a handful of places where the **chameleon** occurs in Europe, although it is extremely rare, and there are only a couple of known specimens; this may (or may not) be attributed to its camouflage skills. It lives in bushes and low trees, and hunts by day; its colour is greenish but obviously variable.

Tortoises, sadly, don't occur in Crete, but the stripe-necked **terrapin** does. Look out for these in any freshwater habitat – Lake Kournás and the Ayía bird sanctuary for example, or even in the cistern at the Zákros palace. There are also **sea turtles** in the Mediterranean: you might be lucky and see one while you're swimming or on a boat, since they sometimes bask on the surface of the water. The one you're most likely to see is the **loggerhead turtle**, which can grow up to a metre long. Crete has important breeding populations on beaches to the west of Haniá, around Mátala, and the largest (more than 350 nests) at Réthymno, but tourism and the development associated with it are threatening their future. Each year, many turtles are injured by motorboats, their nests are destroyed by bikes and jeeps ridden on the beaches, and the newly hatched young die entangled in deckchairs and umbrellas left out at night on the sand. The turtles are easily frightened by noise and lights too, which makes them uneasy cohabitants with freelance campers and nightclubs.

The Greek government has passed **laws** designed to protect the loggerheads, and the Sea Turtle Protection Society of Greece now operates an ambitious conservation programme, but local economic interests tend to prefer a beach full of bodies to a sea full of turtles.

The final group of reptiles are the **snakes**, represented by four species, only one of which is poisonous – the **cat snake**. Even this is back-fanged and therefore extremely unlikely to be able to bite anything as big as a human, so you can relax a bit when strolling round the hillsides; most snakes are very timid and easily frightened anyway. One species worth looking out for is the beautiful **leopard snake**, which is grey with red blotches edged in black. It's fond of basking on the sides of roads and paths.

Only three species of **amphibian** occur in Crete. The **green toad** is smaller than the common toad, with an obvious marbled green and grey back. The **marsh frog** is a large frog, greenish but variable in colour, and very noisy in spring. And **tree frogs** are small, live in trees, and call very loudly at night.

Insects

There are around a million different species of insects in the world, and even in Crete there are probably a few hundred which have yet to be scientifically described or labelled. About a third of all insect species are beetles, and these are very obvious wherever you go. You might see one of the dung beetles rolling a ball of dung along a path like the mythological Sisyphus. If you have time to look closely at bushes and small trees, you might be rewarded with a stick insect or a **praying mantis**, creatures that are rarely seen because of their excellent camouflage.

The **grasshopper** and **cricket** family are well represented, and most patches of grass will hold a few. Grasshoppers produce their chirping noise by rubbing a wing against a leg, but crickets do it by rubbing both wings together. **Cicadas**, which most people think of as a night-calling grasshopper, aren't actually related at all – they're more of a large leaf-hopper. Their continuous whirring call is one of the characteristic sounds of the Mediterranean night, and is produced by the rapid vibration of two membranes, called tymbals, on either side of their body.

Perhaps the most obvious insects are the **butterflies**. Any time from spring through most of summer is good for butterfly-spotting, and there's a second flight of adults of many species in the autumn. Dramatic varieties in Crete include two species of **swallowtail**, easily identified by their large size, yellow and black colouring, and long spurs at the back of the hind wings. **Cleopatras** are large, brilliant yellow butterflies, related to the brimstone of northern Europe, but bigger and more colourful. Look out also for **Cretan Argus** – chocolate brown in colour and only found in the Psilorítis and Dhíkti mountain ranges, it is now thought to be increasingly threatened by human activity.

by Pete Raine and Stephen Roberts

Books

From Homer on, Crete has inspired an exceptionally wide range of literature, and in Nikos Kazantzákis the island also produced one truly world-class author. Though some of it is out of print, most titles are still readily available online. In contrast to the proliferation of ancient history, there is no book in English devoted to modern Cretan history, though there's a good general account included in Hopkins's book on the island (see opposite).

The more specialist titles might also be found at a dedicated travel bookstore or a Greek-interest bookshop: in the UK, try the Hellenic Book Service, in Kentish Town, London (☎020 7267 9499, ⊚hellenicbookservice.com). On Crete, Planet International Bookstore (see p.66) is an excellent source. If you phone or email them, they will post books out to you immediately, trusting you to pay later.

Books marked with the ★ symbol are particularly recommended.

ARCHEOLOGY AND ANCIENT HISTORY

Gerald Cadogan *Palaces of Minoan Crete*. Complete guide to all the major sites, with much more history and general information than the name implies.

John Chadwick *Linear B and related scripts*. A short version of *The Decipherment of Linear B*, in which the whole fascinating story is graphically told by Chadwick, who collaborated with Ventris, the English architect who made the crucial breakthrough. The same author's *Mycenaean World* vividly describes the society revealed by the tablets.

Leonard Cottrell *The Bull of Minos*. Breathless and somewhat dated account of the discoveries of Schliemann and Evans (see box, p.326); easy reading.

Costis Davaras *Guide to Cretan Antiquities*. A fascinating guide by the distinguished archeologist to the antiquities of Crete, from the ancient through to the Turkish eras. Cross-referenced in dictionary form, it has authoritative articles on all the major sites as well as subjects as diverse as Minoan razors and toilet articles, the disappearance of Cretan forests and the career of Venizélos. Widely available at museums on the island.

★**Arthur Evans** *The Palace of Minos*. This four-volume work remains the seminal description of the discovery and excavation of the Knossós palace, and is fascinating to dip into.

Reynold Higgins *Minoan and Mycenaean Art*. Solid introduction to the subject with plenty of illustrations.

★**J. Alexander Macgillivray** *Minotaur: Sir Arthur Evans and the Archaeology of the Minoan Myth*. Outstanding book by a Crete-based archeologist, which demonstrates how Evans fitted the evidence found at Knossós to his own preconception of the Minoans as peaceful, literate and aesthetic second-millennium BC Victorians. A superb read.

★**J.D.S. Pendlebury** *The Archaeology of Crete*. Although published in 1933, this is still the most comprehensive archeological handbook, detailing virtually every site on the island. Pendlebury's *Handbook to the Palace of Minos* remains an excellent guide to the Knossós site by someone who – as curator after Evans's retirement – knew it inside out.

Nikos Psilakis *Byzantine Churches and Monasteries of Crete*. Locally published, this is a superbly illustrated and expert guide to over 150 of Crete's monasteries, churches and convents. As well as interesting background on all the monuments, there's also a fold-out map to locate them.

Paola Pugsley *The Blue Guide*. Excellent, detailed guide to the churches, archeological sites and museums across the island. However, some directions to remoter sights occasionally lack clarity and it is overdue for an update.

Peter Warren *The Aegean Civilizations*. A very good and concise introduction to Minoan and Mycenean Crete by one of the leading modern experts; good illustrations, but in need of a new edition.

R.F. Willetts *Everyday Life in Ancient Crete*. An interesting survey of Minoan daily life as lived in the towns, villages and farms, as well as the palaces.

MODERN HISTORY AND ARCHITECTURE

★**James Angelos** *The Full Castastrophe*. Subtitled "a journey among the new Greek ruins," financial journalist Angelos uses character-driven narratives to bring to life the reality of Greece's current economic collapse. It's all here: the political chicanery, the corruption, the scams, an overburdened patronage system, endemic tax fraud and even the rise of the neo-Nazis. Riveting.

Michele Buonsanti & Alberta Galla *Candia Veneziana – Venetian Itineraries Through Crete*. Useful guide to the under-documented wealth of monuments surviving from

La Serenissima's four and a half centuries of hegemony over the island. Widely available from bookshops on Crete.

Richard Clogg *A Concise History of Greece*. A rigorously historical account of Greek history from its emergence from Ottoman rule to the present day, covering the wider aspects of Crete's struggle for independence and union with Greece.

★ **Adam Hopkins** *Crete, Its Past, Present and People*. Excellent general introduction to Cretan history and society with lots of interesting detail on topics as diverse as the Battle of Crete, daily life and diet, the arrival of mass tourism and medicinal wild herbs.

★ **John Julius Norwich** *Byzantium: the Early Centuries*; *Byzantium: the Apogee*; *Byzantium: Decline and Fall*; *A History of Venice*; *The Middle Sea*. The three volumes of Norwich's history of the Byzantine Empire are terrific narrative accounts, and much can be gleaned from them about Crete in this period. *History of Venice* relates the fascinating story of the rise and fall of the power that ruled Crete for four and a half centuries, while *Middle Sea* charts three thousand years of Mediterranean history, allowing the island's past to be seen in its wider geographical context.

★ **James Pettifer** *The Greeks: the Land and People since the War*. Excellent (if now somewhat dated) introduction to contemporary Greece. Pettifer roams the country and charts the state of the nation's politics, food, family life, religion, tourism and all points in between. Only passing references to Crete, however.

★ **Oliver Rackham & Jennifer Moody** *The Making of the Cretan Landscape*. A classic of its kind, this is an enthralling botanical and anthropological study of the Cretans in their environment, from antiquity to the present day, with sections devoted to the island's geological formation, vegetation, people and settlements. A seasoned champion of the Cretan natural environment, Oliver Rackham died in 2015.

WORLD WAR II

★ **Antony Beevor** *Crete: The Battle and the Resistance*. Relatively short study of the Battle of Crete, with colourful insights into the characters involved. Beevor dissects recent evidence to conclude that defeat was at least in part due to Cretan commander General Freyburg's fatal misinterpretation of an Ultra coded message leading him to divert troops away from the Máleme invasion site, critically weakening the Allied defences.

Alan Clark *The Fall of Crete*. Racy and sensational – but very readable – military history by the late maverick

English politician. Detailed on the battles, and more critical of the command than you might expect from a former cabinet minister.

Wes Davis *The Ariadne Objective*. A fast-moving, novelistic account of the audacious kidnapping of the German commander Kreipe focused on the eccentric, larger-than-life characters (Leigh-Fermor, Moss et al) of the Special Operations Executive who pulled it off.

Patrick Leigh-Fermor *Abducting a General*. Posthumously published account of the kidnap of German general Kreipe by a leading participant. From his night parachute landing on the Katharó plateau to the departure with the captured general from Rodhákino beach a year later, it's a gripping tale. Fermor also gives due credit to the role of the Cretan "mountaineers" in the operation, whose contribution he felt had been downplayed in earlier accounts.

★ **Lew Lind** *Flowers of Rethymnon*. A gripping personal account of his part in the Battle of Crete and subsequent escape by a 19-year-old Australian soldier. The carnage of the battle is rivetingly described, and shining through the horror of it all comes the unflinching bravery of the Cretan villagers who put themselves in danger of German reprisals by helping servicemen trapped on Crete – such as Lind – escape to Egypt.

W. Stanley Moss *Ill Met by Moonlight*. This account of the capture of General Kreipe by one of the participants, largely taken from his diaries of the time, is a good *Boys' Own*-style adventure yarn. Moss also translated Baron von der Heydte's *Daedalus Returned* (o/p), which gives something of the other side of the story.

★ **George Psychoundakis** *The Cretan Runner*. Account of the invasion and resistance by a Cretan participant; Psychoundakis (who died in 2006) was a guide and message-runner for all the leading English-speaking protagonists. Great, although not much appreciated by many of his compatriots, who tend to dismiss him as an English lackey.

Tony Simpson *Operation Mercury: The Battle for Crete, 1941*. A very different way of looking at the subject, putting the campaign into an international context and relying heavily on oral history for details of the combat. Uncompromisingly critical of the command, and far more interesting than straight military history.

Evelyn Waugh *Officers and Gentlemen*; *Diaries*. Both include accounts of the Battle of Crete, and particularly of the horrors of the flight and evacuation.

TRAVEL WRITING

Edward Lear *The Cretan Journal*. Diary of Lear's trip to Crete in 1864, illustrated with his sketches and water-colours. He didn't enjoy himself much.

★ **David MacNeil Doren** *Winds of Crete*. An American and his Swedish wife find enlightenment on Crete in the early 1970s and before the arrival of mass tourism.

An amusing and well-observed travelogue documenting many of the island's customs and curiosities, in addition to some hair-raising brushes with Cretan physicians.

★ **Henry Miller** *The Colossus of Maroussi*. Miller's idiosyncratic account of his travels in Greece on the eve of World War II includes a trip to Crete, where diarrhoea, biting flies and Festós palace all get bit-parts in the epic.

★ **Robert Pashley** *Travels in Crete*. Based on an extensive and punishing journey around Crete in the 1830s, Pashley is the original nineteenth-century British traveller, full of erudite observations, interesting anecdotes and outspoken attitudes. Recently republished in a facsimile edition (two vols.) by the Cambridge University Press.

Dilys Powell *The Villa Ariadne*. The story of the British in Crete, from Arthur Evans to Paddy Leigh Fermor, through the villa at Knossós that linked all of them. Good at bringing the excitement of the early archeological work to life, but rather syrupy in style.

Pandelis Prevelakis *Tale of a Town* (Doric Publications, Athens). English translation of a native's description of life and times in Réthymno during the first quarter of the twentieth century. Widely available at bookshops on the island.

J.E. Hilary Skinner *Roughing It in Crete in 1867*. Great title for this account of another Englishman's adventures, this time with a band of rebels. Interesting on the less glamorous side of the independence struggle, since he spent the whole time searching for food or dodging Turkish patrols.

Christopher Somerville *The Golden Step*. Inspired by an epic (and extreme) long-distance gorge and mountain race from end to end of the island, Somerville set out to hike the same route, much of it along the loosely waymarked Pan-European E4 Footpath. Colourful descriptions of scrapes, scrambles and encounters en route make for an entertaining, perceptive and occasionally poignant tale.

★ **Capt. T.A.B. Spratt** *Travels and Researches in Crete*. Another nineteenth-century Briton who caught the Cretan bug while surveying the island's coastline, and left behind this account of its natural history, geology and archeology.

★ **Patricia Storace** *Dinner with Persephone*. Although not specifically about Crete, this is one of the best books ever written on the Greeks by a foreign author. Storace, an American poet, learned the language and went to live with, and travel among, the Hellenes for a year, delving deep into the psyche of this superficially attractive, but fiendishly complex people. Ideal holiday reading – you'll never look at the Greeks in the same light again.

Peter Trudgill *In Sfakiá*. In the 1970s British student Trudgill travelled to Crete, ending up in Hóra Sfakíon. It was the start of a forty-year love affair during which time the author – now a Greek socio-linguist – has returned annually to the coastal village. An astute and often witty portrait of rugged Sfakiá's customs, legends, history and its equally rugged people.

FICTION

Victoria Hislop *The Island*. The former leper colony of Spinalónga forms the backdrop to this novel about a young woman discovering her Cretan roots. A potentially good story is marred by the cloying and derivative manner of its telling.

Homer *The Iliad* and *The Odyssey*. The first concerns itself, semi-factually, with the Trojan War; the second recounts the hero Odysseus's long journey home, via Crete and seemingly every other corner of the Mediterranean. Homer's accounts were in some ways responsible for the "rediscovery" of Minoan Crete in the nineteenth century, so it seems appropriate to read them here.

★ **Nikos Kazantzákis** *Zorba the Greek*; *Freedom and Death*; *Report to Greco*. Something by the great Cretan novelist and man of letters is essential reading when on Crete. Forget the film that distorted the story's essentials:

Zorba the Greek is a wonderful read on Crete that provides the backdrop to the adventures of one of the most irresistible characters of modern fiction. *Freedom and Death* is just as good, while *Report to Greco* is an autobiographical account of Kazantzákis' early years and later travels.

Ioannis Kondylakis *Patouchas*. The story of a Cretan shepherd on a journey of self-discovery; a wonderfully observed and humorous fictional sketch of Turkish Crete in the nineteenth century by a little-known Cretan author.

Vitzentzos Kornaros (trans. Theodore Stefanides) *Erotokritos*. A beautifully produced English translation of the sixteenth-century Cretan epic poem.

★ **Mary Renault** *The King Must Die*; *The Bull from the Sea*. Stirring accounts of the Theseus legend and Minoan Crete for those who like their history in fictionalized form.

WILDLIFE AND GEOLOGY

Michael Chinerey *Collins Guide to the Insects of Britain and Western Europe*. This doesn't specifically include Greece (there's no comprehensive guide to Greek insects) but it gives a good general background and identification to the main families of insects that you're likely to see.

Charalampos G. Fassoulas *Field Guide to the Geology of Crete*. Excellent introduction to Crete's fascinating geology, explaining the island's geological evolution, paleography and paleontology. Superb colour photos and details of where to find many of the most interesting sites. Widely available at bookshops on the island.

John Fielding & Nicholas Turland *Flowers of Crete*. Coffee-table volume with 1900 colour photos of Cretan flora. A monumental work (in all senses), it runs to nearly 700 pages so is not for the backpack; useful for ID'ing your photos when you get back home.

Bob Gibbons *Travellers' Nature Guides: Greece*. Good general guide to the ecology, flora and fauna of Greece, with a section devoted to Crete.

★ **Anthony Huxley & William Taylor** *Flowers of Greece*. One of the best books for identifying flowers in Crete.

★ **Mullarney, Svensson, Zetterstrom & Grant** *Bird*

Guide to the Birds of Britain and Europe. Outstanding guide to European birds covering most species you're likely to find in Crete. Superbly illustrated, too.

George Sfikas *Wild Flowers of Crete*. Comprehensive illustrated guide to the island's flora.

Paul Whalley *The Mitchell Beazley Pocket Guide to Butterflies* (published in the US as *Butterflies*). A useful identification guide.

HIKING AND TOURING GUIDES

Anavasi *Crete Hiking Maps*. Excellent 1:25.000 scale hikers' map series with maps dedicated to the Lefká Óri, Samariá and Sfakiá, as well as the Psilorítis range and the area around Zákros; more maps are planned. Widely available at bookshops on Crete and from the website.

Freytag & Berndt *Crete Hiking Map*. Booklet and map pack in German, Greek and English describing twenty walks all over the island ranging from a couple of hours to full-day treks; the accompanying large-scale 1:50,000 map is admirably clear. Widely available from bookshops on the island.

★**Jonnie Godfrey & Elizabeth Karslake** *Landscapes of Eastern/Western Crete*. Full of hiking and touring suggestions; both have been recently updated.

Alan Hall *Western Crete: 45 Walks in Kissamos and Sélinos*. A useful, recently updated book with plenty of background detail, covering the extreme west of Crete and detailing more than forty walks of between 5km and 20km, with the majority shorter than 10km.

Loraine Wilson *Crete: The White Mountains*. Thorough and regularly updated guide, written by an experienced trekker, to fifty-plus hikes in the Lefká Óri. Walks range between 3km and 20km, and routes can be linked for extended treks over several days.

FOOD AND DRINK

Konstantinos Lazarakis *The Wines of Greece*. A comprehensive survey of the rapidly changing Greek wine world, detailing what's new and where to find the rising stars.

Marianthi Milona *Culinaria Greece*. Part of the enycyclo-paedic Culinaria series, this is a great book for winter evenings in front of the fire, with plenty of stunning photos of Greek locations and food and drink. There's a chapter devoted to Crete, with articles on olive oil and how it's made, Cretan wine, herbs and teas, plus plenty of recipes.

★**Maria and Nikos Psilakis** *Cretan Cooking*. Highly recommended guide to the Cretan kitchen – if only these dishes were generally available in the island's tavernas. The authors have gathered recipes from all parts of the island and interspersed with them illustrations not only of the food but of rural life past and present.

Language

So many Cretans have been compelled by poverty and other circumstances to work abroad, especially in the English-speaking world, that you'll find someone who speaks some English in almost every village. Add to that the thousands attending language schools or working in the tourist industry – English is the lingua franca of the north coast – and it's easy to see how so many visitors come back having learnt only half a dozen words between them. You can certainly get by this way, even in quite out-of-the-way places, but it isn't very satisfying.

Greek is not an easy language for English-speakers, but it is a beautiful one, and even a brief acquaintance will give you some idea of the debt western European languages owe to it. And the willingness to say even a few words will transform your status from that of *tourístas* to the honourable one of *kséno*, a word which can mean stranger, traveller and guest all rolled into one.

Alphabet and grammar

On top of the usual difficulties of learning a new language, Greek presents the added problem of an entirely separate **alphabet**. Despite initial appearances, this is in practice fairly easily mastered and is a skill that will help enormously if you are going to get around independently (see box opposite). In addition, certain combinations of letters have unexpected results. This book's transliteration system should help you make intelligible noises but you have to remember that the correct **stress** – marked in the book with an accent – is absolutely crucial. With the right sounds but the wrong stress people will either fail to understand you, or else understand something quite different from what you intended.

Greek **grammar** is more complicated still: nouns are divided into three genders, all with different case endings in the singular and in the plural, and all adjectives and articles have to agree with these in gender, number and case. (All adjectives are cited in the neuter form in the following lists.) Verbs are even worse. To begin with at least, the best thing is simply to say what you know the way you know it, and never mind the niceties. If you worry about your mistakes, you'll never say anything.

GREEK WORDS AND PHRASES

ESSENTIALS

Hello	Yiásas/yiásou (polite/ informal) or Hérete
Good morning	Kalíméra
Good evening	Kalíspéra
Goodnight	Kalíníkhta
Please	parakaló
Thank you (very much)	Efharistó (polí)
Yes	né
No	óhi
Certainly	málista
OK, agreed	endáksi
How are you?	Ti kánis/ti kánete?
I'm fine	Kalá íme
And you?	Ke esís?
What's your name?	Pos se léne?
My name is…	Me léne…
I (don't) understand	(Dhen) katalavéno
Speak slower, please	Parakaló, miláte pió sigá
How do you say it in Greek?	Pos léyete sta Eliniká?
I don't know	Dhen kséro
Let's go	Páme
See you tomorrow	Tha se dho ávrio
See you soon	Kalí andhámosi
Goodbye	Adhío
Excuse me, do you speak English?	Parakaló, mípos miláte angliká?
Please help me	Parakaló, na me voithíste
Sorry/excuse me	Signómi

THE GREEK ALPHABET: TRANSLITERATION

Set out below is the Greek alphabet, the system of transliteration used in this book and a brief aid to pronunciation.

Greek	Transliteration	Pronounced
Α, a	a	a as in father
Β, β	v	v as in vet
Γ, γ	y/g	y as in yes when before an e or i; when before consonants or a, o or ou it's a breathy, throaty g
Δ, δ	dh	th as in then
Ε, ε	e	e as in get
Ζ, ζ	z	z sound
Η, η	i	i sound as in ski
Θ, θ	th	th as in theme
Ι, ι	i	i as in bit
Κ, κ	k	k sound
Λ, λ	l	l sound
Μ, μ	m	m sound
Ν, ν	n	n sound
Ξ, ξ	ks	ks sound
Ο, ο	o	shortish o sound
Π, π	p	p sound
Ρ, ρ	r	rolled r sound
Σ, σ, ς	s	s sound
Τ, τ	t	t sound
Υ, υ	i	i sound as in ski
Φ, φ	f	f sound
Χ, χ	h/kh	harsh h sound, like ch in loch
Ψ, ψ	ps	ps as in lips
Ω, ω	o	shortish o sound

Combinations and diphthongs

ΑΙ, αι	e	e as in get
ΑΥ, αυ	av/af	av or af depending on following consonant
ΕΙ, ει	i	i sound as in ski
ΟΙ, οι	i	i sound as in ski
ΕΥ, ευ	ev/ef	ev or ef depending on following consonant
ΟΥ, ου	ou	ou as in tourist
ΓΓ, γγ	ng	ng as in angle
ΓΚ, γκ	g/ng	g as in goat at the beginning of a word, ng in the middle
ΜΠ, μπ	b/mb	b at the beginning of a word, mb in the middle
ΝΤ, ντ	d/nd	d at the beginning of a word, nd in the middle
ΤΣ, τσ	ts	ts as in hits
ΣΙ, σι	sh	sh as in shame
ΤΖ, τζ	ts	j as in jam

Note: An umlaut or dieresis over a letter indicates that the two vowels are pronounced separately; for example *païdhákia* (lamb chops) is pronounced pah-ee-dhakia rather than peh-dhakia.

Cheers!	Stiniyássas!/Yiámas!	**big/small**	megálo/mikró
Mr/Mrs/Miss	Kírios/Kiría/Dhespinís	**cheap/expensive**	ftinó/akrivó
more	perisótero	**hot/cold**	zestó/krío
less	ligótero	**with/without**	mazí/horís
a little	lígo	**quickly/slowly**	grígora/sigá
a lot	polí		

GREEK'S GREEK

There are numerous words and phrases that you will hear constantly, even if you rarely have the chance to use them. These are a few of the most common.

Éla!	Come (literally), but also Speak to me! You don't say! etc.
Oríste?	What can I do for you?
Bros!	Standard phone response
Ti néa?	What's new?
Ti yínete?	What's going on (here)?
Étsi k'étsi	So-so
Ópa!	Whoops! Watch it!
Po-po-po!	Expression of dismay or concern, like French "O la la!"
Pedhí mou	My boy/girl, sonny, friend, etc.
Maláka(s)	Literally "wanker", but often used (don't try it!) as an informal address
Sigá sigá	Take your time, slow down
Kaló taxídhi	Bon voyage

QUESTIONS

To ask a question, it's simplest to start with *parakaló*, then name the thing you want in an interrogative tone.

where?	pou?
how?	pos?
how many?	póssi/pósses?
how much?	póso?
when?	póte?
why?	yatí?
what time…?	ti óra ?
what is/which is…?	ti íne/pió íne..?

ACCOMMODATION

hotel	ksenodhohío
a room	éna dhomátio
We'd like a room	Parakaló, éna dhomátio
for one/two/three people	ya éna/dhío/tría átoma
for one/two/three nights	ya mía/dhío/trís vradhiés
with a double bed	me megálo kreváti
with a shower	me doús
hot water	zestó neró
cold water	krío neró
Can I see it?	Boró na to dho?
Can we camp here?	Boróume na váloume ti skiní edhó?
campsite	kamping/kataskínosi
tent	skiní
youth hostel	ksenodhohío neótitos

SHOPPING AND SERVICES

How much (does it cost)?	póso káni?
What time does it open/close?	Tí óra aníyi/ klíni?
May I have a kilo of oranges?	Parakaló, éna kiló portokália?
to eat/drink	trógo/píno
bakery	foúrnos, psomádhiko

pharmacy	farmakío
post office	tahidhromío
stamps	gramatósima
petrol station	venzinádhiko
bank	trápeza
money	leftá/hrímata
toilet	toualéta
police	astinomía
doctor	iatrós
hospital	nosokomío

ON THE MOVE

airplane	aeropláno
bus	leoforío
car	aftokínito
motorbike, moped	mihanáki, papáki
taxi	taksí
ship	plío/vapóri/karávi
bicycle	podhílato
hitching	otostóp
on foot	me ta pódhia
trail	monopáti
bus station	praktorío leoforíon
bus stop	stási
harbour	limáni
What time does it leave?	Ti óra févyi?
What time does it arrive?	Ti óra ftháni?
How many kilometres?	Pósa hiliómetra?
How many hours?	Pósses óres?
Where are you going?	Pou pas?
I'm going to…	Páo sto…
I want to get off at…	Thélo na katévo sto…
Can you show me the road to…?	Parakaló, o dhrómos ya…?
Where is the bakery?	Parakaló, o foúrnos?
near	kondá
far	makriá

left	aristerá	first	próto
right	dheksiá	second	dhéftero
straight ahead	katefthía	third	tríto
a ticket to…	éna isistírio ya…		
a return ticket	éna isistírio me epistrofí	**TIME AND DAYS OF THE WEEK**	
beach	paralía	now	tóra
cave	spiliá	today	símera
centre (of town)	kéndro	tomorrow	ávrio
church	eklissía	yesterday	khthés
sea	thálassa	Monday	Dheftéra
village	horió	Tuesday	Tríti
		Wednesday	Tetárti
NUMBERS		Thursday	Pémpti
1	énas/éna/mía	Friday	Paraskeví
2	dhío	Saturday	Sávato
3	trís/tría	Sunday	Kiriakí
4	tésseres/téssera	What time is it?	Ti óra íne?
5	pénde	One/two/three o'clock	Mía/dhío/trís óra/óres
6	éksi	Twenty to four	Tésseres pará íkosi
7	eftá	Five past seven	Eftá ke pénde
8	okhtó	Half past eleven	Éndheka ke misí
9	ennéa	half-hour	misí óra
10	dhéka	quarter-hour	éna tétarto
11	éndheka		
12	dhódheka	**MONTHS AND SEASONS**	
13	dhekatrís	You may see Katharévoussa, or hybrid, forms of the	
14	dhekatésseres	months written on timetables or street signs; these are	
20	íkosi	the spoken forms.	
21	íkosi éna	January	Yennáris
30	triánda	February	Fleváris
40	saránda	March	Mártis
50	penínda	April	Aprílis
60	eksínda	May	Maïos
70	evdhomínda	June	Ioúnios
80	ogdhónda	July	Ioúlios
90	enenínda	August	Ávgoustos
100	ekató	September	Septémvris
150	ekatón penínda	October	Októvrios
200	dhiakóssies/ia	November	Noémvris
500	pendakóssies/ia	December	Dhekémvris
1000	hílies/ia	summer schedule	Therinó dhromolóyio
2000	dhío hiliádhes	winter schedule	Himerinó dhromolóyio
1,000,000	éna ekatomírio		

MENU READER

BASICS		katálogo/lísta	menu
aláti	salt	koutáli	spoon
avgá	eggs	kréas	meat
boukáli	bottle	ládhi, eleóladho	olive oil
boútero	butter	lahaniká	vegetables
fayitó	food	lemóni	lemon
(horís) ládhi	(without) oil	olikís aleseos	whole-grain/meal
hortofágos	vegetarian	o logariasmós	the bill
kalambokísio	corn	mahyéri	knife

méli	honey
neró	water
orektiká	starters
pipéri	pepper
piroúni	fork
potíri	glass
psári(a)	fish
psomí	bread
siskalísio psomi	rye bread
sídi	vinegar
skórdho	garlic
thalassiná	seafood
thimárisio	thyme honey; highly prized on Crete
tirí	cheese
yiaoúrti	yoghurt
záhari	sugar

COOKING TERMS

Iliókafto	sun-dried
makaronádha	spaghetti- or pasta-based dish
mayireftá	oven-baked dishes
psitó	roasted
skáras	grilled
sti soúvla	spit-roasted
sto foúrno	baked
tiganitó	pan-fried
tis óras	grilled/fried to order
yemistá	stuffed (squid, vegetables, etc)

STARTERS, SALADS AND MEZÉDHES

angourodomáta saláta	cucumber and tomato salad
avgolémono	egg and lemon soup
bouréki, bourekákia	courgette/zucchini, potato and cheese pie
dákos	barley rusks soaked in oil and tomato, often sprinkled with cheese and oregano
dolmádhes/dolmadhákia	stuffed vine leaves/small stuffed vine leaves
domatosaláta	tomato salad
eliés	olives
fasoládha	bean soup
fáva	purée of split peas with onion
horiátiki (salatá)	Greek salad (with olives, féta, etc)
kalitsoúnia	pies filled with *mizíthra* cheese
keftédhes	meatballs
kolokythakeftedhes	courgette balls (fried)
kolokythákia tiganitá	courgette/zucchini slices fried in batter
kolokithoánthi yemistá	stuffed courgette/zucchini flowers, a delicious Cretan speciality
láhano-karóto saláta	cabbage and carrot salad
maroúli saláta	lettuce salad

THE MINOAN DIET

Like today's islanders, the Minoans ate the wild plants and herbs that grow in the hills and mountains (known by modern Cretans as *hórta*), as well as a variety of grains and pulses. Lovers of **seafood**, they also fished the seas around the island's coast for many of the varieties familiar to modern diners in the island's tavernas: *tsipoúra*, *sargós* and *fangrí* (types of bream) plus *safriós* (mackerel), *okhtapódhi* (octopus) and *ahinosaláta* (sea urchins' eggs). Remains found at many Minoan sites indicate that lobster, crab, oyster, whelks and mussels were also highly regarded.

The Minoans' favourite **meats** (again as today) were sheep and goat, and the Cretan passion for *tsalingária* or *cochlí* (snails) was just as strong three and a half thousand years ago. Duck and partridge were also eaten, although chicken (and their eggs) were unknown in Minoan times. The **olive** was introduced in the Neolithic period and the great *píthoi* oil containers found in the Minoan palaces testify to the importance of oil at all levels of society. The Minoans were probably just as choosy about their olive oil as islanders today and each region – as now – was no doubt renowned for its subtle differences in taste and quality.

Almonds, figs, pears, plums and pomegranates were the Minoans' preferred **fruits**, and their **bread** – cooked on flat dishes using flour with little gluten (raising agent) – would be instantly recognizable to a modern Cretan as the flat *píta*, today a staple throughout Greece. Honey was the main source of sugar in Minoan times, and no doubt *thimárisio* (thyme honey) was as popular then as now. The Minoans were also enthusiastic **wine** drinkers: a four-thousand-year-old winepress discovered at Vathýpetro (see p.77), at the centre of a still-working vineyard, has a fair claim to being the oldest in the world.

melitzanosaláta	aubergine/eggplant dip	apákia	smoked pork loin
melitzánes tiganités	aubergine/eggplant slices fried in batter	biftéki	hamburger
		brizóla	pork or beef chop
paximádhia	twice-baked Cretan rusks softened with water and used in *dákos* or served with *mezédhes*	hirinó	pork
		katsikáki	kid (goat)
		keftédhes	meatballs
		kléftiko	meat, potatoes and veg cooked together in a pot or foil; a Cretan speciality traditionally carried to bandits in hiding
saganáki	fried cheese		
soúpa	soup		
spanakópita/ spanakopitakia	spinach pies/small spinach pies		
taramósalata	fish roe pâté		
tsalingária, cochlí	snails	kókoras krasáto	coq au vin
tyrópita/tyropitákia	cheese pies/small cheese pies	kokorétsi	liver/offal kebab
		kotópoulo	chicken
tzatzíki	yoghurt and cucumber dip	kounéli	rabbit
yígandes	white haricot beans	loukánika	spicy sausages
		moskhári	veal or yearling beef
VEGETABLES		moussaká	aubergine/eggplant, potato and mince pie
anginánes	artichokes		
angoúri	cucumber	païdhákia	lamb chops
bámies	okra	papoutsáki	meat-stuffed version of *imám bayaldí* (see "Vegetables")
briám	ratatouille of courgettes, potatoes, onions, tomato		
		patsás	tripe soup, often served at Easter
domátes	tomatoes		
fakés	lentils	pastítsio	macaroni baked with meat
fasolákia	string beans		
hórta	greens (usually wild)	sikóti	liver
imám bayaldí	stuffed, oven-baked aubergine/eggplant	souvláki	chunks of seasoned meat or fish skewered and chargrilled
kolokithákia	courgette/zucchini		
koukiá	broad beans		
kremídhia	onions	stifádho	meat stew with tomato and onion
ladhéra	vegetables stewed/baked in oil		
		tsalingária	garden snails
melitzána	aubergine/eggplant	tsoutsoukákia	meatballs in tomato sauce
papoutsákia	stuffed aubergine/ eggplant		
		vodhinó	beef
patátes	potatoes	yíros	doner kebab; sliced, spit-roasted seasoned lamb
patátes limonátes	potatoes baked with lemon and oil		
		yiouvétsi	meat casserole with pasta
piperiés	peppers		
radhíkia	wild chicory	**FISH AND SEAFOOD**	
rízi/piláfi	rice (usually with *sáltsa* – sauce)	ahiní	sea urchins; briny orange roe eaten as *ahinosaláta*
saláta	salad	astakós	lobster
spanáki	spinach	barbóunia	red mullet
yemistés	stuffed vegetables	fangrí	sea bream
		garídhes	prawns
MEAT AND POULTRY		gávros	anchovy
agrimí stifádho	braised goat with shallots	glóssa	sole
arnáki me rízi	ragout of lamb with rice	gópa	bogue
arní	lamb	kakaviá	bouillabaisse-style fish stew

kalamária/kalamarákia	squid/baby squid	yaoúrti	yoghurt; superb in Crete and often served with honey as a dessert
kathári	black snapper		
koliós	mackerel		
lavráki	sea bass		
marídhes	whitebait	**CHEESE**	
melanoúri	saddled bream	anthótiros	soft, full-fat unsalted cheese, similar to *mizíthra*
mýdhia	mussels		
okhtapódhi	octopus		
sardhélles	sardines	graviéra	gruyère-type hard cheese
sargós	white bream	kasséri	semi-hard sheep's milk cheese
sinagrídha	dentex		
skáros	parrotfish	kefalotíri	salty, hard sheep's or goat's milk cheese
skorpína	scorpion fish		
skoumbrí	mackerel	ladhotíri	hard cheese matured in oil
soupiá	cuttlefish	manoúri	mild, soft sheep's milk cheese
strídhia	oysters		
tónnos	tuna	mizíthra	sweet or savoury ricotta-style goat's or sheep's milk cheese
tsipoúra	sea bream		
xifías	swordfish		

DESSERTS, FRUIT AND NUTS

DRINKS

baklavá	honey and nut pastry	bíra	beer
banána	banana	frappé	cold instant coffee shaken with condensed milk until it gets a frothy head, served with ice; a Greek institution
bougátsa	creamy cheese pie sprinkled with sugar and cinnamon; a tasty Cretan speciality		
fistíkia	pistachio nuts	gála	milk
fráoules	strawberries	gálakakáo	chocolate milk
galaktobóureko	custard-cream filo pie	gazóza	generic fizzy drink
halvás	sesame-based sweetmeat	hýma (krasí)	wine from the barrel
karidhópita	walnut cake	kafé	coffee
karpoúzi	watermelon	koniák	brandy
kataífi	"angel hair" pastry filled with nuts and/ or almonds	krasí	wine
		áspro	white
		mávro/kókkino	red
kéik	cake	rosé/kokkinéli	rosé
kerásia	cherries	limonádha	lemonade
loukoumádhes	dough fritters served hot with honey or cinnamon	neró metalikó	mineral water
		oúzo	distilled grape spirit; the national drink of Greece
loukoúmia	Turkish delight		
míla	apples	portokaládha	orangeade
milopita/milopitákia	apple pies	tónik	tonic water
pagotó	ice cream	tsáï	tea
pastéli	sesame and honey bar	tsikoudhia/rakí	highly popular grappa-style firewater; the vast majority of islanders make their own which is of course "the best in Crete"
pepóni	melon		
portokália	oranges		
rizógalo	rice pudding		
rodhákino	peach		
síka	(dried) figs		
stafília	grapes	tsípouro	spirit; similar to oúzo

Glossary

acropolis ancient, fortified hilltop

agora market and meeting place of an ancient city

amphora tall, narrow-necked jar for oil or wine

áno upper, as in upper town or village; eg Áno Zákros

apse curved recess at the altar end of a church

Archaic period Late Iron Age, from around 750 BC to the start of the Classical period in the fifth century BC

arsenali arsenals; a term used rather loosely for many Venetian defensive and harbour works

asklepion sanctuary dedicated to Asklepios, the Greek god of healing, where the sick sought cures for their ailments

atrium central altar-court of a Roman house

áyios/ayía/áyii saint or holy (m/f/pl), common place-name prefix (abbrev. Ag. or Ay.): Áyios Nikólaos is St Nicholas; Ayía Triádha is the Holy Trinity

basilica colonnaded "hall-type" church

Byzantine empire created by the division of the Roman Empire in 395 AD, this was the eastern half, ruled from Byzantium or Constantinople (modern Istanbul). There are many Byzantine churches of the fifth to the twelfth century on Crete, and Byzantine art flourished again after the fall of Constantinople in 1453, under Venetian rule, when many artists and scholars fled to the island

central court paved area at the heart of a Minoan palace

Classical period from the end of the Persian Wars in the fifth century BC to the unification of Greece under Philip II of Macedon (338 BC)

dhimarhío town hall (modern usage)

dhomátia rooms for rent in private houses

Dorian civilization that overran the Mycenaeans from the north around 1100 BC, and became their successor throughout much of southern Greece, including Crete

eparhía Greek Orthodox diocese, also the smallest subdivision of a modern province

Eteo-Cretan literally true Cretan, the Eteo-Cretans are believed to have been remnants of the Minoan people who kept a degree of their language and culture alive in isolated centres in eastern Crete as late as the third century BC

Geometric period Post-Mycenaean Iron Age, named for the style of its pottery: beginnings are in the early eleventh century BC with the arrival of Dorian peoples – by the eighth, with the development of representational styles, it becomes known as the Archaic period

Hellenistic period the last and most unified Greek empire, created by Philip II and Alexander the Great in the fourth century BC, finally collapsing with the fall of Corinth to the Romans in 146 BC

hóra main town of a region; literally it means "the place"

horns of consecration Minoan religious symbol imitating the bulls' horns that decorated Minoan palaces and shrines

iconostasis screen between the nave of a church and the altar, often covered in icons

ipnákos Greek version of the siesta, (also called mikró ýpno) which is widely practised in Crete, especially during the hot summer months. It usually lasts from around 1.30pm to 5.30pm with a legal requirement that requires silence from 3–5pm. Many stores and businesses close during these hours

janissary member of the Turkish Imperial Guard: in Crete under the Turks a much-feared mercenary force, often forcibly recruited from the local population

kafenío coffeehouse/café: in a small village the centre of communal life and probably the bus stop, too

kaïki caïque, or medium-sized boat, traditionally wooden. Now used for just about any coast-hopping or excursion boat

kámbos fertile agricultural plateau, usually near the mouth of a river

kapetánios widely used term of honour for a man of local power – originally for guerrilla leaders who earned the title through acts of particular bravado

kástro medieval castle or any fortified hill

káto lower, as in lower town or village; eg Káto Zákros

kernos ancient cult vessel or altar with a number of receptacles for offerings

krater large, two-handled wine bowl

lárnakes Minoan clay coffins

lustral basin a small sunken chamber in Minoan palaces reached by steps; perhaps actually some kind of bath but more likely for purely ritual purification

megaron principal hall of a Mycenaean palace

meltémi north wind that blows across the Aegean in summer (can be vicious in Crete). Its force is gauged by what it knocks over – "tableweather", "chairweather", etc

Minoan Crete's great Bronze Age civilization which dominated the Aegean from about 2500 to 1400 BC

Minos mythical ruler after whom Arthur Evans named Minoan society; more likely the title of a dynasty of priest-kings like the Egyptian "Pharaoh"

moní monastery or convent

Mycenaean mainland civilization centred on Mycenae c.1700–1100 BC: probably responsible for the destruction of Minoan civilization. Mycenaean influence pervaded Crete in the late and post-Minoan periods

Neolithic the earliest era of settlement in Crete, characterized by the use of stone tools and weapons together with basic agriculture

néos, néa, néo new

Neopalatial The zenith of Minoan civilization c.1700–1400BC when the palaces were rebuilt on a luxurious scale following destruction

nomós modern Greek province: Crete is divided into four

odeion small amphitheatre used for performances or meetings

paleós, paleá, paleó old

pallikári Literally "brave man": in Crete a guerrilla fighter, particularly in the struggle for independence from the Turks, also a general term for a tough young man

Panayía the Virgin Mary

paniyíri festival or feast, the local celebration of a holy day

Pantokrátor literally "The Almighty", a stern figure of Christ or God the Father frescoed or in mosaic on the dome of many Byzantine churches

paralía seafront promenade

peak sanctuary mountain-top shrine, often in or associated with a cave, sometimes in continuous use from Neolithic through to Roman times

períptero street kiosk

peristyle colonnade or area surrounded by colonnade, used especially of Minoan halls or courtyards

píthos (pl. píthoi) Large ceramic jar for storing oil, grain etc, very common in the Minoan palaces and used in almost identical form in modern Cretan homes

platía square or plaza. Kentrikí Platía means the main square

Prepalatial The period of Minoan history c.3500–1900BC preceding the era of the palaces

propilea portico or entrance to an ancient building

Protopalatial The period of Minoan history c.1900–1700BC when the first palaces were built

rhyton vessel, often horn-shaped, for pouring libations or offerings

sistrum ancient percussion instrument emitting a maracas or tambourine sound

stele upright stone slab or column, usually inscribed

stoa colonnaded walkway in Classical-era marketplace

theatral area open area found in most of the Minoan palaces with seat-like steps around; may have been a type of theatre or ritual area

tholos conical or beehive-shaped building, especially a Minoan or Mycenaean tomb

Acronyms

ANEL (Anexártitoi Ellines) Right-wing populist and nationalist party, currently a government coalition partner of Syriza

ANEK Anonimí Navtikí Evería Krítis (Shipping Company of Crete Ltd), which runs most ferries between Pireás and Crete, plus many to Italy

ELTA The postal service

EOS Greek Mountaineering Federation, based in Athens with branches in Haniá and Iráklio

EOT Ellinikós Organismós Tourismoú, the National Tourist Organization

KKE The Communist Party, unreconstructed.

KTEL National syndicate of bus companies. The term is also used to refer to bus stations

ND Néa Dhimokratía, the Conservative party

OSE Railway corporation

OTE Telephone company

PASOK Socialist party (Pan-Hellenic Socialist Movement)

SYRIZA (Synaspismós tis Rizopastikís Aristerás) A radical left-wing rainbow coalition including Maoist, Trotskyist and Green elements

XA (Hrisí Avgí or "Golden Dawn") Ultra-nationalist neo-Nazi party

Small print and index

A ROUGH GUIDE TO ROUGH GUIDES

Published in 1982, the first Rough Guide – to Greece – was a student scheme that became a publishing phenomenon. Mark Ellingham, a recent graduate in English from Bristol University, had been travelling in Greece the previous summer and couldn't find the right guidebook. With a small group of friends he wrote his own guide, combining a highly contemporary, journalistic style with a thoroughly practical approach to travellers' needs.

The immediate success of the book spawned a series that rapidly covered dozens of destinations. And, in addition to impecunious backpackers, Rough Guides soon acquired a much broader readership that relished the guides' wit and inquisitiveness as much as their enthusiastic, critical approach and value-for-money ethos.

These days, Rough Guides include recommendations from budget to luxury and cover more than 120 destinations around the globe, as well as producing an ever-growing range of ebooks.

Visit **roughguides.com** to find all our latest books, read articles, get inspired and share travel tips with the Rough Guides community.

Rough Guide credits

Editor: Natasha Foges
Layout: Nikhil Agarwal
Cartography: Ashutosh Bharti
Picture editor: Aude Vauconsant
Proofreader: Stewart Wild
Managing editor: Monica Woods
Assistant editor: Divya Grace Mathew

Production: Jimmy Lao
Cover photo research: Nicole Newman, Roger Mapp
Editorial assistant: Freya Godfrey
Senior pre-press designer: Dan May
Programme manager: Gareth Lowe
Publisher: Keith Drew
Publishing director: Georgina Dee

Publishing information

This tenth edition published June 2016 by
Rough Guides Ltd,
80 Strand, London WC2R 0RL
11, Community Centre, Panchsheel Park,
New Delhi 110017, India
Distributed by Penguin Random House
Penguin Books Ltd, 80 Strand, London WC2R 0RL
Penguin Group (USA), 345 Hudson Street, NY 10014, USA
Penguin Group (Australia), 250 Camberwell Road,
Camberwell, Victoria 3124, Australia
Penguin Group (NZ), 67 Apollo Drive, Mairangi Bay,
Auckland 1310, New Zealand
Penguin Group (South Africa), Block D, Rosebank Office
Park, 181 Jan Smuts Avenue, Parktown North, Gauteng,
South Africa 2193
Rough Guides is represented in Canada by DK Canada, 320
Front Street West, Suite 1400, Toronto, Ontario M5V 3B6
Printed in Singapore
© John Fisher and Geoff Garvey, 2016
Maps © Rough Guides

376pp includes index
A catalogue record for this book is available from the
British Library
ISBN: 978-0-24123-858-5
The publishers and authors have done their best to
ensure the accuracy and currency of all the information
in **The Rough Guide to Crete**, however, they can accept
no responsibility for any loss, injury, or inconvenience
sustained by any traveller as a result of information or
advice contained in the guide.
1 3 5 7 9 8 6 4 2

Help us update

We've gone to a lot of effort to ensure that the tenth
edition of **The Rough Guide to Crete** is accurate and up-
to-date. However, things change – places get "discovered",
opening hours are notoriously fickle, restaurants and
rooms raise prices or lower standards. If you feel we've got
it wrong or left something out, we'd like to know, and if
you can remember the address, the price, the hours, the
phone number, so much the better.

Please send your comments with the subject line
"**Rough Guide Crete Update**" to mail@uk.roughguides
.com. We'll credit all contributions and send a copy of the
next edition (or any other Rough Guide if you prefer) for
the very best emails.

Find more travel information, connect with fellow
travellers and plan your trip on ⓦ roughguides.com.

ABOUT THE AUTHORS

John Fisher was one of the authors of the first ever Rough Guide – to Greece – and has been inextricably linked with the series ever since, much of the time stuck in the office. Now living in London with his wife, Adrienne, and two sons, he is a freelance writer, editor and dispute mediator.

Geoff Garvey first came to Crete as a student of ancient history and progressed from his study of the Minoans to develop a great affection both for the island and its people. When away from Crete he lives in a Spanish mountain village and is co-author of the *Rough Guide to Andalucía*.

Acknowledgements

We are especially grateful for help on this tenth edition to publisher Nikos Karellis in Iráklio, and to Professor Costis Davaras, J. Alexander (Sandy) MacGillivray, and Joseph and Maria Shaw for archeological advice. Information on flora and fauna for this edition was provided by Steve Lenton, Nikos Samaritakis, Steve Daniels and Julia Jones and birding advice by Colin Turvey. Thanks also to Stephen Roberts at the Natural History Museum of Crete and Dr Petros Lyberakis at the University of Crete. We were also greatly assisted by Panos Papadopoulos and the staff of the Greek National Tourist Office in London.

John would like to thank all those who helped along the way including Irene Michalaki, Maria-Ioanna Koutsoudaki, Eva Tsialta, Eleni Vrettou and (as always) Alex Stivanakis in Haniá, Jonny Vlachakis, Frosso Bora and Nikolaos Vrontakis in Réthymno, Giannis Xenakis in Yeoryioúpoli, Phyllis Gousti in Pláka, Judy M. Smith at Grecotel, Petros Marinakis in Fournés, Christoforos Baladimas at the Kallergi Refuge, Elias Kantanoleon in Soúyia, Marilena Kasotaki and Iannis Ieronymakis in Ayía Galini, Eleni Vardaki and Yiannis Polychronakis in Plakiás, Lambros Papoutsakis in Thrónos, Georgia Atsalaki in Kolymbári, Andry Nikolaidou in Kastélli Kissámou, George Lougiakis and Anna

Pamfilou in Paleóhora, Andreas and Katerina Papadakis in Frangokástello, Ioannis Braos and Giorgis Perrakis in Hóra Sfakion, Giorgos Drakoulakis in Omalós, Vangelis and Yiorgos Androulakakis in Loutró and Gerti Vailakaki Schlager in Sarakíniko, Gávdhos. Also to Marc Dubin and, as always, special thanks to A and the two Js for putting up with it.

Geoff would like to thank Yiorgos Saridakis, Yiorgos Margaritakis and Chryssy Karelli in Iráklio, Cliff Cook in Cape Sídheros, Yiorgos Androulakis in Áyios Nikólaos, Yiannis Siganos on the Katharó plateau, Petros Zervakis in Psykhró, Nina Daskalaki and Vangelis Perakis in Eloúnda, Ilse and Michalis Nikitakis in Kamilári, Sylvie Steiner in Mýrtos, Anne Lebrun and Marianna Sardelis in Mókhlos, Nikos Perakis and Ilias Pagiannidis in Káto Zákros, Nikos Voyatzopoulous in Ierápetra, Antonis Stefanakis in Zarós, Lambros Papoutsakis in Thrónos, Katerina Hatzidaki in Xerókambos, Manolis Sergentakis in Kastélli Kissámou, Frosso Bora in Réthymno, Yiannis Lougiakis in Paleohóra, Irene Michalaki and Stavros Badoyiannis in Haniá, Heracles Papadakis in Spíli, and last but by no means least, a special *efharistó para poli* to Stelios Manousakas, Johanne Gaudreau and Maria Manousakas down on the farm in Aryiroúpoli. Finally, a big "thank you" to Han for her help and support in getting the job done.

Readers' updates

Thanks to all the readers who have taken the time to write in with comments and suggestions (and apologies if we've inadvertently omitted or misspelt anyone's name):

Carol Allen, David Authers, Michael Berry, Julia Christofaki, Stelios Chronakis, Francesca Cortellessa, Ruth and Peter Davies, Graham Dean, Jack Edwards, Pierre Forestier, Edna Gallagher, David Hammond, Jane Henchley, Phil Hollowood, Barrie Jones, George Lapidakis, Linda Lashford, Valerie and David Lees, Su McConnel, Huw Morgan, Hanna Nelson, Bernie O'Reilly, Koutras Pashalis, Jonathan Ratty, Carol Scanlon, Carola Scupham, Liz Sharp, Karin Standler, Alec Synge, Eleni Tsioptsia, Adrian Wilkins.

Photo credits

All photos © Rough Guides except the following:
(Key: t-top; c-centre; b-bottom; l-left; r-right)

Index

Maps are marked in grey

R

S

T

Map symbols

The symbols below are used on maps throughout the book

— — ■ ■	Provincial boundary	ⓘ	Information office	Gorge	Gorge	✈	Airport
— — —	Chapter boundary	🅿	Parking	▲	Mountain peak	Ⓗ	Heliport
———	Major road	◆	Point of interest	⌃⌃	Mountain range	★	Bus/taxi stop
———	Minor road	@	Internet access		Cliff	♀	Tree
·-·-·-·	Unpaved road	⋈	Bridge		Hill		Church (town/regional)
———	Pedestrian road	⊤	Fountain	//	Pass		Building
⊓⊓⊓⊓	Steps	♛	Castle	☾	Mosque		Stadium
— —	Ferry route	∴	Archeological site	✡	Synagogue		Park/forest
———	River/coastline	⌂	Mountain hut	⛪	Monastery/convent		Beach
———	Wall	◠	Cave	⊠	Gate		
✉	Post office	☼	Lighthouse	❀	Winery		

Listings key

■	Accommodation
●	Restaurant/café
■	Bar/club/live music
●	Shop